Handbook of Research on Methodologies and Applications of Supercomputing

Veljko Milutinovic
Indiana University, Bloomington, USA

Milos Kotlar
University of Belgrade, Serbia

A volume in the Advances in Systems Analysis, Software Engineering, and High Performance Computing (ASASEHPC) Book Series

Published in the United States of America by
IGI Global
Engineering Science Reference (an imprint of IGI Global)
701 E. Chocolate Avenue
Hershey PA, USA 17033
Tel: 717-533-8845
Fax: 717-533-8661
E-mail: cust@igi-global.com
Web site: http://www.igi-global.com

Library of Congress Cataloging-in-Publication Data

Names: Milutinović, Veljko, editor. | Kotlar, Milos, editor.
Title: Handbook of research on methodologies and applications of
  supercomputing / Veljko Milutinovic and Milos Kotlar, editors.
Description: Hershey, PA : Engineering Science Reference, an imprint of IGI
  Global, [2021] | Includes bibliographical references and index. |
  Summary: "This book offers a variety of perspectives and summarize the
  advances of control flow and data flow super computing, shedding light
  on selected emerging big data applications needing high acceleration
  and/or low power"-- Provided by publisher.
Identifiers: LCCN 2020046761 (print) | LCCN 2020046762 (ebook) | ISBN
  9781799871569 (hardcover) | ISBN 9781799871583 (ebook)
Subjects: LCSH: Supercomputers.
Classification: LCC QA76.88 .H354 2021 (print) | LCC QA76.88 (ebook) |
  DDC 004.1/1--dc23
LC record available at https://lccn.loc.gov/2020046761
LC ebook record available at https://lccn.loc.gov/2020046762

This book is published in the IGI Global book series Advances in Systems Analysis, Software Engineering, and High Performance Computing (ASASEHPC) (ISSN: 2327-3453; eISSN: 2327-3461)

British Cataloguing in Publication Data
A Cataloguing in Publication record for this book is available from the British Library.

All work contributed to this book is new, previously-unpublished material. The views expressed in this book are those of the authors, but not necessarily of the publisher.

For electronic access to this publication, please contact: eresources@igi-global.com.

Advances in Systems Analysis, Software Engineering, and High Performance Computing (ASASEHPC) Book Series

Vijayan Sugumaran
Oakland University, USA

ISSN:2327-3453
EISSN:2327-3461

MISSION

The theory and practice of computing applications and distributed systems has emerged as one of the key areas of research driving innovations in business, engineering, and science. The fields of software engineering, systems analysis, and high performance computing offer a wide range of applications and solutions in solving computational problems for any modern organization.

The **Advances in Systems Analysis, Software Engineering, and High Performance Computing (ASASEHPC) Book Series** brings together research in the areas of distributed computing, systems and software engineering, high performance computing, and service science. This collection of publications is useful for academics, researchers, and practitioners seeking the latest practices and knowledge in this field.

COVERAGE

- Enterprise Information Systems
- Software Engineering
- Computer Networking
- Storage Systems
- Metadata and Semantic Web
- Human-Computer Interaction
- Computer Graphics
- Engineering Environments
- Performance Modelling
- Parallel Architectures

Titles in this Series

For a list of additional titles in this series, please visit: http://www.igi-global.com/book-series/advances-systems-analysis-software-engineering/73689

Impacts and Challenges of Cloud Business Intelligence
Shadi Aljawarneh (Jordan University of Science and Technology, Jordan) and Manisha Malhotra (Chandigarh University, India)
Business Science Reference • © 2021 • 263pp • H/C (ISBN: 9781799850403) • US $195.00

Handbook of Research on Modeling, Analysis, and Control of Complex Systems
Ahmad Taher Azar (Faculty of Computers and Artificial Intelligence, Benha University, Benha, Egypt & College of Computer and Information Sciences, Prince Sultan University, Riyadh, Saudi Arabia) and Nashwa Ahmad Kamal (Faculty of Engineering, Cairo University, Giza, Egypt)
Engineering Science Reference • © 2021 • 685pp • H/C (ISBN: 9781799857884) • US $295.00

Artificial Intelligence Paradigms for Smart Cyber-Physical Systems
Ashish Kumar Luhach (The PNG University of Technology, Papua New Guinea) and Atilla Elçi (Hasan Kalyoncu University, Turkey)
Engineering Science Reference • © 2021 • 392pp • H/C (ISBN: 9781799851011) • US $225.00

Advancements in Model-Driven Architecture in Software Engineering
Yassine Rhazali (Moulay Ismail University of Meknes, Morocco)
Engineering Science Reference • © 2021 • 287pp • H/C (ISBN: 9781799836612) • US $215.00

Cloud-Based Big Data Analytics in Vehicular Ad-Hoc Networks
Ram Shringar Rao (Ambedkar Institute of Advanced Communication Technologies and Research, India) Nanhay Singh (Ambedkar Institute of Advanced Communication Technologies and Research, India) Omprakash Kaiwartya (School of Science and Technology, Nottingham Trent University, UK) and Sanjoy Das (Indira Gandhi National Tribal University, India)
Engineering Science Reference • © 2021 • 312pp • H/C (ISBN: 9781799827641) • US $245.00

Formal and Adaptive Methods for Automation of Parallel Programs Construction Emerging Research and Opportunities
Anatoliy Doroshenko (Institute of Software Systems, Ukraine) and Olena Yatsenko (Institute of Software Systems, Ukraine)
Engineering Science Reference • © 2021 • 279pp • H/C (ISBN: 9781522593843) • US $195.00

701 East Chocolate Avenue, Hershey, PA 17033, USA
Tel: 717-533-8845 x100 • Fax: 717-533-8661
E-Mail: cust@igi-global.com • www.igi-global.com

The following Forewords have been prepared by sincere friends and great minds, whose talents have shaped the scientific face of the Planet, the Nobel Laureates:

- Jerome I Friedman, Nobel Laureate
- Sheldon Glashow, Nobel Laureate
- Stefan Hell, Nobel Laureate
- Tim Hunt, Nobel Laureate
- Jean-Marie Lehn, Nobel Laureate
- Konstantin Novoselov, Nobel Laureate
- Dan Shechtman, Nobel Laureate
- Kurt Wuethrich, Nobel Laureate

Humankind's continuing quests to uncover, understand and utilize the secrets of nature have been greatly enhanced and will be further extended by the power of supercomputers.

- Jerome I. Friedman, Nobel Laureate

Computers have become essential tools for the pursuit of both experimental and theoretical physics, as well as synthetic chemistry, paleontology, the medical sciences, economics the social sciences and so much more. Science, being the most international of all endeavors, will be well served by this important book, which honors the golden anniversary of the creation of Montinegro's Academy of Science.

- Sheldon Glashow, Nobel Laureate

Aim high, stay grounded!

- Stefan Hell, Nobel Laureate

When I became a graduate student in 1964, our lab boasted a mechanical calculator that rang a bell to announce when it had completed a long division and printed the answer on a paper tape. It was powered by electricity, advanced for its age. The Cambridge University computer was called Titan, and we used it to solve simultaneous equations relating to our project about the synthesis of haemoglobin. Both data and program were entered by punched paper tape that one placed in a plastic bag on a hook in the computer lab; if you were lucky and had not made a silly mistake in typing, the results returned the following morning. We dreamed of something more inspiring, we were aware of Dick Tracy's communicating wrist-watch, and amazed by the first Apple computer we encountered in 1979, which, when loaded up with expansion cards made thesis writing a lot easier for our students. But biology really became dependent on computers when we started to sequence DNA and interrogate databases, and teaching began to lean heavily on the graphic capabilities of the Macintosh—a lot of disc swapping required in the early days; assembling lecture notes took weeks, I seem to recall, in the mid-1980s. But DNA is really the thing. Sydney Brenner relates how, when he first laid eyes on the model that Jim Watson and Francis Crick had built, he realised that here before his very eyes was Turing's tape of instructions, the heart of a self-replicating automaton. He spent the rest of his life trying to understand these instructions. Along the way, it was a powerful new computer that allowed Brenner and his collaborators to map the nervous system of the nematode worm, although alas not really to understand how 'The mind of the worm' actually worked. The rate of progress in both hardware and software has been so prodigious that it is possible that artificial intelligence will advance to the point when we really will be able to understand how the worm controls its wriggling and how we recognise our friends. I simply hope for effective simultaneous translation of Japanese and English. It's clear that computers can do anything, as the pioneers already recognised, and it's probably only a matter of time before they can perform any of the kinds of tasks we humans take for granted quicker than blinking. I guess this book represents a stage on this exciting and very important journey.

- Tim Hunt, Nobel Laureate

I wish to congratulate very warmly the Montenegrin Academy of Arts and Sciences on the occasion of its 50th Anniversary and wish the CANU a highly successful future! Science shapes the Future of Mankind. Participate!

- Jean-Marie Lehn, Nobel Laureate

Supercomputers have become a ubiquitous instrument in many areas of science and technology. Very hard to imagine modern physics, biology or chemistry without the use of this versatile tool. The breakthroughs in the development of supercomputers expand the range of problems we can tackle. Supercomputers, as well as specialised computers will undoubtedly contribute significantly to the overall landscape of discoveries in many different disciplines in the future.

- Konstantin Novoselov, Nobel Laureate

Our complex and fast-moving world meets big data issues that call for reliable, efficient analysis and prompt response. A most advanced approach to dealing with these issues is presented in this book where algorithms of Control Flow represent the host architecture of supercomputers and Data Flow represents the acceleration architecture. A comprehensive list of applications is illustrated in the book including natural language processing, medical research, customer-oriented studies and many more.

- Dan Shechtman, Nobel Laureate

I want to commend Dr. Veljko Milutinovic and Dr. Milos Kotlar for having completed this volume in the timely field of supercomputing in these difficult times, and I want to share their optimism regarding its use as a textbook around the world.

- Kurt Wuethrich, Nobel Laureate

Jerome Isaac Friedman (born March 28, 1930) is an American physicist. He won the 1990 Nobel Prize in Physics for work showing an internal structure for protons later known to be quarks.

Sheldon Lee Glashow (born December 5, 1932) is a Nobel Prize-winning American theoretical physicist. He is the Metcalf Professor of Mathematics and Physics at Boston University and Eugene Higgins Professor of Physics, Emeritus, at Harvard University, and is a member of the Board of Sponsors for the Bulletin of the Atomic Scientists. In 1961, Glashow extended electroweak unification models due to Schwinger by including a short range neutral current, the Z0. The resulting symmetry structure that Glashow proposed forms the basis of the accepted theory of the electroweak interactions. For this discovery, Glashow along with Steven Weinberg and Abdus Salam, was awarded the 1979 Nobel Prize in Physics.

These four crisp words of wisdom ac-company the best wishes for the 50th anniversary of the Montenegrin Academy of Sciences and Arts. Stefan W. Hell developed STED fluorescence microscopy, the first lens-based optical microscopy with resolution that is not limited by the diffraction of light.

Sir Richard Timothy Hunt, FRS FMedSci FRSE MAE (born 19 February 1943) is a British biochemist and molecular physiologist. He was awarded the 2001 Nobel Prize in Physiology or Medicine with Paul Nurse and Leland Hartwell for their discoveries of protein molecules that control the division of cells. He received the Nobel Prize in Chemistry for his synthesis of cryptands. (Source: Wikipedia)

Konstantin Sergeevich Novoselov FRS FRSC born 23 August 1974 is a Russian-British physicist, and a Professor at the Centre for Advanced 2D Materials, National University of Singapore. He is also the Langworthy Professor in the School of Physics and Astronomy at the University of Manchester. His work on graphene with Andre Geim earned them the Nobel Prize in Physics in 2010. Konstantin Novoselov was born in Nizhny Tagil, Soviet Union, in 1974. He graduated from the Moscow Institute of Physics and Technology with a MSc degree in 1997, and was awarded a PhD from the Radboud University of Nijmegen in 2004 for work supervised by Andre Geim.

Dan Shechtman is the Philip Tobias Professor of Materials Science at the Technion – Israel Institute of Technology, an Associate of the US Department of Energy's Ames Laboratory, and Professor of Materials Science at Iowa State University. On April 8, 1982, while on sabbatical at the U.S. National Bureau of Standards in Washington, D.C., Shechtman discovered the icosahedral phase, which opened the new field of quasiperiodic crystals. Shechtman was awarded the 2011 Nobel Prize in Chemistry for the discovery of quasicrystals, making him one of six Israelis who have won the Nobel Prize in Chemistry.

Kurt Wüthrich is the Cecil H. and Ida M. Green Professor of Structural Bi-ology at Scripps Research, La Jolla, CA, USA, Professor of Biophysics at the ETH Zürich, Zürich, Switzerland, and Distinguished Senior Professor at the iHuman Institute, ShanghaiTech University, Shanghai, China. For 50 years, Wüthrich groups at the ETH Zürich, at Scripps Research and at the iHuman Institute have used nuclear magnetic resonance spectroscopy (NMR) for research in structural biology. Contributions include the method of protein structure determination with NMR in solution, and the use of the principles of transverse relaxation-optimized spectroscopy (TROSY) for NMR experiments with large supramolecular assemblies. Applications over the years were focused on differentiation in higher organisms, immune suppression and neuropathology. As of April 2019, research using NMR techniques is continued at ShanghaiTech University, with a focus on transmembrane signal transfer by G protein-coupled receptors (GPCRs). At Scripps Research and the ETH Zürich, projects on the general theme "healthcare in the ageing human societies of the 21st century" are pursued, mainly considering the impact of sarcopenia on the human healthspan. Kurt Wüthrich's achievements have been recognized by the Prix Louis Jeantet de Médecine, the Kyoto Prize in Advanced Technology, the Nobel Prize in Chemistry, and by a number of other awards and honorary degrees.

This book is dedicated to the 50th Anniversary of the Montenegrin National Academy of Sciences and Arts (CANU), which represents the central point of the synergies between the Nobel Laureates who contributed the pearls of wisdom and the editors who brought together the authors of chapters, from the world's leading universities at which they lectured in the past. Parts of this book, so far, were used in the educational processes at 40 different universities worldwide. Special thanks are due to: Dragan Vukcevic and Ljubisa Stankovic.

We are immensely grateful to the School of Electrical Engineering, University of Belgrade, Serbia, the Alma Mater of the two co-editors. We are especially thankful both to the institution for its excellent education environment that opened many doors of knowledge, and to colleagues whose help was crucial in a number of important missions: Miroslav Bojovic, the late Georgije Lukatela, Aleksandar Neskovic, Natasa Neskovic, the late Pantelija Nikolic, Jelica Protic, Marija Punt, Sasa Stojanovic, Igor Tartalja, Milo Tomasevic.

List of Contributors

Table of Contents

Detailed Table of Contents

    Miloš Kotlar, School of Electrical Engineering, University of Belgrade, Serbia

In the controlflow paradigm, based on the finite automata theory, one writes a program in order to control the flow of data through the hardware. In the dataflow paradigm, one writes a program in order to configure the hardware. Then, the question is what moves data through the hardware, if that is not a stored program? Ideally, in the dataflow paradigm, data get moved by the voltage difference between the system input and the system output, with flip-flops and register barriers in-between (FPGAs), or without these barriers (referred as ultimate dataflow), possibly but not necessarily, with the computing infrastructure based on the analog hardware. See the references for one specific viewpoint related to the subject.

    Ivan Ratković, Esperanto Technologies, Serbia
    Miljan Djordjevic, University of Belgrade, Serbia

Modern supercomputer designs fall into distinct categories – data and control flow supercomputer design paradigms. Control flow stands as the go-to design philosophy in all von Neumann machines dominating the market thus far. New types of problems demand a different flow mindset – this is where the data flow machines come in play. This chapter introduces control-flow concept as well as its state-of-the-art examples. Introduction section goes over definitions of terms used in succeeding chapters and gives their brief explanations. A brief explanation of supercomputing as a whole given in the Introduction section is then followed by explanations of the data and control flow design philosophies, with real-world examples of both – multi-core, many-core, vector processors, and GPUs in Control Flow Paradigm section. The third section covers real-world processing unit examples, with a rundown of the best standard and low power commercial and supercomputing market representatives.

Chapter 3

Benjamin Berg, Carnegie Mellon University, USA
Mor Harchol-Balter, Carnegie Mellon University, USA

Large data centers composed of many servers provide the opportunity to improve performance by parallelizing jobs. However, effectively exploiting parallelism is non-trivial. For each arriving job, one must decide the number of servers on which the job is run. The goal is to determine the optimal allocation of servers to jobs that minimizes the mean response time across jobs – the average time from when a job arrives until it completes. Parallelizing a job across multiple servers reduces the response time of that individual job. However, jobs receive diminishing returns from being allocated additional servers, so allocating too many servers to a single job leads to low system efficiency. The authors consider the case where the remaining sizes of jobs are unknown to the system at every moment in time. They prove that, if all jobs follow the same speedup function, the optimal policy is EQUI, which divides servers equally among jobs. When jobs follow different speedup functions, EQUI is no longer optimal and they provide an alternate policy, GREEDY*, which performs within 1% of optimal in simulation.

Chapter 4

Bryan Donyanavard, University of California, Irvine, USA
Amir M. Rahmani, University of California, Irvine, USA
Axel Jantsch, TU Wien, Austria
Onur Mutlu, Swiss Federal Institute of Technology in Zurich, Switzerland
Nikil Dutt, University of California, Irvine, USA

Runtime resource management for many-core systems is increasingly complex. The complexity can be due to diverse workload characteristics with conflicting demands, or limited shared resources such as memory bandwidth and power. Resource management strategies for many-core systems must distribute shared resource(s) appropriately across workloads, while coordinating the high-level system goals at runtime in a scalable and robust manner. In this chapter, the concept of reflection is used to explore adaptive resource management techniques that provide two key properties: the ability to adapt to (1) changing goals at runtime (i.e., self-adaptivity) and (2) changing dynamics of the modeled system (i.e., self-optimization). By supporting these self-awareness properties, the system can reason about the actions it takes by considering the significance of competing objectives, user requirements, and operating conditions while executing unpredictable workloads.

Chapter 5

Assefaw Gebremedhin, Washington State University, USA
Mostofa Patwary, NVIDIA, USA
Fredrik Manne, University of Bergen, Norway

The chapter describes two algorithmic paradigms, dubbed speculation and iteration and approximate update, for parallelizing greedy graph algorithms and vertex ordering algorithms, respectively, on multicore architectures. The common challenge in these two classes of algorithms is that the computations involved are inherently sequential. The efficacy of the paradigms in overcoming this challenge is demonstrated via extensive experimental study on two representative algorithms from each class and two Intel multi-core systems. The algorithms studied are (1) greedy algorithms for distance-k coloring (for k = 1 and k = 2) and (2) algorithms for two degree-based vertex orderings. The experimental results show that the paradigms enable the design of scalable methods that to a large extent preserve the quality of solution obtained by the underlying serial algorithms.

Chapter 6

Nenad Korolija, School of Electrical Engineering, University of Belgrade, Serbia
Jovan Popović, Microsoft Development Center, Serbia
Miroslav M. Bojović, School of Electrical Engineering, University of Belgrade, Serbia

This chapter presents the possibilities for obtaining significant performance gains based on advanced implementations of algorithms using the dataflow hardware. A framework built on top of the dataflow architecture that provides tools for advanced implementations is also described. In particular, the authors point out to the following issues of interest for accelerating algorithms: (1) the dataflow paradigm appears as suitable for executing certain set of algorithms for high performance computing, namely algorithms that work with big data, as well as algorithms that include a lot of repetitions of the same set of instructions; (2) dataflow architecture could be configured using appropriate programming tools that can define hardware by generating VHDL files; (3) besides accelerating algorithms, dataflow architecture also reduces power consumption, which is an important security factor with edge computing.

Chapter 7

Christina Pacher, Universität Wien, Austria

This chapter describes a data flow implementation of the image processing algorithms Erosion and Dilation. Erosion and Dilation are basic image processing algorithms which are used to reduce or increase the size of objects in images, respectively, and which are used in a wide number of image processing applications. The chapter first describes the control flow versions of the algorithms in detail. Subsequently, the translation of these algorithms to the Data Flow paradigm is examined, and the details of the data flow implementation as well as possible optimizations are discussed.

Chapter 8

Ilir Murturi, Distributed Systems Group, TU Wien, Austria

In mathematical statistics, an interesting and common problem is finding the best linear or non-linear regression equations that express the relationship between variables or data. The method of least squares (MLS) represents one of the oldest procedures among multiple techniques to determine the best fit line to the given data through simple calculus and linear algebra. Notably, numerous approaches have been proposed to compute the least-squares. However, the proposed methods are based on the control flow paradigm. As a result, this chapter presents the MLS transformation from control flow logic to the dataflow paradigm. Moreover, this chapter shows each step of the transformation, and the final kernel code is presented.

In this chapter a heuristic forest fire model based on cellular automata is presented and realized for efficiency reasons with the DataFlow programming approach. Real-world images taken by satellites are analyzed and used as the basis for simulations. In the presented forest fire model, natural influences like wind strength and direction, burning behavior, as well as different levels of inflammability are considered. The DataFlow implementation on an FPGA-based Maxeler MAX3 Vectis card was compared to a sequential C version executed on an Intel Xeon E5-2650 2.0 GHz CPU. The author obtained speedups of up to 70 for a strong wind situation and 46 for a random wind setting while reducing energy consumption.

The amount of user-generated text available online is growing at an ever-increasing rate due to tremendous progress in enlarging inexpensive storage capacity, processing capabilities, and the popularity of online outlets and social networks. Learning language representation and solving tasks in an end-to-end manner, without a need for human-expert feature extraction and creation, has made models more accurate and much more complicated in the number of parameters, requiring parallelized and distributed resources high-performance computing or cloud. This chapter gives an overview of state-of-the-art natural language processing problems, algorithms, models, and libraries. Parallelized and distributed ways to solve text understanding, representation, and classification tasks are also discussed. Additionally, the importance of high-performance computing for natural language processing applications is illustrated by showing details of a few specific applications that use pre-training or self-supervised learning on large amounts of data in text understanding.

In this review, the authors outline the evidence that emerged some 30 years ago that the mechanisms thought responsible for the deposition of submicron particles in the respiratory region of the lung were inadequate to explain the measured rate of deposition. They then discuss the background and theory of what is believed to be the missing mechanism, namely chaotic mixing. Specifically, they outline how that the recirculating flow in the alveoli has a range of frequencies of oscillation and some of these resonate with the breathing frequency. If the system is perturbed, the resonating frequencies break into chaos, and they discuss a number of practical ways in which the system can be disturbed. The perturbation of fluid particle trajectories results in Hamiltonian chaos, which produces qualitative changes in those trajectories. They end the review with a discussion of the effects of chaotic mixing on the deposition of inhaled particles in the respiratory region of the lung.

Searching for contents in present digital libraries is still very primitive; most websites provide a search field where users can enter information such as book title, author name, or terms they expect to be found in the book. Some platforms provide advanced search options, which allow the users to narrow the search results by specific parameters such as year, author name, publisher, and similar. Currently, when users find a book which might be of interest to them, this search process ends; only a full-text search or references at the end of the book may provide some additional pointers. In this chapter, the author is going to give an example of how a user could permanently get recommendations for additional contents even while reading the article, using present machine learning and artificial intelligence techniques.

Large-scale computing, including machine learning (MI) and AI, offer a great promise in enabling sustainability and resiliency of electric energy systems. At present, however, there is no standardized framework for systematic modeling and simulation of system response over time to different continuous- and discrete-time events and/or changes in equipment status. As a result, there is generally a poor understanding of the effects of candidate technologies on the quality and cost of electric energy services. In this chapter, the authors discuss a unified, physically intuitive multi-layered modeling of system components and their mutual dynamic interactions. The fundamental concept underlying this modeling is the notion of interaction variables whose definition directly lends itself to capturing modular structure needed to manage complexity. As a direct result, the same modeling approach defines an information exchange structure between different system layers, and hence can be used to establish structure for the design of a dedicated computational architecture, including AI methods.

The subgraph isomorphism problem asks whether a given graph is a subgraph of another graph. It is one of the most general NP-complete problems since many other problems (e.g., Hamiltonian cycle, clique, independent set, etc.) have a natural reduction to subgraph isomorphism. Furthermore, there is a variety of practical applications where graph pattern matching is the core problem. Developing efficient algorithms and solvers for this problem thus enables good solutions to a variety of different practical problems. In this chapter, the authors present and experimentally explore various algorithmic refinements and code optimizations for improving the performance of subgraph isomorphism solvers. In particular, they focus on algorithms that are based on the backtracking approach and constraint satisfaction programming. They gather experiences from many state-of-the-art algorithms as well as from their engagement in this field. Lessons learned from engineering such a solver can be utilized in many other fields where backtracking is a prominent approach for solving a particular problem.

Chapter 15
Luiz A. M. Moutinho, University of Suffolk, UK

The chapter is focused on the paradigm shift of artificial intelligence (AI) and marketing evolution. Considering the effects of AI on marketing and AI powered by engagement marketing, why is AI the marketing future? Is AI in marketing merely over-promoted? What can AI do for marketing and how can AI most influence and bring advantages to marketing and transformation of the customer experience through mass personalisation? Some critical impacts of chatbots are highlighted, with explanations of what they can do and how they will change the future of customer engagement. An explanation of how AI products influence and transform the role of product management is given, emphasizing the importance of the human context delivering, along with emerging technologies. Following this is an investigation about AI influencing brand management, and by the end, the issues of the future of AI and robotics are highlighted.

Chapter 16
Victor Potapenko, Florida International University, USA
Malek Adjouadi, Florida International University, USA
Naphtali Rishe, Florida International University, USA

Modeling time-series data with asynchronous, multi-cardinal, and uneven patterns presents several unique challenges that may impede convergence of supervised machine learning algorithms, or significantly increase resource requirements, thus rendering modeling efforts infeasible in resource-constrained environments. The authors propose two approaches to multi-class classification of asynchronous time-series data. In the first approach, they create a baseline by reducing the time-series data using a statistical approach and training a model based on gradient boosted trees. In the second approach, they implement a fully convolutional network (FCN) and train it on asynchronous data without any special feature engineering. Evaluation of results shows that FCN performs as well as the gradient boosting based on mean F1-score without computationally complex time-series feature engineering. This work has been applied in the prediction of customer attrition at a large retail automotive finance company.

Chapter 17
Jakob Salom, Mathematical Institute of Serbian Academy of Sciences and Arts, Serbia

This chapter sheds light on one very important application in the domain of digital economy – mind genomics. Mind genomics is an approach to targeted marketing which reaches each prospect with a different personalized message. This application requires acceleration coming from a data flow accelerator connected to a control flow host. It stresses equally the basic concept and its many applications. Innovation process is a step-by-step process. Once an important step up front is created and a new innovation finds its way into the commercial world, it is difficult to imagine that another dramatical step/leap forward is possible. However, such steps keep happening. Mind genomics is an example of one such step, unthinkable of until only a few years ago. Needs of the users could be served much more effectively not only in business domains or other lucrative domains, but also in the domains of public health, public happiness, public and individual quality of life, public and individual understanding of the environment around, etc.

Chapter 18

The history of neuroscience has tracked with the evolution of science and technology. Today, neuroscience's trajectory is heavily dependent on computational systems and the availability of high-performance computing (HPC), which are becoming indispensable for building simulations of the brain, coping with high computational demands of analysis of brain imaging data sets, and developing treatments for neurological diseases. This chapter will briefly review the current and potential future use of supercomputers in neuroscience.

Chapter 19

Contemporary healthcare systems face growing demand for their services, rising costs, and a workforce. Artificial intelligence has the potential to transform how care is delivered and to help meet the challenges. Recent healthcare systems have been focused on using knowledge management and AI. The proposed solution is to reach explainable and causal AI by combining the benefits of the accuracy of deep-learning algorithms with visibility on the factors that are important to the algorithm's conclusion in a way that is accessible and understandable to physicians. Therefore, the authors propose AI approach in which the encoded clinical guidelines and protocols provide a starting point augmented by models that learn from data. The new structure of electronic health records that connects data from wearables and genomics data and innovative extensible big data architecture appropriate for this AI concept is proposed. Consequently, the proposed technology may drastically decrease the need for expensive software and hopefully eliminates the need to do diagnostics in expensive institutions.

This chapter is an abridged sort of "vision statement" on what supercomputing will be in the future. The main thrust of the argument is that most of the problem lies in the trafficking of data, not the computation.

There needs to be a worldwide effort to put into place a means to move data efficiently and effectively. Further, there likely needs to be a fundamental shift in our model of computation where the computation is stationary and data moves to movement of computation to the data or even as the data is moving.

    Veljko Milutinović, Indiana University, USA
    Miloš Kotlar, School of Electrical Engineering, University of Belgrade, Serbia
    Ivan Ratković, Esperanto Technologies, Serbia
    Nenad Korolija, Independent Researcher, Serbia
    Miljan Djordjevic, University of Belgrade, Serbia
    Kristy Yoshimoto, Indiana University, USA
    Mateo Valero, BSC, Spain

This chapter starts from the assumption that near future 100BTransistor SuperComputers-on-a-Chip will include N big multi-core processors, 1000N small many-core processors, a TPU-like fixed-structure systolic array accelerator for the most frequently used machine learning algorithms needed in bandwidth-bound applications, and a flexible-structure reprogrammable accelerator for less frequently used machine learning algorithms needed in latency-critical applications. The future SuperComputers-on-a-Chip should include effective interfaces to specific external accelerators based on quantum, optical, molecular, and biological paradigms, but these issues are outside the scope of this chapter.

Preface

This book covers the implementation of algorithms of interest for the system and the library software, in the Operating System and/or the Library Bases, both in the Control Flow paradigm (for problems that are best implemented in Control Flow) and in the Data Flow paradigm (for problems that are best implemented in Data Flow). Consequently, this book advocates the need for Hybrid Computing, where the Control Flow part represents the host architecture and Data Flow part represents the acceleration architecture. These (afore mentioned) issues cover the initial eight out of the total of sixteen chapters. The remaining and the final eight chapters cover selected modern applications that are best implemented on a Hybrid Computer, in which the transactional parts (serial code) are implemented on the Control Flow part and the loops (parallel code) on the Data Flow part. These final eight chapters cover two major application domains: The scientific computing, in the widest sense, and the computing for digital economy, in the widest sense.

The rationale behind this book is to summarize the advances of Control Flow and Data Flow Super Computing, and to shed light on selected emerging big data applications needing high acceleration and/or low power. The contributions come from authors affiliated with the major universities in the US and EU. The idea to create this edited volume came around the visiting lectures of the two co-editors at the universities from which the contributing authors were invited. The lectures were on the Data Flow based acceleration of Control Flow Super Computers.

The contributing authors of chapters in Part#1 are experts working on advanced research of interest for the Control Flow paradigm. The contributing authors of chapters in Part#2 are experienced young researchers working on advanced research of interest for the Data Flow paradigm. The contributing authors of Part#3 are working on emerging applications that need badly either the process acceleration or low power, or both. These applications are excellent candidates for Hybrid Machines that synergize Control Flow and Data Flow paradigms. Once the relevant topics were defined, the authors that could provide a proper and a clear treatment of the topics, were invited to contribute. Each chapter could be treated as an independent unit of knowledge. However, the chapters have been lined up in such a manner, so that each previous chapter al-ways defines the know-how needed for a deeper understanding of the later chapters.

The editors have invited eight Nobel Laureates, to share their experiences and wisdom in the form of short one-paragraph forewords, that would shed some wise light on issues they find important. The editors highly appreciate their kindness to help this effort, which is aimed at students of the world's leading universities.

UNIQUE POINTS OF THIS BOOK

A detailed implementation of algorithms on Control Flow and Data Flow paradigms. A presentation of selected emerging applications needing high acceleration and/or low power. An original comparative treatment of Control Flow and Data Flow paradigms. An algorithmic-centric and application-centric treatment of two major computing paradigms.

UNIVERSITIES AT WHICH ELEMENTS OF THIS BOOK WERE USED

This book serves as a textbook to help with Course and/or Workshop Projects at the universities where Professor Milutinovic helps periodically as a Guest Professor or a Workshops Conductor, in close co-operation with Dr. Kotlar. The two of them together taught courses in the past, or do teach courses now/periodically, at the following schools of the US/EU:

- Indiana University
- Purdue University
- Carnegie Melon University
- Temple University
- MIT Media Labs
- University of Massachusetts in Amherst
- Harvard Continuous Education
- NYU Continuous Education
- UCLA Continuous Education
- USC Continuous Education
- ETH Zurich
- EPFL Geneva
- University of Stockholm
- University of Skovde
- University of Heidelberg
- University of Frankfurt
- University of Darmstadt
- University of Stuttgart
- Technical University of Vienna
- Scientific University of Vienna
- Politechnical University of Barcelona
- Politechnical Univeristy of Valencia
- University of Salerno
- University of Siena
- University of Ljubljana
- University of Koper
- University of Zagreb, Ruđer Bošković Institute
- University of Rijeka
- University of Sarajevo

- University of Skopje
- University of Podgorica
- University of Belgrade
- University of Kragujevac
- University o Novi Pazar
- University o Novi Sad
- University o Nis
- University o Skodra
- University o Tirana
- Bogazici University
- Koc University

RELATED COURSE NAMES

This book might be used for different university courses (four related course names):

- Programming for Hybrid Computing
- Programming for DataFlow Computing
- Programming of Emerging Algorithms (for Hybrid, Control Flow, or Data Flow Machines)
- Programming of Emerging Applications (for Hybrid, Control Flow, or Data Flow Machines)

In all these courses, the first four chapters help about the better under-standing of the Control Flow paradigm (especially the paradigm concepts at the Operating System interface to the Data Flow accelerator), the next four chapters help about the better understanding of the Data Flow paradigm (especially the paradigm strengths related to potentials for high acceleration and low power), and the final eight chapters serve as a source of inspiration for two individual programming projects (obligatory), one related to science and engineering (with inspirations found in chapters 9, 10, 11, and 12), and the other one oriented to digital economy and social responsibility (with inspirations found in chapters 13, 14, 15, and 16).

SUPPLEMENTARY MATERIALS FOR THIS BOOK

Editors keep solutions of all our class projects at a publicly accessible web site (URL specified in the book: home/etf/rs/~vm/).

FINAL COMMENTS

1. The contributing authors come from the universities at which the two editors were teaching or do teach courses on the synergy of Data Flow and Control Flow paradigms. Typically, the attending students, professors, researchers, and visiting professionals seeking expertise, would approach the teachers with their applications needing process acceleration and/or low power, and the most brilliant application examples of those were selected for this edited volume (absolutely all contributing

chapters in this volume come from universities at which the two editors of this volume did teach courses for credits that students could use towards their graduation).

2. All chapters in this monograph underwent detailed technical reviews of two editors and/or their affiliated colleagues.

Veljko Milutinović
Indiana University, Bloomington, USA

Miloš Kotlar
University of Belgrade, Serbia
Belgrade, 08 November 2020

Acknowledgment

We are immensely grateful to the School of Electrical Engineering of the of Belgrade, Serbia, the Alma Mater of the two co-editors. We are especially thankful both to the institution for its excellent educational environment that opened many doors of knowledge, and to the colleagues whose help was crucial in a number of important missions. The editors are thankful to Zoran Knezević, Djordje Sijački, Dragoš Cvetković and Gradimir Milovanović of the Serbian Academy of Sciences and Arts (SANU) for suggestions related to this book and for the many wise advices in general. Also to Zoran Marković, Zoran Ognjanović, Miodrag Mihaljević, and Vladisav Jelisavčić of the Mathematical Institute of the Serbian Academy of Sciences and Arts (MISANU), as well as to Zoran Babović, Igor Ikodinović, Goran Rakočević, and Zhilbert Tafa of the MISANU SuperComputing Project. To colleagues all over the World who helped the dissemination of scientific results generated through the MISANU SuperComputing Project (chronologically): Klaus Waldschmidt, Erich Neuhold, Henry Markram, Babak Falsafi, Onur Mutlu, Bozidar Stojadinovic, Schachram Dustdar, Eduard Mehofer, Vladimir Terzija, Violeta Holmes, Vojin Plavsic, Ingi Jonasson, Georgi Gaydadjiev, Gantcho Mantchorov, Massimo De Santo, Roberto Giorgi, Jose Fortes, Jose Carlos Teixeira, Djordje Jovanovic, Milena Djukanovic, Irena Orovic, Danilo Nikolic, Branislav Boricic, Marko Savic, Veljko Vlahovic, Nikola Altiparmakov, Arda Yurdakul, Didem Unat, Petraq Papajorgji, Genci Berati, Jure Jemec, Srdjan Djordjevic, Roman Trobec, Franci Demsar, Uros Cibej, Jurij Mihelic, Saso Tomazic, Anton Kos, Iztok Savnik, Ales Zamuda, Gyula Mester, Bela Marjanovich, Sotiris Nikoletsas, Alkis Konstantellos, Franjo Jovic, Karolj Skala, Liljana Gavrilovska, Marjan Gusev, Osman Unsal, Adrian Crystal, Alan J. Smith, Krste Asanovic, Alex Veidenbaum, Alex Nicolau, Gordana Vunjak, Alan Gottlieb, Anthony Davidson, Howard Moskowitz, Ayhan Irfanoglu, Arun Prakash, Amr Sabry, Yuzhen Ye, Ali Hurson, Zoran Obradovic, Daniela Rus, and Deb Roy. Special thanks go to colleagues from the Montenegrin National Academy of Sciences and Arts: Miomir Dasic, Dragan Vukcevic, Ljubisa Stankovic, and Milojica Jacimovic.

Chapter 1
An Introduction to Controlflow and Dataflow Supercomputing

Miloš Kotlar

School of Electrical Engineering, University of Belgrade, Serbia

ABSTRACT

In the controlflow paradigm, based on the finite automata theory, one writes a program in order to control the flow of data through the hardware. In the dataflow paradigm, one writes a program in order to configure the hardware. Then, the question is what moves data through the hardware, if that is not a stored program? Ideally, in the dataflow paradigm, data get moved by the voltage difference between the system input and the system output, with flip-flops and register barriers in-between (FPGAs), or without these barriers (referred as ultimate dataflow), possibly but not necessarily, with the computing infrastructure based on the analog hardware. See the references for one specific viewpoint related to the subject.

THE CONTROLFLOW ESSENCE

The controlflow paradigm dates back to the times of von Neumann in 1940s (vonNeumann, 1951), when the first machines were implemented based on that paradigm, but its rapid popularity came up with the invention of microprocessors, especially those based on the RISC and MIPS concepts (Hennessy, 1982). In both cases, as already indicated, the essence is in the theory of finite automata.

The more recent advances include a number of architectural advances (e.g., Grujic, 1996; Milenkovic, 2000; Trobec, 2016), technology advances (e.g., Milutinovic1996), extensions of the paradigm (e.g., Babovic, 2016; Gavrilovska, 2010), extensive research in the domains of system software (e.g., Knezevic, 2000), tools for effective code developments (e.g., Trifunovic, 2015), and the ready to use library routines for a plethora of different applications, with a recent stress on Artificial Intelligence, Deep Learning, and Data Mining (e.g., Radivojevic, 2003). These advances span the time from 1990s till today, and are here presented briefly, stressing only the concepts of interest for this edited volume, which all originated from the laboratory that synergizes the contributing authors of this book.

DOI: 10.4018/978-1-7998-7156-9.ch001

Programs predominantly based on the transactional code are well suited for execution on machines implemented using a controlflow architecture. However, controlflow architectures are often times not the best suited for highly parallel code operating on big data, with low power, low volume, and high precision requirements. For such environments, accelerators are needed.

THE DATAFLOW ESSENCE

The dataflow paradigm dates back to the MIT research of professors Dennis and Arvind in 1970s, when the first machines were implemented based on that paradigm, but the machines with a really great potential for speed up and power savings started to appear with the research in and around Maxeler Technologies, in 1990s. In the early MIT research, the essence is in data that flow using standard finite automata hardware underneath, while in the Maxeler research (e.g., see an overview at Milutinovic, 2015), as well as in the early Purdue University research (e.g., Milutinovic, 1987), the essence is in mapping the algorithms into hardware, so that the dataflow process is fully implemented in hardware.

The more recent advances include a number of extensions of the paradigm (e.g., Jovanovic, 2012), extensive research in the domains of system software (e.g., see an overview at Milutinovic, 2015), tools for effective code developments (e.g., Trifunovic, 2015), and the ready to use library routines for large data volumes (e.g., Flynn, 2013). These advances span the time from 1990s till today, and are here presented briefly, stressing only the concepts of interest for this edited volume, which all originated from the laboratory that synergizes the contributing authors of this book.

Programs predominantly based on the highly parallel code are well suited for execution on machines implemented using a dataflow architecture and serving as accelerators. Such accelerators are especially well suited for highly parallel code operating on big data, with low power, low volume, and high precision requirements. For such environments, found in many applications covered in this book, accelerators are an ideal solution. Another type of environment in which the Dataflow paradigm could help is in applications based on approximate computing for low latency (e.g., Milutinovic1980).

CONCLUSION

The major conclusion of this introduction to controlflow and dataflow supercomputing is that the best results are obtained with hybrid computers that synergize the two paradigms. The controlflow part is best used as the host, while the dataflow part is best used as the accelerator. A number of emerging applications are best implemented on hybrid computers.

Further advances in controlflow, dataflow, and hybrid computing need the creativity that is closely coupled with realities in the domains of underlying technologies and emerging applications. One study of creativity utilized in the related research so for could be found, together with related activities in the dissemination domain, in (Blagojevic2017, Bankovic2020).

However, the major challenge is to map efficiently the most sophisticated emerging algorithms and applications onto a properly synergized infrastructure that combines dataflow and controlflow paradigms.

REFERENCES

Arvind, A., Gostelow, K. P., & Plouffe, W. (1977). Indeterminacy, monitors, and dataflow. *Operating Systems Review*, *11*(5), 159–169.

Babovic, Z. B., Protic, J., & Milutinovic, V. (2016). Web performance evaluation for internet of things applications. *IEEE Access: Practical Innovations, Open Solutions*, *4*, 6974–6992.

Banković, M., Filipović, V., Graovac, J., Hadži-Purić, J., Hurson, A. R., Kartelj, A., ... Marić, F. (2020). Teaching graduate students how to review research articles and respond to reviewer comments. []. Elsevier.]. *Advances in Computers*, *116*(1), 1–63.

Blagojević, V., Bojić, D., Bojović, M., Cvetanović, M., Đorđević, J., Đurđević, Đ., ... Milutinović, V. (2017). A systematic approach to generation of new ideas for PhD research in computing. *Advances in Computers*, *104*, 1–31.

Dennis, J. B. (1974). First version of a data flow procedure language. In *Programming Symposium* (pp. 362-376). Springer.

Flynn, M. J., Mencer, O., Milutinovic, V., Rakocevic, G., Stenstrom, P., Trobec, R., & Valero, M. (2013). Moving from petaflops to petadata. *Communications of the ACM*, *56*(5), 39–42.

Gavrilovska, L., Krco, S., Milutinović, V., Stojmenovic, I., & Trobec, R. (Eds.). (2010). *Application and multidisciplinary aspects of wireless sensor networks: concepts, integration, and case studies*. Springer Science & Business Media.

Grujic, A., Tomasević, M., & Milutinovic, V. (1996). A simulation study of hardware-oriented DSM approaches. *IEEE Parallel & Distributed Technology Systems & Applications*, *4*(1), 74–83.

Hennessy, J., Jouppi, N., Przybylski, S., Rowen, C., Gross, T., Baskett, F., & Gill, J. (1982). MIPS: A microprocessor architecture. *ACM SIGMICRO Newsletter*, *13*(4), 17–22.

Jovanović, Ž., & Milutinović, V. (2012). FPGA accelerator for floating-point matrix multiplication. *IET Computers & Digital Techniques*, *6*(4), 249–256.

Knezevic, P., Radnovic, B., Nikolic, N., Jovanovic, T., Milanov, D., Nikolic, M., ... Schewel, J. (2000, January). The architecture of the Obelix-an improved internet search engine. In *Proceedings of the 33rd Annual Hawaii International Conference on System Sciences*. IEEE.

Milenkovic, A., & Milutinovic, V. (2000, August). Cache injection: A novel technique for tolerating memory latency in bus-based SMPs. In *European Conference on Parallel Processing* (pp. 558-566). Springer.

Milutinovic, D., Milutinovic, V., & Soucek, B. (1987). *The honeycomb architecture*. Academic Press.

Milutinovic, V. (1996). *Surviving the design of a 200MHz RISC microprocessor*. IEEE Computer Society Press.

Milutinović, V., Salom, J., Trifunović, N., & Giorgi, R. (2015). *Guide to dataflow supercomputing*. Springer Nature.

Milutinovic, V. M. (1980). Comparison of three suboptimum detection procedures. *Electronics Letters*, *16*(17), 681–683.

Radivojevic, Z., Cvetanovic, M., Milutinovic, V., & Sievert, J. (2003). Data mining: A brief overview and recent IPSI research. *Annals of Mathematics, Computing, and Teleinformatics*, *1*(1), 84–91.

Trifunovic, N., Milutinovic, V., Salom, J., & Kos, A. (2015). Paradigm shift in big data supercomputing: Dataflow vs. controlflow. *Journal of Big Data*, *2*(1), 1–9.

Trobec, R., Vasiljević, R., Tomašević, M., Milutinović, V., Beivide, R., & Valero, M. (2016). Interconnection networks in petascale computer systems: A survey. *ACM Computing Surveys*, *49*(3), 1–24.

Von Neumann, J. (1951). The general and logical theory of automata. Pergamon Press *1951*, 1-41.

Chapter 2
Introduction to Control Flow

Ivan Ratković
 https://orcid.org/0000-0002-0524-7227
Esperanto Technologies, Serbia

Miljan Djordjevic
University of Belgrade, Serbia

ABSTRACT

Modern supercomputer designs fall into distinct categories – data and control flow supercomputer design paradigms. Control flow stands as the go-to design philosophy in all von Neumann machines dominating the market thus far. New types of problems demand a different flow mindset – this is where the data flow machines come in play. This chapter introduces control-flow concept as well as its state-of-the-art examples. Introduction section goes over definitions of terms used in succeeding chapters and gives their brief explanations. A brief explanation of supercomputing as a whole given in the Introduction section is then followed by explanations of the data and control flow design philosophies, with real-world examples of both – multi-core, many-core, vector processors, and GPUs in Control Flow Paradigm section. The third section covers real-world processing unit examples, with a rundown of the best standard and low power commercial and supercomputing market representatives.

INTRODUCTION TO SUPERCOMPUTERS AND THEIR TWO DESIGN PARADIGMS

Supercomputers represent the most powerful computing systems on the planet. First supercomputers were introduced in the 1960s (Cray-1) – the term was broader at that time and the fact that a computer works faster than other general-purpose computers was enough to classify it as a supercomputer (Oyanagi, 2002). Computing has gone so far that chips found in today's pocket devices are more powerful than supercomputers of the past. Initial improvements in supercomputer design involved adding more cores, either general purpose or specialized cores used for highly parallelized task execution. Among the first breakthroughs were the vector machines – processors which operate on whole arrays of data – their single instruction can do as much calculation as a whole program on a normal computer. At the start of

DOI: 10.4018/978-1-7998-7156-9.ch002

the 21st century, general-purpose CPUs become powerful enough to invoke a design philosophy shift in supercomputer architectures – today's supercomputers are built as systems consisting of large amounts of general-purpose market CPUs. With the rapid improvements in GPU power, the latest innovations in supercomputing also take advantage of market class GPUs in order of achieving unparalleled performance gains on specific types of tasks. Unlike general-purpose computers, supercomputers are used for formidable tasks (large scale simulations, weather prediction, cryptanalysis, machine learning, big data problems) which require serious speed and power. Supercomputer's performance is measured in FLOPS (floating-point operations per second) instead of MIPS (million instructions per second) like in general-purpose computers. Today's supercomputers reach up to 100 petaFLOPS and building a supercomputer whose power would be measured in exaFLOPS presents a major challenge of 2020 and beyond.

Out of all applications supercomputers are used for, problems involving manipulating and analyzing massive amounts of data, where normal processing techniques in many cases fail to deliver any results at all, today's so-called big data problems in machine learning and computer vision (deep learning, speech recognition, data mining, genomics, object recognition…), are the primary motivators for dividing supercomputer architecture design philosophies into two classes, those being:

- Control Flow Super Computing Paradigm
- Data Flow Super Computing Paradigm

Computers of the past primarily followed the control flow principle, with programs being executed linearly, in one dimension. With Big Data problems becoming more and more important, with the amount of overall data collected in the past few years surpassing all data collected up to that point, a new approach in computer design was introduced – data flow computing, which essentially differs from the traditional control flow computing in the way program is executed. Unlike control flow, data flow machines use specific hardware capabilities to allow for two-dimensional program execution, in which all task execution is carried out in parallel, while program execution linearity is not guaranteed. With the rise in interest in Machine Learning problems, their high computation cost and only increasing datasets used in trainings, data flow has become increasingly relevant, and for those kinds of applications more important that control flow computing.

CONTROL FLOW PARADIGM

Traditional processing units follow the control flow design philosophy – the emphasis is put on the strict program execution flow which guaranties the instruction execution order predictability. Those processing units aren't limited by power consumption restrains and are often top of the line CISC processors. Today's CPUs are prime examples of control flow architecture in practice – their efficiency is based on caches (instruction and data), data and instruction locality, and branch predictions. Program execution is one dimensional and mostly sequential. Programs executed on these types of machines would be traditional programs with one-dimensional execution.

ISA

ISA, short for Instruction set architecture, stands for an abstract computing model, while its implementations are CPUs, GPUs, etc. ISA of a processor covers all the parts of it which are visible to the programmer. ISA serves as a communication technique between the computer's software and hardware. It defines all of the programmer-visible components and operations of the computer: memory organization – address space and addressability; register set – how many registers of what size and how are they used; instruction set – opcodes (operation selection codes), data types (byte or word), addressing modes (coding schemes to access data). ISAs are most commonly classified into CISC and RISC architectures. Complex Instruction Set Computing (CISC) features complex instructions (many of which are rarely used in most programs) and good code density. Reduced Instruction Set Computing (RISC) features many single-cycle instructions that reduce the clock cycles per instruction and aggressive implementation allowed by simpler instructions which improve clock cycle time. A prime example of ISA is the x86 family of ISAs, developed by Intel on the Intel 8086 microprocessor. The secret of x86's longevity lies in the inertia to change to a different architecture since all of the succeeding processors and software written were tailored toward the x86 architecture. Today, x86 remains on top when it comes to the high-performance (HP) server market, but mid and low range market was overtaken by ARM. A new ISA is on the rise, the open-source RISC-V, which is rapidly overtaking mid and low market from ARM and is attacking the x86 high-end market (Takahashi, 2019).

Multi-Core, Manycore, Vector Processors and GPUs

CPUs can be described as multi-core microprocessors while GPUs are manycore multiprocessors. The following section includes brief descriptions of multi-core, manycore, vector processors and GPUs.

Multi-Core Processors

A multi-core processor is a computer processor integrated circuit with two or more separate processing units on the same chip. They rose in popularity in 1990. when the theories about one core processor dominance became obsolete. Individual processing units are called cores, and each of them executes a program as if it were a separate processing unit. Exploiting instruction-level parallelism attempted at the single-core processors proves to introduce more down-sides than up-sides (Schauer, 2008), so multicore processors take advantage of thread-level parallelism instead. Instruction level parallelism on a single-core processor proves power inefficient. Multicore processor executes a single program by utilizing multithreading, or by separating the task into smaller ones that can be done in parallel on several cores instead of one. Multicore program execution does not guarantee a speedup, the speedup is rather achieved by the problem in hand – so-called embarrassingly parallel programs can utilize the full set of processors as they can be equally and completely separated between all cores. Parallelization of a non-embarrassingly parallel problem often introduces greater programming overhead. This sometimes even go so far as to require redefining the problem's specifications from the ground up. A multicore processor with two cores requires less power to operate than Stwo separate processors (Schauer, 2008). Additional speedup in multicore processors comes from low cache access costs caused by the fact that several processing units share the same die with L1 cache. Main disadvantages of multicore processors are the requirement for a more complex cooling system and the fact that full utilization of a multicore system's power requires writing more sophisticated code. Additional concerns are cache consistency, coherence, and their power consumption (Schauer, 2008) – groups of cores on the same die share a cache, but the problems arise from the shared, higher-order caches.

Manycore Processors

Manycore processors are a special variant of multicore processors, differing from them by the amount of cores featured – they contain vastly greater amounts of cores, from a few tens to a few thousand cores. Multicore processors are often defined as processors featuring between 2 and 8 cores, while manycore processors feature dozens or thousands. Manycore processors sacrifice single-thread performance in order of achieving a higher degree of explicit parallelism and lower power needs. While multicore systems allow for both single thread as well as parallel execution performance, manycore processors focus strictly on highly parallelized task execution. Manycore processors are similar to clusters and vector processors, while GPUs can be taken as processing units similar in nature to manycore processors – they have high throughput and terrible single-thread performance.

Vector Processors

Vector processors or array processors are processors that operate one-dimensional arrays of data, so-called vectors. Their improved performance over regular processors come from the fact that instructions are carried out over arrays instead of single data items. Vector processors become the main processors used for creating supercomputers between 1970. and 1990. after which they were replaced by multicore processors, which saw a massive improvement in performance at that period. To put things into perspective, for under 1000\$ it was possible to buy a laptop in 2011. with clock speed higher than any vector supercomputers in the world. Vector processors use vector instructions that improve code density. Sequential data arrangement helps to handle the data by the hardware in a better way. Vector instruction's bandwidth is reduced. The biggest disadvantages of vector processors are slower memory access and lower startup times caused by their pipeline's lengths. Modern GPUs include an array of shader pipelines which can be considered vector processors. There are two main types of vector processors:

- Classical (traditional) vector processors
- Short vector extension processors

Vector processors are becoming quite interesting in the mobile device and server markets due to their inherently energy-efficient way of exploring data-level parallelism. Traditional vector processors are rarely found in the real-world systems and are primarily used in research. However, short vector extension processors are widespread – Intel's and AMD's advanced vector extension (Intel, 2014).

While vector processors succeeded in the high-performance market in the past, they need a re-tailoring for their potential reappearance in the mobile market (Ratković, 2016). Vector processor designs of the past did not focus on the low power market, which is shaping up as the place of resurfacing for these types of processors (Duric et al., 2015; Ratković et al., 2018; Stanic et al., 2017).

Graphics Processing Units

GPU or a graphics processing unit, is a specialized general-purpose computer peripheral device used for executing computer graphics-based operations. Traditional graphics processing units operate on the image data and write the results to their internal memory, communicate with a display device to display the contents of said memory. Although they existed as specialized graphics circuits in arcade system boards since the 1970s, they were popularized in the 1990s by Nvidia, when their primary functionality consisted of shader calculators. Up until 2005. their primary target audiences were graphics designers and the video game market. The rise in popularity of Big Data problems, specific framework, and tools that allow for general-purpose computing to be carried out on a graphics processing unit were introduced (Intel, 2016a). These frameworks allow the programmer to send the data from the CPU memory to the GPU memory as if it were a picture, and then use GPUs specific highly parallel architecture as the means of executing programs that would otherwise be impossible to execute on a CPU due to its slow performance on these kinds of tasks. Today's general-purpose graphics processing unit software allows programmers to work with ever more complex data structures on a graphics card. On the other hand, today's chip developer efforts are often put toward creating a central processing unit featuring specialized hardware that can be used for advanced graphical processing. Some of the most powerful designs of this sort were demonstrated in January of 2020. by Intel (Intel, 2016a). The biggest issue in CPU-GPU communication is the data transfer between the two and making both of those processing units occupy the same space and therefore reducing the costs of their intercommunication is an obvious goal for these kinds of systems in the future.

Control Flow vs. Data Flow

Control flow and data flow (elaborated in detail later in the book) performance cannot be strictly compared since both design paradigms serve a specific purpose. In general terms, control flow is a go-to architecture for any general-purpose computing, since it's processing units are many orders of magnitude stronger than data flow processing units. Control flow processing units have the advantage of being flexible – they are capable of carrying out a much more diverse set of operations than any data flow processing units. Data flow architectures serve primarily as accelerators for specific types of tasks, being able to spread a simpler task over a larger net of processing units and delivering results that are otherwise impossible to finish on control flow machines due to the time it would take to process the immense amount of data. Control flow machines can be viewed as hosts, while data flow machines are the accelerators added on top of the control flow host for the specific type of load handling – today's big data problems. In essence, those two are incomparable, and the discussion of which is better: several horses or several thousand chickens can be resolved simply – it all depends on the task in hand. The perfect machine is neither strictly control-flow nor data-flow in nature – the perfect machine must combine both of those design philosophies in its different parts to be able to perform at the highest level no matter the given task. The ideal program of the future is separable into the main part requiring strict instruction execution order and the data processing part which can extract the data processing and distribute it onto the hardware accelerators returning the processing result in a non-linear fashion. Control flow remains the go-to hyper capable architecture with the flexibility of executing any set of instructions, while the data problem of the past few years makes the inclusion of the data flow accelerators required in modern machines. One of the AI-based processors which combine both the data and control flow design paradigms is the Habana Goya processor (Wiki Chip, 2018). Special class of data flow processors are the so-called reconfig processors, processors which adjust their hardware to achieve the best performance for the current workload.

STATE OF THE ART CONTROL FLOW PROCESSORS

This chapter provides state of the art overview for different computer markets.

Commercial Market

Modern computing market is dominated by Intel, AMD, Nvidia, and ARM CPUs and GPUs. Some of the top high-end CPUs of 2020 are:

- AMD Ryzen 9 3950X with 16 cores/32 threads, a base clock of 3.5GHz (boost clock 4.7GHz), 64MB of L3 cache memory, and TDP of 105W
- AMD Ryzen Threadripper 3960X with 24 cores/48 threads, a base clock speed of 3.8GHz (boost clock of 4.5GHz), 128MB of L3 cache and TDP of 280W
- Intel Core i5-10600K featuring cornet lake architecture, 6 cores/12 threads, a base frequency of 3.5GHz (boost clock 4.7GHz) and TDP of 128W
- Intel Core i9-10900K featuring cornet lake architecture, 10 cores/20 threads, a base frequency of 3.7GHz (boost frequency of 5.3GHz), 20MB Intel Smart Cache, and TDP of 125W

AMD Ryzen 3900 series processors introduce the Zen 2 architecture, which reduces the processor node size from 12nm to 7nm, support for the new PCIe 4.0 standard on an X570 chipset (AMD, 2017). Intel's newest line of processors, the so-called 10th generation processors, use the Ice Lake processor architecture which reduces the node size from Comet Lake's 14nm to 10nm (Intel, 2019).

Intel's Xeon line of processors is of special importance in the supercomputing commercial market. Xeon processor cores work on lower clock speeds than Intel's desktop CPUs, but they feature many more cores, ECC memory, support bigger caches, and are generally inclined towards highly parallel tasks. Xeon processors are CPUs in the full sense of that word, and don't possess any integrated graphics processing hardware. Later introduced Xeon Phi series contradicts this, as its first-generation Xeon Phi defined coprocessing units, while the following generations' changes pushed Xeon Phi closer to traditional CPUs, resulting in hybrid architectures (Intel, 2016a). Example of a Xeon series CPU is the Intel Xeon E7-8890 v4 which launched in the second quarter of 2016 with 24 cores/48 threads, base core frequency of 2.20GHz, max core frequency of 3.40GHz, 60MB cache and TDP of 165W (Intel, 2016b).

With the Ryzen CPU series, AMD has brought competition back to a stagnant market. While new yearly Intel processors have introduced smaller updates to the previous chips, AMD has pushed the bar for CPU power higher than ever before, surpassing Intel in CPU performance (Gartenberg, 2020). AMD's new chips offer higher speeds and more cores, but Intel's cores remain better when it comes to power consumption (Ou, 2006).

Some of the most powerful standard graphics processing units of 2020 are:

- Nvidia RTX 2080 Ti with Turing (TU102) architecture, 4352 cores, boost clock at 1545MHz, 11GB of GDDR6 14Gbps VRAM, and TDP of 250W (NVIDIA, 2018a)
- Radeon RX 5700 XT featuring Navi 10 architecture, 2560 cores, boost clock at 1755MHz, 8GB of GDDR6 14Gbps VRAM and TDP of 225W (AMD, 2019)

Figure 1. AMD's Zen 2 architecture – each chipset consists of 8 cores split into two groups of 4 cores, manufactured using the 7nm MOSFET. The biggest difference from previous versions of the Zen architecture lies in the decision to separate the I/O hardware to a separate chip manufactured using 12nm MOSFET. Source: Adapted from Ref. (Wiki Chip, 2019).

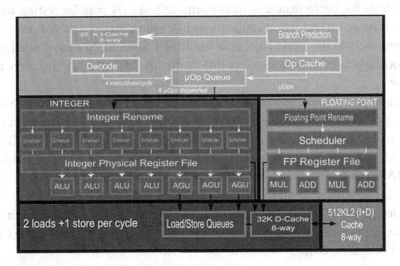

Ray tracing technology has impacted the GPU market over the past couple of years, and Nvidia's top graphics card is marketed as the world's first ray-tracing GPU:

- NVIDIA Quadro RTX 8000 with Turing (TU102) architecture, featuring 4608 CUDA Parallel-processing cores, 576 NVIDIA Tensor cores, 48GB GDDR6 VRAM and TDP of 260W (NVIDIA, 2018b)

Mainstream vector processor solution does not exist, since supercomputers, being their primary use domain, have switched to multicore processors during the 1990s. Vector processors might see a return following the proposals of a modified vector-scalar ARM architecture (Stephens et al., 2017).

Commercial Low Power Market

ARM focuses on designing instruction sets and blueprints for mobile systems-on-a-chip which companies like Apple, Samsung, and Qualcomm license and then use in their mobile devices. Two examples of ARM's top of the line CPUs and GPUs are given bellow:

- ARM Cortex-A77 (CPU) with a max clock of 3.0GHz in phones and 3.3GHz in tablets and laptop devices, 1-4MB of L3 cache, and 1-4 cores per cluster (Design & Reuse, 2020)

- ARM Mali-G77 MP11 (GPU) with 7-16 shader cores, a core clock of 850MHz, 512-4096KiB of L2 cache (ARM Ltd, 2019)

Supercomputing Market

Three lists are of most importance when it comes to supercomputers: TOP500, Green500, and Graph500. They contain the top 500 supercomputers currently operating on the planet ranked by a certain metric: TOP500 is the main list which ranks based on a test featuring a linear equation problem, Green500 is based on the most energy-efficient supercomputers measured as LINPACK FLOPS per watt (Matlis, 2005), Graph500 tests for performance at data-intensive tasks. A popular testing tool is the HPCG benchmark which is based on real-world applications like sparse matrix calculations. Some of the most powerful supercomputers in the world right now are IBM's Summit, Sunway TaihuLight and Tianhe-2A. The design of these three supercomputers differs greatly, and their architectures are described in some detail below.

Summit, with 200 petaFLOPS, was the fastest supercomputer in the world from November 2018 to June 2020. Summit covers the space of two basketball courts and requires 136 miles of cabling. Summit consists of 4,608 nodes, each containing 2 IBM POWER9 CPUs and 6 Nvidia Tesla GPUs. Its 6*16GB HBM2 and 2*8*32GB DDR4 SDRAM is addressable by all CPUs and GPUs. 800 additional gigabytes of non-volatile RAM can be used as a burst buffer or as extended memory (NVIDIA, 2014).

Sunway TaihuLight, with 93 petaFLOPS, was the third-fastest supercomputer in November 2018. 40,960 Chinese-designed SW26010 manycore 64-bit RISC processors each containing 256 cores and additional four auxiliary cores for system management make up a total of 10,649,600 CPU cores across the entire system (Dongarra, 2016).

Tianhe-2A was the fastest supercomputer in the world from June 2013 to June 2016 (33.86 petaFLOPS). 16,000 nodes (each containing two Intel Ivy Bridge Xeon processors and three Xeon Phi coprocessors) or 3,120,000 cores at peak power consumption drain 17.6 megawatts of power.

IBM's Power9 processors are a special line of processors which IBM develops specifically for supercomputers. Power9 is manufactured using the 14nm FinFET process, and its cores work on 4GHz. Power9 processors are based on the open-source Power ISA released in 2016. Power9 processors have 12-24 cores and their different variants can handle bandwidths from 120GB/s to 230GB/s (IBMIT Infrastructure, 2017).

Fugaku

Of special importance is the Japanese Fugaku supercomputer, being the fastest supercomputer at the top of the TOP500 list (Top500, 2020) with an ARM core architecture. Fugaku reaches the high-performance Linpack result of 415.5 petaflops. Fugaku is powered by Fujitsu's 48 core (with 4 assistant cores; all cores are identical) A64FX SoC – ARM developed processor, first to use the ARMv8.2-A Scalable Vector Extension SIMD instruction set with 512-bit vector implementation. Fujitsu A64FX uses 32GB of HBM2 memory with a bandwidth of 1TB per second (Top500, 2020). A64FX is based on 7nm FinFET with 8,786M transistors.

Figure 2. A64FX consists of four Core Memory Groups each one featuring 13 cores (12 regular cores and one assistant core which handles deamon, I/O, etc.; all 13 cores are the same - the assistant core differs only in its function), an L2 cache and a memory controller. A64FX has out-of-order mechanisms in cores, caches and memory controllers, 64KiB L1D, 8MiB L2 cache, and 8GiB of HBM2 memory. A64FX has a mainframe-class RAS for integrity and stability: ECC or duplication for all caches, parity check for execution units, hardware instruction retry, hardware lane recovery for Tofu links, and ~128,440 error check-in total.
Source: Adapted from Ref. (Yoshida, 2018).

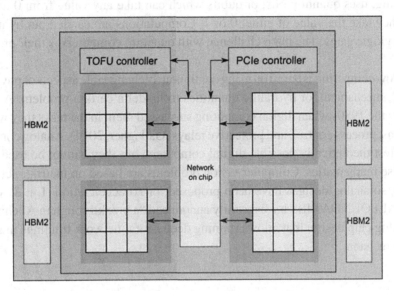

Low Power Market

If Moore's law is to continue, and extremely expensive cooling solutions required to keep it going avoided, hardware design must become oriented towards power and energy efficiency. As frequency scaling has stopped following Moore's law some time ago, new solutions are focusing on achieving faster execution without an increase in power. Low power processors achieve their power efficiency by sacrificing processing power. While regular supercomputers sometimes generate so much heat that they can even be used to heat an entire campus building (Office of Technology Transitions, 2014), low power supercomputers are capable of working under normal air conditioning at room temperature.

IBM Blue Gene is an example of a low power supercomputer which can reach petaFLOPS of power. Blue Gene has topped the Green500 list many times in the past (Blue Gene/Q (three models were developed in total: Blue Gene/L, Blue Gene/P and Blue Gene/Q) took top positions in all three top supercomputing performance lists: TOP500, Graph500 and Green500 in June of 2012).

Blue Gene/Q is the third and final in the series of IBM produced Blue Gene supercomputers. Blue Gene/Q is built from A2 64bit processors – massively multicore processors designed using the POWER ISA v.2.06 specification by IBM. Blue Gene's chip consists of 18 cores that run at 1.6GHz– 16 of which are used for computing, one for interrupts, MPI pacing, and asynchronous I/O, and one which is used as a spare (Ohmacht, 2011). With a total of 65536 processor cores, Blue Gene ranked 17th on the TOP500 list in November of 2011. with 677 TeraFLOPS LINPACK score.

Future Supercomputers

Exascale supercomputers are expected in the next few years, but the farther future of supercomputing promises to be a bit more interesting. New architectures will replace today's designs, and some of the candidates right now are quantum (Ornes, 2019) and analog data flow (Ulmann, 2019).

Quantum computers were first introduced by physicist Paul Benioff in the 1980s when he proposed a quantum mechanical model of the Turing machine. Quantum circuit, the most widely used model in quantum computing, uses quantum bits, or qubits which can take any value from 0 to 1 until they are observed when they take the value of either 0 or 1. Computations are carried out by manipulating qubits with quantum logic gates. The main challenge with quantum computers is their proneness to errors (Scarani, 2012).

Analog data flow computing is based on using continuously changeable aspects of physical phenomena such as electrical, mechanical, or hydraulic quantities to model a certain problem. Analog computers were used up until the 1980s when digital computing surpassed them in the tasks they were designed for – flight simulations, process control, and protective relays (Gallagher, 2014). Analog computers are faster even than the fastest theoretically possible digital computers, but they cannot be used for applications that require precise mathematics. Computer vision problems are based on matrix operations, but don't require precision, so analog designs have been proposed for AI acceleration (Liu & Mullaney, 2020). Imac and GLOBALFOUNDARIES have recently announced "a breakthrough in AI chip" (Cosemans et al., 2019), an analog chip design that allows running deep neural network trainings in analog hardware logic with great precision.

CONCLUSION

This chapter provided an introduction to control-flow computing paradigm. Section I covered the history of supercomputing, Section II introduced the two design paradigms in supercomputing while putting greater emphasis on the control flow paradigm's advantages. Section II also serves as a defining chapter for four different types of processing units. Overview of the regular and supercomputing markets were given in the Section III with detailed covers of the fastest supercomputers currently available on the market.

REFERENCES

AMD. (2017). *Processor Programming Reference (PPR) for AMD Family 17h Model 01h, Revision B1 Processors*. Retrieved August 7, 2020, from https://developer.amd.com/wordpress/media/2017/11/54945_PPR_Family_17h_Models_00h-0Fh.pdf

AMD. (2019). *Radeon™ RX 5700 XT Graphics*. Retrieved August 4, 2020, from https://www.amd.com/en/products/graphics/amd-radeon-rx-5700-xt

ARM Ltd. (2019). *Mali-G77*. Retrieved September 28, 2020, from https://www.arm.com/products/silicon-ip-multimedia/gpu/mali-g77

Cosemans, S., Verhoef, B., Doevenspeck, J., Papistas, I. A., Catthoor, F., Debacker, P., ... Verkest, D. (2019, December). Towards 10000TOPS/W DNN Inference with Analog in-Memory Computing–A Circuit Blueprint, Device Options and Requirements. In *2019 IEEE International Electron Devices Meeting (IEDM)* (pp. 22-2). IEEE. 10.1109/IEDM19573.2019.8993599

Design & Reuse. (2020). *Fourth-Generation, High-Performance CPU Based on DynamIQ Technology*. Retrieved September 28, 2020, from https://www.design-reuse.com/sip/fourth-generation-high-performance-cpu-based-on-dynamiq-technology-ip-48140/

Dongarra, J. (2016). *Report on the sunway taihulight system*. www. netlib. org

Duric, M., Stanic, M., Ratkovic, I., Palomar, O., Unsal, O., Cristal, A., ... Smith, A. (2015, July). Imposing coarse-grained reconfiguration to general purpose processors. In *2015 International Conference on Embedded Computer Systems: Architectures, Modeling, and Simulation (SAMOS)* (pp. 42-51). IEEE. 10.1109/SAMOS.2015.7363658

Gallagher, S. (2014, March 18). *Gears of war: When mechanical analog computers ruled the waves*. Retrieved September 28, 2020, from https://web.archive.org/web/20180908173957/https://arstechnica.com/information-technology/2014/03/gears-of-war-when-mechanical-analog-computers-ruled-the-waves/

Gartenberg, C. (2020, January 6). *AMD's 7nm Ryzen 4000 CPUs are here to take on Intel's 10nm Ice Lake laptop chips*. Retrieved September 28, 2020, from https://www.theverge.com/2020/1/6/21054007/amd-7nm-ryzen-4000-cpu-ces-2020-intel-competition-laptop-processors-zen-2

IBMIT Infrastructure. (2017). *POWER9 processor chip*. Retrieved September 28, 2020, from https://www.ibm.com/it-infrastructure/power/power9

Intel. (2014). *Optimizing performance with Intel Advanced Vector Extensions*. Retrieved August 11, 2020, from https://www.intel.com/content/dam/www/public/us/en/documents/white-papers/performance-xeon-e5-v3-advanced-vector-extensions-paper.pdf

Intel. (2016a). *Intel® Xeon® Processors*. Retrieved September 28, 2020, from https://www.intel.com/content/www/us/en/products/processors/xeon.html

Intel. (2016b). *Intel® Xeon® Processor E7-8890 v4 (60M Cache, 2.20 GHz) Product Specifications*. Retrieved September 28, 2020, from https://ark.intel.com/content/www/us/en/ark/products/93790/intel-xeon-processor-e7-8890-v4-60m-cache-2-20-ghz.htmld

Intel. (2019, August 21). *Intel Expands 10th Gen Intel Core Mobile Processor Family, Offering Double Digit Performance Gains*. Retrieved September 28, 2020, from https://newsroom.intel.com/news/intel-expands-10th-gen-intel-core-mobile-processor-family-offering-double-digit-performance-gains/

Intel. (2020). *Intel CES*. Retrieved August 11, 2020, from https://newsroom.intel.com/press-kits/2020-ces/#gs.d6lufh

Liu, J., & Mullaney, M. (2020, July 8). *Imec and GLOBALFOUNDRIES Announce Breakthrough in AI Chip, Bringing Deep Neural Network Calculations to IoT Edge Devices*. Retrieved September 28, 2020, from https://www.imec-int.com/en/articles/imec-and-globalfoundries-announce-breakthrough-in-ai-chip-bringing-deep-neural-network-calculations-to-iot-edge-devices

Matlis, J. (2005, May 30). *Sidebar: The Linpack Benchmark*. Retrieved September 28, 2020, from https://www.computerworld.com/article/2556400/sidebar--the-linpack-benchmark.html

NVIDIA. (2010). *The Evolution of GPUs for General Purpose Computing*. Retrieved August 14, 2020, from https://www.nvidia.com/content/gtc-2010/pdfs/2275_gtc2010.pdf

NVIDIA. (2014, November). *Summit and Sierra Supercomputers: An Inside Look at the U.S. Department of Energy's New Pre-Exascale Systems*. Retrieved August 4, 2020 from http://www.teratec.eu/actu/calcul/Nvidia_Coral_White_Paper_Final_3_1.pdf

NVIDIA. (2018a). *Graphics Reinvented: NVIDIA GeForce RTX 2080 Ti Graphics Card*. Retrieved August 4, 2020 from https://www.nvidia.com/en-eu/geforce/graphics-cards/rtx-2080-ti/

NVIDIA. (2018b). *Quadro RTX 8000 Graphics Card | NVIDIA Quadro*. Retrieved September 28, 2020, from https://www.nvidia.com/en-us/design-visualization/quadro/rtx-8000/

Office of Technology Transitions. (2014). *NREL's Building-Integrated Supercomputer Provides Heating and Efficient Computing*. Retrieved September 28, 2020, from https://www.energy.gov/technologytransitions/nrels-building-integrated-supercomputer-provides-heating-and-efficient

Ohmacht, M. (2011). *Memory Speculation of the Blue Gene/Q Compute Chip*. Academic Press.

Ornes, S. (2019, December 28). *Quantum Computers Finally Beat Supercomputers in 2019*. Retrieved September 28, 2020, from https://www.discovermagazine.com/the-sciences/quantum-computers-finally-beat-supercomputers-in-2019

Ou, G. (2006, July 17). *Who to believe on power consumption? AMD or Intel?* Retrieved September 28, 2020, from https://www.zdnet.com/article/who-to-believe-on-power-consumption-amd-or-intel/

Oyanagi, Y. (2002). Future of supercomputing. *Journal of Computational and Applied Mathematics*, *149*(1), 147–153. doi:10.1016/S0377-0427(02)00526-5

Ratković, I. (2016). *On the design of power-and energy-efficient functional units for vector processors*. Academic Press.

Ratković, I., Palomar, O., Stanić, M., Ünsal, O. S., Cristal, A., & Valero, M. (2018). Vector processing-aware advanced clock-gating techniques for low-power fused multiply-add. *IEEE Transactions on Very Large Scale Integration (VLSI) Systems*, *26*(4), 639–652.

Scarani, V. (2012). Quantum Computing: A Gentle Introduction. *PhT*, *65*(2), 53.

Schauer, B. (2008). Multicore processors–a necessity. *ProQuest discovery guides*, 1-14.

Stanic, M., Palomar, O., Hayes, T., Ratkovic, I., Cristal, A., Unsal, O., & Valero, M. (2017). An integrated vector-scalar design on an in-order ARM core. *ACM Transactions on Architecture and Code Optimization*, *14*(2), 1–26. doi:10.1145/3075618

Stephens, N., Biles, S., Boettcher, M., Eapen, J., Eyole, M., Gabrielli, G., ... Reid, A. (2017). The ARM scalable vector extension. *IEEE Micro*, *37*(2), 26–39. doi:10.1109/MM.2017.35

Takahashi, D. (2019, December 14). *RISC-V grows globally as an alternative to Arm and its license fees.* Retrieved September 28, 2020, from https://venturebeat.com/2019/12/11/risc-v-grows-globally-as-an-alternative-to-arm-and-its-license-fees/

Top500. (2020, June 22). *News.* Retrieved September 28, 2020, from https://www.top500.org/news/japan-captures-top500-crown-arm-powered-supercomputer/

Ulmann, B. (2019, July 22). *Why Algorithms Suck and Analog Computers are the Future.* Retrieved September 28, 2020, from https://blog.degruyter.com/algorithms-suck-analog-computers-future/

Wiki Chip. (2018). *Goya Microarchitectures.* Retrieved August 7, 2020, from https://en.wikichip.org/wiki/habana/microarchitectures/goya

Wiki Chip. (2019). *Zen 2 - Microarchitectures - AMD.* Retrieved September 28, 2020, from https://en.wikichip.org/wiki/amd/microarchitectures/zen_2

Yoshida, T. (2018, August). Fujitsu high performance CPU for the Post-K Computer. In Hot Chips (Vol. 30). Academic Press.

Chapter 3
Optimal Scheduling of Parallel Jobs With Unknown Service Requirements

Benjamin Berg
Carnegie Mellon University, USA

Mor Harchol-Balter
Carnegie Mellon University, USA

ABSTRACT

Large data centers composed of many servers provide the opportunity to improve performance by parallelizing jobs. However, effectively exploiting parallelism is non-trivial. For each arriving job, one must decide the number of servers on which the job is run. The goal is to determine the optimal allocation of servers to jobs that minimizes the mean response time across jobs – the average time from when a job arrives until it completes. Parallelizing a job across multiple servers reduces the response time of that individual job. However, jobs receive diminishing returns from being allocated additional servers, so allocating too many servers to a single job leads to low system efficiency. The authors consider the case where the remaining sizes of jobs are unknown to the system at every moment in time. They prove that, if all jobs follow the same speedup function, the optimal policy is EQUI, which divides servers equally among jobs. When jobs follow different speedup functions, EQUI is no longer optimal and they provide an alternate policy, GREEDY*, which performs within 1% of optimal in simulation.

1. INTRODUCTION

The Parallelization Tradeoff

Modern data centers are composed of a large number of servers, affording programmers the opportunity to run jobs faster by parallelizing across many servers. To exploit this opportunity, jobs are often designed to run on any number of servers (Delimitrou & Kozyrakis, 2014). Running on additional serv-

DOI: 10.4018/978-1-7998-7156-9.ch003

ers may reduce a job's response time, the time from when the job arrives to the system until it is completed. However, effectively exploiting parallelism is non-trivial. Specifically, one must decide how many servers to allocate to each job in the system at every moment in time. We consider the setting where jobs arrive over time, and the system must choose each job's level of parallelization in order to minimize the mean response time across jobs. In choosing each job's server allocation, one must consider the following tradeoff. Parallelizing an individual job across multiple servers reduces the response time of that individual job. In practice, however, each job receives a diminishing marginal benefit from being allocated additional servers. Hence, allocating too many servers to a single job may decrease overall system efficiency. While a larger server allocation may decrease an individual job's response time, the net effect may be an increase in the overall mean response time across jobs. We therefore aim to design a system which balances this tradeoff, choosing each job's server allocation in order to minimize the mean response time across all jobs. It was shown in (Bienia et al., 2008) that many of the benefits and overheads of parallelization can be encapsulated in a job's speedup function, $s(k)$, which specifies a job's service rate on k servers. If we normalize $s(1)$ to be 1, we see that a job will complete s(k) times faster on k servers than on a single server. In general, it is conceivable that every job will have a different speedup function. However, there are also many workloads (Bienia et al., 2008) where all jobs have the same speedup function, such as when one runs many instances of the same program. It turns out that even allocating servers to jobs which follow a single speedup function is non-trivial. Hence, we will first focus on jobs following a single speedup function before turning our attention to multiple speedup functions. In addition to differing in their speedup functions, different jobs may represent different amounts of computation that must be performed. For example, if a data center is processing search queries, a simple query might require much less processing than a complex query. We refer to the amount of inherent work associated with a job as the job's size. It is common in data centers that job sizes are unknown to the system { users are not required to tell the system anything about the internals of their jobs when they submit them. Hence, we consider the case where the system does not know, at any moment in time, the remaining sizes of the jobs currently in the system.

The question of how to best allocate servers to jobs is commonly referred to as the choice between fine grained parallelism, where every job is parallelized across a large number of servers, and coarse grained parallelism, where the server allocation of each job is kept small. This same tradeoff arises in many parallel systems beyond data centers. For example, (Berg et al., 2017) considers the case of jobs running on a multicore chip. In this case, running on additional cores allows an individual job to complete more quickly, but leads to an inefficient use of resources which could increase the response times of subsequent jobs. Additionally, an operating system might need to choose how to partition memory (cache space) between multiple applications. Likewise, a computer architect may have to choose between fewer, wider bus lanes for memory access, or several narrower bus lanes. In all cases, one must balance the effect on an individual job's response time with the effect on overall mean response time. Throughout this chapter, we will use the terminology of parallelizing jobs across servers, however all of our remarks can be applied equally to any setting where limited resources must be shared amongst concurrently running processes.

Our Model

We assume that jobs arrive into an n server system according to a Poisson Process with rate Λ jobs/second where

$$\ddot{E} := \ddot{e}n \tag{1}$$

for some λ. The random variable X denotes the size of a job, which represents the amount of inherent work associated with a job. We are interested in the common case where the remaining size of each job is unknown to the system at every moment in time. To model this, we assume that each job size, X, is drawn i.i.d. from an exponential distribution with rate μ (which may be unknown to the system). Due to the memoryless property of the exponential distribution, the remaining size of any job in the system is always distributed exponentially with rate μ, regardless of how long the job has been running. Hence, while the system may learn the mean job size over time, the system can never infer that one job has a smaller remaining size than another job. Any job can be run on any subset of the n servers, and running on additional servers increases the service rate that a job receives. Specifically, we define a speedup function, $s : \mathbb{R}_+ \to \mathbb{R}_+$, such that a job running on k servers receives a service rate of s(k) units of work per second. Hence, a job of size X which is parallelized across k servers would complete in X_k seconds, where

$$X_k = \frac{X}{s(k)}$$

In general, the analysis in this chapter will not make use of the specific form of the speedup function. We will, however, make some mild technical assumptions about the speedup function that reflect how parallelizable jobs behave in practice. First, we normalize the service rate that a job receives on a single server to be one unit of work per second, and therefore s(1) = 1. We will assume that the speedup function, $s : \mathbb{R}_+ \to \mathbb{R}_+$, is non-decreasing and concave, in agreement with functions described in (Hill & Marty, 2008). Note that, because servers can be shared between jobs in practice, the speedup function is defined for non-integer server allocations. Finally, we will focus on instances where jobs receive an imperfect speedup and thus s(k) is assumed to be sublinear: $s(k) < k$ for all $k > 1$ and there exists some constant $c > 0$ such that $s(k) < c$ for all $k \geq 0$. When a job runs on less than 1 server, we assume that there is no overhead due to parallelism, and hence the job receives a linear speedup up to 1 server. That is,

$$s(k) = k, \forall 0 \leq k \leq 1$$

An example of a well-known speedup function which obeys the above conditions is Amdahl's law (McCool et al., 2012), which models every job as having a fraction of work, p, which is parallelizable. The speedup factor $s(k)$ is then a function of the parameter p as follows:

$$s\left(k\right) = \frac{1}{\dfrac{p}{k} + 1 - p}, \forall 0 \leq k \leq 1$$

Figure 1 shows Amdahl's law under various values of p. Although Amdahl's law ignores aspects of job behavior, we also see in Figure 1 that several workloads from the PARSEC-3 benchmark (Zhan et al., 2017) follow speedup curves which can be accurately modeled by Amdahl's law. Hence, although our analysis will not rely on the specifics of the speedup function, we will use Amdahl's law in numerical examples. An allocation policy defines, at every moment in time, how many servers are allocated to each job which is currently in the system. Servers are assumed to be identical, and thus any job is capable of running on any server. An allocation policy can therefore allocate any number of servers to any job in the system as long as the total number of servers allocated to all jobs does not exceed n. Furthermore, jobs are assumed to be malleable, meaning a job can change the number of servers it runs on over time. Hence, an allocation policy is free to change the number of servers allocated to each job over time. We will first consider the case where jobs are homogeneous with respect to s - all jobs receive the same speedup due to parallelization. We will then consider the case of heterogeneous jobs which may follow different speedup functions.

Figure 1. Various speedup curves under (a) Amdahl's law and (b) the PARSEC-3 Benchmark. We see that the PARSEC-3 speedup curves are accurately approximated by Amdahl's law; these approximations are shown in (b) in light blue.

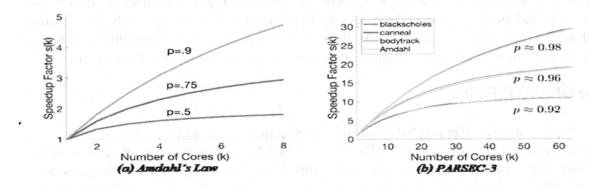

The Problem

The fact that modern parallel jobs are capable of running on any number of servers begs the question of how many servers should be allocated to each job. Let T denote the response time of a job (the time between when the job arrives and when all of its pieces have completed). Our goal is to find and analyze scheduling policies that minimize the mean response time, $\mathbb{E}[T]$, across all jobs. Clearly, $\mathbb{E}[T]$ depends on the allocation policy, the speedup function, s, the arrival rate of jobs into the system, Λ, the mean job size, $\mathbb{E}[X]$, and the number of servers, n. We will denote the mean response time under a particular allocation policy, P, as

$$\mathbb{E}[T]^{P}.$$

We define the average system load, ρ, to be

$$\rho := \frac{\ddot{E}\mathbb{E}[X]}{n}$$

This is equivalently the fraction of time a server is busy when each job is run on a single server. Thus, $\rho < 1$ is a necessary condition for stability, regardless of the allocation policy used. We assume both ρ and $s(\cdot)$ are constant over time. By Little's law, minimizing the mean response time across jobs is equivalent to minimizing the mean number of jobs in the system. Hence, we will frequently consider the number of jobs in the system, N, with the goal of minimizing the mean number of jobs in the system, $\mathbb{E}[N]$. We denote the mean number of jobs in the system under a particular allocation policy, P, to be

$$\mathbb{E}[N]^{P}.$$

The EQUI Policy

EQUI is a policy which first appeared in (Edmonds, 1999). Under EQUI, at all times, the n servers are equally divided among the jobs in the system. Specifically, whenever there are l jobs in the system, each job is parallelized across n / l servers. In Section 3, we prove that EQUI is optimal with respect to mean response time when jobs are homogeneous with respect to speedup (see Theorem 1).

The GREEDY* Policy

We consider the case where jobs follow different speedup functions in Section 4. We show that, when jobs are permitted to have different speedup functions, EQUI is no longer optimal. We also show how to numerically compute the optimal policy, OPT, when jobs follow multiple speedup functions. Since finding OPT is computationally intensive we introduce a simple class of policies, called GREEDY, that performs well by maximizing the departure rate. In Section 4.4, we prove that one policy in this class, GREEDY*, dominates by both maximizing the overall departure rate and deferring parallelizable work (see Theorem 2). When jobs follow multiple speedup functions, GREEDY* achieves a mean response time within 1% of OPT in wide range of simulations.

2. PRIOR WORK

Prior work on exploiting parallelism has traditionally been split between several disparate communities. The SIGMETRICS/Performance community frequently considers scheduling a stream of incoming jobs for execution across several servers with the goal of minimizing mean response time, e.g., (Gupta et al.,

Figure 2. A view of the EQUI policy with various numbers of jobs in the system. At every moment in time, EQUI divides the n = 16 servers equally among the jobs currently in the system.

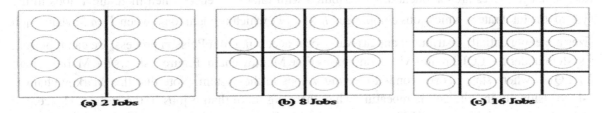

2007; Harchol-Balter et al., 2009; Lu et al., 2011; Nelson & Philips, 1993; Tsitsiklis & Xu, 2011). Job sizes are assumed to be random variables drawn from some general distribution, and arrivals are assumed to occur according to some stochastic arrival process. Typically, it is assumed that each individual job is run on just one server: jobs are not parallelizable. An exception is the work on Fork-Join queues. Here it is assumed that every job is parallelized across all servers (Ko & Serfozo, 2004); the question of finding the optimal level of parallelization is not addressed. This community has also considered systems where the service rate that a job receives can be adjusted over time, but this work has focused on balancing a tradeoff between response time and some other variable such as power consumption (Gandhi et al., 2009) or Goodness of Service (Chaitanya et al., 2008). By contrast, the SPAA/STOC/FOCS community extensively studies the effect of parallelism, however it largely focuses on a single job. More recently, this community has considered the effect of parallelization on the mean response time of a stream of jobs. However, this has been through the lens of competitive analysis, which assumes the job sizes (service times), arrival times, and even speedup curves are adversarially chosen, e.g. (Agrawal et al., 2016; Edmonds, 1999; Edmonds & Pruhs, 2009). Competitive analysis also does not yield closed form expressions for mean response time. We seek to analyze this problem using a more typical queueing theoretic model. Our workloads are drawn from distributions and our analysis yields closed-form expressions for mean response time as well as expressions for the optimal level of parallelization. The advent of moldable jobs which can run on any number of cores has pushed the high performance computing (HPC) systems community to consider how to effectively allocate cores to jobs (Anastasiadis & Sevcik, 1997; Cirne & Berman, 2002; Huang et al., 2013; Srinivasan et al., 2003). These studies tend to be empirical rather than analytical, each looking at specific workloads and architectures, often leading to conflicting results between studies. By contrast, this chapter considers this problem from a stochastic, analytical point of view, deriving optimal scheduling algorithms in a more general model.

3. EQUI: AN OPTIMAL POLICY

In order to effectively parallelize jobs, it makes sense to consider policies where the level of parallelization of each job depends on the state of the system. This may sound discouraging, since systems with state dependent service rates are in general hard to analyze. However, we will show that a very simple policy, EQUI, is both analytically tractable and optimal.

EQUI (Edmonds, 1999) is a generalization of Processor Sharing (Harchol-Balter, 2013) to systems with multiple servers. Under EQUI, whenever there are l jobs in the system, each job runs on n / l

servers. This corresponds to a service rate of $s\left(n\,/\,l\right)$ for each job when there are l jobs in the system. Recall that job sizes are exponentially distributed with rate μ. Hence, when there are l jobs in the system, the total rate at which jobs complete is $l\mu s\left(n\,/\,l\right)$ which is equal to $n\mu$ when $l \geq n$. Because job sizes are exponentially distributed and arrivals occur according to a Poisson process, we can represent a system under the EQUI policy via a continuous time Markov chain. Figure 3 shows the Markov chain for EQUI, where state i corresponds to having i jobs in the system. Note that this Markov chain is 1-Dimensionally infinite and is repeating when there are more than n jobs in the system. Hence, the mean number of jobs under EQUI can be analyzed via standard techniques (Harchol-Balter, 2013; Kleinrock, 1975). It is not immediately clear, however, that EQUI is optimal. Intuitively, EQUI appears to use the smallest degree of parallelism possible for each job without idling servers. While this prevents one from giving a highly inefficient allocation to any job, it seems possible that some policy could improve upon EQUI by exploiting parallelism more aggressively. In Section 3.1 we prove that EQUI is indeed optimal with respect to mean response time when all jobs follow the same speedup function and are exponentially distributed. We then explain the intuition behind this policy in Section 3.2.

3.1 Proving That EQUI Is Optimal

To prove that EQUI is optimal, we first prove a helpful lemma, Lemma 1.

Lemma 1 *For any concave, sublinear function, s, the function* $i \cdot s\left(\dfrac{n}{i}\right)$ *is increasing in* i *for all* $i < n$, *and is non-decreasing in* i *for all* $i \geq n$.

Proof To see that $i \cdot s\left(\dfrac{n}{i}\right)$ is increasing in i when $i < n$, we can consider the following difference for any $\delta > 0$:

Figure 3. Markov chain representing the total number of jobs under EQUI.

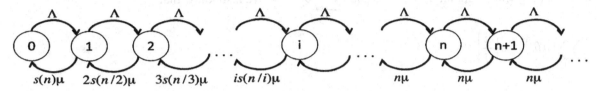

$$i \cdot \left(1 + \delta\right) s \left(\frac{n}{i \cdot \left(1 + \delta\right)} \right) - i \cdot s \left(\frac{n}{i} \right) = i \left(\left(1 + \delta\right) s \left(\frac{n}{i \cdot \left(1 + \delta\right)} \right) - s \left(\frac{n}{i} \right) \right).$$

Since $\frac{n}{i} > 1$, s increases sublinearly, and $\left(1 + \delta\right) s \left(\frac{n}{i \cdot \left(1 + \delta\right)} \right) > s \left(\frac{n}{i} \right)$. Thus

$$i \cdot \left(1 + \delta\right) s \left(\frac{n}{i \cdot \left(1 + \delta\right)} \right) - i \cdot s \left(\frac{n}{i} \right) > 0$$

and $i \cdot s \left(\frac{n}{i} \right)$ is increasing in i. For any $i \geq n$, we have assumed $s \left(\frac{n}{i} \right) = \frac{n}{i}$. Thus,

$$i \cdot s \left(\frac{n}{i} \right) = n, \forall i \geq n,$$

which is non-decreasing in i. We can now prove the optimality of EQUI.

Theorem 1 *Given malleable jobs with exponentially distributed job sizes which all follow the same concave, sublinear speedup function, s,*

$$\mathbb{E}[T]^{EQUI} \leq \mathbb{E}[T]^{P}$$

for any allocation policy P.

Proof Let P be an allocation policy which processes malleable jobs and currently has i active jobs (the system is in state i). In every state, i, P must decide (i) how many jobs, j, to run and (ii) how to allocate the n cores amongst the j jobs. Let $\theta = \left(\theta_1, \theta_2, ..., \theta_j\right)$ denote the fraction of the n servers allocated to each of the j jobs that run while the system is in state i. For example, job 1 receives an allocation of $n\theta_1$ servers and runs at rate $s\left(n\theta_1\right)$ while the system is in state i. Given that each job departs at rate μ when run on a single server, the total rate of departures from state i under P is

$$i \sum\nolimits_{k=1}^{j} s\left(n\theta_k\right) \tag{2}$$

where $0 \langle j \le i, \theta_k \rangle 0$ for all $1 \le k \le j$, and $\sum_{k=1}^{j} \theta_k = 1$. We also know that

$$\frac{1}{j} \sum_{k=1}^{j} s\left(n\theta_k\right) \le s\left(\frac{n}{j}\right)$$

again, by the concavity of s. Hence,

$$\sum_{k=1}^{j} s\left(n\dot{e}_k\right) \le j \cdot s\left(\frac{n}{j}\right), \forall 0 < j \le i, \forall \dot{e} \in \left(0,1\right]^{j}$$

and thus an upper bound on P's total rate of departures from any state is of the form

$$j \cdot s\left(\frac{n}{j}\right)\mu \tag{3}$$

By Lemma 1, $j \cdot s\left(\dfrac{n}{j}\right)$ is non-decreasing in j. Thus, an upper bound on P's rate of departures from any state i is

$$i \cdot s\left(\frac{n}{i}\right)\mu$$

Furthermore, we can see that EQUI achieves this departure rate in every state, i. Hence, (3) is the maximal rate of departures from any state, i. We can now compare the policy P with EQUI. Clearly, the arrival rate in any state i is the same under both policies. If we consider each state i where P has a strictly lower rate of departures than EQUI, we could reduce the rate of departures under EQUI by idling some servers in order to match the rate of departures under P. We call the resulting policy with idle servers P'. Because P' has the same rate of departures and arrivals as P in every state, it is clear that

$$\mathbb{E}\left[N\right]^{P'} = \mathbb{E}\left[N\right]^{P}$$

And hence, by Little's Law,

$$\mathbb{E}\left[T\right]^{P'} = \mathbb{E}\left[T\right]^{P}.$$

However, P' was obtained from EQUI by simply idling servers in some states. It is easy to see that any allocation of these idle servers does not increase mean response time. Hence, we have that

$$\mathbb{E}\left[T\right]^{P'} = \mathbb{E}\left[T\right]^{P} \geq \mathbb{E}\left[T\right]^{EQUI}$$

as desired.

3.2 What Is EQUI Doing?

The above proof provides nice intuition about why EQUI is a good policy. In particular, we proved that in each state, EQUI maximizes the total rate of departures of active jobs. Following a similar argument, it is easy to see that in any state i, EQUI is also maximizing the total service rate of jobs in the system given that there are i jobs. That is, EQUI maximizes the total number of units of work per second completed across all i jobs. Hence, we say that EQUI maximizes system efficiency in every state i. It is not obvious that maximizing system efficiency should lead to the optimal policy. For example, consider the case where jobs have known sizes and the system is given a job of size 1 and a job of size 100. The optimal policy in this case can reduce mean response time by favoring the shorter job, and EQUI in general will not be optimal. In the case of known job sizes, the optimal policy is willing to sacrifice system efficiency in order to reduce the time until the next completion.

In our setting with unknown job sizes, however, EQUI also minimizes the expected time until the next completion. Because all job sizes are drawn i.i.d. from the same exponential distribution, the allocation policy does not have the ability to favor jobs which it believes are shorter. More formally, for any allocation of servers to jobs which results in a total service rate of z, the expected time until the next completion is $1 / z$. Hence, maximizing the total service rate in state i also minimizes the expected time until the next completion. Any policy which favors one job over another is increasing the expected time until the next completion and decreasing system efficiency, which could also have been accomplished by starting with an equal allocation and then idling some servers.

4. MULTIPLE SPEEDUP FUNCTIONS

Thus far, we have assumed that jobs are homogeneous with respect to speedup. In this section, we consider the case where jobs may have different speedup functions, and where the system knows the speedup function for each job. We will see in Section 4.2 that, in the case of multiple speedup functions, EQUI is no longer the optimal policy. In Section 4.3, we propose a class of policies called GREEDY which maximize the departure rate in every state. We then describe the optimal GREEDY policy, GREEDY* in Section 4.4. While GREEDY* is not optimal in general (see Section 4.6), we show that GREEDY* performs near-optimally in a wide range of settings (Sections 4.5 and 4.6).

4.1 Why Multiple Speedup Functions

There are situations in which it would be reasonable to expect all jobs to follow a single speedup function, such as when all jobs are instances of a single application. The PARSEC-3 benchmark provides many examples of workloads for which this is the case (Zhan et al., 2017). In practice, however, it may be the case that there are 2 or more classes of jobs, each with a unique speedup function reflecting the amount of sequential work, number of IO operations, and communication overhead that its jobs will experience when run across multiple servers. We consider the case where jobs may belong to one of two

Figure 4. Heat maps showing the percentage difference in mean response time, $\mathbb{E}[T]$, between (a) EQUI and OPT and between (b) GREEDY* and OPT, in the case of two speedup functions where s_1 and s_2 are Amdahl's law with parameters p_1 and p_2 respectively. Here $\mathbb{E}[X] = \dfrac{1}{2}$ and $\Lambda_1 = \Lambda_2 = 5$. The axes represent different values of p_1 and p_2. GREEDY*, EQUI, and OPT were evaluated numerically using the MDP formulation given in Section 4.5. These heat maps look similar under various values of Λ_1 and Λ_2.

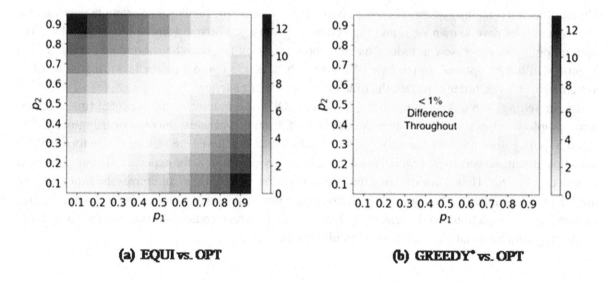

(a) EQUI vs. OPT   **(b) GREEDY* vs. OPT**

classes, each of which has its own speedup function, s_i (the classes may also have different arrival rates, Λ_i, but we assume all job sizes to be exponentially distributed with rate $\mu = 1 / \mathbb{E}[X]$). Without loss of generality, we assume that class 1 jobs are less parallelizable than class 2 jobs, that is

$$s_1(k) \langle s_2(k), \forall k \rangle 1$$

For example, class 1 jobs could follow Amdahl's law with p = .5 while class 2 jobs follow Amdahl's law with p = .75. As usual, our goal is to describe and analyze scheduling policies which minimize overall mean response time across all jobs. We will assume that an allocation policy can differentiate between job classes when making scheduling decisions.

4.2 EQUI Is No Longer Optimal

We have seen that EQUI is optimal when jobs are homogeneous with respect to speedup. One might assume that, since EQUI bases its decisions on the number of jobs in the system rather than the jobs' speedup functions, EQUI could continue to perform well when there are multiple speedup functions. However, it turns out that EQUI's performance is suboptimal even when there are just two speedup functions (see Figure 4). While EQUI's performance is actually close to optimal in the cases where and are similar (is close to in Figure 4), we see that EQUI's performance relative to OPT becomes worse as the difference between the speedup functions increases (p1 is far from p2 in Figure 4).To see why EQUI is suboptimal in this case, recall that EQUI's optimality stems from the fact that it maximizes the rate of departures in every state when jobs follow a single speedup function (see proof of Theorem 1). When jobs are permitted to have different speedup functions, maximizing the rate of departures will require allocating more servers to class 2 jobs and fewer servers to class 1 jobs. Hence, EQUI no longer maximizes the total rate of departures when jobs follow different speedup functions.

4.3 A GREEDY* Class of Policies

Because EQUI fails to maximize the rate of departures when there are multiple speedup functions, we now identify a class of policies that does maximize the total rate of departures of the system. Specifically, we define the GREEDY class of policies to be the class of policies which achieve the maximal total rate of departures in every state.

To describe the policies in GREEDY, we consider any state (x_1, x_2) where there are x_1 class 1 jobs and x_2 class 2 jobs in the system. Attaining the maximal rate of departures can be thought of as a two step process. First, a policy must decide how many servers, a1, to allocate to the x1 class 1 jobs. The remaining $\alpha_2 = n - \alpha_1$ servers will be allocated to class 2 jobs. Second, the policy must decide how to divide the α_1 servers among the class 1 jobs and the α_2 servers among the class 2 jobs. We have seen that, when dividing servers among a set of jobs with a single speedup function, EQUI maximizes the total rate of departures of this set of jobs. For a given choice of a1, the a1 servers should thus be evenly divided among the class 1 jobs and the α_2 servers should be evenly divided among the class 2 jobs in order to maximize the total rate of departures. To find the correct choice of a1, we define $\beta(x_1, x_2)$ to be the maximum rate of departures from the state (x_1, x_2) given that servers will be divided evenly within each class:

$$\beta(x_1, x_2) = \max_{\alpha \in [0,n]} x_1 s_1 \left(\frac{\alpha}{x_1}\right) \mu + x_2 s_2 \left(\frac{n - \alpha}{x_2}\right) \mu. \tag{4}$$

Any policy in GREEDY must then choose α_1 such that

$$\alpha_1 \in \left\{ \alpha : x_1 s_1 \left(\frac{\alpha}{x_1}\right) \mu + x_2 s_2 \left(\frac{n - \alpha}{x_2}\right) \mu = \beta(x_1, x_2) \right\}. \tag{5}$$

This same two-step process will generalize to the case when jobs follow more than 2 speedup functions. Crucially, note that GREEDY is truly a class of policies, since, in a given state, there may be multiple choices of a1 which satisfy (5). That is, there could be multiple allocations which achieve the maximal total rate of departures. For example, consider a system with n = 4 servers. If there are 4 class 1 jobs and 4 class 2 jobs, any choice of results in the maximal rate of departures, . This begs the question of which policy from the GREEDY class achieves the best performance.

4.4 The Best GREEDY Policy: GREEDY*

We now define GREEDY*, a policy which dominates all other GREEDY policies with respect to mean response time. Consider two GREEDY policies, P_1 and P_2. In any state (x_1, x_2), both policies achieve the same maximal rate of departures. However, P_1 might achieve this rate by having a higher departure rate for class 1 jobs and a lower departure rate for class 2 jobs as compared to P_2. If class 1 jobs are less parallelizable than class 2 jobs, we say that P_1 "defers parallelizable work" in this state, which is a strategy that could benefit P_1 in the future. The GREEDY* policy is the GREEDY policy which in all states opts to defer parallelizable work when possible. Specifically, GREEDY* allocates a_1^* servers to class 1 jobs (the less parallelizable class), where a_1^* is the maximum value of a1 satisfying (5). That is,

$$a_1^* \in \left\{ \alpha : x_1 s_1\left(\frac{\alpha}{x_1}\right)\mu + x_2 s_2\left(\frac{n-\alpha}{x_2}\right)\mu = \beta\left(x_1, x_2\right) \right\}.$$

In other words, a_1^* allows GREEDY* to attain the maximal rate of departures while also maximizing the rate at which class 1 jobs are completed. Theorem 2 shows that GREEDY* dominates all other GREEDY policies.

Theorem 2 *For any GREEDY policy, P,*

Proof Consider the performance of GREEDY* and P on the state space $S = \left\{(x_1, x_2) : x_1, x_2 \in \mathbb{N}\right\}$. We will use the technique of precedence relations (see, e.g., (Adan et al., 1994; Bušić et al., 2012)) to compare the mean number of customers, $\mathbb{E}[N]$, under GREEDY* to that under P. This requires that we define a value function for P, $V^P(x_1, x_2)$, and a cost function, $c(x_1, x_2)$. We define the cost of being in state (x_1, x_2) to be

$$c(x_1, x_2) = x_1 + x_2$$

so that the average cost of performing policy P is equal to the mean number of customers, $\mathbb{E}[N]$. We then define $V^P(x_1, x_2)$ to be the asymptotic total difference in the accrued cost under P when starting in state (x_1, x_2) as opposed to some designated reference state (see Appendix 6.1 for details). We require the following lemma which establishes a useful property of V^P.

Lemma 2 *For any GREEDY policy, P, and any $(x_1, x_2) \in S$,*

$$V^P\left(x_1 + 1, x_2\right) > V^P\left(x_1, x_2 + 1\right).$$

Proof See Appendix 6.1 for proof of Lemma 2.

We now prove Theorem 2 by contradiction. We begin by assuming that there exists a GREEDY policy which is optimal in terms of and thus for any GREEDY policy . Since, there exists some state, where P and GREEDY* take different actions. Note that both and must be non-zero in this state, because otherwise there is only one action which will achieve the maximal rate of departures, and P and GREEDY* must therefore take the same action.

We now consider a policy which takes the same action as GREEDY in state, and the same action as P in every other state. We can apply the technique of precedence relations described in (Adan et al., 1994; Bušić et al., 2012) to show that . We start by defining to be the rate of departures of class jobs from the state under policy Q. can now be obtained from P by taking away from the total completion rate of class 2 jobs and adding to the total completion rate of class 1 jobs, where denotes GREEDY*. Theorem 3.1 in (Bušić et al., 2012) tells us that if:

$$\left(\gamma_2^{G^*}\left(x_1, x_2\right) - \gamma_2^P\left(x_1, x_2\right)\right)V^P\left(x_1 - 1, x_2\right) < \left(\gamma_2^P\left(x_1, x_2\right) - \gamma_2^{G^*}\left(x_1, x_2\right)\right)V^P\left(x_1, x_2 - 1\right)$$

To see that this property holds, first note that

$$\left(\gamma_1^{G^*}\left(x_1, x_2\right) - \gamma_1^P\left(x_1, x_2\right)\right) - \left(\gamma_2^P\left(x_1, x_2\right) - \gamma_2^{G^*}\left(x_1, x_2\right)\right)$$

$$= \left(\gamma_1^{G^*}\left(x_1, x_2\right) - \gamma_2^{G^*}\left(x_1, x_2\right)\right) - \left(\gamma_1^P\left(x_1, x_2\right) - \gamma_2^P\left(x_1, x_2\right)\right) = 0$$

since GREEDY* and P have the same (maximal) total rate of departures in every state. Thus,

$$\gamma_1^{G^*}\left(x_1, x_2\right) - \gamma_1^P\left(x_1, x_2\right) = \gamma_2^P\left(x_1, x_2\right) - \gamma_2^{G^*}\left(x_1, x_2\right)$$

By Lemma 2, we know that

$$V^P\left(x_1 - 1, x_2\right) < V^P\left(x_1, x_2 - 1\right).$$

This implies that $\mathbb{E}\left[N\right]^{P'} < \mathbb{E}\left[N\right]^P$ which contradicts our assumption that P is optimal in terms of $\mathbb{E}\left[N\right]$. By Little's Law, we can reformulate this in terms of $\mathbb{E}\left[T\right]$.

While GREEDY* is the best GREEDY policy, it will turn out that it is not optimal (see Section 4.6). Hence, we now turn our attention to computing the optimal policy.

4.5 Computing the Optimal Policy

The optimal policy, OPT, must not only consider the current state of the system when choosing how to determine the best partition (α_1, α_2), but must also consider the probabilities of transitioning to future states as well. To find a policy which balances this tradeoff between performance in the current state and future states, we formulate the problem as a Markov Decision Process (MDP).

We will consider an MDP with state space $S = \left\{ (x_1, x_2) : x_1, x_2 \in N \right\}$, where x_i represents the number of class i jobs in the system. The action space in any state is given by $A = \left\{ (\alpha_1, \alpha_2) : \alpha_1 + \alpha_2 = n \right\}$. Let the arrival rate of class i jobs be given by $\ddot{E}_i$. Given an allocation of α_i servers to x_i type i jobs, it is optimal to run the x_i jobs on these servers using EQUI. Thus, given a state (x_1, x_2) and an action (α_1, α_2), the total departure rate of class i jobs from the system is given by

$$\mu_i(\alpha_i, x_i) := \min\{\alpha_i, x_i\} \cdot \mu \cdot s\left(\max\left\{1, \frac{\alpha_i}{x_i}\right\}\right).$$

We choose the cost function

$$c(x_1, x_2) = x_1 + x_2$$

such that the average cost per period equals the average number of jobs in the system, $\mathbb{E}[N]$. We uniformize the system at rate 1 (always achievable by scaling time) and find that Bellman's optimality equations (Puterman, 1994) for this MDP are given by

$$\mathbb{E}\left[N^{OPT}\right] + V^{OPT}(x_1, x_2) = A^{OPT}(x_1, x_2) + H^{OPT}(x_1, x_2)$$

Where

$$A^{OPT}(x_1, x_2) = c(x_1, x_2) + \Lambda_1\left(V^{OPT}(x_1 + 1, x_2) - V^{OPT}(x_1, x_2)\right)$$
$$+ \Lambda_2\left(V^{OPT}(x_1, x_2 + 1) - V^{OPT}(x_1, x_2)\right), \tag{6}$$

And

$$H^{OPT}(x_1, x_2) = V^{OPT}(x_1, x_2) + \min_{(\alpha_1, \alpha_2) \in A}\left[\begin{array}{l} \mu_1(\alpha_1, x_1)\left(V^{OPT}\left((x_1-1)^+, x_2\right) - V^{OPT}(x_1, x_2)\right) \\ + \mu_2(\alpha_2, x_2)\left(V^{OPT}\left(x_1, (x_2-1)^+\right) - V^{OPT}(x_1, x_2)\right)\end{array}\right]. \tag{7}$$

Here, the value function $V^{OPT}\left(x_1, x_2\right)$ denotes the asymptotic total difference in accrued costs when using the optimal policy and starting the system in state $\left(x_1, x_2\right)$ instead of some reference state. While these equations are hard to solve analytically, the optimal actions can be obtained numerically by defining

$$V_{n+1}^{OPT}\left(x_1, x_2\right) = A_n^{OPT}\left(x_1, x_2\right) + H_n^{OPT}\left(x_1, x_2\right)$$

with $V_0^{OPT}\left(\cdot, \cdot\right) = 0$. Here, A_n^{OPT} and H_n^{OPT} are defined as in (6) and (7), but in terms of V_n^{OPT}. We can then perform value iteration to extract the optimal policy (Lippman, 1973). We use the results of this value iteration to compare the performance of OPT to both EQUI and GREEDY* in Figure 4. Note that using the same MDP formulation when there exists only one speedup function results in a much simpler expression for V^{OPT} which clearly yields EQUI.

4.6 GREEDY* Is Near-Optimal

Surprisingly, even GREEDY* is not optimal for minimizing mean response time as shown in Figure 4 (although it is always within 1% of OPT in the figure). The same intuition that led us to believe that GREEDY* is the best GREEDY policy can be used to explain why GREEDY* is not optimal. We have already seen that deferring parallelizable work is advantageous to GREEDY*. However, we were only comparing GREEDY* to policies which use the maximal overall departure rate. It turns out that the advantage of deferring parallelizable work can be so great that a policy stands to benefit from using a submaximal overall rate of departures, deferring even more parallelizable work than GREEDY*.

5. CONCLUSION

Limitations and Future Work

One limitation of the model described in this chapter is that it assumes that jobs have no internal dependency structure. In reality, as the SPAA community has pointed out, a single job usually consists of multiple interdependent tasks. Hence, the effective speedup a job receives from parallelization may change over time. The problem of how to schedule a stream of jobs which have these dependency structures is open, even in the case of a single processor (Scully et al., 2017). Scheduling these jobs on multiple servers therefore presents an exciting direction for future work. Additionally, it may be interesting to consider the case where the system has some partial information about job sizes. If job sizes were not exponentially distributed, for example, an allocation policy could try to predict a job's remaining size based on how long the job has been running. Similarly, the user may provide the system a noisy estimate of a job's size when submitting the job. In either case, the optimal allocation policy must both maintain system efficiency and also favor the jobs that are likely to have smaller remaining sizes. Although the results of this chapter do not model all of these aspects, they provide a starting point for further research in this area

Summary

This chapter discusses the question of how to allocate servers to jobs in a stochastic model of a data center where jobs have sublinear speedup functions. While it is typical in these data centers for the user to specify the desired number of servers for her jobs, the results of this chapter suggest that allowing the system to schedule jobs can benefit overall mean response time. In the case where all jobs are malleable and follow the same speedup function, we prove that the well-known EQUI policy is optimal given that job sizes are exponentially distributed. When jobs are permitted to have multiple speedup functions, the question of optimal scheduling becomes even harder. We can show that EQUI is no longer optimal for scheduling malleable jobs when jobs follow multiple speedup functions. We see that the optimal policy (OPT) must balance the tradeoff between maximizing the total rate of departures in every state and deferring parallelizable work to preserve future system efficiency. We provide an MDP based formulation of OPT. As an alternative, we define a simple policy, GREEDY*, which can be easily implemented and performs near-optimally in simulation.

REFERENCES

Adan, I., van Houtum, G. J. J. A. N., & van der Wal, J. (1994). Upper and lower bounds for the waiting time in the symmetric shortest queue system. *Annals of Operations Research*, *48*(2), 197–217. doi:10.1007/BF02024665

Agrawal, K., Li, J., Lu, K., & Moseley, B. (2016). Scheduling parallelizable jobs online to minimize the maximum flow time. In *Proceedings of the 28th ACM Symposium on Parallelism in Algorithms and Architectures, SPAA '16*, (pp. 195-205). New York: ACM. 10.1145/2935764.2935782

Anastasiadis, S. V., & Sevcik, K. C. (1997). Parallel application scheduling on networks of workstations. *Journal of Parallel and Distributed Computing*, *43*(2), 109–124. doi:10.1006/jpdc.1997.1335

Berg, B., Dorsman, J.-P., & Harchol-Balter, M. (2017). Towards optimality in parallel scheduling. *Proceedings of the ACM on Measurement and Analysis of Computing Systems*, *1*(2), 1-30.

Bienia, C., Kumar, S., Singh, J. P., & Li, K. (2008). The PARSEC benchmark suite: Characterization and architectural implications. In *Proceedings of the 17th International Conference on Parallel Architectures and Compilation Techniques, PACT '08* (pp. 72-81). New York: ACM. 10.1145/1454115.1454128

Bušić, A., Vliegen, I., & Scheller-Wolf, A. (2012). Comparing Markov chains: Aggregation and precedence relations applied to sets of states, with applications to assemble-to-order systems. *Mathematics of Operations Research*, *37*(2), 259–287. doi:10.1287/moor.1110.0533

Chaitanya, S., Urgaonkar, B., & Sivasubramaniam, A. (2008). Qdsl: A queuing model for systems with differential service levels. *Performance Evaluation Review*, *36*(1), 289–300. doi:10.1145/1384529.1375490

Cirne, W., & Berman, F. (2002). Using moldability to improve the performance of supercomputer jobs. *Journal of Parallel and Distributed Computing*, *62*(10), 1571–1601. doi:10.1016/S0743-7315(02)91869-1

Delimitrou, C., & Kozyrakis, C. (2014). Quasar: Resource-efficient and qos-aware cluster management. *ACM SIGPLAN Notices*, *49*(4), 127–144. doi:10.1145/2644865.2541941

Edmonds, J. (1999). Scheduling in the dark. *Theoretical Computer Science, 235*(1), 109–141. doi:10.1016/ S0304-3975(99)00186-3

Edmonds, J., & Pruhs, K. (2009). Scalably scheduling processes with arbitrary speedup curves. In *Proceedings of the Twentieth Annual ACM-SIAM Symposium on Discrete Algorithms, SODA '09*, (pp. 685-692). New York: ACM. 10.1137/1.9781611973068.75

Gandhi, A., Harchol-Balter, M., Das, R., & Lefurgy, C. (2009). Optimal power allocation in server farms. In *ACM SIGMETRICS Performance Evaluation Review* (Vol. 37, pp. 157–168). ACM.

Gupta, V., Harchol-Balter, M., Sigman, K., & Whitt, W. (2007). Analysis of join-the-shortestqueue routing for web server farms. *Performance Evaluation, 64*(9-12), 1062–1081. doi:10.1016/j.peva.2007.06.012

Harchol-Balter, M. (2013). *Performance Modeling and Design of Computer Systems: Queueing Theory in Action*. Cambridge University Press.

Harchol-Balter, M., Scheller-Wolf, A., & Young, A. R. (2009). Surprising results on task assignment in server farms with high-variability workloads. *Performance Evaluation Review, 37*(1), 287–298. doi:10.1145/2492101.1555383

Hill, M. D., & Marty, M. R. (2008). Amdahl's law in the multicore era. *Computer, 41*(7), 33–38. doi:10.1109/MC.2008.209

Huang, K.-C., Huang, T.-C., Tung, Y.-H., & Shih, P.-Z. (2013). Effective processor allocation for moldable jobs with application speedup model. In *Advances in Intelligent Systems and Applications* (Vol. 2, pp. 563–572). Springer. doi:10.1007/978-3-642-35473-1_56

Kleinrock, L. (1975). Queueing Systems, Volume I: Theory. Wiley.

Ko, S.-S., & Serfozo, R. F. (2004). Response times in M/M/s fork-join networks. *Advances in Applied Probability, 36*(3), 854–871. doi:10.1239/aap/1093962238

Koole, G. M. (2006). Monotonicity in Markov reward and decision chains: Theory and applications. *Foundations and Trends in Stochastic Systems, 1*(1), 1–76. doi:10.1561/0900000002

Lippman, S. A. (1973). Semi-Markov decision processes with unbounded rewards. *Management Science, 19*(7), 717–731. doi:10.1287/mnsc.19.7.717

Lu, Y., Xie, Q., Kliot, G., Geller, A., Larus, J. R., & Greenberg, A. (2011). Join-idle-queue: A novel load balancing algorithm for dynamically scalable web services. *Performance Evaluation, 68*(11), 1056–1071. doi:10.1016/j.peva.2011.07.015

McCool, J., Robison, M., & Reinders, A. (2012). *Structured Parallel Programming: Patterns for Efficient Computation*. Elsevier.

Nelson, R. D., & Philips, T. K. (1993). An approximation for the mean response time for shortest queue routing with general interarrival and service times. *Performance Evaluation, 17*(2), 123–139. doi:10.1016/0166-5316(93)90004-E

Puterman, M. L. (1994). *Markov Decision Processes: Discrete Stochastic Dynamic Programming*. John Wiley & Sons. doi:10.1002/9780470316887

Scully, Z., Blelloch, G., Harchol-Balter, M., & Scheller-Wolf, A. (2017). Optimally scheduling jobs with multiple tasks. *Proceedings of the ACM Workshop on Mathematical Performance Modeling and Analysis*.

Srinivasan, S., Krishnamoorthy, S., & Sadayappan, P. (2003). A robust scheduling strategy for moldable scheduling of parallel jobs. *Proceedings of the IEEE International Conference on Cluster Computing, CLUSTER '03*, 92-99. 10.1109/CLUSTR.2003.1253304

Tsitsiklis, J. N., & Xu, K. (2011). On the power of (even a little) centralization in distributed processing. *Performance Evaluation Review, 39*, 121–132. doi:10.1145/1993744.1993759

Zhan, X., Bao, Y., Bienia, C., & Li, K. (2017). PARSEC3.0: A multicore benchmark suite with network stacks and SPLASH-2X. *ACM SIGARCH Computer Architecture News, 44*(5), 1–16. doi:10.1145/3053277.3053279

APPENDIX 1

Proof of Lemma 2

Lemma 2 *Given any GREEDY policy, P, for any* $(x_1, x_2) \in S$,

$$V^P(x_1 + 1, x_2) > V^P(x_1, x_2 + 1)$$

Proof We begin by defining V_n^P as follows:

$$V_{n+1}^P(x_1, x_2) = A_n^P(x_1, x_2) + I_n^P(x_1, x_2)$$

Where

$$A_n^P(x_1, x_2) = c(x_1, x_2) + \Lambda_1 \left(V_n^P(x_1 + 1, x_2) - V_n^P(x_1, x_2) \right) + \Lambda_2 \left(V_n^P(x_1, x_2 + 1) - V_n^P(x_1, x_2) \right)$$

And

$$I_n^P = \gamma_1^P(x_1, x_2) \left(V_n^P((x_1 - 1)^+, x_2) - V_n^P(x_1, x_2) \right) + \gamma_2^P(x_1, x_2) \left(V_n^P(x_1, (x_2 - 1)^+) - V_n^P(x_1, x_2) \right).$$

and

$$V_0^P(x_1, x_2) = x_1 + x_2 + \frac{x_1}{x_1 + x_2 + 1}$$

for all $(x_1, x_2) \in S$.

Recall that $\gamma_i^P(x_1, x_2)$ denotes the departure rate of class i jobs from state (x_1, x_2) under policy P, $\ddot{E}_i$ denotes the arrival rate of class i jobs, and $c(x_1, x_2) = x_1 + x_2$. From (Puterman, 1994) we know that

$$\lim_{n \to \infty} V_n^P(x_1, x_2) - V_n^P(y_1, y_2) = V^P(x_1, x_2) - V^P(y_1, y_2).$$

Thus, if we can prove that our claim holds for $V_n^P(x_1, x_2)$ for all n ≥ 0, then it must hold for $V^P(x_1, x_2)$ as well (see, for example, (Koole, 2006)). We will now prove that all three of the following properties of V_n^P hold for all n ≥ 0 by induction:

$$V_n^P(x_1 + 1, x_2) > V_n^P(x_1, x_2)$$

$$V_n^P\left(x_1, x_2 + 1\right) > V_n^P\left(x_1, x_2\right)$$

$$V_n^P\left(x_1 + 1, x_2\right) > V_n^P\left(x_1, x_2 + 1\right)$$

Note that the first two properties will be necessary for our proof of the third property, and the lemma follows directly from the third property.

We can easily verify that all three properties hold when n = 0 due to our choice of V_0^P. We now wish to show that if these properties hold for V_n^P, they must hold for V_{n+1}^P.

To prove property 1, we wish to show that

$$V_{n+1}^P\left(x_1 + 1, x_2\right) - V_{n+1}^P\left(x_1, x_2\right)$$

$$= A_n^P\left(x_1 + 1, x_2\right) - A_n^P\left(x_1, x_2\right) + I_n^P\left(x_1 + 1, x_2\right) - I_n^P\left(x_1, x_2\right) > 0$$

We can easily see that

$$A_n^P\left(x_1 + 1, x_2\right) - A_n^P\left(x_1, x_2\right) > 0,$$

since the cost function $c\left(x_1, x_2\right)$ is increasing in x_1 and $V_n^P\left(x_1, x_2\right)$ is increasing in x_1 by the property 1 of the inductive hypothesis. To see that

$$I_n^P\left(x_1 + 1, x_2\right) - I_n^P\left(x_1, x_2\right) > 0,$$

we can expand the terms as follows:

$$I_n^P\left(x_1 + 1, x_2\right) - I_n^P\left(x_1, x_2\right)$$

$$= \gamma_1^P\left(x_1, x_2\right)\left(V_n^P\left(x_1, x_2\right) - V_n^P\left((x_1 - 1)^+, x_2\right)\right) + \gamma_2^P\left(x_1, x_2\right)\left(V_n^P\left(x_1, x_2\right) - V_n^P\left(x_1, (x_2 - 1)^+\right)\right)$$
$$+ \gamma_2^P\left(x_1 + 1, x_2\right)\left(V_n^P\left(x_1 + 1, (x_2 - 1)^+\right) - V_n^P\left(x_1, x_2\right)\right) + \begin{bmatrix} 1 - \gamma_1^P\left(x_1 + 1, x_2\right) \\ -\gamma_2^P\left(x_1 + 1, x_2\right) \end{bmatrix}\begin{bmatrix} V_n^P\left(x_1 + 1, x_2\right) \\ -V_n^P\left(x_1, x_2\right) \end{bmatrix}.$$

Each line here is positive by the inductive hypothesis and the fact that

$$\left(1 - \gamma_1^P\left(x_1 + 1, x_2\right) - \gamma_2^P\left(x_1 + 1, x_2\right)\right) \geq 0$$

since the system was uniformized to one. Thus property 1 holds. The proof of property 2 follows a very similar argument.

To show property 3 we wish to show that

$$V_{n+1}^P \left(x_1 + 1, x_2 \right) - V_{n+1}^P \left(x_1, x_2 + 1 \right)$$

$$= A_n^P \left(x_1 + 1, x_2 \right) - A_n^P \left(x_1, x_2 + 1 \right) + I_n^P \left(x_1 + 1, x_2 \right) - I_n^P \left(x_1, x_2 + 1 \right) > 0$$

We can easily see that

$$A_n^P \left(x_1 + 1, x_2 \right) - A_n^P \left(x_1, x_2 + 1 \right) > 0$$

by the inductive hypothesis. To see that

$$I_n^P \left(x_1 + 1, x_2 \right) - I_n^P \left(x_1, x_2 + 1 \right) > 0,$$

we can expand the terms as follows:

$$I_n^P \left(x_1 + 1, x_2 \right) - I_n^P \left(x_1, x_2 + 1 \right)$$

$$= \gamma_1^P \left(x_1, x_2 + 1 \right) \left[V_n^P \left(x_1, x_2 \right) - V_n^P \left(\left(x_1 - 1 \right)^+, x_2 + 1 \right) \right]$$
$$+ \gamma_2^P \left(x_1 + 1, x_2 \right) \left[V_n^P \left(x_1 + 1, \left(x_2 - 1 \right)^+ \right) - V_n^P \left(x_1, x_2 \right) \right]$$
$$+ \left(\gamma_1^P \left(x_1, x_2 + 1 \right) + \gamma_2^P \left(x_1, x_2 + 1 \right) - \gamma_1^P \left(x_1 + 1, x_2 \right) - \gamma_2^P \left(x_1 + 1, x_2 \right) \right)$$
$$\times \left(V_n^P \left(x_1 + 1, x_2 \right) - V_n^P \left(x_1, x_2 \right) \right) + \left(1 - \gamma_1^P \left(x_1, x_2 + 1 \right) - \gamma_2^P \left(x_1, x_2 + 1 \right) \right)$$
$$\times \left(V_n^P \left(x_1 + 1, x_2 \right) - V_n^P \left(x_1, x_2 + 1 \right) \right).$$

We know, by assumption, that $s_1 \left(k \right) < s_2 \left(k \right)$ for $k > 1$, and thus the coefficient

$$\gamma_1^P \left(x_1, x_2 + 1 \right) + \gamma_2^P \left(x_1, x_2 + 1 \right) - \gamma_1^P \left(x_1 + 1, x_2 \right) - \gamma_2^P \left(x_1 + 1, x_2 \right)$$

is non-negative. Therefore, all terms in this sum are positive by the inductive hypothesis, and property 3 holds.

All three properties therefore hold by induction, and

$$V^P\left(x_1 + 1, x_2\right) > V^P\left(x_1, x_2 + 1\right)$$

as desired.

Chapter 4
Intelligent Management of Mobile Systems Through Computational Self-Awareness

Bryan Donyanavard

University of California, Irvine, USA

Amir M. Rahmani

University of California, Irvine, USA

Axel Jantsch

TU Wien, Austria

Onur Mutlu

Swiss Federal Institute of Technology in Zurich, Switzerland

Nikil Dutt

University of California, Irvine, USA

ABSTRACT

Runtime resource management for many-core systems is increasingly complex. The complexity can be due to diverse workload characteristics with conflicting demands, or limited shared resources such as memory bandwidth and power. Resource management strategies for many-core systems must distribute shared resource(s) appropriately across workloads, while coordinating the high-level system goals at runtime in a scalable and robust manner. In this chapter, the concept of reflection is used to explore adaptive resource management techniques that provide two key properties: the ability to adapt to (1) changing goals at runtime (i.e., self-adaptivity) and (2) changing dynamics of the modeled system (i.e., self-optimization). By supporting these self-awareness properties, the system can reason about the actions it takes by considering the significance of competing objectives, user requirements, and operating conditions while executing unpredictable workloads.

DOI: 10.4018/978-1-7998-7156-9.ch004

INTRODUCTION

Battery powered-devices are the most ubiquitous computers in the world. Users expect the devices to support high performance applications running on same device, sometimes at the same time. The devices support a wide range of applications, from interactive maps and navigation, to web browsers and email clients. In order to meet the performance demands of the complex workloads, increasingly powerful hardware platforms are being deployed in battery-powered devices. These platforms include a number of configurable knobs that allow for a tradeoff between power and performance, e.g., dynamic voltage and frequency scaling (DVFS), core gating, idle cycle injection, etc. These knobs can be set and modified at runtime based on workload demands and system constraints. Heterogeneous manycore processors (HMPs) have extended this principle of dynamic power-performance tradeoffs by incorporating single-ISA, architecturally differentiated cores on a single processor, with each of the cores containing a number of independent tradeoff knobs. All of these configurable knobs allow for a large range of potential tradeoffs. However, with such a large number of possible configurations, HMPs require intelligent runtime management in order to achieve application goals for complex workloads while considering system constraints. Additionally, the knobs may be interdependent, so the decisions must be coordinated. In this chapter, we explore the use of computational self-awareness to address challenges of adaptive resource management in mobile multiprocessors.

Computational Self-awareness

Self-aware computing is a new paradigm that does not strictly introduce new research concepts, but unifies overlapping research efforts in disparate disciplines (Lewis et al., 2016). The concept of self-awareness from psychology has inspired research in autonomous systems and neuroscience, and existing research in fields such as adaptive control theory support properties of self-awareness. This chapter addresses key challenges for achieving computational self-awareness that can make the design, maintenance and operation of complex, heterogeneous systems adaptive, autonomous, and highly efficient. Computational self-awareness is the ability of a computing system to recognize its own state, possible actions and the result of these actions on itself, its operational goals, and its environment, thereby empowering the system to become autonomous (Jantsch et al., 2017). An infrastructure for system introspection and reflective behavior forms the foundation of self-aware systems.

Reflection

Reflection can be defined as *the capability of a system to reason about itself and act upon this information* (Smith, 1982). A reflective system can achieve this by maintaining a representation of itself (i.e., a self-model) within the underlying system, which is used for reasoning. Reflection is a key property of self-awareness. Reflection enables decisions to be made based on both *past* observations, as well as predictions made from past observations. Reflection and prediction involve two types of models: (1) a self-model of the subsystem(s) under control, and (2) models of other policies that may impact the decision-making process. Predictions consider *future* actions, or events that may occur before the next decision, enabling "what-if" exploration of alternatives. Such actions may be triggered by other resource managers running with a shorter period than the decision loop. The top half of Figure 1 shows prediction enabled through reflection that can be utilized in the decision making process of a feedback loop. The main goal of the prediction model is to estimate system behavior based on potential actuation decisions. This type of prediction is most often performed using linear regression-based models (Mück et al., 2015; Pricopi et al., 2013; Annamalai et al., 2013; Singh et al., 2009) due to their simplicity, while others employ a binning-based approach in which metrics sensed at runtime are used to classify workloads into categories (Liu et al., 2013; Donyanavard et al., 2016).

Figure 1. Feedback loop overview. The bottom part of the figure represents a simple observe-decide-act loop. The top part adds the reflection mechanism to this loop, enabling predictions for smart decision making.

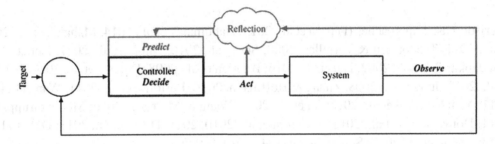

Closed-loop Resource Management in Mobile Systems

Runtime resource management for many-core systems is increasingly challenging due to the complex interaction of: i) integrating hundreds of (heterogeneous) cores and uncore components on a single chip, ii) limited amount of system resources (e.g., power, cores, interconnects), iii) diverse workload characteristics with conflicting constraints and demands, and iv) increasing pressure on shared system resources from data-intensive workloads. As system size and capability scale, designers face a large space of configuration parameters controlled by actuation knobs, which in turn generate a very large number of cross-layer actuation combinations (Zhang & Hoffmann, 2016). Making runtime decisions to configure knobs in order to achieve a simple goal (e.g., maximize performance) can be challenging. That challenge is exacerbated when considering a goal that may change throughout runtime, and consist of conflicting objectives (e.g., maximize performance while minimizing power consumption).

Additionally, ubiquitous mobile devices are expected to be general-purpose, supporting any combination of applications (i.e., workloads) desired by users, often without any prior knowledge of the workload.

Designers face a large space of configuration parameters that often are controlled by a limited number of actuation knobs, which in turn generate a very large number of cross-layer actuation configurations. For instance, Zhang and Hoffman (2016) show that for an 8-core Intel Xeon processor, combining only a handful of actuation knobs (such as clock frequency and Hyperthreading levels) generates over 1000 different actuation configurations; they use binary search to efficiently explore the configuration space for achieving a *single* goal: cap the Thermal Design Power (TDP) while maximizing performance. Searching the configuration space is common practice in many similar single-goal, heuristic-based, runtime resource management approaches (Raghavendra et al., 2008; Choi & Yeung, 2006; Tembey et al., 2010; Vega et al., 2013; Cochran et al., 2011). While there is a large body of literature on ad-hoc resource management approaches for processors using heuristics and thresholds (Deng et al., 2012; Jung et al.,

2008; Ebrahimi et al., 2010; David et al., 2011), rules (Isci et al., 2006; Dhodapkar & Smith, 2002), solvers (Petrica et al., 2013; Hanumaiah et al., 2014), and predictive models (Bitirgen et al., 2008; Dubach et al., 2010, 2013; Donyanavard et al., 2016), there is a lack of formalism in providing guarantees for resource management of complex many-core systems.

Closed-loop systems have been used extensively to improve the state of a system by configuring knobs in order to achieve a goal. Closed-loop systems traditionally deploy an *Observe, Decide* and *Act* (ODA) feedback loop (lower half of Figure 1) to determine the system configuration. In an ODA loop, the observed behavior of the system is compared to the target behavior, and the discrepancy is fed to the controller for decision making. The controller invokes actions based on the result of the Decide stage.

Resource management approaches in the literature can be classified into three main classes:

1. hueristic-based-approaches (Petrica et al., 2013; Hanumaiah et al., 2014; Mahajan et al., 2016; Fu et al., 2011; Teodorescu & Torrellas, 2008; Sui et al., 2016; Gupta et al., 2017; Isci et al., 2006; Dhodapkar & Smith, 2002; Fan et al., 2016; Bitirgen et al., 2008; Dubach et al., 2010, 2013; Deng et al., 2012; Jung et al., 2008; Zhang & Hoffmann, 2016; Bartolini et al., 2011; Wang et al., 2009, 2011; Yan:2016; Lo et al., 2015; Su et al., 2014; Wang & Martinez, 2016; Muthukaruppan et al., 2014; Donyanavard et al., 2016; Ebrahimi et al., 2010, 2011; David et al., 2011; Das et al., 2009, 2013; Chang et al., 2017; Subramanian et al., 2013, 2015),

2. control-theory-based approaches (Maggio et al., 2011; Rahmani et al., 2015, 2017; Mishra et al., 2010; Wu et al., 2004, 2005; Ebrahimi et al., 2009; Ma et al., 2011; Muthukaruppan et al., 2013; Kadjo et al., 2015; Hoffmann, 2011, 2014; Srikantaiah et al., 2009; Kanduri et al., 2016; Haghbayan et al., 2017; Pothukuchi et al., 2016}, and

3. stochastic/machine-learning-based approaches (Gupta et al., 2016; Bitirgen et al., 2008; Dubach et al., 2010; Delimitrou & Kozyrakis, 2014; Ipek et al., 2008). Recent work has combined aspects of machine learning and feedback control (Mishra et al., 2018). In addition, there have been efforts to enable coordinated management in computer systems in various ways (Bitirgen et al., 2008; Raghavendra et al., 2008; Choi & Yeung, 2006; Vardhan et al., 2009; Juang et al., 2005; Wu et al., 2016; Tembey et al., 2010; Vega et al., 2013; Cochran et al., 2011; Dubach et al., 2010; Ebrahimi et al., 2010, 2011; David et al., 2011; Stuecheli et al., 2010; Lee et al., 2010; Das et al., 2009, 2010; Pothukuchi et al., 2018). These works coordinate and control multiple goals and actuators in a non-conflicting manner by adding an ad-hoc component or hierarchy to a controller.

In this chapter, we demonstrate the effectiveness of computational self-awareness in adaptive resource management for mobile processors. The self-aware resource managers discussed are implemented using classical and hierarchical control.

SELF-OPTIMIZATION

Self-optimization is the ability of a system to adapt and act efficiently by itself in the face of *internal stimuli*. We consider internal stimuli as changes related to dynamics in the system's self-model, i.e., model inaccuracy. Internal stimuli does not necessarily include workload itself, but if the self-model is application-dependent, workload changes may be the source of internal stimuli. For example, if the system's self-model is application-dependent, and the executing application changes, a self-optimizing manager will have the ability to reason and act towards achieving the system goal(s) efficiently for the new application. However, if the system's self-model is rigid and the system dynamics used to reason and act are oversimplified, model inaccuracies may lead to undesirable or inefficient decisions when the application changes.

Figure 2. Cluster power vs. operating frequency
(from (Donyanavard et al., 2018))

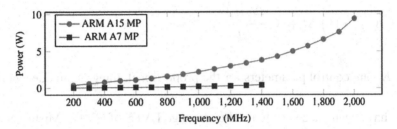

Background and Motivation

Dynamic voltage/frequency scaling (DVFS) has been established as an effective technique to improve the power-efficiency of chip-multiprocessors (CMPs) (Herbert & Marculescu, 2007). In this context, numerous closed-loop control-theoretic solutions for chip power management (Rahmani et al., 2015; Hoffmann, 2011; Mishra et al., 2010; Muthukaruppan et al., 2013; Ma et al., 2011; Wang et al., 2011) have been proposed. These solutions employ *linear control* techniques to limit the power consumption by controlling the CMP operating frequency. However, the relationship between operating frequency and power is often *nonlinear*. Figure 2 illustrates this by showing total power consumed by a 4-core ARM A15 cluster executing a CPU-intensive workload through its entire frequency range (200MHz--2GHz), along with the total power consumed by a 4-core ARM A7 cluster through its frequency range (200MHz--1400MHz). While the A7 cluster frequency-power relationship is almost linear, the A15 cluster's larger frequency range (and more voltage levels) results in a nonlinear relationship. Using a linear model to estimate the behavior of such a system leads to inaccuracies. Inaccurate models result in inefficient controllers, which defeats the very purpose of using control theoretic techniques for power management.

Ideally, control-theoretic solutions should provide formal guarantees, be simple enough for runtime implementation, and handle nonlinear system behavior. Static linear feedback controllers can provide robustness and stability guarantees with simple implementations, while adaptive controllers modify the controller at runtime to adapt to the discrepancies between the expected and the actual system behavior. However, modifying the controller at runtime is a costly operation that also invalidates the formal guarantees provided at design time.

Instead, consider integrating multiple linear models within a single controller implementation in order to estimate nonlinear behavior of DVFS for CMPs. This is a well-established and lightweight adaptive control theoretic technique called *gain scheduling*.

Classical Control

Discrete-time control techniques are the most appropriate to implement control of computer systems. The proportional-integral-derivative (PID) controller is a simple and flexible classical feedback controller that computes control input $u(t)$ based on the error $e(t)$ between the measured output and reference output:

$$u(k) = K_p e(k) + K_i \sum_0^k e(k) \Delta t + K_d \frac{\Delta e(k)}{\Delta t}$$

K_p, K_i, and K_d are control parameters for the proportional, integral, and derivative gains respectively.

PI controllers[1] have been successfully used to manage DVFS of CMPs (Mishra et al., 2010; Wu et al., 2004; Muthukaruppan et al., 2013; Ma et al., 2011; Wang et al., 2011). Mishra et al. (2010) propose the use of PID controllers for VF islands.

The authors model power consumption based on the assumption that the difference relationship between power consumption in successive intervals can be approximated linearly as a function of frequency, which only holds for limited range. Similarly, Hoffman et al. (2011) propose a feedback control technique for power management that includes DVFS, and their transfer function assumes a linear relationship between power and frequency. However, Figure 2 shows that $f \rightarrow P$ becomes nonlinear at higher frequencies. Inaccuracies in linear estimation of nonlinear systems can negatively impact the steady-state error and transient response of the controller. Take for example a system operating under a power budget, or experiencing a thermal emergency -- a DVFS controller designed from an inaccurate model could lead to wasted power or even unnecessary operation at an unsafe frequency.

Consider a DVFS controller for a 4-core CMP with a single frequency domain. The first steps in designing a controller are defining the system and identifying the model. The power consumption of our CMP is not linear across the entire range of supported operating frequencies (200MHz--2GHz), which makes it challenging to model the entire range with a single linear estimation. However, we can divide the measured output (power) for the entire range of frequencies into multiple *operating regions* that exhibit linear behavior. In this example, we identify a model for two different systems: (1) the CMP's behavior through all operating frequencies; (2) the CMP's behavior through a sub-range of the operating frequencies. This specific operating region spans the frequency sub-range of 200MHz--1200MHz. Using these models, we can generate two different $f \rightarrow P$ Single-Input-Single-Output (SISO) PI controllers, and compare them using measured SASO analysis (Hellerstein et al., 2004), focusing on *Accuracy* and *Settling time*. We refer to the full-range controller as Controller 1, and the sub-range controller as Controller 2. Figure 3 displays Controller 1 (Figure 3a) and Controller 2's (Figure 3b) ability to track a dynamic power reference over time for our CMP.

Figure 3. Time plots of two DVFS controllers tracking a dynamic power reference (from (Donyanavard et al., 2018))

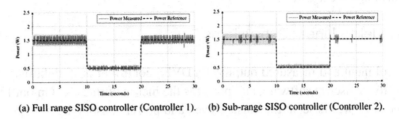

(a) Full range SISO controller (Controller 1).   (b) Sub-range SISO controller (Controller 2).

Accuracy is defined by the steady-state error between the measured output and reference input, e.g., the yellow highlighted region in Figure 3b from 0-10 seconds. We calculate the steady-state error as the mean squared error (MSE) between the measured power and reference power. Both controllers are able to track within 1% of the target power. However, the MSE of Controller 2 is 0.003, while that of Controller 1 is 0.013 -- an order of magnitude larger. This byproduct of model inaccuracy translates into wasted power and undesirable operating frequency, as well as unnecessary changes in the frequency control input (i.e., increased control effort cost).

Settling time is the time it takes to reach sufficiently close to the steady-state value after the reference values are specified, e.g., when the reference changes in Figure 3b at 10 seconds. The settling time of Controller 2 is 40 ms on average, while Controller 1 is more than double on average at 100 ms. Because our actuation periods are 50 ms, this means that our sub-range controller often reaches steady state on its first actuation while the full range controller requires multiple actuation periods to respond to a change in reference.

Identifying operating regions at design time allows us to switch system models at runtime, improving the effectiveness of static controllers.

Figure 4. Modeled and observed behavior of nonlinear full-range system (a) vs. linear operating region (b) (from (Donyanavard et al., 2018))

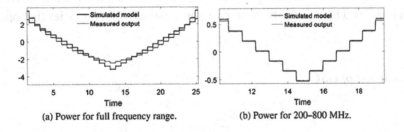

(a) Power for full frequency range.   (b) Power for 200–800 MHz.

Case Study: Designing a Gain Scheduled Controller (GSC) for Power Management

As a demonstrative case study, we target the ODROID-XU3 platform[2] which contains an ARM big. LITTLE based Exynos 5422 Octa-core SoC (Chung et al., 2012) that has heterogeneous multi-processing (HMP) cores. The Exynos platform contains an HMP with two 4-core clusters: the *big* cluster provides high-performance out-of-order cores, while the *little* cluster provides low-power in-order cores. For the purpose of our study, we disable the little cluster (due to its linear behavior) and use only the big cores to emulate a uniform nonlinear CMP[3].

Defining and Modeling Linear Subsystems

Selecting the control input and measured output of a DVFS controller is straightforward. Frequency is the knob available to the user in software, and power is the metric of interest. On our Exynos CMP, the operating frequency of cores is set at the cluster level, and power sensors measure power at the cluster level. A SISO controller is a natural solution, with the entire CMP composing the system under control.

For system identification we generate test waveforms from applications and use statistical black-box methods based on System Identification Theory (Lennart, 1999; Ljung, 2001) for isolating the deterministic and stochastic components of the system to build the model.

Table 1. VF Pairs for ARM A15 in Exynos 5422

Region	Frequency Range (MHz)	Voltage (V)
1	1600 – 2000	1.25
2	1300 – 1500	1.10
3	900 – 1200	1.00
4	200 – 800	0.90

Figure 4a shows a comparison of a simulated model output vs. the measured output over the entire frequency range of our CMP. It is evident that there are ranges for which the estimated behavior differs from that of the actual system behavior. We know that voltage has a nonlinear effect on dynamic power ($P = CV^2 f$). The nonlinear relationship between frequency and voltage pairs through the range of operating frequencies amplifies this effect (Table 1). Table 1 lists all valid VF pairs for the CMP, in which there are only four different voltage levels. Figure 4b shows the measured vs. modeled output when the system is defined by a single operating region grouped by frequencies that operate at the same voltage level.

Figure 5. Block diagram of GSC

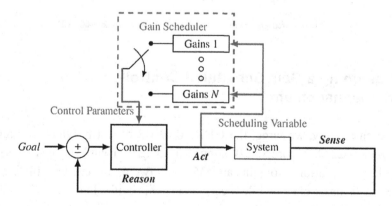

Generating Linear Controllers

We generate a PI controller separately for each operating region using the system models and MATLAB's Control System toolbox. This is a straightforward process for a simple off-the-shelf PI controller.

In the next step, the designed controller is evaluated against disturbance and uncertainties in order to ensure it remains stable at a defined confidence level. Unaccounted elements, modeling limitations, and environmental effects are estimated as model uncertainty in order to check the disturbance rejection of the controller. In our case, we can confirm our controller is robust enough to reject the disturbance from workload variation.

Each controller we design for an operating region is defined by its control parameters K_P and K_I which are stored (in memory) in the gain scheduler (Figure 5). In the gain scheduler, we incorporate logic to determine which gains to provide the controller when invoked.

Implementing Gain Scheduling

The gain scheduler enables us to adapt to nonlinear behavior (Figure 5) by combining multiple linear controllers.

It stores predefined controller gains and is responsible for providing the most appropriate gains based on the operating region in which the system currently resides each time the controller is invoked.

The scheduling variable is the variable used to define operating regions. For our controller, the scheduling variable is frequency as it is simpler to implement in software and has a direct VF mapping (Table 1). Our gain scheduler implements lightweight logic that determines the set of gains based on the system's operating frequency (scheduling variable). Algorithm 1 shows the logic implemented in our gain scheduler with N operating regions where f is the scheduling variable and K_P and K_I are the controller parameters. In addition to the K_P and K_I controller parameters, there is also an *offset*. The *offset* is the mean actuation value for the operating region, and is necessary for providing the control input for the next control period. Algorithm 1 accounts for the transitions between operating regions by applying a full-range linear controller. This method is utilized as the sets of gains for a particular operating region perform poorly outside of that region.

Experiments

Our goal is to evaluate our nonlinear GSC with respect to the state-of-the-art linear controller in terms of both theoretical and observed ability to track power goals on a CMP. Our evaluation is done using the Exynos CMP running Ubuntu Linux[4]. We consider a typical mobile scenario in which one or more multi-threaded applications execute concurrently across the CMP.

Algorithm 1. Gain scheduler implementation

Input: f : frequency, scheduling variable;

Outputs: K_{P_n} , K_{I_n} , $offset_n$: updated controller parameters;

Variables: ref_{prev} , ref_{next} : power reference values for previous and next control periods;

Constants: $Region[N]$: operating regions, defined by mutually exclusive range of frequencies; $K_P[N]$, $K_I[N]$, $offset[N]$: stored controller parameters for each operating region; K_{P_G} , K_{I_G} , $offset_G$: controller parameters for full-range linear controller;

```
if ref_next != ref_prev then
```
$$K_{P_n} = K_{P_G}$$
$$K_{I_n} = K_{I_G}$$
$$offset_n = offset_G$$
```
    return
else
    for i = 1 to N do
        if Region[i].contains(f) then
```
$$K_{P_n} = K_P[i]$$
$$K_{I_n} = K_I[i]$$
$$offset_n = offset[i]$$
```
            return
        end if
    end for
end if
```

Controllers

We designed two DVFS controllers for power management of the CMP: 1) **a linear controller** that estimates the transfer function similarly to (Hoffmann et al., 2011; Mishra et al., 2010);

and our proposed 2) **GSC**. The GSC contains three operating regions (Table 2). We combine the two smallest adjacent Regions, 1 and 2 (Table 1), to create Controller 2.1. Controllers are provided a single power reference for the whole system. The control input is frequency, and the measured output is power, applied to the entire CMP.

The controller is implemented as a Linux userspace process that executes in parallel with the applications. Power is calculated using the on-board current and voltage sensors present on the ODROID board. Power measurements and controller invocation are performed periodically every 50 ms.

Workloads

We developed a custom micro-benchmark used for system identification. The micro-benchmark consists of a sequence of independent multiply-accumulate operations yielding varied instruction-level parallelism. This allows us to model a wide range of behavior in system outputs given changes in the controllable inputs. We test our controllers using three PARSEC benchmarks: bodytrack, streamcluster, and x264. For each case, we execute one multithreaded application instance of the benchmark with four threads, resulting in a fully-loaded CMP. We empirically select three references that we alternate between during execution. ref_1 is 3.5 W, the highest reference and a reasonable power envelope for a mobile SoC. This represents a high-performance mode that maximizes performance under a power budget. ref_2 is 0.5 W, the lowest reference and represents a reduced budget in response to a thermal event. ref_3 is 1.5 W, a middling reference that could represent the result of an optimizer that maximizes energy efficiency. These references are not necessarily trackable for all workloads, but should span at least three different operating regions for each workload. For each case, the applications run for a total of 65 s. After the first 5 s (warm-up period) the controllers are set to ref_1 or 20 s, then changed to ref_2 for 20 s, and to ref_3 for the remaining 20 s.

Controller Design Evaluation

Table 2. Accuracy of the full- (Ctrl 1) and sub-range (Ctrl 2.x) controllers

	Ctrl 1	Ctrl 2.1	Ctrl 2.2	Ctrl 2.3
Freq. Range	200 – 1800	1300 – 1800	900 – 1200	200 – 800
Stable	✓	✓	✓	✓
Accuracy (MSE)	0.1748	0.03089	0.0005382	0.0003701

We used a first-order system, with a target crossover frequency of 0.32. This resulted in a simple controller providing the fastest settling time with no overshoot. Models are generated with a stability focus and uncertainty guardbands of 30%.

All systems are stable according to Robust Stability Analysis. By design all overshoot values are 0.

The settling times of Controllers 2.2 and 2.3 are comparably low at 5 control periods. Controller 2.1 (the most nonlinear operating region) and Controller 1 are slightly higher at 8-9 control periods. The ideal controllers are all very similar in terms of stability, settling time, and overshoot. The primary difference between them is in terms of accuracy. Controllers 2.1-2.3 achieve an order of magnitude better accuracy than Controller 1 (Table 2). This means that the region controllers are equally as responsive as the full-range model in achieving a target value while achieving the value more accurately.

Figure 6. Comparison of GSC with Controller 1
(from (Donyanavard et al., 2018))

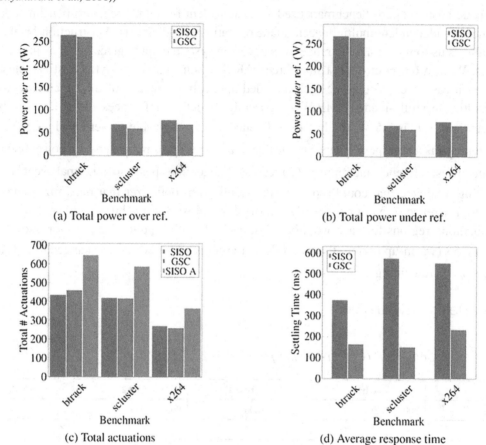

(a) Total power over ref.

(b) Total power under ref.

(c) Total actuations

(d) Average response time

Controller Implementation Evaluation

We now evaluate the effectiveness of our nonlinear control approach implemented in software on the Exynos CMP for multithreaded mobile workloads. Traditional SASO control analysis gives us a way to compare the controllers in theory, but the system-level effects of those metrics are not directly relatable. Therefore, we will compare the runtime behavior of the software controllers using a slightly modified set of metrics: power over target, power under target, number of actuations, and response time. These metrics are shown in Figure 6.

The *power over target* is the total amount of measured power exceeding the reference power throughout execution (Figure 6a). This is the area under the output and above the reference. It represents the amount of power wasted due to inaccuracy, and can also represent unsafe execution above a power cap. Our GSC is able to achieve 12% less power over target than the linear controller for x264 and streamcluster. bodytrack is the most dynamic workload and results in the noisiest power output. In this case the GSC only improves the power over target by 1% compared to the linear controller.

The *power under target* is the total amount of measured power falling short of the reference power throughout execution (Figure 6b). This is the area under the reference and above the output. A lower value translates to improved performance (i.e. lower is better). Similarly to the power over target, our GSC is able to reduce power under target by 12% for x264 and streamcluster, and 1% for bodytrack.

The *number of actuations* is simply a count of how many times the frequency changes throughout execution, and is a measure of overhead (Figure 6c). The GSC's actuation overhead is lower than the linear controller for bodytrack, streamcluster, and x264 by 8%, 1%, and 4% respectively. This is expected, as the controller's resistance to actuation is related to the crossover frequency specified at design time. For the same crossover frequency, the GSC benefits are primarily in the accuracy (power over/under target) and response (settling) time. To illustrate this tradeoff, we performed the same experiments for a full-range linear controller with a target crossover frequency of 0.8 (Controller 1b). We arrived at this value empirically: Controller 1b achieves comparable accuracy to the GSC. However, GSC reduces the actuation overhead by 29% for all workloads compared to Controller 1b.

The *response time* is the average settling time when the target power changes, indicating the controller's ability to respond quickly to changes (Figure 6d). Figure 6d shows the average response time for each workload for both controllers. The GSC is able to improve the response time over Controller 1 by more than 50% in each case. The GSC's overall average response time is 182 ms, which is less than 4 control periods.

The implementation overhead of the GSC w.r.t. the linear controller is negligible: it requires a single execution of Algorithm 1 upon each invocation, and storage for a K_P, K_I, and *offset* value for each operating region. Although workload disturbance plays a significant role in determining the magnitude in imporovement of a nonlinear GSC over a state-of-the-art linear controller, a clear trend exists, and these advantages would increase with the modeled system's degree of nonlinearity.

Summary

Self-models are the core components of self-awareness. In computer systems, system dynamics can be complex. When utilizing a self-model at runtime for reflection, models must be simple and sufficiently accurate. The more accurate the self-model, the more effective the decisions made by a resource manager can be toward achieving a given goal. We propose a simple way to improve the accuracy of self-models for resource managers employing classical controllers: gain scheduling. Gain scheduled control generates multiple controllers based on optimized fixed models for different operating regions of the system, and can deploy the most accurate control at runtime based on the system state. This is an improvement over using a single controller based on a single fixed model with minimal overhead. In our case study, the gain scheduled controller more effectively provides dynamic power management of a single-core processor when compared to a single fixed SISO controller.

Using a static model for resource management may not be sufficient in complex mobile systems: system dynamics may change between applications or devices, and fixed models may not remain accurate over time. In the future, we plan to address such scenarios by identifying and continuously updating models during runtime based on observation, instead of identifying multiple fixed models at design-time to swap out at runtime.

Figure 7. Basic 2×2 MIMO for single-core system. Clock frequency and idle cores are used as control inputs. FPS and power are measured outputs that are compared with reference (i.e., target) values.

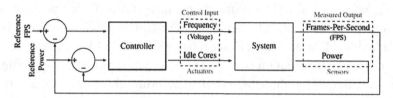

SELF-ADAPTIVITY

Self-adaptivity is the ability of a system to adjust to changes in goals due to external stimuli. For example, if a system experiences a thermal event during a computational sprint and enters an unsafe state, a self-adaptive manager will have the ability to modify the goal from maximizing performance to minimizing temperature.

Motivation and Background

To address self-optimization, we examined a relatively simply use-case in which we deployed a resource manager responsible for controlling a unicore with only a single input and single output. However, modern computer systems incorporate up to hundreds of cores, from datacenters to mobile devices. Modern mobile devices commonly deploy architecturally differentiated cores on a single chip multiprocessor, known as heterogeneous multiprocessors (HMPs). In the case of mobile devices, systems are tasked with the challenge of balancing application goals with system constraints, e.g., a performance requirement within a power budget. Resource managers are required to configure the system at runtime to meet the goal. However, due to workload or operating condition variation, it is possible for goals to change unpredictably at runtime. In this section, we use self-adaptivity to enable a mobile HMP resource manager to adapt to a changing goal, coordinating and prioritizing multiple objectives.

Managing Dynamic System-wide Goals

Controllers may behave non-optimally, or even detrimentally, in meeting a shared goal without knowledge of the presence or behavior of seemingly orthogonal controllers (Rahmani et al., 2018a; Bitirgen et al., 2008; Vega:2013:CUD; Ebrahimi et al., 2009; Ebrahimi et al., 2010; Das et al., 2009). Consider the MIMO controller in Figure 7 that controls a single-core system with two control inputs ($u(t)$) and interdependent measured outputs ($y(t)$). The controller tracks two objectives (frames per second, or FPS, and power consumption) by controlling two actuators (operating frequency and cache size). We implement the MIMO using a Linear Quadratic Gaussian (LQG) controller (Skogestad & Postlethwaite, 2007) similarly to (Pothukuchi et al., 2016):

$$x\bigl(t+1\bigr) = A \times x\bigl(t\bigr) + B \times u\bigl(t\bigr)$$

$$y(t) = C \times x(t) + D \times u(t)$$

where x is the system state, y is the measured output vector, and u is the control input vector.[5]

Figure 8. x264 running on a quad-core cluster controlled by 2×2 MIMOs with different output priorities
(from (Rahmani et al., 2018b))

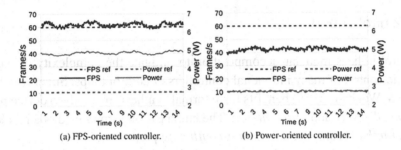

(a) FPS-oriented controller.   (b) Power-oriented controller.

LQG control allows us to specify 1) the relative sensitivity of a system to control inputs, and 2) the relative priority of measured outputs. This is done using 1) a weighted Tracking Error Cost matrix (Q) and 2) a Control Effort Cost matrix (R). The weights are specified during the design of the controller. While this is convenient for achieving a fixed goal, it can be problematic for goals that change over time (e.g., minimizing power consumption before a predicted thermal emergency).

The controller must choose an appropriate trade-off when we cannot achieve both desirable performance and power concurrently. Unfortunately, classical MIMOs fix control weights at design time, and thus *cannot* perform *runtime* tradeoffs that require changing output priorities. Even with constant *reference values*, i.e., desired output values, unpredictable disturbances (e.g., changing workload and operating conditions) may cause the reference values to become unachievable. It is also plausible for the reference values themselves to change dynamically at runtime with system state and operating conditions (e.g., a thermal event).

Let us now consider a more complex scenario: a multi-threaded application running on Linux, executing on a mobile processor, where the system needs to track both the performance (FPS) and power simultaneously. Figure 7 shows the 2×2 MIMO model for this system with operating frequency and the number of active cores as control inputs, and FPS and power as measured outputs.

Both the FPS and power reference values are trackable individually, but not jointly. We implement and compare two different MIMO controllers in Linux to show the effect of competing objectives. One controller prioritizes FPS, and the other prioritizes power. Figure 8 shows the power and performance (in FPS) achieved by each MIMO controller using typical reference values for a mobile device: 60 FPS and 5 Watts. The application is x264, and the mobile processor consists of an ARM Cortex-A15 quad-core cluster. Each MIMO controller is designed with a different Q matrix to prioritize either FPS or power: Figure 8a's controller favors FPS over power by a ratio of 30:1 (i.e., only 1% deviation from the FPS reference is acceptable for a 30% deviation from the power reference), while Figure 8b uses a ratio of 1:30. We observe that neither controller is able to manage changing system goals. Thus, there is a need for a supervisor to autonomously orchestrate the system while considering the significance of competing objectives, user requirements, and operating conditions.

The use of supervisory control presents at least three additional advantages over conventional controllers. First, fully-distributed MIMO or SISO controllers *cannot* address system-wide goals such as power capping. Second, conventional controllers *cannot* model actuation effects that require system-wide perspective, such as task migration. Third, classical control theory *cannot* address problems requiring optimization (e.g., minimizing an objective function) alone (Karamanolis et al., 2005; Pothukuchi et al., 2016).

Supervisory Control Theory

Supervisory control utilizes modular decomposition to mitigate the complexity of control problems, enabling automatic control of many individual controllers or control loops. Supervisory control theory (SCT) (Ramadge & Wonham, 1989) benefits from formal synthesis methods to define principal control properties for *controllability* and *observability*. The emphasis on formal methods in addition to *modularity* leads to *hierarchical consistency* and *non-conflicting* properties.

SCT solves complex synthesis problems by breaking them into small-scale sub-problems, known as modular synthesis. The results of modular synthesis characterize the conditions under which decomposition is effective. In particular, results identify whether a valid decomposition exists.

A decomposition is valid if the solutions to sub-problems combine to solve the original problem, and the resulting composite supervisors are *non-blocking* and *minimally restrictive*. Decomposition also

Figure 9. Supervisory Control structure. Low level control loops are guided by the Supervisory Controller that achieves system-wide goals based on the high-level system model.

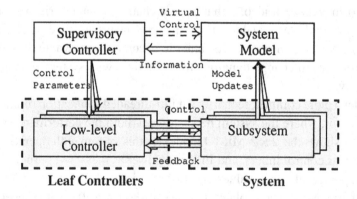

adds robustness to the design because nonlinearities in the supervisor do *not* directly affect the system dynamics.

Figure 9 illustrates how a supervisory control structure can hierarchically manage control loops. As shown in the figure, supervision is vertically decomposed into tasks performed at different levels of abstraction (Thistle, 1996). The supervisory controller is designed to control the high-level *system model*, which represents an abstraction of the system. The *subsystems* compose the pre-existing *system* that does *not* meet the given specifications without the aid of a controller or a supervisor. The *information* channel provides information about the updates in the high-level model to the supervisory controller. Due to the fact that the system model is an abstract model, the controlling channel is an indirect *virtual control channel*. In other words, the control decisions of the supervisory controller will be implemented by controlling the *low-level controller(s)* through *control parameters*. Consequently, the low-level controller(s) can control one or multiple subsystems using the *control* channel and gather information via *feedback*. The changes in the subsystems can trigger *model updates* in the state of the high-level system model. These updates reflect the results of low-level controllers' controlling actions.

The scheme of Figure 9 describes the division of supervision into high-level management and low-level operational supervision. Virtual control exercised via the high-level control channel can be implemented by modifying control parameters to adaptively coordinate the low-level controllers, e.g., by adjusting their objective functions according to the system goal. The combination of horizontal and vertical decomposition enables us to not only physical divide the system into subsystems, but also to logically divide the sub-problems in any appropriate way, e.g., due to varying epochs (control invocation period) or scope. The important requirement of this hierarchical control scheme is control consistency and hierarchical consistency between the high-level model and the low-level system, as defined in the standard Ramadge-Wonham control mechanism (Thistle, 1996)}. For a detailed description of SCT, we refer the reader to (Ramadge & Wonham, 1989; Safonov, 1997; Brandin et al., 1991; Thistle, 1996).

Self-Adaptivity via Supervisory Control

Supervisory controllers are preferable to *adaptive (self-tuning) controllers* for complex system control due to their ability to integrate **logic** with **continuous dynamics**. Specifically, supervisory control has two key properties: i) rapid adaptation in response to abrupt changes in management policy (Hespanha, 2001), and ii) low computational complexity by computing control parameters for different policies **offline**. New policies and their corresponding parameters can be added to the supervisor on demand

Figure 10. Self-adaptivity via gain scheduling in SCT

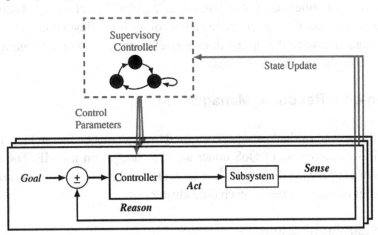

(e.g., by upgrading the firmware or OS), rendering online learning-based self-tuning methods, e.g., least-squares estimation (Åström, 2013), unnecessary.

Figure 11. SPECTR overview

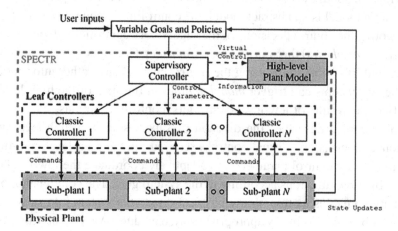

Figure 10 depicts the two mechanisms that enable SCT-based management via low-level controllers: **gain scheduling** and **dynamic references**. Gain scheduling is a nonlinear control technique that uses a set of linear controllers predesigned for different operating regions. Gain scheduling enables the appropriate linear controller based on runtime observations (Leith & Leithead, 2000). Scheduling is implemented by switching between sets of control parameters, i.e., $A_1 \rightarrow A_2$, $B_1 \rightarrow B_2$, $C_1 \rightarrow C_2$, and $D_1 \rightarrow D_2$ in the LQG equations. In this case, the *controller gains* are the values of the control parameters A, B, C, and D. Gains are useful to change objectives at runtime in response to abrupt and sudden changes in management policy. In LQG controllers, this is done by changing priorities of outputs using the Q and R matrices. This is what we call the Hierarchical Control structure, in which local controllers solve specified tasks while the higher-level supervisory controller coordinates the global objective function. In this structure, the supervisory controller receives information from the plant (e.g., the presence of a thermal emergency) or the user/application (e.g., new QoS reference value), and steers the system towards the desired policy using its design logic and high-level model. Thanks to its top-level perspective, the supervisor can update reference values for each low-level controller to either optimize for a certain goal (e.g., getting to the optimum energy-efficient point) or manage resource allocation (e.g., allocating power budget to different cores).

Case Study: On-chip Resource Management

In this section, we design and evaluate a supervisor used to implement a hierarchical resource manager. The use-case requires management of QoS under a power budget on a HMP. The resource manager (SPECTR) consists of a supervisor that guides low-level classical controllers to configure core operating frequency and number of active cores for each core cluster.

Hierarchical System Architecture

Figure 11 depicts a high-level view of SPECTR for many-core system resource management. Either the user or the system software may specify *Variable Goals and Policies*. The *Supervisory Controller* aims to meet system goals by managing the low-level controllers. High-level decisions are made based on the feedback given by the *High-level Plant Model*, which provides an abstraction of the entire system. Various types of *Classic Controllers*, such as PID or state-space controllers, can be used to implement each low-level controller based on the target of each subsystem. The flexibility to incorporate any pre-verified off-the-shelf controllers without the need for system-wide verification is essential for the modularity of this approach. The supervisor provides parameters such as output references or gain values to each low-level controller during runtime according to the system policy. Low-level controller subsystems update the high-level model to maintain global system state, and potentially trigger the supervisory controller to take action. The high-level model can be designed in various fashions (e.g., rule-based or estimator-based (Safonov, 1997; Hespanha, 2001; Morse, 1997)) to track the system state and provide the supervisor with guidelines. We illustrate the steps for designing a supervisory controller using the following experimental case study in which SCT is deployed on a real HMP platform, and we then outline the entire design flow from modeling of the high-level plant to generating the supervisory controller.

Figure 12. SPECTR implementation on the Exynos HMP with two heterogeneous quad-core clusters. Representing a typical mobile scenario with a single foreground application running concurrently with many background applications.

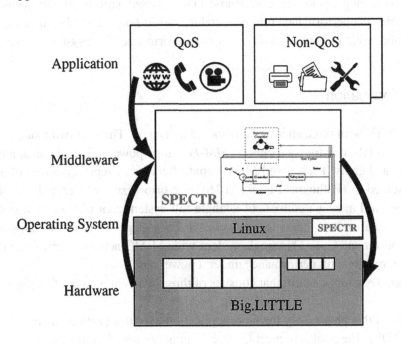

SPECTR Resource Manager

Figure 12 shows an overview of our experimental setup. We target the Exynos platform, which contains an HMP with two quad-core clusters: the **Big** core cluster provides high-performance out-of-order cores, while the **Little** core cluster provides low-power in-order cores. Memory is shared across all cores, so application threads can transparently execute on any core in any cluster. We consider a typical mobile scenario in which a single foreground application (the *QoS application*) is running concurrently with many background applications (the *Non-QoS applications*). This mimics a typical mobile use-case in which gaming or media processing is performed in the foreground in conjunction with background email or social media syncs.

The system goals are twofold: i) meet the QoS requirement of the foreground application while minimizing its energy consumption; and ii) ensure the total system power always remains below the Thermal Design Power (TDP).

The **subsystems** are the two heterogeneous quad-core (*Big* and *Little*) clusters. Each cluster has two actuators: one actuator to set the operating frequency (F_{next} and associated voltage of the cluster; and one to set the number of active cores (AC_{next} on the cluster. We measure the power consumption (P_{curr} of each cluster, and simultaneously monitor the QoS performance (QoS_{curr} of the designated application to compare it to the required QoS (QoS_{ref}.[6]

Supervisory control commands guide the **low-level MIMO controllers** in Figure 12 to determine the number of active cores and the core operating frequency within each cluster.

Supervisory control minimizes the system-wide power consumption while maintaining QoS. In our scenario, the QoS application runs only on the Big cluster, and the supervisor determines whether and how to adjust the cluster's power budget based on QoS measurements.

Gain scheduling is used to switch the priority objective of the low-level controllers.

We define two sets of gains for this case-study: 1) *QoS-based* gains are tuned to ensure that the QoS application can meet the performance reference value, and 2) *Power-based* gains are tuned to limit the power consumption while possibly sacrificing some performance if the system is exceeding the power budget threshold.

Experimental Evaluation

We compare SPECTR with three alternative resource managers. The first two managers use two unco-ordinated 2×2 MIMOs, one for each cluster: *MM-Pow* uses power-oriented gains, and *MM-Perf* uses performance-oriented gains. These fixed MIMO controllers act as representatives of a state-of-the-art solution, as presented in (Pothukuchi et al., 2016), one prioritizing power and the other prioritizing performance. The third manager consists of a single full-system controller (*FS*): a system-wide 4×2 MIMO with individual control inputs for each cluster. FS uses power-oriented gains and its measured outputs are chip power and QoS. This single system-wide MIMO acts as a representative for (Zhang & Hoffmann, 2016), maximizing performance under a power cap.

We analyze an execution scenario that consists of three different phases of execution:

1. **Safe Phase:** In this phase, only the QoS application executes (with an achievable QoS reference within the TDP). The goal is to meet QoS and minimize power consumption.
2. **Emergency Phase:** In this phase, the QoS reference remains the same as that in the Safe Phase while the power envelope is reduced (emulating a thermal emergency). The goal is to adapt to the change in reference power while maintaining QoS (if possible).
3. **Workload Disturbance Phase:** In this phase, the power envelope returns to TDP and background tasks are added (to induce interference from other tasks). The goal is to meet the QoS reference value without exceeding the power envelope.

This execution scenario with three different phases allows us to evaluate how SPECTR compares with state-of-the-art resource managers when facing workload variation and system-wide changes in state (e.g., thermal emergency) and goals.

Evaluated Resource Manager Configurations

We generate stable low-level controllers for each resource manager using the Matlab System Identification Toolbox (MathWorks, 2017).[7] We use the Control Effort Cost matrix (R) to prioritize changing clock frequency over number of cores at a ratio of 2:1, as frequency is a finer-grained and lower-overhead actuator than core count. We generate training data by executing an in-house microbenchmark and varying control inputs in the format of a staircase test (i.e., a sine wave), both with single-input variation and all-input variation. The micro-benchmark consists of a sequence of independent multiply-accumulate operations performed over both sequentially and randomly accessed memory locations, thus yielding various levels of instruction-level and memory-level parallelism. The range of exercised behavior resembles or exceeds the variation we expect to see in typical mobile workloads, which is the target application domain of our case studies.

Experimental Setup

We perform our evaluations on the ARM big.LITTLE-based Exynos SoC (ODROID-XU3 board) as described in our case study (Figure 12). We implement a Linux userspace daemon process that invokes the low-level controllers every 50 ms. When evaluating SPECTR, the daemon invokes the supervisor every 100 ms. We use ARM's Performance Monitor Unit (PMU) and per-cluster power sensors for the performance and power measurements required by the resource managers. The userspace daemon also implements the Heartbeats API (Hoffmann et al., 2013) monitor to measure QoS. By periodically issuing *heartbeats*, the application informs the system about its current performance. The user provides a performance reference value using the Heartbeats API.

To evaluate the resource managers, we use the following benchmarks from the PARSEC benchmark suite (Bienia C., 2011) as QoS applications (i.e., the applications that issue heartbeats to the controller): x264, bodytrack, canneal, and streamcluster. The selected applications consist of the most CPU-bound along with the most cache-bound PARSEC benchmarks, providing varied responses to change in resource allocation. Speedups from $3.2\times$ (streamcluster) to $4.5\times$ (x264) are observed with the maximum resource allocation values compared to the minimum. We also use one of four machine-learning workloads as our QoS application: k-means, KNN, least squares, and linear regression. These four workloads provide a wide range of data-intensive use cases. For all experiments, each QoS application uses four threads. The background (non-QoS) tasks used in the third execution phase are single-threaded microbenchmarks, and have no runtime restrictions, i.e., the Linux scheduler can freely migrate them between and within clusters.

Effectiveness of Self-Adaptivity Through Supervision

We focus our discussion on the x264 benchmark results. Other results are summarized at the end of this section. We use heartbeats to measure the frames per second (FPS) as our QoS metric. Figure 13 shows the measured FPS and power for x264 with respect to their reference values over the course of execution for all of the resource management controllers.

Figure 13. Measured FPS and Power of all four resource managers for three Phases of 5 seconds each, for the x264 benchmark
(from (Rahmani et al., 2018b))

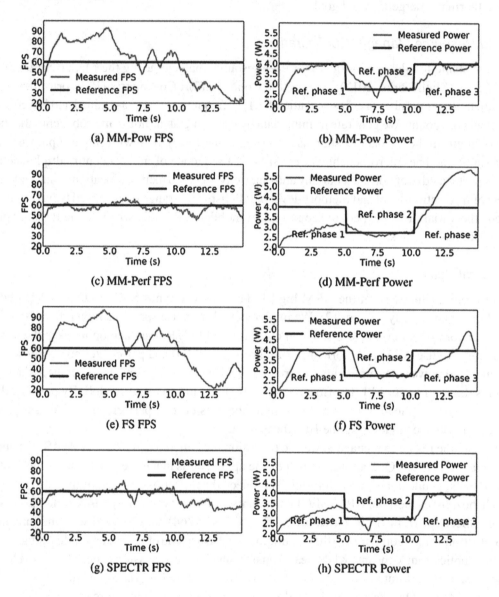

(a) MM-Pow FPS

(b) MM-Pow Power

(c) MM-Perf FPS

(d) MM-Perf Power

(e) FS FPS

(f) FS Power

(g) SPECTR FPS

(h) SPECTR Power

X264 Benchmark

To show the energy efficiency of SPECTR, we study the Safe Phase. The Safe Phase consists of the first 5 seconds of execution during which only the QoS application executes on the Big cluster. In this phase, all controllers are able to achieve the FPS reference value within the power envelope. Figures 14a and 14b show the average steady-state error (%) of QoS and power respectively for each resource manager in Phase 1. Steady-state error is used to define *accuracy* in feedback control systems (Hellerstein et al., 2004). Steady-state error values are calculated as *reference − measured output* . Negative values indicate that the power/QoS **exceeds** the reference value, positive values indicate power savings or failure to meet QoS. We make two key observations. First, both MM-Perf and SPECTR reduce power consumption by 25% (Figure 14b) while maintaining FPS within 10% (Figure 14a) of the reference value. The MM-Perf controller operates efficiently because the reference FPS value is achievable within the TDP threshold. The SPECTR controller similarly operates efficiently: it is able to recognize that the FPS is achievable within TDP and, as a result, lower the reference power. Second, the FS and MM-Pow controllers unnecessarily exceed the reference FPS value and, as a result, consume excessive power. This is because these controllers prioritize meeting the power reference value, consuming the entire available power budget to maximize performance.

Figure 14. Steady-state error for all benchmarks, grouped by phase. A negative value indicates the amount of power/QoS exceeding the reference value (bad), a positive value indicates the amount of power saved (good) or QoS degradation (bad)
(from (Rahmani et al., 2018b)).

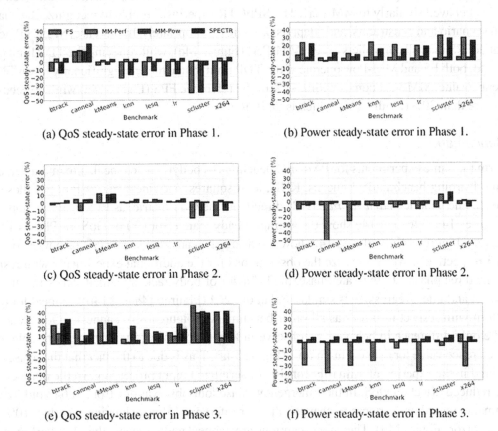

(a) QoS steady-state error in Phase 1.

(b) Power steady-state error in Phase 1.

(c) QoS steady-state error in Phase 2.

(d) Power steady-state error in Phase 2.

(e) QoS steady-state error in Phase 3.

(f) Power steady-state error in Phase 3.

To show SPECTR's ability to adapt to a sudden change in operating constraints, we study the Emergency Phase. The Emergency Phase of execution emulates a thermal emergency, during which, the TDP is lowered to ensure that the system operates in a safe state. This occurs during the second 5-second period of execution in Figure 13. We observe that all controllers are able to react to the change in power reference value and maintain QoS. However, compared to the other controllers, FS has a sluggish reaction (Figure 13f) to the change in power reference, despite the fact that it is designed to prioritize tracking the power output. *Settling time* is a property used to quantify responsiveness of feedback control systems (Hellerstein et al., 2004). Settling time is the time it takes to reach sufficiently close to the steady-state value after the reference values are set. The average settling time for the power output of FS is 2.07 seconds, while SPECTR has an average settling time of 1.28 seconds. The larger size of the state-space ($x(t)$ matrix in LQG equations) and the higher number of control inputs in the 4×2 FS compared to those of 2×2 controllers in SPECTR is the reason for the slow settling time of FS. This is also the reason why SISO controllers are generally faster that MIMOs (Hellerstein et al., 2004).

To show SPECTR's ability to adapt to workload disturbance and changing system goals, we study the Workload Disturbance Phase. The Workload Disturbance Phase occurs in seconds 10-15 of execution in Figure 13. In this phase, 1) the QoS reference value and the power envelope return to the same values as in Phase 1, and 2) we introduce disturbance in the form of background tasks. As a result of the workload disturbance, the QoS reference is *not* achievable within the TDP. We make two observations regarding the steady-state error in Figures 14e and 14f. First, SPECTR behaves similarly to MM-Pow, even though in Phase 1 it behaved similarly to MM-Perf. The SPECTR supervisor is able to recognize the change in execution scenario and constraints, and adapt its priorities appropriately. In this case, SPECTR achieves much higher FPS than all controllers except MM-Perf (Figure 14e), while obeying the TDP limit (Figure 14f). Second, both FS and MM-Pow operate at the TDP limit, but achieve a significantly lower FPS than the reference value. MM-Perf comes within ~5% of the reference FPS (Figure 14e) while exceeding the TDP by more than 30% (Figure 14f), which is undesirable.

Other Benchmarks

We perform the same experiments for PARSEC benchmarks bodytrack, canneal, streamcluster, as well as machine-learning benchmarks k-means, KNN, least squares, and linear regression. For these workloads, we use the generic *heartbeat rate* (HB) directly as the QoS metric, as FPS is not an appropriate metric. Figures 14a, 14c, and 14e show the average steady-state error (%) of QoS for Phases 1, 2, and 3 respectively. Figures 14b, 14d, and 14f show the average steady-state error (%) of power for Phases 1, 2, and 3 respectively. We summarize the observations for the additional experiments with respect to x264 for the three phases. In the Safe Phase, the behavior of bodytrack, streamcluster, k-means, KNN, least squares, and linear regression is similar to that of x264 (Figures 14a and 14b). canneal follows the same pattern with respect to power as all other benchmarks (Figure 14b). canneal's QoS steady-state error is the only difference in behavior we observe in Phase 1. None of the managers are able to meet the QoS reference value for canneal in Phase 1 (Figure 14a). This is due to the fact that the phase of canneal captured in the experiment primarily consists of serialized input processing, so the number of idle cores has reduced affect on QoS. In the Emergency Phase, our observations from x264 hold for nearly all benchmarks regarding response to change in power reference value, achieving less than 10% power steady-state error (Figure 14d). The only exceptions are canneal and k-means: the MM-Perf manager is unable to react to change in TDP for canneal and k-means. The MM-Perf manager lacks a supervisory coordinator and prioritizes performance, and was unable to find a configuration for canneal and k-means that satisfied the QoS reference value within TDP. In the Workload Disturbance Phase, SPECTR, FS, and MM-Pow all achieve near-reference power (Figure 14f). As expected, MM-Perf violates the TDP in all cases, but always achieves the highest QoS (Figure 14e).

We conclude that SPECTR is effective at (1) efficiently meeting multiple system objectives when it is possible to do so, (2) appropriately balancing multiple conflicting objectives, and (3) quickly responding to sudden and unpredictable changes in constraints due to workload or system state.

Overhead Evaluation

To show the overhead of the low-level MIMO controllers, we study their execution time. We measure the MIMO controller execution time to be 2.5 ms, on average, over 30 seconds. The MIMO controller is invoked every 50ms resulting in a 5% overhead, which is experienced by all evaluated controllers. We measure the runtime of the supervisor to be $30\,\mu$s, which is negligible even with respect to the MIMO controller execution time. The supervisor is invoked less frequently than the MIMO controllers ($2\times$ the period in our case), executes in parallel to the workload and MIMO controllers, and simply evaluates the system state in order to determine if the MIMO controller gains need changing. State changes that result in interventions on the low-level controllers occur only due to system-wide changes in the state (e.g., thermal emergency) or goals (e.g., change in performance reference value or execution mode), which are infrequent. When the supervisor needs to change the MIMO gains, it simply points the coefficient matrices to a different set of stored values. In our case study, we have two sets of gains (QoS and power oriented) that are generated when the controllers are designed and stored during system initialization. Changing the coefficient arrays at runtime takes effect immediately, and has no additional overhead.

To show the overhead of SPECTR's supervisory controller, we compare the total execution time of identical workloads with and without SPECTR. With respect to the preemption overhead due to globally managing resources, Linux's HMP scheduler typically maps SCT threads to a core on the low-power Little cluster. Therefore, the SCT threads are executed without preempting the QoS application, which always executes on the Big cluster. We verify the overall impact of the control system overhead by running the benchmarks on two different systems: i) a vanilla Linux setup[8] and ii) vanilla Linux with SPECTR running in the background. For (ii), SPECTR controllers perform all the required computations but do *not* change the system knobs (thus only the SPECTR overhead affects the system). When comparing the QoS of the applications across multiple runs, we verify a negligible average difference of 0.1% between the two systems.

We conclude that the benefits of SPECTR come at a negligible performance overhead.

Summary

Modern mobile systems require intelligent management to balance user demands and system constraints. At any given time, the relative priority of demands and constraints may change based on uncontrollable context, such as dynamic workload or operating condition. A resource manager must be able to autonomously detect such context changes and adapt appropriately. This property is known as self-adaptivity. We demonstrate one way to design a self-adaptive resource manager: using supervisory control theory. Supervisory control theory lends itself well to this challenge due to its high level of abstraction and lightweight implementation. The proposed supervisor successfully adapts to changes when managing quality of service under a power budget for chip multiprocessors. The hierarchy using supervisory control theory represents early exploration of self-adaptivity in the resource management domain, and a slight degree of self-awareness. This approach can be enhanced in one way through the definition and generation of goals. Initial work based on goal-driven autonomy has been done toward this end (Shamsa et al., 2019).

CONCLUSION

We use two forms of computational self-awareness to implement resource managers with simple but effective self-aware components. Systems can be self-aware to varying degrees, and the degree to which self-*X* properties are utilized is case-specific. We demonstrate the use of self-optimization in implementing a DVFS governor for managing power in a processor core. We demonstrate the use of self-adaptivity in implementing a multi-goal resource manager for managing QoS within a power budget in an HMP. Moving forward, as systems scale and configuration spaces grow, computational self-awareness provides a useful abstract tool for tackling various challenges in resource management.

ACKNOWLEDGMENT

This research was partially supported by the National Science Foundation [CCF-1704859].

REFERENCES

Annamalai, Rodrigues, Koren & Kundu. (2013). An opportunistic prediction-based thread scheduling to maximize throughput/watt in AMPs. *Proceedings of the 22nd International Conference on Parallel Architectures and Compilation Techniques*, 63-72. 10.1109/PACT.2013.6618804

Åström, K. J., & Wittenmark, B. (2013). *Adaptive control*. Courier Corporation.

Bartolini, A., Cacciari, M., Tilli, A., & Benini, L. (2011, March). A distributed and self-calibrating model-predictive controller for energy and thermal management of high-performance multicores. In 2011 Design, Automation & Test in Europe (pp. 1-6). IEEE. doi:10.1109/DATE.2011.5763141

Bienia, C. (2011). *Benchmarking modern multiprocessors* [Ph. D. Thesis]. Princeton University.

Bitirgen, R., Ipek, E., & Martinez, J. F. (2008, November). Coordinated management of multiple interacting resources in chip multiprocessors: A machine learning approach. In *2008 41st IEEE/ACM International Symposium on Microarchitecture* (pp. 318-329). IEEE. 10.1109/MICRO.2008.4771801

Brandin, B. A., Wonham, W. M., & Benhabib, B. (1991, August). Discrete event system supervisory control applied to the management of manufacturing workcells. In *Proc. Seventh International Conference on Computer-Aided Production Engineering, Cookeville TN USA* (pp. 527-536). Academic Press.

Chang, K. K., Yağlıkçı, A. G., Ghose, S., Agrawal, A., Chatterjee, N., Kashyap, A., ... Mutlu, O. (2017). Understanding reduced-voltage operation in modern DRAM devices: Experimental characterization, analysis, and mechanisms. *Proceedings of the ACM on Measurement and Analysis of Computing Systems*, *1*(1), 1-42. 10.1145/3078505.3078590

Choi, S., & Yeung, D. (2006, June). Learning-based SMT processor resource distribution via hill-climbing. In *33rd International Symposium on Computer Architecture (ISCA'06)* (pp. 239-251). IEEE. 10.1109/ISCA.2006.25

Chung, H., Kang, M., & Cho, H. D. (2012). *Heterogeneous multi-processing solution of Exynos 5 Octa with ARM big. LITTLE technology*. Samsung White Paper.

Cochran, R., Hankendi, C., Coskun, A. K., & Reda, S. (2011, December). Pack & Cap: adaptive DVFS and thread packing under power caps. In *2011 44th Annual IEEE/ACM International Symposium on Microarchitecture (MICRO)* (pp. 175-185). IEEE. 10.1145/2155620.2155641

Das, R., Ausavarungnirun, R., Mutlu, O., Kumar, A., & Azimi, M. (2013, February). Application-to-core mapping policies to reduce memory system interference in multi-core systems. In *2013 IEEE 19th International Symposium on High Performance Computer Architecture (HPCA)* (pp. 107-118). IEEE. 10.1109/HPCA.2013.6522311

Das, R., Mutlu, O., Moscibroda, T., & Das, C. R. (2009, December). Application-aware prioritization mechanisms for on-chip networks. In *2009 42nd Annual IEEE/ACM International Symposium on Microarchitecture (MICRO)* (pp. 280-291). IEEE. 10.1145/1669112.1669150

Das, R., Mutlu, O., Moscibroda, T., & Das, C. R. (2010). Aérgia: exploiting packet latency slack in on-chip networks. *ACM SIGARCH Computer Architecture News, 38*(3), 106-116.

David, H., Fallin, C., Gorbatov, E., Hanebutte, U. R., & Mutlu, O. (2011, June). Memory power management via dynamic voltage/frequency scaling. In *Proceedings of the 8th ACM international conference on Autonomic computing* (pp. 31-40). 10.1145/1998582.1998590

Delimitrou, C., & Kozyrakis, C. (2014). Quasar: Resource-efficient and QoS-aware cluster management. *ACM SIGPLAN Notices, 49*(4), 127–144. doi:10.1145/2644865.2541941

Deng, Q., Meisner, D., Bhattacharjee, A., Wenisch, T. F., & Bianchini, R. (2012, December). Coscale: Coordinating cpu and memory system dvfs in server systems. In *2012 45th annual IEEE/ACM international symposium on microarchitecture* (pp. 143-154). IEEE.

Dhodapkar, A. S., & Smith, J. E. (2002, May). Managing multi-configuration hardware via dynamic working set analysis. In *Proceedings 29th Annual International Symposium on Computer Architecture* (pp. 233-244). IEEE. 10.1109/ISCA.2002.1003581

Donyanavard, B., Mück, T., Sarma, S., & Dutt, N. (2016, October). SPARTA: Runtime task allocation for energy efficient heterogeneous manycores. In *2016 International Conference on Hardware/Software Codesign and System Synthesis (CODES+ ISSS)* (pp. 1-10). IEEE. 10.1145/2968456.2968459

Donyanavard, B., Rahmani, A. M., Mück, T., Moazemmi, K., & Dutt, N. (2018, March). Gain scheduled control for nonlinear power management in CMPs. In 2018 Design, Automation & Test in Europe Conference & Exhibition (DATE) (pp. 921-924). IEEE. doi:10.23919/DATE.2018.8342141

Dubach, C., Jones, T. M., & Bonilla, E. V. (2013). Dynamic microarchitectural adaptation using machine learning. *ACM Transactions on Architecture and Code Optimization, 10*(4), 1–28. doi:10.1145/2541228.2541238

Dubach, C., Jones, T. M., Bonilla, E. V., & O'Boyle, M. F. (2010, December). A predictive model for dynamic microarchitectural adaptivity control. In *2010 43rd Annual IEEE/ACM International Symposium on Microarchitecture* (pp. 485-496). IEEE. 10.1109/MICRO.2010.14

Ebrahimi, E., Lee, C. J., Mutlu, O., & Patt, Y. N. (2010). Fairness via source throttling: A configurable and high-performance fairness substrate for multi-core memory systems. *ACM SIGPLAN Notices*, *45*(3), 335–346. doi:10.1145/1735971.1736058

Ebrahimi, E., Lee, C. J., Mutlu, O., & Patt, Y. N. (2011). Prefetch-aware shared resource management for multi-core systems. *ACM SIGARCH Computer Architecture News*, *39*(3), 141–152. doi:10.1145/2024723.2000081

Ebrahimi, E., Mutlu, O., Lee, C. J., & Patt, Y. N. (2009, December). Coordinated control of multiple prefetchers in multi-core systems. In *Proceedings of the 42nd Annual IEEE/ACM International Symposium on Microarchitecture* (pp. 316-326). 10.1145/1669112.1669154

Fan, S., Zahedi, S. M., & Lee, B. C. (2016). The computational sprinting game. *ACM SIGARCH Computer Architecture News*, *44*(2), 561–575. doi:10.1145/2980024.2872383

Fu, X., Kabir, K., & Wang, X. (2011, July). Cache-aware utilization control for energy efficiency in multi-core real-time systems. In *2011 23rd Euromicro Conference on Real-Time Systems* (pp. 102-111). IEEE. 10.1109/ECRTS.2011.18

Gupta, U., Ayoub, R., Kishinevsky, M., Kadjo, D., Soundararajan, N., Tursun, U., & Ogras, U. Y. (2017). Dynamic power budgeting for mobile systems running graphics workloads. *IEEE Transactions on Multi-Scale Computing Systems*, *4*(1), 30–40. doi:10.1109/TMSCS.2017.2683487

Gupta, U., Campbell, J., Ogras, U. Y., Ayoub, R., Kishinevsky, M., Paterna, F., & Gumussoy, S. (2016, November). Adaptive performance prediction for integrated GPUs. In *Proceedings of the 35th International Conference on Computer-Aided Design* (pp. 1-8). Academic Press.

Haghbayan, M. H., Miele, A., Rahmani, A. M., Liljeberg, P., & Tenhunen, H. (2017). Performance/reliability-aware resource management for many-cores in dark silicon era. *IEEE Transactions on Computers*, *66*(9), 1599–1612. doi:10.1109/TC.2017.2691009

Hanumaiah, V., Desai, D., Gaudette, B., Wu, C. J., & Vrudhula, S. (2014). STEAM: A smart temperature and energy aware multicore controller. *ACM Transactions on Embedded Computing Systems*, *13*(5s), 1–25. doi:10.1145/2661430

Hellerstein, J. L., Diao, Y., Parekh, S. S., & Tilbury, D. M. (2004). *Feedback control of computing systems* (Vol. 10). Wiley. doi:10.1002/047166880X

Herbert, S., & Marculescu, D. (2007, August). Analysis of dynamic voltage/frequency scaling in chip-multiprocessors. In *Proceedings of the 2007 international symposium on Low power electronics and design (ISLPED'07)* (pp. 38-43). IEEE. 10.1145/1283780.1283790

Hespanha, J. P. (2001, December). Tutorial on supervisory control. *Lecture Notes for the Workshop Control using Logic and Switching for the 40th Conf. on Decision and Contr.*

Hoffmann, H. (2014, July). Coadapt: Predictable behavior for accuracy-aware applications running on power-aware systems. In *2014 26th Euromicro Conference on Real-Time Systems* (pp. 223-232). IEEE.

Hoffmann, H., Maggio, M., Santambrogio, M. D., Leva, A., & Agarwal, A. (2013, September). A generalized software framework for accurate and efficient management of performance goals. In *2013 Proceedings of the International Conference on Embedded Software (EMSOFT)* (pp. 1-10). IEEE. 10.1109/EMSOFT.2013.6658597

Hoffmann, H., Sidiroglou, S., Carbin, M., Misailovic, S., Agarwal, A., & Rinard, M. (2011). Dynamic knobs for responsive power-aware computing. *ACM SIGARCH Computer Architecture News, 39*(1), 199-212.

Ipek, E., Mutlu, O., Martínez, J. F., & Caruana, R. (2008). Self-optimizing memory controllers: A reinforcement learning approach. *ACM SIGARCH Computer Architecture News, 36*(3), 39–50. doi:10.1145/1394608.1382172

Isci, C., Buyuktosunoglu, A., Cher, C. Y., Bose, P., & Martonosi, M. (2006, December). An analysis of efficient multi-core global power management policies: Maximizing performance for a given power budget. In *2006 39th Annual IEEE/ACM International Symposium on Microarchitecture (MICRO'06)* (pp. 347-358). IEEE.

Jantsch, A., Dutt, N., & Rahmani, A. M. (2017). Self-awareness in systems on chip—A survey. *IEEE Design & Test, 34*(6), 8–26. doi:10.1109/MDAT.2017.2757143

Juang, P., Wu, Q., Peh, L. S., Martonosi, M., & Clark, D. W. (2005, August). Coordinated, distributed, formal energy management of chip multiprocessors. In *Proceedings of the 2005 international symposium on Low power electronics and design* (pp. 127-130). 10.1145/1077603.1077637

Jung, H., Rong, P., & Pedram, M. (2008, June). Stochastic modeling of a thermally-managed multi-core system. In *Proceedings of the 45th annual Design Automation Conference* (pp. 728-733). 10.1145/1391469.1391657

Kadjo, D., Ayoub, R., Kishinevsky, M., & Gratz, P. V. (2015, June). A control-theoretic approach for energy efficient CPU-GPU subsystem in mobile platforms. In *2015 52nd ACM/EDAC/IEEE Design Automation Conference (DAC)* (pp. 1-6). IEEE. 10.1145/2744769.2744773

Kanduri, A., Haghbayan, M. H., Rahmani, A. M., Liljeberg, P., Jantsch, A., Dutt, N., & Tenhunen, H. (2016, November). Approximation knob: Power capping meets energy efficiency. In *2016 IEEE/ACM International Conference on Computer-Aided Design (ICCAD)* (pp. 1-8). IEEE. 10.1145/2966986.2967002

Karamanolis, C. T., Karlsson, M., & Zhu, X. (2005, June). Designing Controllable Computer Systems. In HotOS (pp. 9-15). Academic Press.

Lee, C. J., Narasiman, V., Ebrahimi, E., Mutlu, O., & Patt, Y. N. (2010). *DRAM-aware last-level cache writeback: Reducing write-caused interference in memory systems.* Academic Press.

Leith, D. J., & Leithead, W. E. (2000). Survey of gain-scheduling analysis and design. *International Journal of Control, 73*(11), 1001–1025. doi:10.1080/002071700411304

Lennart, L. (1999). *System identification: theory for the user.* PTR Prentice Hall.

Lewis, P. R., Platzner, M., Rinner, B., Tørresen, J., & Yao, X. (2016). *Self-Aware Computing Systems. Natural Computing Series*. Springer. doi:10.1007/978-3-319-39675-0

Liu, G., Park, J., & Marculescu, D. (2013, October). Dynamic thread mapping for high-performance, power-efficient heterogeneous many-core systems. In *2013 IEEE 31st international conference on computer design (ICCD)* (pp. 54-61). IEEE. 10.1109/ICCD.2013.6657025

Ljung, L. (2001, May). Black-box models from input-output measurements. In *IMTC 2001. proceedings of the 18th IEEE instrumentation and measurement technology conference. rediscovering measurement in the age of informatics (cat. no. 01ch 37188)* (Vol. 1, pp. 138-146). IEEE. 10.1109/IMTC.2001.928802

Lo, D., Song, T., & Suh, G. E. (2015, December). Prediction-guided performance-energy trade-off for interactive applications. In *Proceedings of the 48th International Symposium on Microarchitecture* (pp. 508-520). 10.1145/2830772.2830776

Ma, K., Li, X., Chen, M., & Wang, X. (2011, June). Scalable power control for many-core architectures running multi-threaded applications. In *2011 38th Annual International Symposium on Computer Architecture (ISCA)* (pp. 449-460). IEEE. 10.1145/2000064.2000117

Maggio, M., Hoffmann, H., Santambrogio, M. D., Agarwal, A., & Leva, A. (2010, December). Controlling software applications via resource allocation within the heartbeats framework. In *49th IEEE Conference on Decision and Control (CDC)* (pp. 3736-3741). IEEE. 10.1109/CDC.2010.5717893

Mahajan, D., Yazdanbakhsh, A., Park, J., Thwaites, B., & Esmaeilzadeh, H. (2016). Towards statistical guarantees in controlling quality tradeoffs for approximate acceleration. *ACM SIGARCH Computer Architecture News, 44*(3), 66–77. doi:10.1145/3007787.3001144

MathWorks. (2017). *System Identification Toolbox*. Tech. rep. https://www.mathworks.com/products/sysid.html

Mishra, A. K., Srikantaiah, S., Kandemir, M., & Das, C. R. (2010, November). CPM in CMPs: Coordinated power management in chip-multiprocessors. In *SC'10: Proceedings of the 2010 ACM/IEEE International Conference for High Performance Computing, Networking, Storage and Analysis* (pp. 1-12). IEEE. 10.1109/SC.2010.15

Mishra, N., Imes, C., Lafferty, J. D., & Hoffmann, H. (2018). CALOREE: Learning control for predictable latency and low energy. *ACM SIGPLAN Notices, 53*(2), 184–198. doi:10.1145/3296957.3173184

Morse, A. S. (1997). In A. S. Morse (Ed.), *Control using logic-based switching*. Springer. doi:10.1007/BFb0036078

Mück, T., Sarma, S., & Dutt, N. (2015, October). Run-DMC: Runtime dynamic heterogeneous multicore performance and power estimation for energy efficiency. In *2015 International Conference on Hardware/Software Codesign and System Synthesis (CODES+ ISSS)* (pp. 173-182). IEEE. 10.1109/CODESISSS.2015.7331380

Muthukaruppan, T. S., Pathania, A., & Mitra, T. (2014). Price theory based power management for heterogeneous multi-cores. *ACM SIGPLAN Notices, 49*(4), 161–176. doi:10.1145/2644865.2541974

Muthukaruppan, T. S., Pricopi, M., Venkataramani, V., Mitra, T., & Vishin, S. (2013, May). Hierarchical power management for asymmetric multi-core in dark silicon era. In *2013 50th ACM/EDAC/IEEE Design Automation Conference (DAC)* (pp. 1-9). IEEE. 10.1145/2463209.2488949

Petrica, P., Izraelevitz, A. M., Albonesi, D. H., & Shoemaker, C. A. (2013, June). Flicker: A dynamically adaptive architecture for power limited multicore systems. In *Proceedings of the 40th Annual International Symposium on Computer Architecture* (pp. 13-23). 10.1145/2485922.2485924

Pothukuchi, R. P., Ansari, A., Voulgaris, P., & Torrellas, J. (2016, June). Using multiple input, multiple output formal control to maximize resource efficiency in architectures. In *2016 ACM/IEEE 43rd Annual International Symposium on Computer Architecture (ISCA)* (pp. 658-670). IEEE. 10.1109/ISCA.2016.63

Pothukuchi, R. P., Pothukuchi, S. Y., Voulgaris, P., & Torrellas, J. (2018, June). Yukta: multilayer resource controllers to maximize efficiency. In *2018 ACM/IEEE 45th Annual International Symposium on Computer Architecture (ISCA)* (pp. 505-518). IEEE. 10.1109/ISCA.2018.00049

Pricopi, M., Muthukaruppan, T. S., Venkataramani, V., Mitra, T., & Vishin, S. (2013, September). Power-performance modeling on asymmetric multi-cores. In *2013 International Conference on Compilers, Architecture and Synthesis for Embedded Systems (CASES)* (pp. 1-10). IEEE.

Raghavendra, R., Ranganathan, P., Talwar, V., Wang, Z., & Zhu, X. (2008, March). No" power" struggles: coordinated multi-level power management for the data center. In *Proceedings of the 13th international conference on Architectural support for programming languages and operating systems* (pp. 48-59). 10.1145/1346281.1346289

Rahmani, A. M., Donyanavard, B., Mück, T., Moazzemi, K., Jantsch, A., Mutlu, O., & Dutt, N. (2018, March). Spectr: Formal supervisory control and coordination for many-core systems resource management. In *Proceedings of the Twenty-Third International Conference on Architectural Support for Programming Languages and Operating Systems* (pp. 169-183). 10.1145/3173162.3173199

Rahmani, A. M., Haghbayan, M. H., Kanduri, A., Weldezion, A. Y., Liljeberg, P., Plosila, J., ... Tenhunen, H. (2015, July). Dynamic power management for many-core platforms in the dark silicon era: A multi-objective control approach. In *2015 IEEE/ACM International Symposium on Low Power Electronics and Design (ISLPED)* (pp. 219-224). IEEE. 10.1109/ISLPED.2015.7273517

Rahmani, A. M., Haghbayan, M. H., Miele, A., Liljeberg, P., Jantsch, A., & Tenhunen, H. (2016). Reliability-aware runtime power management for many-core systems in the dark silicon era. *IEEE Transactions on Very Large Scale Integration (VLSI). Systems*, 25(2), 427–440.

Rahmani, A. M., Jantsch, A., & Dutt, N. (2018). HDGM: Hierarchical dynamic goal management for many-core resource allocation. *IEEE Embedded Systems Letters*, 10(3), 61–64. doi:10.1109/LES.2017.2751522

Ramadge, P. J., & Wonham, W. M. (1989). The control of discrete event systems. *Proceedings of the IEEE*, 77(1), 81–98. doi:10.1109/5.21072

Safonov, M. G. (1997). Focusing on the knowable. In *Control using logic-based switching* (pp. 224–233). Springer. doi:10.1007/BFb0036098

Shamsa, E., Kanduri, A., Rahmani, A. M., Liljeberg, P., Jantsch, A., & Dutt, N. (2019, March). Goal-driven autonomy for efficient on-chip resource management: Transforming objectives to goals. In 2019 Design, Automation & Test in Europe Conference & Exhibition (DATE) (pp. 1397-1402). IEEE.

Singh, K., Bhadauria, M., & McKee, S. A. (2009). Real time power estimation and thread scheduling via performance counters. *ACM SIGARCH Computer Architecture News*, *37*(2), 46–55. doi:10.1145/1577129.1577137

Skogestad, S., & Postlethwaite, I. (2007). *Multivariable feedback control: analysis and design* (Vol. 2). Wiley.

Smith, B. C. (1982). *Reflection and Semantics in a Procedural Programming Language*. PhD.

Srikantaiah, S., Kandemir, M., & Wang, Q. (2009, December). SHARP control: controlled shared cache management in chip multiprocessors. In *Proceedings of the 42nd Annual IEEE/ACM International Symposium on Microarchitecture* (pp. 517-528). 10.1145/1669112.1669177

Stuecheli, J., Kaseridis, D., Daly, D., Hunter, H. C., & John, L. K. (2010). The virtual write queue: Co-ordinating DRAM and last-level cache policies. *ACM SIGARCH Computer Architecture News*, *38*(3), 72–82. doi:10.1145/1816038.1815972

Su, B., Gu, J., Shen, L., Huang, W., Greathouse, J. L., & Wang, Z. (2014, December). PPEP: Online performance, power, and energy prediction framework and DVFS space exploration. In *2014 47th Annual IEEE/ACM International Symposium on Microarchitecture* (pp. 445-457). IEEE.

Subramanian, L., Seshadri, V., Ghosh, A., Khan, S., & Mutlu, O. (2015, December). The application slowdown model: Quantifying and controlling the impact of inter-application interference at shared caches and main memory. In *2015 48th Annual IEEE/ACM International Symposium on Microarchitecture (MICRO)* (pp. 62-75). IEEE.

Subramanian, L., Seshadri, V., Kim, Y., Jaiyen, B., & Mutlu, O. (2013, February). MISE: Providing performance predictability and improving fairness in shared main memory systems. In *2013 IEEE 19th International Symposium on High Performance Computer Architecture (HPCA)* (pp. 639-650). IEEE.

Sui, X., Lenharth, A., Fussell, D. S., & Pingali, K. (2016). Proactive control of approximate programs. *ACM SIGPLAN Notices*, *51*(4), 607–621. doi:10.1145/2954679.2872402

Tembey, P., Gavrilovska, A., & Schwan, K. (2010, June). A case for coordinated resource management in heterogeneous multicore platforms. In *International Symposium on Computer Architecture* (pp. 341-356). Springer.

Teodorescu, R., & Torrellas, J. (2008). Variation-aware application scheduling and power management for chip multiprocessors. *ACM SIGARCH Computer Architecture News, 36*(3), 363-374.

Thistle, J. G. (1996). Supervisory control of discrete event systems. *Mathematical and Computer Modelling*, *23*(11-12), 25–53. doi:10.1016/0895-7177(96)00063-5

Vardhan, V., Yuan, W., Harris, A. F., Adve, S. V., Kravets, R., Nahrstedt, K., ... & Jones, D. (2009). GRACE-2: integrating fine-grained application adaptation with global adaptation for saving energy. *International Journal of embedded Systems, 4*(2), 152-169.

Vega, A., Buyuktosunoglu, A., Hanson, H., Bose, P., & Ramani, S. (2013, December). Crank it up or dial it down: coordinated multiprocessor frequency and folding control. In *2013 46th Annual IEEE/ACM International Symposium on Microarchitecture (MICRO)* (pp. 210-221). IEEE. 10.1145/2540708.2540727

Wang, X., Ma, K., & Wang, Y. (2011). Adaptive power control with online model estimation for chip multiprocessors. *IEEE Transactions on Parallel and Distributed Systems, 22*(10), 1681–1696. doi:10.1109/TPDS.2011.39

Wang, X., & Martínez, J. F. (2016). ReBudget: Trading off efficiency vs. fairness in market-based multicore resource allocation via runtime budget reassignment. *ACM SIGPLAN Notices, 51*(4), 19–32. doi:10.1145/2954679.2872382

Wang, Y., Ma, K., & Wang, X. (2009). Temperature-constrained power control for chip multiprocessors with online model estimation. *ACM SIGARCH Computer Architecture News, 37*(3), 314-324.

Wu, Q., Deng, Q., Ganesh, L., Hsu, C. H., Jin, Y., Kumar, S., Li, B., Meza, J., & Song, Y. J. (2016). Dynamo: Facebook's data center-wide power management system. *ACM SIGARCH Computer Architecture News, 44*(3), 469–480. doi:10.1145/3007787.3001187

Wu, Q., Juang, P., Martonosi, M., & Clark, D. W. (2004). Formal online methods for voltage/frequency control in multiple clock domain microprocessors. *ACM SIGPLAN Notices, 39*(11), 248–259. doi:10.1145/1037187.1024423

Wu, Q., Juang, P., Martonosi, M., Peh, L. S., & Clark, D. W. (2005). Formal control techniques for power-performance management. *IEEE Micro, 25*(5), 52–62. doi:10.1109/MM.2005.87

Zhang, H., & Hoffmann, H. (2016). Maximizing performance under a power cap: A comparison of hardware, software, and hybrid techniques. *ACM SIGPLAN Notices, 51*(4), 545–559. doi:10.1145/2954679.2872375

ENDNOTES

[1]   Due to the significant stochastic component of computer systems, PI controllers are preferred over PID controllers (Hellerstein et al., 2004).

[2]   https://odroid.com/dokuwiki/doku.php?id=en:odroid-xu3

[3]   We refer to this as the Exynos CMP or CMP throughout.

[4]   Ubuntu 16.04.2 LTS and Linux kernel 3.10.105

[5]   We interchangeably use the terms (*measured output* and *sensor*), as well as the terms (*control input* and *actuator*), as shown in Figure 7.

[6]   The Exynos platform provides only per-cluster power sensors and DVFS; hence our use of cluster-level sensors and actuators.

[7]   We generate the models with a stability focus. All systems are stable according to Robust Stability Analysis. We use Uncertainty Guardbands of 50% for QoS and 30% for power, as in (Pothukuchi et al., 2016).

[8]   Ubuntu 16.04.2 LTS and Linux kernel 3.10.105 (https://dn.odroid.com/5422/ODROID-XU3/Ubuntu/).

Chapter 5
Paradigms for Effective Parallelization of Inherently Sequential Graph Algorithms on Multi-Core Architectures

Assefaw Gebremedhin
Washington State University, USA

Mostofa Patwary
NVIDIA, USA

Fredrik Manne
University of Bergen, Norway

ABSTRACT

The chapter describes two algorithmic paradigms, dubbed speculation and iteration and approximate update, for parallelizing greedy graph algorithms and vertex ordering algorithms, respectively, on multicore architectures. The common challenge in these two classes of algorithms is that the computations involved are inherently sequential. The efficacy of the paradigms in overcoming this challenge is demonstrated via extensive experimental study on two representative algorithms from each class and two Intel multi-core systems. The algorithms studied are (1) greedy algorithms for distance-k coloring (for k = 1 and k = 2) and (2) algorithms for two degree-based vertex orderings. The experimental results show that the paradigms enable the design of scalable methods that to a large extent preserve the quality of solution obtained by the underlying serial algorithms.

DOI: 10.4018/978-1-7998-7156-9.ch005

INTRODUCTION

Greedy graph algorithms—where an optimization problem defined on a graph is solved by processing vertices (or edges) sequentially one at a time, at each step making the "best local" decision—occur frequently in computations. For some graph problems, Minimum Spanning Tree, for instance, a greedy algorithm is indeed the way to get an optimal solution. For NP-hard graph problems that occur as a part in a larger computation, greedy algorithms are often the methods-of-choice as they provide good approximate solutions at low, often linear, runtime. Further, greedy algorithms naturally fit in the framework of *streaming algorithms* (Alon et al., 1999), where input is fed one item at a time.

In some greedy algorithms iterating over vertices, the *order* in which vertices are processed determines the quality of the solution obtained by the greedy algorithm. One may then need to find, for example, a *degree-based ordering*, where the vertices of a graph are ranked such that the vertex at each position is of maximum or minimum degree in a suitably defined induced subgraph. Degree-based ordering techniques may also be needed in their own right as a stand-alone procedure for an independent objective.

These two inter-related classes of algorithms, greedy algorithms and ordering procedures, have one common feature: the computations involved are *inherently sequential*. Existing parallel algorithm design techniques, such as divide-and-conquer, partitioning, pipelining, pointer-jumping, etc, that are commonly discussed in parallel computing books (Jájá, 1992; Grama et al., 2003; Kurzak et al., 2010) fall short as useful guidelines for effectively parallelizing such algorithms. The parallel algorithm developer's "design toolbox" thus needs to be augmented with new techniques, especially in the present era where parallel computing has established itself in the mainstream.

Contributions of This Chapter

This chapter contributes to this goal by focusing primarily on multi-core and multi-threaded architectures. Specifically, the chapter examines two design paradigms that turn out to be effective for parallelizing inherently sequential algorithms. The first paradigm, dubbed SPECULATION and ITERATION, aims at parallelizing greedy algorithms. The second, named Approximate Update, targets parallelization of ordering algorithms.

The key idea in SPECULATION and ITERATION is to:

maximize concurrency by tentatively tolerating potential inconsistencies and then detecting and resolving eventual inconsistencies later, iteratively.

For this approach to be successful (in leading to scalable methods), inconsistencies need to be relatively rare occurrences. We demonstrate that this is in fact the case for practical problems by applying the paradigm to parallelize greedy algorithms for *distance-k coloring* (for $k = 1$ and $k = 2$). We find, for instance, that the inconsistencies discovered in the very first iteration in the resultant parallel coloring algorithms run on moderate-scale computing environments typically involve less than one percent of the total number of vertices for large, sparse graphs. More generally, the number of inconsistencies will depend on the ratio between the number of vertices and threads and the density of the input graph.

The key idea in the APPROXIMATE UPDATE paradigm is to:

minimize synchronization cost by opting for concurrent data structure update with approximate data instead of serialized data structure update with exact data.

Obviously, the solution output by a parallel algorithm designed with this paradigm is *not* guaranteed to be the same as a solution obtained by a sequential algorithm. This is not a major concern, however, since in most computations needing ordering, a slight deviation from the optimal (serial) ordering is not only tolerable but a welcome tradeoff to enable parallelization. We consider in this work the parallelization of two vertex ordering types, known as *Smallest Last* (SL) (Matula, 1968) and *Incidence Degree* (ID) (Coleman and More, 1983), as representatives of our second target class of algorithms. For each of these ordering variants, we study an *approximate degree update* approach for parallelization. We show that the approach gives a scalable method that does not incur too much loss in quality of solution relative to a serial algorithm whereas a method that insists on exact degree update does not scale.

SL and ID ordering and greedy coloring algorithms are closely related: the orderings can be used in an initialization step of the coloring algorithm to reduce the number of colors used. However, SL and ID orderings are also of independent interest because of their use in areas outside coloring, including network analysis and linear solvers.

As platforms for evaluating the scalability of the parallel coloring and ordering algorithms designed using the proposed paradigms, we experiment with two moderate-size (desk-side or desk-top) multi-core systems based on Intel processors. We show that our algorithms generally scale well on both platforms, with varying performance on each.

The remainder of this chapter is organized around the two paradigms. First, this introductory section is wrapped up with a brief review of related work. The second section discusses SPECULATION AND ITERATION and the associated coloring problems, and the third section treats APPROXIMATE UPDATE and the associated ordering problems. The datasets and computing platforms used in the experiments (common to both paradigms) are discussed in the second section.

Related Work

The SPECULATION AND ITERATION design *paradigm* is an outgrowth of a series of previous works in which the focus was the design of parallel algorithms for *specific* graph problems. The basic idea of using speculation for parallelizing greedy graph coloring algorithms was first introduced in Gebremedhin and Manne (2000). There it was used in the context of shared-memory parallelization of coloring algorithms, albeit without iteration. Instead, the conflict resolution phase was carried out just once, serially on one processor. The idea was later enhanced with randomization in Gebremedhin et al. (2002).

Speculation together with iteration formed the core of the framework for parallelizing distance-1 coloring on *distributed-memory* architectures developed in Bozdag et al. (2008). The framework addressed a variety of additional performance requirements entailed by a distributed-memory setting: the input graph needs to be partitioned in a manner that minimizes communication cost; the speculative coloring phase performs better when organized in a coarse-grained fashion with infrequent communications; the coloring of interior and boundary vertices needs to be scheduled carefully; etc. The framework was later extended to distance-2 coloring, where mechanisms for minimizing inter-processor communication in conflict detection and resolution are even more critical (Bozdag et al., 2010).

A *multi-threaded* algorithm for distance-1 coloring derived from the framework of Bozdag et al. (2008) and adapted for shared-memory multi-core architectures has been studied in Catalyurek et al. (2012). In the same work, the architecture-portable, speculation-based multi-threaded algorithm is contrasted with a dataflow-based multi-threaded algorithm custom-designed for the Cray XMT.

Several other recent research activities have successfully used speculation ideas for parallelization (Patwary et al., 2012; Sariyuce et al., 2011, 2012). Initial work on one of the approximate degree updates methods discussed here was presented in Patwary et al. (2011). Although developed in an entirely different context, ideas behind distributed auction algorithms (Zavlanos et al., 2008), broadly interpreted, bear some resemblance to the speculation paradigm discussed here. In yet another different context, the term speculation (or optimistic parallelization) is also used to refer to compiler and/or runtime techniques for automatic parallelization of serial codes (Pingali et al., 2011; Tian et al., 2009).

SPECULATION AND ITERATION

We begin this section with an abstract presentation of the SPECULATION AND ITERATION parallelization paradigm. We then illustrate its use by applying it to parallelize greedy algorithms for graph coloring problems.

Generic Formulation

Suppose the input graph is $G = (V, E)$, the problem of interest involves operations on vertices, and there are p processing units, where $p \ll |V|$. We can formulate the SPECULATION AND ITERATION design technique in a generic fashion as shown in Algorithm 1. There, U denotes the set of "active" vertices.

The approach outlined in Algorithm 1 presupposes that resolving an inconsistency can be achieved via *local* re-evaluations. Intuitively, its viability is directly related to the rate at which the size of U drops from one iteration to the next—the faster the rate, the more viable the approach is. In other words, the approach is effective when the size of eventual inconsistencies discovered in an iteration is relatively small. We showcase the efficacy of this approach using greedy algorithms for *distance-k coloring*, for the cases $k = 1$ and $k = 2$. We proceed by first reviewing the underlying serial greedy coloring algorithms. We then discuss their parallelizations and show performance results. The dataset and platforms used for performance evaluation are discussed prior to the presentation of the performance results.

Algorithm 1. Generic formulation of the Speculation and Iteration parallelization paradigm.

```
Input: Graph G = (V,E) and p processing units
1           U ← V           (U is the set of active vertices);
2           while U is non-empty do
3               Partition U into p nearly equal subsets U₁,...,U_p . and assign
each             subset to a distinct processing unit;
4               Solve the p sub-problems defined by the p subsets in parallel
making          speculative decisions as needed;
5               Check the validity of the p sub-solutions in parallel register-
ing             inconsistencies;
6               Reset U such that it contains only elements needing resolution;
7           end
```

Figure 1. Illustration of a distance-1 and a distance-2 coloring of a graph on nine vertices. The distance-1 coloring example uses three colors with color classes {a,d,e,f,i}; {b,c}; and {g,h}. The distance-2 coloring uses six colors with colors classes {a,i}; {b,f}; {c,d}; {e}; {g}; and {h}.

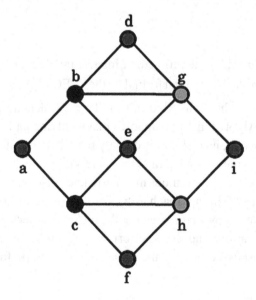

Serial Coloring

A distance-k coloring of a graph $G = (V,E)$ is an assignment of positive integers, called *colors*, to vertices such that any two vertices connected by a path consisting of at most k edges receive different colors. See Figure 1 for an illustration of distance-1 and distance-2 coloring. The objective in the distance-k coloring problem is to minimize the number of colors used. The problem is NP-hard for every fixed integer $k \geq 1$ (Lin and Skiena, 1995).

Algorithms Despite known hardness (including in-approximability) results on distance-1 coloring, previous work has shown that a *greedy* algorithm—an algorithm that visits vertices sequentially in some *order* in each step assigning a vertex the *smallest* permissible color—is quite effective in practice (Coleman and More, 1983). We review in Algorithm 2 an *efficient* formulation of the greedy distance-*k* coloring algorithm.

Algorithm 2. A greedy distance-k coloring algorithm. The color-indexed array forbiddenColors is used to mark impermissible colors to a vertex.

```
Input: Graph G = (V,E)
Output: an array color[v] denoting colors assigned to vertices
1        Initialize forbiddenColors with some value a /∈ V ;
2        for each v ∈ V do
3            for each w ∈ N_k(v) do
4                forbiddenColors[color[w]] ← v;
5            end
6            c ←min{i≥ 1:forbiddenColors[i] ≠ v};
7            color[v] ← c;
8        end
```

In Algorithm 2, and elsewhere in this chapter, $N_k(v)$ denotes the set of distance-*k* neighbors of the vertex *v*. The data structure color is a vertex-indexed array that stores the color of each vertex. The color-indexed array forbiddenColors is used to mark colors that are impermissible to a vertex *v* in a given step of the outer for-loop over vertices. In doing so, the vertex *v* itself is used as a 'stamp' thereby avoiding the need for re-initialization of forbiddenColors in a later step in which another vertex is colored. By the end of the inner for-loop of Algorithm 2, all of the colors that are impermissible to the vertex *v* are recorded in forbiddenColors. In Line 6, the array is scanned from left to right in search of the *lowest* positive index *i* at which a value different from *v* is encountered. The index *i* corresponds to the smallest permissible color *c* to the vertex *v*—and is thus assigned to *v* in Line 7.

The work done in populating the array forbiddenColors is proportional to $d_k(v)$, where $d_k(v)$, denoting "degree-*k*", is the number of edges in the graph induced by the vertices in $N_k(v) \cup \{v\}$. The search for the smallest allowable color *c* (Line 6) terminates after at most $|N_k(v)| + 1$ attempts, since the worst possible scenario is when each of the $|N_k(v)|$ neighbors of *v* uses a distinct color in the sequence $\{1,2,...,|N_k(v)|\}$; otherwise the sequence would contain a permissible color for *v*, allowing earlier termination. Thus, the time complexity of Algorithm 2 is $O\left(|V| \cdot \overline{d_k}\right)$ where $\overline{d_k}$ is the average degree-*k* in the graph. This reduces to $O(|V| \cdot \overline{d_1} = O(|E|)$ for distance-1 coloring. For distance-2 coloring, the expression can be bounded by $O(|E| \cdot \Delta)$, since $\overline{d_2}$ can be bounded by $\overline{d_1} \cdot \Delta$, where Δ is the maximum degree in the graph.

Bounds on Number of Colors We quickly review obvious lower bounds on distance-1 and distance-2 coloring as well as upper bounds on the solution obtained by Algorithm 2 for the two coloring cases. The size of the largest induced clique in *G*, the clique number ω of *G*, is clearly a lower bound on the optimal number of colors needed for distance-1 coloring of *G*. Algorithm 2 in the distance-1 coloring case uses at most $\Delta + 1$ colors, where again Δ is the maximum degree in G. The quantity Δ is a lower bound on the optimal number of colors needed to distance-2 color G. Algorithm 2 in the distance-2 coloring case uses at most $\min\{\Delta^2 + 1, |V|\}$ colors. The stated lower and upper bounds on distance-2 coloring imply that Algorithm 2 in the distance-2 coloring is an $O\left(\sqrt{|V|}\right)$ approximation algorithm (McCormick, 1983).

Ordering The order in which vertices are processed in Algorithm 2 (Line 2) determines the number of colors used by the algorithm. Two ordering techniques known to be particularly effective in reducing number of colors—to values significantly lower than the bound $\Delta + 1$ in the case of distance-1 coloring—are *Smallest Last* (Matula, 1968; Matula et al., 1972) and *Incidence Degree* (Coleman and More, 1983). We use these two ordering techniques in our study of parallel coloring algorithms in this chapter. We defer a discussion of the details of the ordering techniques and their effective parallelization to the Approximate Update section.

Parallelization

We set out to parallelize Algorithm 2 using the SPECULATION AND ITERATION scheme we outlined in Algorithm 1. Let $G = (V,E)$ be the input graph, and p denote the number of available threads (processing units). We partition the vertex set V equally among the p threads. To ensure reasonable load balance, we assume that G is of bounded maximum degree. Our goal is to parallelize Algorithm 2 such that its complexity becomes $O(T_s(|G|)/p)$, where $T_s(|G|)$ is the runtime of the underlying serial algorithm. Algorithm 3 summarizes the key steps of the parallelized version.

The algorithm runs in rounds in an iterative fashion. Each round has two phases each of which is performed in parallel. In the first phase in each round, the current set of vertices to be colored (U) is equally divided among available threads. The threads then concurrently color their respective vertices in a *speculative* manner, paying attention to already available color information. In this phase, two vertices that are distance-k neighbors with each other and are handled by two different threads may be colored concurrently and receive the same color, causing a *conflict*. In the second phase, threads concurrently check the validity of colors assigned to their respective vertices in the current round and identify a set of vertices that needs to be re-colored in the next round to resolve any detected conflicts. The algorithm terminates when every vertex has been colored correctly.

In the event of a conflict, it suffices to re-color only one of the two involved vertices to resolve the conflict. The function $r(\cdot)$ in Line 12 of Algorithm 3 is used to decide which of the two vertices to re-color. There are several choices for the function $r(\cdot)$: one can use, for example, vertex IDs or random numbers associated with each vertex.

On a PRAM (Parallel Random Access Machine (Jájá, 1992)) model, the parallel runtime in each round of Algorithm 3 is bounded by $O(|U| \cdot \overline{d_k}/p)$, assuming the input graph is of bounded maximum degree. Thus, provided that the algorithm terminates after a constant number of iterations, the overall complexity of the parallel algorithm is $O(|V| \cdot \overline{d_k}/p)$.

Algorithm 3. A Speculation and Iteration parallel algorithm for distance-k coloring. The array forbiddenColors is private to each thread.

```
Input: Graph G = (V,E)
Output: An array color indicating colors of vertices
1        UV ;
2          While U ≠ ∅ do
3              for each vertex v ∈ U in parallel do
4                  for each vertex w ∈ Nₖ(v) do
5                          forbiddenColors[color[w]]← v;
6                  end
7                  c ← min{ i ≥ 1: forbiddenColors[i] ≠ v };
8              end
9              R ← ∅   (synchronization);
10              for each vertex v∈U in parallel do
11                  if there exists a vertex w in Nₖ(v) such that
color[v]=color[w]
12                      and r(v)>r(w) then
13                          R← R ∪ {v}            (critical);
14                          Stop search in Nₖ(v);
15                  end
16              end
17              U ← R (synchronization);
18          end
```

Setup for Performance Analysis

Implementation We implemented Algorithm 3, and also the parallel ordering algorithms to be discussed in Section 18, in C++ using *OpenMP*. The algorithms could, however, be implemented in *any* other programming model allowing threading. The performance of the resultant implementations depends on the manner in which tasks (a task in this case is work associated with a vertex) are *scheduled* on threads. OpenMP provides various scheduling options (static, dynamic, guided, runtime). In the results we report in this section and elsewhere in this chapter we use the option *dynamic* since it gave the best performance for a majority of our test cases.

Test platforms We use as our test platforms two moderate-size multi-core systems based on Intel processors. Table 1 gives an overview of the basic architectural features of the platforms along with information on the compilers we used. In all cases, the codes are compiled with -O3 optimization level. To further improve performance in running the codes, we also use compiler provided environment variables for realizing thread affinity (kmp affinity) and mechanisms for realizing non-uniform memory access (numaactl).

Table 1. Summary of architectural features of the two Intel platforms used in our experiments.

	Xeon E7-4850 "Westmere-EX" (Nehalem-based Xeon)	Core i7-860 "Lynnfield" (Nehalem microarch.)
Clock speed	2.0 GHz	2.8 GHz
# of sockets	4	1
Cores/socket	10	4
Threads/socket	20	8
Total cores	40	4
Memory	132 GB	16 GB
L3 cache, shared	20 MB	8 MB
L2 cache/core	256 KB	256 KB
Socket type	LGAa 1567	LGA 1156
Release date	2011	2009
Compiler (GNU, g++)	v 4.8.0	v 4.5.4

Source: See http://ark.intel.com for further information

Notes: ^{a}Land Grid Array

Table 2. Structural properties of the graphs in the testbed.

	$|V|$	$|E|$	Δ	ω		$|V|$	$|E|$	Δ	ω		$|V|$	$|E|$	Δ	ω
er1	262K	2,097K	98	3	g1	262K	2,094K	558	6	b1	262K	2,068K	4,493	35
er2	524K	4,194K	94	3	g2	524K	4,190K	618	6	b2	524K	4,153K	6,342	39
er3	1,049K	8,389K	97	3	g3	1,049K	8,383K	802	6	b3	1,049K	8,318K	9,453	43
er4	2,097K	16,777K	102	3	g4	2,097K	16,768K	1,069	6	b4	2,097K	16,645K	14,066	≥ 51
er5	4,194K	33,554K	109	3	g5	4,194K	33,542K	1,251	6	b5	4,194K	33,341K	20,607	≥ 58

Dataset Our dataset consists of graphs generated using the R-MAT model (Chakrabarti and Faloutsos, 2006). We generated three types of graphs, named er, g and b, using the following R-MAT parameters:

```
er: (0.25,0.25,0.25,0.25) g:(0.45,0.15,0.15,0.25) b:(0.55,0.15,0.15,0.15)
```

These three graph types vary widely in terms of *degree distribution* of vertices and *density of local subgraphs*. Therefore, they represent a wide spectrum of input types posing varying degrees of difficulty for the coloring and ordering algorithms we consider. The er graphs (for *Erdös-Renyi* random graphs) have *normal* degree distribution. The g and b graphs in contrast have skewed-degree distributions and contain many more dense local subgraphs than the er graphs. The g and b graphs differ primarily in the magnitude of maximum vertex degree they contain—the b graphs have much larger maximum degree (see Catalyurek et al. (2012) for an analysis of the structures of similarly generated RMAT graphs).

Table 2 lists the number of vertices, the number of edges, the maximum degree Δ and the clique number ω in each graph in the testbed. Computing the clique number of a graph is an NP-hard problem.

Table 3. Number of iterations and number of vertices colored in each iteration of the distance-1 coloring and distance-2 coloring versions of Algorithm 3 for select runs on the Xeon E5.

	# Threads	D1 Color.		D2 Color.	
		# Rounds	|U| in Each Round	# Rounds	|U| in Each Round
er5	16	2	4,194K → 17	2	4,194K → 394
	24	2	4,194K → 19	2	4,194K → 795
	32	2	4,194K → 44	3	4,194K → 938 → 1
g5	16	2	4,194K → 136	8	4,194K → 2,164 → 151 → 48 → ... 3 → 1
	24	2	4,194K → 119	9	4,194K → 2,209 → 344 → 105 → ... 4 → 2
	32	2	4,194K → 153	10	4,194K → 2,458 → 536 → 187 → ... 3 → 1
b5	16	3	4,194K → 209 → 2	20	4,194K → 11,525 → 2,086 → 1,046 → ... 2 → 1
	24	2	4,194K → 515	26	4,194K → 16,217 → 3,503 → 1,908 → ... 3 → 1
	32	3	4,194K → 377 → 1	24	4,194K → 20,747 → 5,240 → 2,438 → ... 2 → 1

We calculated the clique numbers in Table 2 using fast maximum clique algorithms (exact and heuristic) we implemented (Pattabiraman et al., 2013). For the two graphs b4 and b5, since the execution time of the exact, maximum clique algorithm was high, we settled for a solution provided by the heuristic, which finds a large, but not necessarily a largest clique in a graph. The listed numbers there, 51 and 58, are therefore lower bounds on the clique numbers.

Performance Results

Scalability

As discussed in Section 8, the scheme outlined in Algorithm 3 would scale if the number of *iterations* the algorithm needs to terminate is relatively small. We find that number to be very small indeed in the extensive experiments we carried out with different types of input graphs and levels of concurrency. For the distance-1 coloring version of Algorithm 3, in particular, the number of iterations needed was typically found to be just two or three. Understandably, the distance-2 coloring version needed more iterations to terminate, but still the algorithm typically terminated within at most about two dozen iterations when the highest number of threads are employed.

Furthermore, especially in the distance-1 coloring case, we observed that typically more than 99.9% of the vertices get their final colors in the *first* round! Put in another way, the number of conflicts that arise in the first round was found to be typically less than 0.1%. In the subsequent iterations, the size of conflicts, or the size $|U|$ of the vertices to be recolored, dropped dramatically from one iteration to the next. As an example of these observations, we give in Table 3 the number of iterations and the size of the set U in each iteration in the parallel distance-1 coloring and parallel distance-2 coloring algorithms for three of the largest graphs and select runs on the Xeon E5 machine.

The magnitudes of the number of iterations in Table 3 in general suggest that the Speculation and Iteration approach for parallelizing coloring algorithms is a viable framework. Looking at the numbers,

Figure 2. Speedup of **distance-2 coloring** *on the two platforms and three classes of graphs er, g and b.*

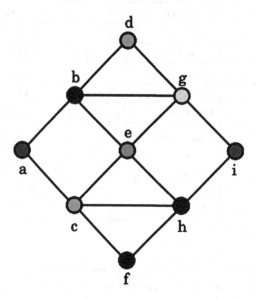

Figure 3. Speedup of **distance-1 coloring** *on the two platforms and the er class of graphs.*

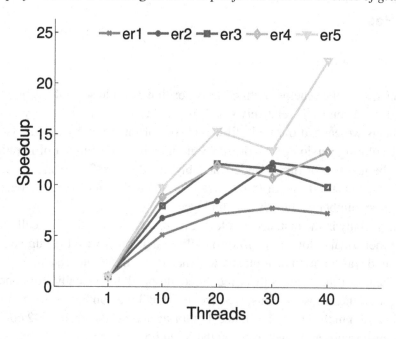

it can be envisioned that best performance in terms of speedup might be attained if one were to stop the

Figure 4. Number of colors used in distance-2 coloring (top) and distance-1 coloring (bottom) while using an approximate SL ordering. The tests are run on the Xeon E7 machine with varying number of threads (1, 10, 20, 30, 40). The lowest bar in each subfigure, labeled lb, shows the lower bounds on the number of colors: Δ in the distance-2 coloring case and ω in the distance-1 coloring case.

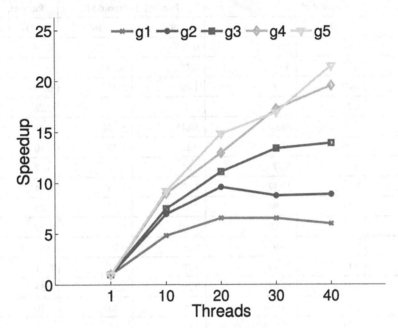

iteration and switch to sequential treatment of U once a predefined cutoff value for $|U|$ has been attained. We do not pursue this line of thought here. We work instead with the basic variant of Algorithm 3, where every iteration is performed in parallel.

Figure 2 shows speedup plots we obtain for the parallel distance-2 coloring algorithm for experiments run on the two test platforms and using all of the graphs in the dataset. In Figure 3 we show analogous results for the distance-1 coloring algorithm, but only for the er graphs in the dataset. We used in these experiments an approximate SL ordering (which we will discuss in Section 18) to reduce the number of colors used. In the plots in figures 2 and 3, the runtimes of the ordering step are, however, excluded for clarity of presentation.

From Figure 2 it can be seen that the distance-2 coloring algorithm scales well across both platforms and all graphs in the testbed. Further, it can be seen from Figure 3 that the scalability in the distance-1 coloring case is poorer than in the distance-2 coloring case, even though the number of iterations the distance-1 coloring algorithm needed was much smaller than what the distance2 coloring algorithm needed. This is because the work involved in distance-1 coloring (which is $O(|E|)$) is substantially less than that in distance-2 coloring (which is $O(|E| \cdot \Delta)$), and hence the algorithm is more sensitive to memory performance.

We point out one difference we observe concerning performance on the Xeon E7 machine compared to performance on the Core i7 machine. In the speedup plots for the Xeon E7 machine in figures 2 and 3 (and elsewhere in this chapter), we report results for up to 40 threads, which amounts to using one

Table 4. Runtime in seconds of the pure sequential algorithms, and of the parallel algorithms when run using one thread, on the **Xeon E7** *machine. For the SL ordering algorithm, two parallelizations are considered: Regular (Reg) and Relaxed (Rel).*

	Sequential			Parallel, 1 Thread SL		Parallel,1 Thread Coloring	
	SL	**D1**	**D2**	**Reg**	**Rel**	**D1**	**D2**
er1	0.21	0.06	1.17	0.33	0.21	0.11	1.66
er2	0.52	0.17	3.12	0.77	0.50	0.31	4.72
er3	1.26	0.49	9.28	1.89	1.23	0.89	14.78
er4	3.46	1.28	23.88	5.30	3.78	2.36	41.09
er5	10.49	3.68	66.00	16.45	10.74	6.44	101.27
g1	0.21	0.06	2.20	0.36	0.20	0.10	2.88
g2	0.49	0.14	5.37	0.81	0.47	0.27	7.63
g3	1.20	0.42	17.17	1.89	1.16	0.74	25.32
g4	3.06	1.13	46.96	4.82	3.17	2.05	70.34
g5	8.24	3.07	123.99	12.46	8.56	5.57	190.39
b1	0.18	0.05	7.89	0.56	0.18	0.08	9.46
b2	0.43	0.11	20.19	1.20	0.43	0.21	25.68
b3	0.87	0.31	69.81	2.50	0.98	0.55	93.78
b4	2.12	0.82	211.64	5.59	2.40	1.50	291.16
b5	5.13	2.05	606.23	13.26	5.89	3.78	860.43

thread per core out of the two available via hyperthreading. We do so because we did not observe any significant further reduction in runtime in going beyond 40 threads. In contrast, for the Core i7 machines, we report results for up to the maximum possible threads, which is 8. This amounts to taking advantage of hyperthreading. As can be seen from the results in figures 2 and 3, some performance gain can be achieved by doing so on these machines. It should be noted here that the *ideal* speedup expected in using two (hyper)threads on a single processor is considerably less than two—it is observed to be at most about 1.5 for most Intel architectures (Barker et al., 2008). In light of this, the decrease in slope of the speedup plots we see in figures 2 and 3 for the segments beyond 4 threads on the Core i7 is in agreement with one's expectation.

In the plots in figures 2 and 3 (and in similar plots in Section 18), the speedups are calculated by normalizing runtimes by the execution time of the relevant parallel algorithm run on *one* thread. This normalizing quantity is not the same as the pure *sequential* algorithm's runtime. In Table 4 we list raw execution times in seconds, on the Xeon E7 machine, of a parallel algorithm run on one thread and of the corresponding sequential algorithm for a number of different algorithms of interest in this chapter. The results relevant for our discussion here are those of the distance-1 coloring and distance-2 coloring algorithms. These are indicated in the table by boldface fonts. We will return to the rest of the data in the table in the Approximate Update section.

Quality of Solution

We have so far presented experimental results on runtime and speedup. We now turn to the quality of the solution obtained by the parallel algorithms.

Previous research has established that the serial greedy distance-k coloring algorithm (Algorithm 2), when employing ordering techniques such as SL, gives near optimal solution on most practically relevant classes of graphs. We find that its parallelization using the speculation paradigm results in runtime speedup without compromising the quality of the solution obtained by the serial algorithm. Figure 4 supports this claim.

The upper row of the figure shows the number of colors the parallel distance-2 coloring version of Algorithm 3 uses while employing an approximate SL ordering for runs conducted on the Xeon E7. In each subfigure, six bars are shown for each graph. The shortest bar shows the maximum degree (Δ) in a graph, which is a lower bound on the optimal number of colors needed to distance-2 color a graph. The remaining five bars correspond to the number of colors used by the parallel algorithm when run using five different numbers of threads: 1, 10, 20, 30 and 40. The lower row of Figure 4 shows entirely analogous results for the parallel distance-1 coloring algorithm. In each subfigure there, the shortest of the six bars shows the clique number (ω) in a graph, which is a lower bound on the optimal number of colors needed to distance-1 color a graph.

We point out two observations from these results. First, it can be seen that the number of colors the parallel algorithm uses remains nearly constant as the number of threads is increased. This is true for both the distance-2 coloring and the distance-1 coloring algorithms. Note here that the number of colors the parallel algorithm uses when one thread is employed (bars labeled *1 thd* in the figures) is the same as the number of colors the *serial* algorithm would have used. Let us call this number C_{1thd}.

Second, it can be seen that the number C_{1thd} is fairly close to the *lower bound* on the optimal solution (bars labeled *lb* in the figures). Since a gap is expected to exist between *the lower bound on the optimal solution* and *the optimal solution*, C_{1thd} would actually be even closer to the optimal solution. Proceeding with comparison against the lower bound nonetheless, we observe that these algorithms do offer low approximation ratios. In the distance-1 coloring case, for instance, the number of colors in each subfigure is observed to be just a small constant γ times the lower bound ω. In the worst cases, γ is observed to be about 3 for the er graphs, 4 for the g graphs, and 2 for the b graphs.

Approximate Update

As mentioned in the Introduction, we use algorithms for obtaining Smallest Last and Incidence Degree orderings as examples to illustrate our second parallelization paradigm, Approximate Update. We begin by reviewing the properties of these orderings and their serial algorithms. Then we discuss their parallelization and present performance results.

Degree-based Vertex Orderings

We define SL and ID ordering in terms of a dynamic degree concept we call *back degree* (Gebremedhin et al., 2013). In an ordering $\pi = v_1, v_2, ..., v_n$ of the vertices of a graph $G = (V, E)$, the *back degree* of the vertex v_i is the number of distance-1 neighbors of v_i in G that are ordered *before* v_i in π.

Algorithm 4. Template for SL and ID Ordering. B is a sparse, two-dimensional array maintaining unordered vertices binned according to their back degrees.

```
Input: Graph G = (V,E)
Output: An ordered list W of the vertices in V
1          For each vertex v ∈ V do
2                  Init b(v);
3                  B[b(v)]← B[b(v)]∪{v};
4          end
5          init i ;
6          While check i do
7                  identify j*, min (or max) index j with B[j] ≠ ∅
8                  Let v be a vertex drawn from B[j*];
9                  W[i]← v;
10                 B[j*] ←B[j*]\{v};
11                 for each vertex w ∈ N₁(v) such that w is in B do
12                         B[b(w)]← B[b(w)]/{w};
13                         update b(w);
14                         B[b(w)]← B[b(w)]∪w};
15                 end
16                 update I;
17        end.
```

An SL ordering π is defined from highest to lowest, v_n to v_1. Initially, the back degree $b(v)$ of every vertex is equal to its degree $d(v,G)$ in G. The last vertex v_n is a vertex with the *smallest* back degree. With v_n determined, the back degree of every distance-1 neighbor of v_n, by definition, is then the original value minus one. The next vertex in the ordering, v_{n-1}, is a vertex with the smallest back degree among the remaining $n-1$ vertices. Suppose the last $n-i-1$ entries of the ordered vertex set have been determined. The ith vertex in the ordering is then a vertex with the *smallest* back degree among the vertices $U = V \setminus \{v_n, v_{n-1}, ..., v_{i+1}\}$ that are yet to be ordered.

An ID ordering π is defined from lowest to highest, v_1 to v_n. Initially, the back degree of every vertex is equal to zero. The first vertex v_1 is a vertex with the *largest* back degree (note that since all back degrees are zero, any one of the vertices would qualify). With v_1 determined, the back degree of every distance-1 neighbor of v_1, by definition, is then the original value plus one. The next vertex in the ordering, v_2, is a vertex with the largest back degree among the remaining $n-1$ vertices. Suppose the first $i-1$ entries of the ordered vertex set have been determined. The ith vertex in the ordering is then a vertex with the *largest* back degree among the vertices $U = V \setminus \{v_1, v_2, ..., v_{i-1}\}$ that are yet to be ordered.

Algorithms

We give in Algorithm 4 a template for an *efficient* implementation of the ordering techniques SL and ID. Table 5 shows how the template is specialized to give SL or ID. The sparse, two-dimensional array B in Algorithm 4 is a vehicle used for arriving at efficient implementation. The array, itself implemented as a vector of vectors with total size $|V|$, is used to maintain vertices that are not yet ordered in *bins* according to their dynamic degrees. Specifically, $B[j]$ stores a set of unordered vertices where each member vertex u has a current back degree $b(u)$ equal to j. The output of Algorithm 4 is given by the ordered list W of the vertices where $W[i]$ stores the ith vertex in the ordering.

We determine the ith vertex in the ordering in constant time by maintaining a pointer to the last element in $B[j^*]$, where j^* is the *smallest* (or *largest*) index j such that $B[j]$ is non-empty. Once the ith vertex v in the ordering is determined (and removed from B), each unordered vertex w adjacent to v is moved from its current bin in B to an appropriate new bin. With suitable pointer techniques the relocation of each vertex can also be performed in constant time (Gebremedhin et al., 2013). Thus the work involved in the ith step of Algorithm 4 is proportional to $d(v,G)$, and the overall complexity of the algorithm is $O(|E|)$.

Applications

The rationale behind the ordering techniques SL and ID in the context of coloring is to bring vertices that are likely to be highly constrained in the choice of colors early in the ordering and thereby reduce the number of colors used. Both of these orderings are highly effective at doing just that. But the use of these orderings is not limited to coloring. For instance, an SL ordering, in reverse order to that obtained by Algorithm 4, can be used to determine *k-cores* (densely connected subgraphs) in social and biological networks. SL ordering, and consequently core computation, is also directly related to the graph-theoretic notions of degeneracy and arboricity (Matula, 1968; Szekeres and Wilf, 1968; Lick and White, 1970; Matula et al., 1972; Matula and Beck, 1983; Gebremedhin et al., 2005).

Table 5. How Algorithm 4 specializes to SL or ID.

	SL	ID
init $b(v)$	$b(v) \leftarrow d(v,G)$	$b(v) \leftarrow 0$
init i	$i \leftarrow |V|$	$i \leftarrow 1$
check i	$i \geq 1$	$i \leq |V|$
identify j^*	$j^* = \min_j\{B[j] \neq \varnothing\}$	$j^* = \max_j\{B[j] \neq \varnothing\}$
update $b(w)$	$b(w) \leftarrow b(w) - 1$	$b(w) \leftarrow b(w) + 1$
update i	$i \leftarrow i - 1$	$i \leftarrow i + 1$

Similarly, an ID ordering obtained by Algorithm 4, when reversed, corresponds to an ordering obtained by the *maximum cardinality search* algorithm (Tarjan and Yannakakis, 1984), which is useful in determining chordality of a graph.

Algorithm 5. A parallel SL ordering algorithm on p threads (Relaxed).

```
Input: Graph G = (V,E)
Output: Output: An ordered list W of the vertices in V
1          for each vertex v ∈ V in parallel do
2          b(v) ← d(v,G);
3          B_{t(v)} [b(v)] ← B_{t(v)} [b(v)] ∪ {v};
4 end
5          i ← |V|;
6          for t = 1 to p in parallel do
7          while i ≥ 0 do
8          Let j* be the smallest index j s.t. B_t [j] ≠∅;
9          Let v be a vertex drawn from B_t [j*];
10         B_t [j*] ← B_t [j*]\{v};
11         for each vertex w ∈ N_1 (v) do
12         if w ∈ B_t then
13         B_t [b(w)] ← B_t [b(w)]\{w};
14         b(w) ← b(w) - 1;
15         B_t [b(w)] ← B_t [b(w)] ∪ {w};
16         end 17            end
18         W [i] ← v          (critical);
19         i ← i - 1          (critical);
20         end
21 end
```

Parallelization

We consider two different approaches for the parallelization of the ordering template depicted in Algorithm 4 (Patwary et al., 2011). The first approach aims at parallelizing the ordering template closely maintaining the serial behavior, while the second approach settles for an approximate solution in favor of increased concurrency, thus falling under the APPROXIMATE UPDATE paradigm. Both approaches apply equally to SL an ID ordering. To simplify presentation, however, we discuss only the SL case here. We denote by $t(v)$ the thread with which the vertex v is initially associated.

The First Approach: Regular The first task this approach parallelizes is the population of the global bin array B. To achieve this, a *local* two-dimensional array B_t is associated with each thread T_t, $1 \leq t \leq p$. The p local arrays are first populated in parallel. Then, the contents are gathered into the global array B, where the parallelization is now switched to run over bins. The remainder of the algorithm mimics the serial algorithm (Algorithm 4). In the serial algorithm, in each step of the while loop, a *single* vertex—a vertex with the *smallest* current dynamic degree $j*$—is ordered and its neighbors' locations updated in B. However, the bin $B[j*]$ could contain *multiple* vertices. The approach *Regular* takes advantage of this opportunity and strives to order such vertices and update their neighborhoods in parallel. This gives rise to a variety of *race* conditions. The approach involves careful handling of these, including the use of frequent *atomic* and *critical* statements. Because of the use of these statements the parallel algorithm behaves much like the serial, resulting in poor scalability (Patwary et al., 2011).

The Second Approach: Relaxed The second approach for parallelizing the SL ordering algorithm abandons the use of the global array B altogether and works only with the local arrays B_t associated with each thread T_t. In updating locations of neighbors of a vertex, a thread T_t checks whether or not the vertex w desired to be relocated is in the thread's local array B_t. If w is indeed in B_t, it is relocated by the same thread. If not, it is simply ignored. In this manner, only *approximate* dynamic degrees are used while computing the *global* ordering. The approach is formalized in Algorithm 5.

Performance Results

The first parallelization approach, Regular, did not scale for a vast majority of the problem-platform combinations in our experiments. As an illustration, we give in Figure 5 speedup plots for the SL-Regular (SL-Reg) algorithm on the two platforms and the er-graphs in the dataset; the results on the other two graph classes (g and b) are similar or worse. In sharp contrast, we found that the approximate update approach RELAXED yielded moderate to excellent speedups as more threads are employed. Figure 6 shows speedup plots for SL-Relaxed (SL-Rel) on the two platforms and all three graph classes.

Figure 5. Speedup results of the parallel ordering algorithm **SL-Regular** *on the two test platforms and for the er class of graphs.*

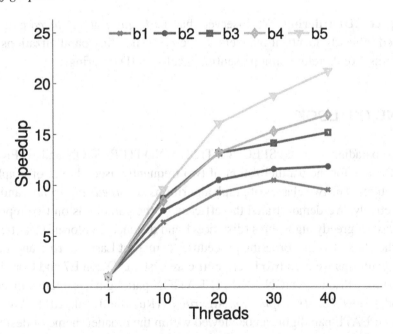

The plots in figures 5 and 6 show speedups wherein runtimes are *normalized* by the parallel algorithm's runtime when one thread is used. Recall that we had provided in Table 4 a summary of the raw compute times in seconds for runs on the Xeon E7 machine of the parallel algorithms on a *single* thread and of the pure sequential algorithms for SL ordering, distance-1 coloring, and distance-2 coloring.

*Figure 6. Speedup results of the parallel **SL-Relaxed** ordering algorithm on the two test platforms and for the three classes of graphs er, g and b.*

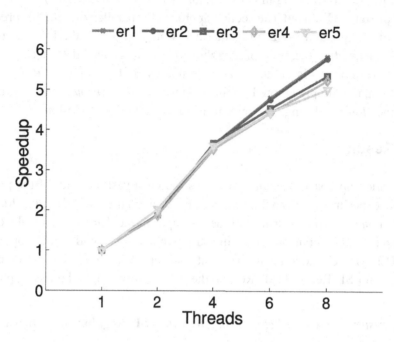

Incidence Degree (ID) ordering: We observed that the *Regular* and *Relaxed* parallelization of ID ordering performed in nearly identical manners as the corresponding parallelizations of SL ordering across both platforms. We therefore omit presenting results on ID ordering.

SUMMARY AND OUTLOOK

We introduced two paradigms, called SPECULATION AND ITERATION and APPROXIMATE UPDATE, that are effective for the parallelization of two frequently used classes of graph algorithms on multi-core architectures. The two classes of graph algorithms are *greedy algorithms* and *vertex ordering procedures*, respectively. We demonstrated the efficacy of the paradigms on two representative algorithms from the class of greedy algorithms (distance-1 and distance-2 coloring) and two representative algorithms from the class of vertex ordering procedures (Smallest Last ordering and Incidence Degree ordering). As test platforms we used two Intel multi-core systems (Xeon E7 and Core i7).

We observe that the SPECULATION AND ITERATION paradigm has interesting connections with the theoretical model called *Local Computation Algorithms* (Rubinfeld et al., 2011). We also note that the APPROXIMATE UPDATE paradigm can be viewed within the broader theme of design of *concurrent data structures* (Shavit, 2011). Both of these connections are worthwhile directions for future research.

ACKNOWLEDGMENT

This work was in part supported by the National Science Foundation Award IIS-1553528.

REFERENCES

Alon, N., Matias, Y., & Szegedy, M. (1999). The space complexity of approximating the frequency moments. *Journal of Computer and System Sciences*, *58*(1), 137–147. doi:10.1006/jcss.1997.1545

Barker, K. J., Davis, K., Hoisie, A., Kerbyson, D. J., Lang, M., Pakin, S., & Sancho, J. C. (2008). A performance evaluation of the Nehalem quad-core processor for scientific computing. *Parallel Processing Letters*, *18*(4), 453–469. doi:10.1142/S012962640800351X

Bozdag, D., Catalyurek, U. V., Gebremedhin, A. H., Manne, F., Boman, E. G., & Ozguner, F. (2010). Distributed-memory parallel algorithms for distance2 coloring and related problems in derivative computation. *SIAM Journal on Scientific Computing*, *32*(4), 2418–2446. doi:10.1137/080732158

Bozdag, D., Gebremedhin, A. H., Manne, F., Boman, E. G., & Catalyurek, U. V. (2008). A framework for scalable greedy coloring on distributed-memory parallel computers. *Journal of Parallel and Distributed Computing*, *68*(4), 515–535. doi:10.1016/j.jpdc.2007.08.002

Catalyurek, U., Feo, J., Gebremedhin, A. H., Halappanavar, M., & Pothen, A. (2012). Graph coloring algorithms for multicore and massively multithreaded architectures. *Parallel Computing*, *38*(10-11), 576–594. doi:10.1016/j.parco.2012.07.001

Chakrabarti, D., & Faloutsos, C. (2006). Graph mining: Laws, generators, and algorithms. *ACM Computing Surveys*, *38*(1), 2. doi:10.1145/1132952.1132954

Coleman, T. F., & More, J. J. (1983). Estimation of sparse Jacobian matrices and graph coloring problems. *SIAM Journal on Numerical Analysis*, *1*(20), 187–209. doi:10.1137/0720013

Gebremedhin, A. H., & Manne, F. (2000). Scalable parallel graph coloring algorithms. *Concurrency (Chichester, England)*, *12*(12), 1131–1146. doi:10.1002/1096-9128(200010)12:12<1131::AID-CPE528>3.0.CO;2-2

Gebremedhin, A. H., Manne, F., & Pothen, A. (2002). Parallel distancek coloring algorithms for numerical optimization. In Proceedings of EuroPar 2002, (vol. 2400, pp. 912–921). Springer.

Gebremedhin, A. H., Manne, F., & Pothen, A. (2005). What color is your Jacobian? Graph coloring for computing derivatives. *SIAM Review*, *47*(4), 629–705. doi:10.1137/S0036144504444711

Gebremedhin, A. H., Nguyen, D., Patwary, M. M. A., & Pothen, A. (2013). ColPack: Software for graph coloring and related problems in scientific computing. *ACM Transactions on Mathematical Software*, *40*(1), 1–31. doi:10.1145/2513109.2513110

Grama, A., Gupta, A., Karypis, G., & Kumar, V. (2003). *Introduction to Parallel Computing*. Pearson.

Jájá, J. (1992). *An Introduction to Parallel Algorithms*. Addison-Wesley.

Kurzak, J., Bader, D., & Dongara, J. (2010). *Scientific Computing with Multicore and Accelerators.* Chapman and Hall/CRC Press. doi:10.1201/b10376

Lick, D. R., & White, A. T. (1970). *k*-degenerate graphs. *Canadian Journal of Mathematics, 22*(5), 1082–1096. doi:10.4153/CJM-1970-125-1

Lin, Y.-L., & Skiena, S. (1995). Algorithms for square roots of graphs. *SIAM Journal on Discrete Mathematics, 8*(1), 99–118. doi:10.1137/S089548019120016X

Matula, D. W. (1968). A max-min theorem for graphs with application to graph coloring. *SIAM Review, 10*, 481–482.

Matula, D. W., & Beck, L. L. (1983). Smallest-last ordering and clustering and graph coloring algorithms. *Journal of the Association for Computing Machinery, 30*(3), 417–427. doi:10.1145/2402.322385

Matula, D. W., Marble, G., & Isaacson, J. (1972). Graph coloring algorithms. In R. Read (Ed.), *Graph Theory and Computing* (pp. 109–122). Academic Press. doi:10.1016/B978-1-4832-3187-7.50015-5

McCormick, S. T. (1983). Optimal approximation of sparse hessians and its equivalence to a graph coloring problem. *Mathematical Programming, 26*(2), 153–171. doi:10.1007/BF02592052

Pattabiraman, B., Patwary, M. M. A., Gebremedhin, A. H., Keng Liao, W., & Choudhary, A. (2013). Fast algorithms for the maximum clique problem on massive sparse graphs. *WAW13, 10th Workshop on Algorithms and Models for the Web Graph.*

Patwary, M. M. A., Gebremedhin, A. H., & Pothen, A. (2011). New multithreaded ordering and coloring algorithms for multicore architectures. *Proceedings of EuroPar 2011, 6853*, 250–262. 10.1007/978-3-642-23397-5_24

Patwary, M. M. A., Refsnes, P., & Manne, F. (2012). Multi-core spanning forest algorithms using disjoint-set data structure. IPDPS 2012, 827–835. doi:10.1109/IPDPS.2012.79

Pingali, K., Nguyen, D., Kulkarni, M., Burtscher, M., Hassaan, M. A., Kaleem, R., Lee, T.-H., Lenharth, A., Manevich, R., M'endez-Lojo, M., Prountzos, D., & Sui, X. (2011). The tao of parallelism in algorithms. In *Proceedings of the 32nd ACM SIGPLAN conference on Programming language design and implementation*, (pp. 12–25). New York, NY: ACM.

Rubinfeld, R., Tamir, G., Vardi, S., & Xie, N. (2011). Fast local computation algorithms. *International Conference on Supercomputing (ICS 2011*, 496–508.

Sariyuce, A. E., Saule, E., & Catalyurek, U. V. (2011). Improving graph coloring on distributed memory parallel computers. *Proc. of HiPC 2011*. 10.1109/HiPC.2011.6152726

Sariyuce, A. E., Saule, E., & Catalyurek, U. V. (2012). Scalable hybrid implementation of graph coloring using MPI and OpenMP. *Proc. IPDPS Workshops and PhD Forum, Workshop on Parallel Computing and Optimization (PCO'12)*. 10.1109/IPDPSW.2012.216

Shavit, N. (2011). Data structures in the multicore age. *Communications of the ACM, 54*(3), 76–84. doi:10.1145/1897852.1897873

Szekeres, G., & Wilf, H. S. (1968). An inequality for the chromatic number of a graph. *Journal of Combinatorial Theory*, *4*(1), 1–3. doi:10.1016/S0021-9800(68)80081-X

Tarjan, R. E., & Yannakakis, M. (1984). Simple linear-time algorithms to test chordality of graphs, test acyclicity of hypergraphs, and selectively reduce acyclic hypergraphs. *SIAM Journal on Scientific Computing*, *13*(3), 566–579. doi:10.1137/0213035

Tian, C., Feng, M., Nagarajan, V., & Gupta, R. (2009). Speculative parallelization of sequential loops on multicores. *International Journal of Parallel Programming*, *37*(1), 508–535. doi:10.100710766-009-0111-z

Zavlanos, M. M., Spesivtsev, L., & Pappas, G. J. (2008). A distributed auction algorithm for the assignment problem. *Proceedings of the 47th IEEE Conference on Decision and Control*, 1212–1217. 10.1109/CDC.2008.4739098

Chapter 6
Introduction to Dataflow Computing

Nenad Korolija
School of Electrical Engineering, University of Belgrade, Serbia

Jovan Popović
Microsoft Development Center, Serbia

Miroslav M. Bojović
School of Electrical Engineering, University of Belgrade, Serbia

ABSTRACT

This chapter presents the possibilities for obtaining significant performance gains based on advanced implementations of algorithms using the dataflow hardware. A framework built on top of the dataflow architecture that provides tools for advanced implementations is also described. In particular, the authors point out to the following issues of interest for accelerating algorithms: (1) the dataflow paradigm appears as suitable for executing certain set of algorithms for high performance computing, namely algorithms that work with big data, as well as algorithms that include a lot of repetitions of the same set of instructions; (2) dataflow architecture could be configured using appropriate programming tools that can define hardware by generating VHDL files; (3) besides accelerating algorithms, dataflow architecture also reduces power consumption, which is an important security factor with edge computing.

BACKGROUND

The 1906 Nobel Prize in Physiology and Medicine was awarded to Camillo Golgi and Ramón y Cajal for having visualized and identified the neuron, the structural and functional unit of the nervous system (Grant, 2007). Since then, it has been discovered that the human brain contains roughly 100 billion neurons and 1000 trillion synapses. Neurons interact through electrochemical signals, also known as actional potentials (AP) or spikes, transmitted from one neuron to the next through synaptic junctions, forming functional and definable circuits which can be organized into larger 'neuronal' networks and anatomical

DOI: 10.4018/978-1-7998-7156-9.ch006

structures. These networks integrate information from multiple brain regions as well as incoming information about the external environment (e.g., sound, light, smell, taste). The result is how we perceive the world, and produce complex behavior and cognitive processes including decision-making and learning (Kandel, 2012); also, with time, these processes modify the structure and function of networks through a process called neuroplasticity (Fuchs & Flugge, 2014).

Understanding how the brain works with the ultimate goal of developing treatments for neurological disease remains one of the greatest scientific challenges of this century. In fact, there is a substantial social and economic burden associated with neurological diseases (Wynford-Thomas & Robertson, 2017). In the US alone, the overall cost of neurological diseases (e.g., stroke, dementia, movement disorders, traumatic brain injury) amounts to nearly $1T, and will dramatically increase in the next few years due to population ageing. Alarmingly, the cost of just dementias and stroke is expected to exceed $600B by 2030 (Gooch, Pracht, & Borenstein, 2017). To tackle this challenge, neuroscientists have developed a battery of increasingly complex tools, which have amplified data storage and computational speed requirements to an unprecedented level, making the use of big data techniques and HPC such as supercomputers a necessity.

In the remainder of this chapter we will briefly review current and future applications of supercomputers in neuroscience, with a focus on computational neural models, brain imaging, and models for brain stimulation. These areas were chosen not only because their advances have been particularly driven by computational approaches, but also because they are highly interconnected. Thereby, understanding how each area is evolving aids prediction of future research trends in the other areas. We also briefly discuss how the next generation of supercomputers might enable further advancements in these areas.

Computational Neural Models

Computational models of neurons and neural networks represent one of the most essential tools that have contributed to the progress of neuroscience. For example, they are used to guide the design of experiments, to quantify relationships between anatomical and physiological data, to investigate the dynamics of systems that cannot be accessed via analytical methods, and to validate estimates made during theoretical derivations. Since the early days of neuronal simulations, a wide range of computational models have been developed ranging from models aimed at describing low-level mechanisms of neural function (e.g., molecular dynamics of ion channels in the neuron) to models of large-scale neuronal networks (Ippen, Eppler, Plesser, & Diesmann, 2017) (see (Fan & Markram, 2019) for a review).

The chosen level of abstraction for a model is based on the scientific question. If focused on subcellular processes (e.g., the transfer of ions underlying changes in membrane voltages that lead to APs), a neuron(s) would be described with detailed multi-compartment models (M. Hines, 1984). Instead, if the question addressed large scale network dynamics, many neurons would be described with one-compartment or few-compartment models that communicate electrically via spikes (Helias et al., 2012; Ippen et al., 2017). Simulators exist for many of these levels, including NEURON (M. L. Hines & Carnevale, 1997), SPLIT (Hammarlund & Ekeberg, 1998), PCSIM (Pecevski, Natschläger, & Schuch, 2009), the NEural Simulation Tool (NEST) (Gewaltig, 2007; van Albada, Kunkel, Morrison, & Diesmann, 2014), and C2 (Ananthanarayanan & Modha, 2007) (see (Helias et al., 2012; Tikidji-Hamburyan, Narayana, Bozkus, & El-Ghazawi, 2017) for a review).

A major challenge when developing such models include the total number of network elements that must be represented. To put the problem into perspective, a 1 mm^3 of brain tissue modeled at the neuronal and synaptic level (Amit & Brunel, 1997; Brunel, 2000; Morrison, Aertsen, & Diesmann, 2007) includes 10^5 neurons and 1 billion synapses (Helias et al., 2012). However, representing neurons in a restricted volume is only part of the problem, as each neuron receives more than half of its inputs from neurons that are not in its vicinity and that can even be located in distant areas (Abeles, 1991; Stepanyants, Martinez, Ferecsko, & Kisvarday, 2009). This issue ultimately severely limits models' predictive power, creating the need for developing models of increasingly larger areas of the brain.

Over the past several decades unprecedented funding has been granted by national brain-research projects supported by the USA, EU, and governments of other developed countries to spur innovative research in this area. Arguably these efforts have transitioned neuroscience from a "small science" to a "big science" approach (i.e., using large multi-discipline teams, with ample resources and competences to tackle the big problems (Markram, 2013)). A general goal of these very ambitious projects has been to build platforms for "simulating the human brain" (Makin, 2019) in a supercomputer. Examples of these projects are the Blue Brain Project in collaboration with IBM, which aims to "develop a digital reconstruction of rodent and eventually human brains by reverse-engineering mammalian brain circuitry" (see for example their reconstruction of a small volume of the rat primary somatosensory cortex (Markram et al., 2015)) and the Human Brain Project (Amunts et al., 2019) (see (Chen et al., 2019) for a review).

Despite these and other substantial efforts, simulations of the whole brain at a neuronal level are not yet feasible, as they would require memory sizes well beyond those available in today's supercomputers. Another bottleneck is represented by the current neural simulators' inefficiency in managing information exchange of neurons across supercomputers nodes. State of the art simulation software and available supercomputers allow simulation of only a small fraction of the human cortex (Jordan et al., 2018; Kunkel et al., 2014). Availability of exascale computers and development of algorithms for optimal processing speed promise to further scale neural networks simulations (Jordan et al., 2018).

Brain Imaging

Another area where supercomputers are enabling advances in brain science is through imaging. A pillar of neuroscience, imaging has greatly contributed to furthering our understanding of brain physiology and disease states. Common imaging technologies include Magnetic Resonance Imaging (MRI; first introduced in 1977), functional Magnetic Resonance Imaging (fMRI, first introduced in 1990 by Bell Laboratories), electroencephalography (EEG, a technique used since the beginning of 1900), and magnetoencephalography (MEG, first introduced in 1970). These techniques have allowed scientists to investigate structure or patterns of activation of different brain areas and develop hypotheses of how specific structural or functional anomalies might lead to emergent pathological behaviors (see (Bowman, 2014) for a review).

Over the years, these technologies have been refined to enable collection of increasingly complex data sets. For example, most state-of-the art medical MRI scans can reach resolutions of around $1.5 \times 1.5 \times 4$mm^3, but ultra-high magnetic field MRI scanners for research purposes have reached a resolution of $80 \times 80 \times 200$μm^3 (Van Reeth, Tham, Tan, & Poh, 2012); fMRI data cycle of acquisition has become faster (increasing from 4s to 1s), and fMRI resolution has increased from 5 mm^3 to 1 mm^3 (Chen et al., 2019). Increases in the size of data sets have not only been driven by these hardware advances, but also by the transition of neuroscience to a big data science which has resulted from the collaborative aspect of the scientific initiatives described in the paragraph above (Li, Guo, & Li, 2019). Typical pre-big data era research data sets collected for example during an fMRI experiment aimed at uncovering which areas of the brain activated during a certain cognitive task were composed of data from tens of subjects, but modern data sets are considerably larger due to the practice of data sharing and integration of multiple data sources (Calhoun & Sui, 2016). Combined with the already high computational power demands that come from the algorithms typically used for analyzing these data sets (which often involve analysis of patterns of activations through different brain areas and subjects via correlation and clustering techniques) one can see how the use of supercomputers is becoming indispensable (Cohen et al., 2017).

Research with EEG, one of the oldest technologies for recording brain electrical activity, has also evolved in a similar direction. Modern scalp EEG systems have evolved from just a few electrodes traditionally used for monitoring changes in signal features in the temporal and/or spectral domain to 256 electrodes when used for research purposes -these high-density EEG systems can be used to build spatio-temporal maps of brain activation (see (Dipietro, Poizner, & Krebs, 2014) for an example). The increased number of electrodes combined with EEG's high temporal resolution (ms) and the easiness of recordings (e.g., due to EEG systems high portability) has led to dramatically increased data set sizes. An area of EEG (and MEG) research where supercomputers may lead to future advancements is source-localization. EEG source localization estimates the location of the brain cells (i.e., neurons that act as electromagnetic dipole sources) from recordings of brain activity made by electrodes placed on the scalp (Dipietro, Plank, Poizner, & Krebs, 2012). Source-localization algorithms require an anatomical model of the subject head and solving a very computationally intensive inverse model problem (Michel & Brunet, 2019). Until very recently, the difficulty in harnessing sufficient computer power had discouraged researchers from attempting this type of analysis on very large data sets, but recently it has been shown how implementations on supercomputers are making this type of analysis more accessible (Delorme et al., 2019).

Brain Stimulation

An emerging application of supercomputers is in the area of brain stimulation. In humans, the invasive technique of deep brain stimulation (DBS) (Herrington, Cheng, & Eskandar, 2016) and noninvasive brain stimulation techniques such as Transcranial Direct Current Stimulation (tDCS) and Transcranial Magnetic Stimulation (TMS) (Brunoni et al., 2012; Klomjai, Katz, & Lackmy-Vallee, 2015; Reed & Cohen Kadosh, 2018) have been successfully used to investigate the functional properties of the nervous system (Polania, Nitsche, & Ruff, 2018) and to treat neurological disorders (Schulz, Gerloff, & Hummel, 2013) such as depression, Parkinson's disease, and chronic pain (see for example (Boccard, Pereira, & Aziz, 2015; Groiss, Wojtecki, Sudmeyer, & Schnitzler, 2009; Liu, Sheng, Li, & Zhang, 2017)). When used to deliver a treatment, these neurostimulation techniques can be administered alone or in conjunction with other treatments. For example, in Parkinson's disease, stimulation techniques could be used adjunctive to drug therapy, and in stroke patients in conjunction with robot-assisted motor therapy (Edwards et al., 2014).

Independent of the technique, understanding how stimulatory fields interact with the neural tissue is a fundamental step in effectively implementing neuromodulation methods (Butson & McIntyre, 2005 ; Wagner, Valero-Cabre, & Pascual-Leone, 2007). Assessing the stimulatory field effects of brain stimulation requires the following computational steps: modeling the human head and brain; modeling stimulation sources; and modeling the tissue-field interactions of stimulation (both in terms of the field-neural cell interactions that drive neuromodulatory effects in the nervous system, and in terms of the biophysical field distributions in the targeted tissue- see Fig. 1). A detailed explanation of this process can be found in the authors' work in (Wagner et al., 2014), which described how to calculate the electromagnetic fields generated during TMS and DBS and their ability to modulate neural activity. To this end the authors used MRI-guided Finite Element Models (FEMs) of the human head based on individual patient anatomy and frequency-dependent tissue impedance properties. The FEM human head models were integrated with models of TMS and DBS sources and the authors subsequently solved for the stimulation field distributions in the targeted brain tissue. The field distributions solutions were then combined with conductance-based compartmental models of neurons, and ultimately used to calculate stimulation thresholds and response dynamics of targeted neurons. Currently, this process is being extended to new neuromodulation techniques and to modeling the response of more complicated cellular and network targets.

The above computational methods guide stimulation dosing, which can be specific for each patient. For example, members of the authors' group are currently developing dosing software for electrosonic stimulation (Wagner & Dipietro, 2018), a new form of noninvasive brain stimulation that combines electrical and ultrasound sources to achieve improved stimulation focality, targeting, and penetration. Electrosonic stimulation is being investigated in clinical trials in patients with Parkinson's disease and chronic pain (such as due to knee osteoarthritis, low back pain, and diabetic neuropathic pain). Many of these studies are being combined with computational studies aimed at optimizing stimulation dosing along a Precision Medicine Initiative trajectory (Ashley, 2015). The National Academies of Science has highlighted Precision Medicine Initiative approaches as an opening for a reductionist data-driven computer-based analysis, adding to the classical hypothetical deductive clinical model and intuition of experienced physicians (Committee on Diagnostic Error in Health Care; Board on Health Care Services; Institute of Medicine; The National Academies of Sciences, 2015).

Figure 1. One can use computational processes to solve for patient specific stimulation doses for non-invasive brain stimulation. The figure depicts TMS cortical current density distributions derived from diffusion tensor imaging-based models. Image adapted from (Wagner, 2006; Wagner, Rushmore, Eden, & Valero-Cabre, 2009).

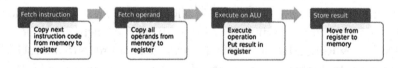

In brain stimulation treatments, personalized modeling might be important not only because different patients have different anatomies (e.g., brain anatomy), but also because neurological disorders often induce changes in brain structure, function, and/or in the electromagnetic properties of the neural tissue (e.g., see mechanisms of central sensitization induced by pain (Latremoliere & Woolf, 2009), or cortical reorganization induced by stroke (Grefkes & Ward, 2014)). For example, a previous study by the authors shows how a brain infarct can affect stimulation (O'Brien et al., 2016). That study compared electromagnetic fields generated during brain stimulation via tDCS, TMS, and Epidural Brain Stimulation (EBS) techniques in a brain with and without focal cortical infarcts. It was shown that changes in electrical properties at stroke boundaries differentially impacted the distribution of stimulation currents in terms of orientation, location, and magnitude (e.g., the impact on current density magnitude was greater for the noninvasive brain stimulation techniques (i.e., tDCS and TMS) than for EBS) (O'Brien et al., 2016). Such effects would need to be taken into account when designing a brain stimulation treatment plan for patients, as they will ultimately alter its efficacy.

The aforementioned computational models require considerable computational resources, which can progressively increase as the level of detail of the model components (e.g., MRI resolution) rises. The growing demand for personalized treatment combined with the mounting use of brain stimulation in the clinic, the increasing urgency of finding effective treatments for neurological diseases, and the growing interest in developing new or optimizing existing brain stimulation technologies are likely to accelerate the use of supercomputers in this area.

CONCLUSIONS

The brain is the world's most sophisticated supercomputer. Unveiling how it works is one of the greatest challenges of this century. This chapter has briefly reviewed how different technologies and their combination have enabled advances in brain science. The cross-pollination of ideas borrowed from neuroscience and supercomputing relies on "Crossdisciplinarization" and "Hybridization" approaches to inspire and generate innovations (Blagojević et al., 2017). Availability of exascale computers and development of faster data processing algorithms are expected to quickly advance different areas of brain sciences. The acceleration of algorithms, via architectural research, could be achieved with one or more of the following general approaches: by introducing improvements into the architecture of a single CPU (e.g., (Milenkovic & Milutinovic, 2000)); by changing the implementation technology (e.g., (V. Milutinovic, 1996)); by changing the computational paradigm at the architectural level (i.e., by switching from control flow to data flow as described for example in (D. Milutinovic, Milutinovic, & Soucek, 1987)); or by introducing a more effective parallel processing into the control flow paradigm (e.g., (Trobec et al., 2016)). In the field of neuroscience, the use of supercomputers is growing and likely to change the trajectory of many research and clinical areas, at a speed that will depend on how much the area relies on computational approaches.

REFERENCES

Abeles, M. (1991). Corticonics: Neural Circuits of the Cerebral Cortex 1st Edition.

Amit, D. J., & Brunel, N. (1997). Model of global spontaneous activity and local structured activity during delay periods in the cerebral cortex. *Cereb Cortex*, 7(3), 237–252. doi:10.1093/cercor/7.3.237

Amunts, K., Knoll, A. C., Lippert, T., Pennartz, C. M. A., Ryvlin, P., Destexhe, A., ... Bjaalie, J. G. (2019). The Human Brain Project-Synergy between neuroscience, computing, informatics, and brain-inspired technologies. *PLoS Biology*, 17(7), e3000344. doi:10.1371/journal.pbio.3000344

Ananthanarayanan, R., & Modha, D. S. (2007). Anatomy of a cortical simulator. Paper presented at the Supercomputing 2007: Proceedings of the ACM/IEEE SC2007 Conference on High Performance Networking and Computing Reno, NV, USA.

Ashley, E. A. (2015). The precision medicine initiative: A new national effort. *Journal of the American Medical Association, 313*(21), 2119–2120. doi:10.1001/jama.2015.3595

Blagojević, V., Bojić, D., Bojović, M., Cvetanović, C., Đorđević, J., Đurđević, D., & Vuletić, P. (2017). *A Systematic Approach to Generation of New Ideas for PhD Research in Computing* (Vol. 104). Elsevier.

Boccard, S. G., Pereira, E. A., & Aziz, T. Z. (2015). Deep brain stimulation for chronic pain. *Journal of Clinical Neuroscience, 22*(10), 1537–1543. doi:10.1016/j.jocn.2015.04.005

Bowman, F. D. (2014). Brain Imaging Analysis. *Annual Review of Statistics and Its Application, 1*, 61–85. doi:10.1146/annurev-statistics-022513-115611

Brunel, N. (2000). Dynamics of sparsely connected networks of excitatory and inhibitory spiking neurons. *Journal of Computational Neuroscience, 8*(3), 183–208. doi:10.1023/a:1008925309027

Brunoni, A. R., Nitsche, M. A., Bolognini, N., Bikson, M., Wagner, T., Merabet, L., ... Fregni, F. (2012). Clinical research with transcranial direct current stimulation (tDCS): Challenges and future directions. *Brain Stimulation, 5*(3), 175–195. doi:10.1016/j.brs.2011.03.002

Butson, C. R., & McIntyre, C. C. (2005). Tissue and electrode capacitance reduce neural activation volumes during deep brain stimulation. *Clinical Neurophysiology, 116*(10), 2490–2500. doi:10.1016/j.clinph.2005.06.023

Calhoun, V. D., & Sui, J. (2016). Multimodal fusion of brain imaging data: A key to finding the missing link(s) in complex mental illness. *Biol Psychiatry Cogn Neurosci Neuroimaging, 1*(3), 230–244. doi:10.1016/j.bpsc.2015.12.005

Chen, S., He, Z., Han, X., He, X., Li, R., Zhu, H., ... Niu, B. (2019). How Big Data and High-performance Computing Drive Brain Science. *Genomics, Proteomics & Bioinformatics, 17*(4), 381–392. doi:10.1016/j.gpb.2019.09.003

Cohen, J. D., Daw, N., Engelhardt, B., Hasson, U., Li, K., Niv, Y., ... Willke, T. L. (2017). Computational approaches to fMRI analysis. *Nature Neuroscience, 20*(3), 304–313. doi:10.1038/nn.4499

Committee on Diagnostic Error in Health Care, & the Board on Health Care Services. Institute of Medicine; The National Academies of Sciences, Engineering, and Medicine (2015). Improving diagnosis in healtcare. Washington (DC): The National Academy Press.

Delorme, A., Majumdar, A., Sivagnanam, S., Martinez-Cancino, K., Yoshimoto, R., & Makeig, S. (2019). The Open EEGLAB portal. Paper presented at the 9th International IEEE/EMBS Conference on Neural Engineering (NER), San Francisco, CA, USA.

Dipietro, L., Plank, M., Poizner, H., & Krebs, H. I. (2012). EEG microstate analysis in human motor corrections. Paper presented at the RAS EMBS International Conference on Biomedical Robotics and Biomechatronics.

Dipietro, L., Poizner, H., & Krebs, H. I. (2014). Spatiotemporal dynamics of online motor correction processing revealed by high-density electroencephalography. *Journal of Cognitive Neuroscience, 26*(9), 1966–1980. doi:10.1162/jocn_a_00593

Edwards, D. J., Dipietro, L., Demirtas-Tatlidede, A., Medeiros, A. H., Thickbroom, G. W., Mastaglia, F. L., ... Pascual-Leone, A. (2014). Movement-generated afference paired with transcranial magnetic stimulation: An associative stimulation paradigm. *Journal of Neuroengineering and Rehabilitation, 11,* 31. doi:10.1186/1743-0003-11-31

Fan, X., & Markram, H. (2019). A Brief History of Simulation Neuroscience. *Frontiers in Neuroinformatics, 13,* 32. doi:10.3389/fninf.2019.00032

Fuchs, E., & Flugge, G. (2014). Adult neuroplasticity: More than 40 years of research. *Neural Plasticity, 541870.* Advance online publication. doi:10.1155/2014/541870

Gewaltig, M. O., & Diesmann, M. (2007). NEST (NEural Simulation Tool). *Scholarpedia, 2*(4), 1430.

Gooch, C. L., Pracht, E., & Borenstein, A. R. (2017). The burden of neurological disease in the United States: A summary report and call to action. *Annals of Neurology, 81*(4), 479–484. doi:10.1002/ana.24897

Grant, G. (2007). How the 1906 Nobel Prize in Physiology or Medicine was shared between Golgi and Cajal. *Brain Research. Brain Research Reviews, 55*(2), 490–498. doi:10.1016/j.brainresrev.2006.11.004

Grefkes, C., & Ward, N. S. (2014). Cortical reorganization after stroke: How much and how functional? *The Neuroscientist, 20*(1), 56–70. doi:10.1177/1073858413491147

Groiss, S. J., Wojtecki, L., Sudmeyer, M., & Schnitzler, A. (2009). Deep brain stimulation in Parkinson's disease. *Therapeutic Advances in Neurological Disorders, 2*(6), 20–28. doi:10.1177/1756285609339382

Hammarlund, P., & Ekeberg, O. (1998). Large neural network simulations on multiple hardware platforms. *Journal of Computational Neuroscience, 5*(4), 443–459. doi:10.1023/a:1008893429695

Helias, M., Kunkel, S., Masumoto, G., Igarashi, J., Eppler, J. M., Ishii, S., ... Diesmann, M. (2012). Supercomputers ready for use as discovery machines for neuroscience. *Frontiers in Neuroinformatics, 6,* 26. doi:10.3389/fninf.2012.00026

Herrington, T. M., Cheng, J. J., & Eskandar, E. N. (2016). Mechanisms of deep brain stimulation. *Journal of Neurophysiology, 115*(1), 19–38. doi:10.1152/jn.00281.2015

Hines, M. (1984). Efficient computation of branched nerve equations. *International Journal of Bio-Medical Computing, 15*(1), 69–76. doi:10.1016/0020-7101(84)90008-4

Hines, M. L., & Carnevale, N. T. (1997). The NEURON simulation environment. *Neural Computation, 9*(6), 1179–1209. doi:10.1162/neco.1997.9.6.1179

Ippen, T., Eppler, J. M., Plesser, H. E., & Diesmann, M. (2017). Constructing Neuronal Network Models in Massively Parallel Environments. *Frontiers in Neuroinformatics, 11,* 30. doi:10.3389/fninf.2017.00030

Jordan, J., Ippen, T., Helias, M., Kitayama, I., Sato, M., Igarashi, J., ... Kunkel, S. (2018). Extremely Scalable Spiking Neuronal Network Simulation Code: From Laptops to Exascale Computers. *Frontiers in Neuroinformatics, 12,* 2. doi:10.3389/fninf.2018.00002

Kandel, E. R. (2012). *Principles of Neural Science* (J. H. Schwartz, T. M. Jessell, S. A. Siegelbaum, & A. J. Hudspeth, Eds.; 5th ed.). McGraw-Hill Education / Medical.

Klomjai, W., Katz, R., & Lackmy-Vallee, A. (2015). Basic principles of transcranial magnetic stimulation (TMS) and repetitive TMS (rTMS). *Annals of Physical and Rehabilitation Medicine, 58*(4), 208–213. doi:10.1016/j.rehab.2015.05.005

Kunkel, S., Schmidt, M., Eppler, J. M., Plesser, H. E., Masumoto, G., Igarashi, J., ... Helias, M. (2014). Spiking network simulation code for petascale computers. *Frontiers in Neuroinformatics, 8*, 78. doi:10.3389/fninf.2014.00078

Latremoliere, A., & Woolf, C. J. (2009). Central sensitization: A generator of pain hypersensitivity by central neural plasticity. *The Journal of Pain, 10*(9), 895–926. doi:10.1016/j.jpain.2009.06.012

Li, X., Guo, N., & Li, Q. (2019). Functional Neuroimaging in the New Era of Big Data. *Genomics, Proteomics & Bioinformatics, 17*(4), 393–401. doi:10.1016/j.gpb.2018.11.005

Liu, S., Sheng, J., Li, B., & Zhang, X. (2017). Recent Advances in Non-invasive Brain Stimulation for Major Depressive Disorder. *Frontiers in Human Neuroscience, 11*, 526. doi:10.3389/fnhum.2017.00526

Makin, S. (2019). The four biggest challenges in brain simulation. *Nature, 571*(7766), S9. doi:10.1038/d41586-019-02209-z

Markram, H. (2013). Seven challenges for neuroscience. *Functional Neurology, 28*(3), 145–151. doi:10.11138/FNeur/2013.28.3.144

Markram, H., Muller, E., Ramaswamy, S., Reimann, M. W., Abdellah, M., Sanchez, C. A., ... Schurmann, F. (2015). Reconstruction and Simulation of Neocortical Microcircuitry. *Cell, 163*(2), 456–492. doi:10.1016/j.cell.2015.09.029

Michel, C. M., & Brunet, D. (2019). EEG Source Imaging: A Practical Review of the Analysis Steps. *Frontiers in Neurology, 10*, 325. doi:10.3389/fneur.2019.00325

Milenkovic, A., & Milutinovic, V. (2000). Cache injection: A novel technique for tolerating memory latency in bus-based SMPs. Paper presented at the European Conference on Parallel Processing, Berlin, Heidelberg.

Milutinovic, D., Milutinovic, V., & Soucek, B. (1987). The Honeycomb Architecture. *Computer, 20*(4), 81–83.

Milutinovic, V. (1996). *Surviving the design of a 200MHz RISC microprocessor*. IEEE Computer Society Press.

Morrison, A., Aertsen, A., & Diesmann, M. (2007). Spike-timing-dependent plasticity in balanced random networks. *Neural Computation, 19*(6), 1437–1467. doi:10.1162/neco.2007.19.6.1437

O'Brien, A. T., Amorim, R., Rushmore, R. J., Eden, U., Afifi, L., Dipietro, L., ... Valero-Cabre, A. (2016). Motor Cortex Neurostimulation Technologies for Chronic Post-stroke Pain: Implications of Tissue Damage on Stimulation Currents. *Frontiers in Human Neuroscience, 10*, 545. doi:10.3389/fnhum.2016.00545

Pecevski, D., Natschläger, T., & Schuch, K. (2009). PCSIM: A Parallel Simulation Environment for Neural Circuits Fully Integrated with Python. Front Neuroinformatics, 3(11).

Polania, R., Nitsche, M. A., & Ruff, C. C. (2018). Studying and modifying brain function with non-invasive brain stimulation. *Nature Neuroscience, 21*(2), 174–187. doi:10.103841593-017-0054-4

Reed, T., & Cohen Kadosh, R. (2018). Transcranial electrical stimulation (tES) mechanisms and its effects on cortical excitability and connectivity. *Journal of Inherited Metabolic Disease*. Advance online publication. doi:10.100710545-018-0181-4

Schulz, R., Gerloff, C., & Hummel, F. C. (2013). Non-invasive brain stimulation in neurological diseases. *Neuropharmacology, 64*, 579–587. doi:10.1016/j.neuropharm.2012.05.016

Stepanyants, A., Martinez, L. M., Ferecsko, A. S., & Kisvarday, Z. F. (2009). The fractions of short- and long-range connections in the visual cortex. *Proceedings of the National Academy of Sciences of the United States of America, 106*(9), 3555–3560. doi:10.1073/pnas.0810390106

Tikidji-Hamburyan, R. A., Narayana, V., Bozkus, Z., & El-Ghazawi, T. A. (2017). Software for Brain Network Simulations: A Comparative Study. *Frontiers in Neuroinformatics, 11*, 46. doi:10.3389/fninf.2017.00046

Trobec, R., Vasiljević, R., Tomašević, M., Milutinović, V., Beivide, R., & Valero, M. (2016). Interconnection networks in petascale computer systems: A survey. [CSUR]. *ACM Computing Surveys, 49*(3), 1–24.

van Albada, S. J., Kunkel, S., Morrison, A., & Diesmann, M. (2014). *Integrating Brain Structure and Dynamics on Supercomputers* (L. Grandinetti, L. Lippert, & N. Petkov, Eds.). Vol. 8603). Springer.

Van Reeth, E., Tham, I. W. K., Tan, C. H., & Poh, C. L. (2012). Super-resolution in magnetic resonance maging: a review. In Concepts in Magnetic Resonance (Vol. Part A 40A. 6, pp. 306–325.).

Wagner, T. (2006). Transcranial Magnetic Stimulation: High Resolution Tracking of the Induced Current Density in the Individual Human Brain. Paper presented at the 12th Annual Meeting of Human Brain mapping, Florence, Italy.

Wagner, T., & Dipietro, L. (2018). Novel methods of transcranial stimulation: electrosonic stimulation. In A. Rezai, P. H. Peckham, & E. Krames (Eds.), *Neuromodulation: Comprehensive Textbook of Principles, Technologies, and Therapies*. Elsevier.

Wagner, T., Eden, U., Rushmore, J., Russo, C. J., Dipietro, L., Fregni, F., ... Valero-Cabre, A. (2014). Impact of brain tissue filtering on neurostimulation fields: A modeling study. *NeuroImage, 85*(Pt 3), 1048–1057. doi:10.1016/j.neuroimage.2013.06.079

Wagner, T., Rushmore, J., Eden, U., & Valero-Cabre, A. (2009). Biophysical foundations underlying TMS: Setting the stage for an effective use of neurostimulation in the cognitive neurosciences. *Cortex, 45*(9), 1025–1034. doi:10.1016/j.cortex.2008.10.002

Wagner, T., Valero-Cabre, A., & Pascual-Leone, A. (2007). Noninvasive human brain stimulation. *Annual Review of Biomedical Engineering, 9*, 527–565. doi:10.1146/annurev.bioeng.9.061206.133100

Wynford-Thomas, R., & Robertson, N. P. (2017). The economic burden of chronic neurological disease. *Journal of Neurology, 264*(11), 2345–2347. doi:10.100700415-017-8632-7

Chapter 7
Data Flow Implementation of Erosion and Dilation

Christina Pacher
Universität Wien, Austria

ABSTRACT

This chapter describes a data flow implementation of the image processing algorithms Erosion and Dilation. Erosion and Dilation are basic image processing algorithms which are used to reduce or increase the size of objects in images, respectively, and which are used in a wide number of image processing applications. The chapter first describes the control flow versions of the algorithms in detail. Subsequently, the translation of these algorithms to the Data Flow paradigm is examined, and the details of the data flow implementation as well as possible optimizations are discussed.

INTRODUCTION

This chapter describes a data flow implementation of the image processing algorithms "erosion" and "dilation". The purpose of these algorithms is to reduce (for erosion) or increase (for dilation) the size of objects in images by removing or adding pixels around their edges. They are also necessary for the image processing algorithms "opening" and "closing", which use sequences of erosion and dilation operations to separate or join objects in images (Phillips, 2000).

Typical use cases for erosion and dilation include the de-noising of images as part of some larger image processing application (e.g. road detection as used by Ming et al. (2017)). But there are also applications outside the domain of image processing: Hanjun & Huali (2010), for example, use erosion and dilation in image rendering for the creation of fake soft shadows.

Image processing algorithms are generally good candidates for implementation as data flow algorithms, as they usually require the same set of operations to be executed for each pixel. In fact there actually exist data flow architectures and hybrid data flow architectures that were designed specifically for working with image processing algorithms; they are highly beneficial for the speed of those algorithms and can even be used for real-time image processing (Quénot & Zavidovique, 1992; Sinha et al., 2002).

DOI: 10.4018/978-1-7998-7156-9.ch007

Like most algorithms, erosion and dilation come in many different flavours. Phillips (2000) offers descriptions of two different versions of each of the algorithms; yet another definition is given by Nixon & Aguado (2012). There are also a great many variants and performance-tuned versions of those algorithms, and/or versions that are tailored to special cases like binary images (e.g. Chen & Haralick (1995) and Cheng (2009)).

The data flow implementation described here is based on one of the versions of erosion and dilation described by Phillips (2000).

The remainder of this chapter will first describe the chosen versions of the algorithms in detail. Subsequently, it will be examined how these algorithms can be translated to the data flow paradigm.

CONTROL FLOW ALGORITHMS

In order to be able to successfully transfer the algorithms to data flow, it is necessary to first understand exactly how the control flow implementations work; for this reason, this section is concerned with a description of erosion and dilation in control flow. It is first necessary to specify some assumptions about the input data, before examining the logic behind the algorithms.

Assumptions

The implementation described here uses the same notion of an image that is employed by Phillips (2000), where each pixel corresponds to one integer number; this basically means that the processed image has only one colour channel (e.g. greyscale). However, the algorithms could just as well be applied to images with three colour channels; it would suffice to perform the operations on each of the colour channels separately and then re-combine the results.

It is also assumed that a pixel value of 0, which is the minimum possible value, denotes the background colour; all pixels with values other than 0 belong to objects. The maximum possible value is assumed to be 255. Of course the algorithms would also work if other values were specified as the minimum and maximum, but it is important that the range of possible values has to be known beforehand since this influences the values of constants in the code, as will be shown below in the discussion of the data flow implementation.

Algorithm Description

The basic idea behind both algorithms is very simple: They iterate over all pixels in the image and choose a new value for each pixel based on its own current value and the current values of its neighbours.

As mentioned above, there are two versions of both erosion and dilation described by Phillips (2000). They differ mainly in their approach to determining the new value: One uses a threshold parameter and changes the value of the current pixel depending on whether or not the number of neighbours with a different value exceeds the threshold, and one uses masks to determine the new value of a pixel. This implementation was based on the mask versions because they translate to data flow very naturally, as will be seen in the discussion of the data flow implementation.

The distinguishing feature of the mask versions is that it is possible to only use some of a pixel's neighbours for the computation of its new value; the purpose of the mask is precisely to specify which of the neighbours will be taken into account.

This is achieved with the following strategy: A 3x3-mask of ones and zeros is "placed over" the pixel in question and its eight neighbours. Pixels that have a 0 in their corresponding mask place will be ignored, pixels with a 1 in their mask place will be used for the computation. An example for this is shown in Figure 1.

Figure 1. Example for how a mask (left) influences the usage of pixel values (right). Values that will be ignored during the computation are marked in grey.

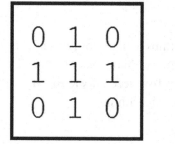 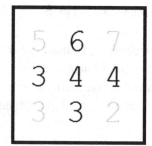

With erosion, which reduces the size of objects, the minimum of all the values that are "activated" by the mask will be chosen as the new value. With dilation on the other hand, which increases object sizes, the maximum of those values will be the pixel's new value.

It can be seen that this approach will achieve the desired results by considering the following: If a pixel lies at an object's edge, it will have a neighbour that has the background colour (which, as defined above, is denoted by the minimum possible value). In the case of erosion, where the minimum of the considered values is chosen, the new value therefore has to be the background colour - the object shrinks.

Similarly considerations apply to dilation: If a background pixel has a neighbour that belongs to an object, that neighbour's value will be greater than the current value, and since this algorithm is looking for the maximum, the object pixel's value will be chosen as the new value, leading to an enlargement of the object.

Different masks lead to different results. This allows the user to control the direction of the operation: it is, for example, possible to perform the erosion or dilation of objects only horizontally, or only vertically. Examples for "horizontal-only" and "vertical-only" masks, and the respective results with erosion and dilation, are shown in Figure 2.

Figure 2. Two possible masks and their results for erosion and dilation

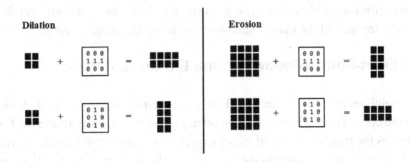

DATA FLOW IMPLEMENTATION

Having examined the theory behind the algorithms, this section is now concerned with how to implement them in data flow. As the structure of the code is very similar for both erosion and dilation, the following explanations will apply to both algorithms; if there are any notable differences, they will be explicitly mentioned.

The implementation described in this section was developed in Maxeler Java via the Maxeler WebIDE (n.d.). Note that the explanations in this text assume the reader to be already familiar with the basics of data flow programming. An introduction to Maxeler Java, including the data flow programming concepts that were used for this implementation, can be found in the tutorial by Maxeler Technologies (2015b).

The required steps for a complete data flow implementation of the erosion and dilation algorithms can be split into four main task groups. First, the data (image and mask values) has to be streamed to the data flow engine; then the 3x3 window around the current pixel has to be extracted in order to obtain the values of its neighbours; subsequently, the pixel's new value has to be determined; and finally, the result has to be streamed back to the CPU. The following subsections will treat the steps required to perform each of those tasks.

Streaming the Data In

In order to get all the data to the data flow engine (DFE), two different strategies are used.

The image data is sent to the DFE as an ordinary input stream, where one value corresponds to one pixel. Mask values, on the other hand, are scalar inputs: They only have to be sent to the DFE once, since their values never change during the course of the computation. As there are only nine mask values, the easiest approach is to send each mask entry to the data flow engine separately, as a single scalar input. On the DFE, those nine inputs are combined into a DFEArray, which will be called *mask* in the following code snippets.

```
DFEVar inStream = io.input("inStream", dfeUInt(32));
DFEVar mask[] = new DFEVar[9];
mask[0] = io.scalarInput("mask0", dfeUInt(32)); //similar procedure for the
other eight mask values
```

This implementation assumes that the image data is streamed in row-wise, as are the mask values. As discussed above, erosion and dilation can be performed in different directions, so it is important that the orientation of the image and the mask match in order to get the desired result.

Extracting an Eight-Point-Window Around the Current Pixel

Working with the neighbours of the current pixel obviously requires knowledge of elements in the data stream other than the current one: It is necessary to open a window into the data stream. For this purpose, Maxeler Java supplies the handy concept of offset expressions, which can help to convert a conceptual offset ("one row to the top, one column to the left" etc.) into the actual offset in the stream. Since the data is streamed in rowwise, the offset expression has to depend on the x dimension of the image, as illustrated in Figure 3.

Figure 3. Part of a possible image. The current pixel (in the center of the eight-point-window) is marked in bold face; the window that has to be opened into the data stream in order to get all the current pixel's neighbours is marked with a shaded background.

```
0 0 0 0 0 0 0 0 0 0 0 0 0 0 0 0 0 0 0 0 0 0 0 0 0 0 0 0 0
0 0 0 0 0 0 0 0 0 0 0 0 5 6 7 0 0 0 0 0 0 0 0 0 0 0 0 0 0
0 0 0 0 0 0 0 0 0 0 0 0 3 4 4 0 0 0 0 0 0 0 0 0 0 0 0 0 0
0 0 0 0 0 0 0 0 0 0 0 0 3 3 2 0 0 0 0 0 0 0 0 0 0 0 0 0 0
0 0 0 0 0 0 0 0 0 0 0 0 0 0 0 0 0 0 0 0 0 0 0 0 0 0 0 0 0
0 0 0 0 0 0 0 ...
```

The following code snippet creates an offset expression that corresponds to an offset of one row and uses it to extract the current pixel's neighbours, which are then stored in the DFEArray called *window*.

```
OffsetExpr nxoffset = stream.makeOffsetParam("nxoffset", 3, nxMax);
DFEVar window[] = new DFEVar[9];
int i = 0;
for (int y=-1; y<=1; y++)
for (int x=-1; x<=1; x++)
window[i++] = stream.offset(inStream, y*nxoffset+x);
```

For pixels on the inside of the image, the above code is all that is necessary to extract the window correctly. However, special care has to be devoted to the cases where a pixel lies directly at the image's edge, because in those cases pixels that are neighbours in the data stream might actually lie on opposite edges of the image - or, for pixels in the top and bottom rows, the required neighbours simply might not exist in the data stream.

To keep track of whether the current pixel is one of those border pixels, first of all a counter chain has to be added.

```
CounterChain chain = control.count.makeCounterChain();
DFEVar ycounter = chain.addCounter(ny, 1);
DFEVar xcounter = chain.addCounter(nx, 1);
```

This counter chain simply keeps track of the row and column number of the current pixel.

Since the dimensions of the image are known, the counter chain can then be used to create flags that store the information about whether the current pixel lies at one of the image edges.

```
DFEVar belowUpperBound = ycounter > 0;
DFEVar aboveLowerBound = ycounter < ny-1;
DFEVar rightOfLeftBound = xcounter > 0;
DFEVar leftOfRightBound = xcounter < nx - 1;
```

The variable belowUpperBound, for example, is true for any pixel that is not part of the top row of the image.

Recognizing the border cases is of course not enough: The implementation also needs to react to them appropriately. The approach that produces the most intuitive results is to treat all values outside the image as „implicit zeros", i.e. they are considered to have the background colour. This means that when performing dilation, the values outside the image will have no impact on the result; with erosion, on the other hand, objects that are placed directly at the image's edge will shrink just the same as objects somewhere in the center of the image.

The next step in the implementation is to introduce a new DFEArray called *values*, which will store the conceptual neighbours of the current pixel including the zeros from outside the image. For each of the entries in this array, a check is performed to see whether its corresponding pixel is still a part of the actual image: If so, the value from the *window* array is copied, if not, a zero is written to that place. The code to determine the entry for *values[0]* is given below to illustrate this procedure (of course different flags have to be checked for each of the entries).

```
values[0] = belowUpperBound & rightOfLeftBound ? window[0]: constant.
var(dfeUInt(32), 0);
```

(Obviously, those two stages - filling *window* and filling *values* - could have been condensed into one single step by checking the flags before using the offset expression to extract values from the stream.)

Determining the New Value and Streaming Back the Result

Now that the values of the current pixel and its neighbours are known, two more steps remain: finding the values that are to be taken into consideration according to the mask, and finding the minimum or maximum among them.

Both of these goals are achieved by the following code (the example code is taken from the erosion algorithm, where the goal is to search for the minimum).

```
DFEVar min = constant.var(dfeUInt(32), 255);
for (int j = 0; j < 9; j++) {
```

```
min = (mask[j] === constant.var(dfeUInt(32), 1)) & (values[j] < min) ?
values[j]: min;
}
```

At first, the variable *min* is set to the maximum possible value, then the code iterates over the entries of *values*. If the mask value in a certain place equals 1 and the corresponding pixel value is smaller than the current value of *min*, then *min* gets updated. Note that this requires the maximum possible value to be known beforehand (in this case it is assumed to be 255). After this, *min* contains what should be the pixel's new value; this result is then simply sent back to the CPU via an output stream.

```
io.output("outStream", min, dfeUInt(32));
```

The code for dilation is analogous: The only difference is that it starts with the variable *max* (instead of *min*) set to 0, which is the minimum possible value, and updates *max* if a larger value is found in a place that is activated by the mask.

An important thing to keep in mind is that while the code shown above for finding the minimum or maximum certainly works, it is nonetheless rather inelegant in data flow programming. The reason for this is that the for-loop in the code snippet actually performs loop unrolling, telling the DFE to carry out the nine comparisons one after the other. As a result, the data flow graph ends up very long and thin, which is generally a bad thing in data flow programming as the goal should be to minimize the distance the data has to travel. A better approach might be to split up the loop so that multiple comparisons can be performed at the same time, leading to a more compact data flow graph and thus a more efficient implementation.

The tutorial by Maxeler Technologies (2015a) offers a detailed explanation of loop unrolling as well as several other methods for dealing with loops in data flow programming.

CONCLUSION

The attentive reader will surely have noticed that the implementations presented in this chapter perform only a very basic version of erosion and dilation. The algorithms can for example not deal correctly with overlapping objects, and neither will they work properly with objects that are only partially visible in the image; the results produced by this implementation will therefore not be very sophisticated.

However, it is precisely because of the simplicity of these algorithms that they provide a very good demonstration of how certain common concepts in image processing can be adapted to the data flow paradigm. Finding adjoining pixels, for example, or finding out whether a pixel lies at the image's edge, are not only crucial tasks for erosion and dilation, but will be necessary in many image processing applications, and the strategies employed here to meet these requirements can be re-used for many other use cases.

REFERENCES

Chen, S., & Haralick, R. (1995). Recursive erosion, dilation, opening, and closing transforms. *IEEE Transactions on Image Processing, 4*(3), 335–345. doi:10.1109/83.366481 PMID:18289983

Cheng, X. (2009). Fast Binary Dilation/Erosion Algorithm Using Reference Points. *2009 International Conference on Networking and Digital Society*, 87-90. 10.1109/ICNDS.2009.102

Hanjun, J., & Huali, S. (2010). Rendering Fake Soft Shadows Based on the Erosion and Dilation. *2010 2nd International Conference on Computer Engineering and Technology, 6*, 234-236.

Maxeler Technologies. (2015a). *Acceleration Tutorial. Loops and Pipelining. Version 2015.1.1*. Author.

Maxeler Technologies. (2015b). *Multiscale Dataflow Programming. Version 2015.1.1*. Author.

Maxeler WebIDE. (n.d.). https://maxeler.mi.sanu.ac.rs

Ming, X., Juan, Z., & Zhijun, F. (2017). Research on unstructured road detection algorithm based on improved morphological operations. *4th International Conference on Smart and Sustainable City*. 10.1049/cp.2017.0104

Nixon, M., & Aguado, A. (2012). *Feature extraction & image processing for computer vision* (3rd ed.). Academic Press.

Phillips, D. (2000). *Image Processing in C*. Electronic Edition.

Quénot, G., & Zavidovique, B. (1992). The ETCA data-flow functional computer for real-time image processing. *Proceedings 1992 IEEE International Conference on Computer Design: VLSI in Computers & Processors*, 492-495. 10.1109/ICCD.1992.276324

Sinha, A., Neogi, S., & Maiti, K. (2002). A reconfigurable data-flow architecture for a class of image processing applications. *ICCSC'02 Conference Proceedings*, 460-463.

Chapter 8
Transforming the Method of Least Squares to the Dataflow Paradigm

Ilir Murturi

https://orcid.org/0000-0003-0240-3834

Distributed Systems Group, TU Wien, Austria

ABSTRACT

In mathematical statistics, an interesting and common problem is finding the best linear or non-linear regression equations that express the relationship between variables or data. The method of least squares (MLS) represents one of the oldest procedures among multiple techniques to determine the best fit line to the given data through simple calculus and linear algebra. Notably, numerous approaches have been proposed to compute the least-squares. However, the proposed methods are based on the control flow paradigm. As a result, this chapter presents the MLS transformation from control flow logic to the dataflow paradigm. Moreover, this chapter shows each step of the transformation, and the final kernel code is presented.

INTRODUCTION

The Method of Least Squares (MLS) is one of the oldest modern statistic methods and a standard regression analysis approach. The well-known technique determines the best fit line to a set of data points and it is used to estimate the parameters. The MLS use can be traced to Greek mathematics, where the predecessor is considered to be Galileo. The first approach towards a modern method description was introduced by the French mathematician Adrien Merie Legendre in 1805, which has been contested by Karl F. Gauss and Pierre S. Laplace. Gauss, in his memoir published in 1809, mentioned that he had discovered MLS and used it at the beginning of 1795 in estimating the orbit of an asteroid. Harter presents in detail the history and pre-history of the MLS (Harter, 1975).

Many opinions exist related to the authorship of the method. Placket presents some conclusions related to how the technique was discovered (Placket, 1972). Over the years, there have been attempts to

DOI: 10.4018/978-1-7998-7156-9.ch008

propose techniques to determine the best fit line to a set of data points. However, the least-squares method is considered the most important among the methods used to find or estimates numerical values to fit a function to a set of given data points. The MLS exists in different variations, and the most well-known ones are Ordinary Least Squares (OLS) and Weighted Least Squares (WLS).

Data collection is essential for any modern system, and often in real-world scenarios, such data may have linear relationships. Therefore, several approaches and platforms utilize MLS to analyze the correlation between various variables or data values (e.g., see (Xu et. al., 2013)). In this context, as well-known data collection platforms are crowdsourcing systems (Murturi et.al, 2015). Data collection from the crowd is an essential part of any crowdsourcing system (Rexha et. al., 2019). Analyzing such data is a way of answering the critical questions for different processes. In crowdsourcing systems, the quality of contributions remains plagued by poor quality, and often such data is often too hard to interpret. Therefore, statistical calculations help explain crowd data into meaningful results or identify the relationships between different data. By calculating the correlation between answers in collected data useful results can be obtained. However, since several MLS implementations exist in the control flow paradigm, we present the implementation and the method's transformation with a straightforward example in this chapter. Note that we do not evaluate the MLS's performance aspects in the dataflow paradigm in this chapter. Beside that, this chapter aims to show the simplicity of transforming control flow logic applications into the dataflow paradigm.

The remainder of this chapter is organized as follows. Section II presents related work regarding the MLS. Section III describes in more detail the method by including the mathematical background. Section IV, showes the implementation of the method in the control flow paradigm. Afterward, the method transforming steps to the dataflow paradigm is described by analyzing the current implementation in CPU code given in C++. Final remarks are given in Section V.

RELATED WORK

The MLS is known to be published for the first time by Adrien Marie Legendre (Legendre, 1805). However, the method was not used as well as no mathematical proof was given. Legendre formulate the problem and starts with the linear equation of the form $E = a + bx + cy + ...$, where the requirement determines unknown variables (x, y) that E decreases to zero or a very small number for each equation. However, such equations are derived without the explicit use of calculus. The equations are generated by multiplying the linear form in the unknowns by the coefficient a, b, c. Each of the unknowns are summed over all the observations and then setting the sums equal to zero (Harter, 1975). When the results produce errors, the proposed approach rejects the equations that produce such error while determining the unknowns from the rest of the equations. On the other side, Puissant, discusses theoretical aspects of the MLS (Puissant, 1805). He also presents an application to the determination of the earth's ellipticity from measures of degrees meridian.

Several research papers use the MLS technique to determine the best fit line to a set of given data points. To compute least squares for the large sparse systems, Shi et al. provide a survey of distributed least squares in distributed networks, sketches the algorithm's skeleton first, and analyzes time-to-completion and communication cost (Shi et al., 2017). Furthermore, the study provides helpful insights into the methods that can be modified to run in a distributed manner to solve linear least-squares. MLS has found extensive usage in various fields and engineering applications in the context of usages. As an example, a recent paper in the Edge and Fog Computing field (Avasalcai et al, 2020) proposes an approach aiming at building the fog infrastructure (Karagiannis et al., 2019). The proposed solution utilizes the MLS to depict the overhead's dependence on the fog network size (i.e., the relationship between the network size and exchanged control messages). Nevertheless, there are many more examples that MLS has been used to determine the relationship between variables (Taneja, 2019). However, in contrast to the mentioned research papers, we present the MLS transformation steps from the control flow paradigm to the dataflow paradigm.

THE METHOD OF LEAST SQUARES

MLS is probably the most well-known technique to determine the best fit line to a set of data points; the proof uses calculus and linear algebra. This chapter refers to the work of Miller (Miller, 2006) and Abdi (Abdi, 2007) for the mathematical background of the method. In the standard formulation, the basic problem is to find the best fit straight line in a given set of N pairs of observations $\left(X_i, Y_i\right)$, for $i \in \left(1, \ldots, N\right)$, where X_i is an independent variable and Y_i is a dependent variable. This set of data points is used to find a function relating the value of the dependent variable Y to the values of an independent variable X. The prediction model is given with one variable and a linear equation:

$$Y' = mX + a \tag{1}$$

The equation involves two parameters where m is the slope of the regression line and a is the y-intercept. The slope of a line is the change in Y over the change in X. The distance $Y - Y'$ between each data point and a potential regression line $Y' = mx + a$ is known as a residual. The fit of a model to a data point is measured by its residual. It is defined as the difference between the actual value of the dependent variable and the value predicted by the model:

$$R_i = Y_i - f\left(x_i, Y'\right) \tag{2}$$

MLS defines the estimation of these parameters through the minimizing the sum of the squares and the model. Further, the method finds the optimal parameter values by minimizing the sum S of the squares:

$$S = \sum_{i=1}^{N} \left(R_i\right)^2 \tag{3}$$

The error associated E, which is the quantity to be minimized is defined as:

$$E = \sum_{i=1}^{N} \left(Y_i - Y_i'\right)^2 = \left[Y_i - \left(mX_i + a\right)\right]^2 \tag{4}$$

Considering the derivative of E concerning m and a and setting them to zero gives so called *normal equations* (see (Abdi, 2007)). After solving the normal equations, the following equations represent least square estimates of m and a as:

$$m = M_y - aM_x \tag{5}$$

$$a = \frac{\sum \left(Y_i - M_Y \right) \left(X_i - M_X \right)}{\sum \left(X_i - M_X \right)^2} \tag{6}$$

Note that M_y and M_x denotes the means of X and Y.

TRANSFORMING AND IMPLEMENTATION DETAILS

Several applications that perform intensive calculations can benefit from the dataflow paradigm (Milutinovic et al., 2015), (Milutinovic et al, 2017). Maxeler DFE technology introduces some differences when compared to the conventional control logic programming model. When Maxeler DFE is used to accelerate an application, it takes some time to transfer the data to and from the DFE. The first step is to analyze implementation and ensure that the data is transferred once during the execution time.

Fortunately, the MLS transformation from the control flow paradigm to the dataflow paradigm is an easy task. As presented in Listing 1, the source code implemented in control flow logic, respectively, in C++, consists of two loops with N iterations. The number of iterations in both loops is defined by the number of pairs X and Y. The pairs' random input data have been generated through a simple random number generator for simplicity reasons. The initialization of the data is realized in the control flow processor. The next step toward translating the method into dataflow hardware is to analyze the possible dependencies between the elements. The elements should not rely on their estimation of any variable with a specific index during iteration in both loops.

Since our implementation has no dependencies on any of the elements, we can start with the MLS translation. Given loops that execute independent iterations could be transformed easily into the dataflow hardware. Moreover, translating the statements written in C++ to the kernel is straightforward, and it requires only removing indexes from array elements.

It is required to define the memory usage in a control flow architecture while in dataflow hardware initialization, we define hardware variables and scalar variables. Listing 2 shows the kernel code for calculating the least squares method that accepts parameter N representing the number of points in the input sequence.

Referring to Listing 2, the kernel has three inputs and one output data streams. These two streams are used for transferring real and imaginary parts of the input sequence points to and from the DFE. In the fifth line, we declare a scalar variable named scalar. In dataflow programming, scalar variables are used when the control flow values do not change during the calculation. In our case, through the scalar value, we initialize the values of hardware variables. In fact, when you need to change the scalar output, it can be changed once per stream, loaded into the chip before starting computation.

Listing 1. Least squares CPU code

```
while(i++ < N){
      xSum = xSum + dataInX[i];
      ySum = ySum + dataInY[i];
      xSecondSum = xSecondSum + pow(dataIn[i],2);
      xySum = xySum + dataInX[i] * dataInY[i];
  }
  //calculate slope and intercept
      slope = (N * xySum - xSum * ySum) /
              (N * xSecondSum - xSum * xSum);
      intercept = (xSecondSum * ySum - xSum * xySum) /
                      (xSecondSum * N - xSum * xSum);
//new fitted values of y-axis
 for(int i = 0; i < N; i++)
      yAxis_fit[i] = slope * dataIn[i] + intercept;
```

Furthermore, the generated data is sent from the CPU to the DFE for computing the MLS on the DFE. Meanwhile, MaxCompiler generates header file PassThrough.h that contains the following method. This communication CPU to the DFE and vice versa is achieved by calling this method in C++, as presented in Listing 3. Note that the SLiC option needs to be enabled for generating the header file by MaxCompiler.

The manager is responsible for taking a stream of values, sending it through the dataflow engine, and returning the same stream. The manager code is given in the Listing 4.

Finally, Figure 1 presents the graphical illustration of the kernel of the MLS generated by MaxCompiler.

CONCLUSION

The dataflow paradigm has already proved its domination comparing to the control flow paradigm in many big computational problems. The approach of modeling a program as a directed graph of data flowing between operations has significantly shortened the time of execution. This chapter presents the transformation steps of least squares method from control flow logic to the dataflow paradigm. In essence, the chapters focuses on the dataflow implementation of the method rather than showing performance results. In the sense of generality, the performance depends on uniform processing and the dependencies between current and previous data processing. Applications with a high number of iterations of loops are considered suitable for transformation in the dataflow paradigm.

ACKNOWLEDGMENT

This work was partially supported by the Research Cluster "Smart Communities and Technologies (Smart CT)" at TU Wien.

Listing 2. Least squares kernel code

```
PassThroughKernel(KernelParameters parameters)
{
    super(parameters);
    // Input
    DFEVar X = io.input("X", dfeUInt(32));
    DFEVar Y = io.input("Y", dfeUInt(32));
    DFEVar scalar = io.scalarInput("scalar", dfeUInt(32));
    // Initialize sum variables
    DFEVar xSum = scalar,
            ySum = scalar,
            x2Sum = scalar,
            xySum = scalar;
    //Calculating sigmas
    xSum = xSum + X;
    ySum = ySum + Y;
    x2Sum = x2Sum + (X * X);
    xySum = xySum + X * Y;
    DFEVar slope, intercept;
    slope = (N * xySum - xSum * ySum) /
            (N * x2Sum - xSum * xSum);
    intercept = (x2Sum * ySum - xSum * xySum) /
                (x2Sum * N - xSum * xSum);
    //to calculate y(fitted) at given x points
    DFEVar result = slope * X + intercept;
    // Output
    io.output("r", result, dfeUInt(32));
}
```

Listing 3. Header file generated by MaxCompiler

```
PassThrough(
        int32_t param_N,
        uint64_t inscalar_PassThroughKernel_scalar,
        const uint32_t *instream_x,
        const uint32_t *instream_y,
        uint32_t *outstream_r);
```

Listing 4. Kernel manager code

```
class PassThroughManager {
  public static void main(String[] args) {
        EngineParameters params = new EngineParameters(args);
        Manager manager = new Manager(params);
        Kernel kernel =
          new PassThroughKernel(manager.makeKernelParameters());
        manager.setKernel(kernel);
        manager.setIO(IOType.ALL_CPU);
        manager.createSLiCinterface();
        manager.build();
  }
}
```

Figure 1. The graphical illustration of the MLS kernel generated by MaxCompiler

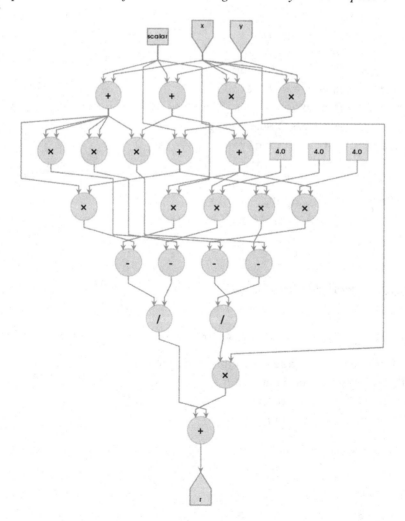

REFERENCES

Abdi, H. (2007). The method of least squares. Encyclopedia of Measurement and Statistics.

Avasalcai, C., Murturi, I., & Dustdar, S. (2020). Edge and fog: A survey, use cases, and future challenges. Fog Computing. *Theory into Practice*, 43–65.

Harter, H. L. (1975). The Method of Least Squares and Some Alternatives. Addendum to Part IV. *International Statistical Review/Revue Internationale de Statistique, 43*(3), 273-278.

Karagiannis, V., Schulte, S., Leitao, J., & Preguiça, N. (2019, May). Enabling fog computing using self-organizing compute nodes. In *2019 IEEE 3rd International Conference on Fog and Edge Computing (ICFEC)* (pp. 1-10). IEEE. 10.1109/CFEC.2019.8733150

Legendre, A. M. (1805). *Nouvelles méthodes pour la détermination des orbites des comètes*. F. Didot.

Miller, S. J. (2006). The method of least squares. *Mathematics Department Brown University, 8*, 1–7.

Milutinovic, V., Kotlar, M., Stojanovic, M., Dundic, I., Trifunovic, N., & Babovic, Z. (2017). *DataFlow Supercomputing Essentials*. Springer.

Milutinović, V., Salom, J., Trifunović, N., & Giorgi, R. (2015). *Guide to dataflow supercomputing*. Springer Nature. doi:10.1007/978-3-319-16229-4

Murturi, A., Kantarci, B., & Oktug, S. F. (2015, October). A reference model for crowdsourcing as a service. In *2015 IEEE 4th International Conference on Cloud Networking (CloudNet)* (pp. 64-66). IEEE. 10.1109/CloudNet.2015.7335281

Plackett, R. L. (1972). Studies in the History of Probability and Statistics. XXIX: The discovery of the method of least squares. *Biometrika, 59*(2), 239–251. doi:10.1093/biomet/59.2.239

Puissant, L. (1805). *Traité de géodésie: ou, Exposition des méthodes astronomiques et trigonométriques, appliquées soit à la mesure de la terre, soit à la confection du canevas des cartes et des plans*. Courcier.

Rexha, B., & Murturi, I. (2019). Applying efficient crowdsourcing techniques for increasing quality and transparency of election processes. *Electronic Government, an International Journal, 15*(1), 107-128.

Shi, L., Zhao, L., Song, W. Z., Kamath, G., Wu, Y., & Liu, X. (2017). *Distributed least-squares iterative methods in networks: A survey*. arXiv preprint arXiv:1706.07098

Taneja, M., Jalodia, N., & Davy, A. (2019). Distributed decomposed data analytics in fog enabled IoT deployments. *IEEE Access: Practical Innovations, Open Solutions, 7*, 40969–40981. doi:10.1109/ACCESS.2019.2907808

Xu, Q., Xiong, J., Huang, Q., & Yao, Y. (2013, October). Robust evaluation for quality of experience in crowdsourcing. In *Proceedings of the 21st ACM international conference on Multimedia* (pp. 43-52). 10.1145/2502081.2502083

Chapter 9
Forest Fire Simulation:
Efficient Realization Based on Cellular Automata

Severin Staudinger
University of Vienna, Austria

ABSTRACT

In this chapter a heuristic forest fire model based on cellular automata is presented and realized for efficiency reasons with the DataFlow programming approach. Real-world images taken by satellites are analyzed and used as the basis for simulations. In the presented forest fire model, natural influences like wind strength and direction, burning behavior, as well as different levels of inflammability are considered. The DataFlow implementation on an FPGA-based Maxeler MAX3 Vectis card was compared to a sequential C version executed on an Intel Xeon E5-2650 2.0 GHz CPU. The author obtained speedups of up to 70 for a strong wind situation and 46 for a random wind setting while reducing energy consumption.

INTRODUCTION

Cellular automata (CA) (Wolfram, 1983) have been introduced in the early 1940s by Stanislaw Ulam and John von Neumann at Los Alamos National Laboratory, New Mexico. Ulam used them to study the growth of crystals, whereas von Neumann modelled a CA-based world of self-replicating robots. While Ulam's CA model is easy to imagine, von Neumann's approach is a complex one and is more or less just a mind game (Shiffman, 2012). Even in a time before powerful computers, Ulam and von Neumann have shown that CA are useful instruments for real-life simulations. Although they were already invented in the early 1940's, cellular automata weren't popular until the invention of Conway's "Game of Life", which was introduced in the work of Gardner (1970). This cellular automaton gained a lot of attention thanks to its ability of generating structures, which literally seem to be living.

The contribution of this chapter is a heuristic forest fire model based on cellular automata. The author's focus is to design an efficient model in order to quickly produce video simulations of the fire propagation. For achieving speedups of up to 70X compared to equivalent software on CPUs, the DataFlow

DOI: 10.4018/978-1-7998-7156-9.ch009

paradigm (Milutinovic et al., 2015) was used. This technology uses so called DFEs (DataFlow Engines) like FPGAs (Field Programmable Gate Arrays). In this paradigm the data is streamed to an accelerator and processed like on an assembly line, meaning that each element is exactly processed like all the others. This fine-granularity makes them well-suited for accelerating the introduced CA-based simulation, since cellular automata offer massive parallelism. Another reason for using DFEs is that they are not only considerably fast for data-intense simulations, but also extremely efficient in energy and space. Therefore, the presented application could be easily used on board of firefighting helicopters in order to navigate the pilot to the most important spot, where the fire should be stopped from further propagating. The consideration of natural influences like wind, burning behavior and inflammability allows the model to make realistic fire propagation predictions, which are useful when wildfires are out of control.

The remainder of this chapter is organized as follows. First, a background on cellular automata is given and related work is discussed. Then, the essence of the forest fire application is presented, and the author explains why the DataFlow paradigm was used. Subsequently, details on the implementation as well as program features are described. After that, the application's performance is evaluated, and the results are discussed. Finally, the last section concludes the chapter and gives an outlook on future work.

BACKGROUND AND RELATED WORK

Cellular automata (CA) are mathematical models, which can be used to realize simulations of natural processes. CA can be described as grids in which individual cells interact with each other in order to form a fluid system (Shiffman, 2012). One major characteristic of CA is taking adjacent cells for each element into account. The set of these surrounding cells is called neighborhood. Most cellular automata use regular or extended "Moore" neighborhoods, but simple ones work with the classic "Von Neumann" neighborhood, in which only the directly surrounding cells are considered (Adamatzky et al., 2008).

In this work the author uses cellular automata in order to simulate the spreading of wildfires. On the one hand, there are several research efforts focusing on fire propagation models based on cellular automata. On the other hand, the high computational effort makes parallelization or use of accelerators necessary. Some research groups use GPUs together with OpenCL (Stone et al., 2010) or CUDA (Manavski et al., 2008). Only few of them use FPGAs (Field Programmable Gate Array) or DataFlow-based approaches.

Back in 2002, four Italian researchers, namely Corsonello, Spezzano, Staino and Talia, published a paper (Corsonello et al., 2002) introducing efficient implementations of cellular automata on FPGAs. They used the low-level language VHDL (Very High Speed Integrated Circuit Hardware Description Language) (Coelho, 1989) to implement a forest fire simulation as well as a thinning algorithm. The runtime of an equivalent software on a general-purpose processor was used as a reference value for the FPGA performance measurements. The reported speedups for the forest fire and thinning algorithm are 24 and 65, respectively.

A few years later the work of van Woudenberg (2006) reported the performance of different cellular automata models in FPGA logic. The author implemented the famous "Game of Life", an HPP model as well as a simplified forest fire simulation. For the implementation itself, the library CAME&L (Cellular Automata Modeling Environment & Library) introduced by Naumov (2004) was used. CAME&L consists of modular components, which are implemented in C++. Van Woudenberg used it to implement some cellular automata which were transformed into FPGA logic with a C++-to-VHDL compiler. Since the communication throughput between the host machine and the FPGA was very limited back in these days, the performance gains were only discussed theoretically.

In 2012, the work of Progias and Sirakoulis (2012) introduced a wildfire spreading model, which was implemented on an Altera Stratic IV FPGA. The performance of the hardware model realized with the hardware language VHDL was compared with a software model implemented in Matlab. Their model was based on a hexagonal grid, which has the advantage of modelling the round shape of a tree cell in a relatively good way. However, the downside of this approach is that a hexagonal grid is not as straightforward to implement compared to a squared one. The authors reported a massive speedup and power reduction achieved by their model. Unfortunately, they also detected slight errors between the models due to rounding errors since their implementations are based on floating point operations, while the model presented in this chapter is based on integers.

Another important contribution to that research topic was the paper of Ntinas et al. (2016), in which the authors compared implementations of wildfire models on GPUs and FPGAs. Their models were based on dynamic "Fuzzy Cellular Automata" (FCA). Their hardware version was implemented with the low-level language VHDL, while the program introduced in this chapter is based on MaxJ (Maxeler Java). The speedups for the most powerful GPU were 81 for the no-wind and 113 for the with-wind test case. The speedups achieved by the FPGA implementation were reported as substantial without mentioning any numbers.

FOREST FIRE SIMULATION APPLICATION

Essence of the Forest Fire Model

In the last decades the climate has been changing drastically, global warming due to human activities seems to be unstoppable. In hot and dry weather periods trees suffer from water shortages and have a higher risk to be ignited due to lightnings or even human negligence. Consequently, there are more forest fires, which are hard to extinguish. Simulations can help fire fighters to be on the right place for stopping the fire before it is propagated over a too large area. These predictions are not only utilized by fire fighters, but they can be also useful for the government to warn people, who are in danger of losing their homes due to the fire.

When it comes to devastating wildfires, people can't afford losing important time when waiting for the fire propagation predictions. However, there are some constraints making quick simulations difficult. One of them is the consideration of many parameters making the model as accurate as possible. Things like forest density, wind direction and strength, as well as inflammability and burning behavior of trees play a major role. Another limiting aspect is the image resolution, which greatly influences the predictions. This means that for very high-resolution pictures the predictions may be highly accurate, but the computations take long. In case of low-resolution images, it is the other way around. Therefore, there is a tradeoff between accuracy and speed.

In order to overcome this tradeoff, the author uses the DataFlow paradigm (Milutinovic et al., 2015). The used accelerators – called DataFlow Engines – can be exactly configured to process data in a given manner and produce a result for an input element in just one tick. Other than in control flow architectures, there is no need for data caching or optimization techniques like branch prediction or speculative execution. As the DFE is set up to process pictures with a fixed resolution, the calculations are not considerably slower when using very high-resolution images. Another benefit of using DFEs is that they are extremely efficient in power and size. To be more precise, when migrating compute-intensive applications from ControlFlow systems to DataFlow ones, the size reduction and power savings are about 20 times (Milutinovic et al., 2015).

This efficiency in power and space makes it even possible to calculate fire propagation simulations directly on board of fire-fighting helicopters. That means the pilots could make new predictions whenever they must refill the water tanks. Thus, the fire propagation simulation video would help figuring out which forest area should be focused on next when combating the fire. When wildfires are out of control every minute counts and fire fighters cannot afford to make any mistakes. Therefore, it is even better to run computer simulations, which can give predictions on the fire propagation and help to develop a strategy to stop wildfires from spreading into critical areas.

IMPLEMENTATION

Software Architecture

For comparing the performance of the forest fire model, the kernel was implemented for DataFlow Engines as well as for CPUs. The input data is based on real satellite images which can be read in at runtime. For experiments it is also possible to make simulations with randomly generated synthetic data.

In the program version presented in this chapter, a tree cell's inflammability is determined by interpreting colors in real satellite pictures, e.g. a wet tree has a dark green shade. These images are reduced in colors by using an explicitly generated color palette based on the satellite image shown in Figure 1. This image represents a typical forest in the context of this implementation.

For satellite images where the forest's density is not completely known, it can be useful to add some noise (empty cells) to the data. Especially in forests with really big trees it is not easy to determine whether there is another tree underneath the larger tree's leaves. To overcome this challenge or to simply experiment with reducing the wood's density the noise consideration was added to the application.

In the presented application the host program, which runs on the CPU, prepares the imported satellite images for the accelerator – the DataFlow Engine. In order to do so, the CPU interprets the color of every pixel in the slightly altered satellite image and determines the resulting flammability. In case of the image in Figure 1, for example, brown cells are not burnable, since they are most likely burned grass or part of the riverbed. After the colors have been successfully interpreted, a user-defined number of randomly chosen tree cells are marked as fire cells. Finally, the data is streamed to the DFE which executes the main algorithm presented in the next section. Since users are interested in the fire behavior rather than the final simulation outcome, the intermediate results, i.e. the calculations of each iteration, have to be streamed back and forth between CPU and DFE. Furthermore, the host program is responsible for exporting and/or visualizing the calculated time steps. The calculations are executed until there are no more burning cells or the used-defined number of iterations is reached.

Figure 1. Satellite image of the Amazon taken from Google Earth. The dark blue lines are parts of the Amazon river. Light cells represent dry trees while brown cells are not burnable since there are assumed to be burned grass or part of the riverbed.
Source: Google Earth (colors reduced)

Algorithm

Although the presented forest fire model is a simplified heuristic one, the produced video simulations show a fairly realistic behavior. The following parameters are considered in the presented model.

- *Inflammability*
- *Burning Behavior*
- *Flying Sparks*
  ◦ Wind direction
  ◦ Wind strength

Unlike simple CA with only two cell states (on/off, dead/alive), there are some more necessary for the presented forest fire simulation. Here, a state has not only to indicate whether a tree is on fire or not, but it also represents how likely a tree is ignited and if so, how long it has been burning already.

The influence of adjacent cells is the main aspect of cellular automata. Particularly for a fire propagation model, the surrounding cells are even more important as they decide whether a cell becomes ignited in the next time step. In very simple models a cell is ignited when at least one of its neighbors is burning. In the presented forest fire simulation, though, it is distinguished between dry and damp wood, since they have different burning behaviors. Anybody, who has a tiled stove or fireplace knows how difficult it is to ignite wood, which is not dry. Therefore, in the presented model a wet tree needs more than just one burning neighbor, while normal dry trees are treated as in simple CA-based forest fire models. Another thing that plays an important role is the burn duration. As a damp tree needs longer to be ignited, it is predicted to burn longer, as the resulting fire is not as hot as for dry wood.

Another important aspect of forest fire simulations is the influence of the wind. When the wind is strong, flying sparks can travel over a long distance. They can ignite trees which are seemingly far away from the fire. Thus, the forest fire can even propagate across rivers or areas which are already burned.

In addition to the already described aspects, the author considers a situation being called "full fire". What is meant by this term is an extremely hot fire occurring when a cell is affected by more than 6 burning trees in its direct neighborhood. This special case can only be induced by directly surrounding neighbors. This means that there is no "full fire" when there are less than 6 burning trees in the inner neighborhood, but more than 6 in the region considered for flying sparks. When it comes to a "full fire" the centered cell burns down quicker, since the resulting fire is assumed to be really strong and hot.

A simplified version of the main algorithm is presented in Figure 2.

Figure 2. Pseudo Code of main algorithm

```
1  Kernel procedure
2    foreach cell do
3      if cell is burnable then
4        neighbors ← # of burning cells in Moore neighborhood ;
5        if neighbors ≥ 6 then
6          cell.status ← full fire ;
7        else
8          if neighbors ≥ neighborThreshold then
9            cell.status ← burning ;
10         else
11           sparks ← # of flying sparks w.r.t. wind settings ;
12           if sparks ≥ sparkThreshold then
13             cell.status ← burning ;
14           end
15         end
16       end
17     else
18       if cell.status = burning then
19         cell.burningRounds-- ;
20       end
21     end
22   end
```

Due to the nature of cellular automata these calculations can be fully parallelized with accelerators like the DataFlow card used for this application. Thus, the simulation can be greatly accelerated by using the DataFlow approach, which is further addressed in the next section.

PERFORMANCE EVALUATION

The test series were done on the Maxeler machine from the Mathematical Institute SANU in Belgrade and on a compute cluster of the University of Vienna. The DataFlow accelerator card used for testing was a Maxeler MAX3 Vectis one, while the used machine for the sequential program version uses Intel Xeon E5-2650 2.0 GHz (Sandy Bridge) CPUs and has 256GB RAM built-in. The compiling was done with MaxCompiler 2015.2 for the DFE version and GCC 4.4.7 for the CPU implementation.

There were multiple tests made for different wind strengths (radius) between 1 (no wind) and 4 (strong wind). In order to obtain a more real-life view on the program performance, runtimes were also measured for random wind strengths. The input data for all tests were randomly generated forests, all having the same ratio of dry and normal trees.

Figure 3. Example simulation. The white circle in the upper right corner indicates the wind directions as well as the strengths (white: no wind, green: weak, yellow: medium, red: strong). In (a) it can be seen how 5 different initial fire cells have formed ring of fires which begin to join in (b). A strong (red) wind in the direction West speeds up the joining process in (c). In (d) the three inner rings have finally joined, and a weak wind slightly accelerates the propagation to the western parts of the forest. The fire even crosses the water where the Amazon River is not so broad.

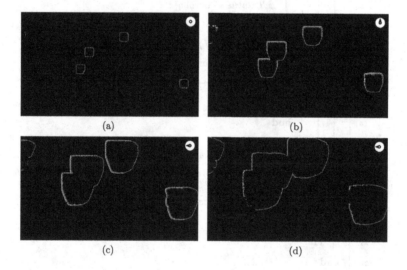

In Figure 3, a simulation for a real-world satellite image is shown. The video visualization was done with the C-library SDL2 (Simple DirectMedia Layer). In Figure 3 it can be observed that the wind acts as an accelerator for the fire. The stronger it is, the faster the fire propagates over the forest. Obviously, the more cells are burned down, the less computations have to be made, since burned cells can't be ignited once again. This fact becomes more important when observing the application's runtime behavior.

Figure 4. Runtime comparison between the CPU implementation (left) and the DFE version (right)

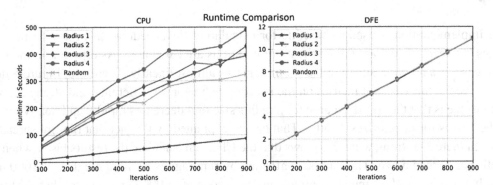

Test Settings

All tests were made with 3 different parameter sets for each wind strength to guarantee a fair parameter test setting. The number of iterations varied between 100 and 900, with a step size of 100. The complete test series were repeated multiple times to ensure that each setting (radius, iteration count, wind directions) is tested for more than one random generated forest. Tests which have converged too early, meaning that they didn't need the configured number of iterations to finish, were removed from the final results. Such tests are invalid, as they cannot be reproduced; thus, averaging of the results would not be possible. Fortunately, there are just a few invalid tests, and therefore, each test run is averaged over a minimum of 8 (out of 9) valid results.

Runtime Behavior

The author observed that the CPU's runtime does not grow linearly for a radius size (wind strength) higher than 1. At first, this seems to be surprising, but it is easily explained by the fact that there are less computations to be made with a greater amount of burned cells. Burning or already burned down cells are processed quickly, as their next state does not depend on their neighbors anymore. As shown in Figure 4, for a no-wind situation, i.e. the radius of size 1, the runtime behavior is almost linear. In this case the amount of burned cells does not have such a great impact, since array accesses within the inner radius 1 Moore neighborhood are much faster than for larger ones. Thus, the calculations are naturally faster when there is no wind to be considered.

The DFE's runtime has a completely different behavior. The runtime is not only equal for each radius size, but it also grows linearly with respect to the number of computed iterations. For a DataFlow Engine it does not matter how many cells are burned, since it cannot adjust itself to the cell's state. The difference between CPU and DFE is that the CPU tries to adjust its computations according to the data, while the DFE is configured to manage a stream of data. This means that input elements are streamed through the DFE and output results are streamed backed to the CPU almost immediately. The DFE produces one result per tick, which is completely independent from the data. Therefore, it is obvious that the runtime is linearly correlated to the number of iterations.

Speedup

The CPU implementation is used as baseline for calculating the speedups. In Figure 5 speedups for radius sizes between 2 and 4 are falling the more iterations are calculated. As reported in the previous section, in case of a no-wind situation the runtime grows almost linearly. Therefore, Figure 5 does not show the curve for this case but focuses on the speedup behavior for different wind strengths. What is interesting to see is that the speedup curve for a radius size of 4 decreases rapidly and nearly falls to the level of the curves for radius sizes 2 and 3. That can be explained by the fact that the fire spreads more quickly when there is a strong wind. It follows that the CPU can calculate the results faster when almost all the cells are burned down. This can be confirmed by running tests with a number of 1000 or more iterations. In these cases, the simulation often converges soon after 900 iterations, while tests for radius sizes of 2 or 3 never converge before 1000 iterations.

Figure 5. Speedup behavior for different wind strengths

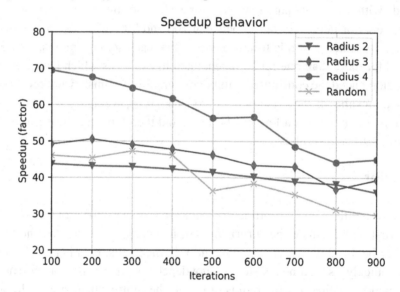

As DataFlow Engines work energy-efficient, the author has not only accelerated the forest fire model greatly, but also shown a way to save electrical energy when doing real-life simulations. Finally, this chapter demonstrated that the DataFlow paradigm is well-suited for accelerating forest fire models based on cellular automata, as the achieved speedups are considerably high.

CONCLUSION AND FUTURE WORK

In this chapter a heuristic fire propagation model based on cellular automata was presented. The model uses an extended Moore neighborhood with a radius corresponding to the wind strength. The main features are the usage of real-world satellite images and the consideration of different environmental factors, such as wind settings, different burning behaviors and levels of inflammability.

The calculations of a forest fire simulation are significantly faster on the Maxeler architecture – compared to the execution time of equivalent CPU code. The speedup for 100 calculated iterations of a strong wind situation (radius 4), random wind and no wind were about 70, 46 and 8, respectively. The speedups for weaker wind strengths, i.e. radius 2 and 3, lay between factors of 44 and 50.

An interesting aspect when evaluating performance was not only the speedup factor, but also the speedup behavior. One insight was that the speedup decreases with the number of calculated iterations. This is the result of faster CPU computations due to less operations necessary when there are more and more cells burned down. The reported variations in speedups are only due to the CPU properties, since the DFE is completely independent from changing values in the data set.

As future work, the following improvements are considered. In the next program version, the user will be able to explicitly set the initial fire cells. Furthermore, a refinement of the model will be considered by taking additional parameters into account; for example, humidity or wood density. One big improvement for long lasting simulations would be the direct export of images for each time step. That would save a lot of resources in the host program due to less necessary memory allocations needed when working with buffers. Finally, the software could be connected to weather stations, which deliver real-time information of environmental data. Thus, the application could help fire fighters to predict wildfire spreads in an extremely fast and accurate way.

ACKNOWLEDGMENT

The author would like to thank Prof. Eduard Mehofer, who helped him creating the software and preparing the manuscript. Special thanks are due to his brother Jakob Staudinger, who suggested some optimizations for the graphical representation. The author is also grateful to Dorian Karafiat for proofreading and refining the paper.

REFERENCES

Adamatzky, A., Alonso-Sanz, R., & Lawniczak, A. (2008). *Automata-2008: Theory and Applications of Cellular Automata*. Luniver Press.

Coelho, D. (1989). *The VHDL Handbook*. Kluwer Academic Publishers. doi:10.1007/978-1-4613-1633-6

Corsonello, P., Spezzano, G., Staino, G., & Talia, D. (2002). Efficient implementation of cellular algorithms on reconfigurable hardware. In *Proceedings 10th Euromicro Workshop on Parallel, Distributed and Network-based Processing* (pp. 211-218). 10.1109/EMPDP.2002.994273

Gardner, M. (1970). Mathematical Games: The fantastic combinations of John Conway's new solitaire game "life". *Scientific American, 223*(4), 120–123. doi:10.1038cientificamerican1070-120

Manavski, S. A., & Valle, G. (2008). CUDA compatible GPU cards as efficient hardware accelerators for Smith-Waterman sequence alignment. *BMC Bioinformatics, 9*(Suppl 2), S10. doi:10.1186/1471-2105-9-S2-S10

Milutinovic, V., Salom, J., Trifunovic, N., & Giorgi, R. (2015). *Guide to DataFlow Supercomputing: Basic Concepts, Case Studies, and a Detailed Example*. Springer Publishing Company, Incorporated. doi:10.1007/978-3-319-16229-4

Naumov, L. (2004). *CAME&L – Cellular Automata Modeling Environment & Library*. Springer Berlin Heidelberg. doi:10.1007/978-3-540-30479-1_76

Ntinas, V. G., Moutafis, B. E., Trunfio, G. A., & Sirakoulis, G. C. (2016). GPU and FPGA Parallelization of Fuzzy Cellular Automata for the Simulation of Wildfire Spreading. In *Parallel Processing and Applied Mathematics* (pp. 560–569). Springer International Publishing. doi:10.1007/978-3-319-32152-3_52

Progias, P., & Sirakoulis, G. C. (2013). An FPGA processor for modelling wildfire spreading. *Mathematical and Computer Modelling*, *57*(5), 1436–1452. doi:10.1016/j.mcm.2012.12.005

Shiffman, D., Fry, S., & Marsh, Z. (2012). *The Nature of Code*. D. Shiffman.

Stone, J. E., Gohara, D., & Shi, G. (2010). OpenCL: A Parallel Programming Standard for Heterogeneous Computing Systems. *Computing in Science & Engineering*, *12*(3), 66–72. doi:10.1109/MCSE.2010.69 PMID:21037981

Van Woudenberg, M. (2006). *Using FPGAs to Speed Up Cellular Automata Computations* [Master's thesis]. University of Amsterdam, Amsterdam, The Netherlands.

Wolfram, S. (1983). Statistical mechanics of cellular automata. *Reviews of Modern Physics*, *55*(3), 601–644. doi:10.1103/RevModPhys.55.601

Chapter 10
High Performance Computing for Understanding Natural Language

Marija Stanojevic
Temple University, USA

Jumanah Alshehri
ⓘD https://orcid.org/0000-0002-0077-7173
Temple University, USA

Zoran Obradovic
Temple University, USA

ABSTRACT

The amount of user-generated text available online is growing at an ever-increasing rate due to tremendous progress in enlarging inexpensive storage capacity, processing capabilities, and the popularity of online outlets and social networks. Learning language representation and solving tasks in an end-to-end manner, without a need for human-expert feature extraction and creation, has made models more accurate and much more complicated in the number of parameters, requiring parallelized and distributed resources high-performance computing or cloud. This chapter gives an overview of state-of-the-art natural language processing problems, algorithms, models, and libraries. Parallelized and distributed ways to solve text understanding, representation, and classification tasks are also discussed. Additionally, the importance of high-performance computing for natural language processing applications is illustrated by showing details of a few specific applications that use pre-training or self-supervised learning on large amounts of data in text understanding.

DOI: 10.4018/978-1-7998-7156-9.ch010

INTRODUCTION

The exponential data explosion requires developing practical tools for efficient and accurate pattern discovery, classification, representation, trend, and anomaly detection in large-scale high dimensional textual data (Szalay & Gray, 2006). For a decade now, IBM has been using high-performance computing (HPC) to analyze text and create intelligent machines. IBM Watson is a supercomputer that famously leveraged language analysis to win a game of Jeopardy (Hemsoth, 2011).

Advances in natural language processing (NLP) are essential for achieving real artificial intelligence. Language is considered one of the most complex human inventions and essential to human intelligence and social integration. Therefore, success in NLP is a prerequisite for fully functioning, artificially intelligent machines.

The industry is currently the largest contributor to NLP development because of its practical importance in handling large amounts of unstructured online data. Understanding public opinion through user-generated text analysis guides more informed decisions, policies, and products. Due to increased use of online social networks, forums, blogs, product reviews, and news comments, it became easy to collect an extensive amount of text needed for understanding opinions and facts about specific topics. Being able to understand those texts fully can shape politics, marketing, and many other fields.

As natural language models have become more complex in recent years, usage of HPC locally or in the cloud has become inevitable in NLP applications. Most novel NLP models are based on neural networks, which forward and backward propagation can be reduced to a vast matrix (tensor) multiplication. Therefore, Graphics Processing Unit (GPU) or Tensors Processing Unit (TPU) hardware is used for faster training. To enhance those models' speed and usability, they are mostly implemented in a distributed manner and expected to run on a high-performance parallel computing system.

Some popular libraries used in implementing and evaluating the most recent natural language models are: NLTK (Loper & Bird, 2002), Gensim (Rehurek & Sojka, 2010), SpaCy (SpaCy, 2020), TensorFlow (Abadi et al., 2016), PyTorch (Paszke et al., 2019), Keras (Chollet, 2017), scikit-learn (Pedregosa, 2011) and all of them support parallel and distributed processing, while most support GPU, and some even run on TPU hardware. Many of those frameworks are easy to learn and have complex neural networks and machine learning modules readily available for use. For those practitioners wanting to create and parallelize their algorithms in python, there is an open-source library, Dask (Dask Development Team, 2019), that natively scales python code. Also, Google has recently developed JAX (Google, 2020), which can transform any python code to allow backpropagation through it. This framework allows an additional training speed up by an innovative combination of operations and simple transformation *pmap,* making the algorithm parallelizable and easy to execute on HPC.

Figure 1. Common NLP Applications

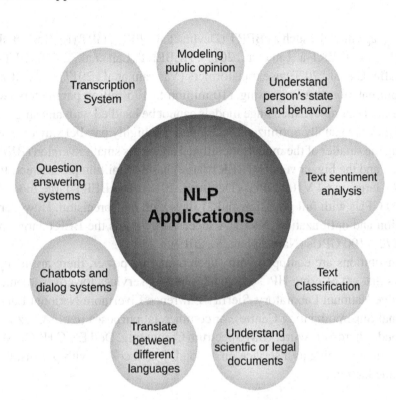

Using those and similar frameworks, people have created data mining and machine learning-based algorithms for different NLP applications. Some of these applications are listed below and summarized in Figure 1.

Some of common NLP applications are:

1. Modeling public opinion from social media and news on different topics (e.g., politics, racism, COVID-19, vaccination);
2. Understand a person's state and behavior (e.g., depression, suicidal thoughts, interest in products, dementia);
3. Sentiment analysis, which goal is to predict the emotion of a given text;
4. Text classification, categorizing text into predefined categories as variables to solve machine learning problems;
5. Understanding and summarizing large amounts of scientific or legal documents;
6. Translation between multiple languages (simultaneously);
7. Chatbots and dialog systems, which can make full-textual conversations with a human agent or another machine;
8. Answering questions automatically, where machines learn how to answer requests coming from humans; and
9. Transcription systems, which aim to teach machines to transcribe voice to text or text to voice.

BACKGROUND

Recent natural language models, such as BERT (Devlin et al., 2018), GPT (Radford et al., 2018), GPT-2 (Radford et al., 2019), ROBERT-a (Liu et al., 2019), ALBERT (Lan et al., 2019), GPT-3 (Brown et al., 2020), and T5 (Raffel C et al., 2020) use transformers (Vaswani et al., 2017) and self-attention mechanisms for text representation learning, using 110 million to 175 billion parameters (weights) to learn from billions of textual examples. Such huge models cannot be handled with any single computer, CPU, or GPU unit, and they are usually optimized and trained in a highly parallel way on a supercomputer.

BERT is among the smaller of the models mentioned above. Its smaller version (BERT base) has 110 million parameters, and the bigger version (BERT large) has 340 million parameters. It takes about 5.4 days to train BERT large on 64 V100 GPUs (Dettmers, 2018). The BERT large model's training takes 34 days on 8 V100 GPUs with full precision and 21 days with half-precision. However, with appropriate parameterization and optimization, NVIDIA successfully trains the BERT large model in only 47 minutes using 1,472 V100 GPUs (Narasimhan, S., 2019).

As very few institutions are equipped with supercomputing power, there are many cloud systems or supercomputers that are offering HPC or supercomputing services for government, academic (e.g., Summit - Oak Ridge National Laboratory, Sierra - Lawrence Livermore National Laboratory, Sunway Taihulight, National Supercomputing Centre), or commercial purposes (e.g., Amazon Web Services - AWS, Google Cloud, Microsoft Azure, IBM Spectrum Computing, Dell EMC HPC). Many commercial solutions offer machine learning as a service on a cloud, which comes with pre-installed software and libraries for machine learning.

PRACTICAL CONSIDERATIONS

Obtaining HPC services to an organization is a crucial decision to make. One must consider many aspects and issues, including privacy, organization utilization, and ways resources would be used. The following are some of the issues involved:

Privacy

- What is the privacy level of that data, and is the user allowed to move the data to external hardware? This question can be problematic for data for which the user has gained unique access. Usually, in such cases, there is a contract that specifies where data can be stored.
- How will HPC hardware store the data, and does the user have options to destroy it entirely? Full data removal should be possible in most of the solutions.

Organization Utilization

- How much do CPU/GPU/storage cost per hour and unit? If the hardware is needed for academic settings, there are many grants and programs through which it can be obtained for free, especially for educational purposes and in smaller amounts. The prices vary between CPU/GPU/TPU units, and they also depend on the amount of RAM given with those processors.

- How much is hard disc space allowed per user? Storage size is rarely the issue in text processing, but some other applications might have this problem.
- How much CPU/GPU computational power exists and can be accessed by one user? This question is one of the significant factors in choosing the right hardware.
- Can the user run multiple processes, and how many of them can be run in parallel? Many of the systems have restrictions on the number of processes that can be run in parallel, and it is essential to understand the level of parallelization.

Resources Usage

- Is there a wall time constraint? There is a restriction on the maximum duration of a process (wall time). If that exists, the user needs to make sure that progress is saved before the wall time ends and that the program can be continued within a new process from the saved file. It is good practice to save progress more often so that it is not lost in a power outage or other hardware issue.
- Is the algorithm parallelizable? Some machine learning algorithms are not parallelizable, or they may be only partially parallelizable. For example, recurrent neural networks (RNN), which were very popular in NLP before transformers, cannot be fully parallelized because of the hidden layer's serial update. The neuron is waiting for the output of the last neuron in the hidden layer.
- Is the implementation well parallelized? A maximum possible amount of parallel processes should be used to save execution time for big applications. Parallelization would depend on computing, RAM size, and network speed between nodes. It is important to balance them in such a way to get the most out of the hardware. A profiler can be used to understand program resource usage better. Also, in many cases, parallelization is not natural, so additional work needs to be done. In most of the frameworks mentioned above, parallelization will take a few additional code lines, but it may require much more work in some other cases.

APPLICATIONS

One of the significant research and industrial goals is to leverage the dynamics of social media content emerging around news articles (NAs), both at publisher websites (news outlets) worldwide and at social networking services such as Twitter, for intelligence and predictive analytics. Social media and NAs play an essential role in documenting daily societal events (Jin et al., 2017; Ramakrishnan et al., 2014; Rekatsinas et al., 2017; Sakaki et al., 2010; Korolov et al., 2016). For example, in NSF supported project "EAGER: Assessing Influence of News Articles on Emerging Events", the Temple Data Analytics and Biomedical Informatics (DABI) team at Temple University is modeling News Articles and Comments collected from more than 1,000 news outlets worldwide. Transforming the streams of social media and comments at thousands of news outlets (NOs) into data signals is the complicated problem addressed in this project. The researchers then use those signals to foretell the imminence of an (important) event, understand opinions about different topics, and develop sound predictive analytics on top of those signals.

This project requires learning a good text representation of formally (news articles) and informally written texts (comments and social media posts). This is a challenging problem which in the given approach utilizes deep learning models based on building blocks called transformers (Vaswani, A et al., 2017), aimed to discover knowledge from ordered sequences of data. Those models are computationally

Figure 2. Proposed framework for classification of short texts from small amount of labeled data

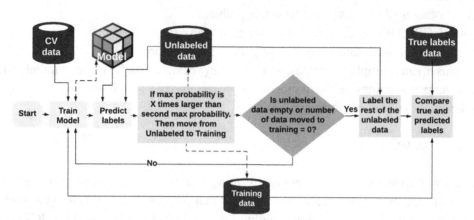

expensive to train and typically require weeks of distributed GPU processing. On the other side, to model complex spatio-temporal networks of user comments in news outlets and social media containing millions of nodes and links, the team formulate a massive optimization problem that requires parallel processing on CPU nodes with large memory. Additionally, multiple available datasets are used to connect news with other kinds of data to get quantitative and qualitative signals for the underlying machine learning problem. One such application studied at DABI laboratory is crime analysis. Those types of complex networks contain spatio-temporal information and, in general, are extremely large. For example, the DABI laboratory study's crime network consists of more than 4.5 million nodes, even when restricted to US data. Both problems are computationally infeasible without relying on high-performance computing resources.

Domain-Adaptation for Representation Learning of News and User Generated Text

When using social media and news comments text to model public opinion or understand events, researchers and industry have a significant constraint because such texts are short and condensed. Additionally, users-generated texts often contain jargon, sarcasm, links, and emoticons that can change the meaning or the tone of the text. To prevail over those challenges and improve accuracy performance, recent papers proposed algorithms for text classification that require millions of labeled documents (Conneau et al., 2016, Zhang et al., 2015, Yang et al., 2016). A vast amount of data needs to be cumulated and labeled to model public opinion and to ensure representation of different views on the same topic. For example, in recent work (Stanojevic et al., 2019), the authors collected 11.75 million unlabeled tweets on gun advocacy.

It is expensive and very time-consuming to label such vast amounts of text. Most universities and corporations do not have the resources to label such amount of data. Even if those efforts are attempted, it can take years to prepare and characterize enough data. Moreover, when the labeling task is too complicated, or the samples are short and have layered meanings, human labels' accuracy is questionable. In those cases, experts need to be employed for characterizing the example meaning. If machine learning models can help with labeling efforts, researchers and practitioners can focus on modeling and interpreting human behavior and opinions.

In (Stanojevic et al., 2019), a self-supervised framework was developed to label vast amounts of unlabeled data with a few thousand labeled examples (Figure 2). While this approach lowered the amount of required labeled data for up to three orders of magnitude, it also resulted in a small drop in prediction accuracy.

To speed up the training module, the most expensive part of the framework was parallelized to use multiple GPU units on HPC. The most expensive training algorithm used was based on convolutional neural networks (CNN). This allowed for more parallelization than recurrent neural networks, which are more commonly used in text processing. The researchers used nodes with 512 GB of RAM, with two NVIDIA Tesla P100 units, each with 12 GB of RAM. Since GPU units generally have much less RAM, neural network-based training module data was fed in small batches leaving enough RAM space to use more prominent architectures with more parameters. Additionally, incremental training was used so that the time complexity did not increase.

When analyzing an event or opinion, the proposed framework focuses on a specific topic (e.g., politics, economy) in which meaning, sentiment, and distributions of phrases change. For example, the word 'liability' is generally perceived as a negative word. However, economists often use it with a neutral sentiment (Loughran, and McDonald, 2011). The results show that the proposed semi-supervised framework with a training module based on CNN architecture performs the best in predicting millions of tweets labels with just 5000 labeled examples.

Modeling Users Content on Social Media to Understand Public Opinion

News and social media data, while abundant, pose many challenges that limit the potential benefits of machine learning based modeling. Some of the main usage constraints are:

1. The demographic information of users is hidden or not given.
2. Content is short and occasionally incomprehensible without context.
3. Manually labeling millions of posts is challenging for any institution.

The first problem can be solved by using information only from users whose demographic information is publicly available. However, as such a pull of users is tiny; the data may contain bias. As a solution to the second and third challenges, automatic systems need to model text into distinct opinions utilizing users' networks and their published content.

The DABI team explored the utilization of topic-specific news data to fine-tune state-of-the-art models, so they can learn to recognize opinion from social media text (Stanojevic et al., 2019). Specifically, influence of news articles was studied with a different bias on models trained to classify Twitter data. Moreover, performance was evaluated on balanced and unbalanced datasets. The experimental studies revealed that the tuning dataset characteristics, such as bias, diversity of vocabulary, and text style, are determining the success of classification models. On the other side, the data volume was less important. Additionally, it was shown that a state-of-the-art algorithm was not robust on an unbalanced twitter dataset, and it exaggerated when predicting the most frequent label.

To learn better representations of text and reduce training time, pre-trained word embeddings WT103 were used as a starting point. These were created on supercomputers by the training state of the art models with freezing layers on large amounts of English text. ULMFiT architecture is used to learn specific word meaning changes in each domain (social media text on specific topics). Despite using model pre-trained on WT103 as a starting point, the algorithm still required GPU training on HPC. The DABI team used 512 GB RAM node with two NVIDIA Tesla P100 units, each with 12 GB of RAM to learn the word meanings when training with differently biased news data and to classify the twitter data.

Classifying User's Comment Relevancy

Users-generated texts, such as blogs, forums, and online news comments, are a rich public opinion poll. Analyzing such data is essential for social scientists, policymakers, and journalists. Many survey-based studies tried to understand users' behavior by characterizing and categorizing comments in online news (Mishne et al., 2006; Ruiz et al., 2011; Weber et al., 2014; Ziegele et al., 2013).

To better reflect the news and comments semantic relation, a categorization was proposed to label comment-article agreement with one of the four categories: relevant, shared entity and category, same category, or irrelevant (Alshehri et al., 2020). Fleiss Kappa statistics (Fleiss, 1971) showed "fair agreement" of native English speakers in categorizing this alignment. This score confirms that comment relevancy labeling is a challenging task.

In this ongoing research, the DABI team proposed using novel powerful deep learning transformer-based models to understand the level of relevance between articles and comments while working with a limited amount of labeled data. A standard word-level embedding model (Doc2Vec) (Mikolov et al., 2013), recurrent neural model language model (Siamese LSTM) (Mueller et al., 2016), and finally, a pre-trained, transformer language model (BERT) (Devlin et al., 2018) were compared. HPC GPU units were used to train and fine-tune BERT on this task, and it achieved up to 26% improvement in accuracy compared to the previous state-of-the-art model based on LSTM (Mullick et al., 2019). These results confirmed the hypothesis that an architecture based on BERT could capture a deeper level of semantic relatedness between comments and news articles.

CONCLUSION

In conclusion, with the rapid advancements in many NLP models, the use of High-Performance Computers resources became a must. Here is a list of some famous applications of HPC in NLP:

- IBM Watson, which used a supercomputer to solve the question-answering problem (Hemsoth, 2011);
- GPT3, the state-of-the-art language model with 175 billion parameters that deceived humans in many cases, trained on a supercomputer (Brown et al., 2020);
- Google translate, which uses big recurrent neural models trained on GPUs (Wu et al., 2016);
- Grammarly, which leverages transformer-based architectures such that training is parallelized on multiple GPUs, for correcting grammar errors (Alikaniotis & Raheja, 2020).
- Facebook, which uses deep learning, trained on HPC to translate and generate its posts in different languages (Facebook Research, 2016).

Those interested in other academic combinations of NLP and HPC can find other applications in content created by Indiana University[1] and University Santiago de Compostela[2].

ACKNOWLEDGMENT

This research was supported in part by the National Science Foundation grant number IIS-1842183; XSEDE grant number IRI20004; National Science Foundation grant number 1625061; and US Army Research Laboratory grant number W911NF-16-2-0189.

REFERENCES

Abadi, M., Barham, P., Chen, J., Chen, Z., Davis, A., Dean, J., . . . Kudlur, M. (2016). Tensorflow: A System for Large-Scale Machine Learning. In *12th {USENIX} Symposium on Operating Systems Design and Implementation ({OSDI} 16)* (pp. 265-283). USENIX.

Alikaniotis, D., & Raheja, V. (2020, May 14). Under the Hood at Grammarly: Leveraging Transformer Language Models for Grammatical Error Correction. *Grammarly Engineering Blog.* https://www.grammarly.com/blog/engineering/under-the-hood-at-grammarly-leveraging-transformer-language-models-for-grammatical-error-correction/

Alshehri, J., Stanojevic, M., Dragut, E., & Obradovic, Z. (2020). (Manuscript submitted for publication). Aligning User Comments to the Content of a News Article. *Work (Reading, Mass.).*

Brown, T. B., Mann, B., Ryder, N., Subbiah, M., Kaplan, J., Dhariwal, P., . . . Agarwal, S. (2020). *Language Models Are Few-Shot Learners.* arXiv Preprint arXiv:2005.14165

Chollet, F. (2017, May 4). Keras-team/keras 2.0.0. *GitHub.* https://github.com/keras-team/keras

Conneau, A., Schwenk, H., Barrault, L., & Lecun, Y. (2017, April). Very Deep Convolutional Networks for Text Classification. In *Proceedings of the 15th Conference of the European Chapter of the Association for Computational Linguistics:* Volume 1, *Long Papers* (pp. 1107-1116). 10.18653/v1/E17-1104

Dask Development Team. (2019, June 25). Dask 2.0.0: Library for Dynamic Task Scheduling. *Dask.* https://dask.org

Dettmers, T. (2020, September 20). TPUs vs GPUs for Transformers (BERT). *Tim Dettmers.* https://timdettmers.com/2018/10/17/tpus-vs-gpus-for-transformers-bert/

Devlin, J., Chang, M. W., Lee, K., & Toutanova, K. (2018). *Bert: Pre-Training of Deep Bidirectional Transformers for Language Understanding.* arXiv Preprint arXiv:1810.04805.

Facebook Research. (2020, May 20). Breaking Down Language Barriers. *Natural Language Processing & Speech.* https://research.fb.com/category/natural-language-processing-and-speech/

Fleiss, J. L. (1971). Measuring Nominal Scale Agreement Among Many Raters. *Psychological Bulletin, 76*(5), 378–382. doi:10.1037/h0031619

Google. (2020, July 26). Google/jax 0.1.52. *GitHub.* https://github.com/google/jax

Hemsoth, N. (2014, April 19). Bringing Natural Language Processing Home. *HPCwire.* https://www. hpcwire.com/2011/06/09/bringing_natural_language_processing_home/

Howard, J., & Ruder, S. (2018, July). Universal Language Model Fine-tuning for Text Classification. In *Proceedings of the 56th Annual Meeting of the Association for Computational Linguistics (Volume 1: Long Papers)* (pp. 328-339). 10.18653/v1/P18-1031

Jin, F., Wang, W., Chakraborty, P., Self, N., Chen, F., & Ramakrishnan, N. (2017, July). Tracking Multiple Social Media for Stock Market Event Prediction. In *Industrial Conference on Data Mining* (pp. 16-30). Springer. 10.1007/978-3-319-62701-4_2

Korolov, R., Lu, D., Wang, J., Zhou, G., Bonial, C., Voss, C., ... Ji, H. (2016, August). On Predicting Social Unrest Using Social Media. In *2016 IEEE/ACM International Conference on Advances in Social Networks Analysis and Mining (ASONAM)* (pp. 89-95). 10.1109/ASONAM.2016.7752218

Lan, Z., Chen, M., Goodman, S., Gimpel, K., Sharma, P., & Soricut, R. (2019, September). ALBERT: A Lite BERT for Self-supervised Learning of Language Representations. In *International Conference on Learning Representations.*

Liu, Y., Ott, M., Goyal, N., Du, J., Joshi, M., Chen, D., . . . Stoyanov, V. (2019). *Roberta: A robustly optimized BERT pretraining approach.* arXiv Preprint arXiv:1907.11692.

Loper, E., & Bird, S. (2002). *NLTK: The Natural Language Toolkit.* arXiv Preprint cs/0205028.

Loughran, T., & McDonald, B. (2011). When Is a Liability Not a Liability? Textual Analysis, Dictionaries, and 10-Ks. *The Journal of Finance, 66*(1), 35–65. doi:10.1111/j.1540-6261.2010.01625.x

Mikolov, T., Sutskever, I., Chen, K., Corrado, G. S., & Dean, J. (2013). Distributed Representations of Words and Phrases and Their Compositionality. In Advances in Neural Information Processing Systems (pp. 3111-3119). Academic Press.

Mishne, G., & Glance, N. (2006, May). Leave a Reply: An Analysis of Weblog Comments. *Third Annual Workshop on the Weblogging Ecosystem.*

Mueller, J., & Thyagarajan, A. (2016, February). Siamese Recurrent Architectures for Learning Sentence Similarity. In *Proceedings of the Thirtieth AAAI Conference on Artificial Intelligence* (pp. 2786-2792). AAAI.

Mullick, A., Ghosh, S., Dutt, R., Ghosh, A., & Chakraborty, A. (2019, April). Public Sphere 2.0: Targeted Commenting in Online News Media. In *European Conference on Information Retrieval* (pp. 180-187). Springer. 10.1007/978-3-030-15719-7_23

Narasimhan, S. (2020, August 26). NVIDIA Clocks World's Fastest BERT Training Time and Largest Transformer Based Model, Paving Path for Advanced Conversational AI. *NVIDIA Developer Blog.* https://developer.nvidia.com/blog/training-bert-with-gpus/

Paszke, A., Gross, S., Massa, F., Lerer, A., Bradbury, J., Chanan, G., . . . Desmaison, A. (2019). Pytorch: An Imperative Style, High-Performance Deep Learning Library. In Advances in Neural Information Processing Systems (pp. 8026-8037). Academic Press.

Pedregosa, F., Varoquaux, G., Gramfort, A., Michel, V., Thirion, B., Grisel, O., ... Vanderplas, J. (2011). Scikit-Learn: Machine Learning in Python. *Journal of Machine Learning Research, 12,* 2825–2830.

Radford, A., Narasimhan, K., Salimans, T., & Sutskever, I. (2018). *Improving Language Understanding by Generative Pre-Training.* Academic Press.

Radford, A., Wu, J., Child, R., Luan, D., Amodei, D., & Sutskever, I. (2019). Language Models are Unsupervised Multitask Learners. *OpenAI blog, 1*(8), 9.

Raffel, C., Shazeer, N., Roberts, A., Lee, K., Narang, S., Matena, M., ... Liu, P. J. (2020). Exploring the Limits of Transfer Learning with a Unified Text-to-Text Transformer. *Journal of Machine Learning Research, 21*(140), 1–67.

Ramakrishnan, N., Butler, P., Muthiah, S., Self, N., Khandpur, R., Saraf, P., ... Kuhlman, C. (2014, August). 'Beating the News' with EMBERS: Forecasting Civil Unrest Using Open Source Indicators. In *Proceedings of the 20th ACM SIGKDD International Conference on Knowledge Discovery and Data Mining* (pp. 1799-1808). 10.1145/2623330.2623373

Rehurek, R., & Sojka, P. (2010). Software Framework for Topic Modelling with Large Corpora. *Proceedings of the LREC 2010 Workshop on New Challenges for NLP Frameworks.*

Rekatsinas, T., Ghosh, S., Mekaru, S. R., Nsoesie, E. O., Brownstein, J. S., Getoor, L., & Ramakrishnan, N. (2017). Forecasting Rare Disease Outbreaks from Open Source Indicators. *Statistical Analysis and Data Mining: The ASA Data Science Journal, 10*(2), 136–150. doi:10.1002am.11337

Ruiz, C., Domingo, D., Micó, J. L., Díaz-Noci, J., Meso, K., & Masip, P. (2011). Public Sphere 2.0? The Democratic Qualities of Citizen Debates in Online Newspapers. *The International Journal of Press/Politics, 16*(4), 463–487. doi:10.1177/1940161211415849

Sakaki, T., Okazaki, M., & Matsuo, Y. (2010, April). Earthquake Shakes Twitter Users: Real-Time Event Detection by Social Sensors. In *Proceedings of the 19th International Conference on World Wide Web* (pp. 851-860). 10.1145/1772690.1772777

SpaCy. (2020, May 19). SpaCy 3.0.0 Industrial-Strength Natural Language Processing in Python. *SpaCy.* https://spacy.io/

Stanojevic, M., Alshehri, J., Dragut, E. C., & Obradovic, Z. (2019, July). Biased News Data Influence on Classifying Social Media Posts. In *Proceedings of NewsIR Workshop @ 42nd International ACM SIGIR Conference on Research and Development in Information Retrieval* (pp. 3-8). Academic Press.

Stanojevic, M., Alshehri, J., & Obradovic, Z. (2019, August). Surveying Public Opinion Using Label Prediction on Social Media Data. In *2019 IEEE/ACM International Conference on Advances in Social Networks Analysis and Mining (ASONAM)* (pp. 188-195). IEEE. 10.1145/3341161.3342861

Szalay, A., & Gray, J. (2006). Science in an Exponential World. *Nature, 440*(7083), 413–414. doi:10.1038/440413a PMID:16554783

Vaswani, A., Shazeer, N., Parmar, N., Uszkoreit, J., Jones, L., Gomez, A. N., . . . Polosukhin, I. (2017). Attention is All You Need. In Advances in Neural Information Processing Systems (pp. 5998-6008). Academic Press.

Weber, P. (2014). Discussions in the Comments Section: Factors Influencing Participation and Interactivity in Online Newspapers' Reader Comments. *New Media & Society*, *16*(6), 941–957. doi:10.1177/1461444813495165

Wu, Y., Schuster, M., Chen, Z., Le, Q. V., Norouzi, M., Macherey, W., . . . Klingner, J. (2016). *Google's Neural Machine Translation System: Bridging the Gap Between Human and Machine Translation.* arXiv Preprint arXiv:1609.08144.

Yang, Z., Yang, D., Dyer, C., He, X., Smola, A., & Hovy, E. (2016, June). Hierarchical Attention Networks for Document Classification. In *Proceedings of the 2016 Conference of the North American Chapter of the Association for Computational Linguistics: Human Language Technologies* (pp. 1480-1489). Academic Press.

Ziegele, M., & Quiring, O. (2013). Conceptualizing Online Discussion Value: A Multidimensional Framework for Analyzing User Comments on Mass-Media Websites. *Annals of the International Communication Association*, *37*(1), 125–153. doi:10.1080/23808985.2013.11679148

ENDNOTES

[1]   http://hpnlp.org/
[2]   http://proxectos.citius.usc.es/hpcpln/index.php/en/

Chapter 11
Deposition of Submicron Particles by Chaotic Mixing in the Pulmonary Acinus:
Acinar Chaotic Mixing

Akira Tsuda
Tsuda Lung Research, USA

Frank S. Henry
Manhattan College, USA

ABSTRACT

In this review, the authors outline the evidence that emerged some 30 years ago that the mechanisms thought responsible for the deposition of submicron particles in the respiratory region of the lung were inadequate to explain the measured rate of deposition. They then discuss the background and theory of what is believed to be the missing mechanism, namely chaotic mixing. Specifically, they outline how that the recirculating flow in the alveoli has a range of frequencies of oscillation and some of these resonate with the breathing frequency. If the system is perturbed, the resonating frequencies break into chaos, and they discuss a number of practical ways in which the system can be disturbed. The perturbation of fluid particle trajectories results in Hamiltonian chaos, which produces qualitative changes in those trajectories. They end the review with a discussion of the effects of chaotic mixing on the deposition of inhaled particles in the respiratory region of the lung.

INTRODUCTION

The primary purpose of the lung is gas exchange. Oxygen-rich air is drawn into the lung by the diaphragm and intercostal muscles, and carbon dioxide and other gasses are rejected with the outgoing air when the muscles relax. This rhythmic, in-and-out, motion of the lungs happens twelve times a minute on average (Weibel, 1984).

DOI: 10.4018/978-1-7998-7156-9.ch011

The anatomy of the lung may be divided into three regions: upper airways (nasal pharynx area), conducting airways (trachea to terminal bronchioles) and the pulmonary acinus (respiratory bronchioles to terminal alveolar ducts). Each region has its own unique anatomy and flow regime (West, 2012). Despite these differences in anatomy and flow type, particles are carried from the mouth to the lung periphery.

For a particle to deposit on the surface of the alveolar blood-air barrier, two things have to occur. First, the particle has to travel with the ambient air through a network of ducts and end up close to the alveolar surface. Second, if the particle is close enough, short-distance forces acting on the particle (e.g., the van der Waals force, electrostatic force, Brownian force, etc. [Friedlander, 1977]) will be sufficient to bring it to the surface.

In the lung physiology literature (e.g., West, 2012; Oberdörster et al. 2007), three mechanisms are typically defined as contributing to particle deposition. These are inertial impaction, gravitational sedimentation, and Brownian motion.

Inertial impaction: describes the situation in which a particle with relatively large mass (typically a relatively large particle, since mass is proportional to the cube of the particle's diameter) cannot follow the curvilinear airflow patterns faithfully; and as a result, it deviates from the airflow streamlines and the particle's own inertia carries it to the surface (Friedlander, 1977). This phenomenon is significant when airflow velocity (U) is large, and thus it occurs predominantly in the upper/large airways. A particle's inertia is consider significant when the Stokes number, $Stk > 1$. The Stokes number, $Stk = \rho_p d^2 U / 18\eta L$, where ρ_p is the particle density, d is the particle diameter, η is the air viscosity, and L is the characteristic length scale.

Sedimentation: particles with large mass are also subject to the external gravitational force, which makes the particles deposit in the direction of gravity (Tsuda et al. 2013). This phenomenon becomes significant when the particle sedimentation velocity (expressed in terms of the terminal velocity $v_s = \rho_p d^2 g / 18\eta$, where g = gravitational acceleration) becomes comparable to, or more than, the airflow velocity. Deposition by sedimentation occurs primarily in the large airways and at the beginning of the acinus.

Brownian motion: the potential for particles to cross flow streamlines and deposit due to Brownian-motion is characterized by the Péclet number, $Pe = UL / D$. A balance between thermal effects and viscous drag exerted on the particle determines the magnitude of the diffusivity, D. Particles with small Péclet numbers are more likely to deposit due to Brownian motion. Particles of very small size (diameters < 0.005 µm) may deposit in the upper/large airways because those small particles have an extremely high diffusivity, and low Péclet numbers. Particles with small mass, which can follow the curvilinear airflow patterns with little inertia/gravitational effects, can enter the pulmonary acinus with the airflow. In this review, we focus on the deposition of particles in the pulmonary acinus, which occupies more than 95% of the lungs in volume (Weibel 1984). We concentrate on particles in the diameter range 0.005 µm to 0.5 µm because particles in this range have been found to deposit preferentially in the acinus (Tsuda et al. 2013). Such particles have diffusivities that are small enough to prevent them from depositing before reaching the acinus but are also light enough to exclude deposition through inertial impaction or sedimentation.

CLASSICAL VIEW

Particle are transported (convected) with the air in a piggy-back fashion all the way from the airway opening to near the alveolar walls. Also, the particle-laden air mixes with the residual gas in the acinus (Tsuda et al. 2013). Thus acinar airflow patterns and the mixing of fresh air with residual gas are very important for particle deposition. The momentum equation for flow of a Newtonian fluid with constant properties and negligible body forces, can be written in Cartesian tensor notation as.

$$\frac{\partial u_i}{\partial t} + \frac{\partial u_j u_i}{\partial x_j} = -\frac{1}{\rho}\frac{\partial p}{\partial x_i} + \nu \frac{\partial^2 u_i}{\partial x_j^2} \tag{1}$$

If we define dimensionless variables as $t' = t / T$, $u_i' = u_i / U$, $x_i' = x_i / L$, and $p' = p / \rho U^2$, where T, U and L are characteristic time, velocity, and length, respectively, then Eq. 1 can be written

$$St \frac{\partial u_i'}{\partial t'} + \frac{\partial u_j' u_i'}{\partial x_j'} = -\frac{\partial p'}{\partial x_i'} + \frac{1}{Re}\frac{\partial^2 u_i'}{\partial x_j'^2} \tag{2}$$

where, $St = L / UT$ is the Strouhal number, and $Re = UL / \nu$ is the Reynolds number

An alternate form of Eq. 2, for oscillatory flow, is gained by multiplying Eq. 2 by Re and introducing the Womersley number, $\alpha = \sqrt{2\pi L^2 / T\nu}$, i.e.,

$$\frac{\alpha^2}{2\pi}\frac{\partial u_i'}{\partial t'} + Re \frac{\partial u_j' u_i'}{\partial x_j'} = -Re\frac{\partial p'}{\partial x_i'} + \frac{\partial^2 u_i'}{\partial x_j'^2} \tag{3}$$

We note that $\alpha^2 = 2\pi St Re$. Also, now, T is the period of oscillation.

In a flow where the Reynolds number is much less than one, the convective terms of Eq. 3 are negligible compared to the other terms. While, the pressure gradient in Eq. 2 is also multiplied by the Reynolds number, it has to be assumed that this term is not negligible as it is the pressure gradient that is driving the flow. In a flow where the Reynolds number is much less than one, the Womersley number is also likely to be less than one (as $\alpha \propto Re$), and hence Eq. 3 can be reduced to

$$Re\frac{\partial p'}{\partial x_i'} = \frac{\partial^2 u_i'}{\partial x_j'^2} \tag{4}$$

In flows where Eq. 4 applies, the direction of the flow is not discernable from inspection of the streamlines; e.g., the upstream streamline pattern for flow over a cylinder would be a mirror image of that of the downstream streamline pattern. This is called a kinematically reversible flow (Taylor 1960). In terms of our cylinder example, it would not be possible to tell if the flow was traveling from left to right or vice versa.

Figure1. Spreading of a bolus of monodisperse aerosols versus depth of volume to which the bolus penetrated (Heyder et al., 1988). The figure demonstrates, experimentally, the presence of kinematical irreversibility in the acinus (Adapted, with permission, from Tsuda, Henry, & Butler, 2013)

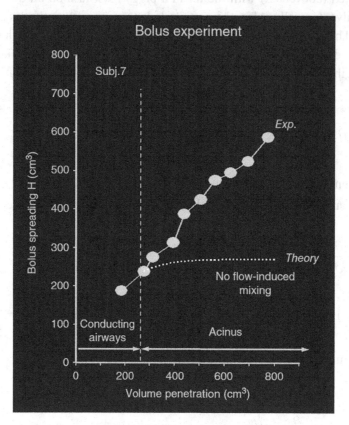

It used to be considered that flow in the lung periphery was perfectly kinematically reversible (Davies, 1972). From this assumption, it followed that particles traveling along streamlines would not deposit (Davies 1972): they would enter alveoli over inspiration and leave over expiration. For particles to deviate from streamlines in a kinematically reversible flow, they must exhibit some intrinsic motion resulting from; for instance, gravitational or diffusional forces. However, in 1988, Heyder et al. showed that the experimental data did not conform to the idea of perfectly kinematically reversible flow in the lung periphery; they found that 1) deposition observed could not be explained by any known deposition mechanisms described above, and 2) deposition increased proportionally as particles penetrated deep into the lungs (Figure 1).

If the flow is not kinematically reversible, the convection terms in Eq. 3 must have some effect on the resulting flow. The Reynolds number at the entrance to the respiratory region of the lung is of the order of 1.0. The Reynolds number is a measure of the importance of inertial transport (convection) over diffusional transport. Thus in the entrance region of the lung, the flow inertia, while small, cannot be ignored. We note that the Womersley number of the flow in the lung periphery is of the order of 0.1; and hence, the flow in this region of the lung can be considered quasi steady.

In 1995, Tsuda et al. showed that the non-zero inertia in the flow in the respiratory region of the lung probably produces chaotic, or convective mixing, and it is believed that such mixing is the mechanism

Figure 2. Rhythmically expanding and contracting alveolated duct model consisting of circular channel surrounded by torus. Q_A, alveolar flow; Q_D, ductal flow; CL, center line; R_D, channel radius; R_A, alveolar radius; L_A, alveolar opening size; γ, opening half angle. (Adapted, with permission, from Tsuda, Henry, & Butler, 1995)

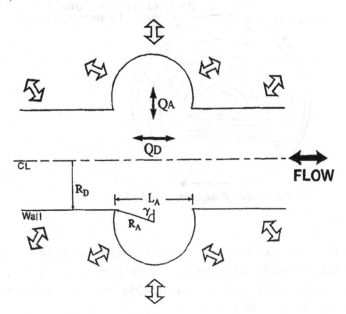

responsible for the experimental findings of Heyder et al. Tsuda et al. (1995) showed that the pathlines of fluid particles, expressed as $x_i = \int u_i dt$, can be highly complex in alveolar flow. They built a very simple alveolated duct model; simple but possessing the basic features of an acinar duct; namely, a thoroughfare central channel surrounded by dead-end side pockets. This geometric model expands and contracts in a self-similar kinematically reversible fashion (Figure 2) so that fluid motion inside the model also should be kinematically reversible according to the classical theory.

COMPUTATIONAL SIMULATION AND HAMILTONIAN CHAOS

The origin of kinematical irreversibility in the alveoli can be explained by the concept of Hamiltonian chaos (Tsuda et al. 2011; Tabor 1989). Basically, this is due to an interplay between two mechanisms operating in the system; the central channel flow and rotation flows inside of the alveolus. Both are cyclic (Figure 3). The frequency of the central channel flow is externally determined by intercostal muscles and diaphragm cyclic motion (controlled by the central nervous system). This frequency represents the breathing frequency (f_{br}). Rotational flows inside of the alveolus are intrinsic to the lung. Fluid in the alveolus (dead-end side pocket) is rotated by the viscous shear force imposed on the alveolar fluid by central channel flow as it passes along an alveolar opening. How strongly and how quickly the alveolar fluid rotates is determined by a balance between shear force exerted by the central channel flow along the alveolar opening and the alveolar wall drag force, which is acting in the opposite directions to the rotation of the alveolar flow. As a result, fluid near the alveolar wall moves more slowly due to the drag

Figure 3. Representative alveolated duct flow. The frequency of the cyclic central channel flow represents breathing frequency (f_{br}), while the frequency of alveolar recirculation flows (f_{alv}) is a family of frequencies. (Adapted, with permission, from Tsuda, Laine-Pearson, & Hydon, 2011)

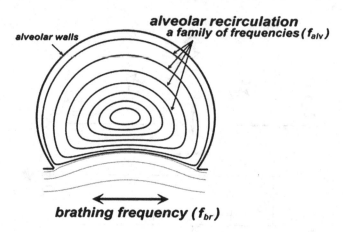

force exerted by the walls, while the fluid at the center of the alveolus moves faster due to being further from the effect of the wall (Figure 4). In other words, the frequency of alveolar recirculation flows (f_{alv}) is a family of frequencies -not one fixed number-, depending on geometric factors such as the alveolar cavity shape and the size of the alveolar opening.

Particles in the alveolus are carried passively with the rotating flow around the alveolar cavity and these paths are called recirculation orbits. The frequency of particle rotation depends on which orbit the particle resides. The motion of a particle depends on the ratio f_{alv}/f_{br}; and this ratio dictates whether or not a particle will follow a chaotic path. When the frequencies f_{alv} and f_{br} resonate (i.e., when the ratio f_{alv}/f_{br} is a rational number), the interaction between the frequencies produces a net drift if the system is perturbed.

Figure 4. Time taken by a fluid element to make one rotation in a model alveolus. The fluid near the alveolar wall moves more slowly due to the drag force exerted by the walls, while the fluid far from the walls (at the center of the alveolus) moves faster (Adapted, with permission, from Karl, Henry, & Tsuda, 2004)

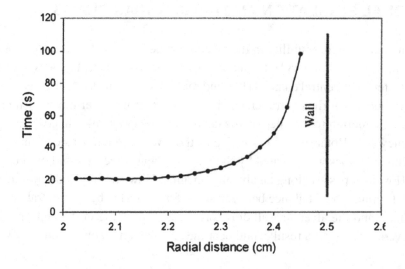

Figure 5. Poincaré sections for a flow with Re=1.0 and α =0.096 (T=3 s). Notice chains of islands surrounded by a sea of chaos. Colors have no significance other than to differentiate between individual orbits. (Adapted, with permission, from Henry, Laine-Pearson, & Tsuda, 2009)

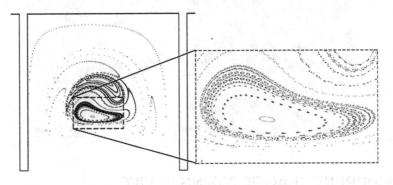

This drift results in Hamiltonian chaos, which produces qualitative changes in those trajectories (Tsuda et al. 2011). Phrased differently, if the system is not perturbed (e.g., the Reynold number is strictly zero), passive particles in the alveoli simply recirculate. In this case, resonance does not produce a qualitative change in particle trajectories: each particle moves back and forth on a single (closed) path forever.

In the lung, the unperturbed situation cannot occur for a number of reasons. For one, Re is never exactly zero, as long as air moves (Tsuda et al., 1995; Henry et al., 2002, 2009); for another, the alveolar walls move, as long as we live (i.e., blood has to perfused to avoid necrosis) (Tsuda et al., 1995; Henry et al., 2002; Laine-Pearson and Hydon 2006); and lastly, small but nonzero geometric hysteresis may exist (Haber et al., 2000; Haber and Tsuda, 2006).

The explanation of the mathematical theory of 'perturbed Hamiltonian dynamical systems' is rather involved, and is beyond the scope of this review. Interested readers are encouraged to read the paper by Tsuda et al. (2011).

The important point here is that f_{alv} is a family of frequencies, the magnitude of which increases as the distance from the wall increases (Figure 4). Hence, in areas of the acinus where the alveolar flow rotates, it is extremely likely that at least one value of f_{alv} resonates with f_{br}. Indeed, Henry et al., 2009, showed that chaotic mixing occurs inside the alveolar space as long as the flow exhibit recirculation, even if the walls do not move. That is, a small but non-zero Reynolds number was enough to perturb the flow and produce chaos (Figure 5).

The strength of chaotic mixing is dependent on the degree of perturbation. For instance, alveoli near the entrance of the acinus create stronger chaotic mixing than those deeper in the acinus due to larger Reynolds number. If alveolar expansion is more or less constant regardless of location along the acinar tree (Weibel 1983), then the ratio between a flow entering into the alveolus (Q_A) and a flow passing by the same alveolus (Q_D) is inversely proportional to Re. Since this ratio Q_A/Q_D is considered as one of the important fluid mechanics parameters to uniquely describe alveolar flow, the ratio Q_A/Q_D, instead of Re (Tsuda et al.1995), is often used in the discussion of chaotic mixing in the pulmonary acinus.

Figure 6. Alveolar recirculation. In many alveoli, circular blue/white color patterns were observed at N = ½. (Bar = 100 µm.) (Adapted, with permission, from Tsuda, Rogers, Hydon, & Butler, 2002)

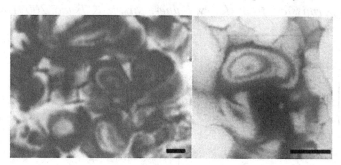

PROOF OF OCURRENT CHAOTIC MIXING *IN VIVO*

The presence of chaotic mixing in the pulmonary acinus was demonstrated experimentally using excised rat lungs (Tsuda et al., 2002). Briefly, using polymerizable viscous fluids of two colors (white & blue), Tsuda et al., 2002, studied the mixing phenomena deep in the lungs. They first filled the lungs with white fluid representing alveolar residual air, then, they ventilated the lungs with blue fluid as a tidal fluid with physiologically relevant ventilatory conditions (e.g., Reynolds number & Womersley parameter were matched to physiological conditions). After letting the two-colors fluids polymerize, they studied blue-white mixing patterns. First, at the end of the first inspiration (Figure 6), most of the large, medium size, and alveolar airways were entirely filled with tidal (blue) fluid with no sign of significant mixing in the acini, but many alveoli (i.e., dead-end pockets) exhibit circular patterns, showing the fluid was indeed recirculating inside the alveoli. After only one breathing cycle (Figure 7), remarkably complex stirring patterns emerged on transverse cross sections of the airways. We performed a box counting analysis (Bassingthwaighte et al., 1994) on transverse cross sections of the airways and found a nearly linear relationship between the overall mean intensity and box size with a slope of about -0.1, showing the color pattern is indeed fractal with a fractal dimension D = 1.1. The facts that 1) the fractal dimension D = 1.1 is invariant throughout the airways from the trachea down to the 12–13th generation (the most distal airways we examined for this analysis) and 2) the front of the tidal fluid represented by the interface of the blue & white colors is enormously stretched by the end of the inspiration sampling millions of alveolar spaces indicate that the observed fractal pattern is a result of chaotic mixing occurring deeper than the 12–13th generation, most likely in the pulmonary acinus.

To quantify the extent of mixing in the acini, we examined the time evolution of mixing patterns on the transverse cross sections of acinar airways (approximately 200µm in diameter) at the end of each breathing cycle for 4 breathing cycles (Figure 8). After the first cycle (N=1 Figure 8), most of the acinar airways appeared predominantly white, with microscopic traces of blue. After the second or the third cycle (N=2, 3 Figure 8), however, a large amount of tidal (blue) fluid appeared on the cross-sectional images, indicating that substantial net axial transport had occurred along the bronchial-acinar tree. The cross-sectional images of acinar airways showed clearly delineated interface patterns with both blue & white fluids being stretched and folded (discussed below). After the fourth cycle (N=4 Figure 8), the clarity of the interface patterns had largely disappeared, and the blue & white patterns changed into smeared (mixed) bluish-white uniformity.

Figure 7. Typical mixing patterns observed on airway cross sections at different locations in the tracheobronchial tree after one ventilatory cycle. The entire transverse cross section of the trachea (A1) was filled with myriad extremely fine blue-white striations, which formed convoluted swirling patterns. Similar patterns were seen on the transverse cross sections of the main stem bronchi (A2). This pattern was consistently seen through the eighth (A8), and even up to the 12th-generation (A12) airways (counted from the trachea). In contrast, the longitudinal airway sections showed much simpler patterns, displaying fine laminae of blue and white striations (see A7 for example; also tested at several other locations). The fact that there were very few complex patterns observed on the longitudinal sections suggests that inertia-based secondary flows such as turbulent eddies were not generated in this experiment. Images bar = 500μm (A1), 500μm (A2), 200μm (A8), 100μm (A12), 100μm (A7). representative of five rat lungs analyzed. (Adapted, with permission, from Tsuda, Rogers, Hydon, & Butler, 2002)

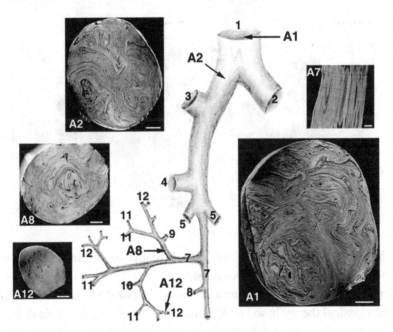

These findings suggest that there may be a specific cycle-by-cycle folding factor f, characteristic of the acinar duct structure. To determine the cycle-by-cycle folding factor f, we analyzed the cross-sectional images of randomly selected acinar airways (approximately 200 μm diameter) for each of $N = $ 1, 2, 3, and 4 (from 12 animals; 3 animals for each cycle number). For each image, we computed the characteristic distance between neighboring blue & white interfaces defined as the harmonic mean wavelength, l_w, obtained by two-dimensional spectral analysis. The time evolution of l_w, normalized by airway diameter, d, showed a sharp decrease from $N = 1$ to $N = 3$, reflecting the decreasing lateral length scales associated with folding. This was followed by a sudden increase in l_w/d at $N = 4$, caused by the diffusive loss of high-frequency components in the pattern. To determine the folding factor f in rat acini, we developed a simple convection-diffusion mathematical model with a parameterized folding factor and fit this to the data. The model represents a simple evolving sine-wave convective pattern, whose wavelength is divided by a folding factor f for each breath cycle, and whose amplitude is allowed

Figure 8. Typical mixing pattern of two colors observed in approximately 200-μm acinar airways of adult rats after ventilatory cycles of N = 1, 2, 3, and 4. (Bars = 100 μm.) (Adapted, with permission, from Tsuda, Rogers, Hydon, & Butler, 2002)

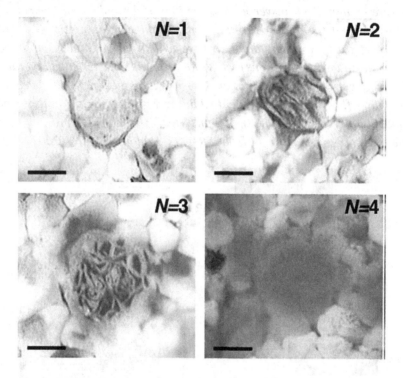

to smooth out by diffusion. We found that a best fit to the data was obtained with a folding factor $f = 2.3$. The significance of this finding is discussed below.

The temporal evolution of convection patterns observed in our study fundamentally differs from the one predicted by the classical theory based on kinematically reversible fluid flow. To illustrate this difference, consider the following two systems. One is kinematically reversible (Figure 9 *Left*) and the other has irreversible stretch and fold convection (Figure 9 *Right*). We introduce a Brownian tracer into both systems and track the evolution of diffusive and convective length scales in both systems. In the kinematically reversible system (Figure 9 *Left*), there is no net convective transport; mixing is therefore characterized by a diffusion distance δ, which increases slowly with time t, that is, $\delta \propto \sqrt{Dt}$, where D is the tracer diffusivity. Significant mixing only occurs when δ becomes of the order of L, the fixed system size, which in our case is a typical alveolar dimension of a few hundred microns. For fine aerosol particles, this process would be very slow because such particles have low diffusivities. By contrast, in the system with stretch-and-fold convection, diffusion and convection interact.

The diffusion length scale δ initially increases as $\sqrt{Dt}$ but asymptotically approaches $\sqrt{D/\alpha}$, where α is the stretching rate. Importantly, however, the length scale over which diffusion must operate to effect mixing is no longer fixed at the system size L, but, because of convective folding, decreases exponentially with cycle number N. This can be expressed as f^{-N}, where f is the characteristic cycle-by-cycle folding factor. In this interaction, mixing is initially very slow, but suddenly increases after a few cycles when the rapidly decreasing folded scales Lf^{-N} become comparable to the asymptotically constant

Figure 9. Comparison of Brownian tracer mixing between a system with pure diffusion and a system with stretch and fold convection and diffusion. (Top) Schematic view of these two systems. (Middle left) The slowly increasing length scale for mixing (δ) in pure diffusion. (Middle right) With stretch and fold convection, δ also increases slowly (but approaches an asymptotic value); by contrast, the folding length scale, w, decreases exponentially rapidly. (Bottom) Representation of the evolving extent of mixing corresponding to diffusion alone and to diffusion coupled with stretch and fold convection. At the time when the two length scales are comparable (vertical dotted line), there is sharp jump in mixing (entropy burst). (Adapted, with permission, from Tsuda, Rogers, Hydon, & Butler, 2002)

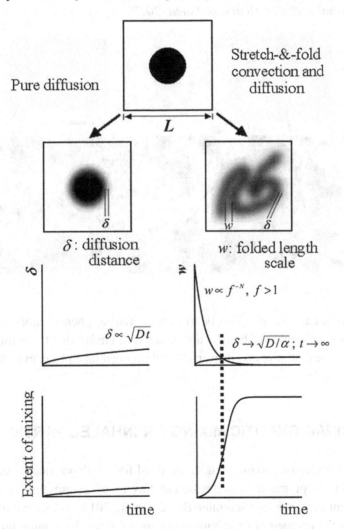

value of diffusion length scale δ (Figure 9 *Bottom Right*). This phenomenon—a sudden increase in mixing that can be described by an equivalent entropy burst (Butler & Tsuda, 1997)—is a characteristic feature of chaotic mixing (Ottino, 1989) and is quantified by the folding factor f. We showed above that in rat acinar airways with diameter of approximately 200 μm, the folding factor f was about 2.3, which means that the lateral length scales over which the complexity of the convective flow patterns is evolving are decreased by more than half at every breath. Equivalently, the complexity of the pattern

Figure 10. The lung parenchyma of the developing lungs in rats at various time points. At 4 days of age in rats, the airways are mostly saccular with smooth-walled primary septa with no visible alveoli (A and D). Acinar structure after the bulk alveolation phase (at 21 days of age in rats), the acinus becomes markedly alveolated, filled with numerous alveoli with a shape similar to, but smaller than, fully developed matured alveoli (B and E). Acinar structure of fully developed adult lungs (at ≥90 days of age in rats) (C and F). (Upper) H&E staining. (Scale bar, 100 μm.) (Lower) SEM imaging, 400×. [Burri noted that there is no noticeable difference in appearance between human immature parenchyma vs. rodent parenchyma, except their size (Burri, 1985)]. [Adapted, with permission, from Semmler-Behnke, Kreyling, Schulz, Takenaka, Butler, Henry, & Tsuda, 2012)

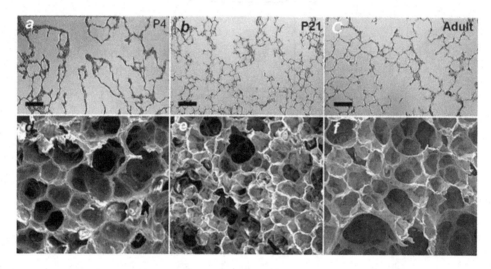

itself more than doubles each breath. This is an exponentiating phenomenon, which in consequence implies that only a modest number of breaths are required to ensure that these mixing lengths become sufficiently small that true diffusive and irreversible mixing can take place, even for aerosols with very low diffusivities.

EFFECTS OF ACINAR CHAOTIC MIXING ON INHALED PARTICLE DEPOSITION

One way to test whether chaotic mixing is indeed crucial for the deposition of submicron particles in the pulmonary acinus is to compared the deposition in the case of the presence of acinar chaotic mixing against a a case without such mixing (Semmler-Behnke et al., 2012). As shown in Figure 10, there are striking differences in the geometry of the lung parenchyma in the developing lungs. Rats at postnatal day 4 (P4) have largely saccular airways with no visible alveoli (Figure 10 A and D), but at postnatal day 21 (P21) the acini show marked alveolation (Figure 10 B and E) with fully shaped, although somewhat smaller, alveoli compared with the adult animal (Figure 10 C and F). The size of the airspace is minimal at ~21 days in the rat, when bulk alveolation and septal thinning have just completed.

Based on this morphological information, we built an alveolar duct model (Figure 11). In the case of very immature lungs (e.g., 0- ~ ½ year old human infants, postnatal 7 days-old or earlier rodent babies), alveoli were too shallow (Figure 11 left) for alveolar recirculation to occur (Figure 12 left); but in the

Figure 11. An alveolar duct model of the developing lungs at various time points. (Adapted, with permission, from Semmler-Behnke, Kreyling, Schulz, Takenaka, Butler, Henry, & Tsuda, 2012)

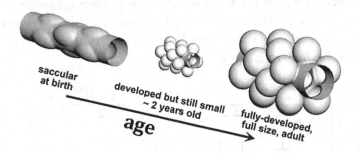

case of slightly older but still immature lungs (e.g., ~ ½-~ 2 years old human infants, postnatal from one week to 3 weeks rodent babies), alveoli were sufficiently deep (Figure 11 middle) to promote recirculation flow inside to the alveoli (Figure 12, middle). In the final stage of lung development (from human toddler, ~ 2 years old, to adult human, or postnatal rats older than 3 weeks to fully-matured adult rats), the shape of acinus does not change but the size increases. Similar to the 2 years old case, alveoli are deep enough (Figure 11 right) to allow recirculation flow to occur inside to the alveolus (Figure 12, right).

Exposing P7, P14, P21, P35 immature Wistar-Kyoto rats and fully-matured adult (P90<) rats to insoluble, radioactively labeled iridium (^{192}Ir) particles of 20 nm and 80 nm, we measured total deposition (Figure 12). We found that total deposition strongly depended on the age of the rats. Though the deposition was generally higher for 20-nm particles compared with 80-nm particles, due to their relatively higher intrinsic diffusivity, the deposition of both 20-nm and 80-nm particles peaked in 21-days-old rats. At

Figure 12. Flow patterns in the alveolar model of the developing lungs. Breathing patterns at various ages were also measured and use for the flow simulation. In awake, spontaneously breathing infant rats the tidal volume (VT), breathing frequency (f), and minute ventilation (MV = VT f) were found to scale allometrically with body weight (BW) to exponents of 1.06, −0.12, and 0.91, respectively. [Adapted, with permission, from Semmler-Behnke M, Kreyling, W.G., Schulz, H., Takenaka, S., Butler, J.P., Henry, F.S., & Tsuda, A. (2012)

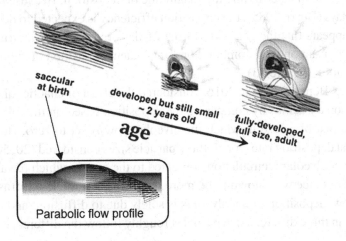

*Figure 13. Total deposition fraction vs. rat age measured immediately after exposure for inhaled 20- and 80-nm particles. Deposition of (Left) 20- and (Right) 80-nm particles peaks in 21-d-old rats, whose acini are largely alveolated already but are still small in size (n = 8 for each age group). n = 16 for age group; *P < 0.05; error bars indicate ± SD. Note that the five chosen age groups represent distinct stages of postnatal acinar structural development (Burri 1985). (Adapted, with permission, from Semmler-Behnke, Kreyling, Schulz, Takenaka, Butler, Henry, & Tsuda, 2012)*

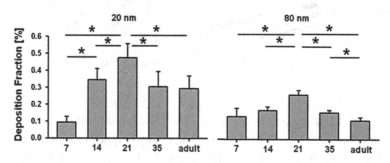

this age, the acini have just completed structural alveolation and septal thinning, and their shapes approximate those of the adult animal, although smaller in size (Figure 10 B and E vs. Figure 10 C and F). Thus, the alveoli at this age may be sufficiently deep to promote rotational flows, and consequent chaotic mixing, as was suggested by the corresponding alveolar shapes in our computational studies (Figure 12, Middle). This finding supports the idea that age-dependent changes in acinar fluid mechanics do indeed play a critical role in determining the fate of inhaled particles (Figure 13). In animals younger than 21 days, the acini have few, relatively shallow, alveoli. Airflows in such acini are shown in computational studies to be simpler and reversible, with a tongue-like Poiseuille flow pattern (Figure 12, Left; and inset). In addition to less-effective diffusional deposition due to the relatively large airspaces in animals younger than 21 days, the absence of chaotic mixing results in less flow-induced mixing. This finding is consistent with our observation of lower deposition fraction in animals younger than 21 days compared with older animals (Figure 13).

In rats of 21 days and older, the acini are fully alveolated, and therefore their airflow patterns are likely rotational and chaotic (Figure 12, Right). These chaotic flow patterns, as noted above, are important in enhancing deposition, but the size of each airspace, through which a particle is transported for deposition, also plays a role in determining the magnitude of deposition. Because alveolar size tends to increase after age 21 days (Burri, 1985), the deposition efficiency is expected to decrease after that age. Overall, therefore, it appears that the geometry of the 21-days-old rat's acinar structure, with its small but fully formed alveoli, is an optimal combination for efficient deposition of submicron particles, and results in a peak deposition (Figure 13).

In a numerical study, Henry & Tsuda, 2016, considered the effect of chaotic mixing on nanoparticle deposition in the pulmonary acinus by comparing the deposition based on the full solution of the flow in a model alveolus to that of a case in which the alveolar flow is set to zero. Henry & Tsuda, 2016, showed (Figure 14) that deposition rates for all three particle sizes considered (20, 50, 80nm) were much higher in the presence of alveolar recirculation compared to the case in which the alveolar flow was set to zero. Further, the difference was shown to be more significant for the less diffusive particles. In the case of no alveolar flow, deposition in the alveolus is solely due to diffusion; and thus, the differences in the deposition rates in three different size particles roughly follow the differences in their diffusivity.

Figure 14. Percentage of particles entering the alveolus that deposit on various regions of the septal surface in a fully developed alveolus (day 21) at generation 0 with and without (w/o) alveolar flow. Blue: deposition on the proximal septa; red: deposition on the primary septa; green: deposition on the distal septa. (Adapted, with permission, from Henry, & Tsuda, 2016)

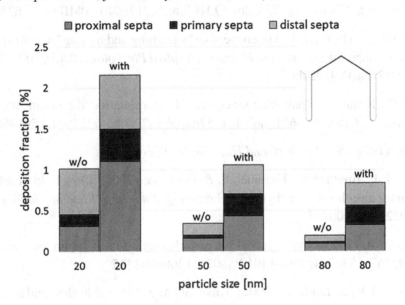

Conversely, in the case with alveolar recirculation, deposition in the alveolus appeared to be greatly enhanced by convective mixing, since the differences in the deposition rates between the three particle sizes did not correspond to the differences in their diffusivity.

SUMMARY

The rate of particle deposition measured experimentally by Heyder et al. (1988) could not be explained by any of the deposition mechanisms known at the time. We have demonstrated that the gas exchange region of the lung, which is necessarily alveolated to increase the surface area for efficient gas exchange, affords the required additional deposition mechanism; namely, chaotic mixing, which occurs inside the alveoli. While this mechanism may be small on an individual alveolus basis, the respiratory region of the lung, which accounts for more than 95% of lung volume, contains hundreds of millions of alveoli. Thus, the deposition cause by chaotic mixing in the gas exchange region of the lungs must plays a crucial role in the deposition of submicron particles, which represent the size range of many important particles; such as, cigarette smoke particles, inhaled bacterial particles, and possible therapeutic drug delivery particles.

REFERENCES

Bassingthwaighte, J. J., Liebovitch, L. S., & West, B. J. (1994). *Fractal Physiology*. Oxford University Press. doi:10.1007/978-1-4614-7572-9

Burri, P. H. (1985) Development and growth of the human lung. In Handbook of Physiology, Section 3: The Respiratory System (pp 1–46). William & Wilkins.

Burri, P. H., Dbaly, J., & Weibel, E. R. (1974). The postnatal growth of the rat lung. I. Morphometry. *The Anatomical Record, 178*(4), 711–730. doi:10.1002/ar.1091780405 PMID:4592625

Butler, J. P., & Tsuda, Λ. (1997). Effect of convective "stretching and folding" to aerosol mixing deep in the lung, assessed by approximate entropy. *Journal of Applied Physiology, 83*(3), 800–809. doi:10.1152/jappl.1997.83.3.800 PMID:9292466

Davies, C. N. (1972). Breathing of half-micron aerosols. II. Interpretation of experimental results. *Journal of Applied Physiology, 35*(5), 605–611. doi:10.1152/jappl.1972.32.5.601 PMID:5064587

Friedlander, S. K. (1977). *Smoke, Dust, and Haze*. Wiley Press.

Haber, S., Butler, J. P., Brenner, H., Emanuel, I., & Tsuda, A. (2000). Flow field in selfsimilar expansion on a pulmonary alveolus during rhythmical breathing. *Journal of Fluid Mechanics, 405*, 243–268. doi:10.1017/S0022112099007375

Haber, S., & Tsuda, A. (2006). Cyclic model for particle motion in the pulmonary acinus. *Journal of Fluid Mechanics, 567*, 157–184. doi:10.1017/S0022112006002345

Henry, F. S., Butler, J. P., & Tsuda, A. (2002). Kinematically irreversible flow and aerosol transport in the pulmonary acinus: A departure from classical dispersive transport. *Journal of Applied Physiology, 92*, 835–845. doi:10.1152/japplphysiol.00385.2001 PMID:11796699

Henry, F.S., Laine-Pearson, F.E., & Tsuda, A. (2009). Hamiltonian chaos in a model alveolus. *Journal of Biomechanical Engineering, 131*, 011006(1)–011006(7).

Henry, F. S., & Tsuda, A. (2016). Onset of alveolar recirculation in the developing lungs and its consequence on nanoparticle deposition in the pulmonary acinus. *Journal of Applied Physiology, 120*(1), 38–54. doi:10.1152/japplphysiol.01161.2014 PMID:26494453

Heyder, J. J. D., Blanchard, J. D., Feldman, H. A., & Brain, J. D. (1988). Convective mixing in human respiratory tract: Estimates with aerosol boli. *Journal of Applied Physiology, 64*(3), 1273–1278. doi:10.1152/jappl.1988.64.3.1273 PMID:3366742

Karl, A., Henry, F. S., & Tsuda, A. (2004). Low Reynolds number viscous flow in an alveolated duct. *Journal of Biomechanical Engineering, 126*(4), 13–19. doi:10.1115/1.1784476 PMID:15543859

Laine-Pearson, F. E., & Hydon, P. E. (2006). Particle transport in a moving corner. *Journal of Fluid Mechanics, 559*, 379–390. doi:10.1017/S0022112006009967

Oberdörster, G., Stone, V., & Donaldson, K. (2007). Toxicology of nanoparticles: A historical perspective. *Nanotoxicology, 1*(1), 2–25. doi:10.1080/17435390701314761

Ottino, J. M. (1989). *The Kinematics of mixing: Stretching, Chaos, and Transport*. Cambridge University Press.

Semmler-Behnke, M., Kreyling, W. G., Schulz, H., Takenaka, S., Butler, J. P., Henry, F. S., & Tsuda, A. (2012). Nanoparticle Delivery in Infant Lungs. *Proceedings of the National Academy of Sciences of the United States of America*, *109*(13), 5092–5097. doi:10.1073/pnas.1119339109 PMID:22411799

Tabor, M. (1989). *Chaos and integrability in nonlinear dynamics*. Wiley Press.

Taylor, G. I. (1960). *Low Reynolds Number Flow (16 mm Film)*. Educational Services Inc.

Tsuda, A., Henry, F. S., & Butler, J. P. (1995). Chaotic mixing of alveolated duct flow in rhythmically expanding pulmonary acinus. *Journal of Applied Physiology*, *79*(3), 1055–1063. doi:10.1152/jappl.1995.79.3.1055 PMID:8567502

Tsuda, A., Henry, F. S., & Butler, J. P. (2013). Particle transport and deposition: Basic physics of particle kinetics. *Comprehensive Physiology*, *3*, 1437–1471. doi:10.1002/cphy.c100085 PMID:24265235

Tsuda, A., Laine-Pearson, F. E., & Hydon, P. E. (2011). Why Chaotic mixing of particles is inevitable in the deep lung. *Journal of Theoretical Biology*, *286*, 57–66. doi:10.1016/j.jtbi.2011.06.038 PMID:21801733

Tsuda, A., Rogers, R. A., Hydon, P. E., & Butler, J. P. (2002). Chaotic mixing deep in the lung. *Proceedings of the National Academy of Sciences of the United States of America*, *99*(15), 10173–10178. doi:10.1073/pnas.102318299 PMID:12119385

Weibel, E. R. (1984). *The pathway for oxygen-structure and function in the mammalian respiratory system*. Harvard University Press.

West, J. B. (2012). *Respiratory Physiology: The essentials* (4th ed.). William & Wilkins.

Chapter 12
Recommender Systems in Digital Libraries Using Artificial Intelligence and Machine Learning:
A Proposal to Create Automated Links Between Different Articles Dealing With Similar Topics

Namik Delilovic
https://orcid.org/0000-0002-3955-8816
Graz University of Technology, Austria

ABSTRACT

Searching for contents in present digital libraries is still very primitive; most websites provide a search field where users can enter information such as book title, author name, or terms they expect to be found in the book. Some platforms provide advanced search options, which allow the users to narrow the search results by specific parameters such as year, author name, publisher, and similar. Currently, when users find a book which might be of interest to them, this search process ends; only a full-text search or references at the end of the book may provide some additional pointers. In this chapter, the author is going to give an example of how a user could permanently get recommendations for additional contents even while reading the article, using present machine learning and artificial intelligence techniques.

INTRODUCTION

Natural Language Processing (NLP) is not a term invented recently. As noted by (Liddy, 2001), research already started in the late 40s in the form of machine translation, which was used to encipher enemy messages. Early machine translation used primitive dictionary look-ups and some word reordering

DOI: 10.4018/978-1-7998-7156-9.ch012

techniques to fit the grammar of the target language. However, after Chomsky's publication *Syntactic Structures,* which made the fields of linguistic and machine translations closer to each other, other application emerged, such as speech recognition. Today when we speak about NLP, we usually refer to it as a discipline of artificial intelligence, and indeed the final goal of NLP is Natural Language Understanding (NLU). The objectives of NLU, as stated by (Liddy, 2001), are:

1. Paraphrase an input text
2. Translate the text into another language
3. Answer questions about the contents of the text
4. Draw inferences from the text

While the increase of memory and processing power led to the rapid development of machine learning (ML) supported Natural Language Processing (NLP) techniques, the ever-increasing amount of data found on the web and technologies which provide faster internet speed (Jelena, 2020) are crucial for the advance of such techniques. This is also the reason the Austria-Forum platform (*Austria-Forum)* which holds over 1.2 million objects in the form of web-books (digital books), documents, images and other multimedia objects is essential for the author's experiments and research. After analysing the usage behaviour of the Austria-Forum users, the author realised that most of the readers (87.34%) come directly from the Google search engine. The different channels and their values are shown in the pie chart of Figure 1. Combining this information with the average number of users from the last 30 days (right plot in Figure 1) the author concludes that out of 7000 daily users, 6000 come from the Google search engine. Even though the platform providers are happy for any channel which leads the user to the content they offer, the fact that the user is utilising the limited Google search option is not satisfying. In section CURRENT STATE the author is going to examine the current state of the Austria-Forum platform and how the users find new contents using essential tools such as navigation, search and browsing, in section FIRST ATTEMPTS the author presents the first version of the linker tool which automatically suggests links for words found in articles. This tool is simple in its implementation and therefore, in section FUTURE IMPLEMENTATIONS the author analyses some current machine learning techniques and proposes a new implementation for the linker tool and finally, in section EVALUATION the author examines the evaluation possibilities for the results which the new linker implementation will provide.

Figure 1. Austria-Forum top channels (left pie chart), number of users per day (right plot) and the average number of users from the last month (right, dashed line)

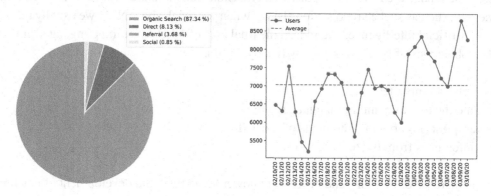

CURRENT STATE

The book *Digitale Bibliotheken* (Endres & Fellner, 2000), presents three different information search and retrieval techniques: navigation, search and browsing. There is also a potential fourth option called Software-Agents and which is related to Artificial Intelligence and Machine Learning. The current state of Austria-Forum also follows this categorisation and provides the first three options which the author is going to describe in the following subsections. The fourth option (Software-Agents) is especially interesting in combination with the Browsing option (see subsection Browsing), which the author partially implemented in Austria-Forum (see section FIRST ATTEMPTS).

NAVIGATION

As mentioned before, there are several ways for a user to find content on the Austria-Forum platform. The most usual method is via Google search, but lacking any control over this tool, it is not relevant for the author's current research. The second most common way is using the entry page of Austria-Forum (see Figure 2); it provides different categories and uses a custom classification schema. In Figure 3 the reader can see the subcategories of the nature category; each of them leads to an index page of the topics belonging to these subcategories (see Figure 4).

Besides the search field, topic categorisation is the most common way for user-navigation in digital libraries and online encyclopaedias such as (*Britannica; Encyclopedia.Com; Springer*). As mentioned before Austria-Forum does not strictly use a hierarchical order to store the articles; the reader can find the same article in multiple categories and subcategories. However, only one physical copy exists on the server (for more details see (Delilovic et al., 2020)). This cross-linking is also the primary reason the platform provider decided against using a standardised classification schema such as the Dewey Decimal Classification, which organizes libraries into distinct classes, divisions and sections (see (Dewey, 1876)).

Figure 2. Austria-Forum entry page

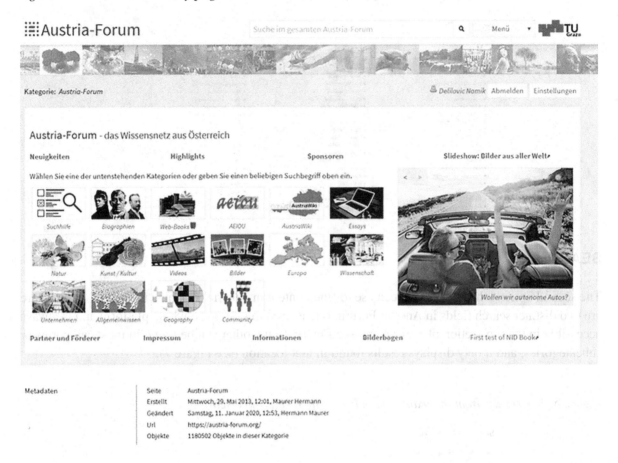

Figure 3. Subcategories inside the Nature category

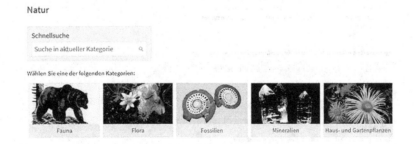

Figure 4. Topic index of the flora subcategory in alphabetical order

SEARCHING

The second option which the reader can use to find content in Austria-Forum is the search field. There are two distinct search fields in Austria-Forum; one is used to search the whole platform and is always accessible in the top section of every page (see Figure 2), the other can be found in most categories or subcategories, and it only displays results found in that location (see Figure 7).

Figure 5. The results from the main search field with a relevance score

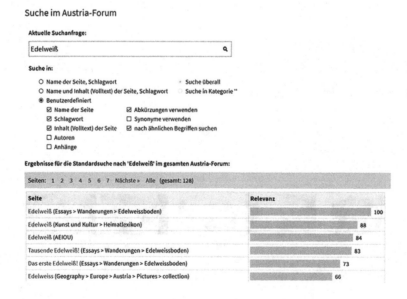

After entering a search term in the main search field, the platform provides the user with a list of search results. A relevance score is attached to each result, which shows how much the search result is relevant in correspondence to the search input (see Figure 5). The main search field allows misspelled entries; this feature is suitable if the user makes some typing mistakes or if the searched topic contains special letters which are not typed by the user. It is possible to enforce a stricter search; if the user surrounds the search term with apostrophes, then only search results which contain the exact search term are retrieved. It is worth to note here that the main search field uses the URL of the page, title, and metadata, which is assigned to each article and web-book inside Austria-Forum, to find the content.

Figure 6. Web-Book Metadata

Title:	Short-Term Load Forecasting by Artificial Intelligent Technologies
Authors:	Wei-Chiang Hong Ming-Wei Li Guo-Feng Fan
Editor:	MDPI
Location:	Basel
Date:	2019
Language:	English
License:	(cc) BY CC BY 4.0
ISBN:	978-3-03897-583-0
Size:	17.0 x 24.4 cm
Pages:	448
Keywords:	Scheduling Problems in Logistics, Transport, Timetabling, Sports, Healthcare, Engineering, Energy Management
Category:	Informatik

Figure 7. Live search results from the Flora category

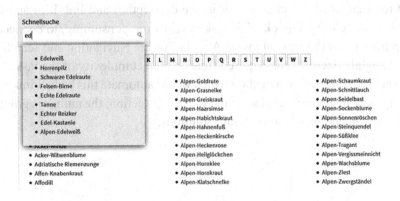

In Figure 6, the reader can see an example of a web-book's metadata file and the information it contains. In Figure 5, the reader can see the advance search options, which give the user the ability to specify which metadata fields should be used for the search, or the ability to search inside the articles/web-books (full-text search). As said before there is another search field visible in most categories or subcategories, it only searches in that location and does not contain any advance search capabilities; also, the input cannot contain typing errors. This search field shows the results in real-time as the user types (see Figure 7).

BROWSING

The term browsing is closely related to hyperlinks which are texts containing links to other textual objects and hypermedia which are links to multimedia objects such as audio, video (Endres & Fellner, 2000) (in this paper they are called links). Links are used every day, and the web without links would be unimaginable. The author of the opinion that browsing as a way of information retrieval is vastly underestimated and not brought to its full potential. Compared to searching, in browsing, users are not required to do any additional tasks, using links as a primitive recommender system, users only decided if they are interested in the recommendation or not. Browsing makes it possible for users to stumble upon content in which they have an interest but have not been aware of it before. The particular issue of information retrieval was already asked around 400 BC by Socrates' student Meno:

How will you enquire, Socrates, into that which you do not know? What will you put forth as the subject of your enquiry? And if you find out what you want, how will you ever know that this is the thing that you did not know? (Endres & Fellner, 2000).

Luckily, browsing might today be the solution for all of Meno's questions mentioned before. There are some potential and realistic issues with browsing, so that for example too many recommendations/links can distract the user (Delilovic et al., 2020) or that wrong recommendation can quickly lead to a frustrated user (Twidale et al., 2008).

Austria-Forum also uses links; they are mostly manually added. One of the major tasks in Austria-Forum is to find relevant words in an article or image description and link it to an existing category, subcategory, related article or web-book. This task is very time-consuming, to connect the words, it is necessary to keep track of all the content inside Austria-Forum. Navigation and search options are also used, but they just slightly decrease the required time and the complexity of the task.

Therefore, the author searched for a method which would automate this task of linking words to other related topics using existing methodologies. In the following section, the author is going to describe the first attempts to tackle this issue and some future solutions.

FIRST ATTEMPTS

In the Browsing subsection, the author mentioned the idea to automate link creation. The benefit of Austria-Forum is that most of the content is locally present, and researchers can for sure rely on its availability (compared to external links which might disappear overnight). On the other side, the challenge is that the content provided in Austria-Forum is not only in textual form but diverse; books, images, videos, user comments, generated geography statistics are only some of these. The author had to narrow the automation to a specific part of the platform. For the first step, the author took the web-books (self-developed implementation of digital books, for more see (Maurer et al., 2019)), and tried to make an automated link suggestion for words found in the books, to the existing topics. These are not complex links, as they only point to a pre-defined list of topics. In the beginning, all of them were still manually created. However, using a simple approach (described in the following text), at least some fundamental tasks have been automated.

Figure 8 shows an overview of the linker's administrator interface. On the far left, the reader can see the topic list, which the tool uses to link with words inside the book. In the middle section, the reader can see the web-book search field with some filtering options; this can find the book on which the automated links should be created and the last section shows the linker-suggested links.

Figure 8. Linker overview

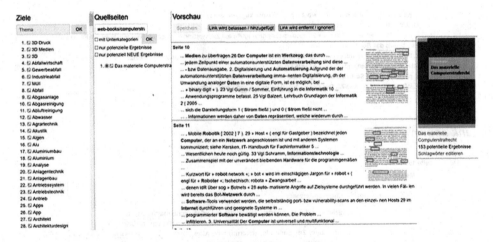

As mentioned before, the far-right section shows the word with potential links; each site also contains a miniaturised representation of the page in the book (see Figure 9).

The linker first analyses the web-book and checks if the words correspond to a provided topic, afterwards, hovering over a miniaturised page, the administrator gets to the place in which he can approve or decline a suggested link, see Figure 10. All link suggestions are per default flagged as declined, all other suggestions which are flagged as accepted, are applied after pressing the save button.

The second step was to add the possibility to interlink any category or subcategory with any article or web-book. In Figure 11, the reader can see an example where the category *biography* is selected as the target category (left side). All articles which contain potential links are displayed in the middle section, in this case, Strauß Johan is selected. Similar to the previous example, the right side shows the link recommendation, which the administrator can either accept or decline. The reader should not get confused that the biography category is in this example at the same time the target and source-destination; the author just took this example, as it is more likely that a biography article will contain other biographies. However arbitrary categories are possible.

Figure 9. Right section of the Linker tool

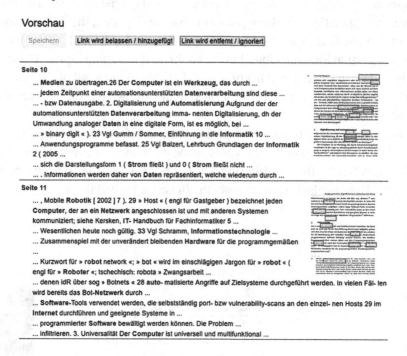

Figure 10. Link approval

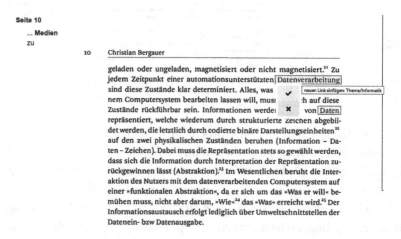

This simple tool makes it possible to interlink existing content and thus provide users with additional suggestions which might interest them. However, the main issue was that it added too many links for each word, making the article unreadable. The problem has been solved by linking only terms in which their potential link destination would not be only the definition of that term (Delilovic et al., 2020).

In the following section, the author proposes an alternative approach for the automated linking process using conventional machine learning techniques.

Figure 11. Linking the biography category with a biography article

FUTURE IMPLEMENTATIONS

There are endless possibilities to improve the linker. However, the focus will be on the goals which on one side will benefit the content provider and their readers, and on the other, they will take minimal time to implement. The following is a list of the base requirements of the future linker:

- **Defined Scope:** Austria-Forum uses Apache JSPWiki (*Apache JSPWiki*) as its base framework, so the articles are stored as *text* files on the server. Text files make any machine learning tasks much more straightforward than handling several format types distributed across the Internet, thus making their availability unreliable. The best place for the next linker will be in the (still under development) new digital library called NID (Networked Interactive Digital Books) which uses the IIIF (International Image Interoperability Framework) as it base. A detailed working principle of the NIDs and the underlying IIIF is described in (Zaka et al., 2020). For this case, it suffices to understand that the future NIDs will provide an environment where different multimedia objects (books, documents, images and others) from various internet sources will be available in a well-defined and structured order. A framework which ensures a specific data structure such as the IIIF is best suited for ML and AI tools. To show that such a scenario is not merely a theory but very realistic, the author recommends reading about an already implemented page classification algorithm which uses ML and the IIIF (Boros et al., 2019).
- **Full Automation:** to be functional, the linker should not require any (or only minimal) inputs. The goal is to save administration time for the cost of less customisation and precision but still not underperforming (e.g. suggesting too many wrong links).
- **Explicit User Information Extraction**: this technique requires gathering direct information from the user. Most of the users in Austria-Forum are browsing anonymously (are not registered),

which makes implicit recommendation obsolete. Using immediate feedback from the user makes it possible to set the links based on their interests dynamically. If, for example, the users read an article about electric cars, they might be more interested in topics such as safety and legal issues, then in the technology behind it (Nemes & Mester, 2017). Explicit information extraction is not always a simple task as users are often not aware of their interests, or are not willing to disclose their interests to the platform due to privacy reasons (Haruna et al., 2017).

- **Context-Aware:** to make intelligent recommendations, the linker should analyse the content inside the articles/web-books. Instead of using specific categories or subcategories, one could switch to a more abstract/uniform model from which all other models are derived (Albini et al., 2019). Context-awareness is often achieved using correlation; this can lead to wrong recommendations if not correctly implemented (Delilovic & Maurer, 2019a).
- **Evaluation**: it should be possible to measure the linker's performance, namely how well it suggests links. As mentioned before, too many wrong link suggestions can lead to user frustration. Having the right evaluation data can help to prevent or widespread such a scenario, and the data can help to make further improvements.

From the list, the reader can see that even when trying to keep the goals as simple as possible, the implementation is still complicated. How to implement a useful recommender system when the users are anonymous? One possibility could be to use cookies to identify users, but they do not represent the user's explicit approval to track their behaviour and probably most users would reject them if they knew their usage (Kristol, 2001). Other methods such as tracking pixels (*Ryte*) or browser fingerprinting (*Electronic Frontier Foundation*) are a grave intrusion into the user's privacy and therefore, out of scope (there is probably a good reason why in the last 15 years, at least 500 English books have been published on the privacy subject (Maurer & Delilovic, 2020)). The way the author tries to handle this issue is to abstract all users and look at them as a single entity. Any future learning algorithms will be applied to this user. An excellent working example of such an algorithm can be observed in the Obelix system, which gathers various page information such as access count, engagement time, bookmarks, page prints, and similar, to achieve an accurate page ranking/recommendation (Knezevic et al., 2000).

This method of user abstraction has many limitations. However, it still allows to apply some user-centric algorithms and not only focus on algorithms which analyse the semantics of content such as the Content-based recommender system (CBRS) explained in the next subsection.

CONTENT-BASED RECOMMENDER SYSTEMS (CBRS)

As mentioned by (Ricci et al., 2015):

Content-based recommender systems (CBRSs) rely on items and user descriptions (content) to build item representations and user profiles to suggest an item similar to those a target user already liked in the past.

This definition perfectly fits into the new linker implementation as on one side; the primary focus relies on content that has to be interlinked using some pre-defined user settings and learning mechanisms gained from simple user feedback. In contrast, another useful feature of CBRS is that it borrows a lot of Natural Language Processing (NLP) mechanisms to use deep content analytics. That is why CBRS is essential for the linker as the idea is to switch from a topic-based to content-based interlinking; not only should it link words to specific topics, but entire articles.

There are two approaches to implement such a recommender system:

- **Top-Down:** focuses on the linguistic understanding of items, similar to how humans analyse the meaning of documents in their natural language.
- **Bottom-Up:** which focuses on the relationship between words and documents in a high-dimensional vector space, this means that each point in the vector space represents a word/text. Analysing the distance between the points, one can decide which articles/words are more related and make an appropriate suggestion to the user (Ricci et al., 2015).

The bottom-up approach uses unsupervised mechanisms (Ricci et al., 2015) to understand the semantics of word/articles and their relationship, thus making it the optimal choice for our future linker tool as it does not require any further actions by the editorial team.

Discriminative Models

To link a specific word in an article of Austria-Forum, the author proposes the use of discriminative models. Discriminative Models (DM) are a part of the bottom-up semantic approach, according to which:

Words that occur in the same context tend to have similar meanings (Ricci et al., 2015).

Applied to the linker, this means if a user reads an article about batteries, all other articles which have the word batteries might interest the user, the same is valid for words within the article. How should the linker decide which words should be analysed? One possibility would be to use a static fill-out form.

To find similarities between documents and words in an unsupervised environment, the author proposes the usage of cosine similarity measures. This method represents each term-context matrix as a vector and measuring the angle between two vectors can determine the relatedness between them. As stated by (Ricci et al., 2015), the major drawback of this method is the so-called *curse of dimensionality,* which occurs when performing a more detailed analysis. This issue will undoubtedly be present in Austria-Forum as it contains thousands of articles which have over 20 sentences; meaning that the dimension of the vector space would be 20 times the one using a classical term-document matrix.

This problem can be solved by using dimensional reduction techniques such as Latent Semantic Indexing (LSI) which transforms a high dimensional space into a low dimensional space (Ricci et al., 2015). However, the dimensional reduction technique is out of scope in this chapter.

EVALUATION

Implementing the new linker without tools to test its performance is of little value. There are two kinds of experiments which can help to test a particular recommender system: online and offline experiments. The offline experiments rely on a few test-subjects which execute a pre-defined set of experiments and are physically close to the observer. Observing the interaction with the system and asking questions can yield valuable data in terms of user satisfaction, quality of recommendation, and others. Offline experiments also have their negative sides: they are expensive and time-consuming, so it is only possible to use a few test-subjects. As the test-subjects are aware of the experiment, the results are often biased and not accurate as online experiments. Fortunately, Austria-Forum has a few thousand users per day, and as said before, most of them are anonymous (unregistered), which makes online experiments a real and cost-effective opportunity. The downside of online experiments is that if done poorly, they can lead to user frustration, thus losing confidence and trust. The optimal approach, according to (Ricci et al., 2015), is to use a combination of offline and online experiments. The first stage is to observe and measure the user interaction on a small number of test subjects (offline experiments) and only proceed to online experiments (with a bigger number of randomly selected users) if the evaluation yields positive results. The tool can be safely deployed for all users if both experiments yield positive results. Additional safety measures such as feedback button (Delilovic & Maurer, 2019b) can be added to respond fast to the users' questions and concerns.

The main experiment should be based on the comparison between the old and new linker tool. To achieve this goal, one has to evaluate both versions with the same set of tests and measures. The primary assumption is that results of offline experiments are the same or similar to results done in a live environment, with the only difference being a possibility to ask the test-subject additional questions explicitly. For this purpose, evaluation attributes from (Ricci et al., 2015) can be adapted and used to develop the linker tool for Austria-Forum:

- **Prediction Accuracy:** how relevant are the link suggestions for the user, thus measuring the number of consumed links and their engagement time. In offline experiments, one can explicitly ask the user about the link relevance.
- **Coverage:** is user-independent and measures the number of suggested topics. The value depends on the user's pre-defined area of interest and the ability of the linker to find relevance within different topics. The coverage evaluation should be evaluated hand in hand with the accuracy factor as full coverage with a small prediction accuracy is not desired.
- **Confidence:** if the linker finds multiple links as potential recommendations, only the one with the best confidence will be visible to the user (Figure 5 shows similar ordering by relevance). The confidence factor should also be part of the offline evaluation process; comparing the user's preferred recommendation list with the linker's confidence list can provide a clear picture of the confidence calculation precision.
- **Trust:** can be determined in offline experiments by directly asking the user whether the recommendation is reasonable. In contrast, for online experiments, the number of followed recommendation (clicked links) can be a valid indicator.
- **Novelty:** depends on the number of recommendations that were not known to the user. This factor is mostly suitable for offline experiments.
- **Serendipity:** depends on the number of recommendations which initiates a *surprise effect* in the user. While an article might already be known to the user, the fact that it is related to the current article might still come as a surprise. In offline experiments, the users can be asked if a recommendation was surprising. In contrast, for online experiments, the geometrical distance between two articles can be used: a recommendation is surprising if the vector representation of two articles is relatively far apart but still consumed (clicked).

- **Diversity:** is the opposite of similarity, the recommender (in case of the linker) presents the user with results which are not directly associated. Such recommendations can lead to positive results but often come at the expense of accuracy. As the goal is to keep the linker simple as possible, such recommendations are obsolete and therefore, out of scope.

- **Utility:** this measurement factor depends on the number of recommendations, which leads to an increase in revenue. Austria-Forum is not revenue driven, all the content is freely available to everyone, and therefore this factor can be excluded for the evaluation.

- **Risk:** is a measurement factor mostly used within platforms which bear a specific risk for the user such as stock markets and is not of much interest for this chapter.

- **Robustness:** is mostly used in recommender systems where the user can influence the recommendation, such as rating items only to increase their ranking. While the users in Austria-Forum can write articles, only articles which have already been approved will be analysed. However, this factor is something which should be considered for future implementation when user-contributed articles get incorporated into the recommender analysis.

- **Privacy:** in our previous text, the author already mentioned that most users in Austria-Forum are not registered and that all users are to be seen as a single abstracted entity. This technique will undoubtedly have adverse effects on the accuracy of the system, but on the other side, it will also mitigate any privacy-related issues.

- **Adaptability:** this measurement depends on the linker's ability to respond to fast-changing environments such as news portals as their content is changing hourly. While one cannot exclude the importance of this measurement, it is still not relevant for this chapter.

- **Scalability:** the ability of the recommender system to scale with an increasing number of items and users is called scalability. Recommender tools which have to analyse more data also require more computation power and memory. In offline experiments, one can ask the test-subjects about their satisfaction with the response time of the platform. In online experiments, one can try to keep within the maximum accepted load time for commercial web pages, which is between 6 or 12 seconds (Ritchie & Roast, 2001). The user read-flow will not be interrupted if one can split the website load-time from the recommender load-time (Austria-Forum's average website load-time is 1 second (*Google Analytics)*). The separation can be achieved using a *generate recommendation* button followed by a *processing* indicator. The final goal is to synchronise the recommender load-time with the current web page load-time.

CONCLUSION

Based on the author's experience with the Austria-Forum information platform, it can be concluded that search and navigation as the primary tools to find multimedia content in digital libraries are not sufficient. With the advance of artificial intelligence and machine learning techniques, more sophisticated approaches such as automated recommender systems have become possible. In this chapter, the author first described a simple link-recommender tool used in the Austria-Forum information platform. Then some future implementation possibilities for the recommender tool have been analysed. They would utilise current machine learning and artificial intelligence techniques. For this task, first the most essential features which the recommender tool must include have been defined. Even those relatively simple goals face several issues. User privacy, scalability, performance, precision and evaluation are only some constraints which must be tackled before the implementation can begin. To satisfy the pre-defined goals, a combination of Content-Based Recommender Systems (CBRS) and a single abstracted user profile have been suggested. Within CBRS, the author proposed the usage of Discriminative Models as they can find the relationship between words and articles, independent of user fingerprints, thus preserving the privacy of users. To achieve better results, user-provided information, such as the current area of interest, can also be utilised. Finally, the author analysed the evaluation possibilities for the future recommender tool. To avoid user dissatisfaction, the combination of offline and online experiments has been proposed. First, a small number of locally available test-subjects would evaluate the tool (offline experiments), and online experiments would only be performed if the offline experiments have yielded positive results.

Combining *implantation* as our primary method of innovation *(Blagojević et al., 2017)* with the proposed AI and ML-based techniques will hopefully lead to a paradigm shift. The mentioned benefits are just the tip of the iceberg. However, after the first results, the author intends to expand to areas such as sentiment analysis, plagiarism tools, neural networks, and others.

ACKNOWLEDGMENT

The author would like to thank Em.Univ.-Prof. Dr.phil. Hermann Maurer for passing on his knowledge, the valuable inputs and all the long but joyful discussions without which this work would not have been possible. Special thanks to Professor Sanela Cejvan Ahmic for proofreading this chapter and thus making it more pleasant to read.

REFERENCES

Albini, A., Mester, G., & Iantovics, L. B. (2019). Unified Aspect Search Algorithm. *Interdisciplinary Description of Complex Systems*, *17*(1), 20–25. doi:10.7906/indecs.17.1.4

Apache JSPWiki. (n.d.). https://jspwiki.apache.org/

Austria-Forum. (n.d.). https://austria-forum.org

Blagojević, V., Bojić, D., Bojović, M., Cvetanović, M., Đorđević, J., Đurđević, Đ., Furlan, B., Gajin, S., Jovanović, Z., Milićev, D., Milutinović, V., Nikolić, B., Protić, J., Punt, M., Radivojević, Z., Stanisavljević, Ž., Stojanović, S., Tartalja, I., Tomašević, M., & Vuletić, P. (2017). A Systematic Approach to Generation of New Ideas for PhD Research in Computing. In A. R. Hurson & V. Milutinović (Eds.), Advances in Computers: Vol. 104. Creativity in computing and dataflow super computing (Vol. 104, pp. 1–31). Academic Press. doi:10.1016/bs.adcom.2016.09.001

Boros, E. E., Toumi, A., Rouchet, E., Abadie, B., Stutzmann, D., & Kermorvant, C. (2019). *Automatic page classification in a large collection of manuscripts based on the International Image Interoperability Framework*. IEEE. https://www.britannica.com/

Delilovic, N., Ebner, M., Maurer, H., & Zaka, B. (2020). Experiences Based on a Major Information Server. *IPSI BgD Transactions on Internet Research*, *16*(1), 68–75.

Delilovic, N., & Maurer, H. (2019a). *A Critical Discussion of Some Current and Future Developments of IT*. Springer International Publishing., doi:10.1007/978-3-030-28005-5_1

Delilovic, N., & Maurer, H. (2019b). A Note Concerning Feedback and Queries for Web Pages. *Journal of Universal Computer Science*, 25(7), 733–739. doi:10.3217/jucs-025-07-0733

Dewey, M. (1876). *A Classification and Subject Index for Cataloguing and Arranging the Books and Pamphlets of a Library*. Kingsport Press, Inc. https://panopticlick.eff.org/

encyclopedia.com. (n.d.). https://www.encyclopedia.com

Endres, A., & Fellner, D. W. (2000). *Digitale Bibliotheken: Informatik-Lösungen für globale Wissens-märkte*. dpunkt-Verlag. https://analytics.google.com/

Haruna, K., Akmar Ismail, M., Suhendroyono, S., Damiasih, D., Pierewan, A., Chiroma, H., & Herawan, T. (2017). Context-Aware Recommender System: A Review of Recent Developmental Process and Future Research Direction. *Applied Sciences (Basel, Switzerland)*, 7(12), 1211. Advance online publication. doi:10.3390/app7121211

Jelena, P. (2020). *5G i samovozeći automobili: XXVI Skup Trendovi razvoja: "Inovacije u modernom obrazovanju"*. Academic Press.

Knezevic, P., Radnovic, B., Nikolic, N., Jovanovic, T., Milanov, D., Nikolic, M., Milutinovic, V., Casselman, S., & Schewel, J. (2000). The architecture of the Obelix-an improved Internet search engine. In R. H. Sprague (Ed.), *Proceedings of the 33rd annual Hawaii international conference on system sciences* (p. 11). IEEE Comput. Soc. 10.1109/HICSS.2000.926873

Kristol, D. M. (2001). HTTP Cookies. *ACM Transactions on Internet Technology*, 1(2), 151–198. doi:10.1145/502152.502153

Liddy, E. D. (2001). *Natural language processing: Encyclopedia of Library and Information Science* (2nd ed.). Marcel Decker, Inc.

Maurer, H., & Delilovic, N. (2020). Ein kritischer Spaziergang durch das Internet. In *Enlightenment Today* (pp. 221–250). Academia Verlag., doi:10.5771/9783896658647-221

Maurer, H., Delilovic, N., & Zaka, B. (2019). Libraries of Interactive Books as Powerful Tool for Information Communication. In *Proceedings of EdMedia + Innovate Learning 2019* (pp. 1353–1359). Association for the Advancement of Computing in Education (AACE). https://www.learntechlib.org/p/210270

Nemes, A., & Mester, G. (2017). Unconstrained evolutionary and gradient descent-based tuning of fuzzy-partitions for UAV dynamic modeling. *FME Transactions*, 45(1), 1–8. doi:10.5937/fmet1701001N

Ricci, F., Rokach, L., & Shapira, B. (2015). *Recommender Systems Handbook*. doi:10.1007/978-1-4899-7637-6

Ritchie, I., & Roast, C. (2001). *Performance, Usability and the Web: Proceedings of the 34th Annual Hawaii International Conference on System Sciences (HICSS-34)* (vol. 5). IEEE Computer Society. https://en.ryte.com/wiki/Tracking_Pixel

Springer. https://www.springer.com/

Twidale, M. B., Gruzd, A. A., & Nichols, D. M. (2008). Writing in the library: Exploring tighter integration of digital library use with the writing process. *Information Processing & Management*, *44*(2), 558–580. doi:10.1016/j.ipm.2007.05.010

Zaka, B., Maurer, H., & Delilovic, N. (2020). Investigating Interaction Activities in Digital Libraries: The Networked Interactive Digital Books Project. *IPSI BgD Transactions on Internet Research*, *16*(1), 75–82.

Chapter 13
Unified Modeling for Emulating Electric Energy Systems:
Toward Digital Twin That Might Work

Marija Ilic
Massachusetts Institute of Technology, USA

Rupamathi Jaddivada
Massachusetts Institute of Technology, USA

Assefaw Gebremedhin
Washington State University, USA

ABSTRACT

Large-scale computing, including machine learning (MI) and AI, offer a great promise in enabling sustainability and resiliency of electric energy systems. At present, however, there is no standardized framework for systematic modeling and simulation of system response over time to different continuous- and discrete-time events and/or changes in equipment status. As a result, there is generally a poor understanding of the effects of candidate technologies on the quality and cost of electric energy services. In this chapter, the authors discuss a unified, physically intuitive multi-layered modeling of system components and their mutual dynamic interactions. The fundamental concept underlying this modeling is the notion of interaction variables whose definition directly lends itself to capturing modular structure needed to manage complexity. As a direct result, the same modeling approach defines an information exchange structure between different system layers, and hence can be used to establish structure for the design of a dedicated computational architecture, including AI methods.

DOI: 10.4018/978-1-7998-7156-9.ch013

INTRODUCTION

This chapter is motivated by a central recognition: electric energy systems could have much better performance than what is achieved today if they are enabled by rich data (appropriately collected and processed) and on-line decision-making based on learning from history and predictions. Taking this recognition a step further, we argue that novel approaches are needed for next generation modeling and computing for managing complex on-going major organizational and technological changes. Clearly, this should not be done from scratch, since there have been major investments in current information technology by entities such as the Pennsylvania-Jersey-Maryland (PJM) independent system operator (ISO), estimated at $800 million (Boston, 2020). This makes it even harder to move forward with the next generation Supervisory Control and Data Acquisition (SCADA) system (Ilic, 2010). An additional subtle challenge comes from the need to almost instantaneously balance supply and demand. This means supporting control and decision making for "guaranteed" Quality of Service (QoS), which is in sharp contrast with Internet protocols where targeting "best efforts" is sufficient. Imagine having to operate a system like Puerto Rico's during a hurricane or an earthquake, when lots of electric system equipment is damaged and disconnected. It is crucial to have a flexible digital twin for simulating such complex systems, both in support of autonomous self-adaptation to the changing conditions and for assessing impact of previously unused technologies and system disturbances, such as intermittent power. This chapter is written with such challenges and opportunities in mind.

Background and History

Computing and simulations in electric power systems enjoy a long history. Generally speaking however, the approach has been rather piece-meal software development for basic applications and computational tasks, such as state estimation (Clements et al., 1981), power flow analysis in a large grid (Stott, 1974), optimal power dispatch for minimizing generation fuel cost when supplying predicted demand (Stott et al., 2009), short circuit analysis (Zhang et al., 1995), and numerical simulation of system response to sudden large equipment failures (Pavella and Murthy, 1994). All of these applications and tasks are used in a feed-forward way with the human-in-the-loop, while relying on local embedded automated feedback to ensure stable and feasible dynamic response in near real-time.

In the early 1970's, utilities worldwide begun to experience major widespread blackouts, and this called for more reliance on computing. These needs motivated active R&D on large-scale numerical methods, such as solving sparse matrix problems (Tinney et al., 1985; Rose, 2012), waveform relaxation for numerical integration of multi-rate differential equations (Ilic et al., 1987), small-signal stability analysis (Verghese et al., 1982) and, more generally, parallel computing for large-scale systems (Betancourt and Alvarado, 1986). In turn, these efforts resulted in computer applications used routinely by control centers for dispatching generation to supply predicted power demand (Fu and Shahidehpour, 2007; Stott, 1974; Cvijic et al., 2018). However, emulation of system dynamics has only been done in an off-line mode for select deterministic scenarios because centralized numerical integration of high-order differential-algebraic equations (DAEs) cannot be done in near real-time (Pavella and Murthy, 1994; Crow and Ilic, 1994). Only a handful of forward-looking utilities have designed a hybrid analog-digital simulators of their own power systems for the purposes of better understanding their performance, particularly during abnormal conditions, and also for simulating potential of system control and protection (Do et al., 2001; Doi et al., 1990).

Preview of Main Contributions

The electric energy ecosystem of our time has a combination of established as well as emerging needs, opportunities and challenges. The long-standing problems of using computing to provide uninterrupted service during extreme events and prevent wide-spread blackouts remains a key need. The root causes of these events have, however, become more complex. In addition to the usual triggers such as transmission lines touching trees and creating cascading outages (Thorp et al., 1998), the causes could be more severe and due to natural disasters causing large number of equipment failures or cyber-security breaches causing malfunctioning of the equipment. Furthermore, there has also been a major change in the type of energy resources, their locations and size (Ilic et al., 2020) and in the nature of loads. Regulatory rules encourage non-utility-owned edge-grid users to supply their own power, participate in electric power trading, etc. The grid itself could control its parameters using fast controllers (Padiyar, 2007). The confluence of all of this unravels a once monolithic system into different subsystems, tightly interacting because of the electrical connections.

Currently, there are no user-friendly computational platforms for emulating dynamics of these systems in response to these various drivers. Because of this, it is hard to understand potential problems and assess candidate solutions. While it is clear that a system would benefit from participation of distributed edge-grid users, there are no standardized modeling and computing frameworks for supporting self-adapting, distributed, and minimally-coordinated electricity services.

The ideas described in this chapter are an attempt to begin to fill this void. In the next section, a multi-layered energy-based framework for modeling electric energy systems is briefly described for completeness (Ilic and Jaddivada, 2018; Ilic and Jaddivada, 2020; Jaddivada, 2020). The fundamental concept underlying this modeling is the one of interaction variables whose definition directly lends itself to capturing the structure needed to manage complexity. In the third section we discuss far-reaching potential of utilizing this modeling framework as the basis for the design of computation architecture. We summarize how the use of interaction variables forms the basis of Dynamic Monitoring and Decision Systems (DyMonDS) framework which conceptualizes the problem as a structured cyber-physical systems problem (Ilic, 2010). Our research has evolved over the past two decades around DyMonDS, including the development of our home-grown computational platform and its use as the basic research tool. We describe more recent attributes of what became Scalable Electric Power System Simulator SEPSS (Ilic et al., 2018).

The idea of using this modeling framework for adaptive computing resource allocation using automata has already been recognized and it awaits further development (Ilic and Jaddivada, 2019a). The new idea introduced in the fourth section concerns plug-and-play automated method for power systems simulations (PAMPS). This is an inherently multi-layered distributed computing approach which presents unique numerical integration challenges because of its interactive nature and the need to compute derivatives of interaction variables accurately and efficiently. While the algorithm finds its use in both distributed control and simulations, in this chapter we focus on the numerical simulations.

In the fifth section we report on our up-to-date experience with numerical integration methods in support of PAMPS. We stress that state-of-the-art in model-based distributed simulations of fast dynamics presents us with many issues, and illustrate these challenges on two typical engineering examples. In the sixth section, we establish the basis for major potential benefits to be drawn from more advanced computational methods, such as algorithmic differentiation (AD) (Griewank and Walther, 2008; Baydin et al., 2017). These methods are briefly summarized and hold the promise of overcoming some key issues in numerical integration of very fast transient processes. We close the chapter with the ideas for next steps and open questions on the way to establishing digital twins of electric power systems.

UNIFIED MULTI-LAYERED MODELING IN ENERGY-POWER DYNAMICAL STATE SPACE

In this section we briefly summarize a recently-introduced unified modeling of electric energy systems as the basis for representing the internal technology-specific local dynamics of core components and their distributed control in terms of their local state variables; and the interaction variables with the rest of the system. Figure 1 reflects the fact that electric energy systems are fundamentally social-ecological systems (SES) whose sustainability can be assessed by understanding core attributes of their resources, users, governance subsystems and their dynamical interactions; determining these core attributes is the foundation for Elinor Ostrom's Nobel prize winning generalized sustainability framework (Ostrom, 2009). Inspired by this work, and based on our modeling of power systems as complex dynamical systems, we introduce multi-layered interactive modeling. At the higher system levels, dynamic interactions between core components shown in Figure 1 are represented using their aggregate variables. Based on this, we study a multi-layered multi-granular modeling of a complex electric energy systems, as shown in Figure 2. Resources and user subsystems are modules, and they interact by means of physical grid and its data-enabled monitoring and control of interactions, and are governed by the industry rules, as shown later in Figure 1.

Next, we summarize for completeness this unified modeling approach and its potential to characterize the input-output dynamical specifications of the core components comprising a social-ecological energy system. The approach is fundamentally based on mapping very complex internal component dynamics into its aggregate state variables in energy-power dynamical state space model (Ilic and Jaddivada, 2018; Ilic and Jaddivada, 2020; Jaddivada, 2020). Notably, depending on the technology and its dynamic properties, its specifications in terms of limits on the ability to interact generally vary with system conditions. Because of this, it is necessary to have interactive information exchange in the online operations, instead of presently-used operating "nomograms" (Papic et al., 2007).

Basic Component Modeling in Energy-power Space

This unified modeling in energy-power space is closely related to the *bond graph* representation which has had a very rich history (Thoma, 2016). Our recent work has been specifically targeted to modular modeling of dynamics for distributed control and optimization of large-scale complex electric energy systems comprising very diverse technologies. As shown in Figure 2, the novel aspect of this modeling is that it starts by representing each component i in its standard state space form (Equations (1), (2) below), with internal states $x_i(t)$, interface variables $r_i(t)$, local primary control $u_i(t)$ and local disturbances $m_i(t)$ which are technology-specific (Ilic and Jaddivada, 2018; Ilic and Jaddivada, 2020).

$$\dot{x}_i(t) = f_{x,i}\left(x_i(t), u_i(t), m_i(t), r_i(t)\right) \tag{1}$$

Figure 1. The core subsystems in a framework for analyzing social-ecological systems (Ostrom, 2009).

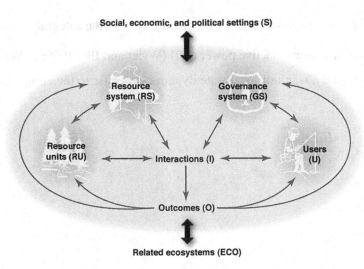

$$\dot{r}_i\big(t\big) = f_{r,i}\Big(x_i\big(t\big), \dot{P}_i\big(t\big), \dot{Q}_i\big(t\big)\Big) \tag{2}$$

Figure 2. Sketch of a new modeling an interconnected system with heterogeneous components (Ilic and Jaddivada, 2018).

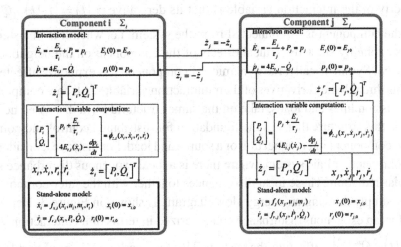

This modeling explicitly shows the general structure of an electric energy system fundamentally based on the following general definition of an interaction variable associated with any component i.

Definition and Structural Properties of Interaction Variables

The Interaction Variable $z_i(t)$ associated with component i is the integral of instantaneous power $\int_0^t P_i(s)\,ds$ and the instantaneous reactive power $Q_i(t)$ (Wyatt and Ilic, 1990; LaWhite and Ilic, 1997). Both of these quantities are a result of local state dynamics specific to the component and are defined as follows:

$$\int_0^t P_i(s)\,ds = \int_0^t p_i(s) + \frac{E_i(s)}{\tau_i}\,ds \tag{3}$$

$$Q_i(t) = \int_0^t 4E_{t,i}(s)\,ds - p_i(t) \tag{4}$$

Here, $E_i, p_i, E_{t,i}$ respectively are the stored energy of the component, its first time derivative and the stored energy in tangent space. τ_i is the time constant of the energy dynamics and can also be interpreted as the ratio of the stored energy and dissipation losses of the component. The details on the definitions of these quantities can be referred to in (Ilic and Jaddivada, 2018; Ilic and Jaddivada, 2020). Important is to note that the interaction variables depend only on local state variables, irrespective of what the connections with rest of the system are.

The key property of the interaction variable is that its derivative $\dot{z}_i(t) = \begin{bmatrix} P_i(t) & \dot{Q}_i(t) \end{bmatrix}^T$ is identically zero when the component is disconnected from the system, i.e. when it is in a stand-alone mode. These derivatives explicitly show dynamical effects of the component on the neighboring component when interconnected. Symmetrically, the dynamics of component i is explicitly affected by the neighboring components through the derivatives of their interaction variables. All core components, including generators, transmission lines and loads, take on the same structural form discussed next (Ilic and Jaddivada, 2018). It is this structure that sets the foundation for distributed control and computing.

Consider a two component interconnection of a source and load. For instance, consider that the source sub-system is a solar photovoltaic system, where there is a local exogenous disturbance seen because of the changes in solar radiation. These local disturbances together with the inter-component interactions can be studied by simply drawing an energy flow diagram as shown in Figure 3. Here, solar radiation can be thought of as an exogenous disturbance characterized in terms of its interaction variable dynamics $\dot{z}_s^m(t) = \begin{bmatrix} P_s^m(t) & \dot{Q}_s^m(t) \end{bmatrix}^T$ affecting the system. The superscript m is used to differentiate the interaction variable dynamics at the interface ports defined as $\dot{z}_s(t) = \begin{bmatrix} P_s(t) & \dot{Q}_s(t)^T \end{bmatrix}$ and $\dot{z}_l(t) = \begin{bmatrix} P_l(t) & \dot{Q}_l(t) \end{bmatrix}^T$ for the source and load sub-systems respectively. The interaction variables as defined in Equations (3) and (4) for both source and load sub-systems, together with the structure-preserving interconnection relations, as will be detailed in the next section, are sufficient for a system operator to operate the interconnected system. The system operator can remain incognizant to internal details as dictated by the more-granular physical lower layer model in Eqn. (1).

Figure 3. Input-output interfacing: Two component system comprising a source and a load.

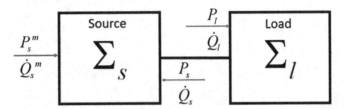

On the other hand, conventional approach of operating these systems is to utilize the internal details of the components defined using the model in Equation 1 with corresponding sub-scripts of s and l, together with algebraic relations stemming from the Kirchhoff's current and voltage laws. For the example under consideration, $m_s(t)$ is the local disturbance seen by source sub-system, whose local primary control is $u_s(t)$. Notably, the high penetration of solar and other intermittent power DERs which are power-electronically-controlled could lead to new electromagnetic instability phenomena already observed in Texas power grid (Adams et al., 2012). The modeling granularity of the dynamics of these components depends on specific technology. These internal physical models quickly become complex and, when interconnected, are also subject to algebraic real and reactive power balance equations, resulting in high-order nonlinear differential algebraic equations (DAE) models (Pai et al., 1995). Because of this complexity, it is very difficult to test components so that the interconnected system dynamics has desired response, say that the system stays stable for certain range of exogenous time-varying disturbances. Notably, this very serious roadblock to innovative deployments by the utilities can be overcome through *distributed computing*.

The most relevant, for purposes of introducing model-based protocols for computing and operating future electric energy systems, are the formulas shown in Figure 2. They represent a closed form mapping of the dynamics of aggregate state variables defined as energy stored in the component $E_i(t)$ and its derivative $p_i(t) = \dot{E}_i(t)$ in terms of internal extended state dynamics $\dot{x}_i(t), \dot{r}_i(t)$ and its interaction variable $\dot{z}_i(t) = \begin{bmatrix} P_i(t) & \dot{Q}_i(t) \end{bmatrix}^T$. Here $E_{t,i}(t)$ is the energy in tangent space and it has the same expression as energy, except the states are replaced by the derivatives of states. The mapping from the physical model into the aggregate states $\begin{bmatrix} E_i(t) & p_i(t) \end{bmatrix}^T$ is shown in the center panel in Figure 2. The fundamental relevance of this model is that any component which knows its own internal dynamics, can design its automation for the ranges of interaction variables it selects. Or, alternatively, the component can enhance its control and internal hardware design to implement its input-output specifications which are given solely as interaction variable specifications.

Unified Multi-layered Dynamical Model of an Interconnected System

The distributed model of each component i in energy-power space described above defines the dynamics of its aggregate variable in energy-power space. Notably, it simply reflects the power conservation law and rate of reactive power conservation law written for the cut-set representing boundary of the component.

$$\dot{E}_i(t) = p_i(t) \tag{5}$$

$$\dot{p}_i(t) = 4E_{t,i}(t) - \dot{Q}_i(t) \tag{6}$$

Figure 2 shows a sketch of the interconnected mathematical model of the small system. General conservation laws (power and rates of change of power) can be written for any level of granularity, by zooming in and zooming out into the system. The dynamics of distributed components is subject to the basic power conservation laws

$$P_i(t) = -\sum_{j \in C_i} P_j(t) \tag{7}$$

$$\dot{Q}_i(t) = -\sum_{j \in C_i} \dot{Q}_j(t) \tag{8}$$

Here, C_i denotes the set of components connected to i. Since each component is characterized in terms of both instantaneous power and rate of change of instantaneous reactive power, it is critical to start by writing generalized Tellegen's Theorem for both instantaneous power and rate of change of instantaneous reactive power (Ilic and Jaddivada, 2018; Penfield et al., 1970). This model cannot be written in standard state space form since it is fundamentally interactive.

MODEL-BASED STRUCTURE OF COMPUTATIONAL PLATFORM

The unified modeling based on first principles supports DyMonDS framework and next generation Supervisory Control and Data Acquisition (SCADA) for monitoring and controlling electric energy systems so that they enable sustainable and resilient service (Ilic, 2010; Ilic and Lessard). Overlaid is the computational platform which processes the information exchange defined using this modeling. Our team has worked for quite some time on applying unified modeling for designing next generation Supervisory Control and Data Acquisition (SCADA) we named Dynamic Monitoring and Decision Systems (DyMoNDS) (Ilic, 2010). The first version of Smart Grid in a Room Simulator (SGRS) was made at Carnegie Mellon University (Wagner et al., 2015). It was used to emulate integration of adaptive load management (ALM) into electricity markets (Joo and Ilic, 2013), to demonstrate potential of transactive energy management (TEM) of small distributed resources in retail markets (Holmberg et al., 2019) as well as for the US ARPA-E project which demonstrates ability of household appliances to participate in fast power balancing (Ilic and Jaddivada, 2019b). At MIT our team has further developed the SGRS into scalable electric power system simulator (SEPSS) which is fundamentally based on the ideas of modular modeling of interactions (Ilic et al., 2018).

The SEPSS simulation platform is based on the conceptual notion of unified multi-layered modeling, which utilizes the structural property that any power system agent needs to send information in terms of derivatives of its interaction variable, and, to, symmetrically, receive information from the rest of the system in terms of derivatives of their interaction variables. This not only ensures privacy but also enhances integration of components to assess a large system and its interconnections. Based on this idea, the SGRS shell makes the first attempt to align the physics-based structure with the partitioning of computing jobs to several processes (Wagner et al., 2015). The shell facilitates allocation of computing resources, sets up the TCP/IP communication channels between different modules and initiates the simulation. The simulation platform is High Level Architecture (HLA)-compatible (Association et al., 2010), allowing integration with third-party software. We have implemented dynamic inter-operability between two simulation platforms: an advanced grid analysis software called NETSSWorks (Ilic and Lang, 2010) and the software platform. The sketch of the components that constitute the simulation platform and its links to external modules is shown in Figure 5 (Holmberg et al., 2019).

Figure 4. Dynamic Monitoring and Decision Systems (DyMonDS) framework (Ilic, 2010)

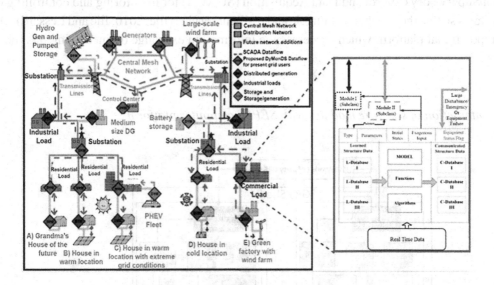

This figure shows interactions that may happen within the system. Here, the module named 'House' is one of the transactive agents, but industrial customers or any other component trading in an energy market can be modeled and treated as such green-colored boxes. Several of these models together constitute a community, and they are either coordinated by a community coordinator or through distributed peer-to-peer decisions. Our simulation platform does not recommend specific architectures for design and in fact is designed to be general enough for testing any given architecture in a rapid manner. Each module in the platform can be plugged in or out without having to change any of the simulation components. These concepts are similar to those proposed in the NIST ACM (Ferraiolo et al., 2001), which characterizes resources and their interfaces.

The simulation platform is still under development, with focus on making the simulations scalable to very large systems, by supporting clustering, aggregation and decomposition according to the physical and organizational structure of an electric power system that is rich in both temporal and spatial scales.

In sharp contrast with the idea of strictly data-enabled self-adaptation and self-optimization of computer architecture in response to workloads experienced (Donyanavard et al., 2020), the approach taken here is to actually define the information that needs to be exchanged between different layers using the unified modeling in energy space, and set the basis for flow control in the computational architecture (Ilic and Jaddivada, 2019a). On the other hand, massive parallel data processing is mainly done by the grid users in parallel, including Machine Learning methods and Model Predictive Control (MPC) and Decisions (Ilic et al., 2019; Lauer et al., 2019; Carvalho et al., 2020). Once this is established, it becomes possible, at later stages, to design a very effective computational architecture which is self-verifying, adjusting and continuously checking its own performance, much the same way as Spiral was introduced for computing Fourier Transformation for signal processing purposes (Puschel et al., 2005). As a matter of fact, the multi-disciplinary approach to conceiving Smart Grid in a Room Simulator (SGRS) was very much motivated by Spiral since we were fortunate to have Franz Franchetti, the key contributor to Spiral, as one of our SGRS team members (Wagner et al., 2015). The unified modeling based on first principles supports Dynamic Monitoring and Decision Systems (DyMonDS) framework and next generation Supervisory Control and Data Acquisition (SCADA) for monitoring and controlling electric energy systems so that they enable sustainable and resilient service (Ilic, 2010; Ilic and Lessard). Overlaid is the computational platform which processes the information exchange defined using this modeling.

Figure 5. Interaction of software modules with SEPSS computer platform
(Holmberg et al., 2019)

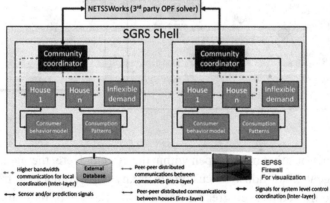

Much work remains to build on this idea of unified modeling for designing dedicated computer platforms for future emulating dynamics of electric energy systems in response to continuous disturbances and events driving changes. In this chapter only the basic idea is presented. In the remainder of this chapter we give several numerical simulation methods needed to actually implement electric energy systems using such computer architecture. As it turns out, state of the art of distributed numerical algorithms that capture fast dynamical interactions taking place within a very complex network system are at their rudimentary stages. We describe next our progress on this problem, illustrate fundamental issues and set the basis for further work.

PLUG-AND-PLAY AUTOMATED METHOD FOR POWER SYSTEMS SIMULATIONS (PAMPS)

The multi-layered model and computational platform structure described here are the first of their kind. While the interconnected system model shown in Figure 2 appears to be in the form of ordinary differential equations (ODE) in terms of energy-power variables while preserving the structure of the system, the modeling is inherently interactive in nature. This is because dynamic maps are needed to transform variables between lower layer and higher layer models at each of the components.

Furthermore, in Figure 2, there is a need to differentiate between the $\dot{z}_i$ that is a result of local energy conversion dynamics and the one that is a function of the interconnection with rest of the system. These quantities are respectively indicated at the top and the bottom of the middle panel in Figure 2, respectively. While these signals are physically the same in case of a feasible interconnection, in context of distributed simulations and/or control, they need to be differentiated. We thus use in what follows the superscript notation "out" and "in", respectively, to differentiate the two quantities. Further, the interaction variables can be modeled at any port of interaction. To differentiate between the local disturbance ports and those that enter the port of interaction, superscripts m and r for these quantities are utilized to avoid confusion.

As evident from Figure 2, the outgoing interaction variables $\dot{z}_i^{r,out}$ depend on both state derivatives and port input derivatives, which in turn evolve as a function of $\dot{z}_i^{r,in}$. These incoming interaction variables, however are a function of interconnection i.e., they depend on $\dot{z}_j^{r,out} \forall j \in C_i$. As a result, the models are of the form $\dot{z}_i^{r,out} = f\left(x_i, \dot{z}_j^{r,out}\right)$, in turn resulting in $\dot{x}_i = f\left(x_i, \dot{x}_j\right)$. To the best of our knowledge these distributed interactive models have not been studied in the literature. Thus, numerical methods need to be devised for distributed simulations of these interactive models, while retaining the ODE structure at the system level.

The multi-layered model proposed here lends itself to distributed computing. However, the hurdle with respect to the interactive nature of the stand-alone models needs to be overcome. By exploiting the unified higher-layer energy space models and exploiting the inherent structure of the system, we propose a novel algorithm referred to as plug-and-play automated method for power system simulations (PAMPS). While the algorithm finds its use in both distributed control and simulations, we focus on the numerical simulations first. The proposed PAMPS approach to distributed simulations would broadly entail following sequence of steps formalized in the Algorithm 1.

PAMPS-based Distributed Simulations

The algorithm begins with the initialization phase (Step 0 in Algorithm 1 where the assignment of the initial values of extended state variables for use by the lower layer model and an assumption on zero incoming interaction variables at initial time.

Next, by using the information of local extended state variables, outgoing interaction variables are computed that would be communicated to the neighbors (Step 1 in Algorithm 1). This dynamic map is abstracted through $\phi_{z,i}$, the expression for which has been shown in Figure 2. Note that this computation would require the knowledge of derivatives of port inputs $\dot{r}_i$ which in turn would depend on the values of the incoming interaction variables $\dot{z}_i^{r,in}$, which has been assumed to be equal to zero in the initialization phase. For the next time step though, this value is computed as a result of interconnection laws in Equations 7 and 8, also included as step 2 in the Algorithm 1.

Algorithm 1. PAMPS algorithm

```
1: Time  t ← 0 . Time initialization
2: while  t ≤ tend  do
3:          for each component  i ∈ N  do          . Parallel implementation
```
4: (Step 0) Given initial extended state space variables: $x_i(0) \leftarrow x_{i,0}$; $r_i(0) \leftarrow r_{i,0}$; and incoming interaction variable dynamics: $\dot{z}_i^{r,in}(t) = 0 \forall t \leq 0$. Initialization

5: (Step 1) Compute outgoing interaction variables as follows and send out to neighbors: $z_i^{r,out}(t) \leftarrow \phi_{z,i}\left(x_i(t), r_i(t), \dot{z}_i^{r,in}(t - \delta t)\right)$

6: (Step 2) Receive outgoing interaction variables communicated by neighbors to obtain incoming interaction variables by establishing interconnection laws:
$$\dot{z}_i^{r,in}(t) \leftarrow -\sum_{j \in C_i} \dot{z}_j^{r,out}(t)$$

7: (Step 3) Compute extended state trajectories:

$$\left[x_i(t + \delta t) \quad r_i(t + \delta t)\right]^T \leftarrow \phi_{x,i}\left(x_i(t), r_i(t), \dot{z}_i^{r,in}(t - \delta t)\right). \text{ All components covered}$$

8: Advance time stamp $t \leftarrow t + \delta t$. Time update

The new values of incoming interaction variables, which are a function of neighbors' state variables are utilized in Step 3 to perform time-stepping of internal states by using an integrator. This map corresponding to the numerical integration is abstracted as $\phi_{x,i}$.

In Figure 2, the dependence of dynamics of extended state $\dot{r}_i$ has been shown to be dependent on $P_i(t)$ implicitly (Ilic and Jaddivada, 2020; Jaddivada, 2020). However, it is actually dependent on $\dot{P}_i(t)$.

We thus introduce additional notation $\dot{\tilde{z}}_i$ to represent the vector $\left[\dot{P}_i \quad \dot{Q}_i\right]^T$ that is to be used in the time-stepping of lower layer extended state variables in Step 3.

There is now a huge disconnect between the steps 2 and 3. To carry out time-stepping of internal states in step 3, the need for estimating $\dot{P}_i^{r,in}$ accurately arises.

This can be done by employing one of the following three alternatives:

- Variant 1: By taking previous historical values of $P_i^{r,in}(t)$ for use in (Step 3)

$$\dot{P}_i^{r,in}(t) = \frac{1}{\delta t}\left(P_i^{r,in}(t) - P_i^{r,in}(t - \delta t)\right) \tag{9}$$

- Variant 2: By revising the (step 1) and (step 2) of the algorithm as follows:

– (step 1)

Previously step 1 of the algorithm made use of the mapping $\phi_{z,i}$ expanded out in Fig. 2. However, for computing $\dot{P}_i^{r,out}(t)$, we propose replacing the first element of $\phi_{z,i}$ with the expression $\dot{p}_i + \dfrac{p_i}{\tau_i}$. Let us call this new map as $\phi_{\tilde{z}_i}$. With this the algorithm's step 1 can be revised as follows:

$$\overset{\dot{}r,out}{\tilde{z}_i}(t) \leftarrow \phi_{\tilde{z}_i}\left(x_i(t), r_i(t), \overset{\dot{}r,in}{\tilde{z}_i}(t - \delta t)\right)$$

– (step 2)

Since the power balancing is a result of generalized Tellegen's theorem. If the real power balances as indicated in Eqn. (7), they should also balance for the rate of change of instantaneous power, thus resulting in following step 2 replacement:

$$\overset{\dot{}r,in}{\tilde{z}_i}(t) \leftarrow -\sum_{j \in C_i} \overset{\dot{}r,out}{\tilde{z}_j}(t)$$

- Variant 3: By assuming historical feasibility of interconnection i.e. $P_i^{r,in}(t - \delta t) = P_i^{r,out}(t - \delta t)$, leading to the following relation (Jaddivada, 2020)

$$\dot{P}_i^{r,in}(t) = \frac{1}{\delta t}\left(P_i^{r,in}(t) - P_i^{r,out}(t - \delta t)\right) \tag{10}$$

Typically, the smaller is the time-step δt the closer would be the trajectories obtained by each of the three variants of derivative estimation, and thus would lead to the faithful emulation of trajectories through distributed simulations. Another strategy for ensuring the error made in estimating the derivative value to fade away with time, is to incorporate an error control strategy as follows. This is made apparent in the discrete time implementation algorithm. Furthermore, the mapping $\phi_{x,i}, \phi_{z,i}$ is could be explicit or an implicit map showing the dependency of variables needed for computing x_i and $z_i^{r,out}$ respectively. The actual relations will be made cleared in the discrete time implementation explained next.

Discrete Time Distributed Implementation

In the continuous time PAMPS algorithm introduced in the previous section, we have focused on differentiating between the outgoing and incoming interaction variables, and explained the dependence of local variables on the interaction variables and vice-versa. However, the algorithm will only be more clear if it is explained in context of discrete time-implementation.

In what follows, we denote timestep T_x for lower-layer state evolution and a timestep T_z for higher-layer energy-space variables computation. Let the associated sample numbers be denoted by k_x and k_z respectively. The time step selection needs to be so that $T_z \ll \tau_i$ and T_x must be smaller than the time constant of the fastest state variable. Note that energy variables evolve at time constant τ_i, which is an aggregate affect of all the local variables, and thus tends to be much slower than the internal state variable evolution. However, for single-state variable components, both lower layer and higher layer models may evolve at the same rates. The discrete time implementation of PAMPS is given in Algorithm 2.

The steps 2.2.1, 2.2.2 or 2.2.3. can in fact be appended with a following error control scheme to reduce the effect of error in estimation of derivative of $P_i^{r,in}$.

$$\dot{z}_i^{r,in}\left[k_z\right] = -\sum_{j \in C_i} \dot{z}_j^{r,out}\left[k_z\right] + \epsilon_i\left[k_z\right] \tag{11}$$

Here $\epsilon_i\left[k_z\right]$ acts as a feedback signal that controls the error made in derivative estimation as sensed by the residual of interconnection laws at the interface. One simple error control scheme is a simple proportional derivative scheme shown under

$$\epsilon_i\left[k_z\right] = -K_d\left(\dot{z}_i^{r,in}\left[k_z - 1\right] + \sum_{j \in C_i} \dot{z}_j^{r,out}\left[k_z\right]\right) - K_p\left(z_i^{r,in}\left[k_z\right] - \sum_{j \in C_i} z_j^{r,out}\left[k_z\right]\right) \tag{12}$$

From these expressions above, clearly $\left|k_d\right| \le 1$ to ensure numerical stability of the updates of $z_i^{r,in}$ while the gain $0 \le k_p \le 1$. The right handed inequality ensures numerical stability while the left hand-sided inequality is a desired property to ensure $\left(z_i^{r,in} - z_i^{r,out}\right)$ decays over continuous time.

PROOF-OF-CONCEPT ILLUSTRATIONS

The different variants of distributed information exchange as required for the estimation of derivative of $P_i^{r,in}$ have been explained in the last two sections in both continuous time domain and discrete time.

Algorithm 2. Multi-rate discrete time distributed simulations

1: $k_z \leftarrow 0, k_x \leftarrow 0$. Time initialization

2: **while** $k_z T_z \leq t_{end}$ **do for** each component $i \in \mathcal{N}$

3: **do** . Parallel implementation

4: (Step 0.0) Initialization at T_x rate: $x_i[k_x] \leftarrow x_{i,0}; r_i[k_x] \leftarrow r_{i,0};$

5: (Step 0.1) Initialization at T_z rate $\dot{z}_i^{r,in}[k_z] \leftarrow 0 \forall k_z \leq 0$

6: (Step 1.1) Compute $\dot{Q}_i^{r,out}[k_z]$ and send it out to neighbors

7: (Step 2.1) Receive from neighbors and apply dynamics of reactive power balance relation

$$\dot{Q}_i^{r,in}[k_z] \leftarrow -\sum_{j \in C_i} \dot{Q}_j^{r,out}[kz]$$

8: Choose one of the three alternatives   . For estimation of $\dot{P}_i^{r,in}[k_z]$

· Variant 1

-       (Step 1.2.1) Compute $P_i^{r,out}[k_z]$ and send it out to neighbors

-       (Step 2.2.1) Receive from neighbors and apply instantaneous power balance equations

$$P_i^{r,in}[kz] \leftarrow -\sum_{j \in C_i} \dot{P}_j^{r,out}[kz]$$

-       Estimate derivative of instantaneous power using historical values

$$\dot{P}_i^{r,in}[k_z] = \frac{1}{T_z}\left(P_i^{r,in}[kz] - P_i^{r,in}[kz-1]\right)$$

· Variant 2

-       (Step 1.2.2) Compute $\dot{P}_i^{r,out}[k_z]$ and send it out to neighbors

-       (Step 2.2.2) Receive from neighbors and apply instantaneous power dynamics balance

equation $\dot{P}_i^{r,in}[k_z] \leftarrow -\sum_{j \in C_i} \dot{P}_j^{r,out}[kz]$

· Variant 3

-       (Step 1.2.3) Compute $P_i^{r,out}[k_z]$ and send it out to neighbors

-       (Step 2.2.3) Receive from neighbors and apply instantaneous power balance equations

$$P_i^{r,in}[kz] \leftarrow -\sum_{j \in C_i} P_j^{r,out}[kz]$$

-       Estimate derivative of instantaneous power assuming feasibility of interconnection

at previous timestep $\dot{P}_i^{r,in}[k_z] = \frac{1}{T_z}\left(P_i^{r,in}[kz] - P_i^{r,out}[kz-1]\right)$

9:       **while** $k_x T_x \leq (k_z + 1) T_z$ **do**

10:       (Step 3.1.) $\left(r_i[k_x + 1] \leftarrow f_r'\left(r_i[k_x], \dot{z}_i^{r,in}[k_z]\right)\right)$

           $x_i[k_x + 1] \leftarrow f_x'\left(x_i[k_x], r_i[k_x + 1]\right)$

11:       (Step 3.2.)

12:       Advance $k_x \leftarrow k_x + 1$

13:       $x_i[k_z + 1] \leftarrow x_i[k_x]; r_i[k_z + 1] \leftarrow r_i[k_x]$. Multi-rate synchronism . All components

considered

14:       Advance $k_z \leftarrow k_z + 1$

Figure 6. Two component - LC-type interconnection

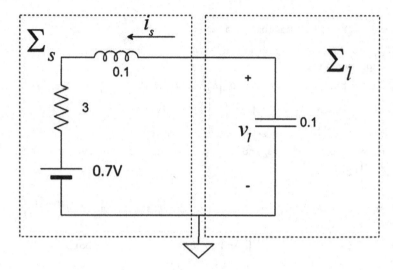

We now take simple examples of two component interconnections to evaluate the dependence of proposed algorithm on the type of distributed information exchange and also on the type of interconnection. The benchmark considered is the response obtained by simulating the interconnected system model in terms of physical variables by eliminating the dependent state variables.

Effect of Information Exchange Type

We first consider a simple two component interconnection shown in Fig. 6 where component 1 is a lossy inductor denoted by R_1, L_1 with a constant voltage source u_1 and let the second component be a lossy capacitor denoted by G_2, C_2.

Figure 7. Multi-layered interactive model and information exchange - LC-type interconnection

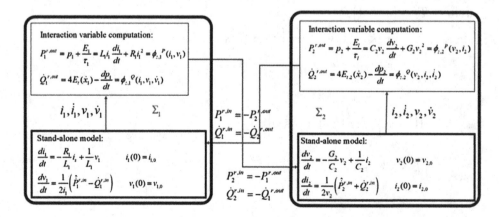

Figure 8. Variation 1-based implementation of PAMPS algorithm on LC interconnection

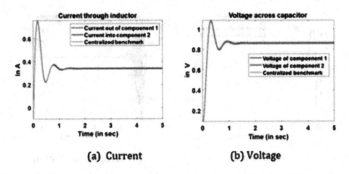

(a) Current (b) Voltage

The multi-layered interactive model for this specific example is shown in Fig. 7. We have implemented Algorithm 2 by choosing a different variant each time to compare the qualitative responses obtained and to understand the propagation of errors in power balancing over a period of time.

For both the variants 1 and 2, similar current and voltage trajectories are obtained as shown in Fig. 8. There is however a significant difference between the two approaches as evident from the error accumulation over time, as seen in Fig. 9. While the shapes of the two plots appear to be the same, the scale can be checked to see that the variant 2 incurs thousand times as large errors as variant 1.

The variant 3 results in a numerically sensitive performance, as evident through high frequency oscillations observed in the error plots in Fig. 10b. Furthermore, the error control gains had to be carefully chosen for this case in contrast to the other two variants.

Figure 9. Error accumulation over time for variants 1 and 2 of PAMPS implementation on LC interconnection

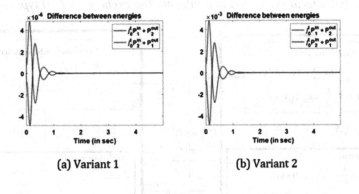

(a) Variant 1 (b) Variant 2

For an LC interconnection, it is known that the symplectic schemes where present values of current and future values of voltage when utilized by component 1, results in energy-preserving numerical scheme (Hairer et al., 2006). Variant 1 is analogous to the symplectic scheme, since the future voltage of component 2 can be computed by component 1, with the knowledge of $\dot{Q}_1^{r,in}$ that is communicated by component 2. The present value of current is available through the value of $P_1^{r,in}$ sent out by the component 2.

Figure 10. Variation3-based implementation of PAMPS algorithm on LC interconnection

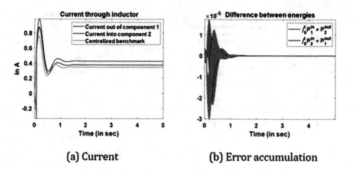

(a) Current   (b) Error accumulation

Figure 11. Variation1-based implementation of PAMPS algorithm on LC interconnection without error control

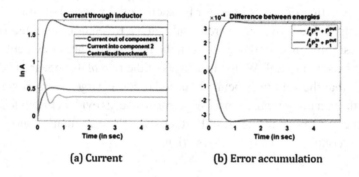

(a) Current   (b) Error accumulation

Figure 12. Multi-layered interactive model and information exchange - CPLtype interconnection

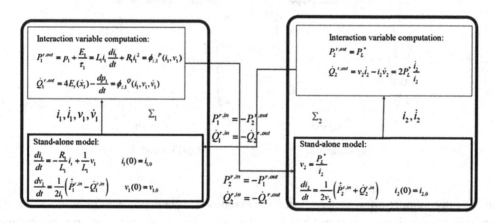

Effect of the Interconnection Type

It has further been noticed that the LC-type interconnection considered in the previous example is bound to work only for when $K_p > 0$. The performance is best when $K_p = 1$. However, when $K_p = 0$, i.e. when the proportional component is absent, we see that the exact simulation responses could not be reproduced as expected. Shown in the Fig. 11 are the corresponding plots.

In contrast, consider another type of interconnection when the component 1 is a lossy inductor with a source voltage serving an ideal power sink. Its distributed modular model is shown in Fig. 12. For this example, it has been observed that variant 1 of PAMPS implementation with or without error control results in the same response shown in Fig. 13.

The constant power load-type interconnection has one of the power variables that is $P_2^{r,in}$ is fixed, while $\dot{Q}_2^{r,in}$ is a free variables and has no dependence on any other variables, since the load component does not have its own dynamics. As a result, any value of $\dot{Q}_2^{r,in}$ sent out by the component 1 is acceptable from the load's perspective and thus there is no need of any error control to reach a consensus as long as the value of $P_1^{r,in} = P_L^*$ is within a range that does not affect dynamic stability of component 1.

Figure 13. Variation1-based implementation of PAMPS algorithm on CPL-type interconnection

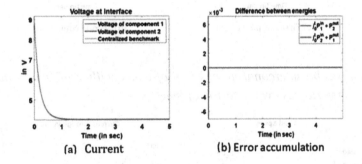

(a) Current   (b) Error accumulation

Feasibility Assessment

Distributed models and simulations render computation of ranges of outgoing interaction variables for given incoming interaction variables. This range is to be a subset of the possible variation of interaction variables for feasibility of the interconnection (Ilic and Jaddivada, 2020; Jaddivada, 2020). For the two component interconnection serving a constant power load varying in time, the limits of the changes in $z_i^{r,in}$ can be estimated ahead of time, given the ranges of P_L^* and $\dot{P}_L^*$.

These bounds are plotted in Figures 14c and 14d (red and yellow plots) for the load profile in Fig. 14a where ranges of P_L^* and $\dot{P}_L^*$ are communicated every 1 second to the component 1. The actual outgoing interaction variables are indicated by blue. Notice that at all times, the outgoing interaction variables lie within the predicted ranges. Thus, we see also through the plots of internal states in Fig. 14b, that there has been no dynamic instability.

Figure 14. Case of a feasible interconnection at all times: Proof-of-concept illustration of validation of conditions on ranges of interaction variables over a period of time

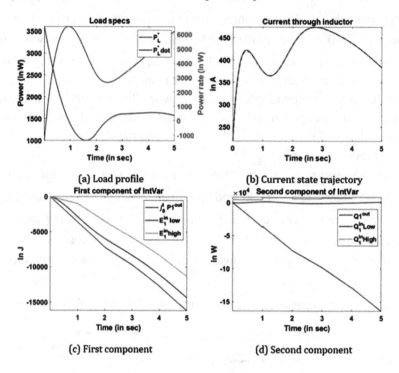

(a) Load profile   (b) Current state trajectory

(c) First component   (d) Second component

Figure 15. Case of a infeasible interconnection: Proof-of-concept illustration of validation of conditions on ranges of interaction variables over a period of time

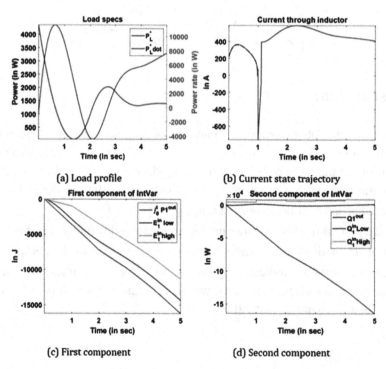

(a) Load profile   (b) Current state trajectory

(c) First component   (d) Second component

Shown in Fig. 15 is the validation of the case when the system is subject to steep changes in power shown in Fig. 15a making the interconnection infeasible after time $t = 0.8$ seconds. While this is not immediately evident through the bounds on first component of interaction variables in Figure. 15c, the dynamic instability can predicted by looking at the the ranges on second component being violated in Figure 15d. Consequently, the internal states show unstable behavior as well as shown in Figure 15b.

In this exercise, we have only validated the energy-based bounds for feasible interconnection. However, distributed computing can also be put to use for ahead-of-time predicting the ranges of incoming interaction variables so that the component takes local preventive or corrective actions to avoid operating closer to the limits.

THE CHALLENGE OF MULTI-LAYERED INTERACTIVE COMPUTING: ACCURATE AND EFFICIENT DERIVATIVES

As introduced in this chapter, the distributed interactive algorithms based on the unified modeling approach lend themselves to parallel distributed computing based on local data processing and information exchange in terms of derivatives of interaction variables information exchange with the rest of the system. This sets the foundations for computational platforms with lots of structure using hybrid computing. Essentially, much data processing specific to technologies and sub-objectives of the distributed subsystems is internalized locally. The information flow in between modules is mainly in terms of derivatives of interaction variables, and this makes it possible to design hybrid computational platforms with well-defined design specifications.

However, as illustrated in the first proof-of-concept simulations of such distributed algorithms, their performance is fundamentally dependent on the accuracy and efficiency of computing derivatives of interaction variables exchanged in between the subsystems. The collaboration of the co-authors of this chapter has opened a new avenue for overcoming this sensitivity. In particular, algorithmic Differentiation (AD), in sharp contrast to finite differencing, provides *exact* derivative information about a function F given in a high-level programming language and it does so with time and space complexity that can be bounded by the complexity of evaluating the function itself. The key idea in algorithmic differentiation is the systematic application of the chain rule of calculus. To that end, the computation of the function F is decomposed into a (typically long) sequence of simple evaluations, e.g., additions, multiplications, and calls to elementary functions such as $sin\left(v\right)$ or $cos\left(v\right)$. The derivatives with respect to the arguments of these simple operations can be easily calculated. A systematic application of the chain rule then yields the derivatives of the entire sequence with respect to the input variables $x \in R^n$.

Modes of AD: AD has two basic modes of operation, called *forward mode* and *reverse mode*. In the forward mode, derivatives are propagated together with the evaluation of the function during the execution of a given code segment. From a mathematical point of view, this can be interpreted as the computation of tangent information in the following way. Assume for a moment that the argument vector x represents the value of a time-dependent path $x\left(t\right) at t = 0$.

Then this time-dependent path defines a tangent $\dot{x} = \left.\dfrac{\partial x(t)}{\partial t}\right|_{t=0}$. Using the forward mode of AD, one computes the resulting tangent $\dot{y}$ obtained for the time-dependent path $F\big(x(t)\big)$ that is well defined if the function F is sufficiently smooth, i.e.

$$\dot{y} = \left.\frac{\partial}{\partial t} F\big(x(t)\big)\right|_{t=0} = \left.F'\big(x(t)\big)\frac{\partial x(t)}{\partial t}\right|_{t=0} = F'(x)\dot{x} = \dot{F}(x,\dot{x})$$

This interpretation also explains the alternative names sometimes used for the forward mode of AD, namely *tangent mode* or *tangent-linear mode*.

Instead of being propagated together with the function evaluation, the derivatives can also be computed backwards starting from the function value y towards the independent variables x after a complete function evaluation. This is called the reverse mode of AD. Much like the mathematical interpretation given earlier for forward mode AD, one can give a similar interpretation for the reverse mode as well. Consider for a given vector $\bar{y} \in R^m$ and a given value $c \in R$ the hyperplane $\{y \in R^m \mid \bar{y}^\top y = c\}$ in the range of F. The hyperplane has the inverse image $\{x \in R^n \mid \bar{y}^\top F(x) = c\}$. By the implicit function theorem, this set is a smooth hypersurface with the normal $\bar{x}^\top = \bar{y}^\top F'(x) \equiv \bar{F}(x,\bar{y})$ at x, provided $\bar{x}^\top$ does not vanish. Geometrically, $\bar{y}$ and $\bar{x}$ can be seen as normals or cotangents.

Over the last several decades, extensive research activities have led to a thorough understanding of the complexities (time as well as memory) of these two basic modes of AD. The forward mode of AD provides one column of the Jacobian $F'(x)$ with a time complexity equal to no more than three function evaluations. The time needed to compute one row of the Jacobian $F'(x)$, e.g., the gradient of a scalar-valued component function of F, is less than four function evaluations using the reverse mode of AD in its basic form. Importantly, this bound for the reverse mode is completely independent of the number of input variables. This is highly attractive in contexts where there are many inputs—e.g., design parameters, neural network weights and the like—and a scalar-valued function such as a scalar loss function to be minimized.

AD Tools: Along with the progress on theoretical foundation, numerous AD software tools have also been developed over the years. Many of these tools have matured to a state where they can be used to provide derivatives for large and unstructured codes. The implementation paradigms underlying most existing AD tools are *source transformation* and *operator overloading*.

When using source transformation to implement AD, a source code that evaluates the function to be differentiated is given to the AD tool together with information as to which variables are the independents and which variables are the dependents. The AD tool then generates a new source code to compute the function as well as the required derivative information. To achieve this, one needs in essence a complete compiler. As a first step, this compiler parses the program to be differentiated to perform analysis, including syntactic and semantic analysis. In a second step, transformation is performed to include the statements for the derivative calculations. In a third step, optimization of the resulting code is carried out to increase performance. Finally, in a fourth step, the extended program is written out in the target programming language.

The technique of operator overloading exploits the capability of programming languages like C++, Fortran 95 and the like to define a new class of variables and to *overload* operators like $+, -, *$ and functions like $sin()$. Using operator overloading, it is rather straightforward to implement a tool for the forward mode AD.

Table 1 gives some representative examples of currently publicly available stand-alone AD tools. The website www.autodiff.org has a more comprehensive list of available AD tools. There is also a burgeoning research activity in AD for domain-specific and emerging languages. Examples include *autodiff* for Halide (Ragan-Kelley et al., 2013), *JuliaDiff* for Julia (Bezanson et al., 2017), and *Clad* as AD tool using Clang and LLVM (Vassilev et al., 2015). *Tangent* (van Merri"enboer et al., 2017) can be used for the algorithmic differentiation of code generated with the scripting language Python.

Table 1. Sample list of stand-alone AD tools.

Language	Tool	Paradigm	Mode
C/C++	ADOL-C	OOL	FM, RM, Taylor arithmetic
	ADIC	ST	FM
	CasADi	OOL	FM, RM
	OpenAD	ST	FM, RM
	Sacado	ST	FM, RM
	TAPENADE	ST	FM, RM
Fortran	ADIFOR	ST	FM
	OpenAD	ST	FM, RM
	TAF	ST	FM, RM
	TAPENADE	ST	FM, RM
Python	ADOL-C	OOL	FM, RM, Taylor arithmetic
	CasADi	OOL	FM, RM
Julia	JuliaDiff	OOL	FM, RM, Taylor arithmetic
MATLAB	AdiMat	ST+OOL	FM, RM
	CasADi	OOL	FM, RM
R	ADOL-C	OOL	FM, RM, Taylor arithmetic
	Madness	OOL	FM, Taylor arithmetic

OOL: operator overloading, ST: source transformation, FM: forward mode, RM: reverse mode.

Exploiting Sparsity in Derivative Computation: For large-scale problems involving vector functions, the underlying Jacobians and Hessians are often very sparse. That is to say, they contain numerous zero entries. Instead of computing all the zero entries with one of the modes of AD as described earlier, one can explicitly exploit the sparsity to make the derivative calculation much more efficient. A well-established way of achieving this efficiency (saving in both storage and time) is using a compress-then-recover strategy. This strategy consists of four steps: (1) determine the sparsity structure of the desired derivative matrix A (Jacobian or Hessian); (2) using graph coloring on an appropriate graph representation of the matrix A, obtain a seed matrix S of much fewer columns (p) than those of A; (3) compute the numerical values of the entries of the compressed matrix $B \equiv AS$; and (4) recover the entries of A from B. This framework has been proven to be an effective technology for computing sparse Jacobian as well as sparse Hessian matrices in a variety of applications (Coleman and Mor´e, 1983; Coleman and Mor´e, 1984; Coleman and Cai, 1986; Gebremedhin et al., 2008, 2009). A comprehensive review and synthesis of the use of graph coloring in derivative computation is available in (Gebremedhin et al., 2005). Efficient star and acyclic coloring algorithms for Hessian computation have been developed in (Gebremedhin et al., 2007), and Hessian recovery algorithms that take advantage of the structures of star and acyclic coloring have been presented in (Gebremedhin et al., 2009). A suite of implementations of various coloring algorithms, recovery methods and graph construction routines (needed in Steps 2 and 4 of the procedure outlined above) is provided in the software package ColPack (Gebremedhin et al., 2013). ColPack is integrated with ADOL-C and has been in distribution since ADOL-C version 2.1.0.

CONCLUSION

In closing, this chapter makes an attempt to establish structural unified modeling for computational platforms needed to emulate dynamics of complex electric energy systems. Such platforms do not exist at present, instead computer applications in support of scheduling resources to supply predictable system demand in this field have been mainly feed-forward off-line and with human-in-the-loop. System dynamics created by such changes in demand and resource scheduling are not simulated on-line because of the overwhelming complexity of high-order ODE models subject to many algebraic constraints. Because of this, the actual utilization of resources is based on the worst-case approach of ensuring acceptable operations for a handful of deterministic scenarios. As new technologies are integrated to meet decarbonization objectives, the renewable resources are highly stochastic. Also, as a direct consequence of climate change, the world is experiencing many more natural disasters than in the past. Providing clean and resilient electricity services over broad ranges of highly-varying and uncertain conditions, requires change of today's operating paradigm from top-down deterministic to a minimally-coordinated distributed self-adaptation of many resources and users, and of the electric power grid itself.

In this chapter we propose that it is indeed possible to evolve today's paradigm into a more flexible and distributed paradigm, and still ensure high QoS. To do so, a more systematic unified modeling is needed for setting information exchange protocols and for data-enabled computing and self-adaptation. Important for this book is the fact that the same unified modeling can and should be used to begin to design computational platforms capable of emulating complex interactions. This is needed to both assess potential effects of different technologies, hardware and software, on system performance, as well as for enabling more flexible operations. A digital twin is needed to emulate evolution of system dynamics at different temporal and spatial granularity. The same computational platform can be used to monitor and indicate feasibility and stability of the system as conditions vary, ultimately enabling its autonomous provision of electricity services. We suggest that while the basic modeling and its use for defining information flows are understood, the self-adaptation and self-organization will require use of

Machine Learning and Artificial Intelligence tools for exact and efficient computing of derivatives. In this chapter we have only illustrated this challenge when attempting to emulate in a distributed way very fast dynamics accurately. Similar challenge examples of the need for accurate computation of various sensitivities of cost functions with respect to active constraints exist in computational platforms relevant for electricity markets. It would be of tremendous value to pursue multi-disciplinary work which furthers the ideas in this chapter to the point of having robust hybrid computational platforms as the basis for scalable digital twins of complex electric energy systems. This chapter reports on the first steps of such collaboration by the co-authors.

REFERENCES

Adams, J., Carter, C., & Huang, S.-H. (2012). Ercot experience with sub-synchronous control interaction and proposed remediation. In *PES T&D 2012* (pp. 1–5). IEEE. doi:10.1109/TDC.2012.6281678

Association, I. S. (2010). IEEE standard for modeling and simulation (m&s) high level architecture (hla)—framework and rules. Institute of Electrical and Electronics Engineers. IEEE Standard, (1516-2010):10–1109.

Baydin, A. G., Pearlmutter, B. A., Radul, A. A., & Siskind, J. M. (2017). Automatic differentiation in machine learning: A survey. *Journal of Machine Learning Research*, *18*(1), 5595–5637.

Betancourt, R., & Alvarado, F. L. (1986). Parallel inversion of sparse matrices. *IEEE Transactions on Power Systems*, *1*(1), 74–81. doi:10.1109/TPWRS.1986.4334846

Bezanson, J., Edelman, A., Karpinski, S., & Shah, V. B. (2017). Julia: A fresh approach to numerical computing. *SIAM Review*, *59*(1), 65–98. doi:10.1137/141000671

Boston, T. (2020). *Private correspondence with Terry Boston, former PJM CEO*. CIRCA.

Carvalho, P. M., Peres, J. D., Ferreira, L. A., Ilic, M. D., Lauer, M., & Jaddivada, R. (2020). Incentive-based load shifting dynamics and aggregators response predictability. *Electric Power Systems Research*, *189*, 106744. doi:10.1016/j.epsr.2020.106744

Clements, K., Krumpholz, G., & Davis, P. (1981). Power system state estimation residual analysis: An algorithm using network topology. *IEEE Transactions on Power Apparatus and Systems*, *PAS-100*(4), 1779–1787. doi:10.1109/TPAS.1981.316517

Coleman & Mor´e. (1983). Estimation of sparse Jacobian matrices and graph coloring problems. *SIAM Journal on Numerical Analysis*, *20*(1), 187–209. doi:10.1137/0720013

Coleman, T. F., & Cai, J.-Y. (1986). The cyclic coloring problem and estimation of sparse Hessian matrices. *SIAM Journal on Algebraic Discrete Methods*, *7*(2), 221–235. doi:10.1137/0607026

Coleman, T. F., & Mor'e, J. J. (1984). Estimation of sparse Hessian matrices and graph coloring problems. *Mathematical Programming*, *28*(3), 243–270. doi:10.1007/BF02612334

Crow, M. L., & Ilic, M. (1994). The waveform relaxation method for systems of differential/algebraic equations. *Mathematical and Computer Modelling*, *19*(12), 67–84. doi:10.1016/0895-7177(94)90099-X

Cvijic, S., Ilic, M., Allen, E., & Lang, J. (2018). Using extended ac optimal power flow for effective decision making. In 2018 IEEE PES Innovative Smart Grid Technologies Conference Europe (ISGT-Europe), (pp. 1–6). IEEE. doi:10.1109/ISGTEurope.2018.8571792

Do, V.-Q., McCallum, D., Giroux, P., & De Kelper, B. (2001). A backward-forward interpolation technique for a precise modeling of power electronics in hypersim. *Proc. Int. Conf. Power Systems Transients*, 337–342.

Doi, H., Goto, M., Kawai, T., Yokokawa, S., & Suzuki, T. (1990). Advanced power system analogue simulator. *IEEE Transactions on Power Systems*, *5*(3), 962–968. doi:10.1109/59.65926

Donyanavard, B., Rahmani, A. M., Jantsch, A., Mutlu, O., & Dutt, N. (2020). *Intelligent management of mobile systems through computational self-awareness.* arXiv preprint arXiv:2008.00095.

Ferraiolo, D. F., Sandhu, R., Gavrila, S., Kuhn, D. R., & Chandramouli, R. (2001). Proposed nist standard for role-based access control. *ACM Transactions on Information and System Security*, *4*(3), 224–274. doi:10.1145/501978.501980

Fu, Y., & Shahidehpour, M. (2007). Fast scuc for large-scale power systems. *IEEE Transactions on Power Systems*, *22*(4), 2144–2151. doi:10.1109/TPWRS.2007.907444

Gebremedhin, A., Manne, F., & Pothen, A. (2005). What color is your Jacobian? Graph coloring for computing derivatives. *SIAM Review*, *47*(4), 629–705. doi:10.1137/S0036144504444711

Gebremedhin, A., Nguyen, D., Patwary, M., & Pothen, A. (2013). ColPack: Software for graph coloring and related problems in scientific computing. *ACM Transactions on Mathematical Software*, *40*(1), 1–31. doi:10.1145/2513109.2513110

Gebremedhin, A., Pothen, A., Tarafdar, A., & Walther, A. (2009). Efficient computation of sparse Hessians using coloring and automatic differentiation. *INFORMS Journal on Computing*, *21*(2), 209–223. doi:10.1287/ijoc.1080.0286

Gebremedhin, A., Pothen, A., & Walther, A. (2008). Exploiting sparsity in Jacobian computation via coloring and automatic differentiation: a case study in a Simulated Moving Bed process. In C. Bischof, M. Bu¨cker, P. Hovland, U. Naumann, & J. Utke (Eds.), *Advances in Automatic Differentiation* (pp. 339–349). Springer. doi:10.1007/978-3-540-68942-3_29

Gebremedhin, A., Tarafdar, A., Manne, F., & Pothen, A. (2007). New acyclic and star coloring algorithms with application to computing Hessians. *SIAM Journal on Scientific Computing*, *29*(3), 1042–1072. doi:10.1137/050639879

Griewank, A., & Walther, A. (2008). *Evaluating Derivatives: Principles and Techniques of Algorithmic Differentiation* (2nd ed.). SIAM. doi:10.1137/1.9780898717761

Hairer, E., Lubich, C., & Wanner, G. (2006). *Geometric numerical integration: structure-preserving algorithms for ordinary differential equations* (Vol. 31). Springer Science & Business Media.

Holmberg, D., Burns, M., Bushby, S., Gopstein, A., McDermott, T., Tang, Y., Huang, Q., Pratt, A., Ruth, M., Ding, F., & ... . (1900). Nist transactive energy modeling and simulation challenge phase ii final report. *NIST Special Publication*, *603*, 2019.

Ilic & Lessard. (n.d.). Distributed coordinated architecture of electrical energy systems for sustainability. *Nature Energy*. (submitted)

Ilic, M., Crow, M., & Pai, M. (1987). Transient stability simulation by waveform relaxation methods. *IEEE Transactions on Power Systems, 2*(4), 943–949. doi:10.1109/TPWRS.1987.4335282

Ilic, M., & Jaddivada, R. (2020). Unified value-based feedback, optimization and risk management in complex electric energy systems. *Optimization and Engineering, 21*(2), 1–57. doi:10.100711081-020-09486-y

Ilic, M., & Jaddivada, R. (2019a). Introducing dymonds-as-a-service (dymaas) for internet of things. HPEC, 1–9.

Ilic, M., & Jaddivada, R. (2019b). Toward technically feasible and economically efficient integration of distributed energy resources. In *2019 57th Annual Allerton Conference on Communication, Control, and Computing (Allerton)*, (pp. 796–803). IEEE. 10.1109/ALLERTON.2019.8919703

Ilic, M., Jaddivada, R., Miao, X., & Popli, N. (2019). Toward multi-layered mpc for complex electric energy systems. In *Handbook of Model Predictive Control* (pp. 625–663). Springer. doi:10.1007/978-3-319-77489-3_26

Ilic, M., & Lang, J. (2010). Netssworks software: An extended ac optimal power flow (ac xopf) for managing available system resources. *AD10-12 Staff Technical Conference on Enhanced Power Flow Models Federal Energy Regulatory Commission.*

Ilic, M. D. (2010). Dynamic monitoring and decision systems for enabling sustainable energy services. *Proceedings of the IEEE, 99*(1), 58–79. doi:10.1109/JPROC.2010.2089478

Ilic, M. D., & Jaddivada, R. (2018). Multi-layered interactive energy space modeling for near-optimal electrification of terrestrial, shipboard and aircraft systems. *Annual Reviews in Control, 45*, 52–75. doi:10.1016/j.arcontrol.2018.04.009

Ilic, M. D., Jaddivada, R., & Korpas, M. (2020). Interactive protocols for distributed energy resource management systems (derms). *IET Generation, Transmission & Distribution, 14*(11), 2065–2081. doi:10.1049/iet-gtd.2019.1022

Ilic, M. D., Jaddivada, R., & Miao, X. Scalable electric power system simulator. In 2018 IEEE PES Innovative Smart Grid Technologies Conference Europe (ISGT-Europe), (pp. 1–6). IEEE. doi:10.1109/ISGTEurope.2018.8571428

Jaddivada, R. (2020). *A unified modeling for control of reactive power dynamics in electrical energy systems* (PhD thesis). Massachusetts Institute of Technology.

Joo, J.-Y., & Ilic, M. D. (2013). Multi-layered optimization of demand resources using lagrange dual decomposition. *IEEE Transactions on Smart Grid, 4*(4), 2081–2088. doi:10.1109/TSG.2013.2261565

Lauer, M., Jaddivada, R., & Ilic, M. Secure blockchain-enabled dymonds de-sign. *Proceedings of the International Conference on Omni-Layer Intelligent Systems*, 191–198. 10.1145/3312614.3312654

LaWhite, N., & Ilic, M. D. (1997). Vector space decomposition of reactive power forperiodic nonsinusoidal signals. *IEEE Transactions on Circuits and Systems. I, Fundamental Theory and Applications*, *44*(4), 338–346. doi:10.1109/81.563623

Ostrom, E. (2009). A general framework for analyzing sustainability of social-ecological systems. *Science*, *325*(5939), 419–422. doi:10.1126cience.1172133 PMID:19628857

Padiyar, K. (2007). *FACTS controllers in power transmission and distribution*. New Age International.

Pai, M., Sauer, P. W., & Lesieutre, B. C. (1995). Static and dynamic nonlinear loads and structural stability in power systems. *Proceedings of the IEEE*, *83*(11), 1562–1572. doi:10.1109/5.481634

Papic, M., Vaiman, M., Vaiman, M., & Povolotskiy, M. (2007). *A new approach to constructing seasonal nomograms in planning and operations environments at idaho power co. In 2007 IEEE Lausanne Power Tech*. IEEE.

Pavella & Murthy. (1994). *Transient stability of power systems: theory and practice*. Academic Press.

Penfield, P., Spence, R., & Duinker, S. (1970). A generalized form of tellegen's theorem. *IEEE Transactions on Circuit Theory*, *17*(3), 302–305. doi:10.1109/TCT.1970.1083145

Puschel, M., Moura, J. M., Johnson, J. R., Padua, D., Veloso, M. M., Singer, B. W., Xiong, J., Franchetti, F., Gacic, A., Voronenko, Y., & ... . (2005). Spiral: Code generation for dsp transforms. *Proceedings of the IEEE*, *93*(2), 232–275. doi:10.1109/JPROC.2004.840306

Ragan-Kelley, J., Barnes, C., Adams, A., Paris, S., Durand, F., & Amarasinghe, S. (2013). Halide: A language and compiler for optimizing parallelism, locality, and recomputation in image processing pipelines. *ACM SIGPLAN Notices*, *48*(6), 519–530. doi:10.1145/2499370.2462176

Rose. (2012). *Sparse Matrices and their Applications: Proceedings of a Symposium on Sparse Matrices and Their Applications, held September 9 10, 1971, at the IBM Thomas J. Watson Research Center, Yorktown Heights, New York, and sponsored by the Office of Naval Research, the National Science Foundation, IBM World Trade Corporation, and the IBM Research Mathematical Sciences Department*. Springer Science & Business Media.

Stott, Jardim, & Alsac. (2009). Dc power flow revisited. *IEEE Transactions on Power Systems*, *24*(3), 1290–1300.

Stott. (1974). Review of load-flow calculation methods. *Proceedings of the IEEE*, *62*(7), 916–929.

Thoma. (2016). *Introduction to bond graphs and their applications*. Elsevier.

Thorp, Seyler, & Phadke. (1998). Electromechanical wave propagation in large electric power systems. *IEEE Transactions on Circuits and Systems. I, Fundamental Theory and Applications*, *45*(6), 614–622.

Tinney, Brandwajn, & Chan. (1985). Sparse vector methods. *IEEE Transactions on Power Apparatus and Systems*, (2): 295–301.

van Merri"enboer, W., & Moldovan. (2017). Tangent: Automatic differentiation using sourcecode transformation in Python. *31st Conference on Neural Information Processing System*.

Vassilev, Vassilev, & Penev, Moneta, & Ilieva. (2015). Clad – Automatic differentiation using Clang and LLVM. *Journal of Physics: Conference Series, 608*(1).

Verghese, Perez-Arriaga, & Schweppe. (1982). Selective modal analysis with applications to electric power systems, part ii: The dynamic stability problem. *IEEE Transactions on Power Apparatus and Systems,* (9): 3126–3134.

Wagner, Bachovchin, & Ilic. (2015). Computer architecture and multi time-scale implementations for smart grid in a room simulator. *IFACPapersOnLine, 48*(30), 233–238.

Wyatt & Ilic. (1990). Time-domain reactive power concepts for nonlinear, nonsinusoidal or nonperiodic networks. In *IEEE International Symposium on Circuits and Systems,* (pp. 387–390). IEEE.

Zhang, Soudi, Shirmohammadi, & Cheng. (1995). A distribution short circuit analysis approach using hybrid compensation method. *IEEE Transactions on Power Systems, 10*(4), 2053–2059.

Chapter 14
A Backtracking Algorithmic Toolbox for Solving the Subgraph Isomorphism Problem

Jurij Mihelič

Faculty of Computer and Information Science, University of Ljubljana, Slovenia

Uroš Čibej

Faculty of Computer and Information Science, University of Ljubljana, Slovenia

Luka Fürst

Faculty of Computer and Information Science, University of Ljubljana, Slovenia

ABSTRACT

The subgraph isomorphism problem asks whether a given graph is a subgraph of another graph. It is one of the most general NP-complete problems since many other problems (e.g., Hamiltonian cycle, clique, independent set, etc.) have a natural reduction to subgraph isomorphism. Furthermore, there is a variety of practical applications where graph pattern matching is the core problem. Developing efficient algorithms and solvers for this problem thus enables good solutions to a variety of different practical problems. In this chapter, the authors present and experimentally explore various algorithmic refinements and code optimizations for improving the performance of subgraph isomorphism solvers. In particular, they focus on algorithms that are based on the backtracking approach and constraint satisfaction programming. They gather experiences from many state-of-the-art algorithms as well as from their engagement in this field. Lessons learned from engineering such a solver can be utilized in many other fields where backtracking is a prominent approach for solving a particular problem.

DOI: 10.4018/978-1-7998-7156-9.ch014

INTRODUCTION

Collecting, organizing, and analysing large amounts of data has emerged as a promising new area of research. Such data often require a structural description, for which graphs are commonly used. Graphs are an essential form of data organization and are emerging in the most surprising applications from chemistry (Agrafiotis et al., 2011; Balaban, 1985; Barnard, 1993), neurology (He & Evans, 2010), social sciences (Carrington, Scott, & Wasserman, 2005), linguistics (Krahmer, Van Erk, & Verleg, 2003), social network analysis (Fan, 2012), and computer vision (Liu & Lee, 2001). Moreover, in these domains graph databases are replacing the traditional relational databases (Batra & Tyagi, 2012). For an extensive review of graph matching for pattern recognition see (Conte, Foggia, Sansone, & Vento, 2004).

From the viewpoint of pattern analysis and recognition, matching graphs and subgraphs is one of the most important tasks in graph processing. The problem of finding instances of a given graph in a larger graph is called *subgraph isomorphism problem*. Given two graphs, namely, a pattern graph and a target graph, the problem is defined as finding a subgraph (corresponding to the pattern graph) in the target graph. Due to the ubiquity of this problem, it has been studied extensively, both from a purely theoretical point of view as well as from a more practical point of view.

A plethora of algorithms for solving the problem exactly exist in the literature. The most widely used and well-known subgraph isomorphism algorithms are Ullmann's algorithm (Ullmann, 1976; Čibej & Mihelič, 2015), VF2 (Cordella, Foggia, Sansone, & Vento, 1999), VF3 (Carletti, Foggia, Saggese, & Vento, 2017), RI (Bonnici, Giugno, Pulvirenti, Shasha, & Ferro, 2013a), Glasgow subgraph solver (McCreesh & Prosser, 2015a), SubSea (Lipets, Vanetik, & Gudes, 2009), FocusSearch (Ullmann, 2010), LAD (Solnon, 2010). Most of them are based on the *backtracking* approach which explores the search tree of possible solutions. As the problem is NP-hard, all such algorithms exhibit exponential running time in the worst case. Nevertheless, in many practical cases, the problem can be quite efficiently solved if advanced techniques of pruning the search tree are employed.

In this paper, we focus on such techniques (intended for backtracking algorithms) which may provide a significant performance boost to algorithms especially if used in combination with others. The techniques are mostly based on heuristic approaches as well as on optimization and tuning of algorithms. They often originate from the field of constraint satisfaction problems and represent a basic approach in the field of algorithm engineering (Muller-Hannemann & Schirra, 2010; McGeoch, 2012). Our approach is systematic (Blagojević et al., 2016) and we strive to give an overview of different issues encountered when developing and engineering efficient backtracking algorithms. The collected experiences can serve as a toolbox for further improvement of algorithms for the subgraph isomorphism problem, as well as guidelines on how to solve similar problems.

In the rest of the chapter, we first formally define the subgraph isomorphism problem and present the main framework of the backtracking approach to solving it. Afterward, we present the backtracking refinement techniques for reduction of both time and space complexity. In the last part, we focus on various search orders, which are one of the most important speedup factors. For each technique, we give a description followed by its experimental evaluation.

SUBGRAPH ISOMORPHISM PROBLEM

We start this section with several definitions of graph theory notions and morphisms. We continue with a description of the definition of several variants of the subgraph isomorphism problem. Then we focus on the algorithmic approach to solving the problem with a focus on the backtracking algorithms. Finally, we present two backtracking-based algorithmic frameworks for solving the problem, namely backward checking and forward checking.

Graph Notions

A pair $G = \left(V_G, E_G \right)$, where $V_G = \left\{ 1, 2, \ldots, n_G \right\}$ is a finite set of *vertices* and $E_G \subseteq V_G \times V_G$ is a set of vertex pairs representing *edges*, is called a *graph*. If edges are unordered or ordered then the graph is undirected or directed, respectively. In this paper we mostly deal with undirected graphs, but our discussion is generally applicable also to the directed ones.

For an undirected graph $G = \left(V_G, E_G \right)$ and a vertex $u \in V_G$ we define

$$\mathcal{N}_G \left(u \right) = \left\{ v \in V_G \mid \left\langle u, v \right\rangle \in E_G \right\}$$

and

$$d_G \left(u \right) = \left| \mathcal{N}_G \left(u \right) \right|$$

as the u is neighborhood and degree, respectively.

Let $H = \left(V_H, E_G \right)$ be a graph. A graph $G = \left(V_G, E_G \right)$ is a subgraph of a graph H if

$$V_G \subseteq V_H \text{ and } E_G \subseteq E_H.$$

If additionally it also holds

$$\forall u, v \in V_G : \left\langle u, v \right\rangle \in E_G \Leftrightarrow \left\langle u, v \right\rangle \in E_H$$

then the graph G is an induced subgraph of the graph H.

Morphisms

Let G and H be two graphs. Oftentimes, the graph G is called a *pattern* and the graph H a *target*. A bijective mapping $\phi : V_G \to V_H$ is called *graph isomorphism* if

$$\forall u, v \in V_G : \left\langle u, v \right\rangle \in E_G \Leftrightarrow \left\langle \phi \left(u \right), \phi \left(v \right) \right\rangle \in E_H.$$

An injective mapping $\phi : V_G \rightarrow V_H$ is called *graph monomorphism* if

$$\forall u, v \in V_G : \langle u, v \rangle \in E_G \Rightarrow \langle \phi(u), \phi(v) \rangle \in E_H.$$

Instead of the term graph monomorphism the term *(ordinary) subgraph isomorphism* is oftentimes used since the mapping ϕ is an isomorphism between G and a subgraph $\phi(G)$ of graph H. Here, $\phi(G)$ represents a subgraph of H to which G is mapped.

Thus, graph monomorphism is an injective mapping preserving adjacency relation where the images of vertices of graph G can have some additional edges in H not present in G. A more strict version of the problem is called *induced subgraph isomorphism* which asks for an injective mapping $\phi : V_G \rightarrow V_H$ where

$$\forall u, v \in V_G : \langle u, v \rangle \in E_G \Leftrightarrow \langle \phi(u), \phi(v) \rangle \in E_H.$$

Consider a simple example in Figure 1 demonstrating the difference between the ordinary and induced version of the subgraph isomorphism.

Figure 1. The left graph G has no induced subgraph isomorphisms in the right graph H while it has six ordinary subgraph isomorphisms. Here, in the latter, the vertices abc of G may map to abc, cba, bca, acb, bac, and cab of H.

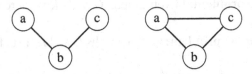

An *automorphism* in a graph G is an isomorphism $G \rightarrow G$, i.e., a neighborhood-preserving permutation of the vertex set of G. For a graph with vertices $\{1,...,n\}$, we will use the notation $a_1 a_2 ... a_n$ to represent the automorphism $\{1 \mapsto a_1, 2 \mapsto a_2, ..., n \mapsto a_n\}$. For example, the graph C_6 in Figure 2 (i.e., the 6-cycle) has 12 automorphisms: 123456, 234561, 345612, 456123, 561234, 612345, 654321, 543216, 432165, 321654, 216543, and 165432.

Figure 2. An example of the cyclic graph C_6 having 12 automorphisms.

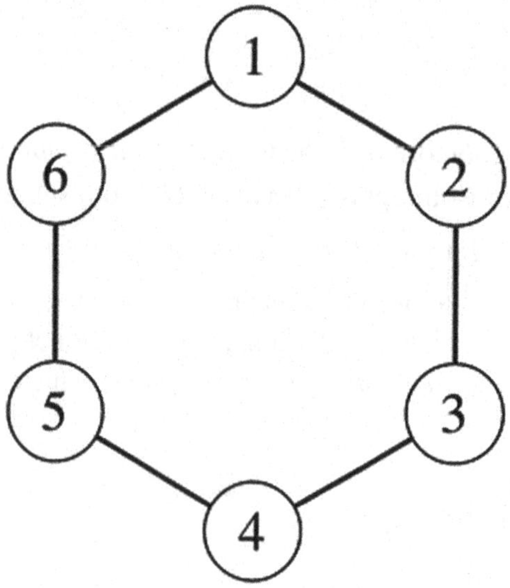

Problem Definitions

Using the morphism definitions in the previous section, we can now define several versions of the subgraph isomorphism problem. Regarding the type of solution sought we have:

- **Decision version of the problem:** Given graphs G and H, is there a subgraph isomorphism between the two?
- **Enumeration version of the problem:** Given graphs G and H, list all the subgraph isomorphisms between the two.
- **Counting version of the problem:** Given graphs G and H, count the number of subgraph isomorphism between the two.

All these problems can be about ordinary or induced subgraph isomorphisms.

To show the NP-completeness of the decision version of the problem, a reduction from the well-known clique or Hamiltonian cycle problems is usually employed (Garey & Johnson, 1979).

Unfortunately, the subgraph isomorphism problem is computationally very difficult, as it is NP-complete (Cook, 1971). Being such a fundamental problem, there are many attempts to overcome this theoretical barrier. To more accurately position our approach in this body of work, we will look at various approaches to dealing with this problem.

Algorithms

The first approach is to reduce the complexity of the problem by restricting input graphs. Polynomial-time exact algorithms exist for trees (Matula, 1978; Valiente, 2002) and some classes of graphs with a bounded treewidth (Gupta & Nishimura, 1996b, 1996a). However, in some cases, such restrictions may not be an acceptable option.

The second approach is to search for approximate solutions (Plantenga, 2013; Liu & Lee, 2001; Fan, 2012). This approach is viable when we allow for a certain amount of error in the results.

Due to the recent growing interest in graph databases, also the specifics of this problem are widely researched (Lee, Han, Kasperovics, & Lee, 2012; Yuan, Wang, Chen, & Wang, 2012; Sun, Wang, Wang, Shao, & Li, 2012; Han, Lee, & Lee, 2013; Messmer & Bunke, 2000). The main advantage for these types of applications is that there is a fixed goal graph (or a fixed set of graphs) and only the pattern graph (the query) changes. The goal graph(s) can thus be preprocessed to speed up the queries.

When all the above approaches are not plausible, exact exponential algorithms remain the only alternative. Recently a growing interest in this type of algorithms has given plenty of theoretical results (Marx & Pilipczuk, 2013; Amini, Fomin, & Saurabh, 2012; Fomin, Jansen, & Pilipczuk, 2012) mainly relating to the fixed-parameter tractability of the problem. Unfortunately, these algorithms do not (yet) have a practical impact, due to their (albeit, in theory, better than brute-force) huge time complexity in practice.

More pragmatical approaches try to find algorithms that might not have any theoretical guarantees but work well in practice. These approaches prune the unpromising parts of the search space, and hope for efficient running time, despite the possibility of exponential worst-case running time. Many successful exact algorithms for the unrestricted graphs are widely used in practice. One of them (still commonly used) was proposed by Ullmann (Ullmann, 1976) more than thirty years ago. He recently proposed a set of improvements to his algorithm and called it FocusSearch (Ullmann, 2010). Similarly to FocusSearch the LAD (Solnon, 2010) algorithm views subgraph isomorphisms as a type of Constrained Satisfaction Problem (CSP) and uses methods from CSP to efficiently find the solution. Other recently proposed algorithms include the first version VF (Cordella et al., 1999) and its improvements VF2 (Cordella, Foggia, Sansone, & Vento, 2004) and VF3 (Carletti et al., 2017). Another straightforward approach with some clever vertex processing ordering is the RI algorithm (Bonnici, Giugno, Pulvirenti, Shasha, & Ferro, 2013b). The latter group of algorithms is modifications of a naïve recursive brute-force search and favor simplicity over sophisticated time-consuming methods to prune the search space. This simplistic approach has proven very efficient in practice.

Backtracking Algorithms

Many of the algorithms for the subgraph isomorphism problem are based on the backtracking approach. Here, the mapping $\phi : V_G \to V_H$ is constructed gradually, on each step one assignment of a vertex $u \in V_G$ is resolved, i.e., $\phi(u)$ is assigned to some $u' \in V_H$. Without loss of generality, we assume (if not otherwise noted) that the vertices of V_G are processed in the order of their labels, i.e., $1, 2, \ldots, n_G$.

A state where some vertices of V_G are already assigned is called a *partial solution*. In particular, on step k, where $1 \leq k \leq n_G$ the algorithm resolves the vertex $k \in V_G$ and constructs a partial solution ϕ_k from ϕ_{k-1}. Here, $\phi_0(u) = \perp$ (i.e., undefined) and $\phi_k(u) = \phi_{k-1}(u)$ for all $u < k$. Finally, $\phi(u) = \phi_{n_G}(u)$.

A *consistency* of a partial solution ϕ_k may be checked by satisfying the following constraints:

Algorithm 1. Pseudocode of the backward checking algorithm for the subgraph isomorphism problem.

Algorithm 1: Backward checking

```
 1 function Search (u)
 2     if u = n_G + 1 then                          /* solution found */
 3         count ← count + 1
 4     else
 5         forall u' ∈ V_H do                       /* try all candidates */
 6             if Check (u, u') then
 7                 φ(u) ← u';
 8                 Search (u + 1)                    /* recurse */
 9         end
10     end
11 function Check (u, u')
12     for v ← 1, 2, ..., u − 1 do
13         if u' = φ(v) then                        /* injectivity */
14             return False
15         if u' ∼_H φ(v) ≢ u ∼_G v then             /* adjacency */
16             return False
17     end
18     return True
```

- **Injectivity:** $\phi(u) \neq \phi(v)$ for each $u, v \in V_G : u \neq v$,
- **Adjacency:** $\langle \phi(u), \phi(v) \rangle \in E_H$ for all $\langle u, v \rangle \in E_G$, and
- **Non-adjacency:** $\langle \phi(u), \phi(v) \rangle \notin E_H$ for all $\langle u, v \rangle \notin E_G$.

The last constraint is only relevant to the induced version of the problem. Notice that, other constraints such as matching of labels of vertices or edges may also be present.

There are two general approaches to how to implement candidate checking in the backtracking algorithms:

- **Backward checking:** When a new candidate target vertex is mapped, check the problem constraints to determine if the partial solution is still valid.
- **Forward checking:** When a new candidate target vertex is mapped, use this new information to update constraints on candidates for not yet mapped vertices.

Backward Checking

Backward checking algorithms proceed as follows. When a new candidate vertex $u' \in V_H$ is mapped to some vertex $u \in V_G$ the consistency of the partial solution is checked: if the check fails then the algorithm backtracks or tries the next candidate otherwise it proceeds to the next vertex of G. When the last vertex is successfully mapped the algorithm finds a subgraph isomorphism.

The pseudo-code of this approach is given in Algorithm 1. Two functions are defined. The first, called Search, recursively implements the backtracking approach. Here, in lines 2 and 3, the algorithm checks if all vertices have been mapped and we have a solution. In line 5 it iterates through all the target vertices and, in line 6, it checks each one if the mapping between a source vertex u and a candidate u' is possible. If the check is successful then mapping ϕ is updated (line 7) and the algorithm recurses (line 8).

The second function, called Check, checks two given vertices u and u' if their mapping complies with the problem constraints. Here, the algorithm iterates through all the source vertices that have already been mapped (line 12). Then it checks whether injectivity (line 13) or topology (line 15) constraints are violated (topology includes adjacency as well as non-adjacency constraint): if they are the check fails, otherwise, it is successful.

Forward Checking

Now, let us turn to a forward-checking variant of backtracking algorithms. Here, whenever a vertex $u \in V_G$ is mapped to $u' \in V_H$, we use this new information to form additional constraints on candidates for vertices not yet mapped. For example, due to injectivity, no vertex in V_G can be mapped to u'. Such additional constraints may be stored in a binary matrix where the u-th row gives the u's candidates.

The pseudo-code of this approach is given in Algorithm 2. It consists of three parts. The first is the function Init which takes care of the initialization of the binary constraint matrix. In the example algorithm it is initialized to all True values which means that, initially, every pattern vertex can be mapped to any target vertex. However, a more elaborate initialization may be used here, e.g. forming the initial constrained relating to degrees of pattern and target vertices; see also the next section for some suggestions on this.

The next function, called Search, is the main backtracking algorithm. It also includes a called to two undefined functions, namely Backup and Restore. Here, the former stores the constraint matrix onto the stack and the latter restores the constraint matrix from the stack.

Finally, the Update function takes care of updating the constraint matrix in order to use the information based on the new mapping of u to u'. The matrix is updated only for the vertices $v > u$, i.e., the vertices that appear later than u in the algorithm processing order. The matrix update technique checks if any relevant True value can be set to False, basically, by checking the injectivity and adjacency constraints.

Algorithm 2. Pseudocode of the forward checking algorithm for the subgraph isomorphism problem.

Algorithm 2: Forward checking

1 **function** Init ()
2 | **for** $u \in V_G, u' \in V_H$ **do** $M[u, u'] \leftarrow$ **True** ;
3 **function** Search (u)
4 | **if** $u = n_G + 1$ **then**   /* solution found */
5 | | $count \leftarrow count + 1$
6 | **else**
7 | | **foreach** $u' \in V_H$ **do**   /* try all candidates */
8 | | | **if** $M[u, u']$ **then**   /* is the candidate suitable */
9 | | | | Backup (M);
10 | | | | Update (u, u');
11 | | | | **if** $\forall v > u \, \exists v' \in V_H : M[v, v']$ **then**
12 | | | | | $\phi(u) \leftarrow u'$;
13 | | | | | Search ($u + 1$)   /* recurse */
14 | | | | **end**
15 | | | | Restore (M);
16 | | | **end**
17 | | **end**
18 | **end**
19 **function** Update (u, u')
20 | **for** $v = u + 1, \ldots, n_G$ **do**   /* not yet processed vertices */
21 | | **forall** $v' \in V_H$ **do**
22 | | | **if** $M[v, v']$ **then**
23 | | | | **if** $v' = u'$ **then**   /* injectivity */
24 | | | | | $M[v, v'] \leftarrow$ **False**
25 | | | | **if** $u' \sim_H v' \not\equiv u \sim_G v$ **then**   /* adjacency */
26 | | | | | $M[v, v'] \leftarrow$ **False**
27 | | | **end**
28 | | **end**
29 | **end**

REFINEMENT TECHNIQUES

In this section, we present several refinement techniques applicable to backtracking algorithms for the subgraph isomorphism problem. In particular, in this section we describe the following refinements:

- **Degree constraints:** Using additional constraints on vertex degrees in order to prune the search tree.
- **Bit arrays:** Code tuning in order to speed up target vertex candidate selection.
- **Parent-based candidate selection:** Tuning technique for faster enumeration of target vertex candidates.
- **Neighborhood adjacency checking:** Search tree pruning via neighborhood checking for adjacent vertices.
- **Arc consistency:** Filtering of target vertex candidates via checking for their support in the neighborhood.
- **Hall's sets:** Employing the all-different constraint to filter candidate vertices.
- **Exploratory equivalence:** Exploiting symmetries in the source graph.

- **Lowering space complexity:** Conservation of memory in the forward checking algorithms.

Some techniques, such as degree constraints and neighborhood adjacency checking, are more related to algorithmic optimization since their goal is usually to prune the search tree as much as possible while other techniques such as bit arrays are more related to code tuning with the goal to speed up the execution without reducing the search space.

Degree Constraints

One approach to pruning the search tree of backtracking algorithms is to derive additional problem constraints. To do this, we start from the basic (and sufficient) constraints given by the problem definition. Then, we derive one or more new constraints which can be used to check if the given partial solution can represent a final solution. The emphasis of derived constraints is on that they can be efficiently checked and if they are not satisfied the search tree can be pruned.

First, let us derive the *vertex degree* constraint, which states that the degree of a vertex $u \in V_G$ is not greater than the degree of the vertex $\phi(u) \in V_H$ that u is mapped to, i.e.,

$$d_G(u) \le d_H(\phi(u)) \text{ for each } u \in V_G.$$

Indeed, due to adjacency constraint, the neighborhood of $u \in V_G$ must be mapped to the neighborhood of $\phi(u)$, i.e., $\phi(\mathcal{N}_G(u)) \subseteq \mathcal{N}_H(\phi(u))$. Moreover, due to injectivity constraint, we have $|\mathcal{N}_G(u)| = |\phi(\mathcal{N}_G(u))|$. Hence, $|\mathcal{N}_G(u)| \le |\mathcal{N}_H(\phi(u))|$ from which the degree constraint is clear. See also Figure 3 for a graphical representation.

Figure 3. Degree constraints derivation: (blue shading) mapping of the neighborhood $\mathcal{N}_G(u)$ of the source vertex $u \in V_G$ to (green shading) the neighborhood $\mathcal{N}_H(\phi(u))$ of the target vertex $\phi(u) \in V_H$.

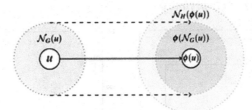

Explicitly storing vertex degrees in the graph data structure enables the algorithm to efficiently check degree constraints. Notice that, in the backward checking algorithms the constraint is easily checked for every new mapping established while in the forward checking algorithms the constraint is included in the preprocessing phase (e.g., initialization of the constraint matrix).

Now we extend a vertex degree constraint to the whole neighborhood of the vertex. First, we define a *neigborhood degree sequence* $Z_G(u)$ for a vertex $u \in V_G$ as an ordered sequence

$$Z_G(u) = (d_G(v))_{v \in \mathcal{N}_G(u)}$$

sorted nonincreasingly. For each vertex $u \in V_G$ (and its mapped vertex $\phi(u) \in V_H$) it must hold

$$Z_G(u) \preceq Z_H(\phi(u)) \tag{1}$$

where $\preceq$ is a relation of lexicographical comparison of two sequences.

To see this, consider $u \in V_G$. Obviously, for each vertex $v \in \mathcal{N}_G(u)$ we have $d_G(v) \leq d_H(\phi(u))$ (using the vertex degree constraints). However, we do not know which vertex from $\mathcal{N}_G(u)$ maps to which vertex from $\mathcal{N}_H(\phi(u))$, but for each $v \in \mathcal{N}_G(u)$ there must be a unique $v' \in \mathcal{N}_H(\phi(u))$ such that $d_G(v) \leq d_H(v')$. Furthermore, checking this for the whole neighborhood corresponds to Equation (1).

To compare the performance of both refinements we performed an experiment with the (backward checking) backtracking algorithm. See Figure 4 for the results of the experimental evaluation on two test scenarios: randomly generated graphs and bounded valence graphs. Both charts show the number of solved instances in a given time: the higher the better. Notice that, using degree constraints slightly improves the performance of the algorithms while neighborhood degree constraints seem to be too much an overhead to improve the total performance of the algorithm.

Figure 4. Results of the experiments for the algorithms using degree constraints on random graphs (left) and bounded valence graphs (right): x-axis specifies time-allowed for solving and y-axis gives the number of solved instances in the given time.

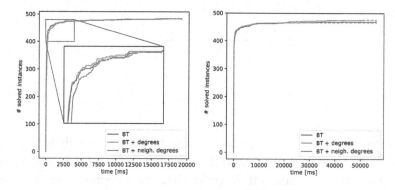

Figure 5. A set of candidates for a vertex $u \in V_G$ is the intersection of neighborhoods of images of already mapped vertices that are neighbors of u. Blue vertices represent the already mapped neighbors of u, green vertices are their images in V_H and green circles are images' neighbourhoods.

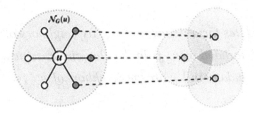

Bit Arrays

The optimization we focus on in this subsection belongs to the code tuning group. In particular, we explore the approaches to represent subsets of vertices of a graph. In what follows we assume vertices are numbered from 1 to n. One approach, oftentimes used in the algorithms, is to represent vertex set with a list where each entry gives the index of a vertex. The size of such a list is, thus, $O(n\log n)$ bits. This approach is also straightforward to implement.

Another approach to representing a vertex subset is to use a *bit array* of length n bits, where the i-th bit of the array corresponds to the membership of the vertex i, e.g., 1 corresponding to members and 0 to nonmembers. Moreover, set operations such as union and intersection, which are oftentimes used in the subgraph-isomorphism backtracking algorithms, can then be efficiently implemented. In particular, set union corresponds to bitwise or, intersection to bitwise and, and difference to bitwise and with not.

Figure 6. The results of experimental evaluation of the backward (left-hand side) and forward (righthand side) checking algorithms with and without the use of bit array: x-axis specifies time-allowed for solving and y-axis gives the number of solved instances in the given time.

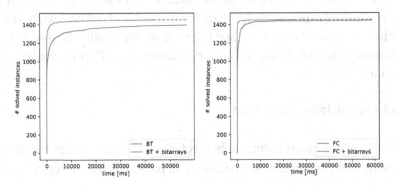

The gain of the latter, thus, is the $O(\log n)$ factor, which in practice usually turns into 32 (or 64) since this is the most common size of the representation of integer values (i.e., vertex indices). Nevertheless, despite space and performance gain steaming from smaller data representation, there may be also performance overhead due to the operations manipulating bits instead of bytes. The approach may also be harder to implement from the ground up, but many algorithmic libraries exist supporting it.

Figure 7. Determining candidates for a vertex $u_k \in V_G$ as neighbors of a vertex assigned to the u_k' parent vertex. Here, the neighborhood of u_k is in the blue circle, some of the vertices may already be processed (dark blue). The candidates in V_H are the neighbors of u_p', which is a vertex that is assigned to u_k is parent vertex u_p.

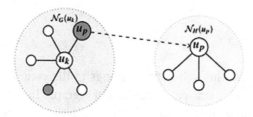

Instead of the adjacency-list representation, graphs can be represented with bit arrays, where for each vertex a bit array stores the set of the vertex's neighbors. Now, to compute the set of candidates for the vertex $u \in V_G$ we consider only the already mapped neighbors of u, i.e., $v \in \mathcal{N}_G(u)$ and $v < u$ (corresponding to the actual search order used), and compute the intersection of neighborhoods to which they are mapped. See also Figure 5 for a graphical representation. More formally, the candidate set for $u \in V_G$ is

$$\bigcap_{v \in \mathcal{N}_G(u), v < u} \mathcal{N}_H\big(\phi(v)\big).$$

An optimization technique may offer some speedups as well as some overheads. To evaluate its practical efficacy, we performed an experiment. We implemented forward and backward checking algorithms, both with and without the use of bit arrays. See Figure 6 for the results. Notice that, in both variants, bit arrays have a positive effect on the algorithm performance. The effect is even a bit more profound in the backward checking algorithm.

Parents-based Candidate Selection

In this section, we describe an algorithmic tuning technique that does not prune the search tree but it enables a faster selection of candidate target vertices for a particular source vertex. Let $\big(u_1, u_2, \ldots, u_{k-1}\big)$, where $u_i \in V_G$ be a partial ordering of vertices and let $u_k \in V_G$ be the next vertex to be assigned ta vertex $u_k' \in V_H$. Moreover, let u_k be adjacent to some vertex $u_p \in V_G$ appearing before u_k in the search order, i.e., $1 \le p < k$. We call such a vertex u_p, a *parent* of u_k. Observe that, u_p has already been matched to some $u_p' \in V_H$ previously in the process.

Figure 8. Filtering based on the selected pattern and target vertices (blue). The neighbors (green) of the pattern vertex are incompatible with the non-neighbors (red) of the target vertex (color online).

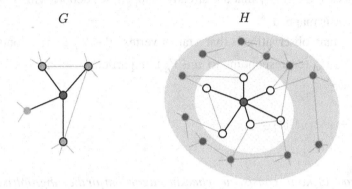

Since a vertex $u_k' \in V_H$ to be assigned to $u_k \in V_G$ must also be adjacent to a vertex $u_p' \in V_H$ that is assigned to $u_p \in V_G$, we may, when checking matching candidates for u_k, iterate only on the neighbors of u_p', i.e., on the vertices $u_k' \in \mathcal{N}_H(u_p')$. See Figure 7 for a graphical representation of parents-based candidate selection.

Notice that, it is possible that u_k does not have a parent, so the algorithm must still check all the vertices. However, in connected graphs the parent almost always exists; in particular, this is true for the RDEG ordering which basically orders the vertices according to the number of parents.

Figure 9 in the next section presents the results of experimental evaluation of parent-based candidate selection in comparisons with several other refinements.

Figure 9. The results of experimental evaluation of several refinements of backward checking: parents-based candidate selection, neighborhood-adjacency checking, and bit arrays code optimization: x-axis specifies time-allowed for solving and y-axis gives the number of solved instances in the given time.

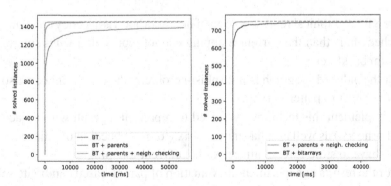

Neighborhood Adjacency Checking

Here, we present a refinement that prunes the search tree. Let $u \in V_G$ and $u' \in V_H$ be the two vertices so that u is mapped to u' (e.g., vertices mapped in the previous step). Another approach to consistency-constraint checking is to actually probe the vertices in the neighborhoods of u and u'. In particular, we check all the vertices $v \in \mathcal{N}_G(u)$ that are already mapped; we denote with $v' \in V_H$ a vertex in the target graph to which v is mapped.

A simple, but important, observation is that a target vertex $v' \in V_G$ (corresponding to $v \in V_G$) must also be adjacent to $u' \in V_H$ (corresponding to $u \in V_G$). In particular, for all $u \in V_G$ and $u' \in V_H$ such that $\phi(u) = u'$ we have

$$\forall v \in \mathcal{N}_G(u) \wedge \phi(v) = v' : (u', v') \in E_H.$$

Algorithm 3. Pseudocode of the arc consistency checking algorithm for the subgraph isomorphism problem.

Algorithm 3: Algorithm for arc consistency checking

```
1   function ArcConsistency(u)
2       change ← True;
3       while change do
4           change ← False;
5           for u ← 1,...,n_G do
6               for v ← 1,...,n_G do
7                   for u' ∈ D'_u do
8                       if φ(u) ← u' has no support for constraints between φ(u)
                            in φ(v) then
9                           D'_u ← D'_u \ {u'};
10                          change ← True;
11                      end
12                  end
13              end
14          end
15      end
```

See also Figure 8 for a graphical representation of neighborhood adjacency checking. If this neighborhood adjacency check fails than the current mapping cannot represent a valid subgraph isomorphism, hence, the algorithm backtracks.

Notice that, for the induced subgraph isomorphism problem, the constraint can also be checked from the viewpoint of the target to pattern graph.

To efficiently implement this technique we need to represent a graph with adjacency lists (for fast iteration of neighborhoods) as well as adjacency matrix (for fast checking of adjacency of two vertices). Moreover, we also have to store inverse images of the current mapping.

See Figure 9 for the results of experimental evaluation of parent-based candidate selection as well as neighborhood adjacency checking (the plot on the left-hand side); we also add the bit arrays refinement for a more in-depth comparison (the right-hand side). Notice, that both parents-based candidate selection, as well as neighborhood adjacency checking refinements, have a profound effect on the algorithm performance. Moreover, a combination of these two refinements performs better than only using bit arrays.

Figure 10. The results of the experimental evaluation of the suggested refinements of forwardchecking algorithms: bit arrays code optimization, arc consistency checking, Hall's sets. On the left-hand side, GCF processing order is used and on the right-hand side the MRV processing order. Here, x-axis specifies time-allowed for solving and y-axis gives the number of solved instances in the given time.

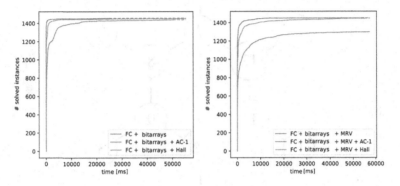

Arc Consistency

In this section, we focus on a refinement suitable for forward checking algorithms. Notice that, at each step of such algorithms we use the information about the current set of candidates for a particular vertex; here, we explore an approach to additionally reduce this set.

Let $\left(\phi\left(u_1\right), \phi\left(u_2\right), \ldots, \phi\left(u_k\right)\right)$ be a partial solution, i.e., target vertices that are mapped to from pattern vertices $u_1, u_2, \ldots, u_k$. We say that a pair of pattern vertices $u \in V_G$ and $v \in V_G$ is *arc consistent* if for all possible mappings of u to $u' \in V_H$ there exists a mapping of v to $v' \in V_H$ satisfying all the constraints between u and v (i.e., adjacency and non-adjacency constraints in our case of the induced subgraph isomorphism problem). If such a mapping from v to v' exists it is called a *support* for the mapping of u to u'.

A partial solution is arc consistent, if all pairs of vertices in the solution are arc consistent. In the course of the backtracking algorithm, all partial solutions and also the final solution must be arc consistent, otherwise, at least one problem constraint is violated.

The main idea of the arc consistency refinement is to purge the candidates of each vertex $u \in V_G$ in order to remove the ones that are not arc consistent. To do this, the algorithm sweeps through all of the elements of the constraint matrix and checks each element, i.e., a candidate vertex u' for u, if there is an arc consistent vertex v with a candidate vertex v'. Hence, the mapping of v to v' represents support for the mapping of u to u'. If no support exists, we can remove the candidate u' for u.

Notice also, since, during the process, we can remove a candidate that is a support for some other vertex, the whole process must be repeated until no change is made. Consequently, the algorithm is of high (although polynomial) computational complexity. The pseudocode is given in Algorithm 3.

In the paper (Čibej & Mihelič, 2015), the authors report that using arc consistency checking may provide a practical speedup to the algorithms but only if used only at the first few steps (i.e., mappings made). Here, we provide experimental results (in the next section) on the variant where arc consistency is used all the way through the algorithm.

Figure 11. A sample host graph.

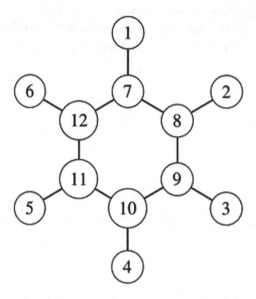

Hall's Sets

The injectivity constraint states that all the mapped vertices must be pairwise distinct. In general constraint satisfaction problems, we call such a constraint *all-different constraint*. Based on these constraints we derive another approach to filtering candidate sets.

First, let us define *Hall's sets*. Let $C_u \subseteq V_H$ be a set of candidates for vertex $u \in V_G$. We call a set $H = \{u_1, u_2, \ldots, u_k\} \subseteq V_G$ a *Hall's set* if the number of candidates for all the vertices from the set H equals to the size of the set H, i.e.,

$$|H| = \left| \bigcup_{u \in H} C_u \right|.$$

All-different constraint tells that k-pattern vertices will be mapped to exactly k-target candidate vertices. Thus, these candidates cannot be used for other pattern vertices (which are not members of the Hall's set). Consequently, we can remove such candidates from the candidate sets of other "non-Hall's" pattern vertices.

Additionally, if we find a subset set of pattern vertices, whose size of the union of candidates is less than the number of vertices, we can backtrack, since all the vertices cannot be mapped, i.e., the condition for backtracking is

$$|H| < \left| \bigcup_{u \in H} C_u \right|.$$

Determining Hall's sets is a computationally daunting task. Instead of this, authors in (McCreesh & Prosser, 2015b) suggest a heuristic approach, which efficiently finds many Hall's sets, but not necessarily all. Their approach is called *counting all-different* and is based on counting the candidates. See the cited paper for details on the approach.

The results of the experimental evaluation are presented in Figure 10. We have performed two experimental scenarios: one with the GCF processing order (the lefthand side) and the other with MRV order (the right-hand side); see the next section for details on the processing orders. In both scenarios, as it can be observed, both refinements (arc consistency checking and Hall's sets) do not provide practical improvement to the algorithm. The overhead costs of computing them are to high to provide practical benefits. Notice that, in both scenarios, we also included bit-arrays-based code optimization.

Exploratory Equivalence

Definition

Exploratory equivalence is a type of equivalence defined on the graph vertex set. In addition to being of independent interest (Mihelič, Fürst, & Čibej, 2014; Čibej, Fürst, & Mihelič, 2019), exploratory equivalence can be employed to deal with automorphisms in the pattern graph. Automorphisms, if ignored, may incur significant overhead in a subgraph isomorphism search algorithm. In particular, given a pattern graph with k automorphisms, a search algorithm that generates all possible neighborhood-consistent vertex-to-vertex mappings between the given pattern graph and the given host graph will discover each occurrence of the pattern graph k times.

For example, an automorphism-unaware algorithm will discover the sole occurrence of the graph $G = C_6$ (Figure 2) in the graph H shown in Figure 11 as many as 12 times, once for each of the 12 automorphisms of G. The automorphism 123456, for instance, corresponds to the G-to-H monomorphism $\{1 \mapsto 7, 2 \mapsto 8, 3 \mapsto 9, 4 \mapsto 10, 5 \mapsto 11, 6 \mapsto 12\}$, the automorphism 234561 corresponds to the monomorphism $\{1 \mapsto 8, 2 \mapsto 9, 3 \mapsto 10, 4 \mapsto 11, 5 \mapsto 12, 6 \mapsto 7\}$, etc.

Before we can formally introduce exploratory equivalence, we have to define a few auxiliary concepts. Let G be a graph with n vertices ($V = \{1, ..., n\}$), and let $Aut(G)$ be the set of automorphisms of G. A set $A \subseteq Aut(G)$ *covers* a set $P \subseteq V$ if for each permutation σ of P there exists an automorphism in A that maps P to $\sigma(P)$.

$$cover(A, P) \equiv \forall \sigma \in Sym(P) \exists a \in A \forall i \in P : \sigma(i) = a(i).$$

Here, $Sym(P)$ denotes the set of all permutations of the set P.

For example, the set of automorphisms of the 6-cycle (Figure 2) covers the set $P = \{1, 3, 5\}$, since it contains an automorphism for each of the 6 permutations of P, automorphism **123456** for permutation 135, automorphism **165432** for permutation 153, automorphism **321654** for permutation 315, automorphism **345612** for permutation 351, automorphism **561234** for permutation 513, and automorphism **543216** for permutation 531. The set $Aut(C_6)$ also covers the set $\{2, 4, 6\}$, as well as all 2-element subsets of the set $\{1 ..., 6\}$ and (trivially) all 1-element subsets of that set.

The *pointwise stabilizer* of a set $A \subseteq Aut(G)$ with respect to the set $P \subseteq V$ is a set of automorphisms in A that fix all vertices in P.

$$PointStab(A, P) = \left\{ a \in A \forall i \in P : a(i) = i \right\}.$$

For example, the pointwise stabilizer of the set $Aut(C_6)$ with respect to the set $\{1, 4\}$ is the set $\{123456, 165432\}$.

Let $\langle P_1, P_2, ..., P_s \rangle$, be a sequence of subsets of V such that $\bigcup_{i=1}^{n} P_i = V$ and $P_i \cap P_j = \varnothing$ for $i \neq j$. Such a sequence will be called an *ordered partition* of V. An ordered partition $\langle P_1, P_2, ..., P_s \rangle$ is *exploratory equivalent* if for all $i \in \{1, ..., s\}$.we have

$$cover(A_{i-1}, P_i) \text{ and } A_i = PointStab(A_{i-1}, P_i),$$

where $A_0 = Aut(G)$. For example, the ordered partition $\langle \{1, 4\}, \{2, 6\}, \{3\}, \{5\} \rangle$ of $V(C_6)$ .is exploratory equivalent because the set $Aut(G)$ covers the set $\{1, 4\}$; the set

$$PointStab(Aut(G), \{1, 4\}) = \{123456, 165432\}$$

covers the set $\{2, 6\}$. etc. The ordered partition $\langle \{1, 3, 5\}, \{2\}, \{4\}, \{6\} \rangle$ is also exploratory equivalent.

An *unordered partition* (or simply a *partition*) of a vertex set V is a set $\{P_1, P_2, ..., P_s\}$ such that $\bigcup_{i=1}^{n} P_i = V$ and $P_i \cap P_j = \varnothing$ for $i \neq j$. A partition $\{P_1, P_2, ..., P_s\}$ is *exploratory equivalent* if there exists a permutation $\sigma : \{1, ..., s\} \to \{1, ..., s\}$ such that the ordered partition $\langle P_{\sigma(1)}, P_{\sigma(2)}, ..., P_{\sigma(s)} \rangle$ is exploratory equivalent.

Exploratory equivalence can be applied to the subgraph isomorphism problem in the following way: if $\{P_1, ..., P_s\}$ is an exploratory equivalent partition of a pattern graph G then for each pair of vertices u and v ($u < v$) of G for which there exists $i \in \{1, ..., s\}$ such that u and v are both members of P_i, we can safely restrict the search for monomorphisms $h : G \to H$ to those that satisfy the restriction $h(u) < h(v)$. A proof of this property can be found in (Fürst, Čibej, & Mihelič, 2015). For example, since $\{\{1, 4\}, \{2, 6\}, \{3\}, \{5\}\}$ is an exploratory equivalent partition of the graph C_6, we can, regardless of the host graph H, generate only those monomorphisms $h : G \to H$ for which $h(1) < h(4)$ and $h(2) < h(6)$ and still be sure that each distinct occurrence of C_6 will be discovered at least once. Alternatively, since $\{\{1, 3, 5\}, \{2\}, \{4\}, \{6\}\}$ is also an exploratory equivalent partition, we could impose the restriction $h(1) < h(3) < h(5)$.

Figure 12. The pattern graphs in our experiments, together with their optimal exploratory equivalent partitions.

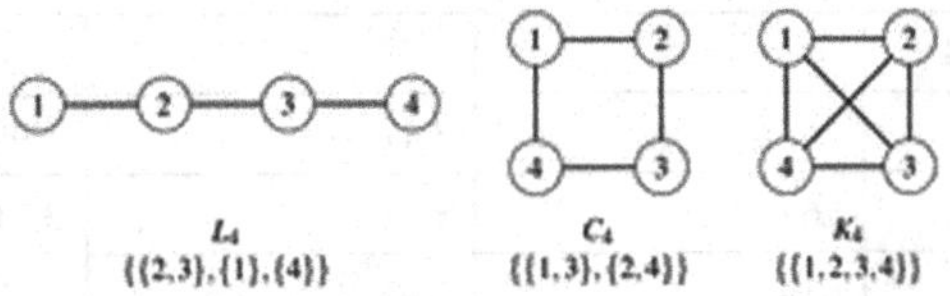

By using the exploratory equivalence to restrict the set of candidate monomorphisms, we can greatly reduce the number of redundant discoveries of pattern graph occurrences while still finding each occurrence at least once. In particular, if $\{P_1, P_2, ..., P_s\}$ (with $P_i = \{v_{i1}) \ v_{i2}, ..., v_{ik_i}\}$ is an exploratory equivalent partition of a graph G then G has $\left(\left|P_1\right|!\left|P_2\right|!...\left|P_s\right|!\right)m$ automorphisms (for some $m \geq 1$) and the same number of monomorphisms between G and each of its occurrences in a graph H, and exactly one in each set of $\left|P_1\right|!\left|P_2\right|!...\left|P_s\right|!$ monomorphisms has the property $h\left(v_{i1}\right) < h\left(v_{i2}\right) < ... < h\left(v_{ik_i}\right)$ for each $i \in \{1, ..., s\}$. The number of discoveries of each occurrence of G is thus reduced by a factor of $\left|P_1\right|!\left|P_2\right|!...\left|P_s\right|!$.

A graph having at least two distinct automorphisms has at least two distinct exploratory equivalent partitions, since the partition composed of singletons is always exploratory equivalent. Let us define the *score* of an exploratory equivalent partition $\mathcal{P} = \{P_1, P_2, ..., P_s\}$ as

$$score\left(\mathcal{P}\right) = \left|P_1\right|!\left|P_2\right|!...\left|P_s\right|!,$$

which, according to the discussion in the preceding paragraph, is exactly the ratio between the number of times each subgraph occurrence is discovered when not using exploratory equivalence and the number of times each occurrence is discovered when the constraints of type $h\left(u\right) < h\left(v\right)$ derived from $\mathcal{P}$ are in effect.

An exploratory equivalent partition with a maximum score can thus be naturally regarded as optimal, and we can define an optimization problem with the goal of finding such a partition of a given graph. As demonstrated in (Čibej et al., 2019), this problem can be solved by a polynomial-time algorithm for certain nontrivial classes of graphs, such as trees and cycles, but for general graphs, such an algorithm is unlikely to exist; we showed that the decision version of the problem is at least as hard as the graph isomorphism problem and is possibly even outside the complexity class NP. For this reason, we turned our attention to heuristic techniques and devised a greedy algorithm that, in practice, produced excellent results despite being suboptimal. Based on the systematic experimental evaluation, the algorithm can be said to find an optimal exploratory equivalent partition for a vast majority of graphs; the cases where it misses an optimum appear to be extremely rare even in theory, let alone in practice.

Table 1. The effects of exploratory equivalence on subgraph isomorphism search: comparing an algorithm that does not use exploratory equivalence with one that does.

H	G	N	t_{naive}	t_{EE}	t_{naive} / t_{EE}
Les Misérables	L_4	26784	3.47	1.94	1.8
|V| = 77	C_4	2672	8.88	3.71	2.4
|E| = 254	K_4	639	7.62	0.77	9.9
US Power Grid	L_4	52556	13.1	8.49	1.5
|V| = 4941	C_4	979	11.6	4.51	2.6
|E| = 6594	K_4	90	6.63	2.36	2.8
David Copperfield	L_4	61254	7.86	4.53	1.7
|V| = 112	C_4	2579	9.36	2.92	3.2
|E| = 425	K_4	58	5.80	0.94	6.2
ca-HepTh	L_4	3850915	483	256	1.9
|V| = 198	C_4	406441	866	245	3.5
|E| = 2742	K_4	78442	667	42.6	15.7
ca-condMath	L_4	4207311	545	305	1.8
|V| = 9877	C_4	239081	627	198	3.2
|E| = 25973	K_4	65592	364	35.8	10.2
ca-CondMat	L_4	50543325	6390	3520	1.8
|V| = 23133	C_4	1505383	9920	2570	3.9
|E| = 93439	K_4	294008	3720	266	14.0

Figure 13. Lowering the space complexity with a list of positions and a stack of snapshots.

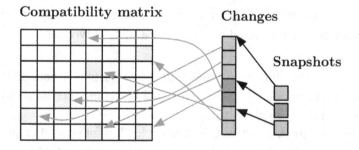

Experimental Results

To see how exploratory equivalence works in practice, we applied two versions of a simple search-plan-based (Rekers & Schürr, 1997; Čibej et al., 2019) subgraph isomorphism search algorithm to a set of real-world benchmark graphs; in particular, we searched for all occurrences of the pattern graphs L_4, C_4, and K_4 (Figure 12) in a set of graphs from the databases KONECT[1] (Kunegis, 2013) and SNAP[2] (Leskovec & Krevl, 2014). The first version of the search algorithm paid no attention to symmetries.

Figure 14. Performance of one variant of the forward checking algorithm with a stack of matrices as well as with a history of changes. Charts show the number of solved instances in a given time limit.

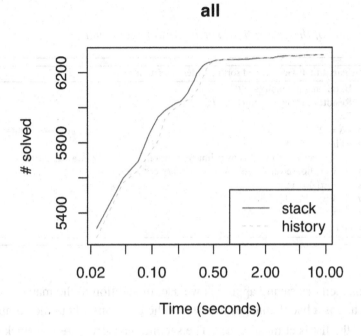

The second derived a set of $h(u) < h(v)$ restrictions from the optimal exploratory equivalent partition of each pattern graph, and continually imposed those restrictions while searching for the occurrences of that graph within the individual host graphs.

Table 1 shows the results of our experimental setup. The column N displays the number of occurrences of the corresponding pattern graph G in the corresponding host graph H. The columns t_{naive} and t_{EE} contain the running times, in milliseconds, of the version that does not employ exploratory equivalence (t_{naive}) and the one that does (t_{EE}). In many cases, as we can see, the ratio between t_{naive} and t_{EE} is close to the theoretical ratio, i.e., the score of an optimal exploratory equivalent partition.

Lowering Space Complexity

In this section, we shift our attention to an optimization of memory usage. In particular, consider forward checking algorithms where a matrix of dimension $n_G \times n_H$ is used for storing mapping candidates for all source vertices. Notice that this matrix has to be saved to and restored from a stack of matrices (see lines 9 and 15 of Algorithm 2. Thus, on the deepest level of recursion, the algorithm may consume up to $O\left(n_G^2 n_H\right)$ of memory.

Here we show how to reduce this to $O\left(n_G n_H\right)$ based on the following observation. For each step (forward) of the algorithm zeros in the matrix remain zeros and only the ones in the matrix may be changed to zeros. Consequently, the upper bound on the number of changes is $n_G n_H$. To reduce memory consumption and at the same time to enable matrix restoring, one only needs to store the history of changes, not the whole matrices.

Algorithm 4. Pseudocode of the generalized sorting order algorithm

---

Algorithm 4: Generalized sorting order algorithm

Data: pattern graph $G = \langle V, E \rangle$
Result: ordering of vertices $ord : \mathbb{N} \to V$
1   $i = 0$;
2   $Vis = \emptyset$;   `// visited vertices`
3   **while** $i < |G|$ **do**
4   A = vertices in $V \setminus Vis$ by primary criterion;   `// candidate se`
5   v = choose vertex from A by secondary criterion;
6      $ord(i) = v$;
7      $Vis = Vis \cup \{v\}$;
8      $i = i+1$;
9   **end**

To implement this memory saving approach we use, in addition to the matrix, two more data structures. The first structure is a list of changes that stores the positions where the compatibility matrix has changed. The size of the list is at most $n_G n_H$. The second data structure is a stack of pointers into the list of changes. Each pointer represents the boundary between two versions of the compatibility matrix. The size of the stack is at most n_G. See Figure 13 for a graphical presentation of the relations among these data structures.

Thus for one change (of the matrix cell containing one), two actions are needed: a change in the matrix, and the addition of its position to the list. To make a backup of the compatibility matrix, one simply pushes the pointer to the last change onto the stack. To backtrack, i.e. to restore the previous matrix, the stack is popped and the corresponding changes are undone.

Notice that the technique also has a positive effect on the algorithm's speed since for each step forward instead of copying the whole matrix only a backup is made. However, there is also a negative performance effect since for each step backward instead of discarding a matrix one must iteratively undo corresponding changes. However, a simple experiment whose results are plotted in Figure 14 shows that the performance difference is negligible.

On the other hand, notice that, memory savings are significant. For example for a pattern graph of 600 vertices and a target graph of 1000 vertices memory consumption with the stack-based approach is about 500 MB, and using the above-described technique only about 1 MB.

SEARCH ORDERS

In this section, we explore various possibilities for vertex orders that are used to process vertices in the backtracking algorithms. Graph theory provides an abundance of features that can be taken into account when sorting the vertices. Our first goal is to devise a generalized framework into which these features can be plugged in. Afterward, we present experimental results of comparison of several orders. We also present two competitive orders from the literature. Finally, we describe heuristic sampling which is a method that samples the input instance in order to determine an efficient vertex order.

Observe that, concerning the correctness of the algorithm, the order may be arbitrary, but concerning the efficiency, it may have a profound impact: even though two vertices (pattern and target vertex) are compatible, their selection may not lead to any subgraph isomorphism. Unfortunately, such bad selections are hard to detect immediately, which leads to an unnecessary exploration of the non-perspective parts of the solution space.

General Framework

Our main focus are static orders, which means that the order of vertices is established before the start of backtracking and it does not change during the execution. Such orders are most widely used in current state-of-the-art solvers. Even though it might seem that the static nature of these orders might make them less efficient, there is an important advantage that makes them competitive with the dynamic orders. There is no overhead of ordering during backtracking. Another important advantage is that at the setup of the algorithm we have plenty of time to examine a wide set of graph properties in order to choose the most suitable one for the graph at hand.

We are going to split the ordering into two phases, each phase will utilize a different criterion:

1. The first phase utilizes a primary criterion that uses topological features of the graph and
2. the second phase uses more local features of the vertices to select the best vertex from the currently available.

These two criteria form a sorting algorithm which is described in more detail in Algorithm 4.

This generalized sorting algorithm represents a suitable framework for a variety of different strategies that can be used to sort the vertices. In what follows we describe a few criteria that we devised to test together on the Ullmans' algorithm.

Primary Criteria

The primary criterion is used to select a candidate set of vertices, from which a single vertex will be selected based on the secondary criterion. In our case, we will use this criterion to include some topological information into the vertex order, but it can be used to get a set of candidates based on various other features of the graph.

- **All vertices:** this criterion is applied when we want to ignore any topology in the graph and use all the vertices as the candidates for the selection. In this case, the secondary criterion is used as the only feature for ordering the vertices.
- **Neighborhood:** this rule chooses the neighbors of the vertices in the set of already visited vertices Vis. If the set Vis .is empty then all the vertices of the graph are candidates for the selection.
- **Maximal subdegree:** we define the *subdegree* of a vertex to be the number of edges from this vertex to the vertices in the set Vis .

Figure 15. The random search strategy vs. a simple degree strategy.

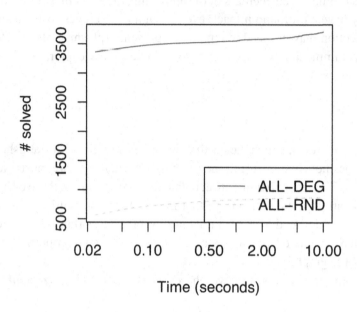

$$d_{Vis}(v) = | \{u \in Vis \mid (v,u) \in E\} |$$

In this case, the candidate set A is the set of all the vertices for further selection by the secondary criterion.

Secondary Criteria

- **Random:** for comparison purposed we used a random selection from the candidate set A.
- **Degree:** The order which was already proposed by Ullmann in (Ullmann, 1976) is the ordering of the pattern vertices by their degree (descending). The logic behind this ordering is that the vertices with the highest degree can usually be mapped to the fewest goal vertices, which reduces the search space already at the top levels of the search tree.
- **Clustering:** Another criterion that can be used for ordering the pattern vertices is the local clustering coefficient. This is a measure that quantifies how close the neighborhood of a vertex is to being a clique. This coefficient for a vertex v_i is computed as:

$$c_i = \frac{\left| \{e_{jk} : e_{jk} \in E \wedge v_j, v_k \in N_i\} \right|}{k_i(k_i - 1)},$$

where N_i is the set of neighbors of v_i and $k_i = |N_i|$. Choosing vertices with a higher clustering coefficient also reduces the search space, because more edges in the neighborhood mean more restrictions to the compatibility matrix.

Figure 16. The best search strategies for Ullman's algorithm.

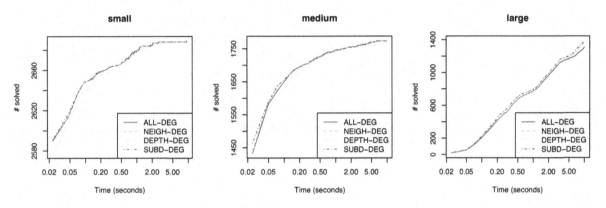

- **Degree-clustering:** A combination of the above two criteria was used, i.e. a simple sum of the vertex degree and the clustering coefficient of the vertex.
- **Eccentricity:** The fourth criterion we are going to use is the eccentricity of a vertex. The eccentricity is simply the greatest distance from the vertex to any other vertex in the graph. With this measure, we are preferring the vertices with lower eccentricity. The logic behind this criterion is that we would like to start the search in the center of the graph, this means that the graph will be fixed in the target graph faster, resulting in a smaller search space.

Experimental Comparison

The experiments were conducted on a well-known test-case library (De Santo, Foggia, Sansone, & Vento, 2003), which was used to evaluate several algorithms, e.g. (Foggia & Sansone, 2001; Foggia, Sansone, & Vento, 2001a, 2001b; Lipets et al., 2009; Solnon, 2010). For our evaluation, we used the test-set of Erdos-Rényi random graphs of various sizes and various densities.

More specifically, we took 6300 test cases altogether. Graphs were generated with different features, one of them being the edge probability of 0.01, 0.05, and 0.1, the second one the sizes target graphs 20, 40, 60, 80, 100, 200, and 400. And the patterns were 20%, 40%, and 60% of the target graph.

To investigate the impact of the size of the problem instance on the running time we grouped these test cases into three groups: small graph (20, 40, 60 nodes - 2700 test cases), medium graph (80, 100 nodes - 1800 test cases), and large graphs (200, 400 nodes - 1800 test cases).

The results are shown in the following manner. The x-axis shows the execution time (log-scale) and the y-axis shows the number of test cases that were solved in time $\leq x$.

For comparison reasons, let us look at a completely random search strategy, to demonstrate the impact that a search strategy has on the overall running time. Figure 15 shows a comparison between ALL-RND and ALL-DEG. Ullmann's algorithm with ALL-DEG managed to solve all the instances in under 10 seconds time, whereas with ALL-RND it solved less than 1000. We exclude the RND criterion from further tests since it is clearly non-competitive.

Figure 17. A random walk in the tree, where the branching at each level gives an estimate of the overall tree size. This is the Knuth's estimation method in a nutshell.

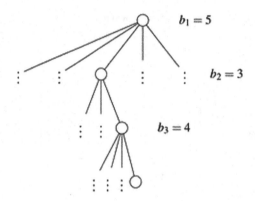

Next, let us have a look at the results of the testing of the classical Ullmann's algorithm with all the 16 remaining strategies. Figure 16 shows the results with the best search strategies for each of the primary criteria. In all cases, the simplest DEG criterion was the best, and surprisingly there are almost no differences between primary criteria. This is a surprising result since other criteria use more information about the graph and should thus obtain a better search strategy. It seems that the main reason (as it will be seen in the UI tests shortly) is the Ullmann's refinement procedure which finds all this information implicitly, so additionally incorporating it into the search strategy does not improve the running times. From the strategies that are not shown in the results, we can highlight the eccentricity, which performed quite badly in combination with all primary criteria.

Alternative Orders

Besides these orders that fall into the category of the above orders, the state-of-the-art solvers use two very efficient orders, which do not fit in the above categorization, namely:

GCF (greatest constraint first) This order is similar to NEIGH-DEG defined above, but equalities are resolved differently. Let M be a set of vertices, with at least one neighbor in the partial order, i.e.,

$$M = \left\{ u \in V_G \setminus U_{k-1} \, \mathcal{N}_G(u) \cap U_{k-1} \neq \varnothing \right\}$$

and the next selected vertex

$$u_k = \underset{u \in V_G \setminus U_{k-1}}{\arg\max} \left(\left| \mathcal{N}_G(u) \cap U_{k-1} \right|, \left| \mathcal{N}_G(u) \cap M \right|, d_G(u) \right).$$

MRV (minimal remaining values) In the forward checking algorithms, we can, for each vertex $u \in V_G$ store its candidate vertices from V_H. Using this information we can, in each state of the search tree, select such a vertex that has a minimum number of candidates. The goal is that the branching of the tree is minimized.

The latter order is not static, which means it changes during the execution of the algorithm. This is its strength, but it also adds some overhead to the running time, which is not the case for static orders.

Heuristic Sampling

In the previous sections, we presented many possibilities for vertex ordering. Oftentimes, it is hard to determine which ordering is the best since the algorithm performance varies highly between different input instances. The ideal scenario would be if we could choose the optimal ordering for a particular input instance. In order to resolve this challenge, researchers have developed methods that can estimate in advance how an order will perform. One of such methods is called *heuristic sampling* and is the focus of this section.

Knuth's Method

Since heuristic sampling is the extension of Knuth's method (Knuth, 1974, 2019), we give a quick description of this interesting approach. In a nutshell, the method traverses the tree by choosing a random path until reaching a leaf of the tree. This random walk yields an estimation S_{est} of the tree size as:

$$S_{est} = 1 + b_1 + b_1 b_2 + b_1 b_2 b_3 + \ldots,$$

where b_i is the number of children the node at depth i has (i.e., the branching rate of that node, see Figure 17). By repeating this random walk and averaging the result, the estimation quickly converges closely to the actual size on many problems.

Our first attempts at using Knuth's method for subgraph isomorphism did not yield satisfactory results. The main reason for this is that the simple sampling assumes a very homogeneous structure of the search-tree. Such structure is present in many classical search problems (such as games and basic combinatorial problems), but it is not present in more complex search problems where the structure varies between branches significantly.

Heuristic Sampling

Heuristic sampling (HS) addresses the issues of Knuth's method. Instead of following a single path in the tree, HS proceeds on many representative paths at the same time. This approach captures better the heterogeneous nature of search trees.

The central concept of HS is a heuristic function $h : N \rightarrow \mathcal{P}$. N being the set of nodes of the search tree and $\mathcal{P}$ being a partially ordered set. This function is called a *stratifier* and it should be designed in such a way to reflect the main characteristics of the nodes in the search tree. Intuitively, it is a function

Algorithm 5. Pseudocode of algorithm for estimating the size of the search tree.

Algorithm 5: estimateSize(G,H,order) - estimating the size of the search tree.
The return value is a list of estimated sizes for each $\alpha \in \mathcal{P}$.

```
1  Q = [root, 1)];
2  sol = {};
3  while |Q| > 0 do
4  │   (n, w) = Q.dequeue;
5  │   sol = sol ∪ {(n,w)};
6  │   Q = Q \ (n,w));
7  │   for m ∈ children of n do
8  │   │   α_m = h(m);
9  │   │   if Q contains an element (s,w_s) with h(s) = α_m then
10 │   │   │   w_s = w_s + 1;
11 │   │   │   with probability w/w_s do s = n;
12 │   │   end
13 │   │   else
14 │   │   │   Q = Q ∪ (m,1);
15 │   │   end
16 │   end
17 end
18 return sol
```

which maps each node into a value that should describe the shape of the subtree rooted at that node. Two nodes mapped to the same value by the stratifier should have similar (similarly sized) subtrees.

With the stratifier given, the method must now find an estimation for the number of nodes for each $\alpha \in \mathcal{P}$. And from such estimations, the entire size of the tree can simply be computed as:

$$S_{est} = \sum_{\alpha} s_{\alpha},$$

where s_{α} is the size of the subtree for α.

In order for HS to be successful on subgraph isomorphism problem, we had to find a suitable stratifier. One which captures the shape of the tree well enough, but also does not degenerate into a function that has to search the entire tree. We chose to use the function

$$h\left(n\right) \to \left(depth\left(n\right), deg\left(n\right)\right),$$

where $depth\left(n\right)$ is the depth at which the node is located and $deg\left(n\right)$ is the number of children the node has. So two nodes will be considered equal if they are at the same depth and they have the same number of children.

The details of the entire procedure are given in Algorithm 5. The method initiates a priority queue, which will serve as the data structure for holding sample nodes of the search tree. The priority of the elements in the queue is $h\left(n\right)$, and the dequeuing removes the element with the maximal value of h. At each step of the iteration, one node is retrieved from the queue and all its children are generated. These children (m) are added to the queue if their $h\left(m\right)$ is not yet present in the queue otherwise the weight of the element in the queue is increased (we found a new instance for this stratum) and the old node in the queue is replaced by the newly found with a probability $\dfrac{w}{w_s}$, where w is the weight of the parent node and w_s is the weight of the newly generated node. A detailed theoretical justification of this method can be found in (Chen, 1992).

Figure 18. The relative error of the Knuth's method on each of the 100 instances.

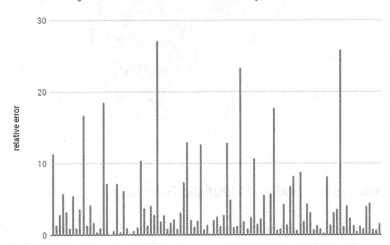

Empirical Evaluation

In order to show the practical potential of these sampling methods, we performed some preliminary tests.

Figure 19. The relative error of heuristic sampling on each of the 100 instances.

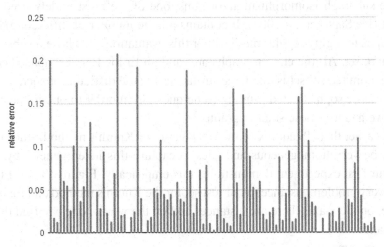

Figure 20. The best orders for each tested instance. Every order is the best on at least one input instance, showing the diversity and importance of predicting the performance for each order.

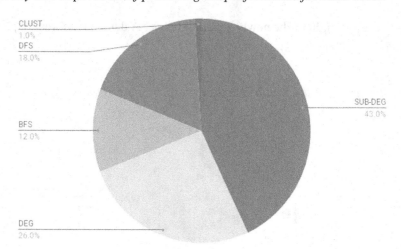

Comparison of Knuth's Method and Heuristic Sampling

Here, our goal is to demonstrate that Knuth's method is not suitable for the subgraph isomorphism problem. To do this, we performed an empirical comparison of both methods. On a chosen set of problem instances, we obtained the exact sizes of the search tree as well as both estimates (i.e., of the Knuth's method and the HS estimate). By showing the large qualitative difference between these two estimates we can justify the dismissal of Knuth's method in our further experiments.

The implementation of this experimental part was done in python, using the igraph library (Csardi & Nepusz, 2006) to tackle the basic graph operations and algorithms. To fully control the execution of the backtracking algorithm, we reimplemented the basic algorithm and we included a few simple pruning techniques. This enabled us to accurately count the tree size and also to implement heuristic sampling since it needs to precisely follow the algorithm it is estimating.

For testing the subgraph isomorphism algorithms, one of the most widely used benchmark set is the Amalfi testset (De Santo et al., 2003). It contains a large number of different graphs, from Erdös-Renyi random graphs to highly regular meshes. For this evaluation, we chose a subset of 100 instances from this benchmark set. All the chosen graphs are random Erdös-Renyi graphs. The main reason for the choice of such a limited subset is that larger instances are too difficult for such a basic backtracking procedure without more sophisticated pruning techniques. So in order to obtain the exact solutions for all the instances, we had to choose smaller graphs.

We mentioned earlier that HS addresses the weaknesses of Knuth's method, since it does not assume the search tree to be very homogeneous and tries to capture this heterogeneity by following several different paths. Our first experiment demonstrates this empirically. Figure 18 and Figure 19 show the relative error on every problem instance in our test set for the Knuth's method and for heuristic sampling respectively. Here, on the *x*-axis there are instances and on the *y*-axis, one can find the relative error of the particular instance.

By relative error we mean

$$\frac{\left|S - S_{est}\right|}{S},$$

where S denotes the search-tree size, and S_{est} denotes the estimated search-tree size. The qualitative difference between the two methods is obvious since the error differs by nearly two orders of magnitude, i.e., the maximal error of HS is 0.2 (20%), whereas the error of the Knuth's method is more than 20. Such errors are unacceptable, so the Knuth's method is omitted from further experiments.

Figure 21. The scatterplot shows the relative difference of the tree size between the best order and worst order on each of the 100 instances. The y-axis is logarithmic.

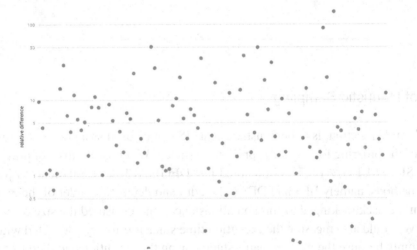

Figure 22. The histogram of relative errors for each prediction (100 instances and 5 orders, i.e. 500 predictions). Two predictions were more than twice the actual number of tree nodes, however most of the predictions were very accurate.

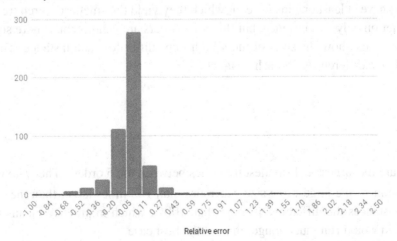

Figure 23. The relative difference between the chosen order and the best order for an instance. In 80% of cases the chosen order in either the best one or within 5% of the best. In one case the chosen order was twice as bad as the best one.

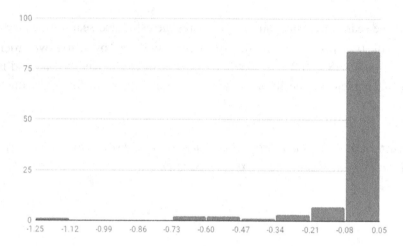

Evaluation of Heuristic Sampling

Our final goal, in this section, is to demonstrate that HS can be used as a practical subroutine for a dynamic choice of the ordering for a specific problem instance. We chose a subset of previously described methods, i.e., SUBD-DEG, ALL-DEG (denoted just DEG), ALL-CLUST (denoted just CLUST) and two classical methods, namely BFS and DFS (a breadth and depth-first order of the graph).

We first ran the backtracking algorithm on all instances and measured the size of the search tree for each of them. We could also measure the execution time since it is nicely correlated with the size of the tree. This is simply because the order remains static during the execution and therefore there is no particular overhead for the computation of different orders. But it is better to choose a machine-independent measure, which makes the evaluation more robust, so the tree size was the most natural choice. To obtain a more reliable number, each estimation was repeated 100 times, and the average was computed.

First, let us demonstrate that these five orders exhibit a large variance in performance on different instances. Figure 20 shows which order was the winner on 100 instances of the benchmark set. We can see that all orders have at least one instance on which they yield the smallest search tree. The clustering order is the winner on only one instance, but the other orders are significantly more successful.

Figure 21 shows also how the sizes of the search trees differ for each instance. The graph shows a scatterplot of relative differences for each instance:

$$\frac{s_{max} - s_{min}}{s_{min}},$$

where s_{max}, s_{min} are the largest and smallest tree sizes between the 5 orders. The y-axis in logarithmic, since in some instances the largest tree size was more than 100 times larger than the smallest one. For the majority of instances the difference is more than 100%, which in practice means that in the worst case, the algorithm would run much longer than in the best case.

Next, we use the heuristic sampling for predicting the tree size for each test instance and each order, altogether 500 predictions. In order to compare the efficiencies between instances, we compute the relative error

$$\frac{|T| - S_{est}}{|T|},$$

where T is the tree size and S_{est} is the estimated size. Figure 22 shows the distribution of these relative errors for the 500 predictions. We can see there are a few predictions that were not that good, but the vast majority of predictions are within 20% of the actual size of the tree.

Since we are investigating if the sampling can be successfully used as a predictor in the backtracking algorithms, the error in the prediction is not the most important factor, What is more important is the ranking accuracy of the method. For each instance, we are interested in finding the best possible order in advance. For this reason, we now show the distribution of the relative difference between the best tree size, and the tree size of the chosen order (both actual, not the predictions):

$$\frac{|T_{best}| - |T_{chosen}|}{|T_{best}|}.$$

The results for this measurement are shown in Figure 23. As we can see, more than 80% of all chosen orders were either exactly the best order or within 5% of the best order. In one instance the predicted winner performed very badly (more than twice the size of the actual best order), but on the rest of the instances, the predictions are very feasible for practical applications.

CONCLUSION

This chapter addressed the subgraph isomorphism problem and presented a toolbox of approaches for improving the performance of backtracking algorithms for this problem. Hard computational problems have a wide variety of approaches to solving them, But, when exact solutions are required, backtracking is by far the most widely used in practice and also the most efficient approach.

However, basic backtracking leads to very inefficient solutions if utilized straightforwardly. To make these algorithms efficient, specific search-tree pruning techniques have to be devised to achieve practically feasible solving times. Besides pruning, it is very important to use good engineering techniques. Certain pruning techniques have a lot of overhead and are useful in practice only if they are very efficiently implemented so that the overhead does not overturn all the gain achieved by the pruning. We presented a set of implementation enhancements that drastically improve the overall performance and without which some of the pruning techniques would be mostly useless.

We focus on the two main flavors of backtracking, namely forward-checking and backward-checking. We also present a set of possible improvements, most of which can be used with any of these two flavors. Some approaches help to prune the search tree while the others belong to the group of algorithmic optimizations or code tuning techniques.

A very promising method that still needs to be fully exploited is the utilization of symmetries. We also presented one concept, i.e. exploratory equivalence, which uses a subset of symmetries and a full evaluation of practical instances will show us how big of an impact this can have in practice. Furthermore, we believe that the concept of exploratory equivalence can further be extended to involve even more instances.

The parameter which in our experience has the most impact on the efficiency is the search order. We devoted a full section to this topic and present a large set of possible orders that can be adapted to a wide variety of input instances.

We also emphasize that when dealing with hard computational problems, no silver bullet exists. Rather, each input instance is a separate challenge and it is very hard to predict which method will be most efficient. We described a method that can serve as such a predictor. Heuristic sampling can be used to probe into the input instance and establish which search order (or other technique) will be the most efficient.

The described approaches are just a subset of possible ways of tackling this problem but we think that such a variety of approaches can serve as a good platform for future enhancements and techniques for new state-of-the-art solvers.

REFERENCES

Agrafiotis, D. K., Lobanov, V. S., Shemanarev, M., Rassokhin, D. N., Izrailev, S., Jaeger, E. P., Alex, S., & Farnum, M. (2011). Efficient Substructure Searching of Large Chemical Libraries: The ABCD Chemical Cartridge. *Journal of Chemical Information and Modeling*, *51*(12), 3113–3130. doi:10.1021/ci200413e PMID:22035187

Amini, O., Fomin, F. V., & Saurabh, S. (2012). Counting subgraphs via homomorphisms. *SIAM Journal on Discrete Mathematics*, *26*(2), 695–717. doi:10.1137/100789403

Balaban, A. T. (1985). Applications of graph theory in chemistry. *Journal of Chemical Information and Computer Sciences*, *25*(3), 334–343. doi:10.1021/ci00047a033

Barnard, J. M. (1993). Substructure searching methods: Old and new. *Journal of Chemical Information and Computer Sciences*, *33*(4), 532–538. doi:10.1021/ci00014a001

Batra, S., & Tyagi, C. (2012). *Comparative analysis of relational and graph databases*. Int'l J. Soft Computing & Engineering.

Blagojević, V., Bojić, D., Bojović, M., Cvetanović, M., Đorđević, J., Đurđević, Đ., ... Vuletić, P. (2016). A systematic approach to generation of new ideas for´ PhD research in computing. *Advances in Computers*, *104*, 1–19.

Bonnici, V., Giugno, R., Pulvirenti, A., Shasha, D., & Ferro, A. (2013). A subgraph isomorphism algorithm and its application to biochemical data. *BMC Bioinformatics*, *14*(Suppl 7), S13. doi:10.1186/1471-2105-14-S7-S13 PMID:23815292

Carletti, V., Foggia, P., Saggese, A., & Vento, M. (2017). Introducing vf3: A new algorithm for subgraph isomorphism. In *International workshop on graphbased representations in pattern recognition* (pp. 128–139). 10.1007/978-3-319-58961-9_12

Carrington, P. J., Scott, J., & Wasserman, S. (2005). *Models and methods in social network analysis.* Cambridge University Press. doi:10.1017/CBO9780511811395

Chen, P. C. (1992). Heuristic sampling: A method for predicting the performance of tree searching programs. *SIAM Journal on Computing, 21*(2), 295–315. doi:10.1137/0221022

Čibej, U., Fürst, L., & Mihelič, J. (2019). A symmetry-breaking node equivalence˘ for pruning the search space in backtracking algorithms. *Symmetry, 11*(10), 1300. doi:10.3390ym11101300

Čibej, U., & Mihelič, J. (2015). Improvements to ullmann's algorithm for the subgraph isomorphism problem. *International Journal of Pattern Recognition and Artificial Intelligence, 29*(07), 1550025. doi:10.1142/S0218001415500251

Conte, D., Foggia, P., Sansone, C., & Vento, M. (2004). Thirty years of graph matching in pattern recongnition. *International Journal of Pattern Recognition and Artificial Intelligence, 18*(3), 265–298. doi:10.1142/S0218001404003228

Cook, S. A. (1971). The complexity of theorem-proving procedures. In *Proc. 3rd annual ACM symposium on theory of computing - stoc '71* (pp. 151–158). ACM Press. 10.1145/800157.805047

Cordella, L. P., Foggia, P., Sansone, C., & Vento, M. (1999). Performance evaluation of the VF graph matching algorithm. In Image analysis and processing, 1999. proceedings. international conference on (pp. 1172–1177). doi:10.1109/ICIAP.1999.797762

Cordella, L. P., Foggia, P., Sansone, C., & Vento, M. (2004, October). A (sub)graph isomorphism algorithm for matching large graphs. *IEEE Transactions on Pattern Analysis and Machine Intelligence, 26*(10), 1367–1372. doi:10.1109/TPAMI.2004.75 PMID:15641723

Csardi, G., & Nepusz, T. (2006). The igraph software package for complex network research. *InterJournal. Complex Systems*, 1695.

De Santo, M., Foggia, P., Sansone, C., & Vento, M. (2003, May). A large database of graphs and its use for benchmarking graph isomorphism algorithms. *Pattern Recognition Letters, 24*(8), 1067–1079. doi:10.1016/S0167-8655(02)00253-2

Fan, W. (2012, March). Graph pattern matching revised for social network analysis. In *Proc. 15th international conference on database theory - ICDT '12* (p. 8). ACM Press. 10.1145/2274576.2274578

Foggia, P., & Sansone, C. (2001). A performance comparison of five algorithms for graph isomorphism. *TC-15 Workshop on Graph- based Representations in Pattern Recognition.*

Foggia, P., Sansone, C., & Vento, M. (2001a). A database of graphs for isomorphism and sub-graph isomorphism benchmarking. *Proc. of the 3rd IAPR TC-15 International Workshop on Graph-based Representations.*

Foggia, P., Sansone, C., & Vento, M. (2001b). A Performance Comparison of Five Algorithm for Graph Isomorphism. *3rd IAPR-TC15 Workshop on Graphbased Representations in Pattern Recognition.*

Fomin, F. V., Jansen, B. M., & Pilipczuk, M. (2012). Preprocessing subgraph and minor problems: when does a small vertex cover help? In *Parameterized and exact computation* (pp. 97–108). Springer. doi:10.1007/978-3-642-33293-7_11

Fürst, L., Čibej, U., & Mihelič, J. (2015). *Maximum exploratory equivalence in trees. 2015 federated conference on computer science and information systems.*

Garey, M. R., & Johnson, D. S. (1979). *Computers and intractability* (Vol. 174). Freeman San Francisco.

Gupta, A., & Nishimura, N. (1996a). Characterizing the complexity of subgraph isomorphism for graphs of bounded path-width. *STACS, 96*, 453–464. doi:10.1007/3-540-60922-9_37

Gupta, A., & Nishimura, N. (1996b). The complexity of subgraph isomorphism for classes of partial *k*-trees. *Theoretical Computer Science, 164*(1), 287–298. doi:10.1016/0304-3975(96)00046-1

Han, W.-S., Lee, J., & Lee, J.-H. (2013). Turboiso: towards ultrafast and robust subgraph isomorphism search in large graph databases. In *Proceedings of the 2013 ACM SIGMOD international conference on management of data* (pp. 337–348). New York: ACM. 10.1145/2463676.2465300

He, Y., & Evans, A. (2010). Graph theoretical modeling of brain connectivity. *Current Opinion in Neurology, 23*(4), 341–350. PMID:20581686

Knuth, D. E. (1974). *Estimating the efficiency of backtrack programs.* Tech. Rep.

Knuth, D. E. (2019). Mathematical preliminaries redux; introduction to backtracking; dancing links (Vol. 4, Fascicle 5). Academic Press.

Krahmer, E., Van Erk, S., & Verleg, A. (2003). Graph-based generation of referring expressions. *Computational Linguistics, 29*(1), 53–72. doi:10.1162/089120103321337430

Kunegis, J. (2013). KONECT: the koblenz network collection. In *Proceedings of the international conference on world wide web companion* (pp. 1343–1350). 10.1145/2487788.2488173

Lee, J., Han, W.-S., Kasperovics, R., & Lee, J.-H. (2012). An in-depth comparison of subgraph isomorphism algorithms in graph databases. In *Proceedings of the 39th international conference on very large data bases* (pp. 133–144). 10.14778/2535568.2448946

Leskovec, J., & Krevl, A. (2014, Jun). *SNAP Datasets: Stanford large network dataset collection.* http://snap.stanford.edu/data

Lipets, V., Vanetik, N., & Gudes, E. (2009). Subsea: An efficient heuristic algorithm for subgraph isomorphism. *Data Mining and Knowledge Discovery, 19*(3), 320–350. doi:10.100710618-009-0132-7

Liu, J., & Lee, Y. T. (2001). Graph-based method for face identification from a single 2D line drawing. *IEEE Transactions on Pattern Analysis and Machine Intelligence, 23*(10), 1106–1119. doi:10.1109/34.954601

Marx, D., & Pilipczuk, M. (2013). *Everything you always wanted to know about the parameterized complexity of subgraph isomorphism (but were afraid to ask).* Academic Press.

Matula, D. W. (1978). Subtree isomorphism in o(n5/2). In P. H. B. Alspach & D. Miller (Eds.), *Algorithmic aspects of combinatorics* (Vol. 2, pp. 91–106). Elsevier. doi:10.1016/S0167-5060(08)70324-8

McCreesh, C., & Prosser, P. (2015a). A parallel, backjumping subgraph isomorphism algorithm using supplemental graphs. In *International conference on principles and practice of constraint programming* (pp. 295–312). 10.1007/978-3-319-23219-5_21

McCreesh, C., & Prosser, P. (2015b). A parallel, backjumping subgraph isomorphism al- gorithm using supplemental graphs. In G. Pesant (Ed.), *Principles and practice of constraint programming* (pp. 295–312). Springer International Publishing. doi:10.1007/978-3-319-23219-5_21

McGeoch, C. C. (2012). *A guide to experimental algorithmics.* Cambridge University Press.

Messmer, B. T., & Bunke, H. (2000, March). Efficient subgraph isomorphism detection: A decomposition approach. *IEEE Transactions on Knowledge and Data Engineering, 12*(2), 307–323. doi:10.1109/69.842269

Mihelič, J., Fürst, L., & Čibej, U. (2014). *Exploratory equivalence in graphs: Definition and algorithms. 2014 federated conference on computer science and information systems.*

Muller-Hannemann, M., & Schirra, S. (Eds.). (2010). *Algorithm engineering: Bridging the gap between algorithm theory and practice.* Springer-Verlag. doi:10.1007/978-3-642-14866-8

Plantenga, T. (2013, February). Inexact subgraph isomorphism in mapreduce. *Journal of Parallel and Distributed Computing, 73*(2), 164–175. doi:10.1016/j.jpdc.2012.10.005

Rekers, J., & Schürr, A. (1997). Defining and parsing visual languages with Layered Graph Grammars. *Journal of Visual Languages and Computing, 8*(1), 27–55. doi:10.1006/jvlc.1996.0027

Solnon, C. (2010, August). AllDifferent-based filtering for subgraph isomorphism. *Artificial Intelligence, 174*(12-13), 850–864. doi:10.1016/j.artint.2010.05.002

Sun, Z., Wang, H., Wang, H., Shao, B., & Li, J. (2012). Efficient subgraph matching on billion node graphs. *Proceedings of the VLDB Endowment International Conference on Very Large Data Bases, 5*(9), 788–799. doi:10.14778/2311906.2311907

Ullmann, J. R. (1976). An Algorithm for Subgraph Isomorphism. *Journal of the Association for Computing Machinery, 23*(1), 31–42. doi:10.1145/321921.321925

Ullmann, J. R. (2010). Bit-vector algorithms for binary constraint satisfaction and subgraph isomorphism. *Journal of Experimental Algorithmics, 15*, 1–6. doi:10.1145/1671970.1921702

Valiente, G. (2002). *Algorithms on Trees and Graphs.* Springer. doi:10.1007/978-3-662-04921-1

Yuan, Y., Wang, G., Chen, L., & Wang, H. (2012, May). Efficient subgraph similarity search on large probabilistic graph databases. *Proc. VLDB Endow., 5*(9), 800–811. 10.14778/2311906.2311908

ENDNOTES

[1]   http://konect.cc/
[2]   https://snap.stanford.edu/data/

Chapter 15
AI Storm ... From Logical Inference and Chatbots to Signal Weighting, Entropy Pooling:
Future of AI in Marketing

Luiz A. M. Moutinho
University of Suffolk, UK

ABSTRACT

The chapter is focused on the paradigm shift of artificial intelligence (AI) and marketing evolution. Considering the effects of AI on marketing and AI powered by engagement marketing, why is AI the marketing future? Is AI in marketing merely over-promoted? What can AI do for marketing and how can AI most influence and bring advantages to marketing and transformation of the customer experience through mass personalisation? Some critical impacts of chatbots are highlighted, with explanations of what they can do and how they will change the future of customer engagement. An explanation of how AI products influence and transform the role of product management is given, emphasizing the importance of the human context delivering, along with emerging technologies. Following this is an investigation about AI influencing brand management, and by the end, the issues of the future of AI and robotics are highlighted.

INTRODUCTION

The most of the smart experts dealing with marketing worldwide surely have already heard quite a lot about Artificial Intelligence Marketing (AI Marketing), which is nowadays significant wave of data-based marketing strategy, and an important of a strong storm ovehelming the entire digital world. Artificial Intelligence enables marketers to create and continuously enhance almost fully personalized consumer experiences, all that with higher cost-efficiency than traditional expensive campaigns and other well-

DOI: 10.4018/978-1-7998-7156-9.ch015

known marketing tools. Within the marketing processes, every interaction a potential buyer or consumer has with a product or solution, repeatedly is utilized for next optimizations. AI capabilities applied to content enable more effective client generation. And personalization help the companies lead ahead of the tomorrow's competitors tomorrow by transforming their consumers' experience and by building a useful Digital Experience Platform (DXP) that will soon become key competitive differentiator. Marketing experts struggle with using AI - to leverage content and to turn data into useful and aplicable insights.

ARTIFICIAL INTELLIGENCE

Looking at 2019, some of the powerful digital companies have enhanced their new product offerings with the ground on the ability to ensure highly relevant and personalised products and content recommendations – let to mention Amazon, Netflix and Spotify. These all arises from (a) AI-based clustering and interpreting of consumer data combined with (b) profile information and demographic data. The mentioned AI-based systems continually adapt to consumers' likes and dislikes and react with new recommendations, all real-time provided. With AI-based solutions, marketers promptly and precisely know what are consumers are feeling, thinking and saying about the each particular brand and product - all in real time. Also, with the avalanche of available social media (and with the AI-based tools to analyse them), marketers can fully and truly understand what consumers are feeling how they are judging them. By using these real-time available data, smart marketers can then quickly modify their messaging or branding for ensuring the highest level of their effectiveness.

AI marketing is a new method where technology achievements are used to improve the consumer experience and also to enlarge the return on investment (ROI) of marketing campaigns. This is enabled by using big data analytics, machine learning, and relevant processes which are providing detailed insights into targeted audiences. Knowing all these about your consumers – partners, you can design new, very effective "consumer touch-points". AI can influence, direct and optimize digital marketing campaignes and, along with that, eliminate the risks caused by human error. Although the much of the digital marketing is still higly dependent on human creations and ingeniosity, an AI program might probably be capable to generate a report using aonly and exclusively available data. However, to deeply connect with your consumers, marketers still need the truly human touch. Empathy, compassion and real-life storytelling are characteristics that AI machines can't emulate - not yet. Namely, AI is not restricted as humans are. And so, respecting still relevant Moore's Law, none can predict what AI will be able to do, even literally tomorrow...

Conversion management solutions based on AI are escalating the next, higher level. Marketing experts are able now to compare sophisticated inbound communication side-by-side against traditionally used metrics, and thus help answer difficult and crucial strategy questions. With AI marketing, there are no longer dilemmas about whether or not a potential consumer is ready for a discussion - the collected data provides the answer.

Machine Learning

Contemporary digital marketing is all about data available in the huge amounts. In the same time, it is more and more visible that marketing for many companies becomes the priority no. 1, as it is strongly linked with the growth of their revenue. Exploiting the unlimited possibilities of AI to enhance the business results is not "a far-horizon" any more, and many companies have already discovered this. Knowing that technology advances rapidly, now it is clear that machine learning (ML) and marketing go firmly hand-in-hand, according to „ CMO'S Guide to AI for Marketing - A comprehensive guide to understanding and using AI for business results" (2019).

Regarding marketing, it is crucial to have a system that quickly (a) identifies trends and (b) actions, all in real-time, and promptly react accordingly, without any additional human input. This specific ability "to learn on the go" is what makes ML highly important in contemporary marketing, as well as in the years to come. The best marketing experts are using ML to (i)understand, (ii) anticipate and (iii) act on the problems their sales potentials are willing to solve much faster and with more clarity than any relevant competitor. Having the clear insight to tailor adequate content, which qualifies the company and satisfies the potential customer for sales to close quickly, is the fuel given by ML-based apps capable of learning - and this is what's most effective for each business deal. Machine learning is enhancing (i) contextual content, (ii) the automation of marketing with crosschannel campaigns in addition, as well as their scoring, (iii) personalization, and (iv) sales forecasting, to significantly higher level of accuracy and speed.

Namely, from practical reasons, of digital transformation, no doubts, early implementation of ML and AI is of the highest importance for the fruitful future business. ML includes the analysis of historical data from various business interactions with consumers, as well as their responses. These combined data will enable the identification of (i) the success factors of marketers / companies communications, and also relevance of (ii) targeting, (iii) offers, (iv) contacts frequency... This should then be used for valuable learning and aplications in future marketing campaigns with the goal to increase the probability of success. All marketers nowadays are more often relying on ML to define more competitive, relevant pricing. ML applications are dealing with price optimization in the wider sense than particular airlines, hotels, and events - to have a bigger picture of pricing scenarios devoted to product and services. ML is applied today to determine pricing elasticity by each product, factoring in (i) channel segment, (ii) customer / consumer segment, (iii) sales period and (iv) the product's position, in an general product pricing strategy.

ML is directing (i) creation, (ii) fine-tuning and (iii) revenue contributions (up-sell / cross-sell) strategies by total automating the entire process. By using ML to qualify the further customer /consumer / clients lists using relevant data from the web, predictive models, including ML, can better predict ideal consumer / buyer profiles. Each sale lead by predictive score becomes for far better predictor of potential new sales, helping sales in prioritizing time, sales efforts and selling strategies. Namely, with the insights that ML provides, businesses can tailor and optimize their marketing efforts, providing a better service for their clients / consumers, and finaly, delivers a more personalized experience. This will help a company to build a loyal, satisfied audience that trusts brand and that will come back to buy more products and services.

Algorithms for ML generate insights applying predictive analytics, and it is then up to individuals to use these insights for relevant activities - or to define rules that allow your AI to acts based on them. For example, it can be defined a rule that establishes when to send emails designated at re-targeting the desired audience, giving a better chance for a higher ROI. Utilizing predictive analytics gives consistently better results across a number of important metrics. For businesses already using predictive analytics, (i) the average profit margin per customer and (ii) customer lifetime value, both are twice as high.

Signal Processing

To researchers working on data and quantitative models, all economic data influencing financial markets are especially challenging. With fast growth of and more available access to these data in digital form, data on finance, economics, and marketing are among the most important and the most tangible for big data applications, due to (i) the relatively clean organization and structure of the data and also (ii) clear application objectives and market demands. However, data-related studies often have different standpoints about the signal processing (SP).

Digital Signal Processors (DSP) take different real-world signals (voice, audio, video, temperature, pressure, or position...), firstly all are digitized, and then mathematically manipulated. Signals have to be processed in the way that the information that they contain can be (a) displayed, (b) analysed and/or (c) converted to another, useful type of signal. For the contrary, in the real-world, analogue products detect the same signals and manipulate them. An analog-to-digital converter then take the real-world signal and modify it into the digital "1's and 0's" format. At that point, the DSP startes with its role - it capture previously digitized information and process it. It then feeds the digitized information back for use in the real world: it does this either (a) digitally, or in (b) an analogue format (by going through a digital-to-analog converter). The entire process happens at very high speeds (Baker, 2003).

By nature similar principles (but far more sophisticated and complicated!) are embedded even to the newest tech advances.

Novel applications of matrix of characteristic values (the matrix of eigenvalues) approach in (i) image description, (ii) feature extraction and (iii) recognition are developing. They introduce the possibility of treating the speech signal graphically with the goal to extract the essential image features, as an elemental step in efficient data-mining appliance in the biometric techniques. The considered object here is the human-voice signal. A proposed frequency spectral evaluation is based on linear predictive coding principle, which has demonstrated (i) the possibility of selecting signal features from the power spectral plot and (ii) entering a matrix in a way similar to its application on images (of written texts, signatures, palm-prints, face geometries or fingerprints). These topics in many cases have already shown a success rate of approx. 98%. The extracted feature-carrying image includes the elements of the matrices to consecutively compute their minimal eigenvalues and introduce a set of characteristic vectors within a class of voices. The required computations can be performed in MATLAB, thus providing speech-signal image recognition in a simple and practical manner.

NATURAL LANGUAGE PROCESSING (NLP)

From recently, in content marketing talks you have probably heard terms as natural language processing (NLP), artificial intelligence and machine learning. All part of that is a part of fast- growing trend to automate (i) content research, (ii) creation and (iii) tracking, enabling marketing experts and teams to create content at large scale.

NLP is a specific part of AI that trains machines to (i) understand human language, (ii) interpret and (iii) lead conversations. This part of AI machine is dependant about the form of input (speech or voice). By exploiting deep learning algorithms, NLP models nowadays are focused on "next sentence prediction", i.e. a set of candidate sentences being ranked by relevance for an unfinished conversation. However, deep learning implementation enables newer models produce results with significant accuracy, since they are more complicated and capable to extract information from the data. This has opened capabilities for a broad range of new applications.

Robots equipped with NLP technology, are able to contribute in customer service, by understanding conversations (still in limited domains) and direct consumers to relevant answers. Emotions analysis helps to analyse conversations and measure satisfaction levels. NLP also helps understand consumers' ideas and intentions, by analysing their conversations and the webpages they visited.

Apps available now can translate whole texts at the semantic level. Developers found the way how to create multi-layered neural networks that function alike human brains. It's a type of ML that actually learns both, (i) the literal and (ii) semantic meaning of text, with the aim of translation that really makes sense to the language speaker. Machine translation is a great tool for marketing content developers working in global markets, where their language is not the first choice spoken; also applies to content created for one country, where many languages are spoken.

Emotion (sentiment) analysis uses ML and NLP to capture and understand the negative or positive connotation induced by a specific text. Some organizations, like IBM, refer to it as "tone analysis". They analyse detected emotions and tone nuances expressed in online content, to predict whether that person is happy, sad, etc.

The combination of (i) machine translation, (ii) speech recognition, (iii) emotion analysis, and (iv) automatic summarization can potentially introduce a greater degree of personalization to marketing content experience.

Social media trends, as well as those within published content, can be very fast identified - with new/adapted content being quickly added to further capitalize on the increased interest.

AI-POWERED TECHNOLOGIES

Speech Recognition

Voice recognition is an AI-powered technology that enables machines to (i) process, (ii) interpret and (iii) respond to human language (Hasrul et al., 2012).

Speech and voice recognition helps to recognise phrases or words and converts them to a machine-readable format. Users can control devices with the help of speech and voice, since the audio and text received by such devices automatically becomes converted into a machine-friendly format. That makes it easier for humans to operate devices without wasting time and effort for operating additional devices such as a mouse, keyboard, etc. This is a major factor promoting the growth of the global speech and voice recognition market and it's anticipated to continue.

Voice-controlled systems are increasingly used in smart cars, smart speakers, and other apps. Voice-controlled and speech-recognition systems are applicable in several industries (the smartphone industry, assistance applications, embedded devices, dictation appliances...). As per the Adobe Analytics Survey, voice recognition used on smart speakers and smartphones today, are mostly used for searching music, maps and directions, weather forecast, news, and others. This indicates, for the near-future, a remarkable speech and voice recognition market growth.

AI is a common term for a seria of technologies that use large datasets for predictions. One of them, the voice recognition, understands what humans are saying. It includes an enormous variety of words, sentence types, and accents. Voice recognition uses AI (i) to turn human speech into text; (ii) then, for analysing that text to assumes what you're saying and how it should respond (namely, when you talk, voice recognition processes your words using past studies, afterwards applies sophisticated ML models to predict what you're saying, looking for the most appropriate respond); (iii) and finally, for delivering a voice or text result. The machine attempts to do this with as high degree of accuracy as possible, although for the time being, it's still not perfect. The continuously machine learns by studying data from all its users, with the aim to improve itself at predicting what the user is saying and what that really means. The process of learning over time results with voice recognition systems getting better by themselves, until they're so accurate, that seem like they understand you perfectly. Until now, enormous enhancements have been made in the accuracy and performance of voice recognition systems — and they are key reasons that we've seen a boom in voice assistants and voice search (Zhang, 2017).

There is the customer-facing technology – the voice assistants, IVRs (interactive voice response) – and then there are elements that are working in the background: speech analytics, voice processing, pattern recognition, voice biometrics and emotion detection are all part of an ecosystem that is aimed at making the experience of interacting with a brand much efficient and effective for consumers (Yacoub et al., 2003; Saeed, 2006).

Then there is the rise of augmented support – speech recognition 'robots' that work in assistance with contact centre agents to monitor interactions with customers and put forward useful information in the heat of discussion. From a consumer standpoint, voice recognition supports and enables voice search and voice assistants on smartphones and smart home devices. That is what allows you to look for directions while driving, tell your phone to call someone, or tell *Alexa* to play a specific song.

Vision / Object Recognition

Computer vision is a field of AI designed to enable computers the visual understanding of the world. Currently computer vision is at large scale used for different purposes as are: event detection, video tracking, object recognition, scene reconstruction, 3D pose and motion estimation, learning, indexing, and image restoration. Computer vision has grown fast, providing thrilling possibilities for the wide spectrum of marketing activities. This technology uses AI and ML to scan images and accurately identify objects and components within them.

Computer vision algorithms can decompose and convert image contents into metadata; these data can then easily stored, organized, and analysed, just alike other data sets. With these capabilities, computer vision, besides (i) recognizing and (ii) identifying image components, can (iii) detect patterns, (iv) respond with triggers like personalized suggestions, (v) overlay virtual images, (vi) enable searchable image sets, etc.

Trading in ecommerce is traditionally all about multiply tagging. Each product has numerous tags, allowing the customer to filter for particular attributes, and also allowing recommendation algorithms to surface related products (these algorithms may also analyse both: behavioural and purchase data).

By it's capabilities, visual recognition software is useful in developing a deeper understanding of consumers. The images and videos a person shares or likes via social media provide insights into what products they like, and in the same time give marketers an insight into other elements of a potential consumer's lifestyle. Highly supported by ML, algorithms can quickly identify unique elements of images; that helps the marketing machine in it's eficacy, i.e. determines what ad should be delivered to whom. Visual search can help also customers in browsing, comparing, and narrowing choices, through image-generated similarities vs. manually attributed classifications. This is minimizing the necesity for consumers to know and understand specific brand jargon and simplifies their "right product" chasing activities. Image detection enables brands to identify the threats and opportunities that influence their business success; they use computer vision to identify brand logos and find good and bad reviews all over the web.

Data generated from browsing using visual cue modifiers might be useful for retailers, who use content management systems (CMS), to trace patterns not visible only through written tagging. For example, two seemingly unrelated products might be purchased together because they have complementary style elements - and the system is enabled to suggest similar pairings in advance.

AI-based software is now capable for visual product discovery, which eliminates the need for most metadata and surfaces similar products based on their visual attributes - as an alternative to a standard filtering system, buyers can select the desired product, and be shown visually similar products.

WHAT CAN AI DO FOR MARKETING? HOW AI INFLUENCES THE MOST AND BRINGS ADVANTAGES TO MARKETING?

In the area of communications: by enabling organic search, voice search, chatbots and higher level of personalisation... In the area of management: by enabling lead scoring, media buying, marketing automation, predictive analytics, propensity modelling, dynamic pricing, ad targeting scoring... In the area of content: by content generation, content curators, chatbots, personalisation... In the area of customers' targeting: by ad targeting scoring, dynamic pricing, propensity modelling, predictive analytics and retargeting... All in all, the most exposed and important roles of AI are by chatbots implementation, and in personalisation, dynamic pricing, predictive analytics...

HUMAN-COMPUTER INTERACTION

Human-computer interaction (HCI) is a multidisciplinary field with the specific focus in computer technology development enabling the interaction between people as users and computers. At the very beginning the designing was focused on computers, but since then the HCI has broadened and the field nowadays integrate almost the whole of information technology.

HCI is studying interaction between humans as users and computers and basically it is mixture of computing, behavioural sciences, design etc. Interaction users-computers is placed at the user interface - both, software plus hardware. The set of resources by which people interact with a system (i.e. a specific machine, device, SW program, or other complex tool) is the HCI. Academic research framework on HCI is combining (i) the experimental methods and (ii) intellectual framework of cognitive psychology, with efficient computer sciences' tools. The research is insisting on a controlled experiment, which brings objective and highly reliable results. HCI is a new branch, a discipline which is firmly connecting cognitive science (the work of a mind) and engineering (the work of computers). As initial results of cognitive engineering, HCI's numerous outputs - models, theories, and frameworks - created a new paradigm for this prospective technology: to empower humans by deeper understanding the way how they think and what they need.

HCIs should be intuitively based, alike direct conversations between two persons - but many of developed products and services haven't satisfied this request. What should be known to satisfy it and design an adequate intuitive communication experience between a person and a machine? The answer is: the adequate mixture of (i) human psychology, (ii) emotional design and (iii) specialized creation processes.

So, HCI is based on (a) deep understanding what does it mean to be a user of a computer (and this is not as simple as it sounds!), and (b) how to design related products and services for their seamlessly integration and interaction. If well-developed, these skills ensure a company the opportunities to create efficient products which therefore sell better.

The evolution of media interfaces is somehow encouraged by HCI research, mainly supported by tools like eye tracking and facial coding. HCI is based on understanding cognitive processes, but allowing ever more intuitive interfaces that decrease user's mental effort and increase satisfaction. Spreading the consistent and influent messages across a plethora of available devices and platforms for marketing experts is among the biggest challenges in the digital era. Brands have access to unlimited number of data on consumer behaviour. HCI have to contextualize that ocean of information for marketers to allow them act properly.

HCI and similar achievements nowadays can help marketing experts and advertisers to offer relevant and personalized content experiences, with the ultimate goal to make more money from described interactions. Namely, HCI can improve content delivery by wider accessibility and higher interactivity. There are now myriad means of connecting consumers with content, and not all are equal. For marketing experts, developing both (a) the optimal means of data collection and (b) making sense of it all, relies on an excellent knowledge about (i) how consumers mainly interact with content, (ii) via which digital platforms they approach to the content and (iii) which end-devices they prefer to access these platforms.

What is necessary to convert HCI principles into practice? A top notch example are facial tracking technologies - the way how marketers (mainly customer experience professionals) are providing content and experiences to potential consumers.

Recent developments in cloud computing, augmented reality (AR) and virtual reality (VR)... combined with general advances in AI, are promising improved, even more seamless HCI... but bringing effectively these developments into reality still remains a challenge (Blagojević, et al., 2017).

Affective Computing

Affective computing (also: emotion AI, or artificial emotional intelligence) by its definition is research and creation of sophisticated products that are able to: (i) clearly discern, (ii) construe (adequately explain and translate), (iii) process, and finaly, (iv) simulate human affects. This an interdisciplinary area is intertwining computation and psychology, with cognitive science. This part of computer science basically arises from Rosalind W. Picard's 1995 article of MIT. The main motivation was to research the possibility to add to machines the emotional intelligence, as well as the possibility provide a sort of empathy. Such a device should (i) identify the emotional status of a human, (ii) adapt its behaviour to the detected state, and (iii) provide appropriate response to detected emotions.

Affective computing changed the face of computing technologies by incorporating emotions in their core, thus extending their capabilities and, consequently, becoming more and more important. In short, the detection of users' emotions currently is the prime aspect of affective computing.

In 1997, Picard defined affective computing as "computing that relates to, arises from, or influences emotions or other affective phenomena." The bottom line of affective computing is: those computers that interact with humans, as the minimum, must have the ability to recognize affect

Picard's ambicious focus is HCI. She have had the ultimate aim for affective computing to "enhance computing machines with the features to (i) identify the emotions captured and (ii) perform them... and somethimes, also for (iii) 'creating and showong' it's own feelings". Besides, the interactivity of the research enables (a) "the people themselves to recognize and better express the emotions they posses at the specific moment" and (b) to enhance machine-supported communications performing among people.

From the time Prof. Picard devised the term "affective computing", she repeatedly says that the goals of AI research during the time have evolved, subtly but sustantially. Picard's work has moved away from perfecting already intelligent machines, towards creating those capable (i) to use of emotional intelligence and (ii) to provide contributions in solving problems. Later her research efforts were re-focused on designing tools that would help computers understand human emotions, but not to mimic them. This change have shifted research away from the initial aim - AI with human-like machine consciousness - that threatened to make "humans unnecessary and obsolete" (Banafa, 2016; Mullin, 2018).

Detecting and Recognizing Emotional Information

Passive sensors that capture data (without interpreting them) are at the very beginning of the process of detecting emotional information of consumers' physical status or how they behave. All collected data are similar to the signals people apply while identify and denote emotions in other human. E.g., a simple videocam can catch one's expression of face, the body attitude, and gestures; a mic is capable to catch the voice and speech. Some specific sensors may identify signs of current feelings which are arising from physiological measurable data as skin temperature...

For recognizing one's emotional information needs is based on recognition the meaningful patterns contained within all collected data. This should be done by using ML tools, i.e. techniques designed specifically to process speech recognition, NLP, or facial expressions detection. The tasks of applied techniques are to produce tags that would in great measure match the tags given by a qualified human observer during an identical or similar circumstances. E.g., when the express of the face of one human is realised in a specific manner (Ekman & Friesen, 1969), then the vision system of a machine should be learnt to tag such face expressions as "smiling" either "delighted" either "happy"... etc. But still, interpretator of results should keep in mind that these tags only can, but not necessarily, express what the watched person is really feels (Ekman, 2013).

The research within affective computing has also the aim to design of AI products that can offer and display inborn affective abilities of such devices and/or that are capable simulating emotions convincingly. The feelings' simulator embedded in a conversational agent is a usable appliance founded on todays existing tech solutions, which is developed to enhance and support human - machine interactive communication (Al Badawi, 2018).

Emotional Speech

Human nervous systems are often bearing with impacts and transformations that may indirectly trigger, even radically, modifications in voice and speech of a person. With the aim to determine person's relevant emotional state, affective technologies are exploiting information about these impacts (Ekman, 1992). E.g., human voice and speech, while a person is happy, surprised or joyful, is higher, louder or sharper etc., with unusual but specific and relevant voice colour and pitch, different than normally. On the contrary, tiredness, or sadness generally bring slow, more quite, and blended speech. It has been found that some emotions can be more easily identified by computation than others. Namely, pattern recognition techniques for emotional speech processing can identify status of peoples' emotions by applying computer analyses of theirs' voice and speech characteristics.

Speech analysis has average accuracy 70 to 80%. That result is qualifying speech analyses as an efficient method of identifying a person's affective state. These systems are overshadowing human accuracy (in this: approx. 60%), but are less precise than systems employing physiological states or facial expressions for emotion detection. Howsoever, due the fact that features of the speech are fully independent of lexical semantics or one's culture, speech analysis techniques are valid candidate also for future studies.

Algorithms

(i) A trustworthy database, (ii) computorised database, or vector space model (based on the idea of similarity), and (iii) a proven classifier i.e. fast and precise feelings identifier - all listed is required to detect and process speech and text, within ML (an application within AI) (Albornoz et al., 2011).

For the time being, the prime classifier aplicable to the space of the set of characteristics (including for the computational recognition of emotions / affects) is LDC (linear discriminant classifier) - where the classification is grounded on the resulting value gained from the linear combination of the values of all particular characteristics given as vectors.

The other often used classifiers are:

- ANN (artificial neural networks). A mathematical model, analogue to biological neural networks, that can deeper understand possible non-lineary events;
- DTA (decision tree algorithms). A replic of the decision-tree model; leaves represent the classification outcome, and branches the conjunction of characteristics that lead to the classification;
- GMM (Gaussian mixture model). A probabilistic model used takes into account sub-groups in the set of characteristics described by the mixture distribution, what allows classification of observations into these sub-groups;
- k-NN (k-nearest neighbour). Classification is based on locating the object, and comparing it with the k-nearest neighbours. The majority vote decides on the classification;
- SVM (support vector machines). A linear classifiers make binary decisions, on which of the two or more possible classes input data belong to;
- HMMs (hidden Markov model). A statistical model; the initial states of features and its transitions within the space are unavailable to be observed directly, but the sets resulting outputs dependent on these statuses are noticeable. These sequences support the predictio of affective state under the classification. HMMs are mostly applied to algorithms for speech recognition.

As it is proved, the emotional state of a person can be classified by a set of majority voting classifiers, but only with enough acoustic evidence available.

Choosing an adequate database for training the classifier is still one of the challenges in detecting emotions based on speech. Most of available databases have been generated from actors - and thus representation only clonned, archetypal emotions. Of course, they are mostly based on the Paul Ekman's Basic Emotions theory, which assumes the presence of six essential emotions (anger, disgust, fear, joy, sadness, surprise), and the others are the simple combination of these listed ones. But naturalistic database, for real-life application, based on observation and analysis of people in their regular surroundings and daily activities, would be valuable. Such database would allow the system (i) to recognize emotions based on their context and (ii) work out the aims and results of the interaction. Such databases would be relevant for authentic real life applications, because they describes states normally occurring during HCI. Creation of such "an emotion database" is a demanding and long-lasting work. but it is a fundamental step in designing a system that will recognize human emotions. Most of the emotion databases on the public disposal include only posed facial expressions. In them, the participants were asked to show specific emotional expressions; in a spontaneous expression database, shown expressions are natural (Neiberg et al., 2006). Spontaneous emotion provocation requires effort in the selection of adequate stimuli - and that can lead to an avalanche of intended emotions. All that requires manual labelling gathered emotions from the side of well educated people - what assure that such databases are highly reliable. On the top of all, perception of the stimuli from the observed person, and the intensity of gained reaction, as well as defining in words of that stimulated reaction, i.e. facial description given by observant, both are by nature genuinelly subjective - so that annotations of experts involved are valuable contribution to the entire validation process.

Human's gestures simply respond to specific emotional stimuli, but they could be complex and meaningful (for instance, while communicating with sign language). People often wave, clap or beckon. When using objects, we show at them, move, touch or handle these. An AI machine can recognize all these gestures, analyse concrete circumstances (taking into account cultural differences, becouse in different communities for the same gestures can have even opposite perceptions), and answer with meaning, as an efficient tool of Human-Computer Interaction.

There are differentiated two main approaches (among the many) in body gesture recognition: (a) 3D-based model (uses facts about specific 3D body details, with the goal to collect a set of personal significant parameters), and (b) an appearance-based model (system utilize pictures and short movies for gestures' immediate contextualization). Hands are in the focus of both described body gesture detection methods.

Emphatic Computing

Incredible nowadays technology designs even empathy (seeing with the eyes, listening with the ears, and feeling with the heart... of an another): the individual is placed in the focus of each experience. Such technology has expanded its range, being applied to entertainment and gaming industry... over news and movies... to education and healthcare systems, marketing... Different studies have proved the influence of emotions in consumers' behaviour and decision-making activities. Empathic media is an umbrella-term relating to all affect-sensitive technologies. That media are engaged to make conclusions about human emotions like feelings, moods, attention, intention... Often they use AI and ML accesses, and are fast-growing in capabilities and applicabilities. Empathic computing today encompasses research activities in virtual reality (VR), augmented reality (AR), mixed reality (MR), immersive virtual reality (IVR), ...

From the physiological side, emotions start in the limbic system: the amygdala produces emotional impulses, then they induce physiological reactions acompanied with emotions, which are reflected as electric activity (face muscles movements, electrodermal activity / galvanic skin response, pupil dilatation, breath and heart rate, blood pressure, brain activity...). Emotions leave a footprints on the body, which are measurable with adequate tools.

Virtual reality (VR) is ideal technology for empathic computing: the main aim of VR is to fully plunge people into simulated experiences.

The final types of empathic computing systems are those that enable a human to share the live experience of others: to allow a person to see what an another human is seeing and to understand the feelings of other in the real time. For instance, augmented reality (AR) is a wearable computing; with body-worn sensors these are two key-technologies for enabling this happen. There are many examples of wearable systems that can live stream video to a remoted collaborator, a few to mention:

- the Google Glass wearable computer (which has a forward facing camera that enables users to share a video of what they are doing - from a cameraman's perspective);
- Jun Rekimoto's JackIn innovation, (an advanced version, shares "360 video" from one user to another who can view the live video in a VR display, and feel like that they are seeing the world from the senders perspective);
- The Empathic Computing Laboratory (ECL), 2018, is going even beyond, by enabling people to share their emotions and non-verbal communication signs; the Empathy Glasses (ECL's project that combines a display mounted on the head, with eye tracking HW and sensors for catching face expression - to enhance collaboration on the distance. By this HW, its remote user can identify the focus where a local user is looking, as well as "local's" feelings - helping so to realize intended tasks and activities...

Brands have trials with "immersive technology" to create „electronic empathy" – by combining digital with experiential marketing, with the aim to share experiences with a wider audience. The threat for brands is that the algorithms companies mainly apply may push them into more and more narrow information "pigeonholes" and thus merge them with bands they in advance agree with. But empathy is about understanding many different standpoints and VR should modify perceptions.

Quantum Cognition

Let start with the quantum mechanics: it is about the behaviour of atoms and their subatoms of which make up all in the known universe - yet great minds are still dealing with a humongous amount of open questions in this „world of the tiny". As a simple example, in the big world, one can know where a train exactly is at the moment on the concrete way from A to B, how fast it is travelling, based on this relevant data, it can be predicted when the train should arrive at the specific station on the route.

If the train is exchanged for an electron, and if regular "big world's"predictive methods are not applicable for its world of the tiny - it is impossible to define the place and momentum of this electron; only the probability that the particle may appear in a specific spot, on its vouyage at a specific rate, can be predicted. Thus, only a vaguely impression of what the electron might be up to is available. In the same way as uncertainty permeate the world of the tiny, it permeates human's decision-making processes. And now about the similarity with quantum mechanics: instead the conservative approach to decision-making processes, the quantum world enables space for "a certain degree" of... uncertainty.

Quantum cognition is a new scientific field, which adopted the concepts of quantum mechanics. It assist psychologists better predict and understand human decision-making processes. It is identified that, while thinking, some human brain regions are included in quantum-like flows / processes (and today's brain scans can effectively highlight them). In short, the 'quantum-based' algorithm of decision-making includes a degree of uncertainty, i.e. a quantum probability in the area of cognition.

PARADIGM SHIFT OF ARTIFICIAL INTELLIGENCE (AI) AND MARKETING EVOLUTION

The Effects of AI on Marketing

If you already have personal experiences as Amazon's buyer, you have probably experienced receiving product suggestions and recommendations based on your past orders and on items you have recently viewed... but the step forward are virtual personal assistants (VPAs) and chatbots, as main examples of AI in practice in the real world of marketing. By such devices AI enables marketers to get real-time insights from collected data, structured as well as unstructured, and that gives brands the power needed to establish personalized and more meaningful interactions with their consumers (Sentance, 2019).

Currently, the outcome of applying AI in marketing by using data science, NLP and predictive analysis is expecting. SW that uses AI now became a basic marketing tool, especially when we are faced with constantly growing quantities of data daily produced within this industry. That provides the efficient opportunity to discover deeper insights to the field, as well as for further marketing's top-noch improvements by implementing data mining, NLP, data analytics and data science.

AI Powered by Engagement Marketing

Applying the predictive analytics and data science enables marketing experts to provide consumers perfectly timed the best offer with the right product and content. And if combined with AI technology, predictive marketing enables marketing experts to fulfill their assignments in real time (Reavie, 2019).

Why AI Is the Marketing Future?

Consumer data explosion. Within the few past years it was visible terrific increase of consumer data; by appliing Internet of things (IoT) devices the world is producing over 2.5 quintillion bytes of data per year; on Twitter there are more than 460K tweets per minute; there are over 3.6 billion searches daily). Data is the fuel for AI. Any serious "manual analyses" are unthinkable (Sullivan, (2018)..

Tempo of marketing. Real-time marketing decisions have to be feeded on live data, as well as conversations (also from chatbots). The number of marketing channels is constantly growing; marketing is acting as a sales function.

Segmentation vs. individual sales. For the consumers' specific segments optimization very complicated algorithms and tools are developed. But the highest level of sophistication is necessary for tools optimizing the segment of individuals!

Is AI in Marketing Merely Over-promoted?

AI in marketing today: high thrill, low implementation rate!

98% marketing experts are seeing benefits from AI, but there are only around 20% of them have already implemented one or more AI solutions, as a core part of their businesses. So, AI enthusiasm vs. implementation is still questionable... And as an example: in the industry-based recent study (2018) only a quarter of all companies use AI in marketing. Just 30% of managers already use AI in their company, only about 25% in their own marketing department. And only 7% already use AI in marketing intensively (Thaliyachira, 2019).

The Rule of Inference

In logic, a rule of inference (or inference rule; or transformation rule) is a logical form that consists a function which (i) takes premises, (ii) analyzes their syntax, and (iii) returns a conclusion / conclusions. Typically, a rule of inference preserves truth, as a semantic property.

Targeted new customer acquisition with inference – also called *logical inference* – is a common AI method that can be used in marketing during prospecting, i.e., the targeted acquisition of new customers.

AI: Transforming the Customer Experience through Mass Personalisation

AI-enabled customer experience consists of:

- predictive offers and web personalisation (self-service discovery),
- chatbots – the new user interface for self-service (increased productivity),
- AI-powered routing and speech-to-text analysis for insights and notification (reduces tension and friction along the buying-tours and make consumers feel happy and stress-free),
- on-time anticipated and well-addressed problems (pre-emptive service - builds professional relationships with quality-minded consumers before they need your services).

It will not be long before AI makes all our shopping decisions („... *that is NOT your colour...*")

Gartner (at the mid of 2019) predicted that by 2021, 15% of all customer service globally interactions will be handled exclusivelly by AI, as an increase of 400% from 2017. By 2022, even 70% of educated employees will daily interact with conversational platforms. This expected growth is the same as the increase in number of employed millennials.

Chatbots have suddenly conquerd the customer service and real-estate industries, but that's probably just the start of their success-story:

- implementation of chatbots can cut business operational costs by up to 30%;
- 85% of consumer interaction by 2021 will be operated without human intermediation;
- 50% of companies plan to spend more on chatbots than on mobile apps;
- 64% of internet users praise 24-hour service as the best role of chatbots;
- 37% of people use a customer service bot to get a quick answer in an emergency;
- 90% of client interaction in banking will be fully automated by 2022.

But – What Chatbots Really Are?

Chatbots are computerised programs using AI to simplify a verity of customer service related tasks.

Chatbots apps help marketers deliver the right content to the right person at the right time. With the opportunity to engage with customer on a direct personal platform, marketers can catch users' attention, initiate conversations and market to customers in a better and more efficient fashion.

What Can Chatbots Do? How They Will Change the Future of Customer Engagement?

Use cases in practice are including: engagement and entertainment, quality for users, generate potential clients and consumers, promote products and services, trainings and educations, customer service as a knowledgebase, online ordering and payment, implementation of loyalty programs...

Always on-hand: should a user face difficulty in content search any time of the day, chatbot offer instant support – and drive customer satisfaction through 24/7 support.

Generate leads: use customer's personal information to create campaigns that guide the customer in the right direction and boost conversation rates – boost conversation rates through customer campaigns.

Improved efficiency: from easy customer interactions to personalised customer service, it helps conduct multiple marketing operations, including product recommendations, in an efficient manner – simplify customer service and interactions and thus operational efficacy.

Blended recommendations with intelligent search... for example, at Alibaba, China, the world's largest e-commerce company and the one of the most valuable tech companies in the world (2018):

- AI-based chatbot backed by DL and NPL, Tmall Smart Selection, helps recommend concrete products to consumers and then direct relevant retailers to enlarge inventory to satisfy the demand;
- AI-based chatbot, Dian Xiaomi, understand over 90 percent of consumer's questions and serves daily over 3.5 million users; its newest version understand a consumer's emotion, and is capable to define priorities and alert customer service employees to act personally when necessary.

Why AI Chatbots Are Gaining Popularity in Customer Service and Support?

Their capabilities and advantages bring to the companies: increased responsiveness, personalized customer service in real time, easy expansion of customer service, cost savings, automated customer relationship... and they are reliable and correct while providing self-service. As an example, beauty retailer *Sephora* (2018) use AI to create an omnichannel retail approach and by investing in AI, the company has created a seamless experience for the customer across both digital and retail outlets.

The example is also Hitachi's *EMIEW3*, a fully humanoid robot, an excellent listener and provider of information for different customer services which through active-learning dialogue data-based AI can learn about information that may change frequently, i.e. such as flight status, and correctly respond to customer enquiries...

Why Is Chatbot Marketing So Appealing to Marketers?

Easy content distribution. Marketers can directly connect with their audiences and deliver content in a timely and efficient manner.

Ubiquity. Billions of people already use messenger app for texting. Digital interactions promote quick and easy marketing.

Personalised approach. Marketers can easily get to know their users and deliver fully personalised and relevant information and experience.

Sales chatbots. They are more than just a novelty - they alleviate bottleneck in sales processes, proactively handle objections or customer concerns without human interaction, improve conversion rates, they are "always on" sales assistant, reduce abandonment and recover lost revenue...

What Is the Future of Chatbots?

The quick adoption of chatbots by satisfied end users has led to the businesses use them more and more - bots produced in ever-advanced AI technologies and with customized SW solutions. Even there are optimistic reports from 2019 that 80–85% of businesses will likely be deploying advanced chatbots by 2020...

Today's chatbots are designed for human speech language understanding, but they are capable to execute many different cognitive services as: speech to text conversion and vice versa, computer vision functions, recognition and translation of languages, content moderation, speaker recognition, text analytics and similar.

Consumer preferences nowadays are favouring chat in comparison with email communication, and many businesses are clearly recognizing the trend. Messaging applications are more and more a second home screen for many, mainly for youngsters, becoming also their ever available and reliable entrance to the internet. And where the youngsters already are, the businesses gladly track them. Companies are planning remarkable invests to develop messaging applications as bots, but also the applications that realize and support almost everything: customer service, online shopping, banking...

Conversations (speech) are the next major step in HCI. Thanks to advances in NLP and ML, the AI-related technologies are getting faster and more accurate - to be viable.

Product Management of AI Products

Building blocks for AI products, according to HBR webinar (McCarthy & Saleh, 2019), are:

- *autonomy* (in self-operation, self-coordination, self-service),
- *optimization* (of performance and diagnostics, and of self-operation)
- *control* (of personalization, and of performance and self-coordination)
- *monitoring* function block (of personalisation, diagnostics and self-service)...

.. and besides traditional, also the novel product management skills (technology and economic trends, cross-cultural knowledge, privacy and regulations, transparency and security, ethical decision-making, autonomy...).

While joining the human context to the emerging technologies needs to be taken into account how the people influence, and how react, to these tech novelties, and also understand how all that correlates with AI. That mean that people in an automated economy should be understood well, that AI should match people's necessities, and that it should be known that data and users can be biased, and that there are limitations of algorithms and while evaluating the ethical aspects.

Product management main resources are machine learning and NLP, considering *all the time correlation between AI and human factor*. But still a lot is to be learnt!

Will AI Replace Product Management Function – and How Should Product Managers Respond?

With continuous development of AI in the age of intelligent products, all major industry verticals will be disrupted, the role of product management as well. AI for product personalization (i.e., building more than 1.5 billion AI agents - one for every person who uses *Facebook* or any of its products!), leveraging artificial intelligence for design, building software using sensor + AI data, self design by AI... are only a few functions which will replace traditional product managers' roles (Boudet et al.,2019).

To "protect" their roles and adapt them to unavoidable avalanche of AI and new market needs, future-oriented product managers should, according to Zinnov *Research and Analysis*, primarily:

- build deep understanding of change forces in the market and the ecosystem (which include engineering service providers, start-ups, universities, expert networks...) with technologies changing consumption models across global markets,
- understand AI impact on the products,
- transform team structure and skill profiles,
- build a data moat and a data ecosystem, and
- orchestrate partnerships to accelerate innovation...

AI Influencing Brand Management

In general, brand is a publicly distinguished product, service or concept that can be easily communicated, marketed and positioned. One of areas of AI implementation in the marketing business is brand management: AI influence systems that aid business decisions through strategic intelligence, focuses on automated solutions requiring less human intervention, visualizes through AI-powered customer experiences, improves recognition, experience, perception and bottom line.

Specifically, at least brand management and several other already mentioned marketing areas can benefit from AI aplications like: AI generated content, voice search, smart content curation, programmatic media buying, propensity modelling, predictive analytics, add targeting, dynamic pricing, chatbots, web and app personalization, re-targeting, predictive customer service... (Sentance, 2019).

Understanding correlations between brand and AI enables providing:

- intelligence-driven product catalogues (identified customer behaviour is used to automatically adapt offerings via catalogue; this include price optimization, content, validity etc., and proposes products re-configurations, all based on deep learning AI functions),
- social networks optimization,
- better market engagement and customer care,
- development of future-oriented decision-wheels, and
- digital media services aimed for achieving higher brand reputation.

AI is giving unprecedented ability to improve brand interaction and rationalize actions that promote brand goals; to avoid a high degree of fluctuation in customer perception; and to help make the brand experience more personalized and predictive. The main tools applied are signal weighting and entropy pooling which improves customer experience, satisfaction, value and competitive advantage. Signal weighting is an indicator that analysis risk through conventional pointers, filters or entropy pooling; signals can be integrated using assigned confidence scores and indicate the probability of brand value scaling up or down. The entropy pooling approach is a theoretical framework to process market views and generalized stress-tests into an optimal "posterior" market distribution, which is then used for risk management and portfolio management (Meucci et al., 2014).

Decision wheel focuses on brand management via customer experience - happy customers create brand loyalty, increasing reputation improving growth. AI improves customer experience by generating personalized recommendations, by building AI-powered application programming interfaces (APIs), by linking business and customers (thus improving perception) and by providing speech recognition and emotional intelligence solutions.

However, brand value over time has cycles of positive and negative trends. With impact of AI, the monitoring provides recommendations identify and mitigate brand impact abnormalities, helping the "control" of brand value by which brand strategy may be better applied. The outcomes are (i) monitoring brand value cycles that generate positive trends, (ii) build up of brand capital, and (iii) defining exposures to high fluctuation events. All that results with (a) increases in brand loyalty, and (b) better isolate the brand against insults which can from time to time occur.

The promise of AI is materializing... however, not all AI is created equal. Some machine learning algorithms are transparent, allowing brands to see how they make decisions, while others are opaque, obscuring the inner logic of models. Still others are transparent yet so convoluted that the results are not easily explainable. This fact highlights the evolving area of explainable AI and how customer insights pros should consider the tradeoffs in risk, accuracy, and applicability when they determine the level of explainability in AI.

AI in marketing brings more brand safety thanks to classification. The AI method of classification can help one of the most important tasks in programmatic advertising. In fact, the technology can learn which pages do not fit the brand and prevent it from being displayed. To do this, the technology solution initially provides information about unwanted websites and environments. On this basis, the AI assesses the advertising environment offered and, in case of doubt, stops the playout. The division into "not brand-safe" takes place via features such as the content of a website or certain keywords.

Social network optimization enables content routing by optimizing information according to demands, traffic volume, users' behaviour etc. Digital media influence brand reputation. Namely, opinions today spread instantaneously; word of mouth and social searches are influental and powerful. Numerous and instant consumer reviews affect reputation. That's why *brands use AI to better control of consumer experiences*, and automation software to simplify labour-intensive tasks.

THE FUTURE OF AI AND ROBOTICS

According to a best-practice insight "Predictive Marketing & Why You Should Look Into It" (2020), predictive marketing, data science and data analytics are among fundamental techniques of AI. But, it is realistic to assume that "better and faster" technologies will soon appear on the horizon, perhaps even based on different philosophy, to replace – and make obsolete – the existing ones. The only thing left for marketing experts who have spawned their positions with the rise of data-driven environment is to be ready for change and to embrace all novelties as a precondition for their own progress.

Personal Digital Twins

Algorithms are all around us, guiding business decisions, social policy and life choices. But the algorithms that organisations use today do not account for individual human objectives, resulting in outcomes that are often detrimental to people and society. The tables are about to turn. B2C marketing professionals need to prepare for a new target audience: the *personal digital twin* (PDT) - a groundbreaking technology.

Digital twin is simply a digital model (as a „physical twin") replicating a concrete, tangeble thing, process, person, place, system and device - of all usable for completing different goals. Such a digital presentation enables providing knowledge about the components and the dynamic behaviour of devices that constitue IoT world during their entire life-time. The ongoing research highlights the following most important characteristics of technological development based on the application of "digital twins": (a) the importance of the connections established by these models between the real and virtual worlds; (b) the establishment of such connections is made possible by the use of sensors which enable the generation of digital data in real time.

CONCLUSION

How the AI Storm in Marketing Influence the Near-future of Marketers (Moutinho, 2019)?

Multidisciplinarity and interdisciplinarity are basics approaches to solve the complex and interblended problems more and more arising in the real world.

A „vertical integration" (namely, according to the science of cognitive, assumptioms and methods within the humanities have to be vertically limited, by a virifiable, measurable truth) obviously labels the adequate priority in hierarchy to the specific scientific field (Bernini & Woods, 2014).

According to Klein's taxonomy research (2010), multidisciplinatity and interdisciplinarity assigns diversed degrees of participation, as well as flexibility of boundaries of the relating disciplinaries. Proximity, contradistinction and aligning among multidisciplinary involved fields largely broaden up cognition and knowledge by their inherent, specific features and supplements, but in the same time all the particular disciplines which contribute leave unaltered. On the contrary, the prominent characteristics of a powerful interdisciplinarity are intense processes of proactive interaction and integration. This can be clearly noticed in the intertwining between creativity methods, i.e. in cross-disciplinarization and adaptation the many traditional with novel scientific fields, like AI, NLP, cognitive computing, affective computing and human-computer interaction.

REFERENCES

Al Badawi, H. S. (2018, September 10). Affective Computing (AI & Emotions). *AI Projects*. Retrieved from https://airesearchprojects.com/2018/09/10/affective-computing-ai-emotions/

Albornoz, E. M., Diego Milone, D., & Rufiner, H. L. (2011, July). Spoken emotion recognition using hierarchical classifiers. *Computer Speech & Language*, *25*, 556–570.

Baker, T. (2003, April 9). *An Introduction to Digital Signal Processors: How to find signals in noise using estimation. A Case Study*. Retrieved from Introduction%20to%20Digital%20Signal%20Processors.pdf

Banafa, A. (2016, June 6). What is Affective Computing? *OpenMind Neweletter: Technology-Digital World*. Retrieved from https://www.bbvaopenmind.com/en/technology/digital-world/what-is-affective-computing/

Bernini, M., & Woods, A. (2014). Interdisciplinarity as cognitive integration: Auditory verbal hallucinations as a case study. *Wiley Interdisciplinary Reviews: Cognitive Science, 5*(5), 603–612. doi:10.1002/wcs.1305 PMID:26005512

Blagojević, V. (2017). A systematic approach to generation of new ideas for PhD research in computing. *Advances in Computers, 104*, 1-31.

Boudet, J. (2019, June 18). The future of personalization—and how to get ready for it. *McKinsey Insights*. Retrieved from https://www.mckinsey.com/business-functions/marketing-and-sales/our-insights/the-future-of-personalization-and-how-to-get-ready-for-it

Ekman, P. (1992, January 1). Facial Expressions of Emotion: New Findings, New Questions. Meeting Report. *Psychological Science*. Retrieved from https://journals.sagepub.com/doi/10.1111/j.1467-9280.1992.tb00253.x

Ekman, P. (2013, July). *Emotional-And-Conversational-Nonverbal-Signals*. Retrieved from https://www.paulekman.com/wp-content/uploads/2013/07/Emotional-And-Conversational-Nonverbal-Signals.pdf

Ekman, P., & Friesen, W. V. (1969). The repertoire of nonverbal behaviour: Categories, origins, usage, and coding. *Semiotica, 1*(1), 49–98. doi:10.1515emi.1969.1.1.49

Hasrul, M. N., Hariharan, M., & Yaacob, S. (2012, April 5). Human Affective (Emotion) behaviour analysis using speech signals: A review. In *2012 International Conference on Biomedical Engineering (ICoBE)*. IEEE. Retrieved from https://ieeexplore.ieee.org/abstract/document/6179008

Klein, J. T. (2010). A taxonomy of interdisciplinarity. In R. Frodeman, J. T. Klein, & C. Mitcham (Eds.), *The Oxford Handbook of Interdisciplinarity* (pp. 15–30). Oxford University Press.

McCarthy, B., & Saleh, T. (2019, November 21). Building the AI-Powered Organization. *Harvard Business Review*. Retrieved from https://hbr.org/webinar/2019/11/building-the-ai-powered-organization

Meucci, A., Ardia, D., & Colasante, M. (2014, June 1). *Quantitative Portfolio Construction and Systematic Trading Strategies Using Factor Entropy Pooling*. EDHEC-Risk Institute. Retrieved from https://risk.edhec.edu/publications/quantitative-portfolio-construction-and-systematic-trading-strategies-using-factor

Moutinho, L. (2019). *AI Storm in Marketing - Paradigm Shift of Artificial Intelligence (AI) and Marketing Evolution*. VIPSI Conference, Budva, Montenegro.

Mullin, M. (2018, October 10). When Robots Feel Our Pain: Rosalind Picard on 'Emotional Intelligence' in a Brave New World. *TheTyee.ca, Newsletter*. Retrieved from https://thetyee.ca/Presents/2018/10/10/Rosalind-Picard-Lecture/

Neiberg, D., Elenius, K., & Laskowski, K. (2006). Emotion recognition in spontaneous speech using GMMs. *Proceedings of Interspeech*.

Picard, R. (1995). *Affective Computing (Abstract)*. MIT Technical Report #321.

Picard, R. (1997). *Affective Computing*. MIT Press.

Reavie, V. (2019, January 17). *Using AI To Drive High-Converting Predictive Marketing*. Forbes Agency Council. Retrieved from /2019/01/17/using-ai-to-drive-high-converting-predictive-marketing/#62807cdd9cd0

Saeed, K. (2006, January). *A Note on Biometrics and Voice Print: Voice-Signal Feature Selection and Extraction–A Burg-Töeplitz Approach*. ResearchGate GmbH. Retrieved from https://www.researchgate.net/publication/228899473_A_Note_on_Biometrics_and_Voice_Print_Voice-Signal_Feature_Selection_and_Extraction-A_Burg-Toeplitz_Approach

Sentance, R. (2019). *15 examples of artificial intelligence in marketing*. Retrieved from https://econsultancy.com/15-examples-of-artificial-intelligence-in-marketing/

Sullivan, L. (2018, July 2). Marketers Struggle With Tying Data To AI Systems. *MediaPost Communications*.

Thaliyachira, C. (2019, December 19). Artificial Intelligence in Marketing. *OMR Industry Journal*. Retrieved from https://www.omrindustryjournal.com/artificial-intelligence-in-marketing/315/

Yacoub, S., Simske, S., Lin, X., & Burns, J. (2003). Recognition of Emotions in Interactive Voice Response Systems. *Proceedings of Eurospeech*, 729–732.

Zhang, X-P. & Wang, F. (2017, April 26). Signal Processing for Finance, Economics, and Marketing - Concepts, framework, and big data applications. *IEEE Signal Processing Magazine*.

Chapter 16
Efficient End–to–End Asynchronous Time–Series Modeling With Deep Learning to Predict Customer Attrition

Victor Potapenko
Florida International University, USA

Malek Adjouadi
Florida International University, USA

Naphtali Rishe
Florida International University, USA

ABSTRACT

Modeling time-series data with asynchronous, multi-cardinal, and uneven patterns presents several unique challenges that may impede convergence of supervised machine learning algorithms, or significantly increase resource requirements, thus rendering modeling efforts infeasible in resource-constrained environments. The authors propose two approaches to multi-class classification of asynchronous time-series data. In the first approach, they create a baseline by reducing the time-series data using a statistical approach and training a model based on gradient boosted trees. In the second approach, they implement a fully convolutional network (FCN) and train it on asynchronous data without any special feature engineering. Evaluation of results shows that FCN performs as well as the gradient boosting based on mean F1-score without computationally complex time-series feature engineering. This work has been applied in the prediction of customer attrition at a large retail automotive finance company.

DOI: 10.4018/978-1-7998-7156-9.ch016

INTRODUCTION

Time-series (TS) data can be classified as synchronous vs. asynchronous, co-cardinal vs. multi-cardinal, and even vs. uneven (Wu et al., 2018). Synchronous TS data are aligned on the time dimension, while asynchronous events are not. Co-cardinal event sequences are aligned on the first and last elements. TS are classified as multi-cardinal if one of the sequences is longer than another. Multi-cardinal sequences are synchronous if the remaining elements are aligned. TS are defined to be even when data points are distributed evenly over time. Unless otherwise specified, we use asynchronous as a general term to describe asynchronous, multi-cardinal, and uneven sequences.

Our instantiation of this problem is a supervised multi-class classification with stationary and TS data. As a case study, we use a dataset comprising more than one million car loan histories. Our TS are asynchronous, multi-cardinal, and uneven. Stationary data is comprised of context data, such as vehicle and customer profiles. The target of the classification task in this case study is the customer attrition classified by type of contract termination within a 6-month horizon. The proposed approach includes database TS data extraction, imbalanced target sampling, time-series dimensionality reduction for XG-Boost models, originally proposed by Chen and Guestrin (2016), that do not support multi-dimensional data, and supervised classification using a Fully Convolutional Network (FCN). (XGBoost is an open-source software library that provides a gradient boosting framework.)

TS extraction is performed with a technique called "streaming updates." The streaming updates method is used to extract value updates as TS data at variable time intervals defined by a frequency of database of field updates. This approach is discussed in Section 3a on Data Extraction. At any given time step, our extracted data is significantly imbalanced towards active accounts that are not terminated. In Section 3b, we outline a sampling approach that mitigates class imbalance in training set and prevents data leakage into the evaluation set by using different sampling techniques designed to simulate real-world conditions.

The input size and frequency of TS varies widely among features extracted with the streaming method. Some features frequently occur at regular time intervals throughout account lifetimes; others only occur a few times at highly irregular intervals. As a result, the products of join operations cause input space to increase dramatically, which leads to high memory and computational requirements for their manipulation and creates the necessity to use imputation techniques to eliminate sparsity. The scope of the present work is limited to the comparison of the non-deep learning approach that uses TS statistics to reduce time dimension, versus the deep learning approach with FCN trained on zero-imputed TS data. In Section 3c, we describe the XGBoost and FCN models. Section 4 outlines evaluation results followed by a discussion in Section 5.

BACKGROUND

Time-series sequences have been modeled with Hidden Markov Models (HMMs) (Rabiner, 1989; Ephraim & Merhav, 2002) and Bayesian Networks (BNs) (Heckerman et al., 1995; Nielsen et al., 2009). However, HMMs and BNs are not designed for asynchronous sequences because they require specification of a constant time interval between consecutive events (Wu et al., 2018). Asynchronous data needs to be reshaped and synchronized to fit HMMs and BNs. TS can be reshaped to synchronicity at the data preprocessing step. Reshaping and synchronization methods often obfuscate original data or create artificial data points that are not initially present in the dataset. This results in information loss and requires imputation techniques that incur significant computational and memory costs when datasets are large, and the degree of synchronicity is low.

Prior research by Wu et al. (2018) classifies asynchronous properties of TS and evaluates sequence synchronization methods and relative time representations by training unmodified Recurrent Neural Networks (RNN) with Long Short-Term Memory (LSTM) cells to perform comparative analysis. Synchronization via state (sync-state) transforms the sequences into synchronous and co-cardinal, but uneven. Synchronization via binning transforms the sequences into synchronous, even, and co-cardinal. Results demonstrate that, depending on the dataset, the sync-state or sync-bin synchronizations produce better results with elision, when all relative timing information is removed. These results are used as a baseline to compare to relative-time representations: Markov, Landmark-any, and Landmark-own. Markov and Landmark-any take the history parameter that defines how many prior values to consider. The Markov relative-time representation does not consider feature values, while the Landmark-any skips the features with zero values. Both Markov and Landmark-any capture bursts of activity. The Landmark-own relative-time representation only assumes some dependence between each of the features by taking relative times between non-zero values of each feature individually. Landmark-own has performed best on AUC on both datasets. (In Machine Learning, AUC is the area under the receiver operating characteristic curve.) However, a sync-bin baseline with elision has outperformed all other models on the PhysioNet dataset based on recall and F1 score. Unmodified LSTM with Landmark-own relative time representation has scored at AUC of 0.6464 on the PhysioNet dataset.

Another approach to modeling multivariate asynchronous data is to represent the problem as Value Missingness; the representation with missing values assumes that missingness is informative. GRU-D (Che et al., 2018) is an RNN-based approach to informative missingness in asynchronous data using modifications to a Gated Recurrent Unit (GRU) (Cho et al., 2014) and masking the data representation. TS are represented by four vectors: feature values, time stamps, missingness indicator, and time interval. GRU cells are modified with a hidden state and input decay terms. The modification aims to capture the property of a feature to return to some default value after a number of steps in the absence of new observations. In GRU-D, the influence of input variables fades away as more missing values are encountered. This model is specific to data with some assumed default values. We cannot make default value and fading influence assumptions uniformly across all sequences in our dataset. The proposed GRU-D model performs at AUC of 0.8370 when evaluated on the PhysioNet dataset that contains 8000 records of intensive care unit (ICU) records.

Phased LSTM (Neil et al., 2016) extends the LSTM unit by adding a time gate. A rhythmic oscillation is specified by three learnable parameters that control the opening and closing of the time gate. Phased LSTM performs updates at irregular time points on asynchronous data. Phased LSTM takes timestamps as a separate input tensor that controls the time gate. This architecture has outperformed LSTMs and Batch-normalized LSTMs on a set of artificial benchmarks, such as the sine wave frequency discrimination at high resolution and asynchronous sampling rates. This architecture does not require any additional preprocessing steps, because it fits asynchronous time-series data by design.

Convolutional Neural Networks (CNN) are state-of-the-art in feature extraction from images. The input structure of a typical CNN allows for multi-dimensional input, which fits the data structure of TS. A Significance-offset Convolutional Network (SOCNN) (Binkowski et al., 2017) uses a representation of asynchronous TS with feature indicator vectors, feature value vectors, and duration vectors. Duration vectors contain values that indicate time elapsed since the previous observation of any feature in the entire feature space. The network scheme consists of significance and offset convolutional subnetworks.

Outputs of subnetworks are combined via the Hadamard Product. This network performs better on asynchronous data when benchmarked against unmodified CNN, ResNet, and LSTM on the same input data, but performs worse on synchronous time-series data.

In recent years, deep learning architectures such as RNNs and CNNs have been adapted to modeling asynchronous TS. By design, RNNs and CNNs ingest multi-dimensional input and can be fit to TS. In our experience, RNNs are challenging to train with asynchronous data due to input sparsity. In our research, we implement an FCN with one-dimensional kernels that differs from a CNN by not using any max-pooling layers and taking advantage of one global average pooling layer that has the advantage of making the model interpretable.

METHODOLOGY

In this section, we describe the methodology we have used to solve the problem of classifying asynchronous TS extracted from the case-study company database, sampled to reduce class imbalance, and modeled with XGBoost and FCN to predict account outcomes within a given time horizon. We use this methodology to predict customer attrition within a 6-month horizon, given the profile and timestamped account activity data stored in the company database.

Data Extraction, Characteristics, and Synchronization

We extract data from a database that contains records of the customer profile, dealer profile, vehicle profile and valuation, vehicle repair orders, account financials, delinquencies, and customer payoff amount requests. All records include two fields ("from" and "to" dates) with timestamps that indicate the time period during which the record is current. This database feature enables the extraction of TS data from a series of database field updates. We categorize data into two major types based on whether or not it changes over time: context data and time-series data.

Context data, such as customer profile, dealer profile, and vehicle profile, does not change over time. Only the latest timestamps are used to extract this type of data. We control for data leakage during exploratory analysis to ensure that this data does not change when the system marks an account as terminated. TS data (such as vehicle valuation, repair orders, account financials, delinquencies, and customer payoff requests) is extracted from the database using a lag function that detects a change in a field value and extracts the changed values along with the change timestamps.

Extracted multivariate daily TS is asynchronous, multi-cardinal, and uneven. Vehicle valuations and account financials are updated frequently and periodically, while repair orders, delinquencies, and customer payoff requests are infrequent and occur sporadically. This asynchronous data form is common in sensors with variable sampling rates. Common integration methods introduce noise by up-sampling or lose information by down-sampling. Both sampling methods adversely affect model performance. In our work, we zero-pad TS for FCN input and reduce dimensionality via calculated TS statistics for input to XGBoost.

Training and Evaluation Sampling

In production, the model does not have access to future data; therefore, providing future data or embedded knowledge about future data during the evaluation phase causes data leakage and low performance on out-of-sample datasets. Given this constraint, we design a sampling process that simulates the feature state available at a specified point in time and computes target values for a specified horizon.

The classification target is represented by termination codes that include active accounts and accounts terminated for various reasons, such as early payoff or scheduled maturity. Training data consists of context data and a set of variable-length TS with termination codes conditioned on a 6-month time horizon. The sampling method for the training dataset is not subject to the same constraints as the evaluation dataset in the production environment if a model trained on such a dataset performs well on evaluation set and in production. We use two different methods for sampling training and evaluation sets. In our case, this allows us to decrease the size of the training dataset, lowering memory complexity, and to mitigate class imbalance, improving classification accuracy.

Our dataset consists of 1.5 million accounts active over five years. Our algorithm splits the dataset into the training and evaluation sets by the split date t_{split}. The algorithm samples the training dataset from the distribution of accounts active between t_0 and t_{split} (Figure 1). The algorithm samples the evaluation dataset from the distribution of accounts active between t_{split} and t_n (Figure 2).

Figure 1. Sample Training Data. Each sample is assigned an
observation_begin_date = contract_open_date. All samples where
contract_open_date > t_{split} are discarded from the training set (sample E). If
termination_date < t_{split} then
observation_end_date = termination_date − (horizon − random_offset) and
target_class = termination_reason_code (samples A and B). Otherwise,
observation_end_date = t_{split} − random_offset) and target_class = 'active' (samples C and
D).

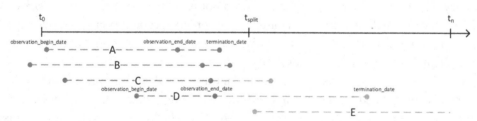

Figure 2. Sample Evaluation Data. Each sample is assigned an observation_begin_date = contract_open_date. All samples where contract_open_date > t_{split} are discarded from the evaluation set (sample E). observation_end_date = t_{split}, and target_class = termination_reason_code if termination_date < $\left(t_{split} - horizon\right)$ (sample C). Otherwise, target_class = 'active' (sample D).

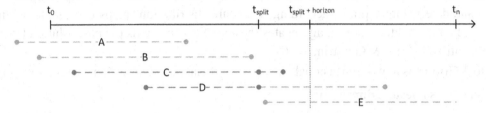

The training set sampling method yields a more class-balanced dataset because it selects all the terminated accounts from the history, while it samples the active accounts only from accounts active at t_{split} timestep. Our experiments show that balanced class distribution has a robust positive impact on model performance. For an account to be classified as terminated, its termination date must occur within the horizon window. We add a random offset to the calculation of observation end-date in order to simulate random sampling and to counter the effects of the timewise-anchored sampling at the known termination date.

The evaluation set sampling method simulates data that the model encounters in production. The observation end-date is the date when the model predicts using all currently active account data available at that time. In our evaluation sampling case, the observation end-date is equal to t_{split} and the classification is made based on whether the termination date occurs within the predetermined time horizon. We use this evaluation data sampling method to extract multiple out-of-sample evaluation splits by altering t_{split}, which allows us to evaluate future model accuracy decay and generate multiple cross-validation splits.

The class imbalance between active and terminated accounts is 10:1 in the evaluation set. In the training set, the imbalance is 1:1.8. When the evaluation set sampling method is applied to sample from the training set, there are two options: sample at fixed intervals and sample at random intervals. The problem of class imbalance remains. The sampling process may miss possibly valuable samples of an underrepresented class, causing the under-sampling of terminated class. A possible downside of the developed sampling methods is data leakage of the active class from the training set where the model learns identities of the class and classifies all previously active accounts as active in all future evaluation sets.

Modeling

XGBoost and TSFresh

We use XGBoost to create a non-deep baseline for the evaluation of our deep modeling approach. XGBoost (Chen & Guestrin, 2016) is an algorithm based on gradient tree boosting (Friedman, 2001). XGBoost algorithm trains an ensemble of decision trees in an additive manner. In most cases, it is computationally infeasible to enumerate all tree structures and their combinations. Trees that result in most improvements in the model are added greedily to an ensemble. XGBoost builds a structure of each decision tree using a greedy algorithm that starts from a single leaf and iteratively adds split branches. Most tree-boosting algorithms use a greedy algorithm that enumerates all possible splits on all features, which makes it computationally demanding when continuous features are present in the data. XGBoost uses an approximate algorithm to reduce computational load. In a nutshell, the approximate algorithm proposes candidate splitting points according to feature distribution, maps continuous features into buckets based on the splitting points, aggregates the statistics, and finds the best solution based on the aggregated statistics (Chen & Guestrin, 2016).

Input to XGBoost is a two-dimensional tensor X with shape (n, m), where n is a total number of samples, and m is a feature dimension.

$$X = \left(x_{0,0}, \ldots, x_{i,j}, x_{i,j+1}, \ldots x_{i+1,j}, x_{i+1,j+1}, x_{n,m} \right),$$

where the element $x_{i,j}$ is a feature j that belongs to sample i and $X \subset \mathbb{R}$. TS has a three-dimensional shape (n, m, t), where t is a time dimension. Therefore, XGBoost does not support TS as input. We perform feature engineering with TSFresh (Christ et al., 2018) to reduce the dimensionality of TS data to XGBoost input dimensions. We concatenate engineered TS and context data to produce a two-dimensional representation of the feature space. We train the XGBoost model on approximately 14000 features, of which 260 features belong to context data, and the remaining features are generated from TS data using TSFresh. (TSFresh is an open-source software library that provides a time-series statistics framework.) Training time is 2.6 hours on a 32-core instance.

We use initial training to eliminate most features based on feature-importance scores provided by XGBoost, with the importance threshold of 100 and the correlation of greater than 0.95. This process returns 367 features. We perform final feature selection using backward feature elimination based on aggregated SHAP values (Shapley Additive Explanations) (Lundberg & Lee, 2017) that assign each feature an importance value for a class prediction of the sample. Our algorithm eliminates one feature with the lowest aggregated SHAP value, and the model is retrained on remaining features at each elimination step until the model accuracy starts to decline significantly. The reason we do not use SHAP on the initial set of 14000 features is the computational and time complexity of calculating the SHAP values and effectively training 14000 models. The feature selection process leaves us with the ten most important features according to the aggregated SHAP values from all classes. We perform parameter tuning on the remaining features via random search sampling from parameter space of the maximum tree depth, learning rate, and number of trees. We set the multi-class logarithmic loss as our evaluation metric for the early stopping based on the evaluation dataset and use softmax (7) as the classification objective function.

Fully Convolutional Network with Context

Fully Convolutional Neural Networks (Wang et al., 2017) have been successfully validated for TS classification on 44 datasets from the University of California, Riverside/University of East Anglia archive. Unlike CNN, FCN does not contain any local pooling layers and uses the Global Average Pooling (GAP) layer instead of the traditional Fully Connected (FC) layer. An FCN consists of three convolutional layers, where each convolutional layer is followed by a batch normalization (BN) layer and a rectified linear unit (ReLU) activation. This structure outputs to a GAP layer, followed by a softmax activation for supervised classification.

Figure 3. Fully Convolutional Network with Context. A basic convolutional block consists of a convolutional layer (i.e., Conv1D (8 x 64) with 64 one-dimensional kernels of size 8), followed by a batch normalization (BN) layer and ReLU activation function. Context data is input into the multilayer perceptron that consists of fully connected layers (i.e., FC (128) with 128 neurons), followed by the ReLU activation function. Outputs of FCN and MLP are inputs to the softmax activation function.

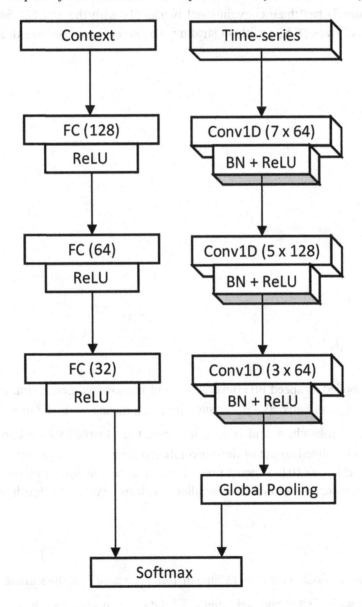

A basic convolution block consists of a convolutional layer, BN, and ReLU, where W and b are the weight and bias vectors:

$$y = W \cdot x + b$$

$$s = BN\left(y\right)$$

$$h = ReLU\left(s\right) \tag{1}$$

Our model (Figure 3) has three convolutional blocks (1) with the {64,128,64} numbers of one-dimensional kernels of sizes {8,5,3} without striding. The kernels are used to extract TS features.

$$\mu_{\mathcal{B}} \leftarrow \frac{1}{m}\sum_{i=1}^{m} y_i \tag{2}$$

$$\sigma_{\mathcal{B}}^2 \leftarrow \frac{1}{m}\sum_{i=1}^{m}\left(y_i - \mu_{\mathcal{B}}\right)^2 \tag{3}$$

$$\hat{y}_i \leftarrow \frac{y_i - \mu_{\mathcal{B}}}{\sqrt{\sigma_{\mathcal{B}}^2 + \epsilon}} \tag{4}$$

$$s_i \leftarrow \gamma\hat{y}_i + \beta \equiv BN_{\gamma\beta}\left(y_i\right) \tag{5}$$

BN (2,3,4,5) is applied to speed up convergence and improve generalization (Wang et al., 2017), where m is the size of mini-batch $\mathcal{B}$, $\mu_{\mathcal{B}}$ is the mini-batch mean, $\sigma_{\mathcal{B}}^2$ is the mini-batch variance, and $\hat{x}_i$ is the normalized mini-batch; γ and β are parameters to be learned via backpropagation; y_i is the scaled, shifted, and normalized output of the convolutional layer over the mini-batch.

ReLU (Hahnloser et al., 2000) is an activation function that has shown to improve the performance of deep neural networks. It prevents saturation of gradients in deep networks by thresholding values at 0 (6).

$$ReLU\left(s\right)_i = \max\left(0, s_i\right) \tag{6}$$

The input of a convolutional layer has a shape of $\left(b, c, l\right)$, where b is the sample batch size, c is the number of channels, and l is the channel length. TS data has an identical shape $\left(n, m, t\right)$, where the samples are equivalent to the batch size, the features to the channels, and the time to the length of each feature. For our XGBoost model, we reduce TS data with TSFresh into the two-dimensional space and concatenate the context data, because the data dimensionalities match. The context and TS data cannot be concatenated for an FCN model because of the dimensionality mismatch. One way to integrate context data into an FCN model is to duplicate context data across the l dimension of a convolution. This method results in added memory complexity because it duplicates over 260 context features in addition to 53 TS features across all time steps of the sample. We integrate context by concatenation of a multi-layer perceptron (MLP) that consists of three FC layers with the {128,64,32} neurons and ReLU activation, each followed by a dropout layer with the rate of 0.2. The output of concatenation of FCN and MLP is connected to the final softmax (7) output layer that normalizes its inputs into a probability distribution over the number of classes K, where h_{n-1} is the output of the last convolutional block.

$$softmax\left(h_{n-1}\right)_i = \frac{e^{h_{n-1_i}}}{\sum_{j=1}^{K} e^{h_{n-1_j}}} \tag{7}$$

The FCN model uses cross-entropy loss function (8) to compute loss and backpropagate gradients throughout the network, where $softmax\left(h_{n-1}\right)_i$ is the output of the softmax function (7) for class i, C is the total number of classes, and t_i is the ground-truth class label.

$$CE = \sum_{i}^{C} t_i \log\left(softmax\left(h_{n-1}\right)_i\right) \tag{8}$$

We implement the FCN model with context using Keras and Tensorflow 2.0. We train this model on a 32-core compute instance with 256 gigabytes of memory. The training set consists of 963,712 records with 260 context features and 53 time-series features, where each feature is limited to the length of 365, corresponding to days in one year. The evaluation set is significantly imbalanced and consists of 456,128 records. We use a data generator to iterate over all instances to conserve disk space by generating zero-filled dense input from the sparse input saved in a file. Tensorflow Dataset API is used to optimize data pipeline by prefetching, shuffling, batching, and caching training and evaluation data at runtime. The caching stores all data generated during the first pass over the dataset into memory. Once we cache the data during the first epoch of training, it occupies 100 gigabytes of memory, including the original sparse dataset. The first epoch training time is 1203 seconds during the first pass over the dataset. The average training time per epoch is 800 seconds with the cached dataset. We train the model with early stopping conditioned on validation loss metric to stop training before the model begins to overfit.

RESULTS

The evaluation dataset is significantly imbalanced because of the small number of contract terminations compared to active contracts at any given time horizon. Additionally, terminations are divided into four subtypes, most of which represent less than 10% of the evaluation dataset. Accuracy is not a reliable model performance measure with imbalanced datasets. If a model classifies all samples as the majority class and misclassifies all minority classes, the accuracy would be misleadingly high.

Table 1a. FCN results

Class	Precision	stdev	Recall	stdev	F1	Stdev
0	0.8741	0.004	0.9934	0.002	0.9299	0.001
1	0.4041	0.011	0.0750	0.012	0.1261	0.017
2	0.6869	0.062	0.1095	0.028	0.1882	0.044
3	0.7005	0.106	0.0068	0.004	0.0133	0.008
4	0.3848	0.007	0.0266	0.003	0.0497	0.005
Mean	0.6101	0.038	0.2423	0.010	0.3468	0.015

Table 1b. XGBoost results

Class	Precision	stdev	Recall	stdev	F1	stdev
0	0.8950	0.002	0.6387	0.006	0.7454	0.003
1	0.1232	0.002	0.4450	0.009	0.1929	0.001
2	0.3923	0.013	0.3563	0.007	0.3734	0.010
3	0.1878	0.021	0.1544	0.015	0.1686	0.011
4	0.3574	0.013	0.0751	0.024	0.1231	0.032
Mean	0.3911	0.010	0.3339	0.012	0.3207	0.011

We evaluate model performance on five out-of-sample datasets that are sampled by shifting the split date one month forward with the time horizon of six months. At each split date, we use the time horizon to determine the contract classification. This procedure simulates real-world conditions, where the model has a task of classifying accounts given the data available up to a point in time. We report results based on the average and standard deviation of model performance across all test splits.

FCN achieves a higher unweighted mean F1-score (Table 1a) than our XGBoost model (Table 1b). F1-score is a harmonic mean of precision and recall. FCN performs much better in terms of precision by classifying the true positives of each target class while capturing less false negatives. FCN recall scores are lower because it captures fewer examples per class than XGBoost. XGBoost captures more true positives than FCN and more false negatives. The standard deviation of the XGBoost model is lower, which suggests that it is more stable over time; however, it is not significant enough to make a definitive judgment.

Precision is more important than recall in our problem domain because of the financial implications of actions taken based on model predictions. If the model predicts an active account to be terminated within the next six months, the company may decide to take action to retain the account, which may include financial incentives or refinancing. These actions have financial consequences. Profits are negatively impacted when a customer terminates their account because of financial incentives based on an incorrect model prediction. When a model has low precision, it is more likely to include more such accounts in a target class.

DISCUSSION

In this paper, we have presented an end-to-end approach for modeling asynchronous time-series data using a deep Fully Convolutional Network with context. We have compared its performance to XGBoost. We have extracted data from a company database as time-series using timestamps to detect field value changes over time. To balance class representation in the training dataset, we have sampled all terminated accounts from three years of account histories using an offset from known target termination date for randomization. This algorithm has captured the accounts that had not been terminated before the train/ evaluation split date.

Our training sampling method effectively discards many samples of the active class by only considering terminated accounts at the points of termination. A possible future direction of this research is to experiment with sampling terminated accounts at the termination, as well as immediately before the termination as active accounts. This possible future approach generates samples around the boundary between active and terminated account states, which may be significant for the model to learn to distinguish the two states with a higher degree of accuracy.

We have reduced the time dimension of our data by computing time-series statistics using TSFresh and performed backward stepwise elimination using SHAP values with XGBoost to select ten most important features. Feature engineering and backward stepwise elimination required for XGBoost was computationally expensive. We have implemented FCN with no computationally-complex feature engineering and obtained similar results with higher mean precision scores than XGBoost.

Our final feature composition and modeling results suggest that most extracted and engineered features have low predictive power. Our goal was to predict which accounts terminate within the next 6-month period, which is a market timing problem. Market timing is an especially tricky problem when information about market participants is sparse. Our dataset contained relatively few data points on the underlying market participants and their states over time, making it a more challenging task. In future work, we plan to explore the effects of additional data sources, time-series data smoothing, data sampling with better representation of active/terminated accounts' boundary, and variants of asynchronous data representation.

ACKNOWLEDGMENT

The authors gratefully acknowledge the support of the National Science Foundation [grant numbers MRI CNS-1532061 and MRI CNS-1920182] and of J.M. Family Enterprises, Inc., and its experts Alfredo Cateriano, Ashley Taylor, Ben Fowler, Arthur Engelman, and Eddie Rivera.

REFERENCES

Binkowski, M., Marti, G., & Donnat, P. (2017). Autoregressive convolutional neural networks for asynchronous time series. *ICML 2017 Time Series Workshop*.

Che, Z., Purushotham, S., Cho, K., Sontag, D., & Liu, Y. (2018). Recurrent neural networks for multivariate time series with missing values. *Scientific Reports*, *8*(1), 6085. doi:10.103841598-018-24271-9 PMID:29666385

Chen, T., & Guestrin, C. (2016). XGBoost: a scalable tree boosting system. In *Proceedings of the 22nd ACM SIGKDD International Conference on Knowledge Discovery and Data Mining* (pp. 785–794). Association for Computing Machinery. 10.1145/2939672.2939785

Cho, K., Merrienboer, B., Gulcehre, C., Bahdanau, D., Bougares, F., Schwenk, H., & Bengio, Y. (2014). Learning phrase representations using RNN encoder-decoder for statistical machine translation. *Proceedings of the 2014 Conference on Empirical Methods in Natural Language Processing*, 1724–1734. 10.3115/v1/D14-1179

Christ, M., Braun, N., Neuffer, J., & Kempa-Liehr, A. W. (2018). Time series feature extraction on the basis of scalable hypothesis tests (TSfresh - a Python package). *Neurocomputing*, *307*, 72–77. doi:10.1016/j.neucom.2018.03.067

Ephraim, Y., & Merhav, N. (2002). Hidden Markov processes. *IEEE Transactions on Information Theory*, *48*(6), 1518–1569. doi:10.1109/TIT.2002.1003838

Friedman, J. (2001). Greedy function approximation: A gradient boosting machine. *Annals of Statistics*, *29*(5), 1189–1232. doi:10.1214/aos/1013203451

Hahnloser, R., Sarpeshkar, R., Mahowald, M., Douglas, R. J., & Seung, H. S. (2000). Digital selection and analog amplification coexist in a cortex-inspired silicon circuit. *Nature*, *405*(6789), 947–951. doi:10.1038/35016072 PMID:10879535

Heckerman, D., Geiger, D., & Chickering, D. M. (1995). Learning Bayesian networks: The combination of knowledge and statistical data. *Machine Learning*, *20*(3), 197–243. doi:10.1007/BF00994016

Lundberg, S. M., & Lee, S. I. (2017). A unified approach to interpreting model predictions. *Advances in Neural Information Processing Systems*, *30*, 4765–4774.

Neil, D., Pfeiffer, M., & Liu, S. (2016). Phased LSTM: accelerating recurrent network training for long or event-based sequences. In *Proceedings of the 30th International Conference on Neural Information Processing Systems* (pp. 3889–3897). Curran Associates Inc.

Nielsen, T. D., & Jensen, F. V. (2009). *Bayesian networks and decision graphs*. Springer Science & Business Media.

Rabiner, L. R. (1989). A tutorial on hidden Markov models and selected applications in speech recognition. *Proceedings of the IEEE*, *77*(2), 257–286. doi:10.1109/5.18626

Wang, Z., Yan, W., & Oates, T. (2017). Time series classification from scratch with deep neural networks: a strong baseline. *2017 International Joint Conference on Neural Networks*, 1578-1585. 10.1109/IJCNN.2017.7966039

Wu, S., Liu, S., Sohn, S., Moon, S., Wi, C., Juhn, Y., & Liu, H. (2018). Modeling asynchronous event sequences with RNNs. *Journal of Biomedical Informatics*, *83*, 167–177. doi:10.1016/j.jbi.2018.05.016 PMID:29883623

KEY TERMS AND DEFINITIONS

Convolutional Neural Network: A type of neural network with an architecture that consists of kernels that learn to perform the matrix convolution operation on inputs to find patterns that have spatial proximity such as images or time-series.

Deep Learning: A subfield of machine learning that specializes in neural network based algorithms that have more than one hidden layer.

Fully Convolutional Network: A type of convolutional network that does not contain any dense layers in its architecture. This type of network only contains layers that are specific to convolutional neural networks, such as convolution, pooling, and batch normalization.

Gated Recurrent Unit: A modification of the long-short term memory unit with fewer parameters and no output gate.

Gradient Tree Boosting: A supervised machine learning algorithm that consists of an ensemble of decision trees.

Long-Short Term Memory Network: A type of recurrent neural network where regular neurons are replaced by long-short term memory units designed to allow deep networks to "remember" inputs over larger number of steps and mitigate the exploding/vanishing gradient problem.

Neural Network: A supervised machine learning algorithm that searches for a function to fit existing data via an iterative training process. Neural Networks are characterized by multiple hidden layers that consist of neurons with activation functions that adjust weights using the backpropagation algorithm and a loss function.

Recurrent Neural Network: A neural network with an added dimension to represent the sequence or time component of sequential or temporal data.

Time-Series Data: Are data points spread across the time dimension. Time-series data is sequential and ordered based on timestamps. Examples include series of event occurrences and temperature measurements over time.

Chapter 17
Mind Genomics With Big Data for Digital Marketing on the Internet

Jakob Salom

Mathematical Institute of Serbian Academy of Sciences and Arts, Serbia

ABSTRACT

This chapter sheds light on one very important application in the domain of digital economy – mind genomics. Mind genomics is an approach to targeted marketing which reaches each prospect with a different personalized message. This application requires acceleration coming from a data flow accelerator connected to a control flow host. It stresses equally the basic concept and its many applications. Innovation process is a step-by-step process. Once an important step up front is created and a new innovation finds its way into the commercial world, it is difficult to imagine that another dramatical step/leap forward is possible. However, such steps keep happening. Mind genomics is an example of one such step, unthinkable of until only a few years ago. Needs of the users could be served much more effectively not only in business domains or other lucrative domains, but also in the domains of public health, public happiness, public and individual quality of life, public and individual understanding of the environment around, etc.

THE CONCEPT

Mind Genomics is an approach to Targeted Marketing, with a number of advantages in comparison with other approaches to Targeted Marketing. In contrast with the Broadband Marketing, where the marketing messages reach all prospects (potential customers) with the same message, the Targeted Marketing reaches each prospect with a different message.

Examples of Broadband Marketing are ads that reach us through radio or TV, through billboards or house faces, through The Internet or direct mail, through newspapers or magazines. The Targeted Marketing is not a recent invention. It existed even ages ago; when a customer appears in a shop of a village, the shop owner, knowing the customer very well, also knows what are the typical shopping desires of

DOI: 10.4018/978-1-7998-7156-9.ch017

that particular customer (as he does for all fellow villagers), and after the customer purchases what he or she came for, the shop owner offers a product (which was not on the customer's list), but is of a kind that this particular customer can't resist buying.

Mind Genomics is a two-phase process. In the first phase, a study is done to determine, what are the basic mind types of customers on the market related to a specific product or service, in a specific geographical region, or on the entire Internet. In the second phase, the Mind Genomics software takes "ambush" at the web site of a specific business (restaurant, medical clinic, school, research lab, etc.), and after the incoming customer finishes the inquiries or purchases about which he/she came for, the Mind Genomics software offers a "value exchange" ("please, click three times on the three multiple choice questions that follow, and you will get something in return (discounts, small awards, more choices, etc.). From the three clicks, the Mind Genomics system knows what is the mind type of the specific customer, and prepares an adequate offer for that customer. As indicated above, it is supposed to be an offer of the kind that the given customer can't reject.

Mind Genomics does not require customers to fill forms and does not trace their behavior, yet the studies have shown that it can provide the increase in sales going from 20% to a high as 100% (Miluti-novic, 2016). This is achieved via value exchange and complex mathematics.

Programs predominantly based on the transactional code are well suited for execution on machines implemented using a Control Flow architecture. However, Control Flow architectures are often times not the best suited for highly parallel code operating on Big Data, with Low Power, Low Volume, and High Precision environments. For such environments, accelerators are absolutely necessary. In general, most of the applications related to digital economy, like Mind Genomics, do need strong accelerators. Programming implementations of Mind Genomics include both the transactional and the parallel code.

1. BASIC FUNCTIONING OF MIND GENOMICS

Marketing can be broadband or targeted. Broadband marketing means that all customers get the same message, via a radio or a TV, Internet or newspapers, billboards or taxicabs. Targeted marketing means that each customer receives a different message, tuned to the real needs and mental characteristics of that particular customer.

Targeted marketing is nothing new; it existed for centuries. For example, in medieval times, in a village shop, where the owner knows all the villagers, which are not many, to some of them the owner offers guns, jewelry to the others. What is new, and originated with the appearance of the Internet, is targeted marketing spanning a huge number of persons unknown to the vendor. This paradigm is referred to by many as modern targeted marketing.

Most approaches to modern targeted marketing imply the following drawbacks:

1. At the entry into the system, customers are asked to fill forms.
2. This is time consuming and represents an attack on the privacy of individuals.
3. During the exploitation, customers are tracked.
4. For example, if bacon is purchased in one store,
5. than when the customer appears at the web portal of another store in the same chain,
6. he/she is again offered bacon, which is annoying.
7. When placing offers to customers, the system is based on socioeconomic principles.

8.   Rich customers are offered one set of things, poor the other.

Mind Genomics, which is the main subject of this chapter, does not have any of the above-mentioned drawbacks. It does not ask the customers to fill forms at the entry into the system, it does not track the customers, nor it divides them along the socioeconomic division lines; yet, it enables the vendor revenues to be much higher.

2. PHASES OF MIND GENOMICS

Mind Genomics is based on sophisticated math, on the notion of value exchange on the top of fast Internet, and on Data Mining. Mind Genomics has the following three production phases:

1.   Micro Science (the phase based on sophisticated math).
2.   Customer Typing (the phase based on value exchange and fast Internet).
3.   Machine Learning (the phase based on Data Mining)

In this context, sophisticated math implies linear regression and related techniques for improving the effects of performed linear regression. Value exchange implies that whenever a customer is asked to do something, he/she must receive an immediate award. Data Mining spans all techniques that can help the system self-learn and adapt to the changing marketing requirements.

In essence, in the first phase, Mind Genomics determines, for a given product or service, in a given geographical region, what the mind types of potential customers (prospects) are; in other words, in the first phase, Mind Genomics determines what the major customer types are, i.e., the "baskets" at which incoming customers are to be placed upon arrival to the web portal or at the door 7kof the vendor. As it will be seen later on, based on the empirically obtained experience, Mind Genomics finds that it is enough to create only three "baskets" i.e., it determines only three customer types, occasionally four.

In the second phase, Mind Genomics waits for a customer to arrive to the web site of the vendor, serves his/her needs, and then, after all customer needs are served properly, offers a value exchange. In this context, value exchange means that the customer is asked to answer three multiple- choice questions, each on a simple 3-point scale, and in return, the customer is offered a compensation for the unexpected effort. (The three additional clicks represent an additional effort which is typically not done without appropriate compensation). The type of compensation used depends on the type of the vendor business. For example, in the case of restaurant business, a free appetizer could be offered (one of several to choose from); in the case of vet clinics, a utility for pets could be offered.

In the third phase, techniques from machine learning in general and Data Mining in particular are used, in order to improve the operation and to make the system more effective.

Mind Genomics can also be treated as a method to implement horizontal segmentation and horizontal segmentation, can be treated as a method to improve market effectiveness. Mind Genomics can be used not only in retail marketing, but also in education, science, or politics, to promote specific new products, services, ideas, opportunities, etc. Mind Genomics combines the general (in the first phase), the specific (in the second phase), and look-ahead (in the third phase).

3. THE INFRASTRUCTURE FRAMEWORK FOR MIND GENOMICS

In most cases, Mind Genomics is used as a software layer on the top of some kind of infrastructure for sales over the Internet. Therefore, a question important for studying Mind Genomics is how to create a site for electronic sales over the Internet. Fundamentals of these issues are well documented by Milutinovic in "Infrastructure for Electronic Business on the Internet".

Basically, there are three major approaches: (a) one for extremely small businesses, including "one-man bands", exemplified by systems like Yahoo! Small Business; (b) one for medium size businesses, pioneered by systems like ecBuilders (Milutinovic, 2001); and (c) for extremely large businesses, exemplified by Microsoft Site Server Commerce Edition.

In the case of "small approaches", creation of an Internet store boils down to filling a form, which is very easy, and could be done by anyone. This is a quick and dirty approach. The good side is that it is easy to make it. The down side is that the capabilities are limited and not any room is left for creativity of the business owner.

In the case of "medium approaches", creation of an Internet store boils down also to filling forms; however, in each step some room is left for the business owner to incorporate creative ideas. This typically means that linking capabilities are provided to other web sites, created by the owner or by the related businesses, worldwide.

In the case of "large approaches", creation of an Internet store boils down to making everything from scratch, which means that the business owner has lots of space for creativity, both in the domain of functionality and in the domain of presentation. Mind Genomics gives the best results if incorporated into the most complex approaches.

In all three cases above, five prerequisites have to be provided: (a) Internet merchant bank account, (b) web space, (c) secure payments certificate, (d) a contract with a provider of online transactions, and (e) electronic shopping cart. Getting an Internet merchant bank account is the responsibility of the business owner. For the other four prerequisites, the approach taken is determined by the selection of the infrastructure to be used. In the case of the "small approaches", everything is fixed and obtainable without the business being able to make selections. In the case of the "medium approaches", the business has an option, to take the defaults or to select its own preferences. In the case of the "large approaches", the business has full freedom in selecting the desired preferences.

For the background information of interest to Mind Genomics research, interested readers are referred to (Moskowitz, 2012; Gabay, 2015; Moskowitz, 2006; Zafeiropoulou, 2015; Olmstead, 2015; Mos, 2013; Columbia, 2015; Cummings, 2015; Carrell, 2015; Oxford, 2015; Milutinovic, 2001).

4. AN EFFICIENT TECHNOLOGICAL SUPPORT FOR MIND GENOMIC

A major question in the implementation of on-line Mind Genomics is "what technological support to select for the on-line Mind Genomics, which is a data-intensive problem?" The answer is: "DataFlow SuperComputing for BigData". References that cover efforts in this domain are: (Antognetti, 1991; Babovic, 2016; Blagojevic, 2017; Dennis, 1974; Furlan, 2012; Flynn, 2013; Grujic, 1996; Gavrilovska, 2010; Hennessy, 1982; Knezevic, 2000; Kotlar, 2018; Milenkovic, 2000; Milutinovic, 1987; Milutinovic, 1996; Milutinovic, 2015; Stojanovic, 2013; Stojkovic, 2017; Stojmenovic, 2012; Trobec, 2016).

The essence of DataFlow SuperComputing is that the code is written to configure the hardware, not to control the flow of data through the hardware. This fact defines its advantages and defines the related programming model.

DataFlow computers, compared to ControlFlow computers, offer speedups of 20 to 200 (even 2000 for some applications), power reductions of about 20, and size reductions of also about 20. However, as indicated, the programming paradigm is different, and has to be mastered.

5. CONCLUSION

In conclusion, this chapter sheds light on yet another important application in the domain of digital economy which requires acceleration coming from a Data Flow accelerator connected to Control Flow host. It stresses equally the basic concept and its many applications.

Innovation process is a step-by-step process. Once an important step up front is created, and a new innovation finds its way into the commercial world, it is difficult to imagine that another dramatical step/leap forward is possible. However, such steps keep happening. Mind Genomics is an example of one such step, unthinkable of until only a few years ago. What are the essential issues, unthinkable of, in Mind Genomics? Here is the answer: Modern targeted marketing methods collect information from users at the entry point into the system, and they cannot be extremely effective unless they track the behavior of the users. What was unthinkable of by the creators of these methods is that the effectiveness could be even higher without any entry point information collection and without any activities related to the tracking of the behavior of the customers. Yet, this is exactly what Mind Genomics is doing, due to a great innovation of Howard Moskowitz, a Harvard alumnus: Mind Genomics includes no information collection and no behavior tracking. It is based on sophisticated mathematics and statistics in its first phase, which refers to market analysis and on the principals of values exchange and fast Internet in its second phase, related to customer typing.

Innovation process rarely makes a lot of sense unless it results in an implementation which enables its sophistication to serve the human needs. A much more desirable scenario is the one in which the innovation creates a revolutionary leap forward of the human wellbeing. Such achievements are possible only with the help of an appropriate enabler technology. That is exactly where the innovation like Mind Genomics needs an innovative technology like MultiScale DataFlow, exemplified in the recent research and developments of another great innovator, Oskar Mencer of Maxeler Technologies, a Stanford alumnus. Mind Genomics and MultiScale DataFlow could synergize in data analytics typical of giants like Google or Yahoo, Facebook or Tweeter, J. P. Morgan or The World Bank. It is absolutely impossible, at this time, to envision all the positive effects for the mankind that a synergy of the two (Mind Genomics and MultiScale DataFlow) could bring up. Needs of the users could be served much more effectively not only in business domains or other lucrative domains, but also in the domains of public health, public happiness, public and individual quality of life, public and individual understanding of the environment around, etc.

Innovation is a process that requires sacrifices, and its success is typically paved by blood, sweat, and tears. In a number of schools of thought, in a number of different cultures, at various times, deep thinkers had created a wisdom which is very applicable both to Mind Genomics and MultiScale DataFlow, and especially to the synergy of the two. This wisdom, in its various incarnations, reads as following: Each great innovation passes through the four inevitable phases. In the first phase, the innovation is ridiculed at. In the second phase, the opponents, sensing that they are slowly losing their grounds, try to kill the innovation, in their conscience or sub-conscience despair, related to the facts that either their lives were tuned to something obsolete, or their business is becoming obsolete. In the third phase, after an undisputable success is reached, many try to arrogate it; often times, that is done very aggressively, and typically by those who were the most aggressive critics in the previous phase. Finally, in the fourth phase, which often times comes after the actors of all the previous phases are already dead, the new generation believes that the innovation has existed forever, maybe even all the way back since the times of the ancient Greeks or Romans. Consequently, developers of great innovations have constantly to think about catalytic mechanisms that would speed up the innovation's flow through initial, painful phases.

We hope this chapter is one such catalytic mechanism, a small one, with elements of a symbiotic stress on the synergy between two innovations that could serve to each other as accelerators through the above-described process.

In this chapter, while reviewing, the author used methodological lessons learned from (Bankovic, 2020).

It also gives some guidelines on the implementation differences coming from various application areas of Mind Genomics, spanning the space from marketing for Internet stores, via the scenario that lift awareness about an educational program or a research topic, till the socially responsible studies.

REFERENCES

A Simulation Study of Hardware-Oriented DSM Approaches. (1996). *IEEE Parallel & Distributed Technology Systems & Applications, 4*(1), 74–83.

Antognetti, P. (1991). *Neural Networks: Concepts Applications, and Implementations*. Prentice Hall.

Aston. (2014). Sentiment Analysis on the Social Networks Using Stream Algorithms. *Journal of Data Analysis and Information Processing, 2*, 60-66.

Babovic, Z. (2016). Web Performance Evaluation for Internet of Things Applications. *IEEE Access: Practical Innovations, Open Solutions, 4*, 6974–6992.

Bankovic, M. (2020). Teaching Graduate Students How to Review Research Articles. *Advances in Computers, 116*, 1-42.

Blagojevic, V. (2017). A Systematic Approach to Generation of New Ideas for PhD Research in Computing. In *Advances in Computers 104* (pp. 1–31). Elsevier.

Carrell, L. (2015). Digital trends shaping the US marketing landscape. *The Guardian*. Available: http://www.theguardian.com/media-network/2015/jun/ 01/trends-us-digital-marketing-landscape

Cummings, K. (2015). *Further Reading | Mindset Segmentation*. Available: http://www.kelliecummings.com/strategies/mindset-segmentation/ further-reading-mindset-segmentation/

Dennis, J. B. (1974). First Version of a Data Flow Procedure Language. In *Programming Symposium*. MIT.

Di, W., Sundaresan, N., Piramuthu, R., & Bhardwaj, A. (2014). Is a Picture Really Worth a Thousand Words?: - on the Role of Images in E-commerce. In *WSDM '14 Proceedings of the 7th ACM international conference on Web search and data mining*. ACM.

Fan, W. (2006, September). Tapping the Power of Text Mining. *Communications of the ACM, 49*(9), 76–82.

Flynn, M. J. (2013). Moving from Petaflops to Petadata. *Communications of the ACM, 56*(5), 39–42.

Furlan, B. (2012). A Survey of Intelligent Question Routing Systems. *The 6ᵗʰ IEEE International Conference on Intelligent Systems*, 14-20.

Future trends and market opportunities in the world's largest 750 cities. (2015). *Oxford Economics.* https://www.oxfordeconomics.com/Media/Default/landing-pages/cities/oe-cities-summary.pdf

Gabay, G., & Moskowitz, H. (2015). Mind Genomics: What Professional Conduct Enhances the Emotional Wellbeing of Teens at the Hospital? *Journal of Psychological Abnormalities in Children, 4*(3).

Garilovska, L. (2010). *Applications and Multidisciplinary Aspects of Wireless Sensor Networks: Concepts, Integration, and Case Studies.* Springer Science and Business Media.

Hennessy, J. (1982). MIPS: A Microprocessor Architecture. *ACM SIGMICRO Newsletter, 13*(4), 17–22.

Jodoin, P.-M. (2013). Meta-tracking for video scene understanding. In *Proceedings on 10th IEEE International Conference on Advanced Video and Signal Based Surveillance (AVSS).* IEEE.

Knezevic, P. (2000). The Architecture of the Obelix – an Improved Internet Search Engine. *Proceedings of the 33rd Annual Hawaii International Conference on System Sciences.*

Kotlar, M., & Milutinovic, V. (2018). Comparing Control Flow and Data Flow for Tensor Calculus: Speed, Power, Complexity, and MTBF. *International Conference on High Performance Computing*, 329-346, 2018.

Milenkovic, A., & Milutinovic, V. (2000). Cache Injection: A Novel Technique for Tolerating Memory Latency in Bus-based SMPs. *European Conference on Parallel Processing*, 558-566.

Milutinovic, D. (1987). The Honeycomb Architecture. *IEEE Computer, 20*(4), 81-83.

Milutinovic, V. (1996). *Surviving the Design of a 200MHz RISC Microprocessor.* IEEE Computer Society Press.

Milutinovic, V. (2001). *Infrastructure for Electronic Business on the Internet. Kluwer Academic Publishers.*

Milutinovic, V. (2015). *Guide to DataFlow SuperComputing.* Springer Nature.

Milutinovic, V., & Salom, J. (2016). *Mind Genomics: Guide to Data Driven Marketing Strategy.* Springer.

Milutinovic, V., & Salom, J. (2016). *Mind Genomics: Guide to Data Driven Marketing Strategy.* Springer.

Moskowitz, H. (2012). Mind genomics: The experimental, inductive science of the ordinary, and its application to aspects of food and feeding. *Physiology & Behavior, 107*(4), 606–613.

Moskowitz, H. (2007). Mind Genomics. *Proceedings of the IPSI-2007*, 1-10.

Moskowitz, H., Gofman, A., Beckley, J., & Ashman, H. (2006). Founding a New Science: Mind Genomics. *Journal of Sensory Studies*, (21), 266–307.

Moss, M. (2013, Feb. 20). The Extraordinary Science of Addictive Junk Food. *The New York Times Magazine*.

Olmstead, M., & Gilbert, J. (2015). In Pursuit of the Perfect Peach: Consumer-assisted Selection of Peach Fruit Traits. *HortScience*, *50*(8), 1202–1212.

Statistical Sampling and Regression: Simple Linear Regression. (2015). *PreMBA Analytical Methods*. Columbia University. Available: http: //ci.columbia.edu/ci/prembatest/c0331/s7/s7_6.html

Stojanovic, S. (2013). Solving Gross Pitaevskii Equation Using Dataflow Paradigm. *The IPSI BgD Transactions on Internet Research, 17*.

Stojkovic, I. (2017). Fast Sparse Gaussian Markov Random Fields Learning Based on Cholesky Factorization. *IJCAI*, 2758–2764.

Stojmenovic, I., & Milutinovic, V. (2012). How to Write Research Articles in Computing and Engineering Disciplines. *Singidunum Journal of Applied Sciences*, *9*(1), 42–50.

Trobec, R. (2016). Interconnection Networks in Petascale Computer Systems: A Survey. *ACM Computing Surveys*, *49*(3), 1–24.

Venkatraman, V. (2014). Predicting Advertising Success Beyond Traditional Measures: New Insights from Neurophysiological Methods and Market Response Modeling. *Social Science Research Network*. https://papers.ssrn.com/sol3/papers.cfm?abstract_id=2498095

Zafeiropoulou, S., & Nadan, J. (2015). Increasing the value of Innovation Consulting Services in the technology age. *Management of Engineering and Technology (PICMET), 2015 Portland International Conference on*, 704-717.

Chapter 18
Supercomputing in the Study and Stimulation of the Brain

Laura Dipietro
Highland Instruments, USA

Seth Elkin-Frankston
U.S. Army Combat Capabilities Development Command Soldier Center, USA

Ciro Ramos-Estebanez
Case Western Reserve University, USA

Timothy Wagner
Harvard-MIT Division of Health Sciences and Technology, Highland Instruments, USA

ABSTRACT

The history of neuroscience has tracked with the evolution of science and technology. Today, neuroscience's trajectory is heavily dependent on computational systems and the availability of high-performance computing (HPC), which are becoming indispensable for building simulations of the brain, coping with high computational demands of analysis of brain imaging data sets, and developing treatments for neurological diseases. This chapter will briefly review the current and potential future use of supercomputers in neuroscience.

BACKGROUND

The 1906 Nobel Prize in Physiology and Medicine was awarded to Camillo Golgi and Ramón y Cajal for having visualized and identified the neuron, the structural and functional unit of the nervous system (Grant, 2007). Since then, it has been discovered that the human brain contains roughly 100 billion neurons and 1000 trillion synapses. Neurons interact through electrochemical signals, also known as actional potentials (AP) or spikes, transmitted from one neuron to the next through synaptic junctions, forming functional and definable circuits which can be organized into larger 'neuronal' networks and anatomical structures. These networks integrate information from multiple brain regions as well as incoming infor-

DOI: 10.4018/978-1-7998-7156-9.ch018

mation about the external environment (e.g., sound, light, smell, taste). The result is how we perceive the world, and produce complex behavior and cognitive processes including decision-making and learning (Kandel, 2012); also, with time, these processes modify the structure and function of networks through a process called neuroplasticity (Fuchs & Flugge, 2014).

Understanding how the brain works with the ultimate goal of developing treatments for neurological disease remains one of the greatest scientific challenges of this century. In fact, there is a substantial social and economic burden associated with neurological diseases (Wynford-Thomas & Robertson, 2017). In the US alone, the overall cost of neurological diseases (e.g., stroke, dementia, movement disorders, traumatic brain injury) amounts to nearly $1T, and will dramatically increase in the next few years due to population ageing. Alarmingly, the cost of just dementias and stroke is expected to exceed $600B by 2030 (Gooch, Pracht, & Borenstein, 2017). To tackle this challenge, neuroscientists have developed a battery of increasingly complex tools, which have amplified data storage and computational speed requirements to an unprecedented level, making the use of big data techniques and HPC such as supercomputers a necessity.

In the remainder of this chapter we will briefly review current and future applications of supercomputers in neuroscience, with a focus on computational neural models, brain imaging, and models for brain stimulation. These areas were chosen not only because their advances have been particularly driven by computational approaches, but also because they are highly interconnected. Thereby, understanding how each area is evolving aids prediction of future research trends in the other areas. We also briefly discuss how the next generation of supercomputers might enable further advancements in these areas.

COMPUTATIONAL NEURAL MODELS

Computational models of neurons and neural networks represent one of the most essential tools that have contributed to the progress of neuroscience. For example, they are used to guide the design of experiments, to quantify relationships between anatomical and physiological data, to investigate the dynamics of systems that cannot be accessed via analytical methods, and to validate estimates made during theoretical derivations. Since the early days of neuronal simulations, a wide range of computational models have been developed ranging from models aimed at describing low-level mechanisms of neural function (e.g., molecular dynamics of ion channels in the neuron) to models of large-scale neuronal networks (Ippen, Eppler, Plesser, & Diesmann, 2017) (see (Fan & Markram, 2019) for a review).

The chosen level of abstraction for a model is based on the scientific question. If focused on subcellular processes (e.g., the transfer of ions underlying changes in membrane voltages that lead to APs), a neuron(s) would be described with detailed multi-compartment models (M. Hines, 1984). Instead, if the question addressed large scale network dynamics, many neurons would be described with one-compartment or few-compartment models that communicate electrically via spikes (Helias et al., 2012; Ippen et al., 2017). Simulators exist for many of these levels, including NEURON (M. L. Hines & Carnevale, 1997), SPLIT (Hammarlund & Ekeberg, 1998), PCSIM (Pecevski, Natschläger, & Schuch, 2009), the NEural Simulation Tool (NEST) (Gewaltig, 2007; van Albada, Kunkel, Morrison, & Diesmann, 2014), and C2 (Ananthanarayanan & Modha, 2007) (see (Helias et al., 2012; Tikidji-Hamburyan, Narayana, Bozkus, & El-Ghazawi, 2017) for a review).

A major challenge when developing such models include the total number of network elements that must be represented. To put the problem into perspective, a 1 mm^3 of brain tissue modeled at the neuronal and synaptic level (Amit & Brunel, 1997; Brunel, 2000; Morrison, Aertsen, & Diesmann, 2007) includes 10^5 neurons and 1 billion synapses (Helias et al., 2012). However, representing neurons in a restricted volume is only part of the problem, as each neuron receives more than half of its inputs from neurons that are not in its vicinity and that can even be located in distant areas (Abeles, 1991; Stepanyants, Martinez, Ferecsko, & Kisvarday, 2009). This issue ultimately severely limits models' predictive power, creating the need for developing models of increasingly larger areas of the brain.

Over the past several decades unprecedented funding has been granted by national brain-research projects supported by the USA, EU, and governments of other developed countries to spur innovative research in this area. Arguably these efforts have transitioned neuroscience from a "small science" to a "big science" approach (i.e., using large multi-discipline teams, with ample resources and competences to tackle the big problems (Markram, 2013)). A general goal of these very ambitious projects has been to build platforms for "simulating the human brain" (Makin, 2019) in a supercomputer. Examples of these projects are the Blue Brain Project in collaboration with IBM, which aims to "develop a digital recon-struction of rodent and eventually human brains by reverse-engineering mammalian brain circuitry" (see for example their reconstruction of a small volume of the rat primary somatosensory cortex (Markram et al., 2015)) and the Human Brain Project (Amunts et al., 2019) (see (Chen et al., 2019) for a review).

Despite these and other substantial efforts, simulations of the whole brain at a neuronal level are not yet feasible, as they would require memory sizes well beyond those available in today's supercomputers. Another bottleneck is represented by the current neural simulators' inefficiency in managing information exchange of neurons across supercomputers nodes. State of the art simulation software and available supercomputers allow simulation of only a small fraction of the human cortex (Jordan et al., 2018; Kunkel et al., 2014). Availability of exascale computers and development of algorithms for optimal processing speed promise to further scale neural networks simulations (Jordan et al., 2018).

BRAIN IMAGING

Another area where supercomputers are enabling advances in brain science is through imaging. A pil-lar of neuroscience, imaging has greatly contributed to furthering our understanding of brain physiol-ogy and disease states. Common imaging technologies include Magnetic Resonance Imaging (MRI; first introduced in 1977), functional Magnetic Resonance Imaging (fMRI, first introduced in 1990 by Bell Laboratories), electroencephalography (EEG, a technique used since the beginning of 1900), and magnetoencephalography (MEG, first introduced in 1970). These techniques have allowed scientists to investigate structure or patterns of activation of different brain areas and develop hypotheses of how specific structural or functional anomalies might lead to emergent pathological behaviors (see (Bow-man, 2014) for a review).

Over the years, these technologies have been refined to enable collection of increasingly com-plex data sets. For example, most state-of-the art medical MRI scans can reach resolutions of around $1.5 \times 1.5 \times 4 mm^3$, but ultra-high magnetic field MRI scanners for research purposes have reached a resolution of $80 \times 80 \times 200 \mu m^3$ (Van Reeth, Tham, Tan, & Poh, 2012); fMRI data cycle of acquisition has become faster (increasing from 4s to 1s), and fMRI resolution has increased from 5 mm^3 to 1 mm^3 (Chen et al., 2019). Increases in the size of data sets have not only been driven by these hardware advances, but also by the transition of neuroscience to a big data science which has resulted from the collaborative aspect of the scientific initiatives described in the paragraph above (Li, Guo, & Li, 2019). Typical pre-big data era research data sets collected for example during an fMRI experiment aimed at uncovering which areas of the brain activated during a certain cognitive task were composed of data from tens of subjects, but modern data sets are considerably larger due to the practice of data sharing and integration of multiple data sources (Calhoun & Sui, 2016). Combined with the already high computational power demands that come from the algorithms typically used for analyzing these data sets (which often involve analysis of patterns of activations through different brain areas and subjects via correlation and clustering techniques) one can see how the use of supercomputers is becoming indispensable (Cohen et al., 2017).

Research with EEG, one of the oldest technologies for recording brain electrical activity, has also evolved in a similar direction. Modern scalp EEG systems have evolved from just a few electrodes traditionally used for monitoring changes in signal features in the temporal and/or spectral domain to 256 electrodes when used for research purposes -these high-density EEG systems can be used to build spatio-temporal maps of brain activation (see (Dipietro, Poizner, & Krebs, 2014) for an example). The increased number of electrodes combined with EEG's high temporal resolution (ms) and the easiness of recordings (e.g., due to EEG systems high portability) has led to dramatically increased data set sizes. An area of EEG (and MEG) research where supercomputers may lead to future advancements is source-localization. EEG source localization estimates the location of the brain cells (i.e., neurons that act as electromagnetic dipole sources) from recordings of brain activity made by electrodes placed on the scalp (Dipietro, Plank, Poizner, & Krebs, 2012). Source-localization algorithms require an anatomical model of the subject head and solving a very computational intensive inverse model problem (Michel & Brunet, 2019). Until very recently, the difficulty in harnessing sufficient computer power had discouraged researchers from attempting this type of analysis on very large data sets, but recently it has been shown how implementations on supercomputers are making this type of analysis more accessible (Delorme et al., 2019).

BRAIN STIMULATION

An emerging application of supercomputers is in the area of brain stimulation. In humans, the invasive technique of deep brain stimulation (DBS) (Herrington, Cheng, & Eskandar, 2016) and noninvasive brain stimulation techniques such as Transcranial Direct Current Stimulation (tDCS) and Transcranial Magnetic Stimulation (TMS) (Brunoni et al., 2012; Klomjai, Katz, & Lackmy-Vallee, 2015; Reed & Cohen Kadosh, 2018) have been successfully used to investigate the functional properties of the nervous system (Polania, Nitsche, & Ruff, 2018) and to treat neurological disorders (Schulz, Gerloff, & Hummel, 2013) such as depression, Parkinson's disease, and chronic pain (see for example (Boccard, Pereira, & Aziz, 2015; Groiss, Wojtecki, Sudmeyer, & Schnitzler, 2009; Liu, Sheng, Li, & Zhang, 2017)). When used to deliver a treatment, these neurostimulation techniques can be administered alone or in conjunction with other treatments. For example, in Parkinson's disease, stimulation techniques could be used adjunctive to drug therapy, and in stroke patients in conjunction with robot-assisted motor therapy (Edwards et al., 2014).

Independent of the technique, understanding how stimulatory fields interact with the neural tissue is a fundamental step in effectively implementing neuromodulation methods (Butson & McIntyre, 2005 ; Wagner, Valero-Cabre, & Pascual-Leone, 2007). Assessing the stimulatory field effects of brain stimulation requires the following computational steps: modeling the human head and brain; modeling stimulation sources; and modeling the tissue-field interactions of stimulation (both in terms of the field-neural cell interactions that drive neuromodulatory effects in the nervous system, and in terms of the biophysical field distributions in the targeted tissue- see Fig. 1). A detailed explanation of this process can be found in the authors' work in (Wagner et al., 2014), which described how to calculate the electromagnetic fields generated during TMS and DBS and their ability to modulate neural activity. To this end the authors used MRI-guided Finite Element Models (FEMs) of the human head based on individual patient anatomy and frequency-dependent tissue impedance properties. The FEM human head models were integrated with models of TMS and DBS sources and the authors subsequently solved for the stimulation field distributions in the targeted brain tissue. The field distributions solutions were then combined with conductance-based compartmental models of neurons, and ultimately used to calculate stimulation thresholds and response dynamics of targeted neurons. Currently, this process is being extended to new neuromodulation techniques and to modeling the response of more complicated cellular and network targets.

The above computational methods guide stimulation dosing, which can be specific for each patient. For example, members of the authors' group are currently developing dosing software for electrosonic stimulation (Wagner & Dipietro, 2018), a new form of noninvasive brain stimulation that combines electrical and ultrasound sources to achieve improved stimulation focality, targeting, and penetration. Electrosonic stimulation is being investigated in clinical trials in patients with Parkinson's disease and chronic pain (such as due to knee osteoarthritis, low back pain, and diabetic neuropathic pain)[1]. Many of these studies are being combined with computational studies aimed at optimizing stimulation dosing along a Precision Medicine Initiative trajectory (Ashley, 2015). The National Academies of Science has highlighted Precision Medicine Initiative approaches as an opening for a reductionist data-driven computer-based analysis, adding to the classical hypothetical deductive clinical model and intuition of experienced physicians (Committee on Diagnostic Error in Health Care; Board on Health Care Services; Institute of Medicine; The National Academies of Sciences, 2015).

In brain stimulation treatments, personalized modeling might be important not only because different patients have different anatomies (e.g., brain anatomy), but also because neurological disorders often induce changes in brain structure, function, and/or in the electromagnetic properties of the neural tissue (e.g., see mechanisms of central sensitization induced by pain (Latremoliere & Woolf, 2009), or cortical reorganization induced by stroke (Grefkes & Ward, 2014)). For example, a previous study by the authors shows how a brain infarct can affect stimulation (O'Brien et al., 2016). That study compared electromagnetic fields generated during brain stimulation via tDCS, TMS, and Epidural Brain Stimulation (EBS) techniques in a brain with and without focal cortical infarcts. It was shown that changes in electrical properties at stroke boundaries differentially impacted the distribution of stimulation currents in terms of orientation, location, and magnitude (e.g., the impact on current density magnitude was greater for the noninvasive brain stimulation techniques (i.e., tDCS and TMS) than for EBS) (O'Brien et al., 2016). Such effects would need to be taken into account when designing a brain stimulation treatment plan for patients, as they will ultimately alter its efficacy.

The aforementioned computational models require considerable computational resources, which can progressively increase as the level of detail of the model components (e.g., MRI resolution) rises. The growing demand for personalized treatment combined with the mounting use of brain stimulation in the clinic, the increasing urgency of finding effective treatments for neurological diseases, and the growing interest in developing new or optimizing existing brain stimulation technologies are likely to accelerate the use of supercomputers in this area.

Figure 1. One can use computational processes to solve for patient specific stimulation doses for non-invasive brain stimulation. The figure depicts TMS cortical current density distributions derived from diffusion tensor imaging-based models.
Image adapted from (Wagner, 2006; Wagner, Rushmore, Eden, & Valero-Cabre, 2009).

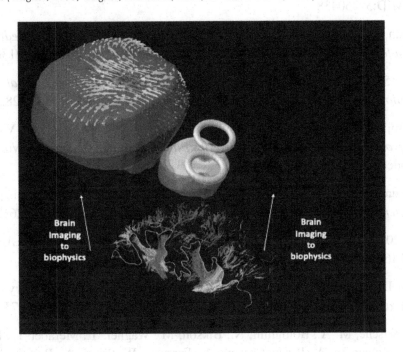

CONCLUSION

The brain is the world's most sophisticated supercomputer. Unveiling how it works is one of the greatest challenges of this century. This chapter has briefly reviewed how different technologies and their combination have enabled advances in brain science. The cross-pollination of ideas borrowed from neuroscience and supercomputing relies on "Crossdisciplinarization" and "Hybridization" approaches to inspire and generate innovations (Blagojević et al., 2017). In the field of neuroscience, the use of supercomputers is growing and likely to change the trajectory of many research and clinical areas, at a speed that will depend on how much the area relies on computational approaches.

REFERENCES

Abeles, M. (1991). Corticonics: Neural Circuits of the Cerebral Cortex. Academic Press.

Amit, D. J., & Brunel, N. (1997). Model of global spontaneous activity and local structured activity during delay periods in the cerebral cortex. *Cerebral Cortex (New York, N.Y.), 7*(3), 237–252. doi:10.1093/cercor/7.3.237 PMID:9143444

Amunts, K., Knoll, A. C., Lippert, T., Pennartz, C. M. A., Ryvlin, P., Destexhe, A., Jirsa, V. K., D'Angelo, E., & Bjaalie, J. G. (2019). The Human Brain Project-Synergy between neuroscience, computing, informatics, and brain-inspired technologies. *PLoS Biology*, *17*(7), e3000344. doi:10.1371/journal. pbio.3000344 PMID:31260438

Ananthanarayanan, R., & Modha, D. S. (2007). Anatomy of a cortical simulator. *Proceedings of the ACM/ IEEE SC2007 Conference on High Performance Networking and Computing*. 10.1145/1362622.1362627

Ashley, E. A. (2015). The precision medicine initiative: A new national effort. *Journal of the American Medical Association*, *313*(21), 2119–2120. doi:10.1001/jama.2015.3595 PMID:25928209

Blagojević, V., Bojić, D., Bojović, M., Cvetanović, C., Đorđević, J., Đurđević, D., & Vuletić, P. (2017). *A Systematic Approach to Generation of New Ideas for PhD Research in Computing* (Vol. 104). Elsevier. doi:10.1016/bs.adcom.2016.09.001

Boccard, S. G., Pereira, E. A., & Aziz, T. Z. (2015). Deep brain stimulation for chronic pain. *Journal of Clinical Neuroscience*, *22*(10), 1537–1543. doi:10.1016/j.jocn.2015.04.005 PMID:26122383

Bowman, F. D. (2014). Brain Imaging Analysis. *Annual Review of Statistics and Its Application*, *1*(1), 61–85. doi:10.1146/annurev-statistics-022513-115611 PMID:25309940

Brunel, N. (2000). Dynamics of sparsely connected networks of excitatory and inhibitory spiking neurons. *Journal of Computational Neuroscience*, *8*(3), 183–208. doi:10.1023/A:1008925309027 PMID:10809012

Brunoni, A. R., Nitsche, M. A., Bolognini, N., Bikson, M., Wagner, T., Merabet, L., Edwards, D. J., Valero-Cabre, A., Rotenberg, A., Pascual-Leone, A., Ferrucci, R., Priori, A., Boggio, P. S., & Fregni, F. (2012). Clinical research with transcranial direct current stimulation (tDCS): Challenges and future directions. *Brain Stimulation*, *5*(3), 175–195. doi:10.1016/j.brs.2011.03.002 PMID:22037126

Butson, C. R., & McIntyre, C. C. (2005). Tissue and electrode capacitance reduce neural activation volumes during deep brain stimulation. *Clinical Neurophysiology*, *116*(10), 2490–2500. doi:10.1016/j. clinph.2005.06.023 PMID:16125463

Calhoun, V. D., & Sui, J. (2016). Multimodal fusion of brain imaging data: A key to finding the missing link(s) in complex mental illness. *Biological Psychiatry: Cognitive Neuroscience and Neuroimaging*, *1*(3), 230–244. doi:10.1016/j.bpsc.2015.12.005 PMID:27347565

Chen, S., He, Z., Han, X., He, X., Li, R., Zhu, H., Zhao, D., Dai, C., Zhang, Y., Lu, Z., Chi, X., & Niu, B. (2019). How Big Data and High-performance Computing Drive Brain Science. *Genomics, Proteomics & Bioinformatics*, *17*(4), 381–392. doi:10.1016/j.gpb.2019.09.003 PMID:31805369

Cohen, J. D., Daw, N., Engelhardt, B., Hasson, U., Li, K., Niv, Y., Norman, K. A., Pillow, J., Ramadge, P. J., Turk-Browne, N. B., & Willke, T. L. (2017). Computational approaches to fMRI analysis. *Nature Neuroscience*, *20*(3), 304–313. doi:10.1038/nn.4499 PMID:28230848

Committee on Diagnostic Error in Health Care, & the Board on Health Care Services. Institute of Medicine; The National Academies of Sciences, E., and Medicine. (2015). Improving diagnosis in healtcare. Washington, DC: The National Academy Press.

Delorme, A., Majumdar, A., Sivagnanam, S., Martinez-Cancino, K., Yoshimoto, R., & Makeig, S. (2019). *The Open EEGLAB portal.* Paper presented at the 9th International IEEE/EMBS Conference on Neural Engineering (NER), San Francisco, CA.

Dipietro, L., Plank, M., Poizner, H., & Krebs, H. I. (2012). *EEG microstate analysis in human motor corrections.* Paper presented at the RAS EMBS International Conference on Biomedical Robotics and Biomechatronics. 10.1109/BioRob.2012.6290832

Dipietro, L., Poizner, H., & Krebs, H. I. (2014). Spatiotemporal dynamics of online motor correction processing revealed by high-density electroencephalography. *Journal of Cognitive Neuroscience, 26*(9), 1966–1980. doi:10.1162/jocn_a_00593 PMID:24564462

Edwards, D. J., Dipietro, L., Demirtas-Tatlidede, A., Medeiros, A. H., Thickbroom, G. W., Mastaglia, F. L., Krebs, H. I., & Pascual-Leone, A. (2014). Movement-generated afference paired with transcranial magnetic stimulation: An associative stimulation paradigm. *Journal of Neuroengineering and Rehabilitation, 11*(1), 31. doi:10.1186/1743-0003-11-31 PMID:24597619

Fan, X., & Markram, H. (2019). A Brief History of Simulation Neuroscience. *Frontiers in Neuroinformatics, 13*, 32. doi:10.3389/fninf.2019.00032 PMID:31133838

Fuchs, E., & Flugge, G. (2014). Adult neuroplasticity: More than 40 years of research. *Neural Plasticity, 541870*, 1–10. Advance online publication. doi:10.1155/2014/541870 PMID:24883212

Gewaltig, M. O., & Diesmann, M. (2007). NEST (NEural Simulation Tool). *Scholarpedia, 2*(4), 1430. doi:10.4249cholarpedia.1430

Gooch, C. L., Pracht, E., & Borenstein, A. R. (2017). The burden of neurological disease in the United States: A summary report and call to action. *Annals of Neurology, 81*(4), 479–484. doi:10.1002/ana.24897 PMID:28198092

Grant, G. (2007). How the 1906 Nobel Prize in Physiology or Medicine was shared between Golgi and Cajal. *Brain Research. Brain Research Reviews, 55*(2), 490–498. doi:10.1016/j.brainresrev.2006.11.004 PMID:17306375

Grefkes, C., & Ward, N. S. (2014). Cortical reorganization after stroke: How much and how functional? *The Neuroscientist, 20*(1), 56–70. doi:10.1177/1073858413491147 PMID:23774218

Groiss, S. J., Wojtecki, L., Sudmeyer, M., & Schnitzler, A. (2009). Deep brain stimulation in Parkinson's disease. *Therapeutic Advances in Neurological Disorders, 2*(6), 20–28. doi:10.1177/1756285609339382 PMID:21180627

Hammarlund, P., & Ekeberg, O. (1998). Large neural network simulations on multiple hardware platforms. *Journal of Computational Neuroscience, 5*(4), 443–459. doi:10.1023/A:1008893429695 PMID:9877024

Helias, M., Kunkel, S., Masumoto, G., Igarashi, J., Eppler, J. M., Ishii, S., Fukai, T., Morrison, A., & Diesmann, M. (2012). Supercomputers ready for use as discovery machines for neuroscience. *Frontiers in Neuroinformatics, 6*, 26. doi:10.3389/fninf.2012.00026 PMID:23129998

Herrington, T. M., Cheng, J. J., & Eskandar, E. N. (2016). Mechanisms of deep brain stimulation. *Journal of Neurophysiology, 115*(1), 19–38. doi:10.1152/jn.00281.2015 PMID:26510756

Hines, M. (1984). Efficient computation of branched nerve equations. *International Journal of Bio-Medical Computing, 15*(1), 69–76. doi:10.1016/0020-7101(84)90008-4 PMID:6698635

Hines, M. L., & Carnevale, N. T. (1997). The NEURON simulation environment. *Neural Computation, 9*(6), 1179–1209. doi:10.1162/neco.1997.9.6.1179 PMID:9248061

Ippen, T., Eppler, J. M., Plesser, H. E., & Diesmann, M. (2017). Constructing Neuronal Network Models in Massively Parallel Environments. *Frontiers in Neuroinformatics, 11*, 30. doi:10.3389/fninf.2017.00030 PMID:28559808

Jordan, J., Ippen, T., Helias, M., Kitayama, I., Sato, M., Igarashi, J., Diesmann, M., & Kunkel, S. (2018). Extremely Scalable Spiking Neuronal Network Simulation Code: From Laptops to Exascale Computers. *Frontiers in Neuroinformatics, 12*, 2. doi:10.3389/fninf.2018.00002 PMID:29503613

Kandel, E. R. (2012). *Principles of Neural Science* (J. H. Schwartz, T. M. Jessell, S. A. Siegelbaum, & A. J. Hudspeth, Eds.; 5th ed.). McGraw-Hill Education / Medical.

Klomjai, W., Katz, R., & Lackmy-Vallee, A. (2015). Basic principles of transcranial magnetic stimulation (TMS) and repetitive TMS (rTMS). *Annals of Physical and Rehabilitation Medicine, 58*(4), 208–213. doi:10.1016/j.rehab.2015.05.005 PMID:26319963

Kunkel, S., Schmidt, M., Eppler, J. M., Plesser, H. E., Masumoto, G., Igarashi, J., Ishii, S., Fukai, T., Morrison, A., Diesmann, M., & Helias, M. (2014). Spiking network simulation code for petascale computers. *Frontiers in Neuroinformatics, 8*, 78. doi:10.3389/fninf.2014.00078 PMID:25346682

Latremoliere, A., & Woolf, C. J. (2009). Central sensitization: A generator of pain hypersensitivity by central neural plasticity. *The Journal of Pain, 10*(9), 895–926. doi:10.1016/j.jpain.2009.06.012 PMID:19712899

Li, X., Guo, N., & Li, Q. (2019). Functional Neuroimaging in the New Era of Big Data. *Genomics, Proteomics & Bioinformatics, 17*(4), 393–401. doi:10.1016/j.gpb.2018.11.005 PMID:31809864

Liu, S., Sheng, J., Li, B., & Zhang, X. (2017). Recent Advances in Non-invasive Brain Stimulation for Major Depressive Disorder. *Frontiers in Human Neuroscience, 11*, 526. doi:10.3389/fnhum.2017.00526 PMID:29163106

Makin, S. (2019). The four biggest challenges in brain simulation. *Nature, 571*(7766), S9. doi:10.1038/d41586-019-02209-z PMID:31341313

Markram, H. (2013). Seven challenges for neuroscience. *Functional Neurology, 28*(3), 145–151. doi:10.11138/FNeur/2013.28.3.144 PMID:24139651

Markram, H., Muller, E., Ramaswamy, S., Reimann, M. W., Abdellah, M., Sanchez, C. A., Ailamaki, A., Alonso-Nanclares, L., Antille, N., Arsever, S., Kahou, G. A. A., Berger, T. K., Bilgili, A., Buncic, N., Chalimourda, A., Chindemi, G., Courcol, J.-D., Delalondre, F., Delattre, V., ... Schurmann, F. (2015). Reconstruction and Simulation of Neocortical Microcircuitry. *Cell, 163*(2), 456–492. doi:10.1016/j.cell.2015.09.029 PMID:26451489

Michel, C. M., & Brunet, D. (2019). EEG Source Imaging: A Practical Review of the Analysis Steps. *Frontiers in Neurology, 10*, 325. doi:10.3389/fneur.2019.00325 PMID:31019487

Morrison, A., Aertsen, A., & Diesmann, M. (2007). Spike-timing-dependent plasticity in balanced random networks. *Neural Computation, 19*(6), 1437–1467. doi:10.1162/neco.2007.19.6.1437 PMID:17444756

O'Brien, A. T., Amorim, R., Rushmore, R. J., Eden, U., Afifi, L., Dipietro, L., Wagner, T., & Valero-Cabre, A. (2016). Motor Cortex Neurostimulation Technologies for Chronic Post-stroke Pain: Implications of Tissue Damage on Stimulation Currents. *Frontiers in Human Neuroscience, 10*, 545. doi:10.3389/fnhum.2016.00545 PMID:27881958

Pecevski, D., Natschläger, T., & Schuch, K. (2009). PCSIM: A Parallel Simulation Environment for Neural Circuits Fully Integrated with Python. *Front Neuroinformatics, 3*(11).

Polania, R., Nitsche, M. A., & Ruff, C. C. (2018). Studying and modifying brain function with non-invasive brain stimulation. *Nature Neuroscience, 21*(2), 174–187. doi:10.103841593-017-0054-4 PMID:29311747

Reed, T., & Cohen Kadosh, R. (2018). Transcranial electrical stimulation (tES) mechanisms and its effects on cortical excitability and connectivity. *Journal of Inherited Metabolic Disease, 41*(6), 1123–1130. Advance online publication. doi:10.100710545-018-0181-4 PMID:30006770

Schulz, R., Gerloff, C., & Hummel, F. C. (2013). Non-invasive brain stimulation in neurological diseases. *Neuropharmacology, 64*, 579–587. doi:10.1016/j.neuropharm.2012.05.016 PMID:22687520

Stepanyants, A., Martinez, L. M., Ferecsko, A. S., & Kisvarday, Z. F. (2009). The fractions of short- and long-range connections in the visual cortex. *Proceedings of the National Academy of Sciences of the United States of America, 106*(9), 3555–3560. doi:10.1073/pnas.0810390106 PMID:19221032

Tikidji-Hamburyan, R. A., Narayana, V., Bozkus, Z., & El-Ghazawi, T. A. (2017). Software for Brain Network Simulations: A Comparative Study. *Frontiers in Neuroinformatics, 11*, 46. doi:10.3389/fninf.2017.00046 PMID:28775687

van Albada, S. J., Kunkel, S., Morrison, A., & Diesmann, M. (2014). *Integrating Brain Structure and Dynamics on Supercomputers* (Vol. 8603). Springer. doi:10.1007/978-3-319-12084-3_3

Van Reeth, E., Tham, I. W. K., Tan, C. H., & Poh, C. L. (2012). Super-resolution in magnetic resonance imaging: a review. In Concepts in Magnetic Resonance (Vol. Part A 40A. 6, pp. 306–325.). Academic Press.

Wagner, T. (2006). *Transcranial Magnetic Stimulation: High Resolution Tracking of the Induced Current Density in the Individual Human Brain.* Paper presented at the 12th Annual Meeting of Human Brain mapping, Florence, Italy.

Wagner, T., & Dipietro, L. (2018). Novel methods of transcranial stimulation: electrosonic stimulation. In A. Rezai, P. H. Peckham, & E. Krames (Eds.), *Neuromodulation: Comprehensive Textbook of Principles, Technologies, and Therapies.* Elsevier. doi:10.1016/B978-0-12-805353-9.00137-6

Wagner, T., Eden, U., Rushmore, J., Russo, C. J., Dipietro, L., Fregni, F., Simon, S., Rotman, S., Pitskel, N. B., Ramos-Estebanez, C., Pascual-Leone, A., Grodzinsky, A. J., Zahn, M., & Valero-Cabre, A. (2014). Impact of brain tissue filtering on neurostimulation fields: A modeling study. *NeuroImage, 85*(Pt 3), 1048–1057. doi:10.1016/j.neuroimage.2013.06.079 PMID:23850466

Wagner, T., Rushmore, J., Eden, U., & Valero-Cabre, A. (2009). Biophysical foundations underlying TMS: Setting the stage for an effective use of neurostimulation in the cognitive neurosciences. *Cortex*, *45*(9), 1025–1034. doi:10.1016/j.cortex.2008.10.002 PMID:19027896

Wagner, T., Valero-Cabre, A., & Pascual-Leone, A. (2007). Noninvasive human brain stimulation. *Annual Review of Biomedical Engineering*, *9*(1), 527–565. doi:10.1146/annurev.bioeng.9.061206.133100 PMID:17444810

Wynford-Thomas, R., & Robertson, N. P. (2017). The economic burden of chronic neurological disease. *Journal of Neurology*, *264*(11), 2345–2347. doi:10.100700415-017-8632-7 PMID:29038885

ENDNOTE

[1] Research reported in this publication are or were supported in part by the National Institute of Health NIA (Award Number R44AG055360), NIDDK (Award Number DK117710), and NCCIH (Award Number AT008637A). The content is solely the responsibility of the authors and does not necessarily represent the official views of the National Institutes of Health.

Chapter 19
An Experimental Healthcare System:
Essence and Challenges

Miroslav M. Bojović
School of Electrical Engineering, University of Belgrade, Serbia

Veljko Milutinović
School of Electrical Engineering, University of Belgrade, Serbia

Dragan Bojić
School of Electrical Engineering, University of Belgrade, Serbia

Nenad Korolija
School of Electrical Engineering, University of Belgrade, Serbia

ABSTRACT

Contemporary healthcare systems face growing demand for their services, rising costs, and a workforce. Artificial intelligence has the potential to transform how care is delivered and to help meet the challenges. Recent healthcare systems have been focused on using knowledge management and AI. The proposed solution is to reach explainable and causal AI by combining the benefits of the accuracy of deep-learning algorithms with visibility on the factors that are important to the algorithm's conclusion in a way that is accessible and understandable to physicians. Therefore, the authors propose AI approach in which the encoded clinical guidelines and protocols provide a starting point augmented by models that learn from data. The new structure of electronic health records that connects data from wearables and genomics data and innovative extensible big data architecture appropriate for this AI concept is proposed. Consequently, the proposed technology may drastically decrease the need for expensive software and hopefully eliminates the need to do diagnostics in expensive institutions.

DOI: 10.4018/978-1-7998-7156-9.ch019

1. PROBLEM DEFINITION

Recent healthcare systems have been focused on using knowledge management in such a way so as to achieve clinical advice based on multiple items of patient data (Morr, 2010). Most of them consist of three parts: the knowledge base, an inference engine, and a mechanism to communicate. Another approach which does not use a knowledge base uses a form of Artificial intelligence (AI) called machine learning, which allows computers to learn from past experiences and/or find patterns in clinical data.

Artificial intelligence has the potential to transform healthcare organizations and healthcare services. As longevity increases, healthcare systems face growing demand for their services (population ageing, patient expectations, lifestyle choices, and the never ending cycle of innovation), rising the costs and requiring a workforce that is struggling to meet the needs of the patients. AI in healthcare can support significant improvements in Self-care/Prevention/Wellness, Triage and Diagnosis, Diagnostics, Clinical Decision Support, Care Delivery, Chronic Care Management, etc. The number of data sources in healthcare services has grown rapidly as a result of widespread use of mobile, wearable sensors technologies and implants, which has flooded healthcare area with a huge amount of data and changed our understanding of human biology and of how medicines work, enabling personalized and real-time treatment for all. Therefore, the high volume of diversified medical data analysis based on traditional methods becomes non promising solution.

Exploiting AI eliminates the need for writing rules and for expert input. However, since systems based on machine learning cannot explain the reasons for their conclusions, most clinicians do not use them directly for diagnoses, for reliability and accountability reasons. Nevertheless, they can be useful as post-diagnostic systems, for suggesting patterns for clinicians to look into in more depth. Advances in a form of AI called deep learning mean that algorithms can generate layers of abstract features that enable computers to recognize complicated concepts (such as a diagnosis) by building on simpler ones that are accessible in the data. This enables them to learn discriminative features automatically and to create approximate highly complex relationships. Such algorithms have been around for some time now, but the recent expansion of datasets and computational resources have enabled a series of breakthrough improvements that could now be applied to augment healthcare provision.

To reach that goal it is necessary to propose an extensible big data architecture for healthcare applications formed by separate components for storing, processing, and analyzing the high amount of data.

2. EXISTING TECHNOLOGIES FOR HEALTHCARE SYSTEMS

Computers are utilized in healthcare for decades (Korolija, 2013), (Korolija, 2019). Contemporary healthcare systems tend to utilize the technology advancements for reducing costs and producing suggestions with higher accuracies. Many of them are based on AI. There are many AI methods. Most of them are oriented towards producing better results, but using decision trees, a health care professional could follow the decisions that the computer made, enabling him to change the decision by adjusting the path that the computer has taken. However, in general case, decision trees do not produce the same quality output as those methods that do not reveal the decision process. Recent advances in big data processing enable high quality decisions, while at the same time healthcare professionals are not eliminated from the process of making decisions.

2.1. Contemporary Healthcare Systems

In most contemporary healthcare systems, healthcare professionals are expected to make rational decisions, weighing up available knowledge and making choices about patients' needs. In some cases, computers could aid in estimating the probability of diseases based on measured parameters of a patient (Wilson, 2000), (Arenson, 2000), (McLane, 2005). However, based on the knowledge about healthcare needs that both computers and human professions have, they might come to the opposite conclusions. Typically, a healthcare professional is responsible for making a decision. However, the knowledge used by computers, as well as the decision policies, are usually closed to computers, so that the computers act as black boxes. On the other hand, it would be beneficial if healthcare professions could navigate through the decision process, as authoritative medical knowledge could intersects with knowledge from other sources.

2.2. Artificial Intelligence

Cognitive systems could act as if they understand, reason, and learn, helping people expand their knowledge base and improve the productivity. It also deepens the expertise of professionals. Cognitive computing can impact the field of health care more than we ever thought possible (Chaudhry, 2008).

According to the Barcelona Declaration for the Proper Development and Usage of Artificial Intelligence in Europe (Steels, 2018), AI methodologies can be divided into two fundamentally different categories: knowledge-based AI and data-driven AI. Knowledge-based AI consists in "an attempt to model human knowledge in computational terms, starting in a top-down fashion from human self-reporting of what concepts and knowledge individuals use to solve problems or answer queries in a domain of expertise, including common sense knowledge", and "formalizes and operationalizes this knowledge in terms of software. It rests primarily on highly sophisticated but now quite standard symbolic computing technologies and has already had a huge impact" (Steels, 2018). Data-driven AI, on the other hand, is characterized by "starting in a bottom-up fashion from large amounts of data of human activity, which are processed with statistical machine learning methods (Blagojević, 2017) in order to abstract patterns that can then be used to make predictions, complete partial data, or emulate human behaviour in similar conditions in the past. Data-driven AI requires big data and very substantial computing power to reach adequate performance levels" (Steels, 2018). Knowledge-based methodologies are well established, but less able to exploit large volumes of data, and to automatically build a knowledge model by generalizing from data themselves. In fact, knowledge models often remain human-developed. Knowledge acquisition and formalization is thus a "bottleneck", which consumes development time and requires a significant initial effort. On the other hand, data-driven methodologies are currently receiving a lot of attention, thanks to the large amount of data available in electronic form, to the availability of powerful computing architectures, and to the significant advancement of machine learning techniques that are able to extract characteristic features and to identify patterns from data with a high level of accuracy (Montani, 2019).

In a recent research study (Chen, 2017) have observed that the knowledge-based approach to clinical decision support is limited in scale, due to the lack of evidence in some domains as well as to the cost of human knowledge authoring processes. On the contrary, taking advantage of the accumulated clinical data, stored, e.g., in electronic patient records, powerful data-driven clinical decision support systems can be implemented, possibly leading to more effective outcomes in practice.

2.3. Big Data Technologies

It is known that humans generate an enormous amount of health-related data. Reports say data from the U.S. healthcare system alone reached, in 2011, 150 exabytes (Raghupathi, 2014). They range from personal fitness trackers and mobile apps to electronic medical records and genomic and clinical research (Kos, 2015), (Trifunovic, 2015). However, much of this information is discarded. Many patients do not even have access to their own data. On the other side, patients would benefit if healthcare professionals could harness the best expertise from all doctors, reaching remote regions and matching more patients than ever. Cognitive health should bring together individual and clinical research from a diverse range of healthcare sources to redefine healthcare professionals decision path to better health.

For the big data scientists, there are opportunities to exploit vast amount of data. By discovering associations, patterns and trends within the data, big data analytics could improve healthcare, save millions of lives and lower healthcare costs at the same time. Thus, big data analytics applications in healthcare could benefit from the explosion in data and extract insights for making better decisions.

3. PROPOSED SOLUTION

The innovative contribution of this project is to propose an extensible big data architecture for healthcare applications formed by several components capable of storing, processing, and analyzing the high amount of data. Improvements in data, processing power and algorithms are rapidly changing what is feasible. The scope and quality of healthcare data produced and the potential to link datasets are opening new possibilities. Both the quality and consistency of data are improving as more data are machine generated. Electronic wearables produce new types of longitudinal data. Genomics data are becoming more accessible as the costs of sequencing and bioinformatic techniques have significantly reduced. The new structure of Electronic Health Records (EHRs) that can connect longitudinal data and genomics data will be proposed in this project. The main idea is to reach explainable and causal AI by combining the benefits of the accuracy of deep-learning algorithms with visibility on the factors that are important to the algorithm's conclusion, in a way that is accessible to physicians and other practitioners, as in rules-based systems, enabled by richer data and improved computing. Therefore, we propose AI in healthcare as a synergy of two concepts, where encoding clinical guidelines and/or existing clinical protocols provides a starting point, which then can be augmented by models that learn from data and demonstrate the distinctive properties of AI, the ability to perform tasks in complex environments without constant user guidance and improving performance by learning from experience.

This transition from rules drawn up by experts to systems that learn from data would be exemplified and proven by applications to triage patients, applications to support clinical decision making. The AI therefore incorporates two concepts starting with rules based approaches, but increasingly introduces the capacity to learn by training a specific task on large datasets.

The proposed AI Healthcare System has the potential to transform healthcare organizations and healthcare services, and meet the current and future society needs in worldwide.

4. ANALYSIS OF THE PROPOSED SOLUTION

By 2050, 1 in 6 people will be over the age of 65, in Europe and North America, this will be 1 in 4. This demographic shift, combined with rapid urbanization, modernization, globalization and accompanying changes in risk factors and lifestyles, means chronic conditions will be more common, and an increasingly comorbid population's demand for healthcare will increase (Revision, 2019). Managing patients with complex needs is typically more expensive, especially in conditions when health systems are already stretched. It also adds complexity to information flows, as large volumes of healthcare data no longer sit primarily in hospital. It also requires a different set of skills and a strong culture of collaboration between physicians across specialties.

In this context, financial sustainability is a core challenge for European healthcare systems. In 2018, healthcare expenditure in France, Germany, Italy, Spain and the UK ranged between 8.8 and 11.2 percent of the GDP and are expected to continue rising. Healthcare spending as a share of GDP has been growing since 1990, outpacing average wage growth and the growth of GDP itself (Porter, 2008).

Without major structural and transformational change, healthcare systems will struggle to find the funding needed to address growing demand, whilst maintaining or improving standards of care, access and patient experience. Staff shortages and skill gaps are also limiting healthcare systems' ability to cater to this increasing demand.

AI has the potential to transform the way care is delivered and to help meet the challenges set out above. Investment in AI in healthcare is increasing at pace across the world, particularly in North America, Europe and Asia.

The proposed system defines a new structure of Electronic Health Record that can connect longitudinal data and genomics data. The data integration allows us to develop the "digital twin" of the patient. The another innovative contribution of this project is an extensible big data architecture appropriate for this AI concept.

The proposed AI Healthcare System, where encoding clinical guidelines and/or existing clinical protocols provides a starting point, which then can be augmented by deep learning models that learn from data and demonstrate the distinctive properties of AI, which also open new routes to delivering better, faster and more cost-effective care, and may have a greater focus on prevention and promoting wellness.

5. IMPLEMENTATION GUIDELINES

The first goal in the project is to develop the "digital twin" of the patient and define an Electronic Health Record (EHR), defining which data should be relevant and how that data could be collected. Therefore state of the art mobile wearables and the amount and quality of available genomics sources will be selected. The longitudinal data from selected wearables and the available genomics data will be analyzed and classified. As a result of that analyze and classification, a new structure of EHR that can connect that data will be proposed. The next step is estimation of the amount of data, based on defined EHR structure. Storing, processing and analyzing such high amount of data is serious challenge. Big data architectures will be analyzed, and an extensible big data architecture which can satisfy the requirements be proposed. The next activity of the project is definition of an synergistic concept of AI in healthcare. The main idea is to reach explainable and causal AI by combining the benefits of the accuracy of deep-learning algorithms with visibility on the factors that are important to the algorithm's conclusion in a way that is accessible to physicians and other practitioners, as in rules-based systems, enabled by richer data and improved computing. This transition from rules drawn up by experts to systems that learn from data will be exemplified and proven by selected application to support clinical decision making. The healthcare domain expertise is expected for knowledge based rules for selected application and clinical decision making as general. The necessary activities in implementing the proposed solution are shown in the Table 1.

Table 1. Activities in implementing the proposed solution

No.	Activity	Description of the Activity
1.	Mobile wearables selection	State of the art mobile wearables will be selected
2.	Genomics data sources selection	Available genomics sources will be selected.
3.	Analysis of Health Record	The Health Record domain expertise
4.	Analysis of data from state of the art wearables	The amount and quality of data from state of the art wearables will be analyzed. Based on that analysis, a set of wearables data will be chosen as an input for Electronic Health Record.
5.	Analysis of available genomics data	The amount and quality of available genomics data will be analyzed, and respective set of genomics data will be chosen as an input for Electronic Health Record.
6.	Definition of an Electronic Health Record	A new structure of Electronic Health Record (EHR) will be defined. It will connect longitudinal data from wearables and genomics data. This data integration allows to develop the "digital twin" of the patient. Based on defined EHR, the amount of data will be estimated. This activity can be partially interleaved with activities 3., 4. and 5., but must be finalized before final definition of a big data architecture and definition of AI synergistic concept.
7.	Definition of an extensible big data architecture	An extensible big data architecture for healthcare applications will be proposed. It is formed by several components capable of storing, processing, and analyzing the high amount of data. This activity can be partially interleaved with activity 3.
8.	Clinical guidelines	Clinical guidelines domain expertise
9.	Existing clinical protocols	Existing clinical protocols domain expertise
10.	Definition of an synergistic concept of AI in healthcare	An AI in healthcare, as a synergy of two concepts, will be proposed. Clinical guidelines or existing clinical protocols provides a starting point, which then can be augmented by models that learn from data. The healthcare domain expertise is expected for knowledge based rules for selected application and clinical decision making as general. The transition from rules drawn up by experts to systems that learn from data will be exemplified and proven by selected application to support clinical decision making.

6. CONCLUSION

This chapter challenges contemporary healthcare systems facing growing demand for their services, associated with rising costs and a workforce. Artificial Intelligence methods are often exploited in a sub-optimal manner. Automatically generated decisions using AI usually eliminate healthcare professions from making decisions, or produce human trackable decision path with lower precision in generated decisions.

The proposed solution is to transform how care is delivered in order to reach explainable and causal AI by combining the benefits of the accuracy of deep-learning algorithms with visibility on the factors that are important to the algorithm's decision process. These factors represent the encoded clinical guidelines and protocols that serve as a starting point, which is then augmented by models that learn from data. Authors believe that the proposed technology may drastically decrease the need for expensive software and expensive diagnostics.

This chapter has briefly reviewed how combination of different AI technologies supported by big data technologies has enabled significant advances in healthcare systems. The combination of ideas and technologies is based on "Adaptation" and "Hybridization" approaches to inspire and generate innovations (Blagojević, 2017). It could also be considered as creativity based on "Implantation" (Blagojević, 2017), since computers as a new resource are applied to the problem that existed for ages.

REFERENCES

Arenson, R. L., Andriole, K. P., Avrin, D. E., & Gould, R. G. (2000). Computers in imaging and health care: Now and in the future. *Journal of Digital Imaging*, *13*(4), 145–156. doi:10.1007/BF03168389 PMID:11110253

Blagojević, V., Bojić, D., Bojović, M., Cvetanović, M., Đorđević, J., Đurđević, Đ., ... Milutinović, V. (2017). A systematic approach to generation of new ideas for PhD research in computing. [). Elsevier.]. *Advances in Computers*, *104*, 1–31.

Chaudhry, B. (2008). *Computerized clinical decision support: will it transform healthcare?* Academic Press.

Chen, J. H., Alagappan, M., Goldstein, M. K., Asch, S. M., & Altman, R. B. (2017). Decaying relevance of clinical data towards future decisions in data-driven inpatient clinical order sets. *International Journal of Medical Informatics*, *102*, 71–79.

El Morr, C., & Subercaze, J. (2010). Knowledge management in healthcare. In *Handbook of research on developments in e-health and telemedicine: Technological and social perspectives* (pp. 490–510). IGI Global. doi:10.4018/978-1-61520-670-4.ch023

Korolija, N., Djukic, T., Milutinovic, V., & Filipovic, N. (2013). *Accelerating Lattice-Boltzman method using Maxeler dataflow approach. The IPSI BgD Transactions on Internet Research*, *34*.

Kos, A., Tomažič, S., Salom, J., Trifunovic, N., Valero, M., & Milutinovic, V. (2015). New benchmarking methodology and programming model for big data processing. *International Journal of Distributed Sensor Networks*, *11*(8), 271752.

McLane, S. (2005). Designing an EMR planning process based on staff attitudes toward and opinions about computers in healthcare. *CIN: Computers, Informatics. Nursing*, *23*(2), 85–92. PMID:15772509

Montani, S., & Striani, M. (2019). Artificial intelligence in clinical decision support: A focused literature survey. *Yearbook of Medical Informatics*, *28*(1), 120.

Porter, M. E. (2008). Value-based health care delivery. *Annals of Surgery*, *248*(4), 503–509.

Raghupathi, W., & Raghupathi, V. (2014). Big data analytics in healthcare: Promise and potential. *Health Information Science and Systems, 2*(1), 3.

Steels, L., & López de Mantaras, R. (2018). The Barcelona declaration for the proper development and usage of artificial intelligence in Europe. *AI Communications, 31*(6), 485–494. doi:10.3233/AIC-180607

Trifunovic, N., Milutinovic, V., Salom, J., & Kos, A. (2015). Paradigm shift in big data supercomputing: Dataflow vs. controlflow. *Journal of Big Data, 2*(1), 1–9.

Wilson, R. (2000). *Using computers in health information systems. In Design and Implementation of Health Information System.* World Health Organization.

Chapter 20
What Supercomputing Will Be Like in the Coming Years

Mehmet Dalkilic
Indiana University, Bloomington, USA

ABSTRACT

This chapter is an abridged sort of "vision statement" on what supercomputing will be in the future. The main thrust of the argument is that most of the problem lies in the trafficking of data, not the computation. There needs to be a worldwide effort to put into place a means to move data efficiently and effectively. Further, there likely needs to be a fundamental shift in our model of computation where the computation is stationary and data moves to movement of computation to the data or even as the data is moving.

INTRODUCTION

Indiana University has had a history of possessing some of the most powerful supercomputers for of any University world-wide. So, it is fitting to do exercise some visioning into the future of supercomputing holds for faculty who routinely use a supercomputer. The newest supercomputer, named Big Red 200 (BR200), coinciding with Indiana University's 200th, anniversary is among the first next-generation supercomputer based on HPE's Cray Shasta architecture. BR200 operates at nearly 6 petaFlops which, at the time of this writing, makes it the 32nd most powerful supercomputer in operation world-wide and the most powerful university-owned and operated AI supercomputer in the U.S.

A Simple Observation From Feynman

Richard Feynman (1918-1988) was a Nobel winning physicist who worked not only in physics, but in other areas as well, *i.e.*, computing (Feynman et al., 1998). In this work, he makes a prescient prediction which we will paraphrase where *t* is time:

DOI: 10.4018/978-1-7998-7156-9.ch020

$$\lim_{t \to \infty} \frac{Computation_t\left(Data\right)}{Move_t\left(Data\right)} = 0$$

This means, in words, as scientists move toward building increasingly more powerful computing machines, the time to move the data will be the limiting factor, not the time of the computation. This problem was seen several years back *e.g.*, (Coughlin, 2018). A projected timeline showing the disparity between the growth of data in zettabytes

Figure 1. Amount of data produced and predicted vs. when current machine learning and AI algorithms were developed. It is estimated that all of human speech every spoken could be captured with ~42 zettabytes.

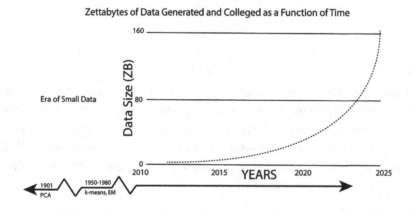

and when the current, most popular AI/ML algorithms were created is shown in Figure 1. The difference is startling when one realizes that the most popular data reduction technique, PCA (Principle Component Analysis) is 120 years old. Even with Moore's Law still reasonably true, for the next couple of years, the fact remains that data growth will continue. The traditional means of moving data to the computation rather than moving (multiple) computations to the data will have to change. The infrastructure that researchers currently have moves data at nearly 2/3 the speed of light for short distances, but, almost amusingly, using *physical* transportation of the data remains faster than sending it electronically. What does this mean for the supercomputer?

Monolithic Supercomputer

This inundation of data might mean that the standard, monolithic supercomputer's days are number except for specialized types of computation, *e.g.*, weather. With the resurgence of AI/ML pervading almost every STEM discipline, and many non-STEM disciplines as well, more and more people demand access to computation for a myriad of purposes with <u>one thing in common</u>—big data. Outside of those who use supercomputers, there is a misconception that computation is the limiting factor. This fact is significant because it is the public who will decide what to fund—an easily understandable, yet more powerful, supercomputer or infrastructure to shuttle data more effectively, or even wholly new architectures where computation is done on the data as it is moved. What will it be? Though Quantum Computing is lurking around the corner, there remain physical limitations and real differences in how they compute. Adopting this new loop-less model will take some time if not just for the physicality of the machine. Additionally, many standard desktops are nearing a dozen cores with memory that is relatively cheap. In the authors' own work optimizing Indiana University's public transportation with every bus generating ~200GB of data from sensors sending signals ever second or so and laser data for passengers entering and existing a bus, the authors were able to generate a semester's schedule for the entire campus using only a standard desktop with 6 cores in a matter of a few minutes (Zimmer et al., 2018) This points to another conundrum—what will be the use of a supercomputer if users have something akin at their disposal. With a new focus on GPU (graphical processing units) and their evidently intimate tie to deep learning algorithms, supercomputers, as they are now, the authors believe still have some legs for the foreseeable future. As data eventually overwhelms computation, there will be coming forth, new models—different from the traditional Von Neuman where data will become the bottleneck. The authors imagine a future where it is computation that will become moveable and, perhaps, even indistinguishable from data. Other questions remain that make the vision more complicated—How is data going to be stored? Will SQL remain the dominant language of data management? How will researchers keep track of provenance (how the data was generated—its lineage as it were)? As languages change, it is becoming increasingly difficult to recapitulate computation done only a few years ago—how do scientists confirm the outcome of a computation that used a decommissioned supercomputer in a data format that does not exist anymore?

CONCLUSION

In the end, the authors believe so long as the public supports the supercomputer and so long as there are identifiable uses, *e.g.*, weather, bioinformatics, the supercomputer will be present in some form for some time. But it is clear that there are competitors on the horizon that will deal with the explosion of data that Feynman about a half-century ago saw himself and forces scientists to rethink what a supercomputer is.

REFERENCES

Coughlin, T. (2018). *175 Zettabytes By 2025*. https://www.forbes.com/sites/tomcoughlin/2018/11/27/175-zettabytes-by2025/#e301d7454597

Feynman, R. P., & Hey, J. G. (1998). *Feynman Lectures on Computation*. Addison-Wesley Longman Publishing Co.

Zimmer, K., Kurban, H., Jenne, M., Keating, L., Maull, P., & Dalkilic, M. M. (2018). Using Data Analytics to Optimize Public Transportation on a College Campus. 2018 *IEEE 5th International Conference on Data Science and Advanced Analytics*, 460-469.

Chapter 21
The Ultimate Data Flow for Ultimate Super Computers-on-a-Chip

Veljko Milutinović
Indiana University, USA

Miloš Kotlar
School of Electrical Engineering, University of Belgrade, Serbia

Ivan Ratković
 https://orcid.org/0000-0002-0524-7227
Esperanto Technologies, Serbia

Nenad Korolija
Independent Researcher, Serbia

Miljan Djordjevic
University of Belgrade, Serbia

Kristy Yoshimoto
Indiana University, USA

Mateo Valero
BSC, Spain

ABSTRACT

This chapter starts from the assumption that near future 100BTransistor SuperComputers-on-a-Chip will include N big multi-core processors, 1000N small many-core processors, a TPU-like fixed-structure systolic array accelerator for the most frequently used machine learning algorithms needed in bandwidth-bound applications, and a flexible-structure reprogrammable accelerator for less frequently used machine learning algorithms needed in latency-critical applications. The future SuperComputers-on-a-Chip should include effective interfaces to specific external accelerators based on quantum, optical, molecular, and biological paradigms, but these issues are outside the scope of this chapter.

INTRODUCTION

Appropriate interfaces to memory and standard I/O, as well as to the Internet and external accelerators, are absolutely necessary, as depicted in the attached figure. Also, the number of processors in Figure 1, could be additionally increased if appropriate techniques are used, like cache injection and cache splitting

DOI: 10.4018/978-1-7998-7156-9.ch021

(Milutinovic, 1996). Finally, a higher speed could be achieved if some more advanced technology is used, like GaAs (Fortes, 1986; Milutinovic et al., 1986). Figure 1 is further explained with data in Table 1.

Figure 1. Generic structure of a future SuperComputer-on-a-Chip with 100 Billion Transistors.

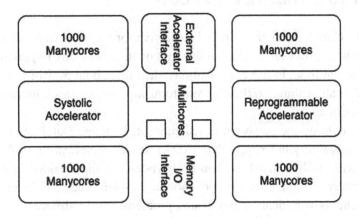

Table 1. Basically, current efforts include about 30 billion transistors on a chip, and this article advocates that, for future 100 billion transistor chips, the most effective resources to include are those based on the dataflow principle. For some important applications, such resources bring significant speedups, that would fully justify the incorporation of additional 70 billion transistors. The speedups could be, in reality, from about 10x to about 100x, and the explanations follow in the rest of this article.

Chip Hardware Type	Estimated Transistor Count
One Manycore with Memory	3.29 million
4000 Manycores with Memory	11 800 million (Techpowerup, 2020)
One Multicore with Memory	1 billion (Williams, 2019)
4 Multicore with Memory	4 billion
One Systolic Array	<1 billion (Fuchs et al., 1981)
One Reprogrammable Ultimate Dataflow	<69 billion (Xilinx, 2003)
Interface to I/O with external Memory	<100 million
Interface to External Accelerators	<100 million
TOTAL	<100 billion

Since the first three structures (multi-cores, many-cores, and TPU) are well elaborated in the open literature, this article focuses only on the fourth type of architecture, and elaborates on an idea referred to as the Ultimate DataFlow, that offers specific advantages, but requires a more advanced technology, other than today's FPGAs.

In addition, some of the most effective power reduction techniques are not applicable to FPGAs, which is another reason that creates motivation for research leading to new approaches for mapping of algorithms onto reconfigurable architectures. Consequently, the novel approach, referred to as Ultimate DataFlow, is described next.

INTRODUCTION TO UNTIMATE DATAFLOW

The architectures like Google TPU are extremely effective for the most frequent Tensor Calculus and related algorithms to which they are tuned, but these algorithms, in many important applications, burn only about 50% of the run time. In these applications, the other about 50% of run time gets burned by a huge number of other algorithms, so their architectural support requires a lot more flexible and fully reconfigurable architecture.

This article sheds light on the newly proposed concept, Ultimate DataFlow for BigData, offering flexibility and reconfigurability in DeepAnalytics (DA) and MachineLearning (ML).

Some of the problems in DA and ML are bandwidth-bound, while the others are latency bound. The bandwidth-bound problems could, for many applications, be solved successfully using the FPGA-based DataFlow systems. The most critical latency-bound problems need a different in-memory computing technology. The Ultimate DataFlow implies elements of internal analog processing, which brings potentials, that are first presented, and then explained through an adequate elaboration.

POTENTIALS OF ULTIMATE DATAFLOW

The Ultimate DataFlow approach offers an effective solution for latency-bound problems, with the following improvement potentials over the FPGA-based solutions:

1. Up to about 2000 in speed up,
2. Up to about 200 in transistor count,
3. Up to about 80 (20x4) in power reduction, and
4. Up to about 2 in data precision.

With the above in mind, this position article covers the issues related to the potentials of the concept, using the programming model utilized in numerous FPGA-based DataFlow engines.

The existing DataFlow approaches are still far away from the ideal Ultimate DataFlow, but for specific Machine Learning and BigData applications, they still do achieve considerable speedups over ControlFlow machines, especially for some specific BigData problems. Consequently, the drive for new technology-supported architectural solutions is not too strong these days. However, for research missions, like those around Mubadala and IMEC, or Esperanto and IPSI, innovative solutions are badly needed.

What is good, however, about the existing DataFlow approaches, is that their DataFlow programming models are directly applicable to the case of the Ultimate DataFlow, so the continuity of existing experiences and the already developed software products could be maintained and improved.

For precision, the ratio 2x was quoted above, since the approach could benefit from approximate computing, due to its data format flexibility, as explained later. It is well suited also for *bloat16*, a possible new standard for tensor applications.

ELABORATIONS OF POTENTIALS OF ULTIMATE DATAFLOW

For power, the ratio 80x was quoted, for two reasons: First, ControlFlow machines like Intel or NVidia operate on up to 4GHz or even higher frequencies, while the current FPGAs operate on about 200MHz, which makes the ratio of about 20x, when it comes to dissipation. Second, an additional 4x one could get from operating at the 2x lower voltage. Both factors together result in the total improvement ratio of 80x.

For transistor count, the ratio of 200x was quoted, for the following reason: If one looks up the Intel microprocessor floor plan, one finds out that only about 0.5% of the area is dedicated to Arithmetic and Logic, making the above quoted 1/200x ratio.

For speedup, the frequently quoted numbers are: (a) 20x as the lowest number on speedup in recent publications of the authors of this article, (b) 200x as the highest number ever reported by the same authors, and (c) 2000x was quoted for the reason, that has nothing to do with existing DataFlow implementations, but has a lot to do with Ultimate DataFlow, as elaborated later; (d) even 20000x could be hoped for some applications, as explained next.

In Ultimate DataFlow, the speedup depends predominantly on the contribution of loops to the overall execution time:

- If loops contribute with more than 99.95% to the overall run time, then one can hope for a speedup of 2000x.
- If one looks up some of the applications on the list of current DataFlow successes in Machine Learning for BigData, one finds out that in many cases the contribution of loops was well over 99.995%, which is why the potentials of Ultimate DataFlow could reach even 20000x.

EXPLANATIONS OF THE ULTIMATE DATAFLOW CONCEPT

The Ultimate DataFlow, as a concept, is built on the following two premises (each one with 4 sub-premises):

1. Compiler does the following:

    a. Separates effectively spatial and temporal data, to satisfy the requirements of the Nobel Laureate Ilya Prigogine, since that action lowers the entropy of a computer system, meaning that the rest of the compiler could do a much better optimization job (lower entropy brings more order into the optimization process and consequently better optimization opportunities).

    b. Maps the execution graph in the way that makes sure that edges are of the minimal length, which brings consistency with the observations of Nobel Laureate Richard Feynman, related to trade-offs between speed and power.

    c. Enables one to go to a lower precision, for what is not of ultimate importance, and consequently to save on resources, that could be reinvested into what is of ultimate importance, following the approximate computing wisdom of Nobel Laureate Daniel Kahneman.

    d. Enables one to trade between latency and precision, which, in latency-tolerant applications, brings more precision with less resources, and in latency-intolerant applications, brings less latency, in exchange for a lower precision, thus following the wisdom of Nobel Laureate Tom Hunt, and analogies with his findings related to birth, life, reproduction, and death of cells.

None of the FPGA-based dataflow compilers, as far as we know, does any of the above.

2.   Hardware consists of the following:

   a.   An analog DataPath of the honeycomb structure, to which one could effectively map the execution graphs corresponding to loops. Analog functional units could leverage low-precision computation.

   b.   A DataPath clocked at a much lower frequency, and hopefully not clocked at all, if the analog path is not unacceptably long, so it is literally the voltage difference between input and output, that moves data through the execution graph.

   c.   A digital memory is on the side of the DataPath, so that computing parameters could be kept non-volatile, and temporary results could be stored more effectively.

   d.   The I/O connecting the host and the dataflow is much faster.

Unfortunately, FPGAs offer none of the above today! Consequently, the FPGA technology is today only the least bad solution on the road to the ultimate goal!

In conclusion, the benefits of the Ultimate DataFlow approach will become fully achievable only once the semiconductor and the compiler technologies become capable of supporting the above specified two sets of requirements. References leading to the above conclusion are spreading four decades of the research of one of the co-authors (Flynn et al., 2013; Hurson & Milutinovic, 2017; Jovanović & Milutinović, 2012; Milutinovic et al., 1987; Milutinovic, 1995; Milutinović et al., 2015; Trifunovic & Milutinovic, 2016; Trifunovic et al., 2015; Trobec et al., 2016). The future is in in-memory analog AI accelerators, as explained in the recent effort of (Cosemans et al., 2019). Another viewpoint of the related issues could be found in (Reuther et al., 2019).

EXPERIENCES IN EDUCATION AND RESEARCH

About 4000 students world-wide have used the dataflow machine at the Mathematical Institute of the Serbian Academy of Sciences (https://maxeler.mi.sanu.ac.rs/), and these students come from universities like: MIT, Harvard, Princeton, Yale, Columbia, NYU, Purdue, University of Indiana in Bloomington, University of Michigan in Ann Arbor, Ohio State, Georgia Tech, CMU, FIU, FAU, etc (in the USA), ETH, EPFL (in Switzerland), UNIWIE, TUWIEN (in Austria), Karlsruhe, Heidelberg (in Germany), Manchester, Bristol, Cambridge, Oxford (in England), and, of course, from the leading schools of Belgrade: ETF, MATF, FON, FFH. They attended the hands-on workshops of classes for one, two, three, or six credits.

As far as research efforts with students, they were asked to compare a real ControlFlow Multicore, a real Controlflow ManyCore, a real FPGA-based DataFlow, and a theoretical Ultimate DataFlow machine based on an analog Sea-of-Gates architecture. Especially intensive was the students-oriented research effort at the University of Indiana, since early 2016, through courses on DataFlow SuperComputing (for BigData) and Software Engineering Management (with Creativity Methods), plus through the undergraduate research effort called UROC.

Two UROC students have contributed significantly to programming that demonstrates the potentials of Ultimate DataFlow. Students in Siena, Salerno, Barcelona, and Valencia contributed to the development of related concepts.

The Belgrade University graduate and undergraduate students helped determine the best distribution of transistors over resources, for a possible effort based on a 100 billion transistor chip.

CONCLUSION

Ultimate DataFlow concept is a secure bet when it comes to the future of supercomputing, but is still unreachable due to the limitations of available hardware.

ACKNOWLEDGMENT

The authors are thankful to Lars Zetterberg of KTH, Henry Markram of EPFL, Roberto Giorgi of the University of Siena, and Anton Kos of the University of Ljubljana, for their eyes opening discussions related to the topic of ICT.

REFERENCES

Cosemans, S., Verhoef, B., Doevenspeck, J., Papistas, I. A., Catthoor, F., Debacker, P., ... Verkest, D. (2019, December). Towards 10000TOPS/W DNN Inference with Analog in-Memory Computing–A Circuit Blueprint, Device Options and Requirements. In *2019 IEEE International Electron Devices Meeting (IEDM)* (pp. 22-2). IEEE. 10.1109/IEDM19573.2019.8993599

Flynn, M. J., Mencer, O., Milutinovic, V., Rakocevic, G., Stenstrom, P., Trobec, R., & Valero, M. (2013). Moving from petaflops to petadata. *Communications of the ACM*, *56*(5), 39–42. doi:10.1145/2447976.2447989

Fortes, J. A. (1986, January). A High-Level Systolic Architecture for GaAs. In *Proc. 19th Ann. Hawaii Int'l Conf. System Sciences* (pp. 253-258). Academic Press.

Fuchs, H. J., Whelan, D., Jackson, J., H. Niimi, Y., Goncalves, N., & Gharachorloo, N. (1981, January 1). *A million transistor systolic array graphics engine*. Retrieved October 11, 2020, from https://link. springer.com/article/10.1007/BF00932064

Hurson, A. R., & Milutinovic, V. (2017). *Creativity in Computing and DataFlow SuperComputing*. Academic Press.

Jovanović, Ž., & Milutinović, V. (2012). FPGA accelerator for floating-point matrix multiplication. *IET Computers & Digital Techniques*, *6*(4), 249–256. doi:10.1049/iet-cdt.2011.0132

Milenkovic, A., & Milutinovic, V. (2000, August). Cache injection: A novel technique for tolerating memory latency in bus-based SMPs. In *European Conference on Parallel Processing* (pp. 558-566). Springer. 10.1007/3-540-44520-X_76

Milutinovic, D., Milutinovic, V., & Soucek, B. (1987). *The honeycomb architecture*. Academic Press.

Milutinovic, V. (1988). *A Comparison of Suboptimal Detection Algorithms*. Suboptimal Algorithms for Data Analytics.

Milutinovic, V. (1995). *Splitting Spatial and Temporal Localities for Entropy Minimiation*. Academic Press.

Milutinovic, V. (1996). The split temporal/spatial cache: Initial performance analysis. *SCIzzL*, *5*(March), 63–69.

Milutinovic, V., Fura, D., & Helbig, W. (1986). An introduction to GaAs microprocessor architecture for VLSI. *Computer, 19*(3), 30–42. doi:10.1109/MC.1986.1663177

Milutinović, V., Salom, J., Trifunović, N., & Giorgi, R. (2015). *Guide to dataflow supercomputing*. Springer Nature. doi:10.1007/978-3-319-16229-4

Reuther, A., Michaleas, P., Jones, M., Gadepally, V., Samsi, S., & Kepner, J. (2019). Survey and benchmarking of machine learning accelerators. doi:10.1109/HPEC.2019.8916327

Techpowerup. (2020, September 16). *NVIDIA GeForce GTX 1080 Ti Specs*. Retrieved October 11, 2020, from https://www.techpowerup.com/gpu-specs/geforce-gtx-1080-ti.c2877

Trifunovic, N., & Milutinovic, V. (2016). The Appgallery. Maxeler. com for BigData SuperComputing. *Journal of Big Data*.

Trifunovic, N., Milutinovic, V., Salom, J., & Kos, A. (2015). Paradigm shift in big data supercomputing: Dataflow vs. controlflow. *Journal of Big Data, 2*(1), 1–9. doi:10.118640537-014-0010-z

Trobec, R., Vasiljevic, R., Tomasevic, M., & Milutinovic, V. (2016). *Interconnection Networks for PetaComputing*. Academic Press.

Williams, A. (2019, August 21). *Largest Chip Ever Holds 1.2 Trillion Transistors*. Retrieved October 11, 2020, from https://hackaday.com/2019/08/21/largest-chip-ever-holds-1-2-trillion-transistors/

Xilinx. (2003, December 8). *Revolutionary Architecture for the Next Generation Platform FPGAs*. Retrieved October 11, 2020, from https://m.eet.com/media/1081699/XIL.PDF

Conclusion

A SUMMARY OF EMERGING APPLICATIONS USING BIG DATA, COMPLEX ALGORITHMS, AND NEEDING ACCELERATION

If applications deal with Big Data, use complex algorithms, and need acceleration, the best solution is to utilize is: Hybrid Architectures (Kotlar, 2018; Milutinovic, 2015), based on a Control Flow host (Grujic, 1996; Milutinovic, 1996; Trobec, 2016), and a Data Flow accelerator (Flynn, 2013; Milenkovic, 2000; Milutinovic, 1987).

Examples of such applications could be found in a number of emerging fields: in scientific computing (e.g., Stojanovic, 2013, 2017), in digital economy (e.g., Knezevic, 2000. Milutinovic, 2016), in artificial intelligence (e.g., Antognetti, 1991; Furlan, 2012), and in data mining (Antognetti, 1991; Kotlar, 2018).

A selected subset of the above-mentioned application was selected and presented in a coherent way (Stojmenovic, 2012). Each contribution was presented in a way that shows clearly why it needs acceleration. In some cases, in addition to the acceleration, other important requirements are also placed before the programmers: Low Power, Small Volume, High Precision, etc.

SUMMARY

This book has been proven useful as a secondary textbook for master level classes, open also to senior undergraduate students, as well as Ph.D. students. Examples of emerging applications is where students look for inspiration related to their homework assignments.

This book also has strong elements of a monograph, since the emerging applications, as well as the related Control Flow and Data Flow concepts, where chosen from the past research of the two editors, which was sponsored by the industry of the USA and the European collaborative research projects.

This book also has a value coming from the fact that it synergizes the teaching experiences of the editors and the research experiences of their colleagues form universities in the USA and Europe, where they delivered lectures, but also were able to learn a lot about the state-of-the-art research of their hosts.

Veljko Milutinović
Indiana University in Bloomington, USA

REFERENCES

Antognetti, P. (1991). *Neural networks: concepts, applications and implementations*. Prentice Hall Professional Technical Reference.

Flynn, M. J., Mencer, O., Milutinovic, V., Rakocevic, G., Stenstrom, P., Trobec, R., & Valero, M. (2013). Moving from petaflops to petadata. *Communications of the ACM, 56*(5), 39–42.

Furlan, B., Nikolic, B., & Milutinovic, V. (2012, September). A survey of intelligent question routing systems. In *2012 6th IEEE International Conference Intelligent Systems* (pp. 14-20). IEEE.

Grujic, A., Tomasevíc, M., & Milutinovic, V. (1996). A simulation study of hardware-oriented DSM approaches. *IEEE Parallel & Distributed Technology Systems & Applications, 4*(1), 74–83.

Knezevic, P., Radnovic, B., Nikolic, N., Jovanovic, T., Milanov, D., Nikolic, M., ... Schewel, J. (2000, January). The architecture of the Obelix-an improved internet search engine. In *Proceedings of the 33rd Annual Hawaii International Conference on System Sciences* (pp. 11-pp). IEEE.

Kotlar, M., & Milutinovic, V. (2018, June). Comparing controlflow and dataflow for tensor calculus: speed, power, complexity, and MTBF. In *International Conference on High Performance Computing* (pp. 329-346). Springer.

Milenkovic, A., & Milutinovic, V. (2000, August). Cache injection: A novel technique for tolerating memory latency in bus-based SMPs. In *European Conference on Parallel Processing* (pp. 558-566). Springer.

Milutinovic, D., Milutinovic, V., & Soucek, B. (1987). *The honeycomb architecture*. Academic Press.

Milutinovic, V. (1996). *Surviving the design of a 200MHz RISC microprocessor*. IEEE Computer Society Press.

Milutinovic, V., & Salom, J. (2016). *Mind Genomics: A Guide to Data-Driven Marketing Strategy*. Springer.

Milutinović, V., Salom, J., Trifunović, N., & Giorgi, R. (2015). *Guide to dataflow supercomputing*. Springer Nature.

Stojanović, S., Bojić, D., & Milutinović, V. (2013). Solving Gross Pitaevskii equation using dataflow paradigm. *The IPSI BgD Transactions on Internet Research, 17*.

Stojkovic, I., Jelisavcic, V., Milutinovic, V., & Obradovic, Z. (2017, August). Fast Sparse Gaussian Markov Random Fields Learning Based on Cholesky Factorization. In IJCAI (pp. 2758-2764). Academic Press.

Stojmenović, I., & Milutinović, V. (2012). How to write research articles in computing and engineering disciplines. *Singidunum Journal of Applied Sciences, 9*(1), 42-50.

Trobec, R., Vasiljević, R., Tomašević, M., Milutinović, V., Beivide, R., & Valero, M. (2016). Interconnection networks in petascale computer systems: A survey. *ACM Computing Surveys, 49*(3), 1–24.

Appendix: Birds of a Feather

In this section, the editors give room to selected researchers to share thir specific views, of current importance.

Editors, Veljko Milutinović and Miloš Kotlar

IS SUPERCOMPUTING A MATTER OF SUPERPOWERS?

Massimo De Santo, University of Salerno, Italy

It's a very long time since I first met supercomputing. It was in far 1987 when I started trafficking with "transputers", the final result of a PanEuropean research effort aimed to develop the basic building block of a fully reconfigurable and scalable parallel computer [1]. I was a young Ph.D. student working to something that appeared like an impossible dream: managing the complexity of handwritten character recognition, with a machine powerful enough to dominate the ever-growing number of matrixes implied by our newborn thinning algorithms. We worked hard for two exhausting months with no results. The basic idea of "transputers supercomputing" was that the single transputer represented a complete Von Neumann autonomous unit and that you can put together and assemble in a fully customizable architecture a variable number of units, connecting them through four high-speed links. [2] This idea in the following years would be subsumed in the "multicore approach".

We tried and tried, increasing the number of transputers but our so hardly devised algorithms did not converge. We added more and more power with no results.

As always happens in novels, and sometimes in real life, the solution came by one night sudden "illumination": I visualized the flow of information in my mind and clearly realized that the problem was in the way we uploaded and shared data among transputers and not (only) in the sheer number of them.

Simply changing the shape of the links could be the boost we needed. So, while my tremble hands re-arranged the tiny connectors of these "transistor computers", to finally achieve success, I learned that supercomputing was not (only) a matter of brute force but instead a new thinking question [3].

"Power is nothing without Control" claims one very famous advertising of the past [4]. In the following years, my research interests changed. Among other things, I explored the multimedia world, where image processing is a fundamental step and the ability of supercomputing a lifesaving need. In the last ten years, I landed on the multidisciplinary world of ICT for Cultural Heritage where I met Big Data and non-relational databases, Ontologies, and Neural Networks [5]. In each and every of these research realms, I envisioned the needs of power and control, the lesson I learned such a long time ago. Finally, I can say that generalization and multi-disciplinarism have always been the leading principles in my experience with supercomputing. Directions that I'm going to use again, I'm sure, in my future years in this beautiful realm that is Computer Science Research.

References

[1] Hey, A. J. (1990). Supercomputing with transputers—past, present and future. *ACM SIGARCH Computer Architecture News*, *18*(3b), 479-489.

[2] Chianese, A.; De Santo, M.; Vento M. "TAP: Trasputer Array Processor." *Iasted Symphosium on Computers and their Applications* Zurigo Acta Press Pag.55-58 ISBN:9780000000002

[3] https://www.pirelli.com/global/en-ww/life/power-is-nothing-without-control-celebrates-25-years

[4] Chianese, A., Cordella, L. P., De Santo, M., Marcelli, A., & Vento, M. (1988, January). A preliminary approach to the design and evaluation of a reconfigurable architecture for computer vision. In *9th International Conference on Pattern Recognition* (pp. 724-725). IEEE Computer Society.

[5] Clarizia, F., Colace, F., De Santo, M., Lombardi, M., Pascale, F., Santaniello, D., & Tuker, A. (2020). A multilevel graph approach for rainfall forecasting: A preliminary study case on London area. *Concurrency and Computation: Practice and Experience*, *32*(8), e5289.

DATA SCIENCE TECHNOLOGIES AND APPLICATIONS

Borko Furht, Florida Atlantic University, Boca Raton, Florida, USA

We recently received an award from U.S. National Science Foundation on the topic: A Graduate Traineeship in Data Science Technologies and Applications. This award is $ 2.4 millions for 5-year project [1].

Data science and analytics is an emerging transdisciplinary area comprising computing, statistics, and various application domains including medicine, nursing, industry and business applications among others. A significant shortcoming of the current graduate curricula in the U.S. is that scientists and engineers are well trained in their own areas of specialty but lack the integrative knowledge needed for new scientific discoveries and industry applications made possible by data science and analytics. The National Science Foundation Research Traineeship award to Florida Atlantic University will address these shortcomings by proposing a new model of convergence education through experimental learning. Transdisciplinary education brings integration of different disciplines in a harmonious manner to construct new knowledge and uplift the student to higher domains of cognitive abilities and sustained knowledge and skills. The traineeship anticipates providing a unique and comprehensive training opportunity for one hundred sixty graduate students (160), including forty five (45) funded trainees. Thirty faculty members from five colleges and ten departments will participate in the program. The program has the potential to have a significant impact on training practices for future data science professionals.

Appendix:

Primary training elements of the curriculum will include the development of normalization courses, the creation of different testbeds for the various application domains, boot-camps, in-depth elective courses, and professional workshops. Normalization courses will be used to address various background of students entering the program. The convergent research themes will focus on three data science and analytics areas: (i) medical and healthcare applications, (ii) industry applications, and (iii) data science and AI technologies. To address these, the goal is to create a curriculum for graduate students in data science and analytics, where each course will be developed by at least two faculty members from two different disciplines. In order to integrate research and training, multiple testbeds for different application domains will be developed in a newly created Data Science and Artificial Intelligence Laboratory. Each testbed, which relates to a research project, will include a computer platform, software tools, and a set of learning modules. Research projects will be formulated jointly with industry partners who are members of the NSF Industry/University Cooperative Research Center CAKE at FAU [1]. The program will produce graduates with technical depth [2] and understanding of data science technologies and applications.

References

[1] http://cake.fiu.edu/
[2] Blagojević, V., Bojić, D., Bojović, M., Cvetanović, M., Đorđević, J., Đurđević, Đ., ... & Milutinović, V. (2017). A systematic approach to generation of new ideas for PhD research in computing. In *Advances in computers* (Vol. 104, pp. 1-31). Elsevier.

HIGH-PERFORMANCE COMPUTING

Violeta Holmes, Huddersfield University, England, UK

High-performance Computing (HPC) and Big Data are technologies vital for advancements in science, business and industry [Holmes, 2016]. HPC combines computing power of supercomputers and computer clusters, and parallel and distributed processing techniques for solving complex computational problems. An HPC system can be defined as a collection of the world's most powerful supercomputers [Top500], or as any computer system larger than a regular desktop PC used for modelling and simulation. They range from a desktop computing with an accelerator, through clusters of servers and data centres, up to high-end custom supercomputers. HPC is used typically to process numerical and largely static data, whilst Big Data requires processing of various data, both structured and unstructured, such as text, geospatial and numerical data. HPC and e-infrastructure are drivers of economic growth and societal well-being. Modelling and simulation have come to complement theory and experiment as a key component of the scientific method, and many of our scientific findings and technological advances rely on models simulated on high performance computers. "It costs £500,000 to do each physical test of a car crash, and it's not repeatable. It costs £12 to run a virtual simulation of a car crash, and its fully repeatable, so it can be used to optimise the design of a vehicle." Andy Searle, Head of Computer Aided Engineering, Jaguar Land Rover. The digital revolution of the past two decades has led to unprecedented demands for high-performance data-processing systems. More recently, real-time HPC systems have appeared which can assist humans in instantaneous decision taking. Combining HPC computational models with real-time data in order to aid in urgent decision making, such as a part of disaster response, moves HPC well beyond traditional computational workloads [Brown, 2019].

The performance of HPC systems is increasing, as the Top500 list demonstrates year-on year, approaching exascale, capable of calculating at least 10exp18 floating point operations per second (1 exaFLOPS). The new top system Fugaku's (Top500 June 2020) is capable of high computational performance of 415.5 petaFLOPS. The demand for computational power is rising at an even greater rate. It is anticipated that the HPC will continue to be a vital technology, and demand for greater computing power will continue. Synergy of AI, HPC and Big Data paradigms will enable new insights and ways the research and development is undertaken.

References

[Brown, 2019] Brown, N. "Workshop on HPC for Urgent Decision Making (UrgentHPC)", 2019, SC19, Denver, USA.

[Holmes, 2016] Holmes, V. & Newall, M., 2016, "HPC and the Big Data challenge", In: Safety and Reliability. 36, 3, p. 213-224 12 p. [Top500] TOP500.org

APPLICATIONS OF SUPERCOMPUTING FOR INFRASTRUCTURE OF THE FUTURE

Ayhan Irfanoglu and Arun Prakash, Purdue University, West Lafayette, Indiana, USA

From early day mechanical calculators to modern day supercomputers and to potentially quantum computers of tomorrow, computing has seen an explosive growth in almost all fields for human endeavor. In one generation we moved from slide rules and punch cards to running simulations on advanced supercomputers. On many fronts, the separation between real world and its simulation has narrowed to such a level that we can now transfuse them in various forms such as augmented reality, digital twins, real-time integrity monitoring, active control and adaptation.

In the field of Structural Engineering, computing has had a big impact on how engineers design and analyze structures such as buildings, bridges, dams, and really every infrastructure facility that we have come to rely upon. This impact is evident in how the skylines of our major cities around the World have evolved over the past few decades with ever taller or longer structures designed and constructed with immense engineering precision. Advances in computer modelling and simulation have allowed engineers to take on the challenges of designing and constructing such structures with more confidence than ever before (Ewins, 2016). Large infrastructure projects such as tall buildings and iconic bridges have to be analyzed and designed to withstand a multitude of hazards, both natural (such as earthquakes, floods, windstorms) and man-made (such as impact, blast, fire). For example, engineers have been able to fine tune the dynamic response of structures to such threats by leveraging non-linear structural response using high-fidelity computer models which take ever shortening time. What now takes days to run on the most powerful supercomputer clusters of today were impossibilities yesterday. Tomorrow, they might need only an instant.

The ability to conduct such computational analyses with confidence has also had a great impact on higher education (Fernández et al., 2019). In Structural Engineering, education has evolved from the study of linear structural systems to deep dives into how the laws of physics and mechanics come together to hold our structures together and how to ensure that the computer models reflect this reality with reasonable and justifiable assumptions to provide not only just the best estimates but also associated uncertainties.

Structures of the future are likely to be even more tightly bound with computing where they are not only continuously monitored using sensors but also actively respond and adapt to threats, environmental conditions, and use alterations based on computer models that can optimize their behavior. Even today, there are instances around the world of such 'actively controlled' structures and this trend is likely to grow. With the explosion of big data, machine learning and high-fidelity modeling, simulation and control (Ichimura et al., 2020) of our structures, it is not unfathomable that the infrastructure of tomorrow will be ubiquitously instrumented, adaptable and resilient to almost any threat they face. For example, the stationary structures we are so used to could become controlled shape-shifting structures, with mechanisms that could be activated to increase safety margins when threats develop or, simply, to improve the utility of the structure for its occupants. To overcome the challenges of future we need strong collaboration between different branches of engineering, material and environmental sciences, computational sciences and other fields. While the experts may have their own domain-specific sandpits in their proverbial backyards, the common playground where challenges will be studied and solutions explored together is going to be the computational environment the supercomputers will afford them.

References

Álvaro Fernández, Camino Fernández, José Ángel Miguel-Dávila, Miguel Ángel Conde, Vicente Matellán, Supercomputers to improve the performance in higher education: A review of the literature, Computers & Education, Volume 128, 2019, Pages 353-364.

Tsuyoshi Ichimura, Kohei Fujita, Takuma Yamaguchi, Muneo Hori, Lalith Wijerathne, and Naonori Ueda. 2020. Fast Multi-Step Optimization with Deep Learning for Data-Centric Supercomputing. In Proceedings of the 2020 4th International Conference on High Performance Compilation, Computing and Communications (HP3C 2020). Association for Computing Machinery, New York, NY, USA, 7–13. DOI:https://doi.org/10.1145/3407947.3407949

Ewins, DJ, Exciting vibrations: the role of testing in an era of supercomputers and uncertainties, Meccanica, volume 51, number 12, pages 3241-3258, 2016.

PHOTONICS AND SUPERCOMPUTING

Brana Jelenkovic, Serbian Academy of Sciences and Arts, Belgrade, Serbia

Optics have proved to be the best means for ultrafast data transmission, and data processing. There are number of advantages of optics and photonics vs VLSI technology. Optical components have low transmission loss and large bandwidth, they are immune to electromagnetic interference, capable of sending signals to adjacent fibers without interference and cross talks. Photons have been extensively applied in proof-in-principle demonstrations of supercomputing. Optical data processing can also be done in parallel, but faster and less expensive.

Photonics in computers meant, until recently, replacement of a transistor as the basic computing element, with all optical elements for switching and logic. But, as long as the underlying technology for optical circuits is the silicon photonics, there are still remaining issues, how to avoid light-to-electronics and electronics-to-light conversions in the design of all-optical computers. The speed of optical processing is limited by the speed of electronic input and output. Under such approach and technology, the best that optics can do to be useful, is to accomplish the same goals as digital electronics, reducing speed energy consumption and heat generation, in a more efficient manner [1]

Recently, Chinese researchers presented a scalable chip, that did not rely on silicon photonics [2]. Here, photons contained in the optical source are treated as individual computation carriers like the current in electronic computers. Their optical computer works differently from standard ones, it cannot be programmed, but was able to solve the problem in a way that suggests future versions could outpace even the fastest supercomputers. Built-in photonic computer was able to efficiently solve complex computer science challenge, called the subset sum problem. This problem is hard to solve efficiently in time with conventional computers. Because their approach could fairly simply be scaled up to much bigger instances of the problem, authors believe that they invention is a step towards "photonic supremacy," mimicking the term "quantum supremacy" used to denote the point at which quantum computers outperform classical ones. Remarkably, for developing the three-dimensional waveguide network for their chip, they used rather simple, cheaper technology, based on a femto-second laser direct writing technique: the network of wave-guides channel photons through the processor as well as a series of junctions that get the light beams to split, pass each other, or converge.

Note that some claimed advantages of photons vs electrons, that photons do not interact with one another and that light beams may pass through one another without distorting the information, were challenged recently in the work showing photons interactions in strong nonlinear media [3].

References

[1] H. John Caulfield and Shlomi Dolev, *Why future supercomputing requires optics*, Nature Photonics **4**, pages261–263 (2010).

[2] Xiao-Yun Xu *et al.*, *A scalable photonic computer solving the subset sum problem*, Sci. Adv. 6 1, (2020).

[3] S. H. Cantu, A. V. Venkatramani, W. Xu, Leo Zhou, B. Jelenković, M. D. Lukin and V. Vuletić, *Repulsive photons in a quantum nonlinear medium*, Nature Physics 16, 921–925 (2020)

SUPERCOMPUTING ESSENTIALS

Aleksandar Kavcic, CMU, Pittsburgh, Pennsylvania, USA

The second half of the 20th century spurred tremendous advances in data storage technology. The storage of choice were magnetic data storage devices (tapes, floppies, discs). However, today we are witnessing a shift away from magnetic storage to solid state storage. Mobile phones and many laptops use solid state storage devices. Magnetic devices are still used to store large volumes of data (cloud storage). Magnets definitely have some advantages, since they are far more stable over time, but they have one big disadvantage, they require moving parts to magnetize the medium and read it back. Solid state (electronic) devices seem to be winning the market battle in hand-held devices because they are smaller and shock-resistant. The question is whether magnets can come back. If technology can be invented that could magnetize small magnetic domains without the need to utilize moving parts (spindles, motors, etc.) magnets could win. Future will tell. In the related research and development processes, creativity in science and engineering is of a crucial importance [Blagojevic2017, Kavcic2020].

References

[Kavcic2020] https://patents.justia.com/inventor/aleksandar-kavcic

[Blagojevic2017] Blagojević, V., Bojić, D., Bojović, M., Cvetanović, M., Đorđević, J., Đurđević, Đ., ... & Milutinović, V. (2017). A systematic approach to generation of new ideas for PhD research in computing. In Advances in computers (Vol. 104, pp. 1-31). Elsevier.

1988-2020: A JOURNEY FROM ATOMS TO TRANSISTORS WITH GLOBAL IMPACT

Gerhard Klimeck, Purdue University, West Lafayette, Indiana, USA

1988 Supriyo Datta introduced me to Quantum Transport in an electrical engineering graduate class at Purdue [Datta]. It was fascinating to begin to understand devices that are defined on critical dimensions of 5nm; AND there was a real chance that Moore's law could scale to such dimensions. Datta established the Non-Equilibrium Green Function (NEGF) methodology as a sound foundational basis for understanding electronic devices [Datta05]. However, "everyone" in the field believed that NEGF is too complex and computationally expensive to be useful. Indeed, the practical use of NEGF and wide dissemination required dramatic breakthroughs as well as technical innovations of the type categorized by Blagojevic [Blagojevic] that I am hoping to highlight here.

1994-98 at Texas Instruments within the first industrial "Nanoelectronics" research group our team was charged with accurately predicting and optimizing performances of real resonant tunneling diodes based on a non-parameterized, physics-based theory. Ultimate success while using NEGF was enabled by three breakthroughs: 1) we developed multi-scale physics or matrix partitioning approaches to treat the critically important, spatially extended contacts and the central device with the required accuracy on equal footing [Klimeck95, Lake97]. 2) we demonstrated that the typical view of a continuum matter must be abandoned, and an atomistic device representation is required [Bowen97]. 3) we developed an intuitive interactive graphical user interface (GUI) that let experimentalists explore the design space in seconds and over the lunch hour, and the GUI was dynamically generated from the internal, rapidly changing model requirements [Klimeck98]. Alongside these breakthroughs we pursued somewhat plannable technical developments. We developed accurate atomistic tight-binding representations of III-V materials, adopted efficient algorithms for partial matrix inversions from other fields, developed memory conserving meshing techniques, efficient spectral analysis techniques, and object-oriented recursive techniques (in C, F77, F90, before C++ was stable) to make NEGF feasible for realistically extended quantum devices. On state-of-the-art workstations our NEMO software delivered results to experimentalists interactively in seconds and in batch model over lunch or over-night. High fidelity, foundational, theoretical questions required a few days runtime. While we were strongly encouraged to use supercomputers these turned out to be useless due to a lack of consistent and continuous access. We could get answers faster on a network of workstations than with supercomputers.

In 1998 I joined the High-Performance-Computing group at NASA, JPL, Caltech, where Thomas Sterling was building the first Beowulf clusters [Sterling97]. These machines were despised by the general HPC community but offered affordable and accessible supercomputing for engineers. Given their availability we now faced the challenge to build scalable application software rapidly that could demonstrate the superior FLOPs/$ capabilities of the new cluster computers. Atomistic nanoelectronic modeling in 3D (NEMO-3D) required intense sparse matrix-vector multiplications and by 2000 we demonstrated the first multi-million electronic structure calculations for arbitrary 3D quantum dot geometries [Klimeck02]. Given the need to enable application engineers to utilize modeling software we also prototyped web-based tool deployments with WIGLAF (A Web Interface Generator and Legacy Application Façade) [Cwik02]. However, there was no institutional drive or need to make this a massive effort.

In 1995 Mark Lundstrom at Purdue began to create the Purdue University Network Computing Hub (PUNCH) which offered web-form-based access to sophisticated simulation tools [Kapadia97]. The concept was very innovative, created its own infrastructures when there were no open source web servers and enabled the rapid sharing of research-based simulation tools. Experimentalists ran the existing tools to explain experiments and faculty used the tools for teaching. The user experience, however, was more like what your bank still offers you today in 2020 in terms of data visualization – you click a button, retrieve some data, and if you want do something with it, you need to download it. Engineers need end-to-end integrated simulation and data integrations to pursue concepts and ideas rapidly as our NEMO work had demonstrated.

In 2002 The US National Science Foundation (NSF) was open to receive a proposal to take PUNCH to the national and global level and to support the newly created nanoHUB. Mark Lundstrom, Supriyo Datta, and I envisioned global impact of simulation tools in research and education through sharing of research-based codes with a team of 6 Universities and with very strong Purdue support. While web-portals were hip at the time, we were facing dramatic challenge after winning the proposal and creating the Network for Computational Nanotechnology. On the technical side we needed to overcome three significant challenges: 1) web middleware that could host fully interactive Graphical User Interfaces to powerful simulation engines (Rick Kennell – [Middleware]) on long latency networks, 2) a system that enables device-oriented graduate students without web or GUI knowledge to create intuitive and interactive GUIs rapidly - developed by Michael McLennan with the Rappture framework [Kennell10] and 3) reliable middleware that can run jobs on remote clusters reliably [Zentner11]. While the technical problems were addressed rapidly in 2005-08 the social perception challenges continue to persist. We continued to face perceptions that "portals cannot support large scale education", "portals cannot be used for (real) research", and "What is the benefit for a researcher to share their 'crown jewel' simulation tools?". We showed rapid deployment of research codes and rapid adoption into classrooms (6 months adoption rate from publication to first time use in classrooms) and we showed significant impact on research [Madhavan13]. I kept telling my audiences that these tools are the "real publications" since they enable the duplication of published simulation results. Finally, in 2016 the Web of Science began to list nanoHUB tools as proper publications and Google Scholar followed suit. I believe it is fair to say that we created the first end-to-end user scientific computing computing cloud. Today nanoHUB has about 20,000 annual simulation users and over 2 million visitors that come for lectures and tutorial on nanotechnology.

In parallel to the nanoHUB work my research group continued to push the NEMO tool suites into full 3D quantum transport for realistic devices [Steiger11]. We won a Gordon Bell Prize honorable mention to create the first peta-scale engineering code in 2011 [Luisier11], deployed NEMO-based apps into nanoHUB and various Industry partners helped us to get us to a stage where NEMO5 is now the state-of-the art quantum transport engine. Industry has embraced the use of massively parallel HPC for device simulation and continues to partner with Academia to bring in the latest approaches and software developments. Today Moore's law has reached the point of critical device lengths of 5nm and NEMO helps the semiconductor Industry [Stettler19] to design today's transistors and is being commercialized with Silvaco [Silvaco].

In summary my journey has taken me from intellectual curiosity of what might happen in 5nm quantum devices to today's 5nm transistors. This journey involved somewhat plannable technical developments and conceptual, non-predictable innovations. The teams I played with ultimately reached widespread global impact through dissemination beyond papers and HPC demonstrations. We continued to ask the bigger questions. I encourage any graduate student to ask themselves how to make a difference at any time of their career adventures. Making a difference for others defines the better questions, defines immediate technical challenges, and through collaborations these questions just might create a stroke of genius.

References

[Datta] Supriyo Datta, *Quantum Phenomena*:Modular Series on Solid State Devices, Vol 8 ISBN 978-0-201-07956-2

[Datta05] Supriyo Datta, *Quantum Transport: Atom to Transistor* ISBN 978-0-521-63145-7

[Blagojevic] V. Blagojevic, D. Bojić, M. Bojović, M. Cvetanović, J. Đorđević, Đ. Đurđević, B. Furlan, S. Gajin, Z. Jovanović, D. Milićev, V. Milutinović, B. Nikolić, J. Protić, M. Punt, Z. Radivojević, Ž. Stanisavljević, S. Stojanović, I. Tartalja, M. Tomašević, P. Vuletić, Chapter One - A Systematic Approach to Generation of New Ideas for PhD Research in Computing, Advances in Computers, Elsevier, Volume 104, 2017, Pages 1-31, ISSN 0065-2458, ISBN 9780128119556, https://doi.org/10.1016/bs.adcom.2016.09.001.

[Klimeck95] Gerhard Klimeck, Roger Lake, R. Bowen, William Frensley, Ted Moise, "Quantum Device Simulation with a Generalized Tunneling Formula" Appl. Phys. Lett., Vol. 67, p.2539 (1995); doi: 10.1063/1.114451

[Lake97] Roger Lake, Gerhard Klimeck, R. Bowen, Dejan Jovanovic,
"Single and multiband modeling of quantum electron transport through layered semiconductor devices", J. of Appl. Phys. 81, 7845 (1997);doi: 10.1063/1.365394

[Bowen97] R. Bowen, Gerhard Klimeck, Roger Lake, William Frensley, Ted Moise,
"Quantitative Simulation of A Resonant Tunneling Diode"
J. of Appl. Phys. 81, 3207 (1997); doi: 10.1063/1.364151

[Klimeck98] Gerhard Klimeck, Daniel Blanks, Roger Lake, R. Bowen, Chenjing Fernando, Manhua Leng, William Frensley, Dejan Jovanovic, Paul Sotirelis,
"Writing Research Software in a Large Group for the NEMO Project"
VLSI Design, Vol 8, p 79 (1998);doi:10.1155/1998/35374

[Sterling97] M. Patrick Goda, Thomas Sterling, and Gregoire S. Winckelmans, 1997 ACM Gordon Bell Prize.

[Klimeck02] Gerhard Klimeck, Fabiano Oyafuso, Timothy Boykin, R. Bowen, Paul Allmen,
"Development of a Nanoelectronic 3-D (NEMO 3-D) Simulator for Multimillion Atom Simulations and Its Application to Alloyed Quantum Dots (INVITED)"
Computer Modeling in Engineering and Science (CMES) Volume 3, No. 5 pp 601-642 (2002)

[Cwik02] Thomas A. Cwik, Akos Czikmantory, Gerhard Klimeck, Fabiano Oyafuso, Hook Hua, Edward S. Vinyard, "WIGLAF (A Web Interface Generator and Legacy Application Façade)", Oct. 8, 2002, NTR 30842, JPL New Technology Report.

[Kapadia97] N. H. Kapadia, J. A. B. Fortes and M. S. Lundstrom, "The Semiconductor Simulation Hub: a network-based microelectronics simulation laboratory," *Proceedings of the UGIM Symposium, Microelectronics Education for the Future. Twelfth Biennial University/Government/Industry Microelectronics Symposium (Cat. No.97CH36030)*, Rochester, NY, USA, 1997, pp. 72-77, doi: 10.1109/UGIM.1997.616686.

[Middleware] https://nanohub.org/about/middleware

[Kennell10] R. Kennell and M. McLennan, "HUBzero: A Platform for Dissemination and Collaboration in Computational Science and Engineering" in *Computing in Science & Engineering*, vol. 12, no. 02, pp. 48-53, 2010. doi: 10.1109/MCSE.2010.41

[Zentner11] Lynn Zentner, Steven Clark, Krishna Madhavan, Swaroop Shivarajapura, Victoria Farnsworth, Gerhard Klimeck, "Automated Grid-Probe System to Improve End-To-End Grid Reliability for a Science Gateway", Proceedings of TeraGrid 2011 conference. July 18-21, 2011, Salt Lake City, ACM proceedings, ISBN: 978-1-4503-0888-5;doi:10.1145/2016741.2016789

[Madhavan13] Krishna Madhavan, Michael Zentner, Gerhard Klimeck, "Learning and research in the cloud", Nature Nanotechnology 8, 786–789 (2013); doi:10.1038/nnano.2013.231

[Luisier11] Mathieu Luisier, Timothy Boykin, Gerhard Klimeck, "Atomistic nanoelectronic device simulations with sustained performances up to 1.44 PFlop/s", Finalist in ACP/IEEE in Gordon Bell Prize Competition (5 finalists) Supercomputing Nov. 2011, IEEE Proceedings, E-ISBN: 978-1-4503-0771-0

[Steiger11] Sebastian Steiger, Michael Povolotskyi, Hong-Hyun Park, Tillmann Kubis, Gerhard Klimeck, "NEMO5: A Parallel Multiscale Nanoelectronics Modeling Tool", IEEE Transactions on Nanotechnology, Vol. 10, Issue: 6, Page(s): 1464 - 1474, Nov. 2011; doi:10.1109/TNANO.2011.2166164

[Stettler19] M. Stettler *et al.*, "State-of-the-art TCAD: 25 years ago and today," *2019 IEEE International Electron Devices Meeting (IEDM)*, San Francisco, CA, USA, 2019, pp. 39.1.1-39.1.4, doi: 10.1109/IEDM19573.2019.8993451.

[BusinessWire18] https://www.businesswire.com/news/home/20180824005025/en/Silvaco-Purdue-Team-Bring-Scalable-Atomistic-TCAD

SUPERCOMPUTING APPLIED TO DIGITAL LIBRARIES

Hermann Maurer, Technical University of Graz, Austria

In the past there have been tremendous efforts to replace current libraries, small and large, by replacing them by digitized versions of the books. This provides some obvious advantage: (a) Books are accessible 24 hours a day, 7 days a week; (b) Searching in a digitized book is often supported by new techniques, from electronic table of contents to full text searching; (c) registered users may leave bookmarks to return later to the last point where they stopped reading, or to particularly interesting spots.

It is surprising that current technologies of digitization and upcoming methods due to the use of supercomputing have been largely ignored in digital libraries. For this reason, a team lead by Hermann Maurer introduced the concept of NID: Networked Interactive Digital material, see [1], and or first unfinished examples [2]. The main advantages of NID libraries are: Links can be made at any point to a page to some other spot in the same or a different book or some location on the WWW; conversely, WWW pages can point to any book in such a NID book; there is a group hierarchy: books can be read anonymously, or when one is registered notes and more can be added just for private purposes, or for a well-defined group of users, or for the public. Books use the IIIF format [3], so that books from some of the largest scientific libraries of the work, like Stanford, can be included, even on the same screen, next to a page from an NID book; annotations can be added anywhere, visible to well-defined groups and can be any multimedia material: text, sound, video, other books, experiments, etc. Discussion forums can be started on any point, and can be any multimedia material: text, sound, video, whole other books, experiments, e-Learning units., etc. Searching is supported whenever the book allows the production of readable PDF files.

There is one major weakness: while one link from any place to a book to any place of another book based on the same word is possible, this is almost impossible in a large digital library with say a million books: After all, in a library of one million books we are looking at some 10^{12} or even more words. Thus, linkage would not just require substantial effort, it would be entirely confusing for the reader, since most words on most pages will point to hundreds of other books. Thus, at the moment, only standard AI methods are used to support the manual creation of some meaningful links, excluding many words as much too "generic" are used, and continuously improved.

However, the real future is different. Users concentrating on a special issue such as "dangers of Lithium" should, by deep language analysis of million zillion of book pages point only to those that seem closely related (since they outline a similar attitude, or the exact opposite). This will only be possible by creative [4] using of advanced language understanding techniques not feasible without supercomputers.

Generalization [4]: By generalizing searching. **Specialization:** By concentrating on language analysis to understand the meaning of a segment of text**; Revitalization:** By extracting only pertinent words or phrases from book pages**; Implantation:** By replacing simple search techniques by methods based on true language understanding**; or Hybridization:** By combining reading with communication and combination with non-textual media.

References

[1] Libraries of Interactive Books as Powerful Tool for Information Communication (with Namik Delilovic and Bilal Zaka); Proceedings of ED-Media 2019, AACE (2019), 1353- 1359

[2] https://austria-forum.org/af/User/Maurer%20Hermann/NID-Servers

[3] https://iiif.io/

[4] Blagojević, V., Bojić, D., Bojović, M., Cvetanović, M., Đorđević, J., Đurđević, Đ., ... & Milutinović, V. (2017). A systematic approach to generation of new ideas for PhD research in computing. In Advances in computers (Vol. 104, pp. 1-31). Elsevier.

SUPERCOMPUTERS IN WEATHER AND ENVIRONMENTAL PREDICTION

Fedor Mesinger, Serbian Academy of Sciences and Arts, Belgrade, Serbia

As I write these words, in 2020, it is precisely 70 years since the publication of the paper by Charney, Fjørtoft, and von Neumann (1950), in which the first successful result of "numerical weather prediction" (NWP) was shown to general public. Of course this was only possible following many crucial steps that made this "successful result" achievable (e.g., Phillips 2001). Success of the forecasts made was understandably rather limited, and they were not really forecasts, being produced after the fact and not in real time.

Although the progress in usability and power of computers took off and continued until this day unimpeded, progress in the skill of NWP was hardly visible for at least the next two decades or so. Perhaps the main reason was that while the basic fluid equations were well understood, solving these equations for the atmosphere presented problems beyond those of discrete mathematics. Observations of the basic atmospheric variables are available only at some points; and when they are somehow mapped to a discrete set of grid points, what the grid point values represent is not obvious. Impact of processes for which fundamental equations are not available, such as clouds, turbulent transfers, need to be represented, "parameterized", in terms of variables for which we do have fundamental equations.

A discovery of Arakawa (1966), in its later more general form referred to as "a stunning and somewhat mysterious achievement" by Salmon (2004), was a major milestone in approaches to the design of what is today named "dynamical cores" of NWP models. But many other steps enabled continued progress, led to aptly referred to by Bauer, Thorpe and Brunet (2015) as "The quiet revolution of numerical weather prediction". The ever more powerful supercomputers were a crucial ingredient enabling that progress. Numerous major NWP centers today use systems that execute computations beyond petaflop (10^{15} floating point operations) per second.

With the dependence of major NWP and now environmental prediction centers thus on cutting edge supercomputers, and participation of large teams of scientists and code specialists in the design of prediction models, an unavoidable feature of major centers is that decisions on basic dynamical core approaches are made years before results of the road taken are known.

A good illustration of how this can be problematic might be the abandonment of the so-called eta vertical coordinate by a major NWP center in 2006, even though later on following a not too complex removal of its problem discovered by Gallus and Klemp (2000), done by (Mesinger et al. 2012, see also Mesinger and Veljovic 2017) a result was obtained perhaps just about extraordinary. In a situation of a major impact of the Rocky Mountains topographic barrier, the Eta model members driven by those of the European Centre for Medium-Range Weather Forecasts (EC) ensemble members, repeatedly achieved better 250 hPa jet-stream wind placement scores for all of its 21 members, according to several verification scores. This was done with the Eta members using about the same resolution as their EC driver members, and was demonstrated to have come largely as a result of the choice of the eta as opposed to the almost universally used terrain-following coordinates. Note the statement of a recent review of the numerical methods for the atmosphere and ocean by Côté et al. (2015) "Although spectral transform methods are being predicted to be phased out, the current spectral model at the European Centre for Medium-Range Weather Forecasts ... is the benchmark to beat, and it is not clear that any of the new developments are ready to replace it".

References

Arakawa, A., 1966: Computational design for long-term numerical integration of equations of fluid motion: Two dimensional incompressible flow. Part I. *Journal of Computational Physics*, 1(1), 119–143.

Bauer, P., Thorpe, A., and Brunet, G., 2015: The quiet revolution of numerical weather prediction. *Nature*, 525, 47-55.

Charney, J. G., Fjørtoft, R., and von Neumann, J., 1950: Numerical integration of the barotropic vorticity equation. *Tellus*, 2, 237–254.

Côté, J., Jablonowski, C., Bauer, P., and Wedi, N., 2015: Numerical methods of the atmosphere and ocean. *Seamless prediction of the Earth system: From minutes to months*. World Meteorological Organization, WMO-No. 1156, 101–124.

Gallus, W. A. Jr., and Klemp, J. B., 2000: Behavior of flow over step orography. *Monthly Weather Review,* 128(4), 1153–1164.

Mesinger, F., and Veljovic, K., 2017: Eta vs. sigma: Review of past results, Gallus-Klemp test, and large-scale wind skill in ensemble experiments. *Meteorology and Atmospheric Physics,* 129, 573-593.

Mesinger, F., and Veljovic K., 2020: Topography in weather and climate model: Lessons from cut-cell Eta vs. European Centre for Medium-Range Weather Forecasts experiments. *Journal of the Meteorological Society of Japan*, 98(5), in press.

Mesinger, F., Chou, S. C., Gomes. J., Jovic, D., Bastos, P., Bustamante, J. F., Lazic, L., Lyra, A. A., Morelli, S., Ristic, I., and Veljovic, K., 2012: An upgraded version of the Eta model. *Meteorology and Atmospheric Physics,* 116, 63–79.

Phillips, N., 2001: A review of theoretical questions in the early days of NWP. *50th Anniversary of Numerical Weather Prediction Commemorative Symposium*, Book of Lectures. Potsdam, 9-10 March 2000, A. Spekat, Ed., Europ. Meteorol. Soc., 13-28.

Salmon, R., 2004: Poisson-Bracket approach to the construction of energy- and potential-enstrophy-conserving algorithms for the shallow-water equations. *Journal of the Atmospheric Sciences,* 61(16), 2016–2036.

SUPERCOMPUTERS AND THE FUTURE OF BIOINFORMATICS

Nenad Mitic, School of Mathematics, University of Belgrade, Serbia

Throughout history, supercomputers have always been synonymous with the machine with the highest data processing speed, the largest possible memory size, the largest physical dimensions and the highest price. On the other hand, supercomputers are associated with solving problems that require high-performance calculations. One of the areas in which the use of supercomputers enables the opening of new horizons is Bioinformatics. Today, solving biological problems is at the top of the priority of supercomputer application. For example, the first two problems from the top of the list of projects in which the most powerful supercomputer was engaged at the time of writing this text (www.top500.org, June 2020) belong to the field of Bioinformatics [Riken2020]). Bioinformatics problems are characterized by a large amount of data ("big data") and a large number of possibilities/variants for processing this data, which often results in an enormous number of different algorithms whose application is being attempted. Today, supercomputers are used in a large number of problems in Bioinformatics ([Segal2015], [Suplatov2019]), but the real challenges still lie ahead. In the last 50 years, science fiction has been the generator of a large number of new ideas from various fields that have been quickly realized in real life. The cult series "Star Trek" shows a large number of Bioinformatics applications that await us in the near or distant future: personal medicine ("Tricorder" for complete medical diagnostics and determination of therapy/drugs), complete genetic image of a person ("Teleporter" - conversion individuals in a set of digital data and its recreating at the target destination), determination of potentially dangerous viruses and organisms and their removal, sample analysis and determination of species taxonomy (human, Klingon, clone, synthetic creature, alien species, ...), etc. All these ideas basically have the same Bioinformatics basis - in the first step the possibility of decoding the complete genome of any organism, including small differences that bring individuality, and creating database of these data. Knowledge of the complete genome

includes knowledge of the effect of interactions between its constituents (e.g., protein-protein interactions). The data from such database will enable the realization of the previously mentioned applications, possibly on personal computers and not necessarily on supercomputers (although today's desktops are more powerful than former supercomputers, with the expectation that the same trend will continue in the future regardless of the possible introduction of quantum computers). However, the use of supercomputers will be necessary for efficient model development as a basis for these applications due to the large amount of available data [NCBIStatistic2020], (still) insufficient knowledge of mechanisms and a large number of possible interactions in genomes, and the need for parallel execution due to lack of precise methods for for solving the problem. The resources needed to effectively precisely decoding the genomes of a large number of living organisms and store them in a database exceed the currently available capabilities in all computer centers in the world, but it is expected that this gap in the future will gradually narrow with the development of new supercomputers. Additionally, due to the need to develop software and methods that would respond to the challenges that are posed, proper education is needed that enhances creativity of students as future researchers and teaches them how to present properly the results of their work [Blagojevic2017, Bankovic2020])"

References

[Bankovic2020] Bankovic, M., et al,: Teaching graduate students how to review research articles and respond to reviewer comments, Advances in Computers, Elsevier, Vol. 116, 2020, pp. 1-63

[Blagojevic2017] Blagojević, V., Bojić, D., Bojović, M., Cvetanović, M., Đorđević, J., Đurđević, Đ., ... & Milutinović, V. (2017). A systematic approach to generation of new ideas for PhD research in computing. In Advances in computers (Vol. 104, pp. 1-31). Elsevier.

[NCBIStatistic2020] NCBI GenBank - available data: https://www.ncbi.nlm.nih.gov/genbank/statistics/

[Riken2020] Projects in Riken Center for Computational Science https://www.r-ccs.riken.jp/en/fugaku/outcome (September 2020)

[Segal2015] Segall S. R., Cook, S. J., and Zhang, Q. (Eds).: Research and Applications in Global Supercomputing, pp. 149-241, IGI Global 2015.

[Suplatov2019] Suplatov, D., et al.: High-Performance Hybrid Computing for Bioinformatic Analysis of Protein Superfamilies, in Supercomputing, 5th Russian Supercomputing Days, 2019, V. Voevodin, S. Sobolev (Eds.), pp. 249-264, Springer 2019

ADVANCES IN SUPERCOMPUTING

Michael Resch, HLRC, University of Stuttgart, Germany

As Moore's law comes to an end the increase in computing speed will slow down over the next years. As a result, supercomputers tend to live longer without becoming obsolete. Consequently, we face the wonderful situation that software can finally start to catch up. Supercomputing will be much more productive in the years ahead as scientists and industry can finally optimize codes for stable architectures. The level of sustained performance will increase. Power management will be optimized to further reuse both financial and environmental costs.

At the same time supercomputing becomes ubiquitous being available to people and systems in many more ways than today. This allows computer simulations and applications of artificial intelligence to become part of our everyday live. People will have their lives controlled and steered by systems that are much faster and more reliable in their decisions. However, we will see an erosion of trust in computers as these better decisions are not understood by the users and lack all humanity. As a result, people will seek to establish computer ethics trying to operationalize ethical concepts they were familiar with over the last 2500 years. These attempts will fail and will force us to rethink ethics of computers.

References

Nagel, Wolfgang E.; Kröner, Dietmar B.; Resch, Michael M. (Eds.), "High Performance Computing in Science and Engineering ?18", Transactions of the High Performance Computing Center Stuttgart, Springer, Berlin ? Heidelberg ? New York, 2019

Michael Resch, Andreas Kaminski, The Epistemic Importance of Technology in Computer Simulation and Machine Learning, Minds and Machines (2019), 29:9-27 https://doi.org/10.1007/s11023-019-09496-5

SUPERCOMPUTING ESSENTIALS

Julio Sahuquillo, University of Valencia, Spain

Supercomputing is demanding each time more and more throughput in general purpose processors. To address this fact, processor manufactures include simultaneous multithreading (SMT) cores in their server systems.

These processors, however, introduce a high intra-core interference which which make difficult these SMT cores to scale. The main reason is that these cores were designed to improve the utilization of the functional units, and present a limited fetch bandwidth. Scalability in the number of supported threads could be achieved by designing these cores from scratch to improve fetch and commit bandwidth.

Current processors use each time more and more space devoted to cache space. To increase the storage capacity, new high-density CMOS compatible technologies have been used like eDRAM and racetrack. However, most efforts have focused on the L2 and or the L3 caches. Future processors will integrate these technologies into the pipeline (e.g. as first-level caches) in order to provide a high cache bandwidth and support a high number of threads.

References

Z. Sun, X. Bi, W. Wu, S. Yoo, and H. Li. Array Organization and Data Management Exploration in Racetrack Memory. IEEE Transactions on Computers, 65(4), 2016.

R. Venkatesan, V. J. Kozhikkottu, M. Sharad, C. Augustine, A. Ray- chowdhury, K. Roy, and A. Raghu-nathan. Cache Design with Domain Wall Memory. IEEE Transactions on Computers, 65(4): 2016.

Blagojević, V., Bojić, D., Bojović, M., Cvetanović, M., Đorđević, J., Đurđević, Đ., ... & Milutinović, V. (2017). A systematic approach to generation of new ideas for PhD research in computing. In Advances in computers (Vol. 104, pp. 1-31). Elsevier.

Maximizing on-chip parallelism in Proceedings 22ndAnnual International Symposium on Computer Architecture, 1995, pp.392

A. Snavely and D. M. Tullsen, S. J. Eggers, and H. M. Levy, Simultaneous mul-tithreading: Maximizing on-chip parallelism,=E2=80=9D inProceedings 22ndAnnual International Symposium on Computer Architecture, 1995, pp.392=E2=80=93403.[2] A. Snavely and S. K. Sadasivam, B. W. Thompto, R. Kalla and W. J. Starke, "IBM Power9 Processor Architecture," in IEEE Micro, vol. 37, no. 2, pp. 40-51, Mar.-Apr. 2017, doi: 10.1109/MM.2017.40.

Appendix:

Blagojevic, V., et al, "A Systematic Approach to Generation of New Ideas for PhD Research in Computing," Advances in Computers, Elsevier, Vol. 104, 2016, pp. 1-19.

DEW, FOG AND CLOUD COMPUTING TOWARDS THE GLOBAL RAINBOW SERVICE (SMART SERVICE SYSTEM-SSS)

Karolj Skala and Zorislav Šojat, Ruđer Bošković Institute, Zagreb, Croatia

Modern day "computing", in its widest sense as "constructed/programmed machine action", fosters for a huge community of involved participants from almost the entire spectrum of human endeavour, and, consequently puts huge *Ecological Responsibility* into the hands of Computer Science and Computer Scientists.

For computing and data processing there are individual computers, clusters, HPC, grids, and, finally, the clouds. For pure data communication there is the Internet, and for the Human-understandable Information Communication for example the World Wide Web. The rapid development of hand-held mobile devices with high computational capabilities and Internet connectivity enabled certain parts of Clouds to be "lowered" into so called "thin clients". This led to development of the Fog-Computing Paradigm as well as development of the so-called "Internet of Things (IoT)" and "Internet of Everything (IoE)" concepts.

With the rapid development of fixed and mobile sensor, effector and complex control devices, many without and some with Internet connectivity, the tendency becomes that the most significant amount of information processing all around us is done on the lowest possible level, outright connected to the physical environment and mostly directly controlling our human immediate surroundings. These "embedded" information processing devices we find in everything (cars, air-conditioners, lighting, vending machines, traffic-controls...), and also in comprehensive products all over the industry. These devices, which are neither at the Cloud/Fog edge, nor even at the mobile edge or even the edge of Internet, but rather at the physical edge of computing, are the basis of the *Dew Computing Paradigm* [1] [2].

The Dew Computing Paradigm is primarily oriented towards the physical-edge, human environment control devices, where human control of the environment must take precedence over possible higher-level requests, or at least be coordinated with them, without disturbing the immediate human environment [3]. This is the reason why in *Dew-Computing* there are two *basic notions*, which do not exist in the rest of the hierarchy, in the Fog and in the Cloud: *self-sufficiency* and *co-operation* [4] [5].

For further development of our civilisation as a nature-human-machine inhabitable eco-system, it is essential to explore the realm of possibilities of Dew Computing, and solve the basic problems of integration of the "dew" level with the higher service levels in the Dew-Fog-Cloud hierarchy. This will necessitate both horizontal scalability, in all layers, as well as vertical scalability throughout the emerging Rainbow Service Ecosystem.

Horizontal scalability [6] is an approach to increasing capacity that relies on connecting multiple hardware or software entities so they work as a single logical distributed service unit. Horizontal scalability is often referred to as scaling out and extends the functional ability of a system layer. Horizontal scalability can be contrasted with vertical scalability, which increases capacity by adding to the service more complex resources and function abilities for advanced applications.

Figure 1. Vertical Distributed Rainbow Smart Service System [8]

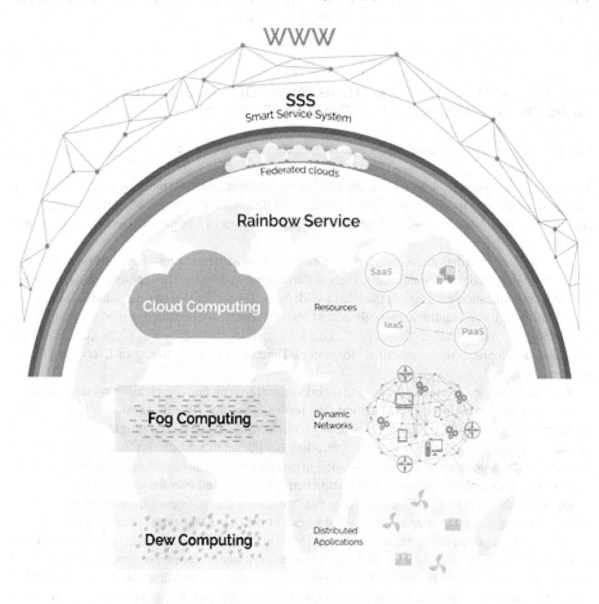

Figure 2. Artificial intelligence as an upgrade of Nature and Human Intelligence

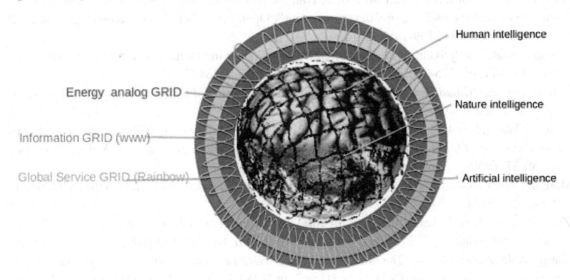

When the distributed Cloud-Fog-Dew service architecture is adopted, a Cloud server and many Dew servers will cooperate as a distributed application to provide controls or services. Several Clouds in symbiosis result in a Cloud federation, interconnecting the cloud service environments. Such federated Cloud services, supported by HPC, federated Fog services and federated Dew services will provide global *Rainbow services*; based on the vertical service hierarchy that provides direct services connection to a user [7] [8].

The tendency of our future is the usage of three global grids: the Energy Grid, the Information Grid (www) and the Smart Service System (SSS) or Rainbow Grid. The emerging nature-human-machine ecosystem, the Rainbow Ecosystem [9], integrating all the mentioned three grids with ecologically aware cooperation with nature, will define the future technical civilization and the infrastructure for the development of Nature-Human-Machine Intelligence on Earth, marking a new Industrial revolution of Ecological Sustainability.

However, in view of all the social, political, economical and ecological problems we face, most of them due to our own civilisation's behaviour, any viable future we want to attain will necessitate huge efforts in the fields of Education and, specifically Creativity. Proper stimulation and coordination, within a Cybernetical Ecological model framework, and with the prerequisite of Appropriateness, of both Revolutionary Creativity, for the necessary paradigm-shifting breakthroughs, and Evolutionary Creativity, for non-paradigm-shifting improvements of existing solutions, [10] are essential to attain the global paradigm shift towards Local Economy and Global Ecology. Otherwise we, as a civilisation, have low chances of further viability.

References

[1] Karolj Skala, Zorislav Šojat: *"Cloud, Fog and Dew Computing: A Distributed Hierarchy"*, DOI: 10.13140/RG.2.2.26021.52963, 2015.

[2] Karolj Skala, Davor Davidović, Enis Afgan, Ivan Sović, Zorislav Šojat: *"Scalable distributed computing hierarchy: cloud, fog and dew computing"*, Open Journal of Cloud Computing (OJCC), 2 (1). pp. 16-24. ISSN 2199-1987, 2016.

[3] Zorislav Šojat, Karolj Skala, "The dawn of Dew: Dew Computing for advanced living environment", MIPRO 2017, pp. 375-380, DOI:10.23919/MIPRO.2017.7973447, 2017.

[4] Yingwei Wang, *"Cloud-dew architecture"*, International Journal of Cloud Computing, vol. 4, no. 3, pp. 199–210, 2015.

[5] Yingwei Wang, Karolj Skala, Andy Rindos, Marjan Gušev, Shuhui Yang, Yi Pan: *"Dew Computing and Transition of Internet Computing Paradigms"*, ZTE Communications 2017, Vol. 15, Issue (4), pp. 30-37, DOI: 10.3969/j.issn.1673-5188.2017.04.004, 2017.

[6] Margaret Rouse: *"horizontal scalability (scaling out)"*, http://go.techtarget.com/r/53592267/4004705 [8/9/2020, 20:41].

[7] Zorislav Šojat, Karolj Skala, *"Views on the Role and Importance of Dew Computing in the Service and Control Technology"*, MIPRO 2016, pp. 175-179, DOI: 10.1109/MIPRO.2016.7522131, 2016.

[8] Karolj Skala, Zorislav Šojat, *"The Rainbow Global Service Ecosystem"*, Proceedings of the 3rd International Workshop on Dew Computing (DewCom 2018), IEEE DewCom STC, Toronto, Canada, pp. 25-30, 2018.

[9] Zorislav Šojat, *"From Dew Over Cloud Towards the Rainbow - Ecosystem of the Future: Nature — Human — Machine"*, Intelligence in Big Data Technologies - Beyond the Hype, Chapter 1, Advs in Intelligent Syst., Computing, Vol. 1167, Springer Nature, Singapore, ISBN 978-981-15-5284-7, 2020.

[10] V. Blagojević, D. Bojić, M. Bojović. M. Cvetanović, J. Đorđević. Đ. Đurđević. B. Furlan, S. Gajin, Z. Jovanović, D.Milićev, V. Milutinović, B. Nikolić, J. Protić, M. Punt, Z. Radivojević, Ž. Stanisavljević, S. Stojanović, I. Tartalja, P. Vuletić: *"A Systematic Approach to Generation of New Ideas for PhD Research in Computing"*, Creativity in Computing and DataFlow SuperComputing, Advances in Computers, Volume 104, Pages 1-31, DOI: 10.1016/bs.adcom.2016.09.001, 2017.

ADVANCES IN SCIENCE AND ENGINEERING

Per Stenstrom, Chalmers University of Technology, Goteborg, Sweden

The main theme of this textbook, that outlines general approaches for how we make advances in science and engineering, is needless to say both important and fascinating. I do fully agree, that the ten themes of idea generation mentioned capture well how ideas can be born inspired from work being done to advance our knowledge.

However, in my view, fundamental to idea generation is ultimately the background and the intellectual preferences of ideas of individuals. Individuals who choose a research career typically make choices based on curiosity. They typically select, without a strategy, the scientific areas of intellectual interest and narrow them down into topics where their hearts pond because of intellectual curiosity, again typically with no strategy. That is, in my view, the heart of the research process. A few examples from my own personal development are useful for reference.

First, out of high school, I was interested in Math and Physics, full stop. But I realized that doing it in the framework of an engineering curriculum would pragmatically give me better job opportunities. I often think whether that was the best choice for me to trade off curiosity for pragmatic reasons. Anyway, I studied Electrical Engineering and was confronted with a number of exciting areas: Control theory, Electrical measurement and Computer engineering. As I was in love with demonstrating results, building my first computer in my early 20s, made me make my choice to dive into Computer Engineering.

In my first job, I worked on how to encode human speech compactly and started to research compression techniques and was intellectually in love with that. I will pick up on that later. When being enrolled as a PhD student in the 80s, I proposed to my advisor to pick cache coherence as my PhD topic. My advisor told me that the fundamental problems in this area were already solved. I persevered and showed my advisor that me being in intellectual love with cache coherence led me to make important contributions in this area.

Another example: My early interest in compression techniques made me realize how to use that to build more powerful computers and led to a research agenda leading to many breakthroughs over the years and to spin-out a company that offers products to build faster and more energy-efficient computers.

In closing, the moral is that idea generation is, in my view, a human activity in which an individual is predominantly driven from curiosity and brings her/his background to solve a problem in a potentially novel and groundbreaking way.

CAN SUPERCOMPUTER SEE THE COVID-19?

Radovan Stojanovic, University of Montenegro and MECOnet, Podgorica, Montenegro

There is now a sufficient evidence to conclude that the COVID-19 virus can often be spread with aerosols through a close contact with an infected person or through inhaling respiratory droplets from him. How, then, can we identify the particles that may contain the virus?

The answer lies in the use of an artificial, third eye, consisting of an ultra-fast camera, a laser beam and a supercomputer. Microdroplets or aerosols are a particles that are 1-100 micrometers in size, invisible to the human eye, which are, however, visible to the camera and laser when special scattering techniques are applied. The ocular device should be in the form of a headband or a cap, capable of emitting a laser beam, receiving stray light, and detecting virus-containing particles. In addition, using a similar non-contact measurement principle, the eye must detect the temperature of a person nearby.

Why do we need a supercomputer here? The camera must be ultra-fast and have an ultra-high resolution, around 10,000 frames/sec and 10Kx10K pixels. Algorithms for image processing, feature extraction, classification and decision making are very demanding, mimicking the segment of the brain responsible for processing of the vision information. In fact, we are dealing with big data during a "thunderstorm". Through bio-feedback, we are alerted to danger through the sound in the headphones.

Our supercomputer should not only be ultra-fast and work with big data, but together with the sensors, it should have low consumption, be charged from a small battery. The design problems are challenging in this case.

In conclusion, it should be noted that by using super sensors and supercomputers, we can create an intelligent artificial eye that can detect COVID-19 or other dangerous particles in the air.

References

1. Vladimir Blagojević, Veljko Milutinović et all, A Systematic Approach to Generation of New Ideas for PhD Research in Computing
2. R. Stojanovic, A. Skraba, and B. Lutovac, A Headset Like Wearable Device to Track COVID-19 Symptoms, in 2020 9th Mediterranean Conference on Embedded Computing (MECO) Proccedings, Budva, Montenegro, Jun. 2020, pp. 14.

SUPERCOMPUTING IN SOCIAL SCIENCES AND HUMANITIES

Veljko Milutinovic, Nemanja Trifunovic, and Petar Trifunovic, School of Electrical Engineering, University of Belgrade, Serbia; Milica Matic, School of Medicine, University of Belgrade, Serbia.

The major challenges for supercomputing in social studies are in the domain of economy, from micro to macro, from the national leveles to the global levels. The higher the number of professionals in economy with solid backgrounds in computng and mathematics, the higher the chances that the economies on all leveles be held on healthy legs. Consequently, this short viewpoint text advocates the need for computer and mathematics experts to create interests for research in the domain of economy in particular and social studies in general. A good sign telling that the awareness of these issues is on the rise is contained in the fact that the number of start-up companies in the domain of supercomputing for digital economy is constantly increasing.

Supercomputing is also crucial for the further development of the general field of humanities in general, and heritage preservation in particular. The amount of the accumulated knowledge of the homosapiens is huge, while on the other hand, understanding of that knowledge and understanding of the impact of that knowledge is higly limited. Supercomputing offers effective mechanisms for uncovering of hidden knowledge, for finding important correlations between data, and for effective decision making on issues of crucial importance. These goals are effectively reached by the existing artificial intelligence theories and the existing machine learning software; however, these mechanisms need strong supercomputers.

An important group of supercomputing applications is in public health, medicine, biomedicine, and scientific experimenting that synergizes medicine and physics (https://github.com/milicamatic/supercomputing/blob/main/README.md).

The authors of this viewpoint strongly beleive that the optimal solution for the architecture of the needed supercomputers on a chip implies the following: (A) N multi-core processors, (B) 1000N many-core processors, (C) A fixed systolic array tuned to up to M most frequently used machine learning algorithms that contribute to about 50% of the run time, and (D) A reconfigurable FPGA structure that implements the dataflow paradigm for an extremely large number of current and future algorithms that appear less frequently in the current and future application, but do contribute to about 50% of the run time. In the last case, technological advances would be needed that enable the advantages of the dataflow paradigm to blossom at their maxima [Trifunovic2015].

Finally, it is the human creativity that has the major role in further developments of the issues mentioned here. Of special importance are the methods that enhance creativity like in [Blagojevic2017] and the presentation of the results of creative research activities [Bankovic2020]. Consequently, education that enhances creativity should represent the foundations on all levels of the national education systems, from kindergarden and preschools, to elementary and secondary schools. Results like those presented in [Knezevic2000, Milutinovic1996, Milutinovic1987] are possible only with strong educational systems, and esspecially in developing countries, since the talent is equally spread all over the planet, but opportunites for talent developments are not.

References

Banković, Milan, et al. "Teaching graduate students how to review research articles and respond to reviewer comments." *Advances in Computers*. Vol. 116. No. 1. Elsevier, 2020. 1-63.

Blagojević, V., Bojić, D., Bojović, M., Cvetanović, M., Đorđević, J., Đurđević, Đ., ... & Milutinović, V. (2017). A systematic approach to generation of new ideas for PhD research in computing. In Advances in computers (Vol. 104, pp. 1-31). Elsevier.

Knezevic, P., Radnovic, B., Nikolic, N., Jovanovic, T., Milanov, D., Nikolic, M., ... & Schewel, J. (2000, January). The architecture of the Obelix-an improved internet search engine. In Proceedings of the 33rd Annual Hawaii International Conference on System Sciences (pp. 11-pp). IEEE.

Milutinovic, V. *Surviving the design of a 200MHz RISC microprocessor*. IEEE Computer Society Press, Washington DC, USA, 1996.

Milutinovic, D., V. Milutinovic, and B. Soucek. "The honeycomb architecture." (1987): 81-83.

Trifunovic, Nemanja, et al. "Paradigm shift in big data supercomputing: dataflow vs. controlflow." Journal of Big Data 2.1 (2015): 1-9.

FROM ZUSE TO SUPERCOMPUTER

Klaus Waldschmidt, Goethe University, Frankfurt/Main, Germany

About eighty years ago Konrad Zuse (1) presented his Computer Z3 to the DLR, a german space agency. This was the first modern digital computer, free programmable and with floating point arithmetic. This presentation in 1941 opened the start to our modern digital world. The Z3 was built with about 2000 relais, operated with a clock frequency of ca. 5 Hz and had a performance of 1 Flop. In contrast, modern supercomputer operate with several Ghz and have a performance of ca.150 Pflops. No other artificial technical device can compare with such an increase in performance. The reasons for this incredible evolution is a unique synergism of technology and architecture.

First of all, Moore`s law of exponential increase in transistor count on a chip (doubling of transistor count in about two years), massive parallelism (instruction level and multicore parallelism) and implementing dataflow by field programming devices (FPGA).

What is coming next? Quantum computing, Memristive-Computing, Non-Silicon-based-Technology or quite new paradigms? Next generations will give the answer.

Decades ago, Konrad Zuse (2,3) proposed the idea of modelling the universe as a big digital computer. I will say: The universe migrate more and more in our modern supercomputer world.

References

(1) Zuse, K. Der Computer – Mein Lebenswerk Springer Verlag 1984

(2) Zuse K. Rechnender Raum- Schriften zur Datenverarbeitung Band 1 Vieweg Verlag Braunschweig 1969

(3) Gardner, M Das gespiegelte Universum Vieweg Verlag Braunschweig 1967

DIFFERENT ARCHITECTURAL APPROACHES FOR SUPERCOMPUTING

Kristy Yashimoto, Indiana University, Bloomington, Indiana, USA

I now strongly believe that the future of supercomputing on a 100Billion transistor chip is in the synergy of the following architectural structures: (A) K MultiCore processors, (B) 1000K ManyCore processors, (C) One fixed systolic array for the N most frequently used Tensor Calculus algorithms in AI, and (D) One reconfigurable dataflow engine for the less frequent AI algorithms. Of course, proper interfaces are needed for memory, I/O, Internet, and external accelerators (e.g., quantum, optical, biological, molecular, etc...). It will be interesting to see, among the many creative options, which one will prove to be the most effective in the future [1, 2].

References

[1] Blagojević, V., Bojić, D., Bojović, M., Cvetanović, M., Đorđević, J., Đurđević, Đ., ... & Milutinović, V. (2017). A systematic approach to generation of new ideas for PhD research in computing. In Advances in computers (Vol. 104, pp. 1-31). Elsevier.

[2] Kotlar, M., & Milutinovic, V. (2018, June). Comparing controlflow and dataflow for tensor calculus: speed, power, complexity, and MTBF. In *International Conference on High Performance Computing* (pp. 329-346). Springer, Cham.

AREA OF AUTOMATIC CONTROL

Stanislaw H. Żak, Purdue University, West Lafayette, Indiana, USA

The one who has tools, rules! A supercomputer is a game changing tool of power. Thanks to supercomputers what was only imagined in the past is now a reality. Take for example population-based optimization algorithms. For a long time, these methods were just a class of exotic optimization techniques with no significant implementations. Now population-based optimization methods are being used to design sophisticated machines, such as electric motors and generators with unreasonable effectiveness. Today, we have new complete theories awaiting an advent of more powerful computers. For example, finite dimensional linear system theory is being used successfully in controlling chemical, biological, engineering as well economic processes [1]. However, the control of these processes would be much improved if we could use their infinite dimensional models [2], which calls for more powerful super-computers. This, on the other hand, requires a new approach to the way we teach and do research in the area of computation [3,4]. Finally, we are now at the juncture where we need to consider the ethical and moral implications of the way we use supercomputers.

References

[1] S. H. Żak, Systems and Control, Oxford, New York, 2003

[2] S. Rolewicz, Functional Analysis and Control Theory: Linear Systems, Springer Science+Business Media Dordrecht, 1987

[3] A. R. Hurson and V. Milutinović, Academic Press and Elsevier, Cambridge, MA, 2020

[4] Blagojević, V., Bojić, D., Bojović, M., Cvetanović, M., Đorđević, J., Đurđević, Đ., ... & Milutinović, V. (2017). A systematic approach to generation of new ideas for PhD research in computing. In Advances in computers (Vol. 104, pp. 1-31). Elsevier.

SUPERCOMPUTERS AND CRYPTANALYSIS

Miodrag Živković, School of Mathematics, University of Belgrade, Serbia

Cryptanalysis is very important throughout the history, see [1]. Cryptanalysis demands as much as possible computation power, so it is one of the most important applications of supercomputing. During the WW2 Colossus, special top secret computer, is used to break German ciphers [2], before the first non-secret computer was built.

The block algorithm DES (Data Encryption Standard) Developed in the early 1970s at IBM based on Lucifer, the algorithm with 128 bit long key. DES key length is only 56 bits. This fact raised concerns about the security of DES: brute force attack needs to check possible keys to determine the right one, if one knows a cipher text and the corresponding plain text [3]. It seems that the key length is carefully chosen, so that this brute force attack can be performed only by somebody having enough powerful supercomputer. Advance in technology a few decades later made DES obsolete.

Stream cipher algorithm (see [4], for example) uses PRNG (*pseudorandom number generator*, a finite state automaton) to obtain a sequence of key sequence bits, which is used to transform plaintext bit into corresponding cipher text bit , where addition is modulo . If the initial state of PRNG is the key for this algorithm, and if the key length is bits, then the brute force known plaintext attack needs to check possible keys. If a PRNG is a simple LFSR (*linear feedback shift register*) of length , then can be linearly expressed in terms of key bits, so the attack of complexity is possible, where is some polynomial.

The combination of two LFSRs and (of lengths and , respectively) can be used as a PRNG, where is *irregularly clocking* (see [4], Clock-Controlled Generator). The brute force attack of complexity on such a PRNG can be replaced by a substantially more efficient attack of complexity [5,6]. The attack is based on considering all possible initial states of , and trying to determine the corresponding initial states of Hence, cryptanalytic attack uses the combination of the knowledge of the algebraic structure of PRNG, and the supercomputer power to check the all initial states of a sub generator. This type of attack can be obviously generalized, making it possible to attack generators with hidden algebraic structure: by traversing all the possible values of some of its state component, and determining the rest of state by low complexity algebraic attack.

For the implementation of the presented notions, it is crucial that students are educated in the way that enhances creativity [7, 8].

References

[1] David Kahn, The Codebreakers: The Story of Secret Writing, Macmillan, 1967

[2] Copeland, B. Jack, ed.: Colossus: The Secrets of Bletchley Park's Codebreaking Computers, Oxford University Press, 2006

[3] Hellman, M. and W. Diffie, Special Feature Exhaustive Cryptanalysis of the NBS Data encryption standard, Computer, Vol. 10 (6), 1977

[4] H.C.A. van Tilborg, S. Jajodia (Eds.): Encyclopedia of Cryptography and Security, Springer, 2011

[5] Jovan Dj. Golic, Luke O'Connor, Embedding and Probabilistic Correlation Attacks on Clock-Controlled Shift Registers, In Advances in Cryptology: EuroCrypt 94, Berlin: Lecture Notes in Computer Science, 1994, 230-243

[6] M. Zivkovic, An Algorithm for the Initial State Reconstruction of the Clock-Controlled Shift Register, IEEE Trans. Inform. Theory 37 (1991), no. 5, 1488-1490

[7] Bankovic, M., et al,: Teaching graduate students how to review research articles and respond to reviewer comments, Advances in Computers, Elsevier, Vol. 116, 2020, pp. 1-63

[8] Blagojević, V., Bojić, D., Bojović, M., Cvetanović, M., Đorđević, J., Đurđević, Đ., ... & Milutinović, V. (2017). A systematic approach to generation of new ideas for PhD research in computing. In Advances in computers (Vol. 104, pp. 1-31). Elsevier.

Compilation of References

IBMIT Infrastructure. (2017). *POWER9 processor chip*. Retrieved September 28, 2020, from https://www.ibm.com/it-infrastructure/power/power9

McCool, J., Robison, M., & Reinders, A. (2012). *Structured Parallel Programming: Patterns for Efficient Computation*. Elsevier.

Milutinovic, V. (1995). *Splitting Spatial and Temporal Localities for Entropy Minimiation*. Academic Press.

Intel. (2014). *Optimizing performance with Intel Advanced Vector Extensions*. Retrieved August 11, 2020, from https://www.intel.com/content/dam/www/public/us/en/documents/white-papers/performance-xeon-e5-v3-advanced-vector-extensions-paper.pdf

Milutinovic, V. (1996). The split temporal/spatial cache: Initial performance analysis. *SCIzzL*, *5*(March), 63–69.

Tsitsiklis, J. N., & Xu, K. (2011). On the power of (even a little) centralization in distributed processing. *Performance Evaluation Review*, *39*, 121–132. doi:10.1145/1993744.1993759

Agrawal, K., Li, J., Lu, K., & Moseley, B. (2016). Scheduling parallelizable jobs online to minimize the maximum flow time. In *Proceedings of the 28th ACM Symposium on Parallelism in Algorithms and Architectures, SPAA '16*, (pp. 195-205). New York: ACM. 10.1145/2935764.2935782

Intel. (2016a). *Intel® Xeon® Processors*. Retrieved September 28, 2020, from https://www.intel.com/content/www/us/en/products/processors/xeon.html

Milutinovic, V., Fura, D., & Helbig, W. (1986). An introduction to GaAs microprocessor architecture for VLSI. *Computer*, *19*(3), 30–42. doi:10.1109/MC.1986.1663177

Huang, K.-C., Huang, T.-C., Tung, Y.-H., & Shih, P.-Z. (2013). Effective processor allocation for moldable jobs with application speedup model. In *Advances in Intelligent Systems and Applications* (Vol. 2, pp. 563–572). Springer. doi:10.1007/978-3-642-35473-1_56

Intel. (2019, August 21). *Intel Expands 10th Gen Intel Core Mobile Processor Family, Offering Double Digit Performance Gains*. Retrieved September 28, 2020, from https://newsroom.intel.com/news/intel-expands-10th-gen-intel-core-mobile-processor-family-offering-double-digit-performance-gains/

Intel. (2020). *Intel CES*. Retrieved August 11, 2020, from https://newsroom.intel.com/press-kits/2020-ces/#gs.d6lufh

Kleinrock, L. (1975). Queueing Systems, Volume I: Theory. Wiley.

Reuther, A., Michaleas, P., Jones, M., Gadepally, V., Samsi, S., & Kepner, J. (2019). Survey and benchmarking of machine learning accelerators. doi:10.1109/HPEC.2019.8916327

Hill, M. D., & Marty, M. R. (2008). Amdahl's law in the multicore era. *Computer, 41*(7), 33–38. doi:10.1109/MC.2008.209

Intel. (2016b). *Intel® Xeon® Processor E7-8890 v4 (60M Cache, 2.20 GHz) Product Specifications*. Retrieved September 28, 2020, from https://ark.intel.com/content/www/us/en/ark/products/93790/intel-xeon-processor-e7-8890-v4-60m-cache-2-20-ghz.htmld

Techpowerup. (2020, September 16). *NVIDIA GeForce GTX 1080 Ti Specs*. Retrieved October 11, 2020, from https://www.techpowerup.com/gpu-specs/geforce-gtx-1080-ti.c2877

Harchol-Balter, M., Scheller-Wolf, A., & Young, A. R. (2009). Surprising results on task assignment in server farms with high-variability workloads. *Performance Evaluation Review, 37*(1), 287–298. doi:10.1145/2492101.1555383

Liu, J., & Mullaney, M. (2020, July 8). *Imec and GLOBALFOUNDRIES Announce Breakthrough in AI Chip, Bringing Deep Neural Network Calculations to IoT Edge Devices*. Retrieved September 28, 2020, from https://www.imec-int.com/en/articles/imec-and-globalfoundries-announce-breakthrough-in-ai-chip-bringing-deep-neural-network-calculations-to-iot-edge-devices

Trifunovic, N., & Milutinovic, V. (2016). The Appgallery. Maxeler. com for BigData SuperComputing. *Journal of Big Data*.

Harchol-Balter, M. (2013). *Performance Modeling and Design of Computer Systems: Queueing Theory in Action*. Cambridge University Press.

Matlis, J. (2005, May 30). *Sidebar: The Linpack Benchmark*. Retrieved September 28, 2020, from https://www.computerworld.com/article/2556400/sidebar--the-linpack-benchmark.html

NVIDIA. (2010). *The Evolution of GPUs for General Purpose Computing*. Retrieved August 14, 2020, from https://www.nvidia.com/content/gtc-2010/pdfs/2275_gtc2010.pdf

Puterman, M. L. (1994). *Markov Decision Processes: Discrete Stochastic Dynamic Programming*. John Wiley & Sons. doi:10.1002/9780470316887

Trobec, R., Vasiljevic, R., Tomasevic, M., & Milutinovic, V. (2016). *Interconnection Networks for PetaComputing*. Academic Press.

Nelson, R. D., & Philips, T. K. (1993). An approximation for the mean response time for shortest queue routing with general interarrival and service times. *Performance Evaluation, 17*(2), 123–139. doi:10.1016/0166-5316(93)90004-E

NVIDIA. (2014, November). *Summit and Sierra Supercomputers: An Inside Look at the U.S. Department of Energy's New Pre-Exascale Systems*. Retrieved August 4, 2020 from http://www.teratec.eu/actu/calcul/Nvidia_Coral_White_Paper_Final_3_1.pdf

Williams, A. (2019, August 21). *Largest Chip Ever Holds 1.2 Trillion Transistors*. Retrieved October 11, 2020, from https://hackaday.com/2019/08/21/largest-chip-ever-holds-1-2-trillion-transistors/

AMD. (2017). *Processor Programming Reference (PPR) for AMD Family 17h Model 01h, Revision B1 Processors*. Retrieved August 7, 2020, from https://developer.amd.com/wordpress/media/2017/11/54945_PPR_Family_17h_Models_00h-0Fh.pdf

Bušić, A., Vliegen, I., & Scheller-Wolf, A. (2012). Comparing Markov chains: Aggregation and precedence relations applied to sets of states, with applications to assemble-to-order systems. *Mathematics of Operations Research, 37*(2), 259–287. doi:10.1287/moor.1110.0533

Lippman, S. A. (1973). Semi-Markov decision processes with unbounded rewards. *Management Science, 19*(7), 717–731. doi:10.1287/mnsc.19.7.717

NVIDIA. (2018a). *Graphics Reinvented: NVIDIA GeForce RTX 2080 Ti Graphics Card.* Retrieved August 4, 2020 from https://www.nvidia.com/en-eu/geforce/graphics-cards/rtx-2080-ti/

Xilinx. (2003, December 8). *Revolutionary Architecture for the Next Generation Platform FPGAs.* Retrieved October 11, 2020, from https://m.eet.com/media/1081699/XIL.PDF

Chaitanya, S., Urgaonkar, B., & Sivasubramaniam, A. (2008). Qdsl: A queuing model for systems with differential service levels. *Performance Evaluation Review, 36*(1), 289–300. doi:10.1145/1384529.1375490

NVIDIA. (2018b). *Quadro RTX 8000 Graphics Card | NVIDIA Quadro.* Retrieved September 28, 2020, from https://www.nvidia.com/en-us/design-visualization/quadro/rtx-8000/

Office of Technology Transitions. (2014). *NREL's Building-Integrated Supercomputer Provides Heating and Efficient Computing.* Retrieved September 28, 2020, from https://www.energy.gov/technologytransitions/nrels-building-integrated-supercomputer-provides-heating-and-efficient

Srinivasan, S., Krishnamoorthy, S., & Sadayappan, P. (2003). A robust scheduling strategy for moldable scheduling of parallel jobs. *Proceedings of the IEEE International Conference on Cluster Computing, CLUSTER '03,* 92-99. 10.1109/CLUSTR.2003.1253304

Anastasiadis, S. V., & Sevcik, K. C. (1997). Parallel application scheduling on networks of workstations. *Journal of Parallel and Distributed Computing, 43*(2), 109–124. doi:10.1006/jpdc.1997.1335

Ohmacht, M. (2011). *Memory Speculation of the Blue Gene/Q Compute Chip.* Academic Press.

Ko, S.-S., & Serfozo, R. F. (2004). Response times in M/M/s fork-join networks. *Advances in Applied Probability, 36*(3), 854–871. doi:10.1239/aap/1093962238

Ornes, S. (2019, December 28). *Quantum Computers Finally Beat Supercomputers in 2019.* Retrieved September 28, 2020, from https://www.discovermagazine.com/the-sciences/quantum-computers-finally-beat-supercomputers-in-2019

Gupta, V., Harchol-Balter, M., Sigman, K., & Whitt, W. (2007). Analysis of join-the-shortestqueue routing for web server farms. *Performance Evaluation, 64*(9-12), 1062–1081. doi:10.1016/j.peva.2007.06.012

Ou, G. (2006, July 17). *Who to believe on power consumption? AMD or Intel?* Retrieved September 28, 2020, from https://www.zdnet.com/article/who-to-believe-on-power-consumption-amd-or-intel/

Cirne, W., & Berman, F. (2002). Using moldability to improve the performance of supercomputer jobs. *Journal of Parallel and Distributed Computing, 62*(10), 1571–1601. doi:10.1016/S0743-7315(02)91869-1

Oyanagi, Y. (2002). Future of supercomputing. *Journal of Computational and Applied Mathematics, 149*(1), 147–153. doi:10.1016/S0377-0427(02)00526-5

Ratković, I. (2016). *On the design of power-and energy-efficient functional units for vector processors.* Academic Press.

Zhan, X., Bao, Y., Bienia, C., & Li, K. (2017). PARSEC3.0: A multicore benchmark suite with network stacks and SPLASH-2X. *ACM SIGARCH Computer Architecture News, 44*(5), 1–16. doi:10.1145/3053277.3053279

Lu, Y., Xie, Q., Kliot, G., Geller, A., Larus, J. R., & Greenberg, A. (2011). Join-idle-queue: A novel load balancing algorithm for dynamically scalable web services. *Performance Evaluation, 68*(11), 1056–1071. doi:10.1016/j.peva.2011.07.015

Ratković, I., Palomar, O., Stanić, M., Ünsal, O. S., Cristal, A., & Valero, M. (2018). Vector processing-aware advanced clock-gating techniques for low-power fused multiply-add. *IEEE Transactions on Very Large Scale Integration (VLSI) Systems, 26*(4), 639–652.

Scarani, V. (2012). Quantum Computing: A Gentle Introduction. *PhT*, *65*(2), 53.

Scully, Z., Blelloch, G., Harchol-Balter, M., & Scheller-Wolf, A. (2017). Optimally scheduling jobs with multiple tasks. *Proceedings of the ACM Workshop on Mathematical Performance Modeling and Analysis*.

AMD. (2019). *Radeon™ RX 5700 XT Graphics*. Retrieved August 4, 2020, from https://www.amd.com/en/products/graphics/amd-radeon-rx-5700-xt

Gandhi, A., Harchol-Balter, M., Das, R., & Lefurgy, C. (2009). Optimal power allocation in server farms. In *ACM SIGMETRICS Performance Evaluation Review* (Vol. 37, pp. 157–168). ACM.

Schauer, B. (2008). Multicore processors–a necessity. *ProQuest discovery guides*, 1-14.

Stanic, M., Palomar, O., Hayes, T., Ratkovic, I., Cristal, A., Unsal, O., & Valero, M. (2017). An integrated vector-scalar design on an in-order ARM core. *ACM Transactions on Architecture and Code Optimization*, *14*(2), 1–26. doi:10.1145/3075618

Stephens, N., Biles, S., Boettcher, M., Eapen, J., Eyole, M., Gabrielli, G., ... Reid, A. (2017). The ARM scalable vector extension. *IEEE Micro*, *37*(2), 26–39. doi:10.1109/MM.2017.35

Takahashi, D. (2019, December 14). *RISC-V grows globally as an alternative to Arm and its license fees*. Retrieved September 28, 2020, from https://venturebeat.com/2019/12/11/risc-v-grows-globally-as-an-alternative-to-arm-and-its-license-fees/

Top500. (2020, June 22). *News*. Retrieved September 28, 2020, from https://www.top500.org/news/japan-captures-top500-crown-arm-powered-supercomputer/

Ulmann, B. (2019, July 22). *Why Algorithms Suck and Analog Computers are the Future*. Retrieved September 28, 2020, from https://blog.degruyter.com/algorithms-suck-analog-computers-future/

Wiki Chip. (2018). *Goya Microarchitectures*. Retrieved August 7, 2020, from https://en.wikichip.org/wiki/habana/microarchitectures/goya

Wiki Chip. (2019). *Zen 2 - Microarchitectures - AMD*. Retrieved September 28, 2020, from https://en.wikichip.org/wiki/amd/microarchitectures/zen_2

Yoshida, T. (2018, August). Fujitsu high performance CPU for the Post-K Computer. In Hot Chips (Vol. 30). Academic Press.

ARM Ltd. (2019). *Mali-G77*. Retrieved September 28, 2020, from https://www.arm.com/products/silicon-ip-multimedia/gpu/mali-g77

Berg, B., Dorsman, J.-P., & Harchol-Balter, M. (2017). Towards optimality in parallel scheduling. *Proceedings of the ACM on Measurement and Analysis of Computing Systems*, *1*(2), 1-30.

Fortes, J. A. (1986, January). A High-Level Systolic Architecture for GaAs. In *Proc. 19th Ann. Hawaii Int'l Conf. System Sciences* (pp. 253-258). Academic Press.

Bienia, C., Kumar, S., Singh, J. P., & Li, K. (2008). The PARSEC benchmark suite: Characterization and architectural implications. In *Proceedings of the 17th International Conference on Parallel Architectures and Compilation Techniques, PACT '08* (pp. 72-81). New York: ACM. 10.1145/1454115.1454128

Cosemans, S., Verhoef, B., Doevenspeck, J., Papistas, I. A., Catthoor, F., Debacker, P., ... Verkest, D. (2019, December). Towards 10000TOPS/W DNN Inference with Analog in-Memory Computing–A Circuit Blueprint, Device Options and Requirements. In *2019 IEEE International Electron Devices Meeting (IEDM)* (pp. 22-2). IEEE. 10.1109/IEDM19573.2019.8993599

Fuchs, H. J., Whelan, D., Jackson, J., H. Niimi, Y., Goncalves, N., & Gharachorloo, N. (1981, January 1). *A million transistor systolic array graphics engine.* Retrieved October 11, 2020, from https://link.springer.com/article/10.1007/BF00932064

Delimitrou, C., & Kozyrakis, C. (2014). Quasar: Resource-efficient and qos-aware cluster management. *ACM SIGPLAN Notices, 49*(4), 127–144. doi:10.1145/2644865.2541941

Design & Reuse. (2020). *Fourth-Generation, High-Performance CPU Based on DynamIQ Technology.* Retrieved September 28, 2020, from https://www.design-reuse.com/sip/fourth-generation-high-performance-cpu-based-on-dynamiq-technology-ip-48140/

Hurson, A. R., & Milutinovic, V. (2017). *Creativity in Computing and DataFlow SuperComputing.* Academic Press.

Dongarra, J. (2016). *Report on the sunway taihulight system.* www. netlib. org

Koole, G. M. (2006). Monotonicity in Markov reward and decision chains: Theory and applications. *Foundations and Trends in Stochastic Systems, 1*(1), 1–76. doi:10.1561/0900000002

Adan, I., van Houtum, G. J. J. A. N., & van der Wal, J. (1994). Upper and lower bounds for the waiting time in the symmetric shortest queue system. *Annals of Operations Research, 48*(2), 197–217. doi:10.1007/BF02024665

Duric, M., Stanic, M., Ratkovic, I., Palomar, O., Unsal, O., Cristal, A., ... Smith, A. (2015, July). Imposing coarse-grained reconfiguration to general purpose processors. In *2015 International Conference on Embedded Computer Systems: Architectures, Modeling, and Simulation (SAMOS)* (pp. 42-51). IEEE. 10.1109/SAMOS.2015.7363658

Edmonds, J., & Pruhs, K. (2009). Scalably scheduling processes with arbitrary speedup curves. In *Proceedings of the Twentieth Annual ACM-SIAM Symposium on Discrete Algorithms, SODA '09,* (pp. 685-692). New York: ACM. 10.1137/1.9781611973068.75

Gallagher, S. (2014, March 18). *Gears of war: When mechanical analog computers ruled the waves.* Retrieved September 28, 2020, from https://web.archive.org/web/20180908173957/https://arstechnica.com/information-technology/2014/03/gears-of-war-when-mechanical-analog-computers-ruled-the-waves/

Milutinovic, D., Milutinovic, V., & Soucek, B. (1987). *The honeycomb architecture.* Academic Press.

Edmonds, J. (1999). Scheduling in the dark. *Theoretical Computer Science, 235*(1), 109–141. doi:10.1016/S0304-3975(99)00186-3

Gartenberg, C. (2020, January 6). *AMD's 7nm Ryzen 4000 CPUs are here to take on Intel's 10nm Ice Lake laptop chips.* Retrieved September 28, 2020, from https://www.theverge.com/2020/1/6/21054007/amd-7nm-ryzen-4000-cpu-ces-2020-intel-competition-laptop-processors-zen-2

Milutinovic, V. (1988). *A Comparison of Suboptimal Detection Algorithms.* Suboptimal Algorithms for Data Analytics.

A Simulation Study of Hardware-Oriented DSM Approaches. (1996). *IEEE Parallel & Distributed Technology Systems & Applications, 4*(1), 74–83.

Abadi, M., Barham, P., Chen, J., Chen, Z., Davis, A., Dean, J., . . . Kudlur, M. (2016). Tensorflow: A System for Large-Scale Machine Learning. In *12th {USENIX} Symposium on Operating Systems Design and Implementation ({OSDI} 16)* (pp. 265-283). USENIX.

Abdi, H. (2007). The method of least squares. Encyclopedia of Measurement and Statistics.

Abeles, M. (1991). Corticonics: Neural Circuits of the Cerebral Cortex 1st Edition.

Abeles, M. (1991). Corticonics: Neural Circuits of the Cerebral Cortex. Academic Press.

Adamatzky, A., Alonso-Sanz, R., & Lawniczak, A. (2008). *Automata-2008: Theory and Applications of Cellular Automata*. Luniver Press.

Adams, J., Carter, C., & Huang, S.-H. (2012). Ercot experience with sub-synchronous control interaction and proposed remediation. In *PES T&D 2012* (pp. 1–5). IEEE. doi:10.1109/TDC.2012.6281678

Agrafiotis, D. K., Lobanov, V. S., Shemanarev, M., Rassokhin, D. N., Izrailev, S., Jaeger, E. P., Alex, S., & Farnum, M. (2011). Efficient Substructure Searching of Large Chemical Libraries: The ABCD Chemical Cartridge. *Journal of Chemical Information and Modeling*, *51*(12), 3113–3130. doi:10.1021/ci200413e PMID:22035187

Al Badawi, H. S. (2018, September 10). Affective Computing (AI & Emotions). *AI Projects*. Retrieved from https://airesearchprojects.com/2018/09/10/affective-computing-ai-emotions/

Albini, A., Mester, G., & Iantovics, L. B. (2019). Unified Aspect Search Algorithm. *Interdisciplinary Description of Complex Systems*, *17*(1), 20–25. doi:10.7906/indecs.17.1.4

Albornoz, E. M., Diego Milone, D., & Rufiner, H. L. (2011, July). Spoken emotion recognition using hierarchical classifiers. *Computer Speech & Language*, *25*, 556–570.

Alikaniotis, D., & Raheja, V. (2020, May 14). Under the Hood at Grammarly: Leveraging Transformer Language Models for Grammatical Error Correction. *Grammarly Engineering Blog*. https://www.grammarly.com/blog/engineering/under-the-hood-at-grammarly-leveraging-transformer-language-models-for-grammatical-error-correction/

Alon, N., Matias, Y., & Szegedy, M. (1999). The space complexity of approximating the frequency moments. *Journal of Computer and System Sciences*, *58*(1), 137–147. doi:10.1006/jcss.1997.1545

Alshehri, J., Stanojevic, M., Dragut, E., & Obradovic, Z. (2020). (Manuscript submitted for publication). Aligning User Comments to the Content of a News Article. *Work (Reading, Mass.)*.

Amini, O., Fomin, F. V., & Saurabh, S. (2012). Counting subgraphs via homomorphisms. *SIAM Journal on Discrete Mathematics*, *26*(2), 695–717. doi:10.1137/100789403

Amit, D. J., & Brunel, N. (1997). Model of global spontaneous activity and local structured activity during delay periods in the cerebral cortex. *Cereb Cortex*, *7*(3), 237–252. doi:10.1093/cercor/7.3.237

Amunts, K., Knoll, A. C., Lippert, T., Pennartz, C. M. A., Ryvlin, P., Destexhe, A., ... Bjaalie, J. G. (2019). The Human Brain Project-Synergy between neuroscience, computing, informatics, and brain-inspired technologies. *PLoS Biology*, *17*(7), e3000344. doi:10.1371/journal.pbio.3000344

Ananthanarayanan, R., & Modha, D. S. (2007). Anatomy of a cortical simulator. Paper presented at the Supercomputing 2007: Proceedings of the ACM/IEEE SC2007 Conference on High Performance Networking and Computing Reno, NV, USA.

Ananthanarayanan, R., & Modha, D. S. (2007). Anatomy of a cortical simulator. *Proceedings of the ACM/IEEE SC2007 Conference on High Performance Networking and Computing*. 10.1145/1362622.1362627

Annamalai, Rodrigues, Koren & Kundu. (2013). An opportunistic prediction-based thread scheduling to maximize throughput/watt in AMPs. *Proceedings of the 22nd International Conference on Parallel Architectures and Compilation Techniques*, 63-72. 10.1109/PACT.2013.6618804

Antognetti, P. (1991). *Neural Networks: Concepts Applications, and Implementations*. Prentice Hall.

Apache JSPWiki. (n.d.). https://jspwiki.apache.org/

Arenson, R. L., Andriole, K. P., Avrin, D. E., & Gould, R. G. (2000). Computers in imaging and health care: Now and in the future. *Journal of Digital Imaging, 13*(4), 145–156. doi:10.1007/BF03168389 PMID:11110253

Arvind, A., Gostelow, K. P., & Plouffe, W. (1977). Indeterminacy, monitors, and dataflow. *Operating Systems Review, 11*(5), 159–169.

Ashley, E. A. (2015). The precision medicine initiative: A new national effort. *Journal of the American Medical Association, 313*(21), 2119–2120. doi:10.1001/jama.2015.3595

Association, I. S. (2010). IEEE standard for modeling and simulation (m&s) high level architecture (hla)—framework and rules. Institute of Electrical and Electronics Engineers. IEEE Standard, (1516-2010):10–1109.

Aston. (2014). Sentiment Analysis on the Social Networks Using Stream Algorithms. *Journal of Data Analysis and Information Processing, 2*, 60-66.

Åström, K. J., & Wittenmark, B. (2013). *Adaptive control.* Courier Corporation.

Austria-Forum. (n.d.). https://austria-forum.org

Avasalcai, C., Murturi, I., & Dustdar, S. (2020). Edge and fog: A survey, use cases, and future challenges. Fog Computing. *Theory into Practice*, 43–65.

Babovic, Z. (2016). Web Performance Evaluation for Internet of Things Applications. *IEEE Access: Practical Innovations, Open Solutions, 4*, 6974–6992.

Babovic, Z. B., Protic, J., & Milutinovic, V. (2016). Web performance evaluation for internet of things applications. *IEEE Access: Practical Innovations, Open Solutions, 4*, 6974–6992.

Baker, T. (2003, April 9). *An Introduction to Digital Signal Processors: How to find signals in noise using estimation. A Case Study.* Retrieved from Introduction%20to%20Digital%20Signal%20Processors.pdf

Balaban, A. T. (1985). Applications of graph theory in chemistry. *Journal of Chemical Information and Computer Sciences, 25*(3), 334–343. doi:10.1021/ci00047a033

Banafa, A. (2016, June 6). What is Affective Computing? *OpenMind Neweletter: Technology-Digital World.* Retrieved from https://www.bbvaopenmind.com/en/technology/digital-world/what-is-affective-computing/

Bankovic, M. (2020). Teaching Graduate Students How to Review Research Articles. *Advances in Computers, 116*, 1-42.

Banković, M., Filipović, V., Graovac, J., Hadži-Purić, J., Hurson, A. R., Kartelj, A., ... Marić, F. (2020). Teaching graduate students how to review research articles and respond to reviewer comments. []. Elsevier.]. *Advances in Computers, 116*(1), 1–63.

Barker, K. J., Davis, K., Hoisie, A., Kerbyson, D. J., Lang, M., Pakin, S., & Sancho, J. C. (2008). A performance evaluation of the Nehalem quad-core processor for scientific computing. *Parallel Processing Letters, 18*(4), 453–469. doi:10.1142/S012962640800351X

Barnard, J. M. (1993). Substructure searching methods: Old and new. *Journal of Chemical Information and Computer Sciences, 33*(4), 532–538. doi:10.1021/ci00014a001

Bartolini, A., Cacciari, M., Tilli, A., & Benini, L. (2011, March). A distributed and self-calibrating model-predictive controller for energy and thermal management of high-performance multicores. In 2011 Design, Automation & Test in Europe (pp. 1-6). IEEE. doi:10.1109/DATE.2011.5763141

Bassingthwaighte, J. J., Liebovitch, L. S., & West, B. J. (1994). *Fractal Physiology*. Oxford University Press. doi:10.1007/978-1-4614-7572-9

Batra, S., & Tyagi, C. (2012). *Comparative analysis of relational and graph databases*. Int'l J. Soft Computing & Engineering.

Baydin, A. G., Pearlmutter, B. A., Radul, A. A., & Siskind, J. M. (2017). Automatic differentiation in machine learning: A survey. *Journal of Machine Learning Research*, *18*(1), 5595–5637.

Bernini, M., & Woods, A. (2014). Interdisciplinarity as cognitive integration: Auditory verbal hallucinations as a case study. *Wiley Interdisciplinary Reviews: Cognitive Science*, *5*(5), 603–612. doi:10.1002/wcs.1305 PMID:26005512

Betancourt, R., & Alvarado, F. L. (1986). Parallel inversion of sparse matrices. *IEEE Transactions on Power Systems*, *1*(1), 74–81. doi:10.1109/TPWRS.1986.4334846

Bezanson, J., Edelman, A., Karpinski, S., & Shah, V. B. (2017). Julia: A fresh approach to numerical computing. *SIAM Review*, *59*(1), 65–98. doi:10.1137/141000671

Bienia, C. (2011). *Benchmarking modern multiprocessors* [Ph. D. Thesis]. Princeton University.

Binkowski, M., Marti, G., & Donnat, P. (2017). Autoregressive convolutional neural networks for asynchronous time series. *ICML 2017 Time Series Workshop*.

Bitirgen, R., Ipek, E., & Martinez, J. F. (2008, November). Coordinated management of multiple interacting resources in chip multiprocessors: A machine learning approach. In *2008 41st IEEE/ACM International Symposium on Microarchitecture* (pp. 318-329). IEEE. 10.1109/MICRO.2008.4771801

Blagojević, V. (2017). A systematic approach to generation of new ideas for PhD research in computing. *Advances in Computers, 104*, 1-31.

Blagojević, V., Bojić, D., Bojović, M., Cvetanović, M., Đorđević, J., Đurđević, Đ., Furlan, B., Gajin, S., Jovanović, Z., Milićev, D., Milutinović, V., Nikolić, B., Protić, J., Punt, M., Radivojević, Z., Stanisavljević, Ž., Stojanović, S., Tartalja, I., Tomašević, M., & Vuletić, P. (2017). A Systematic Approach to Generation of New Ideas for PhD Research in Computing. In A. R. Hurson & V. Milutinović (Eds.), Advances in Computers: Vol. 104. Creativity in computing and dataflow super computing (Vol. 104, pp. 1–31). Academic Press. doi:10.1016/bs.adcom.2016.09.001

Blagojevic, V. (2017). A Systematic Approach to Generation of New Ideas for PhD Research in Computing. In *Advances in Computers 104* (pp. 1–31). Elsevier.

Blagojević, V., Bojić, D., Bojović, M., Cvetanović, C., Đorđević, J., Đurđević, D., & Vuletić, P. (2017). *A Systematic Approach to Generation of New Ideas for PhD Research in Computing* (Vol. 104). Elsevier.

Blagojević, V., Bojić, D., Bojović, M., Cvetanović, M., Đorđević, J., Đurđević, Đ., ... Milutinović, V. (2017). A systematic approach to generation of new ideas for PhD research in computing. *Advances in Computers*, *104*, 1–31.

Blagojević, V., Bojić, D., Bojović, M., Cvetanović, M., Đorđević, J., Đurđević, Đ., ... Vuletić, P. (2016). A systematic approach to generation of new ideas for ′ PhD research in computing. *Advances in Computers*, *104*, 1–19.

Boccard, S. G., Pereira, E. A., & Aziz, T. Z. (2015). Deep brain stimulation for chronic pain. *Journal of Clinical Neuroscience*, *22*(10), 1537–1543. doi:10.1016/j.jocn.2015.04.005

Bonnici, V., Giugno, R., Pulvirenti, A., Shasha, D., & Ferro, A. (2013). A subgraph isomorphism algorithm and its application to biochemical data. *BMC Bioinformatics*, *14*(Suppl 7), S13. doi:10.1186/1471-2105-14-S7-S13 PMID:23815292

Boros, E. E., Toumi, A., Rouchet, E., Abadie, B., Stutzmann, D., & Kermorvant, C. (2019). *Automatic page classification in a large collection of manuscripts based on the International Image Interoperability Framework.* IEEE. https://www.britannica.com/

Boston, T. (2020). *Private correspondence with Terry Boston, former PJM CEO.* CIRCA.

Boudet, J. (2019, June 18). The future of personalization—and how to get ready for it. *McKinsey Insights.* Retrieved from https://www.mckinsey.com/business-functions/marketing-and-sales/our-insights/the-future-of-personalization-and-how-to-get-ready-for-it

Bowman, F. D. (2014). Brain Imaging Analysis. *Annual Review of Statistics and Its Application, 1,* 61–85. doi:10.1146/annurev-statistics-022513-115611

Bozdag, D., Catalyurek, U. V., Gebremedhin, A. H., Manne, F., Boman, E. G., & Ozguner, F. (2010). Distributed-memory parallel algorithms for distance2 coloring and related problems in derivative computation. *SIAM Journal on Scientific Computing, 32*(4), 2418–2446. doi:10.1137/080732158

Bozdag, D., Gebremedhin, A. H., Manne, F., Boman, E. G., & Catalyurek, U. V. (2008). A framework for scalable greedy coloring on distributed-memory parallel computers. *Journal of Parallel and Distributed Computing, 68*(4), 515–535. doi:10.1016/j.jpdc.2007.08.002

Brandin, B. A., Wonham, W. M., & Benhabib, B. (1991, August). Discrete event system supervisory control applied to the management of manufacturing workcells. In *Proc. Seventh International Conference on Computer-Aided Production Engineering, Cookeville TN USA* (pp. 527-536). Academic Press.

Brown, T. B., Mann, B., Ryder, N., Subbiah, M., Kaplan, J., Dhariwal, P., . . . Agarwal, S. (2020). *Language Models Are Few-Shot Learners.* arXiv Preprint arXiv:2005.14165

Brunel, N. (2000). Dynamics of sparsely connected networks of excitatory and inhibitory spiking neurons. *Journal of Computational Neuroscience, 8*(3), 183–208. doi:10.1023/a:1008925309027

Brunoni, A. R., Nitsche, M. A., Bolognini, N., Bikson, M., Wagner, T., Merabet, L., ... Fregni, F. (2012). Clinical research with transcranial direct current stimulation (tDCS): Challenges and future directions. *Brain Stimulation, 5*(3), 175–195. doi:10.1016/j.brs.2011.03.002

Burri, P. H. (1985) Development and growth of the human lung. In Handbook of Physiology, Section 3: The Respiratory System (pp 1–46). William & Wilkins.

Burri, P. H., Dbaly, J., & Weibel, E. R. (1974). The postnatal growth of the rat lung. I. Morphometry. *The Anatomical Record, 178*(4), 711–730. doi:10.1002/ar.1091780405 PMID:4592625

Butler, J. P., & Tsuda, A. (1997). Effect of convective "stretching and folding" to aerosol mixing deep in the lung, assessed by approximate entropy. *Journal of Applied Physiology, 83*(3), 800–809. doi:10.1152/jappl.1997.83.3.800 PMID:9292466

Butson, C. R., & McIntyre, C. C. (2005). Tissue and electrode capacitance reduce neural activation volumes during deep brain stimulation. *Clinical Neurophysiology, 116*(10), 2490–2500. doi:10.1016/j.clinph.2005.06.023

Calhoun, V. D., & Sui, J. (2016). Multimodal fusion of brain imaging data: A key to finding the missing link(s) in complex mental illness. *Biol Psychiatry Cogn Neurosci Neuroimaging, 1*(3), 230–244. doi:10.1016/j.bpsc.2015.12.005

Carletti, V., Foggia, P., Saggese, A., & Vento, M. (2017). Introducing vf3: A new algorithm for subgraph isomorphism. In *International workshop on graphbased representations in pattern recognition* (pp. 128–139). 10.1007/978-3-319-58961-9_12

Carrell, L. (2015). Digital trends shaping the US marketing landscape. *The Guardian.* Available: http: //www.theguardian.com/media-network/2015/jun/ 01/trends-us-digital-marketing-landscape

Carrington, P. J., Scott, J., & Wasserman, S. (2005). *Models and methods in social network analysis.* Cambridge University Press. doi:10.1017/CBO9780511811395

Carvalho, P. M., Peres, J. D., Ferreira, L. A., Ilic, M. D., Lauer, M., & Jaddivada, R. (2020). Incentive-based load shifting dynamics and aggregators response predictability. *Electric Power Systems Research, 189,* 106744. doi:10.1016/j.epsr.2020.106744

Catalyurek, U., Feo, J., Gebremedhin, A. H., Halappanavar, M., & Pothen, A. (2012). Graph coloring algorithms for multicore and massively multithreaded architectures. *Parallel Computing, 38*(10-11), 576–594. doi:10.1016/j.parco.2012.07.001

Chakrabarti, D., & Faloutsos, C. (2006). Graph mining: Laws, generators, and algorithms. *ACM Computing Surveys, 38*(1), 2. doi:10.1145/1132952.1132954

Chang, K. K., Yağlıkçı, A. G., Ghose, S., Agrawal, A., Chatterjee, N., Kashyap, A., ... Mutlu, O. (2017). Understanding reduced-voltage operation in modern DRAM devices: Experimental characterization, analysis, and mechanisms. *Proceedings of the ACM on Measurement and Analysis of Computing Systems, 1*(1), 1-42. 10.1145/3078505.3078590

Chaudhry, B. (2008). *Computerized clinical decision support: will it transform healthcare?* Academic Press.

Cheng, X. (2009). Fast Binary Dilation/Erosion Algorithm Using Reference Points. *2009 International Conference on Networking and Digital Society,* 87-90. 10.1109/ICNDS.2009.102

Chen, J. H., Alagappan, M., Goldstein, M. K., Asch, S. M., & Altman, R. B. (2017). Decaying relevance of clinical data towards future decisions in data-driven inpatient clinical order sets. *International Journal of Medical Informatics, 102,* 71–79.

Chen, P. C. (1992). Heuristic sampling: A method for predicting the performance of tree searching programs. *SIAM Journal on Computing, 21*(2), 295–315. doi:10.1137/0221022

Chen, S., & Haralick, R. (1995). Recursive erosion, dilation, opening, and closing transforms. *IEEE Transactions on Image Processing, 4*(3), 335–345. doi:10.1109/83.366481 PMID:18289983

Chen, S., He, Z., Han, X., He, X., Li, R., Zhu, H., ... Niu, B. (2019). How Big Data and High-performance Computing Drive Brain Science. *Genomics, Proteomics & Bioinformatics, 17*(4), 381–392. doi:10.1016/j.gpb.2019.09.003

Chen, T., & Guestrin, C. (2016). XGBoost: a scalable tree boosting system. In *Proceedings of the 22nd ACM SIGKDD International Conference on Knowledge Discovery and Data Mining* (pp. 785–794). Association for Computing Machinery. 10.1145/2939672.2939785

Che, Z., Purushotham, S., Cho, K., Sontag, D., & Liu, Y. (2018). Recurrent neural networks for multivariate time series with missing values. *Scientific Reports, 8*(1), 6085. doi:10.103841598-018-24271-9 PMID:29666385

Choi, S., & Yeung, D. (2006, June). Learning-based SMT processor resource distribution via hill-climbing. In *33rd International Symposium on Computer Architecture (ISCA'06)* (pp. 239-251). IEEE. 10.1109/ISCA.2006.25

Cho, K., Merrienboer, B., Gulcehre, C., Bahdanau, D., Bougares, F., Schwenk, H., & Bengio, Y. (2014). Learning phrase representations using RNN encoder-decoder for statistical machine translation. *Proceedings of the 2014 Conference on Empirical Methods in Natural Language Processing,* 1724–1734. 10.3115/v1/D14-1179

Chollet, F. (2017, May 4). Keras-team/keras 2.0.0. *GitHub.* https://github.com/keras-team/keras

Christ, M., Braun, N., Neuffer, J., & Kempa-Liehr, A. W. (2018). Time series feature extraction on the basis of scalable hypothesis tests (TSfresh - a Python package). *Neurocomputing, 307*, 72–77. doi:10.1016/j.neucom.2018.03.067

Chung, H., Kang, M., & Cho, H. D. (2012). *Heterogeneous multi-processing solution of Exynos 5 Octa with ARM big. LITTLE technology.* Samsung White Paper.

Čibej, U., Fürst, L., & Mihelič, J. (2019). A symmetry-breaking node equivalenceˇ for pruning the search space in back-tracking algorithms. *Symmetry, 11*(10), 1300. doi:10.3390ym11101300

Čibej, U., & Mihelič, J. (2015). Improvements to ullmann's algorithm for the subgraph isomorphism problem. *International Journal of Pattern Recognition and Artificial Intelligence, 29*(07), 1550025. doi:10.1142/S0218001415500251

Clements, K., Krumpholz, G., & Davis, P. (1981). Power system state estimation residual analysis: An algorithm using network topology. *IEEE Transactions on Power Apparatus and Systems, PAS-100*(4), 1779–1787. doi:10.1109/TPAS.1981.316517

Cochran, R., Hankendi, C., Coskun, A. K., & Reda, S. (2011, December). Pack & Cap: adaptive DVFS and thread packing under power caps. In *2011 44th Annual IEEE/ACM International Symposium on Microarchitecture (MICRO)* (pp. 175-185). IEEE. 10.1145/2155620.2155641

Coelho, D. (1989). *The VHDL Handbook.* Kluwer Academic Publishers. doi:10.1007/978-1-4613-1633-6

Cohen, J. D., Daw, N., Engelhardt, B., Hasson, U., Li, K., Niv, Y., ... Willke, T. L. (2017). Computational approaches to fMRI analysis. *Nature Neuroscience, 20*(3), 304–313. doi:10.1038/nn.4499

Coleman, T. F., & Cai, J.-Y. (1986). The cyclic coloring problem and estimation of sparse Hessian matrices. *SIAM Journal on Algebraic Discrete Methods, 7*(2), 221–235. doi:10.1137/0607026

Coleman, T. F., & Mor'e, J. J. (1984). Estimation of sparse Hessian matrices and graph coloring problems. *Mathematical Programming, 28*(3), 243–270. doi:10.1007/BF02612334

Coleman, T. F., & More, J. J. (1983). Estimation of sparse Jacobian matrices and graph coloring problems. *SIAM Journal on Numerical Analysis, 1*(20), 187–209. doi:10.1137/0720013

Committee on Diagnostic Error in Health Care, & the Board on Health Care Services. Institute of Medicine; The National Academies of Sciences, E., and Medicine. (2015). Improving diagnosis in healtcare. Washington, DC: The National Academy Press.

Committee on Diagnostic Error in Health Care, & the Board on Health Care Services. Institute of Medicine; The National Academies of Sciences, Engineering, and Medicine (2015). Improving diagnosis in healtcare. Washington (DC): The National Academy Press.

Conneau, A., Schwenk, H., Barrault, L., & Lecun, Y. (2017, April). Very Deep Convolutional Networks for Text Classification. In *Proceedings of the 15th Conference of the European Chapter of the Association for Computational Linguistics: Volume 1, Long Papers* (pp. 1107-1116). 10.18653/v1/E17-1104

Conte, D., Foggia, P., Sansone, C., & Vento, M. (2004). Thirty years of graph matching in pattern recongnition. *International Journal of Pattern Recognition and Artificial Intelligence, 18*(3), 265–298. doi:10.1142/S0218001404003228

Cook, S. A. (1971). The complexity of theorem-proving procedures. In *Proc. 3rd annual ACM symposium on theory of computing - stoc '71* (pp. 151–158). ACM Press. 10.1145/800157.805047

Cordella, L. P., Foggia, P., Sansone, C., & Vento, M. (1999). Performance evaluation of the VF graph matching algorithm. In Image analysis and processing, 1999. proceedings. international conference on (pp. 1172–1177). doi:10.1109/ICIAP.1999.797762

Cordella, L. P., Foggia, P., Sansone, C., & Vento, M. (2004, October). A (sub)graph isomorphism algorithm for matching large graphs. *IEEE Transactions on Pattern Analysis and Machine Intelligence*, *26*(10), 1367–1372. doi:10.1109/TPAMI.2004.75 PMID:15641723

Corsonello, P., Spezzano, G., Staino, G., & Talia, D. (2002). Efficient implementation of cellular algorithms on reconfigurable hardware. In *Proceedings 10th Euromicro Workshop on Parallel, Distributed and Network-based Processing* (pp. 211-218). 10.1109/EMPDP.2002.994273

Coughlin, T. (2018). *175 Zettabytes By 2025*. https://www.forbes.com/sites/tomcoughlin/2018/11/27/175-zettabytes-by2025/#e301d7454597

Crow, M. L., & Ilic, M. (1994). The waveform relaxation method for systems of differential/algebraic equations. *Mathematical and Computer Modelling*, *19*(12), 67–84. doi:10.1016/0895-7177(94)90099-X

Csardi, G., & Nepusz, T. (2006). The igraph software package for complex network research. *InterJournal. Complex Systems*, 1695.

Cummings, K. (2015). *Further Reading | Mindset Segmentation*. Available: http: //www.kelliecummings.com/strategies/mindset-segmentation/ further-reading-mindset-segmentation/

Cvijic, S., Ilic, M., Allen, E., & Lang, J. (2018). Using extended ac optimal power flow for effective decision making. In 2018 IEEE PES Innovative Smart Grid Technologies Conference Europe (ISGT-Europe), (pp. 1–6). IEEE. doi:10.1109/ISGTEurope.2018.8571792

Das, R., Ausavarungnirun, R., Mutlu, O., Kumar, A., & Azimi, M. (2013, February). Application-to-core mapping policies to reduce memory system interference in multi-core systems. In *2013 IEEE 19th International Symposium on High Performance Computer Architecture (HPCA)* (pp. 107-118). IEEE. 10.1109/HPCA.2013.6522311

Das, R., Mutlu, O., Moscibroda, T., & Das, C. R. (2009, December). Application-aware prioritization mechanisms for on-chip networks. In *2009 42nd Annual IEEE/ACM International Symposium on Microarchitecture (MICRO)* (pp. 280-291). IEEE. 10.1145/1669112.1669150

Das, R., Mutlu, O., Moscibroda, T., & Das, C. R. (2010). Aérgia: exploiting packet latency slack in on-chip networks. *ACM SIGARCH Computer Architecture News, 38*(3), 106-116.

Dask Development Team. (2019, June 25). Dask 2.0.0: Library for Dynamic Task Scheduling. *Dask*. https://dask.org

David, H., Fallin, C., Gorbatov, E., Hanebutte, U. R., & Mutlu, O. (2011, June). Memory power management via dynamic voltage/frequency scaling. In *Proceedings of the 8th ACM international conference on Autonomic computing* (pp. 31-40). 10.1145/1998582.1998590

Davies, C. N. (1972). Breathing of half-micron aerosols. II. Interpretation of experimental results. *Journal of Applied Physiology*, *35*(5), 605–611. doi:10.1152/jappl.1972.32.5.601 PMID:5064587

De Santo, M., Foggia, P., Sansone, C., & Vento, M. (2003, May). A large database of graphs and its use for benchmarking graph isomorphism algorithms. *Pattern Recognition Letters*, *24*(8), 1067–1079. doi:10.1016/S0167-8655(02)00253-2

Delilovic, N., Ebner, M., Maurer, H., & Zaka, B. (2020). Experiences Based on a Major Information Server. *IPSI BgD Transactions on Internet Research*, *16*(1), 68–75.

Delilovic, N., & Maurer, H. (2019a). *A Critical Discussion of Some Current and Future Developments of IT.* Springer International Publishing., doi:10.1007/978-3-030-28005-5_1

Delilovic, N., & Maurer, H. (2019b). A Note Concerning Feedback and Queries for Web Pages. *Journal of Universal Computer Science, 25*(7), 733–739. doi:10.3217/jucs-025-07-0733

Delorme, A., Majumdar, A., Sivagnanam, S., Martinez-Cancino, K., Yoshimoto, R., & Makeig, S. (2019). The Open EEGLAB portal. Paper presented at the 9th International IEEE/EMBS Conference on Neural Engineering (NER), San Francisco, CA, USA.

Delorme, A., Majumdar, A., Sivagnanam, S., Martinez-Cancino, K., Yoshimoto, R., & Makeig, S. (2019). *The Open EEGLAB portal.* Paper presented at the 9th International IEEE/EMBS Conference on Neural Engineering (NER), San Francisco, CA.

Deng, Q., Meisner, D., Bhattacharjee, A., Wenisch, T. F., & Bianchini, R. (2012, December). Coscale: Coordinating cpu and memory system dvfs in server systems. In *2012 45th annual IEEE/ACM international symposium on microarchitecture* (pp. 143-154). IEEE.

Dennis, J. B. (1974). First Version of a Data Flow Procedure Language. In *Programming Symposium*. MIT.

Dennis, J. B. (1974). First version of a data flow procedure language. In *Programming Symposium* (pp. 362-376). Springer.

Dettmers, T. (2020, September 20). TPUs vs GPUs for Transformers (BERT). *Tim Dettmers.* https://timdettmers.com/2018/10/17/tpus-vs-gpus-for-transformers-bert/

Devlin, J., Chang, M. W., Lee, K., & Toutanova, K. (2018). *Bert: Pre-Training of Deep Bidirectional Transformers for Language Understanding.* arXiv Preprint arXiv:1810.04805.

Dewey, M. (1876). *A Classification and Subject Index for Cataloguing and Arranging the Books and Pamphlets of a Library.* Kingsport Press, Inc. https://panopticlick.eff.org/

Dhodapkar, A. S., & Smith, J. E. (2002, May). Managing multi-configuration hardware via dynamic working set analysis. In *Proceedings 29th Annual International Symposium on Computer Architecture* (pp. 233-244). IEEE. 10.1109/ISCA.2002.1003581

Di, W., Sundaresan, N., Piramuthu, R., & Bhardwaj, A. (2014). Is a Picture Really Worth a Thousand Words?: - on the Role of Images in E-commerce. In *WSDM '14 Proceedings of the 7th ACM international conference on Web search and data mining.* ACM.

Dipietro, L., Plank, M., Poizner, H., & Krebs, H. I. (2012). EEG microstate analysis in human motor corrections. Paper presented at the RAS EMBS International Conference on Biomedical Robotics and Biomechatronics.

Dipietro, L., Plank, M., Poizner, H., & Krebs, H. I. (2012). *EEG microstate analysis in human motor corrections.* Paper presented at the RAS EMBS International Conference on Biomedical Robotics and Biomechatronics. 10.1109/BioRob.2012.6290832

Dipietro, L., Poizner, H., & Krebs, H. I. (2014). Spatiotemporal dynamics of online motor correction processing revealed by high-density electroencephalography. *Journal of Cognitive Neuroscience, 26*(9), 1966–1980. doi:10.1162/jocn_a_00593

Doi, H., Goto, M., Kawai, T., Yokokawa, S., & Suzuki, T. (1990). Advanced power system analogue simulator. *IEEE Transactions on Power Systems, 5*(3), 962–968. doi:10.1109/59.65926

Donyanavard, B., Rahmani, A. M., Jantsch, A., Mutlu, O., & Dutt, N. (2020). *Intelligent management of mobile systems through computational self-awareness.* arXiv preprint arXiv:2008.00095.

Donyanavard, B., Rahmani, A. M., Mück, T., Moazemmi, K., & Dutt, N. (2018, March). Gain scheduled control for nonlinear power management in CMPs. In 2018 Design, Automation & Test in Europe Conference & Exhibition (DATE) (pp. 921-924). IEEE. doi:10.23919/DATE.2018.8342141

Donyanavard, B., Mück, T., Sarma, S., & Dutt, N. (2016, October). SPARTA: Runtime task allocation for energy efficient heterogeneous manycores. In *2016 International Conference on Hardware/Software Codesign and System Synthesis (CODES+ ISSS)* (pp. 1-10). IEEE. 10.1145/2968456.2968459

Do, V.-Q., McCallum, D., Giroux, P., & De Kelper, B. (2001). A backward-forward interpolation technique for a precise modeling of power electronics in hypersim. *Proc. Int. Conf. Power Systems Transients*, 337–342.

Dubach, C., Jones, T. M., Bonilla, E. V., & O'Boyle, M. F. (2010, December). A predictive model for dynamic micro-architectural adaptivity control. In *2010 43rd Annual IEEE/ACM International Symposium on Microarchitecture* (pp. 485-496). IEEE. 10.1109/MICRO.2010.14

Dubach, C., Jones, T. M., & Bonilla, E. V. (2013). Dynamic microarchitectural adaptation using machine learning. *ACM Transactions on Architecture and Code Optimization*, 10(4), 1–28. doi:10.1145/2541228.2541238

Ebrahimi, E., Lee, C. J., Mutlu, O., & Patt, Y. N. (2010). Fairness via source throttling: A configurable and high-performance fairness substrate for multi-core memory systems. *ACM SIGPLAN Notices*, 45(3), 335–346. doi:10.1145/1735971.1736058

Ebrahimi, E., Lee, C. J., Mutlu, O., & Patt, Y. N. (2011). Prefetch-aware shared resource management for multi-core systems. *ACM SIGARCH Computer Architecture News*, 39(3), 141–152. doi:10.1145/2024723.2000081

Ebrahimi, E., Mutlu, O., Lee, C. J., & Patt, Y. N. (2009, December). Coordinated control of multiple prefetchers in multi-core systems. In *Proceedings of the 42nd Annual IEEE/ACM International Symposium on Microarchitecture* (pp. 316-326). 10.1145/1669112.1669154

Edwards, D. J., Dipietro, L., Demirtas-Tatlidede, A., Medeiros, A. H., Thickbroom, G. W., Mastaglia, F. L., ... Pascual-Leone, A. (2014). Movement-generated afference paired with transcranial magnetic stimulation: An associative stimulation paradigm. *Journal of Neuroengineering and Rehabilitation*, 11, 31. doi:10.1186/1743-0003-11-31

Ekman, P. (1992, January 1). Facial Expressions of Emotion: New Findings, New Questions. Meeting Report. *Psychological Science*. Retrieved from https://journals.sagepub.com/doi/10.1111/j.1467-9280.1992.tb00253.x

Ekman, P. (2013, July). *Emotional-And-Conversational-Nonverbal-Signals*. Retrieved from https://www.paulekman.com/wp-content/uploads/2013/07/Emotional-And-Conversational-Nonverbal-Signals.pdf

Ekman, P., & Friesen, W. V. (1969). The repertoire of nonverbal behaviour: Categories, origins, usage, and coding. *Semiotica*, 1(1), 49–98. doi:10.1515emi.1969.1.1.49

El Morr, C., & Subercaze, J. (2010). Knowledge management in healthcare. In *Handbook of research on developments in e-health and telemedicine: Technological and social perspectives* (pp. 490–510). IGI Global. doi:10.4018/978-1-61520-670-4.ch023

encyclopedia.com. (n.d.). https://www.encyclopedia.com

Endres, A., & Fellner, D. W. (2000). *Digitale Bibliotheken: Informatik-Lösungen für globale Wissensmärkte*. dpunkt-Verlag. https://analytics.google.com/

Ephraim, Y., & Merhav, N. (2002). Hidden Markov processes. *IEEE Transactions on Information Theory*, 48(6), 1518–1569. doi:10.1109/TIT.2002.1003838

Facebook Research. (2020, May 20). Breaking Down Language Barriers. *Natural Language Processing & Speech*. https://research.fb.com/category/natural-language-processing-and-speech/

Fan, S., Zahedi, S. M., & Lee, B. C. (2016). The computational sprinting game. *ACM SIGARCH Computer Architecture News*, *44*(2), 561–575. doi:10.1145/2980024.2872383

Fan, W. (2006, September). Tapping the Power of Text Mining. *Communications of the ACM*, *49*(9), 76–82.

Fan, W. (2012, March). Graph pattern matching revised for social network analysis. In *Proc. 15th international conference on database theory - ICDT '12* (p. 8). ACM Press. 10.1145/2274576.2274578

Fan, X., & Markram, H. (2019). A Brief History of Simulation Neuroscience. *Frontiers in Neuroinformatics*, *13*, 32. doi:10.3389/fninf.2019.00032

Ferraiolo, D. F., Sandhu, R., Gavrila, S., Kuhn, D. R., & Chandramouli, R. (2001). Proposed nist standard for role-based access control. *ACM Transactions on Information and System Security*, *4*(3), 224–274. doi:10.1145/501978.501980

Feynman, R. P., & Hey, J. G. (1998). *Feynman Lectures on Computation*. Addison-Wesley Longman Publishing Co.

Fleiss, J. L. (1971). Measuring Nominal Scale Agreement Among Many Raters. *Psychological Bulletin*, *76*(5), 378–382. doi:10.1037/h0031619

Flynn, M. J. (2013). Moving from Petaflops to Petadata. *Communications of the ACM*, *56*(5), 39–42.

Flynn, M. J., Mencer, O., Milutinovic, V., Rakocevic, G., Stenstrom, P., Trobec, R., & Valero, M. (2013). Moving from petaflops to petadata. *Communications of the ACM*, *56*(5), 39–42.

Foggia, P., & Sansone, C. (2001). A performance comparison of five algorithms for graph isomorphism. *TC-15 Workshop on Graph- based Representations in Pattern Recognition*.

Foggia, P., Sansone, C., & Vento, M. (2001b). A Performance Comparison of Five Algorithm for Graph Isomorphism. *3rd IAPR-TC15 Workshop on Graphbased Representations in Pattern Recognition*.

Foggia, P., Sansone, C., & Vento, M. (2001a). A database of graphs for isomorphism and sub-graph isomorphism benchmarking. *Proc. of the 3rd IAPR TC-15 International Workshop on Graph-based Representations*.

Fomin, F. V., Jansen, B. M., & Pilipczuk, M. (2012). Preprocessing subgraph and minor problems: when does a small vertex cover help? In *Parameterized and exact computation* (pp. 97–108). Springer. doi:10.1007/978-3-642-33293-7_11

Friedlander, S. K. (1977). *Smoke, Dust, and Haze*. Wiley Press.

Friedman, J. (2001). Greedy function approximation: A gradient boosting machine. *Annals of Statistics*, *29*(5), 1189–1232. doi:10.1214/aos/1013203451

Fu, X., Kabir, K., & Wang, X. (2011, July). Cache-aware utilization control for energy efficiency in multi-core real-time systems. In *2011 23rd Euromicro Conference on Real-Time Systems* (pp. 102-111). IEEE. 10.1109/ECRTS.2011.18

Fuchs, E., & Flugge, G. (2014). Adult neuroplasticity: More than 40 years of research. *Neural Plasticity*, *541870*. Advance online publication. doi:10.1155/2014/541870

Furlan, B. (2012). A Survey of Intelligent Question Routing Systems. *The 6th IEEE International Conference on Intelligent Systems*, 14-20.

Fürst, L., Čibej, U., & Mihelič, J. (2015). *Maximum exploratory equivalence in trees. 2015 federated conference on computer science and information systems*.

Future trends and market opportunities in the world's largest 750 cities. (2015). *Oxford Economics*. https://www.oxfordeconomics.com/Media/Default/landing-pages/cities/oe-cities-summary.pdf

Fu, Y., & Shahidehpour, M. (2007). Fast scuc for large-scale power systems. *IEEE Transactions on Power Systems*, 22(4), 2144–2151. doi:10.1109/TPWRS.2007.907444

Gabay, G., & Moskowitz, H. (2015). Mind Genomics: What Professional Conduct Enhances the Emotional Wellbeing of Teens at the Hospital? *Journal of Psychological Abnormalities in Children*, 4(3).

Gardner, M. (1970). Mathematical Games: The fantastic combinations of John Conway's new solitaire game "life". *Scientific American*, 223(4), 120–123. doi:10.1038cientificamerican1070-120

Garey, M. R., & Johnson, D. S. (1979). *Computers and intractability* (Vol. 174). Freeman San Francisco.

Garilovska, L. (2010). *Applications and Multidisciplinary Aspects of Wireless Sensor Networks: Concepts, Integration, and Case Studies*. Springer Science and Business Media.

Gavrilovska, L., Krco, S., Milutinović, V., Stojmenovic, I., & Trobec, R. (Eds.). (2010). *Application and multidisciplinary aspects of wireless sensor networks: concepts, integration, and case studies*. Springer Science & Business Media.

Gebremedhin, A. H., Manne, F., & Pothen, A. (2002). Parallel distancek coloring algorithms for numerical optimization. In Proceedings of EuroPar 2002, (vol. 2400, pp. 912–921). Springer.

Gebremedhin, A. H., & Manne, F. (2000). Scalable parallel graph coloring algorithms. *Concurrency (Chichester, England)*, 12(12), 1131–1146. doi:10.1002/1096-9128(200010)12:12<1131::AID-CPE528>3.0.CO;2-2

Gebremedhin, A. H., Manne, F., & Pothen, A. (2005). What color is your Jacobian? Graph coloring for computing derivatives. *SIAM Review*, 47(4), 629–705. doi:10.1137/S0036144504444711

Gebremedhin, A. H., Nguyen, D., Patwary, M. M. A., & Pothen, A. (2013). ColPack: Software for graph coloring and related problems in scientific computing. *ACM Transactions on Mathematical Software*, 40(1), 1–31. doi:10.1145/2513109.2513110

Gebremedhin, A., Pothen, A., Tarafdar, A., & Walther, A. (2009). Efficient computation of sparse Hessians using coloring and automatic differentiation. *INFORMS Journal on Computing*, 21(2), 209–223. doi:10.1287/ijoc.1080.0286

Gebremedhin, A., Pothen, A., & Walther, A. (2008). Exploiting sparsity in Jacobian computation via coloring and automatic differentiation: a case study in a Simulated Moving Bed process. In C. Bischof, M. Bücker, P. Hovland, U. Naumann, & J. Utke (Eds.), *Advances in Automatic Differentiation* (pp. 339–349). Springer. doi:10.1007/978-3-540-68942-3_29

Gebremedhin, A., Tarafdar, A., Manne, F., & Pothen, A. (2007). New acyclic and star coloring algorithms with application to computing Hessians. *SIAM Journal on Scientific Computing*, 29(3), 1042–1072. doi:10.1137/050639879

Gewaltig, M. O., & Diesmann, M. (2007). NEST (NEural Simulation Tool). *Scholarpedia*, 2(4), 1430.

Gooch, C. L., Pracht, E., & Borenstein, A. R. (2017). The burden of neurological disease in the United States: A summary report and call to action. *Annals of Neurology*, 81(4), 479–484. doi:10.1002/ana.24897

Google. (2020, July 26). Google/jax 0.1.52. *GitHub*. https://github.com/google/jax

Grama, A., Gupta, A., Karypis, G., & Kumar, V. (2003). *Introduction to Parallel Computing*. Pearson.

Grant, G. (2007). How the 1906 Nobel Prize in Physiology or Medicine was shared between Golgi and Cajal. *Brain Research. Brain Research Reviews*, 55(2), 490–498. doi:10.1016/j.brainresrev.2006.11.004

Grefkes, C., & Ward, N. S. (2014). Cortical reorganization after stroke: How much and how functional? *The Neuroscientist*, 20(1), 56–70. doi:10.1177/1073858413491147

Griewank, A., & Walther, A. (2008). *Evaluating Derivatives: Principles and Techniques of Algorithmic Differentiation* (2nd ed.). SIAM. doi:10.1137/1.9780898717761

Groiss, S. J., Wojtecki, L., Sudmeyer, M., & Schnitzler, A. (2009). Deep brain stimulation in Parkinson's disease. *Therapeutic Advances in Neurological Disorders*, *2*(6), 20–28. doi:10.1177/1756285609339382

Grujic, A., Tomasevíc, M., & Milutinovic, V. (1996). A simulation study of hardware-oriented DSM approaches. *IEEE Parallel & Distributed Technology Systems & Applications*, *4*(1), 74–83.

Gupta, U., Campbell, J., Ogras, U. Y., Ayoub, R., Kishinevsky, M., Paterna, F., & Gumussoy, S. (2016, November). Adaptive performance prediction for integrated GPUs. In *Proceedings of the 35th International Conference on Computer-Aided Design* (pp. 1-8). Academic Press.

Gupta, A., & Nishimura, N. (1996a). Characterizing the complexity of subgraph isomorphism for graphs of bounded path-width. *STACS*, *96*, 453–464. doi:10.1007/3-540-60922-9_37

Gupta, A., & Nishimura, N. (1996b). The complexity of subgraph isomorphism for classes of partial k-trees. *Theoretical Computer Science*, *164*(1), 287–298. doi:10.1016/0304-3975(96)00046-1

Gupta, U., Ayoub, R., Kishinevsky, M., Kadjo, D., Soundararajan, N., Tursun, U., & Ogras, U. Y. (2017). Dynamic power budgeting for mobile systems running graphics workloads. *IEEE Transactions on Multi-Scale Computing Systems*, *4*(1), 30–40. doi:10.1109/TMSCS.2017.2683487

Haber, S., Butler, J. P., Brenner, H., Emanuel, I., & Tsuda, A. (2000). Flow field in selfsimilar expansion on a pulmonary alveolus during rhythmical breathing. *Journal of Fluid Mechanics*, *405*, 243–268. doi:10.1017/S0022112099007375

Haber, S., & Tsuda, A. (2006). Cyclic model for particle motion in the pulmonary acinus. *Journal of Fluid Mechanics*, *567*, 157–184. doi:10.1017/S0022112006002345

Haghbayan, M. H., Miele, A., Rahmani, A. M., Liljeberg, P., & Tenhunen, H. (2017). Performance/reliability-aware resource management for many-cores in dark silicon era. *IEEE Transactions on Computers*, *66*(9), 1599–1612. doi:10.1109/TC.2017.2691009

Hahnloser, R., Sarpeshkar, R., Mahowald, M., Douglas, R. J., & Seung, H. S. (2000). Digital selection and analog amplification coexist in a cortex-inspired silicon circuit. *Nature*, *405*(6789), 947–951. doi:10.1038/35016072 PMID:10879535

Hairer, E., Lubich, C., & Wanner, G. (2006). *Geometric numerical integration: structure-preserving algorithms for ordinary differential equations* (Vol. 31). Springer Science & Business Media.

Hammarlund, P., & Ekeberg, O. (1998). Large neural network simulations on multiple hardware platforms. *Journal of Computational Neuroscience*, *5*(4), 443–459. doi:10.1023/a:1008893429695

Hanjun, J., & Huali, S. (2010). Rendering Fake Soft Shadows Based on the Erosion and Dilation. *2010 2nd International Conference on Computer Engineering and Technology*, *6*, 234-236.

Hanumaiah, V., Desai, D., Gaudette, B., Wu, C. J., & Vrudhula, S. (2014). STEAM: A smart temperature and energy aware multicore controller. *ACM Transactions on Embedded Computing Systems*, *13*(5s), 1–25. doi:10.1145/2661430

Han, W.-S., Lee, J., & Lee, J.-H. (2013). Turboiso: towards ultrafast and robust subgraph isomorphism search in large graph databases. In *Proceedings of the 2013 ACM SIGMOD international conference on management of data* (pp. 337–348). New York: ACM. 10.1145/2463676.2465300

Harter, H. L. (1975). The Method of Least Squares and Some Alternatives. Addendum to Part IV. *International Statistical Review/Revue Internationale de Statistique*, *43*(3), 273-278.

Haruna, K., Akmar Ismail, M., Suhendroyono, S., Damiasih, D., Pierewan, A., Chiroma, H., & Herawan, T. (2017). Context-Aware Recommender System: A Review of Recent Developmental Process and Future Research Direction. *Applied Sciences (Basel, Switzerland), 7*(12), 1211. Advance online publication. doi:10.3390/app7121211

Hasrul, M. N., Hariharan, M., & Yaacob, S. (2012, April 5). Human Affective (Emotion) behaviour analysis using speech signals: A review. In *2012 International Conference on Biomedical Engineering (ICoBE)*. IEEE. Retrieved from https://ieeexplore.ieee.org/abstract/document/6179008

Heckerman, D., Geiger, D., & Chickering, D. M. (1995). Learning Bayesian networks: The combination of knowledge and statistical data. *Machine Learning, 20*(3), 197–243. doi:10.1007/BF00994016

Helias, M., Kunkel, S., Masumoto, G., Igarashi, J., Eppler, J. M., Ishii, S., ... Diesmann, M. (2012). Supercomputers ready for use as discovery machines for neuroscience. *Frontiers in Neuroinformatics, 6*, 26. doi:10.3389/fninf.2012.00026

Hellerstein, J. L., Diao, Y., Parekh, S. S., & Tilbury, D. M. (2004). *Feedback control of computing systems* (Vol. 10). Wiley. doi:10.1002/047166880X

Hemsoth, N. (2014, April 19). Bringing Natural Language Processing Home. *HPCwire*. https://www.hpcwire.com/2011/06/09/bringing_natural_language_processing_home/

Hennessy, J. (1982). MIPS: A Microprocessor Architecture. *ACM SIGMICRO Newsletter, 13*(4), 17–22.

Hennessy, J., Jouppi, N., Przybylski, S., Rowen, C., Gross, T., Baskett, F., & Gill, J. (1982). MIPS: A microprocessor architecture. *ACM SIGMICRO Newsletter, 13*(4), 17–22.

Henry, F.S., Laine-Pearson, F.E., & Tsuda, A. (2009). Hamiltonian chaos in a model alveolus. *Journal of Biomechanical Engineering, 131*, 011006(1)–011006(7).

Henry, F. S., Butler, J. P., & Tsuda, A. (2002). Kinematically irreversible flow and aerosol transport in the pulmonary acinus: A departure from classical dispersive transport. *Journal of Applied Physiology, 92*, 835–845. doi:10.1152/japplphysiol.00385.2001 PMID:11796699

Henry, F. S., & Tsuda, A. (2016). Onset of alveolar recirculation in the developing lungs and its consequence on nanoparticle deposition in the pulmonary acinus. *Journal of Applied Physiology, 120*(1), 38–54. doi:10.1152/japplphysiol.01161.2014 PMID:26494453

Herbert, S., & Marculescu, D. (2007, August). Analysis of dynamic voltage/frequency scaling in chip-multiprocessors. In *Proceedings of the 2007 international symposium on Low power electronics and design (ISLPED'07)* (pp. 38-43). IEEE. 10.1145/1283780.1283790

Herrington, T. M., Cheng, J. J., & Eskandar, E. N. (2016). Mechanisms of deep brain stimulation. *Journal of Neurophysiology, 115*(1), 19–38. doi:10.1152/jn.00281.2015

Hespanha, J. P. (2001, December). Tutorial on supervisory control. *Lecture Notes for the Workshop Control using Logic and Switching for the 40th Conf. on Decision and Contr.*

He, Y., & Evans, A. (2010). Graph theoretical modeling of brain connectivity. *Current Opinion in Neurology, 23*(4), 341–350. PMID:20581686

Heyder, J. J. D., Blanchard, J. D., Feldman, H. A., & Brain, J. D. (1988). Convective mixing in human respiratory tract: Estimates with aerosol boli. *Journal of Applied Physiology, 64*(3), 1273–1278. doi:10.1152/jappl.1988.64.3.1273 PMID:3366742

Hines, M. (1984). Efficient computation of branched nerve equations. *International Journal of Bio-Medical Computing, 15*(1), 69–76. doi:10.1016/0020-7101(84)90008-4

Hines, M. L., & Carnevale, N. T. (1997). The NEURON simulation environment. *Neural Computation, 9*(6), 1179–1209. doi:10.1162/neco.1997.9.6.1179

Hoffmann, H. (2014, July). Coadapt: Predictable behavior for accuracy-aware applications running on power-aware systems. In *2014 26th Euromicro Conference on Real-Time Systems* (pp. 223-232). IEEE.

Hoffmann, H., Maggio, M., Santambrogio, M. D., Leva, A., & Agarwal, A. (2013, September). A generalized software framework for accurate and efficient management of performance goals. In *2013 Proceedings of the International Conference on Embedded Software (EMSOFT)* (pp. 1-10). IEEE. 10.1109/EMSOFT.2013.6658597

Hoffmann, H., Sidiroglou, S., Carbin, M., Misailovic, S., Agarwal, A., & Rinard, M. (2011). Dynamic knobs for responsive power-aware computing. *ACM SIGARCH Computer Architecture News, 39*(1), 199-212.

Holmberg, D., Burns, M., Bushby, S., Gopstein, A., McDermott, T., Tang, Y., Huang, Q., Pratt, A., Ruth, M., Ding, F., & ... . (1900). Nist transactive energy modeling and simulation challenge phase ii final report. *NIST Special Publication, 603*, 2019.

Howard, J., & Ruder, S. (2018, July). Universal Language Model Fine-tuning for Text Classification. In *Proceedings of the 56th Annual Meeting of the Association for Computational Linguistics (*Volume 1*: Long Papers)* (pp. 328-339). 10.18653/v1/P18-1031

Ilic & Lessard. (n.d.). Distributed coordinated architecture of electrical energy systems for sustainability. *Nature Energy.* (submitted)

Ilic, M. D., Jaddivada, R., & Miao, X. Scalable electric power system simulator. In 2018 IEEE PES Innovative Smart Grid Technologies Conference Europe (ISGT-Europe), (pp. 1–6). IEEE. doi:10.1109/ISGTEurope.2018.8571428

Ilic, M., & Jaddivada, R. (2019a). Introducing dymonds-as-a-service (dymaas) for internet of things. HPEC, 1–9.

Ilic, M., & Jaddivada, R. (2019b). Toward technically feasible and economically efficient integration of distributed energy resources. In *2019 57th Annual Allerton Conference on Communication, Control, and Computing (Allerton),* (pp. 796–803). IEEE. 10.1109/ALLERTON.2019.8919703

Ilic, M., & Lang, J. (2010). Netssworks software: An extended ac optimal power flow (ac xopf) for managing available system resources. *AD10-12 Staff Technical Conference on Enhanced Power Flow Models Federal Energy Regulatory Commission.*

Ilic, M. D. (2010). Dynamic monitoring and decision systems for enabling sustainable energy services. *Proceedings of the IEEE, 99*(1), 58–79. doi:10.1109/JPROC.2010.2089478

Ilic, M. D., & Jaddivada, R. (2018). Multi-layered interactive energy space modeling for near-optimal electrification of terrestrial, shipboard and aircraft systems. *Annual Reviews in Control, 45*, 52–75. doi:10.1016/j.arcontrol.2018.04.009

Ilic, M. D., Jaddivada, R., & Korpas, M. (2020). Interactive protocols for distributed energy resource management systems (derms). *IET Generation, Transmission & Distribution, 14*(11), 2065–2081. doi:10.1049/iet-gtd.2019.1022

Ilic, M., Crow, M., & Pai, M. (1987). Transient stability simulation by waveform relaxation methods. *IEEE Transactions on Power Systems, 2*(4), 943–949. doi:10.1109/TPWRS.1987.4335282

Ilic, M., & Jaddivada, R. (2020). Unified value-based feedback, optimization and risk management in complex electric energy systems. *Optimization and Engineering, 21*(2), 1–57. doi:10.100711081-020-09486-y

Ilic, M., Jaddivada, R., Miao, X., & Popli, N. (2019). Toward multi-layered mpc for complex electric energy systems. In *Handbook of Model Predictive Control* (pp. 625–663). Springer. doi:10.1007/978-3-319-77489-3_26

Ipek, E., Mutlu, O., Martínez, J. F., & Caruana, R. (2008). Self-optimizing memory controllers: A reinforcement learning approach. *ACM SIGARCH Computer Architecture News*, *36*(3), 39–50. doi:10.1145/1394608.1382172

Ippen, T., Eppler, J. M., Plesser, H. E., & Diesmann, M. (2017). Constructing Neuronal Network Models in Massively Parallel Environments. *Frontiers in Neuroinformatics*, *11*, 30. doi:10.3389/fninf.2017.00030

Isci, C., Buyuktosunoglu, A., Cher, C. Y., Bose, P., & Martonosi, M. (2006, December). An analysis of efficient multi-core global power management policies: Maximizing performance for a given power budget. In *2006 39th Annual IEEE/ACM International Symposium on Microarchitecture (MICRO'06)* (pp. 347-358). IEEE.

Jaddivada, R. (2020). *A unified modeling for control of reactive power dynamics in electrical energy systems* (PhD thesis). Massachusetts Institute of Technology.

Jájá, J. (1992). *An Introduction to Parallel Algorithms*. Addison-Wesley.

Jantsch, A., Dutt, N., & Rahmani, A. M. (2017). Self-awareness in systems on chip—A survey. *IEEE Design & Test*, *34*(6), 8–26. doi:10.1109/MDAT.2017.2757143

Jelena, P. (2020). *5G i samovozeći automobili: XXVI Skup Trendovi razvoja: "Inovacije u modernom obrazovanju"*. Academic Press.

Jin, F., Wang, W., Chakraborty, P., Self, N., Chen, F., & Ramakrishnan, N. (2017, July). Tracking Multiple Social Media for Stock Market Event Prediction. In *Industrial Conference on Data Mining* (pp. 16-30). Springer. 10.1007/978-3-319-62701-4_2

Jodoin, P.-M. (2013). Meta-tracking for video scene understanding. In *Proceedings on 10th IEEE International Conference on Advanced Video and Signal Based Surveillance (AVSS)*. IEEE.

Joo, J.-Y., & Ilic, M. D. (2013). Multi-layered optimization of demand resources using lagrange dual decomposition. *IEEE Transactions on Smart Grid*, *4*(4), 2081–2088. doi:10.1109/TSG.2013.2261565

Jordan, J., Ippen, T., Helias, M., Kitayama, I., Sato, M., Igarashi, J., ... Kunkel, S. (2018). Extremely Scalable Spiking Neuronal Network Simulation Code: From Laptops to Exascale Computers. *Frontiers in Neuroinformatics*, *12*, 2. doi:10.3389/fninf.2018.00002

Jovanović, Ž., & Milutinović, V. (2012). FPGA accelerator for floating-point matrix multiplication. *IET Computers & Digital Techniques*, *6*(4), 249–256.

Juang, P., Wu, Q., Peh, L. S., Martonosi, M., & Clark, D. W. (2005, August). Coordinated, distributed, formal energy management of chip multiprocessors. In *Proceedings of the 2005 international symposium on Low power electronics and design* (pp. 127-130). 10.1145/1077603.1077637

Jung, H., Rong, P., & Pedram, M. (2008, June). Stochastic modeling of a thermally-managed multi-core system. In *Proceedings of the 45th annual Design Automation Conference* (pp. 728-733). 10.1145/1391469.1391657

Kadjo, D., Ayoub, R., Kishinevsky, M., & Gratz, P. V. (2015, June). A control-theoretic approach for energy efficient CPU-GPU subsystem in mobile platforms. In *2015 52nd ACM/EDAC/IEEE Design Automation Conference (DAC)* (pp. 1-6). IEEE. 10.1145/2744769.2744773

Kandel, E. R. (2012). *Principles of Neural Science* (J. H. Schwartz, T. M. Jessell, S. A. Siegelbaum, & A. J. Hudspeth, Eds.; 5th ed.). McGraw-Hill Education / Medical.

Kanduri, A., Haghbayan, M. H., Rahmani, A. M., Liljeberg, P., Jantsch, A., Dutt, N., & Tenhunen, H. (2016, November). Approximation knob: Power capping meets energy efficiency. In *2016 IEEE/ACM International Conference on Computer-Aided Design (ICCAD)* (pp. 1-8). IEEE. 10.1145/2966986.2967002

Karagiannis, V., Schulte, S., Leitao, J., & Preguiça, N. (2019, May). Enabling fog computing using self-organizing compute nodes. In *2019 IEEE 3rd International Conference on Fog and Edge Computing (ICFEC)* (pp. 1-10). IEEE. 10.1109/CFEC.2019.8733150

Karamanolis, C. T., Karlsson, M., & Zhu, X. (2005, June). Designing Controllable Computer Systems. In HotOS (pp. 9-15). Academic Press.

Karl, A., Henry, F. S., & Tsuda, A. (2004). Low Reynolds number viscous flow in an alveolated duct. *Journal of Biomechanical Engineering, 126*(4), 13–19. doi:10.1115/1.1784476 PMID:15543859

Klein, J. T. (2010). A taxonomy of interdisciplinarity. In R. Frodeman, J. T. Klein, & C. Mitcham (Eds.), *The Oxford Handbook of Interdisciplinarity* (pp. 15–30). Oxford University Press.

Klomjai, W., Katz, R., & Lackmy-Vallee, A. (2015). Basic principles of transcranial magnetic stimulation (TMS) and repetitive TMS (rTMS). *Annals of Physical and Rehabilitation Medicine, 58*(4), 208–213. doi:10.1016/j.rehab.2015.05.005

Knezevic, P., Radnovic, B., Nikolic, N., Jovanovic, T., Milanov, D., Nikolic, M., Milutinovic, V., Casselman, S., & Schewel, J. (2000). The architecture of the Obelix-an improved Internet search engine. In R. H. Sprague (Ed.), *Proceedings of the 33rd annual Hawaii international conference on system sciences* (p. 11). IEEE Comput. Soc. 10.1109/HICSS.2000.926873

Knezevic, P. (2000). The Architecture of the Obelix – an Improved Internet Search Engine. *Proceedings of the 33rd Annual Hawaii International Conference on System Sciences.*

Knezevic, P., Radnovic, B., Nikolic, N., Jovanovic, T., Milanov, D., Nikolic, M., ... Schewel, J. (2000, January). The architecture of the Obelix-an improved internet search engine. In *Proceedings of the 33rd Annual Hawaii International Conference on System Sciences*. IEEE.

Knuth, D. E. (2019). Mathematical preliminaries redux; introduction to backtracking; dancing links (Vol. 4, Fascicle 5). Academic Press.

Knuth, D. E. (1974). *Estimating the efficiency of backtrack programs.* Tech. Rep.

Korolija, N., Djukic, T., Milutinovic, V., & Filipovic, N. (2013). *Accelerating Lattice-Boltzman method using Maxeler dataflow approach. The IPSI BgD Transactions on Internet Research, 34.*

Korolov, R., Lu, D., Wang, J., Zhou, G., Bonial, C., Voss, C., ... Ji, H. (2016, August). On Predicting Social Unrest Using Social Media. In *2016 IEEE/ACM International Conference on Advances in Social Networks Analysis and Mining (ASONAM)* (pp. 89-95). 10.1109/ASONAM.2016.7752218

Kos, A., Tomažič, S., Salom, J., Trifunovic, N., Valero, M., & Milutinovic, V. (2015). New benchmarking methodology and programming model for big data processing. *International Journal of Distributed Sensor Networks, 11*(8), 271752.

Kotlar, M., & Milutinovic, V. (2018). Comparing Control Flow and Data Flow for Tensor Calculus: Speed, Power, Complexity, and MTBF. *International Conference on High Performance Computing,* 329-346, 2018.

Krahmer, E., Van Erk, S., & Verleg, A. (2003). Graph-based generation of referring expressions. *Computational Linguistics, 29*(1), 53–72. doi:10.1162/089120103321337430

Kristol, D. M. (2001). HTTP Cookies. *ACM Transactions on Internet Technology, 1*(2), 151–198. doi:10.1145/502152.502153

Kunegis, J. (2013). KONECT: the koblenz network collection. In *Proceedings of the international conference on world wide web companion* (pp. 1343–1350). 10.1145/2487788.2488173

Kunkel, S., Schmidt, M., Eppler, J. M., Plesser, H. E., Masumoto, G., Igarashi, J., ... Helias, M. (2014). Spiking network simulation code for petascale computers. *Frontiers in Neuroinformatics*, *8*, 78. doi:10.3389/fninf.2014.00078

Kurzak, J., Bader, D., & Dongara, J. (2010). *Scientific Computing with Multicore and Accelerators*. Chapman and Hall/CRC Press. doi:10.1201/b10376

Laine-Pearson, F. E., & Hydon, P. E. (2006). Particle transport in a moving corner. *Journal of Fluid Mechanics*, *559*, 379–390. doi:10.1017/S0022112006009967

Lan, Z., Chen, M., Goodman, S., Gimpel, K., Sharma, P., & Soricut, R. (2019, September). ALBERT: A Lite BERT for Self-supervised Learning of Language Representations. In *International Conference on Learning Representations*.

Latremoliere, A., & Woolf, C. J. (2009). Central sensitization: A generator of pain hypersensitivity by central neural plasticity. *The Journal of Pain*, *10*(9), 895–926. doi:10.1016/j.jpain.2009.06.012

Lauer, M., Jaddivada, R., & Ilic, M. Secure blockchain-enabled dymonds de-sign. *Proceedings of the International Conference on Omni-Layer Intelligent Systems*, 191–198. 10.1145/3312614.3312654

LaWhite, N., & Ilic, M. D. (1997). Vector space decomposition of reactive power for periodic nonsinusoidal signals. *IEEE Transactions on Circuits and Systems. I, Fundamental Theory and Applications*, *44*(4), 338–346. doi:10.1109/81.563623

Lee, C. J., Narasiman, V., Ebrahimi, E., Mutlu, O., & Patt, Y. N. (2010). *DRAM-aware last-level cache writeback: Reducing write-caused interference in memory systems*. Academic Press.

Lee, J., Han, W.-S., Kasperovics, R., & Lee, J.-H. (2012). An in-depth comparison of subgraph isomorphism algorithms in graph databases. In *Proceedings of the 39th international conference on very large data bases* (pp. 133–144). 10.14778/2535568.2448946

Legendre, A. M. (1805). *Nouvelles méthodes pour la détermination des orbites des comètes*. F. Didot.

Leith, D. J., & Leithead, W. E. (2000). Survey of gain-scheduling analysis and design. *International Journal of Control*, *73*(11), 1001–1025. doi:10.1080/002071700411304

Lennart, L. (1999). *System identification: theory for the user*. PTR Prentice Hall.

Leskovec, J., & Krevl, A. (2014, Jun). *SNAP Datasets: Stanford large network dataset collection*. http://snap.stanford.edu/data

Lewis, P. R., Platzner, M., Rinner, B., Tørresen, J., & Yao, X. (2016). *Self-Aware Computing Systems. Natural Computing Series*. Springer. doi:10.1007/978-3-319-39675-0

Lick, D. R., & White, A. T. (1970). *k*-degenerate graphs. *Canadian Journal of Mathematics*, *22*(5), 1082–1096. doi:10.4153/CJM-1970-125-1

Liddy, E. D. (2001). *Natural language processing: Encyclopedia of Library and Information Science* (2nd ed.). Marcel Decker, Inc.

Lin, Y.-L., & Skiena, S. (1995). Algorithms for square roots of graphs. *SIAM Journal on Discrete Mathematics*, *8*(1), 99–118. doi:10.1137/S089548019120016X

Lipets, V., Vanetik, N., & Gudes, E. (2009). Subsea: An efficient heuristic algorithm for subgraph isomorphism. *Data Mining and Knowledge Discovery*, *19*(3), 320–350. doi:10.100710618-009-0132-7

Liu, G., Park, J., & Marculescu, D. (2013, October). Dynamic thread mapping for high-performance, power-efficient heterogeneous many-core systems. In *2013 IEEE 31st international conference on computer design (ICCD)* (pp. 54-61). IEEE. 10.1109/ICCD.2013.6657025

Liu, Y., Ott, M., Goyal, N., Du, J., Joshi, M., Chen, D., . . . Stoyanov, V. (2019). *Roberta: A robustly optimized BERT pretraining approach*. arXiv Preprint arXiv:1907.11692.

Liu, J., & Lee, Y. T. (2001). Graph-based method for face identification from a single 2D line drawing. *IEEE Transactions on Pattern Analysis and Machine Intelligence, 23*(10), 1106–1119. doi:10.1109/34.954601

Liu, S., Sheng, J., Li, B., & Zhang, X. (2017). Recent Advances in Non-invasive Brain Stimulation for Major Depressive Disorder. *Frontiers in Human Neuroscience, 11*, 526. doi:10.3389/fnhum.2017.00526

Li, X., Guo, N., & Li, Q. (2019). Functional Neuroimaging in the New Era of Big Data. *Genomics, Proteomics & Bioinformatics, 17*(4), 393–401. doi:10.1016/j.gpb.2018.11.005

Ljung, L. (2001, May). Black-box models from input-output measurements. In *IMTC 2001. proceedings of the 18th IEEE instrumentation and measurement technology conference. rediscovering measurement in the age of informatics (cat. no. 01ch 37188)* (Vol. 1, pp. 138-146). IEEE. 10.1109/IMTC.2001.928802

Lo, D., Song, T., & Suh, G. E. (2015, December). Prediction-guided performance-energy trade-off for interactive applications. In *Proceedings of the 48th International Symposium on Microarchitecture* (pp. 508-520). 10.1145/2830772.2830776

Loper, E., & Bird, S. (2002). *NLTK: The Natural Language Toolkit*. arXiv Preprint cs/0205028.

Loughran, T., & McDonald, B. (2011). When Is a Liability Not a Liability? Textual Analysis, Dictionaries, and 10-Ks. *The Journal of Finance, 66*(1), 35–65. doi:10.1111/j.1540-6261.2010.01625.x

Lundberg, S. M., & Lee, S. I. (2017). A unified approach to interpreting model predictions. *Advances in Neural Information Processing Systems, 30*, 4765–4774.

Ma, K., Li, X., Chen, M., & Wang, X. (2011, June). Scalable power control for many-core architectures running multi-threaded applications. In *2011 38th Annual International Symposium on Computer Architecture (ISCA)* (pp. 449-460). IEEE. 10.1145/2000064.2000117

Maggio, M., Hoffmann, H., Santambrogio, M. D., Agarwal, A., & Leva, A. (2010, December). Controlling software applications via resource allocation within the heartbeats framework. In *49th IEEE Conference on Decision and Control (CDC)* (pp. 3736-3741). IEEE. 10.1109/CDC.2010.5717893

Mahajan, D., Yazdanbakhsh, A., Park, J., Thwaites, B., & Esmaeilzadeh, H. (2016). Towards statistical guarantees in controlling quality tradeoffs for approximate acceleration. *ACM SIGARCH Computer Architecture News, 44*(3), 66–77. doi:10.1145/3007787.3001144

Makin, S. (2019). The four biggest challenges in brain simulation. *Nature, 571*(7766), S9. doi:10.1038/d41586-019-02209-z

Manavski, S. A., & Valle, G. (2008). CUDA compatible GPU cards as efficient hardware accelerators for Smith-Waterman sequence alignment. *BMC Bioinformatics, 9*(Suppl 2), S10. doi:10.1186/1471-2105-9-S2-S10

Markram, H. (2013). Seven challenges for neuroscience. *Functional Neurology, 28*(3), 145–151. doi:10.11138/FNeur/2013.28.3.144

Markram, H., Muller, E., Ramaswamy, S., Reimann, M. W., Abdellah, M., Sanchez, C. A., ... Schurmann, F. (2015). Reconstruction and Simulation of Neocortical Microcircuitry. *Cell, 163*(2), 456–492. doi:10.1016/j.cell.2015.09.029

Marx, D., & Pilipczuk, M. (2013). *Everything you always wanted to know about the parameterized complexity of subgraph isomorphism (but were afraid to ask).* Academic Press.

MathWorks. (2017). *System Identification Toolbox.* Tech. rep. https://www.mathworks.com/products/sysid.html

Matula, D. W. (1968). A max-min theorem for graphs with application to graph coloring. *SIAM Review, 10,* 481–482.

Matula, D. W. (1978). Subtree isomorphism in o(n5/2). In P. H. B. Alspach & D. Miller (Eds.), *Algorithmic aspects of combinatorics* (Vol. 2, pp. 91–106). Elsevier. doi:10.1016/S0167-5060(08)70324-8

Matula, D. W., & Beck, L. L. (1983). Smallest-last ordering and clustering and graph coloring algorithms. *Journal of the Association for Computing Machinery, 30*(3), 417–427. doi:10.1145/2402.322385

Matula, D. W., Marble, G., & Isaacson, J. (1972). Graph coloring algorithms. In R. Read (Ed.), *Graph Theory and Computing* (pp. 109–122). Academic Press. doi:10.1016/B978-1-4832-3187-7.50015-5

Maurer, H., Delilovic, N., & Zaka, B. (2019). Libraries of Interactive Books as Powerful Tool for Information Communication. In *Proceedings of EdMedia + Innovate Learning 2019* (pp. 1353–1359). Association for the Advancement of Computing in Education (AACE). https://www.learntechlib.org/p/210270

Maurer, H., & Delilovic, N. (2020). Ein kritischer Spaziergang durch das Internet. In *Enlightenment Today* (pp. 221–250). Academia Verlag., doi:10.5771/9783896658647-221

Maxeler Technologies. (2015a). *Acceleration Tutorial. Loops and Pipelining. Version 2015.1.1.* Author.

Maxeler Technologies. (2015b). *Multiscale Dataflow Programming. Version 2015.1.1.* Author.

Maxeler WebIDE. (n.d.). https://maxeler.mi.sanu.ac.rs

McCarthy, B., & Saleh, T. (2019, November 21). Building the AI-Powered Organization. *Harvard Business Review.* Retrieved from https://hbr.org/webinar/2019/11/building-the-ai-powered-organization

McCormick, S. T. (1983). Optimal approximation of sparse hessians and its equivalence to a graph coloring problem. *Mathematical Programming, 26*(2), 153–171. doi:10.1007/BF02592052

McCreesh, C., & Prosser, P. (2015a). A parallel, backjumping subgraph isomorphism algorithm using supplemental graphs. In *International conference on principles and practice of constraint programming* (pp. 295–312). 10.1007/978-3-319-23219-5_21

McGeoch, C. C. (2012). *A guide to experimental algorithmics.* Cambridge University Press.

McLane, S. (2005). Designing an EMR planning process based on staff attitudes toward and opinions about computers in healthcare. *CIN: Computers, Informatics. Nursing, 23*(2), 85–92. PMID:15772509

Messmer, B. T., & Bunke, H. (2000, March). Efficient subgraph isomorphism detection: A decomposition approach. *IEEE Transactions on Knowledge and Data Engineering, 12*(2), 307–323. doi:10.1109/69.842269

Meucci, A., Ardia, D., & Colasante, M. (2014, June 1). *Quantitative Portfolio Construction and Systematic Trading Strategies Using Factor Entropy Pooling.* EDHEC-Risk Institute. Retrieved from https://risk.edhec.edu/publications/quantitative-portfolio-construction-and-systematic-trading-strategies-using-factor

Michel, C. M., & Brunet, D. (2019). EEG Source Imaging: A Practical Review of the Analysis Steps. *Frontiers in Neurology, 10,* 325. doi:10.3389/fneur.2019.00325

Mihelič, J., Fürst, L., & Čibej, U. (2014). *Exploratory equivalence in graphs: Definition and algorithms. 2014 federated conference on computer science and information systems.*

Mikolov, T., Sutskever, I., Chen, K., Corrado, G. S., & Dean, J. (2013). Distributed Representations of Words and Phrases and Their Compositionality. In Advances in Neural Information Processing Systems (pp. 3111-3119). Academic Press.

Milenkovic, A., & Milutinovic, V. (2000). Cache injection: A novel technique for tolerating memory latency in bus-based SMPs. Paper presented at the European Conference on Parallel Processing, Berlin, Heidelberg.

Milenkovic, A., & Milutinovic, V. (2000). Cache Injection: A Novel Technique for Tolerating Memory Latency in Bus-based SMPs. *European Conference on Parallel Processing*, 558-566.

Milenkovic, A., & Milutinovic, V. (2000, August). Cache injection: A novel technique for tolerating memory latency in bus-based SMPs. In *European Conference on Parallel Processing* (pp. 558-566). Springer.

Miller, S. J. (2006). The method of least squares. *Mathematics Department Brown University*, 8, 1–7.

Milutinovic, D. (1987). The Honeycomb Architecture. *IEEE Computer, 20*(4), 81-83.

Milutinovic, D., Milutinovic, V., & Soucek, B. (1987). *The honeycomb architecture*. Academic Press.

Milutinovic, D., Milutinovic, V., & Soucek, B. (1987). The Honeycomb Architecture. *Computer, 20*(4), 81–83.

Milutinovic, V. (1996). *Surviving the design of a 200MHz RISC microprocessor*. IEEE Computer Society Press.

Milutinovic, V. (1996). *Surviving the Design of a 200MHz RISC Microprocessor*. IEEE Computer Society Press.

Milutinovic, V. (2001). *Infrastructure for Electronic Business on the Internet. Kluwer Academic Publishers*.

Milutinovic, V. (2015). *Guide to DataFlow SuperComputing*. Springer Nature.

Milutinovic, V. M. (1980). Comparison of three suboptimum detection procedures. *Electronics Letters, 16*(17), 681–683.

Milutinovic, V., Kotlar, M., Stojanovic, M., Dundic, I., Trifunovic, N., & Babovic, Z. (2017). *DataFlow Supercomputing Essentials*. Springer.

Milutinovic, V., & Salom, J. (2016). *Mind Genomics: Guide to Data Driven Marketing Strategy*. Springer.

Milutinović, V., Salom, J., Trifunović, N., & Giorgi, R. (2015). *Guide to dataflow supercomputing*. Springer Nature.

Milutinovic, V., Salom, J., Trifunovic, N., & Giorgi, R. (2015). *Guide to DataFlow Supercomputing: Basic Concepts, Case Studies, and a Detailed Example*. Springer Publishing Company, Incorporated. doi:10.1007/978-3-319-16229-4

Ming, X., Juan, Z., & Zhijun, F. (2017). Research on unstructured road detection algorithm based on improved morphological operations. *4th International Conference on Smart and Sustainable City*. 10.1049/cp.2017.0104

Mishne, G., & Glance, N. (2006, May). Leave a Reply: An Analysis of Weblog Comments. *Third Annual Workshop on the Weblogging Ecosystem*.

Mishra, A. K., Srikantaiah, S., Kandemir, M., & Das, C. R. (2010, November). CPM in CMPs: Coordinated power management in chip-multiprocessors. In *SC'10: Proceedings of the 2010 ACM/IEEE International Conference for High Performance Computing, Networking, Storage and Analysis* (pp. 1-12). IEEE. 10.1109/SC.2010.15

Mishra, N., Imes, C., Lafferty, J. D., & Hoffmann, H. (2018). CALOREE: Learning control for predictable latency and low energy. *ACM SIGPLAN Notices, 53*(2), 184–198. doi:10.1145/3296957.3173184

Montani, S., & Striani, M. (2019). Artificial intelligence in clinical decision support: A focused literature survey. *Yearbook of Medical Informatics, 28*(1), 120.

Morrison, A., Aertsen, A., & Diesmann, M. (2007). Spike-timing-dependent plasticity in balanced random networks. *Neural Computation, 19*(6), 1437–1467. doi:10.1162/neco.2007.19.6.1437

Morse, A. S. (1997). In A. S. Morse (Ed.), *Control using logic-based switching*. Springer. doi:10.1007/BFb0036078

Moskowitz, H. (2007). Mind Genomics. *Proceedings of the IPSI-2007*, 1-10.

Moskowitz, H. (2012). Mind genomics: The experimental, inductive science of the ordinary, and its application to aspects of food and feeding. *Physiology & Behavior, 107*(4), 606–613.

Moskowitz, H., Gofman, A., Beckley, J., & Ashman, H. (2006). Founding a New Science: Mind Genomics. *Journal of Sensory Studies*, (21), 266–307.

Moss, M. (2013, Feb. 20). The Extraordinary Science of Addictive Junk Food. *The New York Times Magazine.*

Moutinho, L. (2019). *AI Storm in Marketing - Paradigm Shift of Artificial Intelligence (AI) and Marketing Evolution.* VIPSI Conference, Budva, Montenegro.

Mück, T., Sarma, S., & Dutt, N. (2015, October). Run-DMC: Runtime dynamic heterogeneous multicore performance and power estimation for energy efficiency. In *2015 International Conference on Hardware/Software Codesign and System Synthesis (CODES+ ISSS)* (pp. 173-182). IEEE. 10.1109/CODESISSS.2015.7331380

Mueller, J., & Thyagarajan, A. (2016, February). Siamese Recurrent Architectures for Learning Sentence Similarity. In *Proceedings of the Thirtieth AAAI Conference on Artificial Intelligence* (pp. 2786-2792). AAAI.

Muller-Hannemann, M., & Schirra, S. (Eds.). (2010). *Algorithm engineering: Bridging the gap between algorithm theory and practice.* Springer-Verlag. doi:10.1007/978-3-642-14866-8

Mullick, A., Ghosh, S., Dutt, R., Ghosh, A., & Chakraborty, A. (2019, April). Public Sphere 2.0: Targeted Commenting in Online News Media. In *European Conference on Information Retrieval* (pp. 180-187). Springer. 10.1007/978-3-030-15719-7_23

Mullin, M. (2018, October 10). When Robots Feel Our Pain: Rosalind Picard on 'Emotional Intelligence' in a Brave New World. *TheTyee.ca, Newsletter.* Retrieved from https://thetyee.ca/Presents/2018/10/10/Rosalind-Picard-Lecture/

Murturi, A., Kantarci, B., & Oktug, S. F. (2015, October). A reference model for crowdsourcing as a service. In *2015 IEEE 4th International Conference on Cloud Networking (CloudNet)* (pp. 64-66). IEEE. 10.1109/CloudNet.2015.7335281

Muthukaruppan, T. S., Pricopi, M., Venkataramani, V., Mitra, T., & Vishin, S. (2013, May). Hierarchical power management for asymmetric multi-core in dark silicon era. In *2013 50th ACM/EDAC/IEEE Design Automation Conference (DAC)* (pp. 1-9). IEEE. 10.1145/2463209.2488949

Muthukaruppan, T. S., Pathania, A., & Mitra, T. (2014). Price theory based power management for heterogeneous multi-cores. *ACM SIGPLAN Notices, 49*(4), 161–176. doi:10.1145/2644865.2541974

Narasimhan, S. (2020, August 26). NVIDIA Clocks World's Fastest BERT Training Time and Largest Transformer Based Model, Paving Path for Advanced Conversational AI. *NVIDIA Developer Blog.* https://developer.nvidia.com/blog/training-bert-with-gpus/

Naumov, L. (2004). *CAME&L – Cellular Automata Modeling Environment & Library.* Springer Berlin Heidelberg. doi:10.1007/978-3-540-30479-1_76

Neiberg, D., Elenius, K., & Laskowski, K. (2006). Emotion recognition in spontaneous speech using GMMs. *Proceedings of Interspeech.*

Neil, D., Pfeiffer, M., & Liu, S. (2016). Phased LSTM: accelerating recurrent network training for long or event-based sequences. In *Proceedings of the 30th International Conference on Neural Information Processing Systems* (pp. 3889–3897). Curran Associates Inc.

Nemes, A., & Mester, G. (2017). Unconstrained evolutionary and gradient descent-based tuning of fuzzy-partitions for UAV dynamic modeling. *FME Transactions, 45*(1), 1–8. doi:10.5937/fmet1701001N

Nielsen, T. D., & Jensen, F. V. (2009). *Bayesian networks and decision graphs*. Springer Science & Business Media.

Nixon, M., & Aguado, A. (2012). *Feature extraction & image processing for computer vision* (3rd ed.). Academic Press.

Ntinas, V. G., Moutafis, B. E., Trunfio, G. A., & Sirakoulis, G. C. (2016). GPU and FPGA Parallelization of Fuzzy Cellular Automata for the Simulation of Wildfire Spreading. In *Parallel Processing and Applied Mathematics* (pp. 560–569). Springer International Publishing. doi:10.1007/978-3-319-32152-3_52

O'Brien, A. T., Amorim, R., Rushmore, R. J., Eden, U., Afifi, L., Dipietro, L., ... Valero-Cabre, A. (2016). Motor Cortex Neurostimulation Technologies for Chronic Post-stroke Pain: Implications of Tissue Damage on Stimulation Currents. *Frontiers in Human Neuroscience, 10*, 545. doi:10.3389/fnhum.2016.00545

Oberdörster, G., Stone, V., & Donaldson, K. (2007). Toxicology of nanoparticles: A historical perspective. *Nanotoxicology, 1*(1), 2–25. doi:10.1080/17435390701314761

Olmstead, M., & Gilbert, J. (2015). In Pursuit of the Perfect Peach: Consumer-assisted Selection of Peach Fruit Traits. *HortScience, 50*(8), 1202–1212.

Ostrom, E. (2009). A general framework for analyzing sustainability of social-ecological systems. *Science, 325*(5939), 419–422. doi:10.1126cience.1172133 PMID:19628857

Ottino, J. M. (1989). *The Kinematics of mixing: Stretching, Chaos, and Transport*. Cambridge University Press.

Padiyar, K. (2007). *FACTS controllers in power transmission and distribution*. New Age International.

Pai, M., Sauer, P. W., & Lesieutre, B. C. (1995). Static and dynamic nonlinear loads and structural stability in power systems. *Proceedings of the IEEE, 83*(11), 1562–1572. doi:10.1109/5.481634

Papic, M., Vaiman, M., Vaiman, M., & Povolotskiy, M. (2007). *A new approach to constructing seasonal nomograms in planning and operations environments at idaho power co. In 2007 IEEE Lausanne Power Tech*. IEEE.

Paszke, A., Gross, S., Massa, F., Lerer, A., Bradbury, J., Chanan, G., . . . Desmaison, A. (2019). Pytorch: An Imperative Style, High-Performance Deep Learning Library. In Advances in Neural Information Processing Systems (pp. 8026-8037). Academic Press.

Pattabiraman, B., Patwary, M. M. A., Gebremedhin, A. H., Keng Liao, W., & Choudhary, A. (2013). Fast algorithms for the maximum clique problem on massive sparse graphs. *WAW13, 10th Workshop on Algorithms and Models for the Web Graph.*

Patwary, M. M. A., Refsnes, P., & Manne, F. (2012). Multi-core spanning forest algorithms using disjoint-set data structure. IPDPS 2012, 827–835. doi:10.1109/IPDPS.2012.79

Patwary, M. M. A., Gebremedhin, A. H., & Pothen, A. (2011). New multithreaded ordering and coloring algorithms for multicore architectures. *Proceedings of EuroPar 2011, 6853*, 250–262. 10.1007/978-3-642-23397-5_24

Pavella & Murthy. (1994). *Transient stability of power systems: theory and practice*. Academic Press.

Pecevski, D., Natschläger, T., & Schuch, K. (2009). PCSIM: A Parallel Simulation Environment for Neural Circuits Fully Integrated with Python. Front Neuroinformatics, 3(11).

Pedregosa, F., Varoquaux, G., Gramfort, A., Michel, V., Thirion, B., Grisel, O., ... Vanderplas, J. (2011). Scikit-Learn: Machine Learning in Python. *Journal of Machine Learning Research, 12*, 2825–2830.

Penfield, P., Spence, R., & Duinker, S. (1970). A generalized form of tellegen's theorem. *IEEE Transactions on Circuit Theory, 17*(3), 302–305. doi:10.1109/TCT.1970.1083145

Petrica, P., Izraelevitz, A. M., Albonesi, D. H., & Shoemaker, C. A. (2013, June). Flicker: A dynamically adaptive architecture for power limited multicore systems. In *Proceedings of the 40th Annual International Symposium on Computer Architecture* (pp. 13-23). 10.1145/2485922.2485924

Phillips, D. (2000). *Image Processing in C.* Electronic Edition.

Picard, R. (1995). *Affective Computing (Abstract).* MIT Technical Report #321.

Picard, R. (1997). *Affective Computing.* MIT Press.

Pingali, K., Nguyen, D., Kulkarni, M., Burtscher, M., Hassaan, M. A., Kaleem, R., Lee, T.-H., Lenharth, A., Manevich, R., M'endez-Lojo, M., Prountzos, D., & Sui, X. (2011). The tao of parallelism in algorithms. In *Proceedings of the 32nd ACM SIGPLAN conference on Programming language design and implementation*, (pp. 12–25). New York, NY: ACM.

Plackett, R. L. (1972). Studies in the History of Probability and Statistics. XXIX: The discovery of the method of least squares. *Biometrika, 59*(2), 239–251. doi:10.1093/biomet/59.2.239

Plantenga, T. (2013, February). Inexact subgraph isomorphism in mapreduce. *Journal of Parallel and Distributed Computing, 73*(2), 164–175. doi:10.1016/j.jpdc.2012.10.005

Polania, R., Nitsche, M. A., & Ruff, C. C. (2018). Studying and modifying brain function with non-invasive brain stimulation. *Nature Neuroscience, 21*(2), 174–187. doi:10.103841593-017-0054-4

Porter, M. E. (2008). Value-based health care delivery. *Annals of Surgery, 248*(4), 503–509.

Pothukuchi, R. P., Ansari, A., Voulgaris, P., & Torrellas, J. (2016, June). Using multiple input, multiple output formal control to maximize resource efficiency in architectures. In *2016 ACM/IEEE 43rd Annual International Symposium on Computer Architecture (ISCA)* (pp. 658-670). IEEE. 10.1109/ISCA.2016.63

Pothukuchi, R. P., Pothukuchi, S. Y., Voulgaris, P., & Torrellas, J. (2018, June). Yukta: multilayer resource controllers to maximize efficiency. In *2018 ACM/IEEE 45th Annual International Symposium on Computer Architecture (ISCA)* (pp. 505-518). IEEE. 10.1109/ISCA.2018.00049

Pricopi, M., Muthukaruppan, T. S., Venkataramani, V., Mitra, T., & Vishin, S. (2013, September). Power-performance modeling on asymmetric multi-cores. In *2013 International Conference on Compilers, Architecture and Synthesis for Embedded Systems (CASES)* (pp. 1-10). IEEE.

Progias, P., & Sirakoulis, G. C. (2013). An FPGA processor for modelling wildfire spreading. *Mathematical and Computer Modelling, 57*(5), 1436–1452. doi:10.1016/j.mcm.2012.12.005

Puissant, L. (1805). *Traité de géodésie: ou, Exposition des méthodes astronomiques et trigonométriques, appliquées soit à la mesure de la terre, soit à la confection du canevas des cartes et des plans.* Courcier.

Puschel, M., Moura, J. M., Johnson, J. R., Padua, D., Veloso, M. M., Singer, B. W., Xiong, J., Franchetti, F., Gacic, A., Voronenko, Y., & ... . (2005). Spiral: Code generation for dsp transforms. *Proceedings of the IEEE, 93*(2), 232–275. doi:10.1109/JPROC.2004.840306

Quénot, G., & Zavidovique, B. (1992). The ETCA data-flow functional computer for real-time image processing. *Proceedings 1992 IEEE International Conference on Computer Design: VLSI in Computers & Processors*, 492-495. 10.1109/ICCD.1992.276324

Rabiner, L. R. (1989). A tutorial on hidden Markov models and selected applications in speech recognition. *Proceedings of the IEEE, 77*(2), 257–286. doi:10.1109/5.18626

Radford, A., Narasimhan, K., Salimans, T., & Sutskever, I. (2018). *Improving Language Understanding by Generative Pre-Training*. Academic Press.

Radford, A., Wu, J., Child, R., Luan, D., Amodei, D., & Sutskever, I. (2019). Language Models are Unsupervised Multitask Learners. *OpenAI blog, 1*(8), 9.

Radivojevic, Z., Cvetanovic, M., Milutinovic, V., & Sievert, J. (2003). Data mining: A brief overview and recent IPSI research. *Annals of Mathematics, Computing, and Teleinformatics, 1*(1), 84–91.

Raffel, C., Shazeer, N., Roberts, A., Lee, K., Narang, S., Matena, M., ... Liu, P. J. (2020). Exploring the Limits of Transfer Learning with a Unified Text-to-Text Transformer. *Journal of Machine Learning Research, 21*(140), 1–67.

Ragan-Kelley, J., Barnes, C., Adams, A., Paris, S., Durand, F., & Amarasinghe, S. (2013). Halide: A language and compiler for optimizing parallelism, locality, and recomputation in image processing pipelines. *ACM SIGPLAN Notices, 48*(6), 519–530. doi:10.1145/2499370.2462176

Raghavendra, R., Ranganathan, P., Talwar, V., Wang, Z., & Zhu, X. (2008, March). No" power" struggles: coordinated multi-level power management for the data center. In *Proceedings of the 13th international conference on Architectural support for programming languages and operating systems* (pp. 48-59). 10.1145/1346281.1346289

Raghupathi, W., & Raghupathi, V. (2014). Big data analytics in healthcare: Promise and potential. *Health Information Science and Systems, 2*(1), 3.

Rahmani, A. M., Donyanavard, B., Mück, T., Moazzemi, K., Jantsch, A., Mutlu, O., & Dutt, N. (2018, March). Spectr: Formal supervisory control and coordination for many-core systems resource management. In *Proceedings of the Twenty-Third International Conference on Architectural Support for Programming Languages and Operating Systems* (pp. 169-183). 10.1145/3173162.3173199

Rahmani, A. M., Haghbayan, M. H., Kanduri, A., Weldezion, A. Y., Liljeberg, P., Plosila, J., ... Tenhunen, H. (2015, July). Dynamic power management for many-core platforms in the dark silicon era: A multi-objective control approach. In *2015 IEEE/ACM International Symposium on Low Power Electronics and Design (ISLPED)* (pp. 219-224). IEEE. 10.1109/ISLPED.2015.7273517

Rahmani, A. M., Haghbayan, M. H., Miele, A., Liljeberg, P., Jantsch, A., & Tenhunen, H. (2016). Reliability-aware runtime power management for many-core systems in the dark silicon era. *IEEE Transactions on Very Large Scale Integration (VLSI). Systems, 25*(2), 427–440.

Rahmani, A. M., Jantsch, A., & Dutt, N. (2018). HDGM: Hierarchical dynamic goal management for many-core resource allocation. *IEEE Embedded Systems Letters, 10*(3), 61–64. doi:10.1109/LES.2017.2751522

Ramadge, P. J., & Wonham, W. M. (1989). The control of discrete event systems. *Proceedings of the IEEE, 77*(1), 81–98. doi:10.1109/5.21072

Ramakrishnan, N., Butler, P., Muthiah, S., Self, N., Khandpur, R., Saraf, P., ... Kuhlman, C. (2014, August). 'Beating the News' with EMBERS: Forecasting Civil Unrest Using Open Source Indicators. In *Proceedings of the 20th ACM SIGKDD International Conference on Knowledge Discovery and Data Mining* (pp. 1799-1808). 10.1145/2623330.2623373

Reavie, V. (2019, January 17). *Using AI To Drive High-Converting Predictive Marketing.* Forbes Agency Council. Retrieved from /2019/01/17/using-ai-to-drive-high-converting-predictive-marketing/#62807cdd9cd0

Reed, T., & Cohen Kadosh, R. (2018). Transcranial electrical stimulation (tES) mechanisms and its effects on cortical excitability and connectivity. *Journal of Inherited Metabolic Disease.* Advance online publication. doi:10.100710545-018-0181-4

Rehurek, R., & Sojka, P. (2010). Software Framework for Topic Modelling with Large Corpora. *Proceedings of the LREC 2010 Workshop on New Challenges for NLP Frameworks.*

Rekatsinas, T., Ghosh, S., Mekaru, S. R., Nsoesie, E. O., Brownstein, J. S., Getoor, L., & Ramakrishnan, N. (2017). Forecasting Rare Disease Outbreaks from Open Source Indicators. *Statistical Analysis and Data Mining: The ASA Data Science Journal, 10*(2), 136–150. doi:10.1002am.11337

Rekers, J., & Schürr, A. (1997). Defining and parsing visual languages with Layered Graph Grammars. *Journal of Visual Languages and Computing, 8*(1), 27–55. doi:10.1006/jvlc.1996.0027

Rexha, B., & Murturi, I. (2019). Applying efficient crowdsourcing techniques for increasing quality and transparency of election processes. *Electronic Government, an International Journal, 15*(1), 107-128.

Ricci, F., Rokach, L., & Shapira, B. (2015). *Recommender Systems Handbook.* doi:10.1007/978-1-4899-7637-6

Ritchie, I., & Roast, C. (2001). *Performance, Usability and the Web: Proceedings of the 34ᵗʰ Annual Hawaii International Conference on System Sciences (HICSS-34)* (vol. 5). IEEE Computer Society. https://en.ryte.com/wiki/Tracking_Pixel

Rose. (2012). *Sparse Matrices and their Applications: Proceedings of a Symposium on Sparse Matrices and Their Applications, held September 9 10, 1971, at the IBM Thomas J. Watson Research Center, Yorktown Heights, New York, and sponsored by the Office of Naval Research, the National Science Foundation, IBM World Trade Corporation, and the IBM Research Mathematical Sciences Department.* Springer Science & Business Media.

Rubinfeld, R., Tamir, G., Vardi, S., & Xie, N. (2011). Fast local computation algorithms. *International Conference on Supercomputing (ICS 2011,* 496–508.

Ruiz, C., Domingo, D., Micó, J. L., Díaz-Noci, J., Meso, K., & Masip, P. (2011). Public Sphere 2.0? The Democratic Qualities of Citizen Debates in Online Newspapers. *The International Journal of Press/Politics, 16*(4), 463–487. doi:10.1177/1940161211415849

Saeed, K. (2006, January). *A Note on Biometrics and Voice Print: Voice-Signal Feature Selection and Extraction–A Burg-Töeplitz Approach.* ResearchGate GmbH. Retrieved from https://www.researchgate.net/publication/228899473_A_Note_on_Biometrics_and_Voice_Print_Voice-Signal_Feature_Selection_and_Extraction-A_Burg-Toeplitz_Approach

Safonov, M. G. (1997). Focusing on the knowable. In *Control using logic-based switching* (pp. 224–233). Springer. doi:10.1007/BFb0036098

Sakaki, T., Okazaki, M., & Matsuo, Y. (2010, April). Earthquake Shakes Twitter Users: Real-Time Event Detection by Social Sensors. In *Proceedings of the 19th International Conference on World Wide Web* (pp. 851-860). 10.1145/1772690.1772777

Sariyuce, A. E., Saule, E., & Catalyurek, U. V. (2011). Improving graph coloring on distributed memory parallel computers. *Proc. of HiPC 2011.* 10.1109/HiPC.2011.6152726

Sariyuce, A. E., Saule, E., & Catalyurek, U. V. (2012). Scalable hybrid implementation of graph coloring using MPI and OpenMP. *Proc. IPDPS Workshops and PhD Forum, Workshop on Parallel Computing and Optimization (PCO'12).* 10.1109/IPDPSW.2012.216

Schulz, R., Gerloff, C., & Hummel, F. C. (2013). Non-invasive brain stimulation in neurological diseases. *Neuropharmacology*, *64*, 579–587. doi:10.1016/j.neuropharm.2012.05.016

Semmler-Behnke, M., Kreyling, W. G., Schulz, H., Takenaka, S., Butler, J. P., Henry, F. S., & Tsuda, A. (2012). Nanoparticle Delivery in Infant Lungs. *Proceedings of the National Academy of Sciences of the United States of America*, *109*(13), 5092–5097. doi:10.1073/pnas.1119339109 PMID:22411799

Sentance, R. (2019). *15 examples of artificial intelligence in marketing*. Retrieved from https://econsultancy.com/15-examples-of-artificial-intelligence-in-marketing/

Shamsa, E., Kanduri, A., Rahmani, A. M., Liljeberg, P., Jantsch, A., & Dutt, N. (2019, March). Goal-driven autonomy for efficient on-chip resource management: Transforming objectives to goals. In 2019 Design, Automation & Test in Europe Conference & Exhibition (DATE) (pp. 1397-1402). IEEE.

Shavit, N. (2011). Data structures in the multicore age. *Communications of the ACM*, *54*(3), 76–84. doi:10.1145/1897852.1897873

Shi, L., Zhao, L., Song, W. Z., Kamath, G., Wu, Y., & Liu, X. (2017). *Distributed least-squares iterative methods in networks: A survey.* arXiv preprint arXiv:1706.07098

Shiffman, D., Fry, S., & Marsh, Z. (2012). *The Nature of Code*. D. Shiffman.

Singh, K., Bhadauria, M., & McKee, S. A. (2009). Real time power estimation and thread scheduling via performance counters. *ACM SIGARCH Computer Architecture News*, *37*(2), 46–55. doi:10.1145/1577129.1577137

Sinha, A., Neogi, S., & Maiti, K. (2002). A reconfigurable data-flow architecture for a class of image processing applications. *ICCSC'02 Conference Proceedings*, 460-463.

Skogestad, S., & Postlethwaite, I. (2007). *Multivariable feedback control: analysis and design* (Vol. 2). Wiley.

Smith, B. C. (1982). *Reflection and Semantics in a Procedural Programming Language*. PhD.

Solnon, C. (2010, August). AllDifferent-based filtering for subgraph isomorphism. *Artificial Intelligence*, *174*(12-13), 850–864. doi:10.1016/j.artint.2010.05.002

SpaCy. (2020, May 19). SpaCy 3.0.0 Industrial-Strength Natural Language Processing in Python. *SpaCy*. https://spacy.io/

Springer. https://www.springer.com/

Srikantaiah, S., Kandemir, M., & Wang, Q. (2009, December). SHARP control: controlled shared cache management in chip multiprocessors. In *Proceedings of the 42nd Annual IEEE/ACM International Symposium on Microarchitecture* (pp. 517-528). 10.1145/1669112.1669177

Stanojevic, M., Alshehri, J., Dragut, E. C., & Obradovic, Z. (2019, July). Biased News Data Influence on Classifying Social Media Posts. In *Proceedings of NewsIR Workshop @ 42nd International ACM SIGIR Conference on Research and Development in Information Retrieval* (pp. 3-8). Academic Press.

Stanojevic, M., Alshehri, J., & Obradovic, Z. (2019, August). Surveying Public Opinion Using Label Prediction on Social Media Data. In *2019 IEEE/ACM International Conference on Advances in Social Networks Analysis and Mining (ASONAM)* (pp. 188-195). IEEE. 10.1145/3341161.3342861

Statistical Sampling and Regression: Simple Linear Regression. (2015). *PreMBA Analytical Methods*. Columbia University. Available: http://ci.columbia.edu/ci/prembatest/c0331/s7/s7_6.html

Steels, L., & López de Mantaras, R. (2018). The Barcelona declaration for the proper development and usage of artificial intelligence in Europe. *AI Communications*, *31*(6), 485–494. doi:10.3233/AIC-180607

Stepanyants, A., Martinez, L. M., Ferecsko, A. S., & Kisvarday, Z. F. (2009). The fractions of short- and long-range connections in the visual cortex. *Proceedings of the National Academy of Sciences of the United States of America*, *106*(9), 3555–3560. doi:10.1073/pnas.0810390106

Stojanovic, S. (2013). Solving Gross Pitaevskii Equation Using Dataflow Paradigm. *The IPSI BgD Transactions on Internet Research, 17*.

Stojkovic, I. (2017). Fast Sparse Gaussian Markov Random Fields Learning Based on Cholesky Factorization. *IJCAI*, 2758–2764.

Stojmenovic, I., & Milutinovic, V. (2012). How to Write Research Articles in Computing and Engineering Disciplines. *Singidunum Journal of Applied Sciences*, *9*(1), 42–50.

Stone, J. E., Gohara, D., & Shi, G. (2010). OpenCL: A Parallel Programming Standard for Heterogeneous Computing Systems. *Computing in Science & Engineering*, *12*(3), 66–72. doi:10.1109/MCSE.2010.69 PMID:21037981

Stott. (1974). Review of load-flow calculation methods. *Proceedings of the IEEE, 62*(7), 916–929.

Stott, Jardim, & Alsac. (2009). Dc power flow revisited. *IEEE Transactions on Power Systems*, *24*(3), 1290–1300.

Stuecheli, J., Kaseridis, D., Daly, D., Hunter, H. C., & John, L. K. (2010). The virtual write queue: Coordinating DRAM and last-level cache policies. *ACM SIGARCH Computer Architecture News*, *38*(3), 72–82. doi:10.1145/1816038.1815972

Su, B., Gu, J., Shen, L., Huang, W., Greathouse, J. L., & Wang, Z. (2014, December). PPEP: Online performance, power, and energy prediction framework and DVFS space exploration. In *2014 47th Annual IEEE/ACM International Symposium on Microarchitecture* (pp. 445-457). IEEE.

Subramanian, L., Seshadri, V., Ghosh, A., Khan, S., & Mutlu, O. (2015, December). The application slowdown model: Quantifying and controlling the impact of inter-application interference at shared caches and main memory. In *2015 48th Annual IEEE/ACM International Symposium on Microarchitecture (MICRO)* (pp. 62-75). IEEE.

Subramanian, L., Seshadri, V., Kim, Y., Jaiyen, B., & Mutlu, O. (2013, February). MISE: Providing performance predictability and improving fairness in shared main memory systems. In *2013 IEEE 19th International Symposium on High Performance Computer Architecture (HPCA)* (pp. 639-650). IEEE.

Sui, X., Lenharth, A., Fussell, D. S., & Pingali, K. (2016). Proactive control of approximate programs. *ACM SIGPLAN Notices*, *51*(4), 607–621. doi:10.1145/2954679.2872402

Sullivan, L. (2018, July 2). Marketers Struggle With Tying Data To AI Systems. *MediaPost Communications*.

Sun, Z., Wang, H., Wang, H., Shao, B., & Li, J. (2012). Efficient subgraph matching on billion node graphs. *Proceedings of the VLDB Endowment International Conference on Very Large Data Bases*, *5*(9), 788–799. doi:10.14778/2311906.2311907

Szalay, A., & Gray, J. (2006). Science in an Exponential World. *Nature*, *440*(7083), 413–414. doi:10.1038/440413a PMID:16554783

Szekeres, G., & Wilf, H. S. (1968). An inequality for the chromatic number of a graph. *Journal of Combinatorial Theory*, *4*(1), 1–3. doi:10.1016/S0021-9800(68)80081-X

Tabor, M. (1989). *Chaos and integrability in nonlinear dynamics*. Wiley Press.

Taneja, M., Jalodia, N., & Davy, A. (2019). Distributed decomposed data analytics in fog enabled IoT deployments. *IEEE Access: Practical Innovations, Open Solutions, 7*, 40969–40981. doi:10.1109/ACCESS.2019.2907808

Tarjan, R. E., & Yannakakis, M. (1984). Simple linear-time algorithms to test chordality of graphs, test acyclicity of hypergraphs, and selectively reduce acyclic hypergraphs. *SIAM Journal on Scientific Computing, 13*(3), 566–579. doi:10.1137/0213035

Taylor, G. I. (1960). *Low Reynolds Number Flow (16 mm Film)*. Educational Services Inc.

Tembey, P., Gavrilovska, A., & Schwan, K. (2010, June). A case for coordinated resource management in heterogeneous multicore platforms. In *International Symposium on Computer Architecture* (pp. 341-356). Springer.

Teodorescu, R., & Torrellas, J. (2008). Variation-aware application scheduling and power management for chip multi-processors. *ACM SIGARCH Computer Architecture News, 36*(3), 363-374.

Thaliyachira, C. (2019, December 19). Artificial Intelligence in Marketing. *OMR Industry Journal.* Retrieved from https://www.omrindustryjournal.com/artificial-intelligence-in-marketing/315/

Thistle, J. G. (1996). Supervisory control of discrete event systems. *Mathematical and Computer Modelling, 23*(11-12), 25–53. doi:10.1016/0895-7177(96)00063-5

Thoma. (2016). *Introduction to bond graphs and their applications*. Elsevier.

Thorp, Seyler, & Phadke. (1998). Electromechanical wave propagation in large electric power systems. *IEEE Transactions on Circuits and Systems. I, Fundamental Theory and Applications, 45*(6), 614–622.

Tian, C., Feng, M., Nagarajan, V., & Gupta, R. (2009). Speculative parallelization of sequential loops on multicores. *International Journal of Parallel Programming, 37*(1), 508–535. doi:10.100710766-009-0111-z

Tikidji-Hamburyan, R. A., Narayana, V., Bozkus, Z., & El-Ghazawi, T. A. (2017). Software for Brain Network Simulations: A Comparative Study. *Frontiers in Neuroinformatics, 11*, 46. doi:10.3389/fninf.2017.00046

Tinney, Brandwajn, & Chan. (1985). Sparse vector methods. *IEEE Transactions on Power Apparatus and Systems*, (2): 295–301.

Trifunovic, N., Milutinovic, V., Salom, J., & Kos, A. (2015). Paradigm shift in big data supercomputing: Dataflow vs. controlflow. *Journal of Big Data, 2*(1), 1–9.

Trobec, R. (2016). Interconnection Networks in Petascale Computer Systems: A Survey. *ACM Computing Surveys, 49*(3), 1–24.

Trobec, R., Vasiljević, R., Tomašević, M., Milutinović, V., Beivide, R., & Valero, M. (2016). Interconnection networks in petascale computer systems: A survey. *ACM Computing Surveys, 49*(3), 1–24.

Tsuda, A., Henry, F. S., & Butler, J. P. (1995). Chaotic mixing of alveolated duct flow in rhythmically expanding pulmonary acinus. *Journal of Applied Physiology, 79*(3), 1055–1063. doi:10.1152/jappl.1995.79.3.1055 PMID:8567502

Tsuda, A., Henry, F. S., & Butler, J. P. (2013). Particle transport and deposition: Basic physics of particle kinetics. *Comprehensive Physiology, 3*, 1437–1471. doi:10.1002/cphy.c100085 PMID:24265235

Tsuda, A., Laine-Pearson, F. E., & Hydon, P. E. (2011). Why Chaotic mixing of particles is inevitable in the deep lung. *Journal of Theoretical Biology, 286*, 57–66. doi:10.1016/j.jtbi.2011.06.038 PMID:21801733

Tsuda, A., Rogers, R. A., Hydon, P. E., & Butler, J. P. (2002). Chaotic mixing deep in the lung. *Proceedings of the National Academy of Sciences of the United States of America*, *99*(15), 10173–10178. doi:10.1073/pnas.102318299 PMID:12119385

Twidale, M. B., Gruzd, A. A., & Nichols, D. M. (2008). Writing in the library: Exploring tighter integration of digital library use with the writing process. *Information Processing & Management*, *44*(2), 558–580. doi:10.1016/j.ipm.2007.05.010

Ullmann, J. R. (1976). An Algorithm for Subgraph Isomorphism. *Journal of the Association for Computing Machinery*, *23*(1), 31–42. doi:10.1145/321921.321925

Ullmann, J. R. (2010). Bit-vector algorithms for binary constraint satisfaction and subgraph isomorphism. *Journal of Experimental Algorithmics*, *15*, 1–6. doi:10.1145/1671970.1921702

Valiente, G. (2002). *Algorithms on Trees and Graphs*. Springer. doi:10.1007/978-3-662-04921-1

van Albada, S. J., Kunkel, S., Morrison, A., & Diesmann, M. (2014). *Integrating Brain Structure and Dynamics on Supercomputers* (L. Grandinetti, L. Lippert, & N. Petkov, Eds.). Vol. 8603). Springer.

van Merri"enboer, W., & Moldovan. (2017). Tangent: Automatic differentiation using sourcecode transformation in Python. *31st Conference on Neural Information Processing System*.

Van Reeth, E., Tham, I. W. K., Tan, C. H., & Poh, C. L. (2012). Super-resolution in magnetic resonance maging: a review. In Concepts in Magnetic Resonance (Vol. Part A 40A. 6, pp. 306–325.).

Van Reeth, E., Tham, I. W. K., Tan, C. H., & Poh, C. L. (2012). Super-resolution in magnetic resonance maging: a review. In Concepts in Magnetic Resonance (Vol. Part A 40A. 6, pp. 306–325.). Academic Press.

Van Woudenberg, M. (2006). *Using FPGAs to Speed Up Cellular Automata Computations* [Master's thesis]. University of Amsterdam, Amsterdam, The Netherlands.

Vardhan, V., Yuan, W., Harris, A. F., Adve, S. V., Kravets, R., Nahrstedt, K., ... & Jones, D. (2009). GRACE-2: integrating fine-grained application adaptation with global adaptation for saving energy. *International Journal of embedded Systems*, *4*(2), 152-169.

Vassilev, Vassilev, & Penev, Moneta, & Ilieva. (2015). Clad – Automatic differentiation using Clang and LLVM. *Journal of Physics: Conference Series*, *608*(1).

Vaswani, A., Shazeer, N., Parmar, N., Uszkoreit, J., Jones, L., Gomez, A. N., . . . Polosukhin, I. (2017). Attention is All You Need. In Advances in Neural Information Processing Systems (pp. 5998-6008). Academic Press.

Vega, A., Buyuktosunoglu, A., Hanson, H., Bose, P., & Ramani, S. (2013, December). Crank it up or dial it down: co-ordinated multiprocessor frequency and folding control. In *2013 46th Annual IEEE/ACM International Symposium on Microarchitecture (MICRO)* (pp. 210-221). IEEE. 10.1145/2540708.2540727

Venkatraman, V. (2014). Predicting Advertising Success Beyond Traditional Measures: New Insights from Neurophysiological Methods and Market Response Modeling. *Social Science Research Network*. https://papers.ssrn.com/sol3/papers.cfm?abstract_id=2498095

Verghese, Perez-Arriaga, & Schweppe. (1982). Selective modal analysis with applications to electric power systems, part ii: The dynamic stability problem. *IEEE Transactions on Power Apparatus and Systems*, (9): 3126–3134.

Von Neumann, J. (1951). The general and logical theory of automata. Pergamon Press *1951*, 1-41.

Wagner, Bachovchin, & Ilic. (2015). Computer architecture and multi time-scale implementations for smart grid in a room simulator. *IFACPapersOnLine*, *48*(30), 233–238.

Wagner, T. (2006). Transcranial Magnetic Stimulation: High Resolution Tracking of the Induced Current Density in the Individual Human Brain. Paper presented at the 12th Annual Meeting of Human Brain mapping, Florence, Italy.

Wagner, T., & Dipietro, L. (2018). Novel methods of transcranial stimulation: electrosonic stimulation. In A. Rezai, P. H. Peckham, & E. Krames (Eds.), *Neuromodulation: Comprehensive Textbook of Principles, Technologies, and Therapies*. Elsevier.

Wagner, T., Eden, U., Rushmore, J., Russo, C. J., Dipietro, L., Fregni, F., ... Valero-Cabre, A. (2014). Impact of brain tissue filtering on neurostimulation fields: A modeling study. *NeuroImage*, *85*(Pt 3), 1048–1057. doi:10.1016/j.neuroimage.2013.06.079

Wagner, T., Rushmore, J., Eden, U., & Valero-Cabre, A. (2009). Biophysical foundations underlying TMS: Setting the stage for an effective use of neurostimulation in the cognitive neurosciences. *Cortex*, *45*(9), 1025–1034. doi:10.1016/j.cortex.2008.10.002

Wagner, T., Valero-Cabre, A., & Pascual-Leone, A. (2007). Noninvasive human brain stimulation. *Annual Review of Biomedical Engineering*, *9*, 527–565. doi:10.1146/annurev.bioeng.9.061206.133100

Wang, Y., Ma, K., & Wang, X. (2009). Temperature-constrained power control for chip multiprocessors with online model estimation. *ACM SIGARCH Computer Architecture News, 37*(3), 314-324.

Wang, X., Ma, K., & Wang, Y. (2011). Adaptive power control with online model estimation for chip multiprocessors. *IEEE Transactions on Parallel and Distributed Systems*, *22*(10), 1681–1696. doi:10.1109/TPDS.2011.39

Wang, X., & Martínez, J. F. (2016). ReBudget: Trading off efficiency vs. fairness in market-based multicore resource allocation via runtime budget reassignment. *ACM SIGPLAN Notices*, *51*(4), 19–32. doi:10.1145/2954679.2872382

Wang, Z., Yan, W., & Oates, T. (2017). Time series classification from scratch with deep neural networks: a strong baseline. *2017 International Joint Conference on Neural Networks*, 1578-1585. 10.1109/IJCNN.2017.7966039

Weber, P. (2014). Discussions in the Comments Section: Factors Influencing Participation and Interactivity in Online Newspapers' Reader Comments. *New Media & Society*, *16*(6), 941–957. doi:10.1177/1461444813495165

Weibel, E. R. (1984). *The pathway for oxygen-structure and function in the mammalian respiratory system*. Harvard University Press.

West, J. B. (2012). *Respiratory Physiology: The essentials* (4th ed.). William & Wilkins.

Wilson, R. (2000). *Using computers in health information systems. In Design and Implementation of Health Information System*. World Health Organization.

Wolfram, S. (1983). Statistical mechanics of cellular automata. *Reviews of Modern Physics*, *55*(3), 601–644. doi:10.1103/RevModPhys.55.601

Wu, Y., Schuster, M., Chen, Z., Le, Q. V., Norouzi, M., Macherey, W., ... Klingner, J. (2016). *Google's Neural Machine Translation System: Bridging the Gap Between Human and Machine Translation*. arXiv Preprint arXiv:1609.08144.

Wu, Q., Deng, Q., Ganesh, L., Hsu, C. H., Jin, Y., Kumar, S., Li, B., Meza, J., & Song, Y. J. (2016). Dynamo: Facebook's data center-wide power management system. *ACM SIGARCH Computer Architecture News*, *44*(3), 469–480. doi:10.1145/3007787.3001187

Wu, Q., Juang, P., Martonosi, M., & Clark, D. W. (2004). Formal online methods for voltage/frequency control in multiple clock domain microprocessors. *ACM SIGPLAN Notices*, *39*(11), 248–259. doi:10.1145/1037187.1024423

Wu, Q., Juang, P., Martonosi, M., Peh, L. S., & Clark, D. W. (2005). Formal control techniques for power-performance management. *IEEE Micro, 25*(5), 52–62. doi:10.1109/MM.2005.87

Wu, S., Liu, S., Sohn, S., Moon, S., Wi, C., Juhn, Y., & Liu, H. (2018). Modeling asynchronous event sequences with RNNs. *Journal of Biomedical Informatics, 83*, 167–177. doi:10.1016/j.jbi.2018.05.016 PMID:29883623

Wyatt & Ilic. (1990). Time-domain reactive power concepts for nonlinear, nonsinusoidal or nonperiodic networks. In *IEEE International Symposium on Circuits and Systems*, (pp. 387–390). IEEE.

Wynford-Thomas, R., & Robertson, N. P. (2017). The economic burden of chronic neurological disease. *Journal of Neurology, 264*(11), 2345–2347. doi:10.100700415-017-8632-7

Xu, Q., Xiong, J., Huang, Q., & Yao, Y. (2013, October). Robust evaluation for quality of experience in crowdsourcing. In *Proceedings of the 21st ACM international conference on Multimedia* (pp. 43-52). 10.1145/2502081.2502083

Yacoub, S., Simske, S., Lin, X., & Burns, J. (2003). Recognition of Emotions in Interactive Voice Response Systems. *Proceedings of Eurospeech*, 729–732.

Yang, Z., Yang, D., Dyer, C., He, X., Smola, A., & Hovy, E. (2016, June). Hierarchical Attention Networks for Document Classification. In *Proceedings of the 2016 Conference of the North American Chapter of the Association for Computational Linguistics: Human Language Technologies* (pp. 1480-1489). Academic Press.

Yuan, Y., Wang, G., Chen, L., & Wang, H. (2012, May). Efficient subgraph similarity search on large probabilistic graph databases. *Proc. VLDB Endow., 5*(9), 800–811. 10.14778/2311906.2311908

Zafeiropoulou, S., & Nadan, J. (2015). Increasing the value of Innovation Consulting Services in the technology age. *Management of Engineering and Technology (PICMET), 2015 Portland International Conference on*, 704-717.

Zaka, B., Maurer, H., & Delilovic, N. (2020). Investigating Interaction Activities in Digital Libraries: The Networked Interactive Digital Books Project. *IPSI BgD Transactions on Internet Research, 16*(1), 75–82.

Zavlanos, M. M., Spesivtsev, L., & Pappas, G. J. (2008). A distributed auction algorithm for the assignment problem. *Proceedings of the 47th IEEE Conference on Decision and Control*, 1212–1217. 10.1109/CDC.2008.4739098

Zhang, X-P. & Wang, F. (2017, April 26). Signal Processing for Finance, Economics, and Marketing - Concepts, framework, and big data applications. *IEEE Signal Processing Magazine*.

Zhang, H., & Hoffmann, H. (2016). Maximizing performance under a power cap: A comparison of hardware, software, and hybrid techniques. *ACM SIGPLAN Notices, 51*(4), 545–559. doi:10.1145/2954679.2872375

Zhang, Soudi, Shirmohammadi, & Cheng. (1995). A distribution short circuit analysis approach using hybrid compensation method. *IEEE Transactions on Power Systems, 10*(4), 2053–2059.

Ziegele, M., & Quiring, O. (2013). Conceptualizing Online Discussion Value: A Multidimensional Framework for Analyzing User Comments on Mass-Media Websites. *Annals of the International Communication Association, 37*(1), 125–153. doi:10.1080/23808985.2013.11679148

Zimmer, K., Kurban, H., Jenne, M., Keating, L., Maull, P., & Dalkilic, M. M. (2018). Using Data Analytics to Optimize Public Transportation on a College Campus. 2018 *IEEE 5th International Conference on Data Science and Advanced Analytics*, 460-469.

About the Contributors

Malek Adjouadi received the B.S. degree in Electrical Engineering from Oklahoma State University and the M.S. and PhD degrees in Electrical Engineering from the University of Florida. He is currently the Ware Professor with the Department of Electrical and Computer Engineering, Florida International University. He is the Founding Director of the Center for Advanced Technology and Education funded by the National Science Foundation since 1993. His research interests are in image and signal processing, assistive technology to help persons with visual disabilities, and brain research with a focus on Alzheimer's disease and epilepsy.

Dragan Bojić received a Ph.D. degree in Electrical Engineering and Computer Science from the University of Belgrade in 2001. He is a professor at the School of Electrical Engineering, University of Belgrade. His research interests include formal languages and parsing, software engineering techniques and tools, and e-learning.

Miroslav Bojović is with the School of Electrical Engineering, University of Belgrade, Serbia. His PhD in Computer Engineering from the University of Belgrade was announced as the best in the school in 1988. He teaches database systems. He held talks at prestigious Universities, including: UCLA, Purdue, and Brown, as well as in companies: McDonnell Douglasand Boeing, Medsite, and Medec. MobilePDR, the project he led was awarded as the best software product in the USA in the field of medical information system software for year 2004. His research interests include database systems, software engineering, and fault tolerant computing.

Uroš Čibej received his doctoral degree in Computer Science from the University of Ljubljana in 2007. Currently, he is with the Laboratory of Algorithmics at the Faculty of Computer and Information Science where he teaches various courses and is involved in research and industrial projects. His research interests include computational models, halting probability, graph algorithms, graph compression, graph symmetries and computational complexity.

Mehmet Dalkilic works in Data Science, Big Data, Analytics, and AI/ML. He was the first faculty in the Luddy School of Informatics, Computing, and Engineering. He co-created the computational biology graduate program and is currently the Director of the Data Science Undergraduate Program.

Namik Delilovic attended the Polytechnic High School in Zavidovici (Bosnia), got his B.Sc. degree in Mobile Computing from the University of Applied Sciences Upper Austria and his M.Sc. degree in

Software Engineering and Management at Graz University of Technology. He did an Erasmus stay at the Bosphorus University (Turkey), worked for several companies including Samsung Mobile Austria and he received the Samsung Best Mobiler award in Seoul (South Korea). His primary interest and research area at the Institute of Interactive Systems and Data Science is in Machine Learning and Natural Language Processing.

Bryan Donyanavard is an Assistant Professor of Computer Science at San Diego State University. His work focuses on applying principles of computational self-awareness to the runtime management of energy-efficient cyber-physical systems. He received his BS and MS in Computer Engineering from UC Santa Barbara, and his PhD in Computer Science from UC Irvine. He previously spent time as a researcher at TU Munich and Ericsson.

Miljan Đorđević is currently pursuing a bachelor's degree in Computer Engineering and Information Theory at the Faculty of Electrical Engineering, University of Belgrade. He was a Web developer at CSA Yazilim ve Danişmanık Hizmetleri, Istanbul, Turkey and a machine learning intern at Microsoft Development Center Serbia, Belgrade, Serbia.

Nikil Dutt is a Distinguished Professor of CS, Cognitive Sciences, and EECS at UC Irvine.

Seth Elkin-Frankston received his Ph.D. in Anatomy and Neurobiology from Boston University School of Medicine. His graduate work focused on understanding how different brain areas interact to process visual information to develop techniques that could provide lasting changes to visual performance. After completing a post-doctoral fellowship in Paris, Seth worked in industry where he developed and led a breadth of Government funded research programs. Seth is presently a Cognitive Scientist at the U.S. Army CCDC Soldier Center in Natick, MA.

Luka Fürst received his M.Sc. and Ph.D. degrees in computer science from the University of Ljubljana in 2007 and 2013, respectively. He works as an assistant professor at the University of Ljubljana, Faculty of Computer and Information Science. His research areas include algorithms and data structures (with a particular emphasis on graph algorithms), software engineering, and computer programming education.

Assefaw Gebremedhin is an associate professor in the School of Electrical Engineering and Computer Science at Washington State University, where he leads the Scalable Algorithms for Data Science (SCADS) Lab. His current research interests include: data science and AI, network science, high-performance computing, and applications in cyber security, energy systems, and bioinformatics. In 2016, Assefaw received the National Science Foundation CAREER Award for work on fast and scalable combinatorial algorithms for data analytics. He earned his PhD and MS in Computer Science from the University of Bergen, Norway and his BS in Electrical Engineering from Addis Ababa University, Ethiopia.

Mor Harchol-Balter is the Bruce J. Nelson Professor of Computer Science at Carnegie Mellon. She received her Ph.D. from U.C. Berkeley in 1996 under the direction of Manuel Blum. She joined CMU in 1999, and served as the Head of the PhD program from 2008-2011. Mor is a Fellow of both ACM and IEEE. She is a recipient of the McCandless Junior Chair, the NSF CAREER award, and several teaching awards, including the Herbert A. Simon Award and Spira Teaching Award. She is a recipient of dozens of Industrial Faculty Awards including multiple awards from Google, Microsoft, IBM, EMC, Facebook, Intel, Yahoo!, and Seagate. Mor's work focuses on designing new resource allocation policies, including load balancing policies, power management policies, and scheduling policies, for distributed systems. Mor is heavily involved in the SIGMETRICS / PERFORMANCE research community, where she has received many paper awards (SIGMETRICS 19, PERFORMANCE 18, INFORMS APS 18, EUROSYS 16, MASCOTS 16, SIGMETRICS 03, SIGMETRICS 96). She is also the author of a popular textbook, "Performance Analysis and Design of Computer Systems," published by Cambridge University Press, which bridges Operations Research and Computer Science. Mor is best known for her enthusiastic keynote talks (recent examples: QTNA 19, YEQT 18, MIT LIDS 17, CANQUEUE 16, SIGMETRICS 16, ICDCS 15, GREENMETRICS 14) and her many PhD students, most of whom are professors at top academic institutions.

Frank Henry has spent more than 40 years in academia and began his current position at Manhattan College in 2010. His main research interest is the application of numerical methods to the study of biofluid flows.

Marija Ilić has retired as a Professor Emerita at Carnegie Mellon University. She is currently a Senior Staff in the Energy Systems Group 73 at the MIT Lincoln Laboratory, and a Senior research Scientist at MIT Institute for Data, Systems and Society (IDSS)/LIDS. She is an IEEE Life Fellow. She was the first recipient of the NSF Presidential Young Investigator Award for Power Systems signed by late President Ronald Regan. In addition to her academic work, she is the founder of New Electricity Transmission Software Solutions, Inc. (NETSS, Inc.). She has co-authored several books on the subject of large-scale electric power systems, and has co-organized an annual multidisciplinary Electricity Industry conference series at Carnegie Mellon (https://www.ece.cmu.edu/~electriconf) with participants from academia, government, and industry.

Rupamathi Jaddivada is currently a postdoctoral researcher at Massachusetts Institute of technology after receiving her doctoral degree from the Dept. of Electrical Engineering and Computer Science in 2020 from the same institution. Her doctoral research investigated the usage of reactive power dynamics for better analysis and control design of complex electric energy systems. Her research interests include control, optimization, and numerical methods applied to complex systems. Jaddivada received her Master of Science degree in Electrical and Computer Engineering from Carnegie Mellon University in 2015, and a Bachelor of Technology degree from Jawaharlal Nehru Technological University, India in 2014.

Axel Jantsch graduated from TU Wien in Computer Science. Between 1992-2014 he was with KTH (Royal Institute of Technology) in Stockholm working with Systems on Chip, Networks on Chip and Embedded Systems. Since 2014 he is with TU Wien focusing his research on Systems on Chip, Self-Aware Cyber-Physical systems and Embedded Machine Learning.

Nenad Korolija is with the School of Electrical Engineering, University of Belgrade, Serbia. He received a PhD degree in electrical engineering and computer science in 2017. His interests and experiences are strongly related to high performance computer architectures. During 2008, he worked on DTA architecture as a part of the HIPEAC FP7 project at the University of Siena, Italy. In 2013, he was an intern at Google Inc., Mountain View, CA, USA. In 2017, he was working on dataflow architectures in Maxeler Ltd., London.

Miloš Kotlar received his BSc (2016) and MSc (2017) degrees in Electrical and Computer Engineering from the University of Belgrade, School of Electrical Engineering, Serbia. He is a Ph.D. candidate at School of Electrical Engineering, University of Belgrade. General research fields includes implementation of energy efficient tensor implementations using the dataflow paradigm (FPGA and ASIC accelerators) as well as meta learning approaches for anomaly detection tasks.

Fredrik Manne is a professor in the Department of Informatics at the University of Bergen, Norway. His main research interests are in parallel and distributed computing, and more specifically in combinatorial scientific computing and self-stabilizing algorithms.

Jurij Mihelič received his doctoral degree in Computer Science from the University of Ljubljana in 2006. Currently, he is with the Laboratory of Algorithmics, Faculty of Computer and Information Science, University of Ljubljana, Slovenia, as an assistant professor. His research interests include algorithm engineering, experimental algorithmics, system software and programming languages.

Veljko Milutinovic (1951) received his PhD from the University of Belgrade in Serbia, spent about a decade on various faculty positions in the USA (mostly at Purdue University and more recently at the University of Indiana in Bloomington), and was a co-designer of the DARPAs pioneering GaAs RISC microprocessor on 200MHz (about a decade before the first commercial effort on that same speed) and was a co-designer also of the related GaAs Systolic Array (with 4096 GaAs microprocessors). Later, for almost three decades, he taught and conducted research at the University of Belgrade in Serbia, for departments of EE, MATH, BA, and PHYS/CHEM. His research is mostly in datamining algorithms and dataflow computing, with the emphasis on mapping of data analytics algorithms onto fast energy efficient architectures. Most of his research was done in cooperation with industry (Intel, Fairchild, Honeywell, Maxeler, HP, IBM, NCR, RCA, etc...). For 10 of his books, forewords were written by 10 different Nobel Laureates with whom he cooperated on his past industry sponsored projects. He published 40 books (mostly in the USA), he has over 100 papers in SCI journals (mostly in IEEE and ACM journals), and he presented invited talks at over 400 destinations worldwide. He has well over 1000 Thomson-Reuters WoS citations, well over 1000 Elsevier SCOPUS citations, and about 4000 Google Scholar citations. His Google Scholar h index is equal to 30. He is a Life Fellow of the IEEE since 2003 and a Member of The Academy of Europe since 2011. He is a member of the Serbian National Academy of Engineering and a Foreign Member of the Montenegro National Academy of Sciences and Arts.

Luiz Moutinho (BA, MA, PhD, MAE, FCIM) is Visiting Professor of Marketing at Suffolk Business School, Faculty of Arts, Business and Applied Social Science, University of Suffolk, Ipswich, England, and at The Marketing School, Portugal and Adjunct Professor at University of South Pacific, Suva, Fiji. During 2015 - 2017 he was professor of BioMarketing and Futures Research at the DCU Business School, Dublin City University, Ireland. This was the first Chair in the world on both domains - BioMarketing and Futures Research. Previously, and for 20 years, he had been appointed as the Foundation Chair of Marketing at the Adam Smith Business School, University of Glasgow, Scotland. In 2017 Luiz Moutinho received a degree of Professor Honoris Causa from the University of Tourism and Management Skopje, FYR of Macedonia. In 2020 he was elected as the member of The Academia Europaea. Professor Moutinho completed his PhD at the University of Sheffield in 1982. He has been a Full Professor for 29 years and has held Visiting Professorship positions at numerous universities worldwide. He is the Founding Editor-in-Chief of the Journal of Modelling in Management (JM2) and Co-editor-in-Chief of the Innovative Marketing Journal. His main areas of research interest encompass marketing, management and tourism futurecast, artificial intelligence, biometrics and neuroscience in marketing, evolutionary algorithms, human-computer interaction, the use of artificial neural networks in marketing, modelling processes of consumer behaviour, futures research. Professor Moutinho has over 155 articles published in refereed academic journals, 34 books and 15,539 academic citations, the h-index of 57 and the i10-index of 212 (Google Scholar, Sept. 2020).

Ilir Murturi is a university assistant and PhD student at the Distributed Systems Group of the Institute of Information Systems Engineering. After receiving his bachelor's degree in 2011, he started working as an intern in Robert Bosch GmbH, at the Division of Electrical Vehicles and Hybrid Systems, Germany. In 2015, he received his master's degree in Computer Engineering at the University of Prishtina where he continued his career as a university assistant. In 2018, he joined the Distributed Systems Group.

Onur Mutlu is a Professor of Computer Science at ETH Zurich. He is also a faculty member at Carnegie Mellon University, where he previously held the Strecker Early Career Professorship. His current broader research interests are in computer architecture, systems, hardware security, and bioinformatics. A variety of techniques he, along with his group and collaborators, has invented over the years have influenced industry and have been employed in commercial microprocessors and memory/storage systems. He obtained his PhD and MS in ECE from the University of Texas at Austin and BS degrees in Computer Engineering and Psychology from the University of Michigan, Ann Arbor. He started the Computer Architecture Group at Microsoft Research (2006-2009), and held various product and research positions at Intel Corporation, Advanced Micro Devices, VMware, and Google. He received the IEEE Computer Society Edward J. McCluskey Technical Achievement Award, ACM SIGARCH Maurice Wilkes Award, the inaugural IEEE Computer Society Young Computer Architect Award, the inaugural Intel Early Career Faculty Award, US National Science Foundation CAREER Award, Carnegie Mellon University Ladd Research Award, faculty partnership awards from various companies, and a healthy number of best paper or "Top Pick" paper recognitions at various computer systems, architecture, and hardware security venues. He is an ACM Fellow "for contributions to computer architecture research, especially in memory systems", IEEE Fellow for "contributions to computer architecture research and practice", and an elected member of the Academy of Europe (Academia Europaea). His computer architecture and digital logic design course lectures and materials are freely available on YouTube, and his research group makes a wide variety of software and hardware artifacts freely available online. For more information, please see his webpage at https://people.inf.ethz.ch/omutlu/.

Zoran Obradovic is a Distinguished Professor and a Center director at Temple University, an Academician at the Academia Europaea (the Academy of Europe) and a Foreign Academician at the Serbian Academy of Sciences and Arts. He mentored 45 postdoctoral fellows and Ph.D. students, many of whom have independent research careers at academic institutions (e.g. Northeastern Univ., Ohio State Univ,) and industrial research labs (e.g. Amazon, Facebook, Hitachi Big Data, IBM T.J.Watson, Microsoft, Yahoo Labs, Uber, Verizon Big Data, Spotify). Zoran is the editor-in-chief at the Big Data journal and the steering committee chair for the SIAM Data Mining conference. He is also an editorial board member at 13 journals and was the general chair, program chair, or track chair for 11 international conferences. His research interests include data science and complex networks in decision support systems addressing challenges related to big, heterogeneous, spatial and temporal data analytics motivated by applications in healthcare management, power systems, earth and social sciences. His studies were funded by AFRL, DARPA, DOE, KAUST, NIH, NSF, ONR, and the PA Department of Health and industry. For more details see https://www.dabi.temple.edu/zoran-obradovic

Mostofa Patwary is a senior deep learning research scientist at the Applied Deep Learning Research team at NVIDIA. Mostofa's research interests span in the areas of natural language processing, scalable deep learning, HPC, and algorithm engineering. Prior to joining NVIDIA, Mostofa worked on scaling large language models and the predictability of scaling deep learning applications at Baidu's Silicon Valley AI Lab. Mostofa also made significant contributions in developing large-scale code for several core kernels in machine learning capable of running on supercomputers.

Jovan Popović is a Senior Program Manager at the Microsoft Development Center Serbia. He received an PhD degree in electrical engineering and computer science from the University of Belgrade in 2016. He is a software practitioner specialized in cloud computing, big data analytics, software engineering, and web application development. Before, he was with the School of Electrical Engineering, University of Belgrade.

Victor Potapenko received the B.B.A. degree in International Finance and Marketing and M.B.A. in Finance from the University of Miami, and the M.S. in Computer Science from the Nova Southeastern University. He is currently a PhD candidate at the College of Engineering and Computing, Florida International University. His research interests are in time series modeling, deep learning, and artificial intelligence.

Amir M. Rahmani is the founder of Health SciTech Group (healthscitech.org) at the University of California, Irvine (UCI). He is an Assistant Professor of Computer Science and Nursing (joint appointment) at UCI, and is also a life-time adjunct professor (Docent) at the Department of Future Technologies of University of Turku, Turku, Finland. Prior to joining UCI, he was an EU Marie Curie Global Fellow in the Computer Science Department of UCI and in the Institute of Computer Technology of TU Wien, Vienna, Austria. He has worked as a visiting researcher in the department of Industrial and Medical Electronics of KTH Royal Institute of Technology, Stockholm, Sweden. He received his Ph.D. from the IT department at University of Turku, Finland, and M.Sc. from ECE department at University of Tehran. He also received MBA jointly from Turku School of Economics and European Institute of Innovation & Technology (EIT) Digital. He is the recipient of the Nokia Foundation's Research Excellence Award (2 consecutive years), Ulla Tuominen Foundation's research excellence award, UTU's Teacher of the Year candidate, UTU's Rector awarded life-time Docent title, the European Union's awarded Global Marie Curie Fellowship, and UCI Faculty Innovation Fellowship. His work spans ubiquitous computing, wearable technology, applied machine learning, bio-signal processing, health informatics, and fog/edge computing. His research interests include novel sensing, computation, communication and networking paradigms, applied to healthcare/medical and wellbeing applications. He is the associate editor of the ACM Transactions on Computing for Healthcare and International Journal of Big Data Analytics in

Healthcare, and has served as a guest editor in several prestigious journals such as IEEE JBHI, ACM/ Springer MONET, Elsevier FGCS, Elsevier JPDS, Springer Supercomputing, and Elsevier JASC.

Ciro Ramos-Estebanez, MD, PhD, MBA, is a physician-scientist with positions at the University of Illinois at Chicago (School of Medicine) and Case Western Reserve University in Cleveland. **Clinical Training:** Ciro has completed extensive clinical training including a full Internal Medicine residency (Albert Einstein College of Medicine), a Neurology residency (Harvard Medical School), and Neuro-Critical Care fellowship at the University of Miami (Trauma Center, Critical care unit, and Miami Spine Project). **Basic Neuroscience and Translational Research:** Ciro earned a European Union International Doctor of Philosophy.

Ivan Ratkovic received the B.S. and M.S. degrees in electrical engineering and computer science from the University of Belgrade, Belgrade, Serbia, and the Ph.D. degree in computer architecture from the Polytechnic University of Catalonia, Barcelona, Spain. He was with the BSC Microsoft Research Center, Barcelona, the Barcelona Supercomputing Center, Barcelona, and the Berkeley Wireless Research Center, Berkeley, CA, USA. He is currently a CPU Research and Development Engineer with Esperanto Technologies. His current research interests include low-power design, computer architecture, vector and single instruction, multiple data processors, digital arithmetic, VLSI design flows, and embedded systems.

Naphtali Rishe is a Professor of Computer Science and the inaugural Outstanding University Professor at Florida International University in Miami. Rishe is the Director of National Science Foundation's Industry-University Cooperative Research Center for Advanced Knowledge Enablement, a consortium of FIU, Florida Atlantic University, and University of Greenwich (UK). Rishe has been awarded $55 million in grants. Rishe has published 6 books, 400 papers, and has been awarded 21 U.S. patents. Rishe's geographic data management system, TerraFly, has been featured in FOX TV News, New York Times, USA Today, NPR, Science and Nature journals and in the National Science Foundation's annual report to Congress. More about Dr. Rishe at http://cake.fiu.edu/Rishe/.

Jakob Salom received BSc. at School of Electrical Engineering Most distinguished software development results: Domestic Payment System (all ex-Yugoslavia payments in dinars) considered the best in the world; first on-line e-banking started in 1988; establishing e-banking in Hypo-Alpe-Adria bank Serbia. Since 2015 a consultant in the fields of Data warehousing, data archiving and data mining; DataFlow High Performance Computing on Maxeler computers; Implementing Mind Genomics in marketing.

Akira Tsuda, Ph.D., is a bioengineer working on lung physiology. His research interest is on the intersection of lung biology and engineering. For many years, he has explored both theoretical/computational and experimental aspects of the health effects of air polluting particles.

Mateo Valero Cortes is the director of the Barcelona Supercomputing Center. His research encompasses different concepts within the field of computer architecture, a discipline in which he has published more than 700 papers in journals, conference proceedings and books. Valero has received numerous awards, including the Eckert–Mauchly Award in 2007, for "extraordinary leadership in building a world class computer architecture research center, for seminal contributions in the areas of vector computing and multithreading, and for pioneering basic new approaches to instruction-level parallelism."

Kristy Yoshimoto completed a B.S. degree in Computer Science from the Luddy School of Informatics, Computing, and Engineering at Indiana University. During her academic career, she was acknowledged as a Founders Scholar and a member of the Dean's List. Under the guidance of Professor Veljko Milutinovic and Dr. Milos Kotlar, she developed a program to show the efficiency of running a process on an accelerator. Her current research interests include multi-factor authentication and supercomputing.

Index

E

efficiency 6, 13, 18-19, 27, 34, 51, 62, 68-71, 73, 122, 125, 158, 199, 202, 231, 242, 244, 261

Electronic Health Records 301, 304

exploratory equivalence 208, 216, 225-229, 242, 244-245

F

FPGA 1, 3, 123-124, 132, 312, 316-317

Fully Convolutional Network 268-269, 274-275, 279, 281

Fully Convolutional Neural Network 268

G

Gated Recurrent Unit 270, 281

gradient boosting 268-269, 280

Gradient Tree Boosting 273, 281

graph coloring 74, 76-77, 93-94, 202-204

graph theory 94, 208, 210, 230, 242

Graphics Processing Unit 5, 9, 134

H

Hamiltonian chaos 145, 149, 151, 160

High Performance Computing 23, 70, 96, 133, 288

high-performance computing 102, 133-134, 138, 290, 296

horizontal segmentation 282, 284

hybrid computing 1-2, 199

I

IIIF 171

image processing 106, 112-113, 206

Interactive Multi-layered Platforms 179

K

knowledge management 301-302, 307

L

latency 2-3, 67, 70, 104, 288, 312, 314-315, 317

least-squares 57, 114-115, 121

Long-Short Term Memory Network 281

low power 2, 5, 8, 11, 13, 68-69, 71, 283

M

machine learning 6, 44, 66-67, 133-139, 141, 143, 162-164, 171, 175, 179, 188, 203, 248-250, 262, 264, 268, 270, 280-281, 284, 302-303, 310, 312, 314-315, 318

Maxeler Java 106, 109-110, 124

memory 3, 7-10, 12-13, 16, 19, 41, 49, 59, 61, 67-69, 72, 81, 85, 94, 98, 104, 117, 131, 138, 163, 175, 200, 217, 229-230, 269-270, 272, 277, 281, 288, 292, 311-312, 316-317

Mind Genomics 282-288

mixing 145, 147-148, 151-156, 158-161

ML 162-163, 171, 179, 249, 251-252, 255-257, 262, 310, 314

ML and AI for Electric Energy Systems 179

Moore neighborhood 122, 129-130

multicore 7-8, 11, 13, 16, 18-19, 35-36, 68, 70-74, 93-94, 316

multi-core architectures 74, 77, 92

multi-core processor 7

Multithreaded architectures 74

N

Natural Language Processing 133-134, 141-143, 162-163, 172, 177, 250, 280

Networked Interactive Digital Books 162, 171, 178

neural network 14-15, 103, 200, 268, 281, 297

neuromodulation 99-100, 105, 293-294, 299

neuronal networks 97, 290-291

Neuroscience 42, 97-98, 101-105, 290-292, 295-299

NID 162, 171

NLP 134-135, 137, 140-141, 143, 162-163, 172, 250-251, 255, 259, 262, 265

O

OpenMP 81, 94

orbit 114, 145, 150

P

parallel computing 1, 75, 93-94, 134, 180

parallelism 7-8, 18-20, 23-24, 34, 51, 61, 94, 123, 206

particles 145-146, 148-151, 154, 156-159, 161

Performance Modeling 18, 35-36

personalisation 247, 253, 260, 262

Picard 254-255, 266-267

power consumption 6, 8, 10, 12, 16, 23, 43, 45-46, 54-55, 60, 63, 96

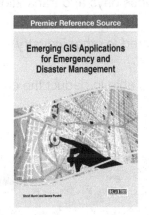

IGI Global's Transformative Open Access (OA) Model:
How to Turn Your University Library's Database Acquisitions Into a Source of OA Funding

Well in advance of Plan S, IGI Global unveiled their OA Fee Waiver (Read & Publish) Initiative. Under this initiative, librarians who invest in IGI Global's InfoSci-Books and/or InfoSci-Journals databases will be able to subsidize their patrons' OA article processing charges (APCs) when their work is submitted and accepted (after the peer review process) into an IGI Global journal.

How Does it Work?

Step 1: **Library Invests in the InfoSci-Databases:** A library perpetually purchases or subscribes to the InfoSci-Books, InfoSci-Journals, or discipline/subject databases.

Step 2: **IGI Global Matches the Library Investment with OA Subsidies Fund:** IGI Global provides a fund to go towards subsidizing the OA APCs for the library's patrons.

Step 3: **Patron of the Library is Accepted into IGI Global Journal (After Peer Review):** When a patron's paper is accepted into an IGI Global journal, they option to have their paper published under a traditional publishing model or as OA.

Step 4: **IGI Global Will Deduct APC Cost from OA Subsidies Fund:** If the author decides to publish under OA, the OA APC fee will be deducted from the OA subsidies fund.

Step 5: **Author's Work Becomes Freely Available:** The patron's work will be freely available under CC BY copyright license, enabling them to share it freely with the academic community.

Note: *This fund will be offered on an annual basis and will renew as the subscription is renewed for each year thereafter. IGI Global will manage the fund and award the APC waivers unless the librarian has a preference as to how the funds should be managed.*

Hear From the Experts on This Initiative:

"I'm very happy to have been able to make one of my recent research contributions *freely available* along with having access to the *valuable resources* found within IGI Global's InfoSci-Journals database."

— **Prof. Stuart Palmer,**
Deakin University, Australia

"Receiving the support from IGI Global's OA Fee Waiver Initiative *encourages me to continue my research work without any hesitation*."

— **Prof. Wenlong Liu,** College of Economics and Management at Nanjing University of Aeronautics & Astronautics, China

Printed in the United States
by Baker & Taylor Publisher Services